**PRINCIPLES
OF OBJECT-ORIENTED
ANALYSIS AND DESIGN**

A *James Martin* BOOK

THE JAMES MARTIN BOOKS
currently available from Prentice Hall

- Application Development Without Programmers
- Building Expert Systems
- Communications Satellite Systems
- Computer Data-Base Organization, Second Edition
- Computer Networks and Distributed Processing: Software, Techniques, and Architecture
- Data Communication Technology
- DB2: Concepts, Design, and Programming
- Design and Strategy of Distributed Data Processing
- An End User's Guide to Data Base
- Fourth-Generation Languages, Volume I: Principles
- Fourth-Generation Languages, Volume II: Representative 4GLs
- Fourth-Generation Languages, Volume III: 4GLs from IBM
- Future Developments in Telecommunications, Second Edition
- Hyperdocuments and How to Create Them
- IBM Office Systems: Architectures and Implementations
- IDMS/R: Concepts, Design, and Programming
- Information Engineering, Book I: Introduction and Principles
- Information Engineering, Book II: Planning and Analysis
- Information Engineering, Book III: Design and Construction
- An Information Systems Manifesto
- Local Area Networks: Architectures and Implementations
- Managing the Data-Base Environment
- Object-Oriented Analysis and Design
- Principles of Data-Base Management
- Principles of Data Communication
- Principles of Object-Oriented Analysis and Design
- Recommended Diagramming Standards for Analysts and Programmers
- SNA: IBM's Networking Solution
- Strategic Information Planning Methodologies, Second Edition
- System Design from Provably Correct Constructs
- Systems Analysis for Data Transmission
- Systems Application Architecture: Common User Access
- Systems Application Architecture: Common Communications Support: Distributed Applications
- Systems Application Architecture: Common Communications Support: Network Infrastructure
- Systems Application Architecture: Common Programming Interface
- Technology's Crucible
- Telecommunications and the Computer, Third Edition
- Telematic Society: A Challenge for Tomorrow
- VSAM: Access Method Services and Programming Techniques

with Carma McClure

- Action Diagrams: Clearly Structured Specifications, Programs, and Procedures, Second Edition
- Diagramming Techniques for Analysts and Programmers
- Software Maintenance: The Problem and Its Solutions
- Structured Techniques: The Basis for CASE, Revised Edition

ON INFORMATION TECHNOLOGY

Video education courses are available on these topics through James Martin Insight, Inc., 1751 West Diehl Road, Naperville, IL 60563-9099 (tel: 708-983-4808 or 800-526-0452).

Database

- AN END USER'S GUIDE TO DATABASE
- PRINCIPLES OF DATABASE MANAGEMENT (second edition)
- COMPUTER DATABASE ORGANIZATION (third edition)
- MANAGING THE DATABASE ENVIRONMENT (second edition)
- DATABASE ANALYSIS AND DESIGN
- VSAM: ACCESS METHOD SERVICES AND PROGRAMMING TECHNIQUES
- DB2: CONCEPTS, DESIGN, AND PROGRAMMING
- IDMS/R: CONCEPTS, DESIGN, AND PROGRAMMING

Security

- SECURITY, ACCURACY, AND PRIVACY IN COMPUTER SYSTEMS

Telecommunications

- TELECOMMUNICATIONS AND THE COMPUTER (third edition)
- COMMUNICATIONS SATELLITE SYSTEMS

Distributed Processing

- COMPUTER NETWORKS AND DISTRIBUTED PROCESSING
- DESIGN AND STRATEGY FOR DISTRIBUTED DATA PROCESSING

Office Automation

- IBM OFFICE SYSTEMS: ARCHITECTURES AND IMPLEMENTATIONS
- TCP/IP NETWORKING: ARCHITECTURE, ADMINISTRATION, AND PROGRAMMING

Networks and Data Communications

- PRINCIPLES OF DATA COMMUNICATION
- TELEPROCESSING NETWORK ORGANIZATION
- SYSTEMS ANALYSIS FOR DATA TRANSMISSION
- DATA COMMUNICATION TECHNOLOGY
- DATA COMMUNICATION DESIGN TECHNIQUES
- SNA: IBM's NETWORKING SOLUTION
- LOCAL AREA NETWORKS: ARCHITECTURES AND IMPLEMENTATIONS (second edition)
- OFFICE AUTOMATION STANDARDS
- DATA COMMUNICATION STANDARDS
- COMPUTER NETWORKS AND DISTRIBUTED PROCESSING: SOFTWARE, TECHNIQUES, AND ARCHITECTURE

Society

- THE COMPUTERIZED SOCIETY
- TELEMATIC SOCIETY: A CHALLENGE FOR TOMORROW
- TECHNOLOGY'S CRUCIBLE
- VIEWDATA AND THE INFORMATION SOCIETY

SAA: Systems Application Architecture

- SAA: COMMON USER ACCESS
- SAA: COMMON COMMUNICATIONS SUPPORT: DISTRIBUTED APPLICATIONS
- SAA: COMMON COMMUNICATIONS SUPPORT: NETWORK INFRASTRUCTURE
- SAA: COMMON PROGRAMMING INTERFACE

PRINCIPLES OF OBJECT-ORIENTED ANALYSIS AND DESIGN

JAMES MARTIN

P T R PRENTICE HALL
Englewood Cliffs, New Jersey 07632

Library of Congress Cataloging-in-Publication Data
MARTIN, JAMES (date)
　　Principles of object-oriented analysis and design / by James Martin.
　　　p.　cm.
　　"A James Martin book."
　　Includes bibliographical references and index.
　　ISBN 0-13-720871-5
　　1. Object-oriented programming (Computer science)　I. Title.
　　QA76.64.M38　1993
　　005.1 ' 1—dc20　　　　　　　　　　　　　　　　92-31822
　　　　　　　　　　　　　　　　　　　　　　　　　　　　CIP

Editorial/production supervision: *Kathryn Gollin Marshak*
Liaison: *Mary P. Rottino*
Jacket design: *Lundgren Graphics*
Pre-press buyer: *Mary Elizabeth McCartney*
Manufacturing buyer: *Susan Brunke*

Copyright © 1993 by James Martin and James J. Odell

Published by P T R Prentice Hall
Prentice-Hall, Inc.
A Paramount Communications Company
Englewood Cliffs, New Jersey 07632

All rights reserved. No part of this book may be
reproduced, in any form or by any means,
without permission in writing from the publisher.

The publisher offers discounts on this book when ordered
in bulk quantities. For more information, contact:
　　Corporate Sales Department
　　P T R Prentice Hall
　　113 Sylvan Avenue
　　Englewood Cliffs, NJ 07632
　　Phone 201-592-2863; Fax 201-592-2249

Printed in the United States of America

10　9　8　7　6　5　4　3

ISBN 0-13-720871-5

Prentice-Hall International (UK) Limited, *London*
Prentice-Hall of Australia Pty. Limited, *Sydney*
Prentice-Hall Canada Inc., *Toronto*
Prentice-Hall Hispanoamericana, S.A., *Mexico*
Prentice-Hall of India Private Limited, *New Delhi*
Prentice-Hall of Japan, Inc., *Tokyo*
Simon & Schuster Asia Pte. Ltd., *Singapore*
Editora Prentice-Hall do Brasil, Ltda., *Rio de Janeiro*

TO CORINTHIA

CONTENTS

Preface   xv

Index of Basic Concepts   xix

PART I OVERVIEW

1 OO: An Integrating Paradigm   3

*A Software Revolution 4; Killer Technologies 5;
Integrating the Killer Technologies 6; Taking the Blinders Off 12;
All Types of Computing 13; The Integrating Paradigm 14;
References 15*

2 Basic Concepts   17

*What is an Object? 17; What Is an Object Type? 18;
Operations 19; Methods 19; Encapsulation 19; Requests 21;
BLOBs 23; What Is a Class? 23; Inheritance 24;
Perception and Reality 24; Self-Contained Creatures 28;
Nature's Building Blocks 29; References 30*

3 Why Object-Oriented?   31

*Characteristics of OO Techniques 31;
Summary of the Benefits of OO Technology 32;
Different Benefits 36; Reusability 39;
More Like Hardware Engineering 40; Orderly Behavior 41;
Reliability Needs Simplicity 42; Program Complexity Metrics 42;
Great Rolling Snowballs of Code 43; Enhanced Creativity 44;
Immediate Feedback 45; The Bad News 45;
A Change in the Way We Think 46; References 46*

PART II MODELS AND DIAGRAMS

4 Basic Guidelines 51

*End User Involvement Must Be Enhanced 51;
The OO Models Must Be Easy for End Users to Understand 51;
OO Diagrams Should Be Executable 52;
OO Techniques Should Facilitate Enterprise Redesign 52;
Enterprise Models Should Be "Intelligent" 53;
OO Techniques Should Be as Automated as Possible 53;
The Emphasis Should Be on OO-CASE Tools Not OO
Programming Languages 53;
OO Development Needs Diagramming Standards 54;
OO Diagramming Standards Must Be as Easy to Learn as
Possible by Conventional Systems People 55;
A Repository is Needed for OO Analysis and Design 55;
The Principle of Occam's Razor Should Be Applied to Object
Types 56; Skilled Analysis Is Essential 56;
Enterprisewide Analysis Is Needed 57; Reference 57*

5 OO Models 59

*Models of Reality 59; Tools 60; Two Aspects of an OO Model 61;
The Similarity of Analysis and Design 62;
Information Engineering 64; Accommodation of Old Systems 66*

6 Categorizing Objects 69

*Generalization Hierarchies 71; Fern Diagrams 72;
Benefits of Fern Diagrams 73; Types and Instances 73;
Box Diagrams 74; Complete and Incomplete Sets of Subtypes 75;
An Object Can Be an Instance of Multiple Subtypes 75;
Objects Categorized in Various Ways 77;
How to Determine What Should Be a Subtype 79*

7 Relationships Among Object Types 81

*Entities and Objects 81; Data Models 82;
Object-Relationship Diagrams 82; Attributes 83; Instances 83;
Cardinality Constraints 83; Labeling of Lines 86;
Reading Associations Like Sentences 87; Subtypes 87;
Arrows Indicating Subtypes 88; Composed-of Diagrams 89;
Subtyping Versus Composed-of Diagrams 93;
Subtyping and Composition on the Same Diagram 94;
Occam's Razor at Work 95; Overview Diagrams 96;
Summary 101; References 101*

8   State and State Changes   *103*

*State Lifecycles 103; State-Transition Diagrams 104;
Substates 105; Reusability in State Transitions 106;
Complex State-Transition Diagrams 107;
Finite-State Machines 107; Multiple Simultaneous States 108;
Events 109; Reference 109*

9   Events, Triggers, and Operations   *111*

*Events 111; A Sequence of Operations 111;
Events and Operations 112; Events and State Changes 113;
The Linking of Operations 114; Cause-and-Effect Isolation 114;
Preconditions and Postconditions 115;
Clear Modularization 117; Clock Events 117;
External Sources of Events 117; Types of Events 118;
Trigger Rules 119; Multiple Triggers 120;
Control Conditions 121; The Basic Construct of Event Diagrams 122;
Simultaneous Operations 123;
Operation Subtypes and Supertypes 124;
Event Subtypes and Supertypes 125; Hierarchical Schemas 127;
Object-Flow Diagrams 128; Reference 132*

10   Rules   *133*

*Rules Expressed in English 133;
Declarative Versus Procedural Statements 134;
Making Business Knowledge Explicit 135;
Rules Linked to Diagrams 136; Categories of Rules 137;
Stimulus/Response Rules 137; Operation Condition Rules 140;
Conditions for Executing an Operation 141;
Executable Diagrams 142;
Rules Attached to Other OO Diagrams 143;
The Programmer as Lawyer 143; The Inference Engine 145;
Unnecessary Rules 150; Visible and Nonvisible Rules 150;
Traceability 151; Changing How Business Are Run 151;
References 154*

11   How the Diagrams Interrelate   *155*

*Linking Activities and State Changes 158;
Rules Linked to Diagrams 166*

12   Basic Concepts of OO Design   *169*

*The Self-Contained Viewpoint of the Object 170; Class 171;
From Operations to Methods 172; Class Inheritance 174;
Classes High in the Hierarchy 176; Selecting a Method 176;
Polymorphism 181; "Same As, Except . . ." 182; References 186*

13 Responsibility-Driven Design 187

*Responsibilities 187; Responsibilities and Collaborators 188;
Classes Are Actors 188; CRC Cards 188;
Thinking Like an Object 189; Finding the Right Wording 191;
Contracts 191; Public and Private Responsibilities 193;
Subtypes 193; Objects Composed of Objects 193;
Class-Communication Diagrams 195;
Legacy Applications 197; Combining Cards and CASE 197;
References 199*

14 OO Workshops with End Users 201

*The Best of Computers and People 202;
Repository, Not Paper 206; The Executive Sponsor 207;
The Facilitator 207; The Scribe 209; Facilitator Training 210;
Who Attends the JRP Workshop? 210; A Gelled Team 211;
Workshop Duration 212; Group Dynamics 212; Open Issues 213;
The Five-Minute Rule 213; The Workshop Room 213;
Training the Participants 215; Wall Charting 216; Summary 216;
References 217*

15 Methods Creation 219

*Increasing the Power of Languages 219;
Procedural Versus Nonprocedural Techniques 221;
Procedural Techniques 223; Action Diagrams 225;
Code Generation with Action Diagrams 226;
Avoidance of Procedural Design 229; Report Generators 231;
Screen and Dialog Painters 231; Default Options 231;
Declarative Language 231; Rules 233; Inference Engine 235;
Event Diagrams 235; Decision Trees and Tables 235;
Declarative Tables 235; English 237; Class Libraries 239;
Summary 239; References 239*

16 Object-Oriented Information Engineering 241

*Information Engineering 241; Divide and Conquer 246;
Goals of Information Engineering 247; Enterprise Planning 249;
Business Area Analysis 251; System Design 252;
Construction 253; Analysis for Reusability 253;
Enterprisewide Implementation 255; Human Coordination 256;
References 258*

PART III TOOLS

17 Object-Oriented Programming Languages 261

*The Genesis of OO Technology 261; Smalltalk 261;
The Evolution from Untyped to Typed Languages 262;
User-Defined Types (UDTs) 263;
Abstract Data Types (ADTs) 263; Objects and Requests 265;
Inheritance and Polymorphism 266;
Canceling Inherited Features 269;
Characteristics of OO Languages 269;
Pure Versus Hybrid OO Languages 270;
Enforcement of Discipline 272;
Interpreters Versus Compilers 273; Pointers 274;
Static Versus Dynamic Binding 275;
Avoidance of CASE Statements 276;
Languages and Environments 277; References 277*

18 OO-CASE Tools 281

*A Variety of Tools 282; Pure OO And Hybrid CASE 283;
Categories of CASE Tools 283; Insightful Models 284;
Design Synthesis and Code Generation 285;
Code Generators 287; Instant CASE 287;
Precision in Diagramming 288;
Diagrams for OO Development 289; Repository 290;
More Than a Dictionary 290; Intelligence in the Repository 292;
Documentation 292; Consistency Among Diagrams 293;
Consistency Among Different Projects 293;
Maximum Reusability 294;
Three Sources of Reusable Components 297;
The Future of CASE 298; References 299*

19 Object-Oriented Databases 301

*A Brief History of Database Development 302;
Active Databases 308; Knowledgebases 308;
Object-Oriented Databases 308; A Unified Conceptual Model 309;
OO Database Architecture 311; Development with OODB 312;
Three Approaches to Building OODBs 313;
Data Independence Versus Encapulation 314;
OODB Will Not Completely Replace RDB 314;
Complexity of Data Structure 314; Performance 315;
Avoiding Redundancy 315; Differences Between RDB and OODB 316;
Summary 319; References 320*

20 Future Tools for Reliable Software 321

True Engineering of Software 321;
Mathematics and Programming 323;
Up-Front Verification 326;
Preconditions and Postconditions 326;
Illegal to Bypass the Controls 327; Immediate Feedback 327;
The Problem with Programming Languages 327;
From Model to Chips 328; A Combination of Disciplines 330;
References 331

21 Standards for Object Interaction 333

The Object Management Group 333;
The OMG Object Model 334;
Object Management Architecture 335;
The Object Request Broker (ORB) 337;
Diverse ORB Implementations 338; Operations 341;
Object Interfaces 341; Interface Definition Language 341;
The ORB Repositories 342; ORBs and OODB 342;
Multiple ORBs 342; Interface to Non-OO Software 344;
References 345

PART IV EPILOGUE

22 The Future of Software 349

Introduction 349; Optical Disks 350;
The Need for Power Tools 350;
Evolution of Software Production 351;
Inhuman Use of Human Beings 352; Chain Reaction 353;
Repository Standards 354; Packaged Software 355;
Reusability 357; Formal Methods 358; Parallelism 362;
Networks and Distribution of Objects 363;
Intercorporate Computer Interaction 364;
Speed of Interaction 365; The Need for Fast Development 366;
International Standards for Reusable Classes 367;
Code Generation from the Enterprise Model 367;
The Evolution of Programming Techniques 368;
Pyramids of Complexity 371; References 371

PART V APPENDIX

A Recommended Diagramming Standards 375

*A Natural Way to Think About Systems 375;
Conventional Diagrams 376; Object-Oriented Diagrams 377;
Square-Cornered and Round-Cornered Boxes 377;
Reality and Information About Reality 377;
External Objects and Operations 382; Lines and Arrows 383;
Class Communication Diagram 383; Cardinality Constraints 383;
Labeling of Lines 387; Object-Relationship Diagrams 387;
Composed-of Diagrams 388; Subtypes and Supertypes 389;
Fern Diagrams 390; Types and Instances 391;
Triangle Arrows for Subtyping 392; Events 392;
Clock Events 394; Control Conditions 394; Triggers 394;
Parallel Processing 396;
Omitting Events and Control Conditions 396; States 397;
Mutual Exclusivity 399; Subtype Boxes 399;
Nonmutually Exclusive Subtypes 400;
Multiple Sets of Subtypes 400; Expansion and Contraction 402;
Using Windows to Achieve Clarity 403; Reference 403*

Index 405

PREFACE

In the next ten years we will see an explosive growth in the power of computers, especially that of workstations, LAN servers, and machines that exploit parallel (concurrent) processing. The demands for new software will be immense. Unless a revolution occurs in the way software is built, the software industry will cripple the potential of the computer hardware industry.

The revolution is likely to come from object-oriented techniques combined with integrated-CASE tools, code generators, CASE repositories, class libraries, formal methods, and techniques for managing software development that encourage the maximum reuse of software design and components. Object-oriented programming, by itself, is insufficient. The power of object-oriented technology lies primarily in OO modeling, analysis, and design—the subjects of this book.

Most enterprises (except very small ones) need redesigning today in order to take advantage of new technology and networks, streamline procedures, eliminate redundancy and bureaucracy, and empower the employees to add more value. Business process redesign is the most important function of I.S. departments. To redesign the value chains of an enterprise, the chains need to be modeled. Object-oriented modeling is the best way to do this. The models should reflect the business policies and rules, and OO tools should allow these to be translated into operational systems as automatically as possible. When the business policies change (which happens constantly), the business systems should be regenerated quickly to reflect the change.

Information engineering, as it is generally practiced today, has taken us far beyond the mess-making techniques of the previous decade. However, it needs to be revamped so that it helps to achieve mass reusability in software, to create models for redesigning the enterprise, and to create systems that can be quickly changed to reflect changing business policies. This requires object-oriented information engineering with an object-oriented repository.

The primary technical skills of business systems analysts will be object-oriented modeling, analysis, and design—the subjects of this book.

Object-oriented modeling, analysis, and design need a clear diagrammatic language which is as easy as possible to teach both to business people (end users) and to the millions of I.S. professionals steeped in an earlier culture. To maximize communication, this language should be a standard and should be the basis of object-oriented CASE tools. In order to minimize the culture-change difficulties, it should resemble the diagrammatic language that analysts already use.

The Appendix of this book describes recommended diagramming standards which multiple vendors are using for building object-oriented CASE tools. This diagrammatic language has been extensively refined by usage in the field.

The Object Management Group has done immensely valuable work in establishing the vocabulary of OO technology, an OO reference model, the concept of the Object Request Broker, and de facto standards for enabling OO systems to interact with one another. We must all support the OMG in helping to achieve the communication which is essential in a future OO world. This book attempts to adopt OMG's vocabulary and model of OO technology.

OO technology is the most important software evolution of the 1990s. It is destined to change not only the way we build software, but the way software intercommunicates over worldwide multivendor networks. OO modeling will change the way we design business processes and the way we think about enterprises. It will change the way enterprises interact with one another because computers in one corporation will be on line to computers in other corporations, interacting in real time. A much higher level of business automation is evolving, and this will change the patterns of world commerce.

Every I.S. professional concerned about his career must fully understand the subject matter of this book.

To make this book appeal to a wide audience, it attempts to avoid the acronyms of the computer industry. Human vocabulary contains less than 25,000 words, but the *Acronyms, Initialisms, and Abbreviations Dictionary* has 300,000 entries.

The acronym OO for "object oriented" is visually appealing and easily remembered. So, it will be used throughout the book.

ACKNOWLEDGMENTS The source of much knowledge about object-oriented technology is the Object Management Group (OMG). They have established the vocabulary and set the standards for the OO revolution. It is vital that the entire software industry follows the guidelines of the OMG. (OMG Standards are discussed in Chapter 21.) Precise definition of the terms used in OO analysis and design is very important. It is necessary that the computer industry agree on these definitions. The terms used in this book are based on those recommended by the Object Management Group (OMG) [3, 4] and the Object-Oriented Database Task Group (OODBTG) [1, 2]. We have sometimes reworded these definitions to achieve tutorial clarity.

Much of the information in this book is an extension of that in an earlier book, *Object-Oriented Analysis and Design,* which I co-authored with James J. Odell, who has continued to help shape my views on OO principles.

Much knowledge is drawn from consultants in James Martin and Co., Reston, VA, who have been using OO techniques in practice and extending the frontiers of OO information engineering. I am particularly grateful to Kevin Murphy and Franz Van Assche for their contributions.

In making videotaped seminars on OO technology for James Martin Insight, Naperville, IL, the following were particularly informative: Michael D. Williams and K. C. Branscomb of IntelliCorp, David A. Taylor of Taylor Consulting, Mary E. S. Loomis of Versant Object Technology, James J. Odell of James Odell Associates, Chris Stone of the OMG, Charles Hazeltine of NCR, Charles Duff of the White Water Group, Keith Short of Texas Instruments, James Cerrato of ADT, Tim Andrews of ONTOS, Inc., Franz Van Assche, Ward Cunningham, and Prof. Tony Hoare of Oxford University. I thank each of them very much.

A special thank you goes to Tony Hoare for commenting on Chapter 20, concerned with ultra-reliable software.

IntelliCorp has created a CASE tool that helps automate the techniques described in this book. I would like to thank Gary Fine, Mike Williams, Conrad Bok, and Richard Treitel for their help in refining the ideas.

Special thanks to Dr. Andrea Matthies for word processing, editing, and valiantly improving my use of English.

James Martin

REFERENCES

1. Otis, Allen, Craig Thompson and Bill Kent, ed. (1991) *ODM Reference Model,* Object-Oriented Databases Task Group (X3 ANSI/SPARC), Technical Report OODB 89-01R7, April 30, 1991.

2. Perez, Edward and Mark Sastry, ed. (1991) *ODM Glossary,* Object-Oriented Databases Task Group (X3 ANSI/SPARC), Technical Report OODB 91-07R1, July 5, 1991.

3. Soley, Richard Mark, ed. (1990) *Object Management Architecture Guide,* Object Management Group, Document 90.9.1, November 1, 1990.

4. OMG, *The OMG Object Model,* OMG Document Number 91.9.1.

INDEX OF BASIC CONCEPTS

The basic concepts, principles, and terms explained in this book are listed below along with the page on which they are introduced or defined. A complete index appears at the end of the book.

Abstract Data Types (ADTs)	263
Action Diagrams	225
Attributes	83
BLOB (Binary Large OBject)	23
Business Area Analysis	251
Cardinality Constraints	83
Class	171
Contracts	191
CRC Cards	188
Data Models	82
Encapsulation	19
Event Diagrams	235
Events	109
Fern Diagrams	72
Formal Methods	323
Generalization Hierarchies	71
I-CASE	282
Inference Engine	10
Inheritance	24

Instances	83
Legacy Applications	197
Method	24
Metrics, Program Complexity	42
Multiple Inheritance	24
Object	19
Object Management Architecture	335
Object Management Group	333
Object-Oriented Databases (Object Databases)	308
Object Request Broker (ORB)	337
Object Type	23
Occam's Razor	56
OMG Object Model	334
OO-CASE	294
Parallelism	362
Polymorphism	181
Postconditions and Preconditions	115
Relational Database	305
Repository	8
Requests	21
Reusability	39
Rules	133
Scribe	209
Subtypes	87
User-Defined Types (UDTs)	263

PART I OVERVIEW

1 OO: AN INTEGRATING PARADIGM

In making a videotaped series about the material in this book, I opened with shots of babies learning about their world [1]. They were discovering objects, such as blocks, containers, binoculars, and a television remote control. Their brains were playfully trying to categorize the objects. Different types of blocks and containers could be stacked and inserted. The babies learned about the behavior of objects—a rattle makes a noise, lego blocks clip together, and binoculars do nothing interesting if put to your ear. The baby shots were intercut with clips of a systems analyst explaining how he discovered and categorized objects in a bank. His analysis led to much better software.

We have a natural way of organizing our knowledge about the world. From earliest childhood we learn to categorize and make sense of an amazing mass of knowledge. The techniques that are so natural to human thinking should be applied to systems thinking.

Readers of this book will not be learning an arcane and difficult formalism but rather learning to analyze the world in a way that seems natural to human thinking. Object-oriented analysis enables us to build better systems and also makes the process easier. Particularly important, it improves communication with end users and business people.

My cat is object-oriented. She thinks of the world in terms of objects and how they behave. A ball of silver paper behaves differently than a mouse when she zaps it. It has different methods. She learns what messages cause objects such as her owner to behave in a desired way.

> The models built during object-oriented analysis provide a more natural way to think about systems.

The Object Management Group is an industry-funded group that is creating important standards (which will be discussed later). It comments

> ... the biggest point of the object revolution [is] to reduce the semantic gap between the models we use in computer programming languages and database management systems, and the conceptual models we use in thinking about the world normally [2].

Object-oriented analysis and design bring a surprising number of advantages (described in Chapter 3). They caused Bill Gates, the richest man in the computer industry, to proclaim, "'Object-oriented' is going to be the most important emerging software technology of the 1990s."

A SOFTWARE REVOLUTION

One of the most urgent concerns in the computer industry today is the need to create software and corporate systems much faster and at lower cost. To put the ever-growing power of computers to good use, we need software of *much* greater complexity. Although more complex, this software also needs to be more reliable. High quality is essential in software development, as poor quality wastes money.

The need for better software development applies both within the software industry itself and within enterprises of all types that develop their own computer applications. I.S. (Information Systems) organizations need to create and modify applications much faster. If applications take two or three years to build with an application backlog of several years, businesses cannot create applications or react to competitive thrusts nearly quickly enough. The vital ability for dynamic change is lost.

The means of achieving the quantum leap in Fig. 1.1 is probably now within sight. Instead of one technique, a combination of many tools and techniques is needed.

Object-oriented techniques allow software to be constructed of *objects* that have a specified behavior. Objects themselves can be built out of other objects,

---

In software we need a quantum leap in

- Complexity
- Reliability
- Design Capability
- Flexibility
- Speed of Development
- Ease of Change

Figure 1.1

that in turn can be built out of objects. This resembles complex machinery being built out of assemblies, subassemblies, sub-subassemblies, and so on.

Systems analysis in the object-oriented world is done by analyzing the objects in an environment and the events that interact with those objects. Software design is done by reusing existing object classes and, when necessary, building new classes. In modeling an enterprise, the analysts should identify its object types, its events, the operations that cause those objects to behave in certain ways, and the rules that govern the operations.

Throughout the history of engineering, a principle seems to emerge—*great engineering is simple engineering.* Ideas that become too cumbersome, inflexible, and problematic tend to be replaced with newer, conceptually cleaner ideas that have an aesthetic simplicity. When a programmer's diagram looks like a tangled mess, the time has come to rethink the entire program.

Software constantly runs the danger of becoming cumbersome, inflexible, and problematic. The linkages tend to multiply as new features are added and as users request changes. Unless the designers have conceptual clarity, they will weave a tangled web.

> Object-oriented techniques simplify the design of complex systems.

Systems can be visualized as a collection of objects with each object being in one of many specified states. The operations that change the state are relatively simple. Objects are built out of other objects. Systems are built out of proven components with standard-format requests invoking the operations of the component.

The term software industrial revolution has been used to describe the move to an era when software will be compiled out of reusable components. Components will be built out of other components and vast libraries of such components will be created. We must progress from an era of monolithic software packages, where one vendor builds the whole package, to an era in which software is assembled from components and packages from many vendors—just as computers or cars are assembled from components from many vendors. The components will become increasingly complex internally but simple to interact with. They will be black boxes that we do not look inside.

KILLER TECHNOLOGIES

Object-oriented techniques alone cannot provide the magnitude of change needed. They must be combined with other software technologies. Object-oriented techniques have existed for two decades, but the early techniques were mainly concerned with coding in languages such as Smalltalk and C++. Meanwhile, other powerful technologies have evolved, such as CASE tools, code generators, repository-based development, the inference engine, and artificial intelligence techniques. Object-oriented techniques become very powerful when combined with these other technologies.

Figure 1.2 lists a set of *killer technologies* for software development. The synergistic *combination* of these technologies will bring a revolution in software. This will require teamwork, education, and good management along with cooperation among software companies. Standards now evolving will aid this cooperation. Box 1.1 describes the software killer technologies.

Killer Technologies for Software Development

- CASE and I-CASE
- Visual Programming
- Code Generators
- Repository and Repository Coordinator
- Repository-Based Methodologies
- Information Engineering
- Object-Oriented Databases
- Nonprocedural Languages
- Formal Mathematically-Based Methods
- Inference Engines
- Client-Server Technology
- Class Libraries which maximize reusability
- Object-Oriented Analysis and Design

Figure 1.2

INTEGRATING THE KILLER TECHNOLOGIES

Any one of the killer technologies in Fig. 1.2 is powerful. However, a software industrial revolution will not come from one of those technologies alone but all of them integrated into an object-oriented framework.

Software, like machines, will be built from reusable components. Designers will not need to know the internal workings of the components. A designer of a video-cassette recorder would not design it transistor by transistor but out of high-level components. One chip may contain a hundred-thousand transistors. In a similar way, there should be high-level software components, some containing a hundred-thousand lines of code and designed to have zero errors.

BOX 1.1   Killer technologies for software development

- **CASE (Computer-Aided Software Engineering).** Particularly important to the future of software development is the growth of the CASE industry. CASE tools are the software industry's equivalent of CAD (computer-aided design) tools for such activities as circuit layout and chip design.

  > CASE tools employ graphic representations on the screen to help automate the planning, analysis, design, and generation of software.

- **I-CASE (Integrated CASE).** A particularly important facility of CASE tools is the code generator. Code generators should be as powerful and efficient as possible. The term I-CASE is used to mean integrated CASE, in which the tools for all stages of the lifecycle link together and drive a code generator.

  > I-CASE refers to a CASE toolset that supports all lifecycle stages including complete code generation, with a single logically consistent repository.

- **Visual Programming.** Visual programming is a form of CASE that expresses the design of programs with graphics, color, and possibly sound. Objects are represented in visual form and may be thought of as physical machines that transition from state to state.

  > *Visual programming* allows developers to enter, understand, think of, run, debut, and manipulate programs using primarily pictorial notations.

- **Code Generators.** Whenever possible, programs should be generated automatically from high-level designs, specifications, or images on a CASE screen. Code can be generated from decision tables, rules, action diagrams, diagrams of events, state transition diagrams, representations of objects and their properties and relationships, and so on.

(Continued)

BOX 1.1   *(Continued)*

> *Code generators* produce code with no syntax errors from high-level designs, charts, or specifications.

  Ideal code generators would generate code as fast as designers can think and allow them to execute it.

- **Repository.** CASE tools employ a repository, which some vendors call an encyclopedia, to store the knowledge that they help the analyst create. The planning tools put information in a repository that can be used by modeling or analysis tools. These, in turn, put information in a repository that can be used by the design tools. In addition, the design tools put information in a repository that can be used to generate code. The repository provides a seamless interface among the tools in the I-CASE toolset. I-CASE tools employ a *single, nonredundant repository.* Though logically nonredundant, physically it may employ a distributed database. Repository coordinator software uses many rules to ensure integrity of the information in the repository.

> The *repository* is a mechanism for defining, storing, and managing information about an enterprise, its data and systems.
>
> The *repository coordinator* applies methods to the data in the repository to ensure that the data and their CASE representations have consistency and integrity.

- **Repository-Based Methodologies.** Efficient software development will increasingly be repository based. An ever-growing repository stores models, specifications, designs, and reusable constructs from which software is built. Methodologies for systems development now relate to building a comprehensive collection of knowledge in a repository, where the repository drives the generation of code. A growing collection of reusable constructs are stored in the repository.

> A *repository-based methodology* is designed to take full advantage of an I-CASE toolset and to maximize reusability.

  Particularly important are repository-based methodologies for high-speed development.

BOX 1.1 *(Continued)*

- **Information Engineering.** Information engineering applies repository-based development to an entire enterprise to integrate the planning, design, and construction of systems that need to interoperate across the enterprise. It creates a model of the enterprise and attempts to redesign the enterprise information systems to be as effective as possible.

  > *Information engineering* applies integrated modeling and design techniques to the enterprise as a whole (or to a large section of the enterprise) rather than to merely one project.

- **Object-Oriented Databases.** An object-oriented database is an intelligent database. It supports the object-oriented paradigm, storing data and operations, rather than just data. It is designed to be physically efficient in storing complex objects. It can prevent access to the data except via the stored operations.

  > An *object-oriented database* is designed to store object data and methods with techniques that are efficient for object-oriented processing.

  A CASE repository should be an object-oriented database (even when the CASE tools do not support object-oriented analysis, design, or programming).

- **Nonprocedural Languages.** With procedural languages (such as COBOL and C) we instruct the computer as to the sequence of operations it must execute. With nonprocedural languages, we define the results that we require. An interpreter or compiler generates the code.

  > *Nonprocedural languages* define what is wanted, rather than how it is programmed.

  Many fourth-generation languages (such as Focus and Natural) contain both procedural and nonprocedural elements.

- **Formal Mathematically-Based Methods.** Mathematical techniques have been used for creating specifications of provable correctness and for

(Continued)

BOX 1.1 *(Continued)*

proving the correctness of programs. Examples of mathematically based methods include the Z specification language and the OCCAM programming language.

> *Formal methods* are used to guarantee that programs perform as intended, with zero errors.

Formal methods are appropriate for creating the building blocks (classes) of object-oriented systems.

- **Inference Engine.** An inference engine operates with a collection of rules about an area of knowledge. It selects rules and effectively chains them together to perform inferential reasoning. It may use forward chaining (input-directed reasoning) or backward chaining (goal-directed reasoning) or both. It enables a computer to make complex deductions without an application program. It is the primary technique used in artificial intelligence software.

> An *inference engine* is software that makes deductions from facts and rules by using techniques of logical inference.

- **Client-Server Technology.** The computer world increasingly requires software that runs on multiple computers, such as LAN-server systems, cooperative systems, distributed computing, and parallel computers. Client-server computing can be described as a software relationship as follows.

> A *client* is a software module that requests an operation.
>
> A *server* is a software module that responds to that request.

Clients and servers can run on separate machines arranged in almost any configuration.

- **Class Libraries.** A class library contains reusable implementation of object types. Its intent should be to achieve the maximum degree of reusability in software development. Class-library software should help developers find, adapt, and use the classes they need.

BOX 1.1 *(Continued)*

> A *class* is a software implementation of an object type. A class can have many subclasses.

- **Object-Oriented Analysis and Design.** The object-oriented analyst views the world as objects with data structures and methods as well as events that trigger operations that change the state of objects. Operations occur as objects make requests of other objects. The analyst creates diagrams of the object structures and events that change the objects. The designer's model is similar to the analyst's model but is taken into enough detail to create code.

    Object-oriented analysis and design attempt to achieve mass reusability of object classes.

> *Object-oriented analysis and design* model the world in terms of objects that have properties and behavior, as well as events that trigger operations that change the state of the objects. Objects interact formally with other objects.

A video-cassette recorder (VCR) has many components that are themselves objects, with specific operations, communicated with by specific requests. A lower-level object type, such as a circuit board, may be used in many different VCR models. The circuit board itself is built from components such as chips. To assemble a VCR, a complex bill of materials is used. Similarly, software needs a bill of materials; it should be assembled from many types of objects.

Instead of thinking in terms of loops, program steps, and procedural code, software designers will think about objects and how the objects can be accessed and modified. Some objects will become highly complex, because they are built out of objects that are built out of objects and so on. Repositories with vast numbers of object designs will become available. Designers will have tools for finding the necessary object types and reusing and extending their behavior as appropriate. Analysts will create diagrams of events, triggers, and operations that cause objects to behave in certain ways. Business people will learn to think in terms of events, triggers, and operations that change the state of objects. Databases will contain complex objects and allow them to be manipulated only with specifically defined operations. This will help prevent misuse of data or violations of integrity.

The *methods* that objects use should be created with powerful techniques, such as declarative statements, decision tables, diagrams, rule-based inferencing, nonprocedural languages, and CASE-tool code generators.

Client-server techniques will allow objects to interact with other objects in separate machines. Object-oriented design is the key to massively distributed computing.

TAKING THE BLINDERS OFF

Software developers often become deeply immersed in one technology. They have such interesting and difficult problems to solve with that technology that they do not have time to learn other software technologies. They are like horses going around with blinders on. We talk about COBOL bigots, information engineering bigots, LISP bigots, professors who understand only formal methods, and so on. The bigots of one technology often pour scorn on the other technologies. What we need for a software industrial revolution is integration of killer technologies, not isolated bigots. This requires vision and education. We must constantly ask: How do we educate the blindered specialists? Software developers need to be moved from one technology to another, so that they grasp the power of integrating technologies.

Many of the early CASE tools were built *without* an understanding of object-oriented technologies. Today, the combination of object-oriented techniques with I-CASE and repository-based development can clearly change the world of software development. Similarly, fourth-generation languages and nonprocedural languages were built without an object-oriented viewpoint. These languages could be more powerful if redesigned for object-oriented development.

The inferencing tools of the artificial-intelligence community evolved from *rule-based* to *frame-based,* where a frame is, essentially, an object type and the *methods* used by the object type are those of rule processing.

The early client-server software was primarily built without object-oriented techniques. It is now clear that the best—and in the long run perhaps the only practical—way to organize client-server interaction is with object-oriented design. An object from the client software sends a request to an object from the server software, and the latter executes one or more methods and responds.

The CASE repository is vitally important for integrating the various tools. The repository itself is (or should be) an object-oriented database. Even tools that do not support object-oriented analysis and design employ an object-oriented repository. Such repositories will contain objects of ever-increasing complexity as objects are built out of other objects, that in turn can be built of other objects.

The corporate I.S. (Information Systems) organization has a variety of tools and techniques available to obtain the advantages of OO analysis and development. Currently, none of the tools are perfect or fully integrated, but some spectacular examples exist of success with OO methodologies. Exciting new OO-CASE tools have immense potential, and can evolve greatly, with growing libraries of objects and templates.

The object-oriented viewpoint is a major paradigm shift, requiring system developers to think about the world in a different way. The diagrams used should be a natural extension of what is already familiar.

The main obstacle is people—not tools. A major effort is needed to reeducate the I.S. professionals, so that they understand the advantages and employ the techniques. The move to OO, with widespread reusability of design and code generation, must be made by management. Reaping the benefits of OO techniques requires management understanding and commitment.

ALL TYPES OF COMPUTING

Object-oriented techniques are sometimes thought of in terms of what can be done with OO programming languages, such as C++ and Smalltalk. This is too restricted a viewpoint. Methods can be created with *any* appropriate technique. Sometimes, procedural languages, such as C, COBOL, and FORTRAN, are used. At other times, nonprocedural languages, such as SQL and report generators, are appropriate. Functional languages, such as LISP, solve other problems. Methods may also be implemented with an inference engine and rule-based processing or the techniques of artificial intelligence and PROLOG. Methods may be diagrammed with either action diagrams or declarative techniques.

The object-oriented approach can encompass all of the other techniques for programming. In general, the most powerful techniques must be used, which usually means employing a CASE tool for analysis and design with an integrated code generator and perhaps an inference engine.

Object-oriented programming has substantially improved software development, but does not *by itself* bring the massive improvement needed by the computer industry. Object-oriented techniques must be combined with every aspect of software automation available.

OO techniques will change

- the entire software industry
- the way application packages are sold
- the way we use computers
- the way we use networks
- the way we analyze systems
- the way we design systems
- the way we use CASE tools
- the way we re-engineer corporations
- the job of all I.S. professionals

THE INTEGRATING PARADIGM

The software industrial revolution will gain power as object-oriented techniques spread, and we have large libraries of object classes. The libraries will link to CASE repositories so that new classes can be quickly assembled from existing classes. Most software tools will shift to using the object-oriented paradigm.

While this software revolution gathers momentum, we will see parallel computers spreading—machines with not one but many processors. A desktop workstation should have many processor chips. A LAN (local area network) server should use parallel processing. Mainframes and supercomputers will eventually be highly parallel machines.

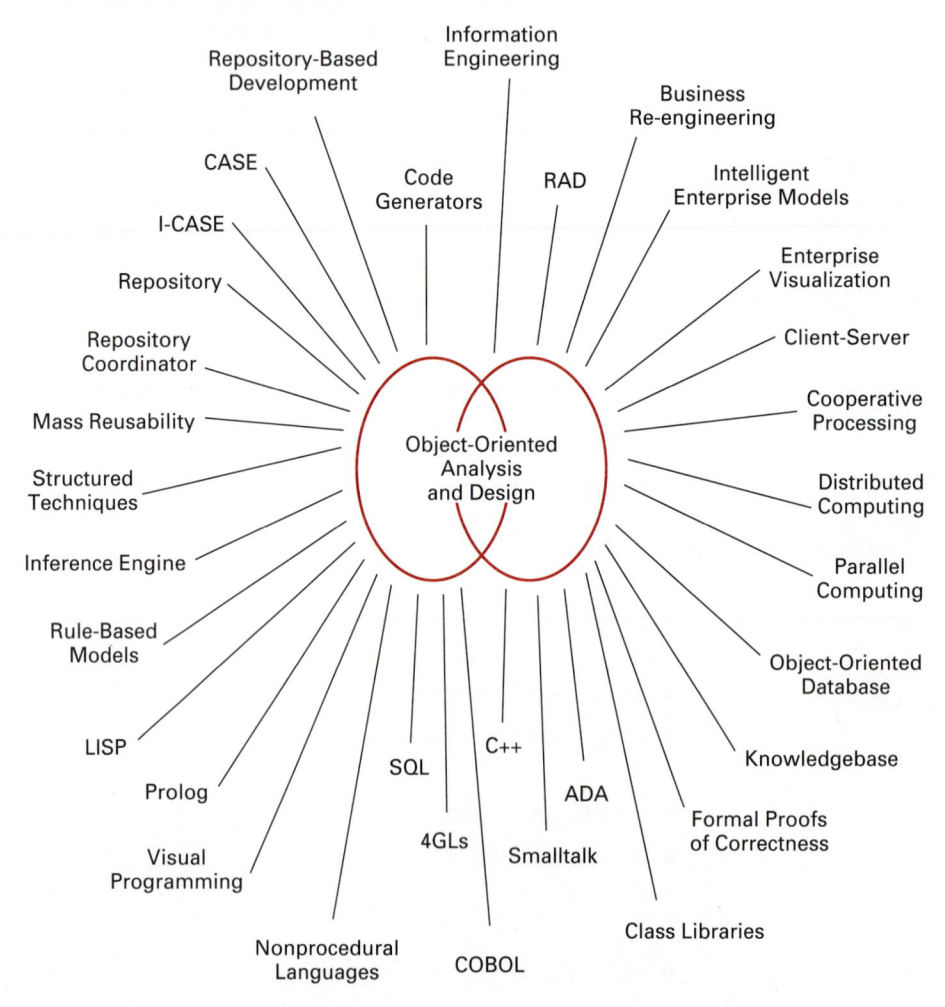

Figure 1.3 Object-oriented analysis and design should integrate and be used with the other powerful software technologies.

Object-oriented software will allow separate objects to run on separate processors simultaneously. Object-oriented design, with CASE tools and code generators, is the key to building software for powerful parallel machines.

Object-oriented analysis and design is a general way of viewing software that will integrate all of the killer technologies (shown in Fig. 1.3) and make them more effective. This integration will cause a software industrial revolution. As this is recognized, the software industry will build the tools and standards that facilitate the integration. The sooner object-oriented analysis and design become widespread, the sooner software creation will progress from a cottage industry to an engineering discipline.

> Object-oriented modeling and design are an integrating paradigm that should tie together all the powerful tools and techniques for software creation.

Object-oriented analysis and design are fundamentally different from structured analysis and design. Given their power and potential, their use must soon become widespread. To make this happen, OO techniques should be made compatible with what most systems analysts already know and practice. Powerful tools are needed to speed acceptance. The OO standards emerging from the Object Management Group (discussed in Chapter 21) should become widely understood. Much education is needed to spread the best techniques as stated in the manifesto in Box 1.2.

We need to build software as complex and trustworthy as jumbo jets or the worldwide telephone network and as rich as a legal library or an art historian's archives. One day, software of vast complexity, flexibility, and richness will be delivered on gigabyte optical disks. This software should be developed with object-oriented analysis and design.

Many computer industry authorities have failed to understand the power of OO technology. Some (including high-powered advisors to the Department of Defense) are saying that OO techniques are the latest fad. To the contrary, OO techniques are a fundamental way of thinking and will change the whole computer industry. The Object-Oriented Manifesto in Box 1.2 should be widely publicized.

REFERENCES

1. Martin, James. Videotape. James Martin Insights, Naperville, IL, 1991.
2. Object Management Group, *The OMG Object Model,* OMG Document Number 91.9.1.

BOX 1.2   An Object-Oriented Manifesto

- All computer analysts and designers should be trained in OO techniques.
- All universities, technical colleges, and business schools should teach OO thinking.
- All organizations involved with software should fully support the evolving standards from the Object Management Group.
- All CASE tool vendors should upgrade their tools to support OO modeling, design, and code generation.
- Repository standards should evolve to support OO modeling, design, and code generation.
- There should be industrywide acceptance of the OO diagramming standards described in this book (see Appendix).
- All enterprises with an I.S. organization should create OO models of their operations with a view toward thorough redesign of business processes and better communication between I.S. and business people.
- Software vendors should evolve rapidly toward distributed object architectures.
- Software vendors should cooperate to create reusable class libraries and multivendor software (as opposed to monolithic software).

2 BASIC CONCEPTS

The fundamental ideas that underlie object-oriented technology include

- Objects and classes (a class being the implementation of an object type)
- Methods
- Requests
- Inheritance
- Encapsulation

These notions, described in this chapter, are the basis of object-oriented software.

WHAT IS AN OBJECT? From a very early age, we form concepts. Each concept is a particular idea or understanding we have of our world. The concepts we acquire allow us to make sense of and reason about the things in our world. These things to which our concepts apply are called *objects*. An object might be real or abstract, such as the examples below:

- an invoice
- an organization
- a shape in a program for drawing (such as MacDraw)
- a screen with which a user interacts
- a field or node on the screen of a CASE tool
- a mechanism in a robotic device
- an entire engineering drawing

- a component on an engineering drawing
- a grouping of text and pictures used in a newspaper layout
- an airplane
- an airline reservation
- an airline flight
- an icon on a screen that a user points to and "opens"
- an order-filling process

In OO analysis and design, we are interested in the behavior of the object. If we are building software, OO software modules are based on object types. The software implementing the object contains data structures and operations that express the behavior of the object. The operations are coded as *methods*. The OO software representation of the object is thus a collection of *data types and methods,* packaged together.

> An *object* is any thing, real or abstract, about which we store data and those operations that manipulate the data.

An object may be composed of other objects. These objects, in turn, may be composed of objects—just as a machine is composed of subassemblies and its subassemblies composed of other subassemblies. This intricate structure of objects allows very complex objects to be defined.

WHAT IS AN OBJECT TYPE?

The concepts we possess apply to specific kinds of objects. For example, **Employee** applies to those objects that are persons employed by some organization. An instance of **Employee** is one specific person. In object-oriented analysis, these concepts are called *object types;* their instances are called *objects*.

> An *object type* is a category of object.
> An *object* is an instance of an object type.

The database world defines *entity types* such as **Customer, Employee,** and **Part.** There are many *instances* of each entity type. For example, *instances* of **Employee** are Fred Collins, Margot Finkelstein, and so on. Similarly, the object-oriented world defines *object types* and *instances* of object types. For example, an object type might be **Invoice** and an *object* might be Invoice #51783.

The term object, however, is fundamentally different from the term entity. *Entity* is concerned merely with the data. We typically store one record only for each entity. *Object* is concerned with both the data and the methods with which the data is manipulated. The data for one object may include multiple, associated record types. In the OO world, the data structure and operations for each object type are packaged together. The data structure cannot be accessed or manipulated except with the operations that are part of the object type.

OPERATIONS

Operations are used to read or manipulate the data of an object. The operations in an object type reference *only* the data structures of that object type. They should not directly access the data structures of another object. To use the data structure of another object, they must send a message to that object.

An object is thus a *thing* with its properties represented by data types and its behavior represented by operations.

An operation associated with the object type Invoice might be one that computes the total of an invoice. Another might transmit the invoice to a customer. Another might check periodically to see whether the invoice has been paid and add interest to it if it has not.

METHODS

When operations are encoded in software, they are referred to as *methods*.

> *Methods* specify the way in which operations are encoded in software.

ENCAPSULATION

Packaging data and operations together is called *encapsulation*. The object hides its data from other objects and allows the data to be accessed via its own operations. This is called *information hiding*. Encapsulation protects an object's data from corruption. If all programs could access the data in any way users wished, the data could easily be corrupted or misused. Encapsulation protects the object's data from arbitrary and unintended use.

Encapsulation hides the details of its internal implementation from the users of an object. Users understand what operations may be requested of the object but do not know the details of how the operation is performed. All the specifics of the object's data and the coding of its operations are tucked out of sight.

> *Encapsulation* is the result (or act) of hiding the implementation details of an object from its user.

Encapsulation is important, because it separates how an object behaves from how it is implemented. This allows object implementations to be modified without requiring the applications that use them to be modified also.

It is easier to modify programs using encapsulation, because one object type is modified at a time. If an object type is changed, only the operations and data structures associated with that object type are affected and usually only *some* of those operations and data structures. The object type's behavior can be changed and tested, independently of other object types.

Figure 2.1 illustrates an object. The data structure at the center can be used only with the operations in the outer ring.

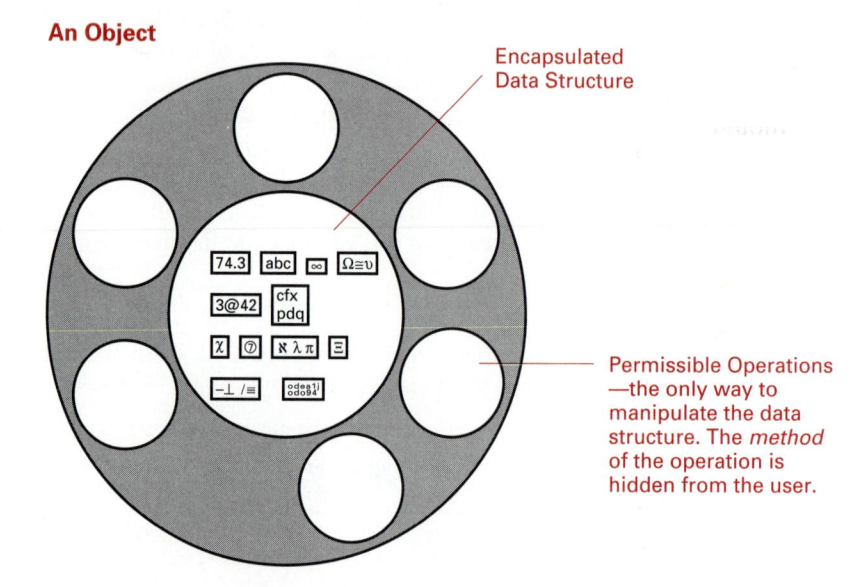

An Object

Figure 2.1 Each object encapsulates a data structure and operations. A *data structure* is at the core of an object. The object is manipulated by *operations* that implement permitted operations. The data structure may be used *only* with those methods. This restriction of access is called *encapsulation.* Encapsulation protects the data from corruption.

A VCR (video cassette recorder) is an example of an object. It has certain specified types of behavior. A **Sony AH-8500 VCR** is an *object type,* and an individual machine might be an *instance of this type.* All machines of that type have the same *operations.* The VCR contains many complex components most of which themselves contain components, but you do not need to know about them.

The electronics or its data cannot be accessed directly. (It states CAUTION. DO NOT OPEN, RISK OF ELECTRIC SHOCK.) You can use only the specified operations. Encapsulation prevents interference with the internals and also hides the complexity of the components. You are concerned only with the behavior of the VCR as described in its manual.

This object type has many operations, such as playback, recording, loading and unloading a cassette, setting the timer, audio dubbing, and tape counter functions. The data in the object cannot be used except with these operations. Telephone messages cannot be recorded on the VCR or its timer used to work the coffee machine.

REQUESTS

To make an object do something, we send it a *request*. This request causes an operation to be invoked. The operation performs the appropriate method and, optionally, returns a response. The message that constitutes the request contains the name of the object, the name of an operation, and sometimes a group of parameters.

Object-oriented programming is a form of modular design in which the world is thought of in terms of objects, operations, methods, and messages passed among those objects as illustrated in Fig. 2.2. A message is a *request* to carry out the indicated *operation* on a given object and return the result. Consequently, OO implementations refer to messages as *requests*.

> A *request* asks that a specified operation be invoked using one or more objects as parameters.

Objects can be very complex, because objects can be built of other objects, these in turn can be built out of other objects, and so on. Someone using the object does not need to know its internal complexity, only how to communicate with it and how it responds.

For example, you may communicate with your VCR by sending it *requests* from a hand-held controller. It responds by taking some action and displaying responses on its display. All objects of the type **Sony AH-8500 VCR** are controlled using the same kind of *interface*. The requests from your hand-held controller will not communicate with a **JVC HR-S6600 VCR**, because it requires a different type of interface.

A user of an office tool can mouse-click on the icon that represents an address-book object. The object responds by displaying a scrollable list of names on the screen. The user can employ different operations for interacting with this list—scrolling to a portion of the list and pointing to a particular person's name. The software then highlights the name. At this point, the user may request the person's address, add information, or drag the name across the screen to a telephone icon, thereby requesting the software to look up the phone number and dial it.

When object X sends a request to object Y, an operation of object X invokes an operation of object Y resulting in the data of object Y being manipulated in some way. Object Y may then return a value to object X.

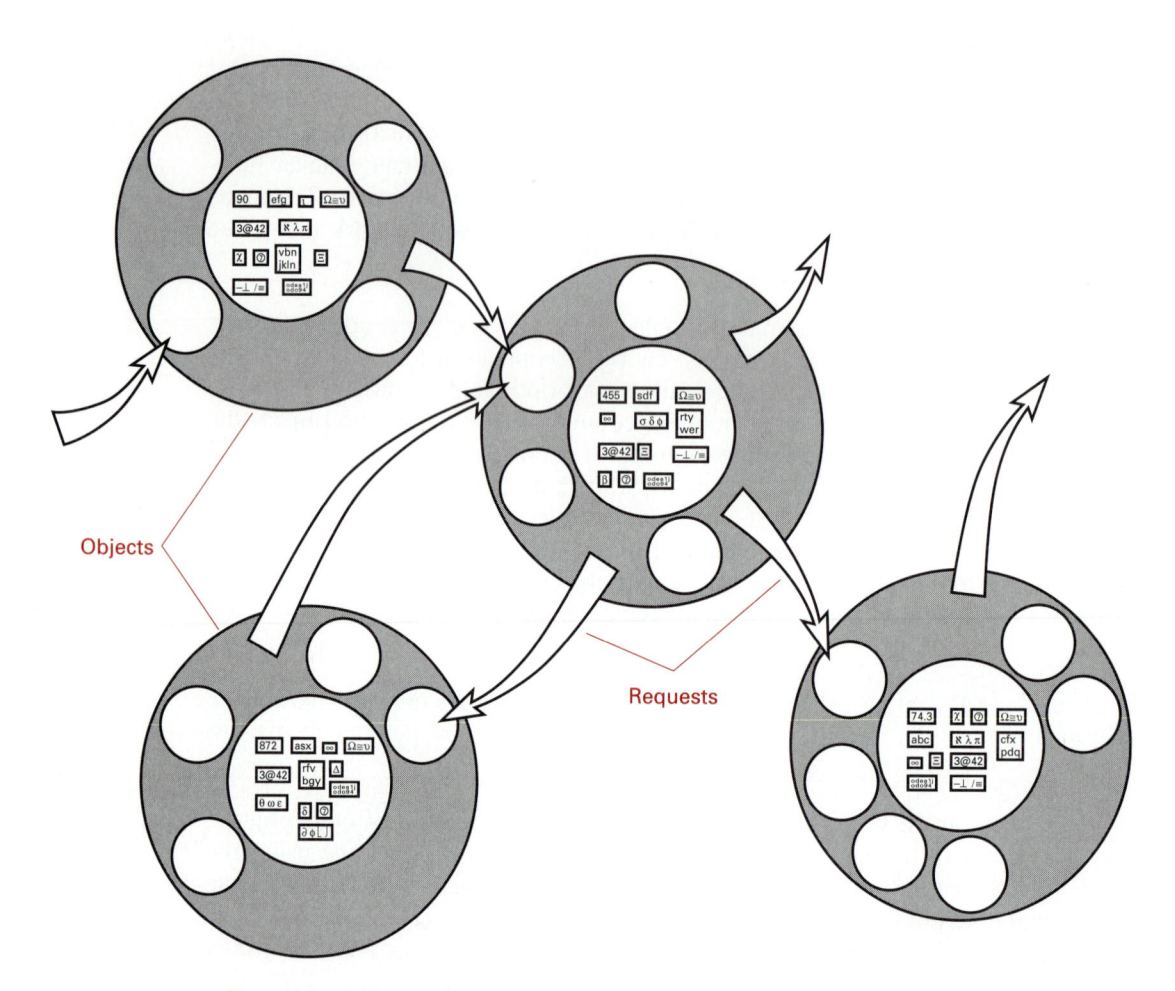

Figure 2.2 Objects communicate with requests. A *request* is a message specifying that an indicated operation be carried out using one or more objects—and, optionally, returning a result.

For example, consider an instance of the object type **Cylinder**. We can send a request to obtain the height of a **Cylinder** object. The height operation returns its stored height value. Additionally, we can send a request to obtain the **Cylinder** object's volume. The volume operation uses the following method to compute and return the object's **volume** value:

PI * CYLINDER.RADIUS**2 * CYLINDER.HEIGHT.

A request to a **Portfolio** object might be for its current valuation, and an operation for accomplishing this computation is invoked.

A request to a robot vehicle might be

VEHICLE 71 MOVE TO BIN 18.

Here the object is Vehicle 71, the operation is Move To, and the parameter for that method is Bin 18.

Some of the newer OO implementations paraphrase this request in a different manner:

MOVE TO (VEHICLE 71, BIN 18).

In this way, a request is not a message restricted *to* one recipient object but *for* multiple objects. Therefore, the user is not required to know which object is the recipient and which are the supporting parameters.

BLOBs   Today's computers can store large strings of bits that represent images, diagrams, speech, or possibly music or video. These are objects referred to with the acronym BLOB (Binary Large OBject). BLOBs have operations which enable them to be displayed or used. Compaction techniques are used, for example, so that images or sound can be stored in a smaller number of bits. The BLOB may have operations that enable it to be displayed on different screens. It may have operations for security, such as enciphering and deciphering. In image processing, images may be processed with low resolution when searching for an image, and with high resolution for final display.

The growing acceptance of image processing will increase the importance of object-oriented databases that can handle large binary objects efficiently. We will send requests to BLOBs telling them to display themselves, encipher themselves, link together for editing, and so on. In an OO database, an Invoice could be maintained in a handwritten graphic form along with the customer's spoken instructions—as well as an alphanumeric record. The handwritten graphic image is one object; the spoken instructions is another object; the alphanumeric record yet another. Together, they can compose a single Invoice object.

WHAT IS A CLASS?   The term *class* refers to the software implementation of an object type.

Object type is a conceptual notion. It specifies a family of objects without stipulating *how* they are implemented. Object types are specified during OO analysis. The details of *classes* are determined in OO design.

In the Modula programming language, object types are implemented as *modules,* while Ada uses the word *package.* In object-oriented languages, object types are implemented as *classes.*

> A *class* is an implementation of an object type. It has a *data structure* and *methods* that specify the operations which may be used with that data structure.

The class implementation specifies the data structure for each of its objects (see Fig. 2.1). For example, an **Employee** class might include data about exemptions, position, salary, phone extension, and so on. In addition, each class defines a set of permissible operations that allow access to and modification of object data. An **Employee** class might include operations such as hire, promote, and change phone extension for an **Employee** class. Details of the class include the specification of each *method*. The term *method,* then, refers to the specification that describes an operation.

Figure 2.1 draws an object as though the operation were part of an object. In software, the method is stored once, and all objects of a given class share it.

We need large *libraries of classes* that can be employed by an analyst or designer.

INHERITANCE

A high-level concept can be specialized into lower-level concepts. An object type can have subtypes. For example, the object type **Person** may have subtypes **Civilian** and **Military Person**. **Military Person** may have subtypes **Officer** and **Enlisted Person**. **Officer** may have subtypes **Lieutenant**, **Captain**, and **Major** and also subtypes such as **Marine** or **Engineer**, and **Officer on Active Service** or **Officer on nonActive Service**. There is a hierarchy of object types, subtypes, sub-subtypes, and so on.

A class implements the object type. A subclass *inherits* properties of its parent class; a sub-subclass inherits properties of the subclasses, and so on. The subclass inherits data types and methods—it also has methods and sometimes data types of its own.

Figure 2.3 shows a class and subclass. The subclass has the same methods as its superclass but also has method G. Sometimes, a class inherits properties of more than one superclass. This is called *multiple inheritance.*

PERCEPTION AND REALITY

With software we play games with reality. We can make something appear to have a certain behavior when in reality it is different. We can create a simple interface to something complex and hide the complexity.

The term *transparent* is used to mean that something appears not to exist when, in fact, it does. Many of the complex mechanisms in data storage or transmission are hidden, so that the programmers do not have to understand or even know about them. Programmers can use a logical record, for example, in which

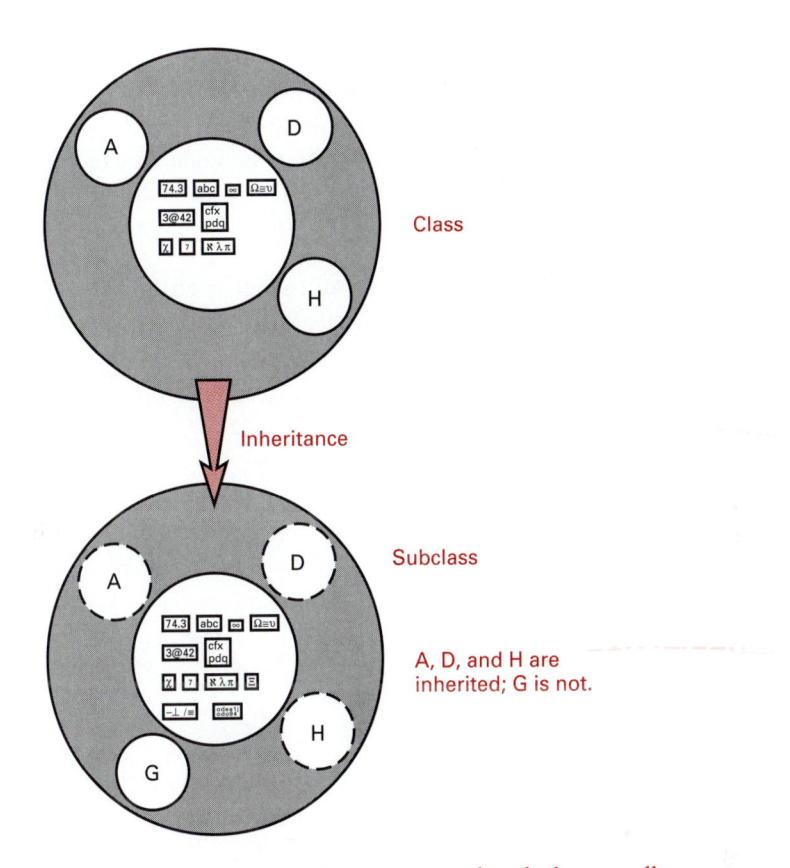

Figure 2.3 A class can have its own data structure and methods—as well as inherit them from its superclass.

some fields may be hidden, and the complexities of the physical structure are hidden.

Conversely, when the word *virtual* is used to refer to storage, transmission circuits, and other facilities, it indicates that a specified item *appears* to exist to the programmer or user when, in reality, it does not exist in that form. We talk about virtual storage and virtual circuits.

> Something *virtual* appears to exist but in reality does not.
>
> Something *transparent* appears not to exist when in reality it does.

In OO implementations, an object is perceived as being a package of data and operations that can be performed on these data. It encapsulates the data and operations. Reality is different. The procedures are not stored in each object. This would be very wasteful, because the same procedure would have to be stored many times. Instead, the software examines each request that refers to an object and has a selection mechanism for finding the code to execute. The *method* is part of the class—not part of the *object.* The method may not even be part of the class; it may be part of a higher-level class in the class hierarchy. The software can find it.

Figure 2.4 illustrates the difference between how we perceive objects and how the software actually operates. Only by using transparent and virtual

When a request is received, the software determines what objects it refers to and what methods will be used.

The user of an object perceives it as a package of data and procedures that can be performed on those data. It appears as though the object does its own thing.

Encapsulated Data Structure

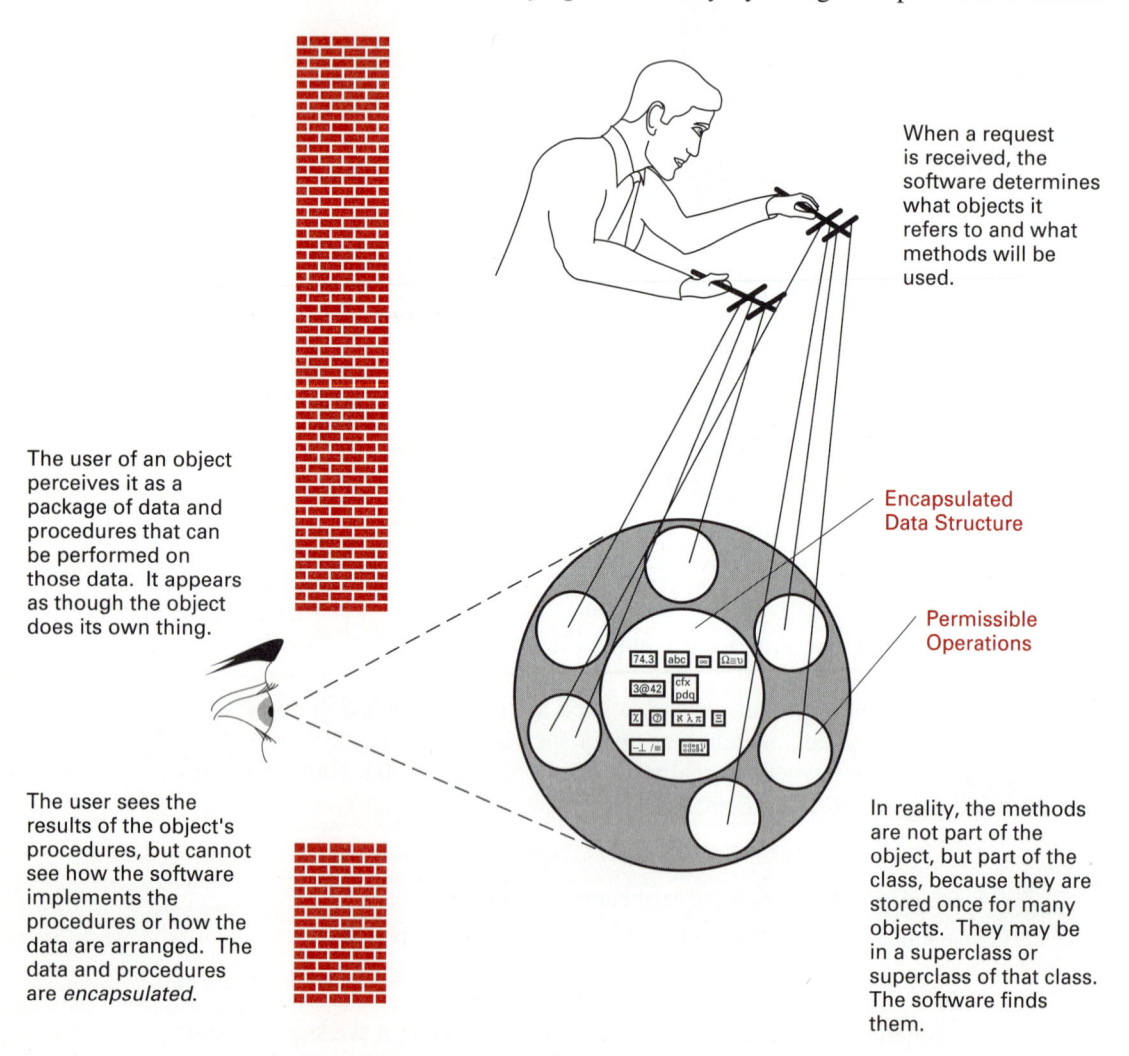

Permissible Operations

The user sees the results of the object's procedures, but cannot see how the software implements the procedures or how the data are arranged. The data and procedures are *encapsulated.*

In reality, the methods are not part of the object, but part of the class, because they are stored once for many objects. They may be in a superclass or superclass of that class. The software finds them.

Figure 2.4 The difference between how we may perceive objects and how the software operates.

Chap. 2   Basic Concepts   27

mechanisms can we succeed in building structures of the complexity we need.

Objects may communicate with objects: existing in one software package or in different packages; located in a processor or multiple processors; or scattered across a worldwide network (see Fig. 2.5). Programmers need not know the

We perceive object-oriented software as consisting of objects receiving requests and sending responses. The request specifies what objects are to carry out what operations.

Objects may be
• in the same software module
• in separate software modules
• on separate processors
• on separate machines
• scattered across a worldwide network

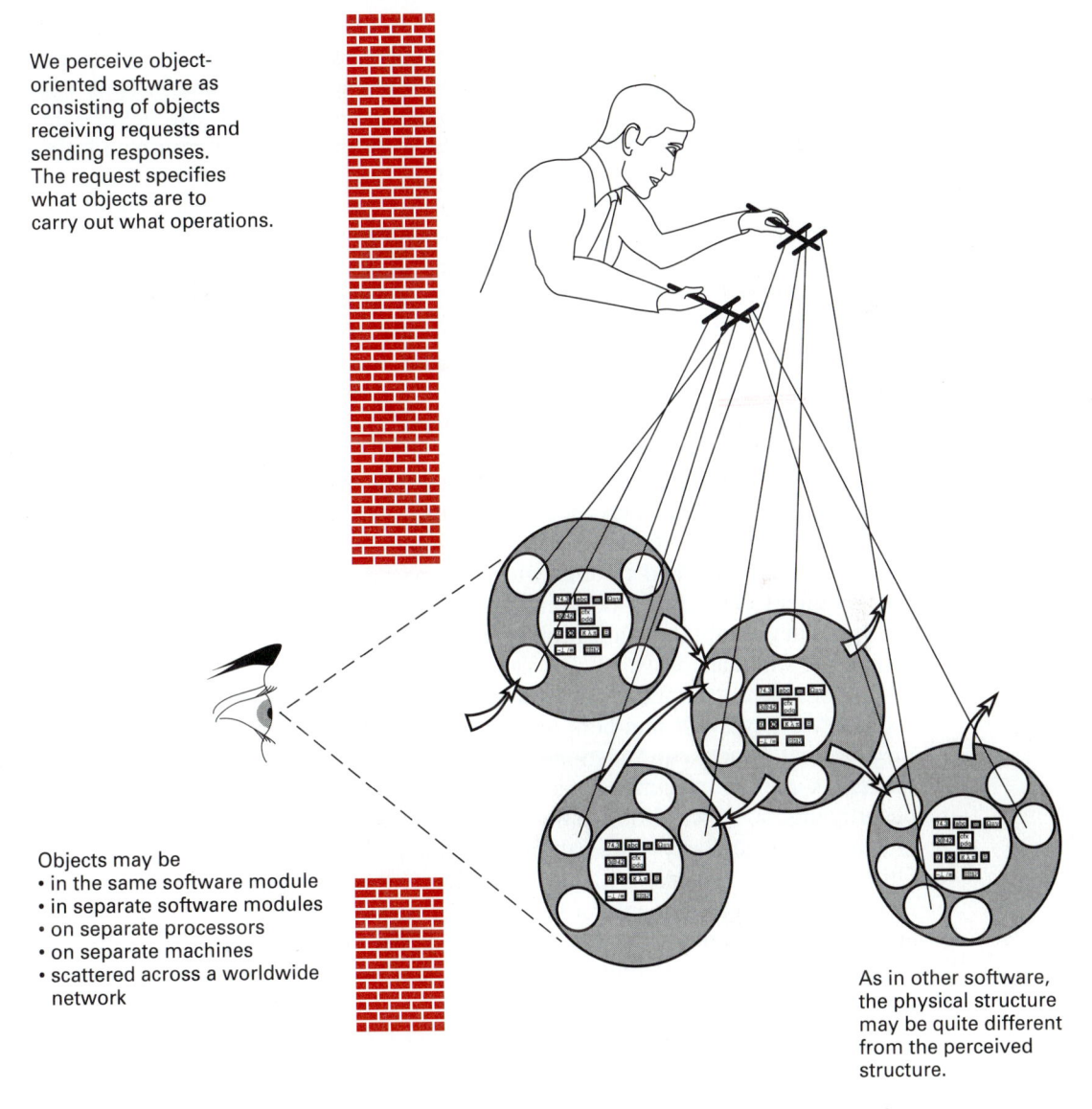

As in other software, the physical structure may be quite different from the perceived structure.

Figure 2.5 We often perceive that objects communicate. In reality, the OO software's selection mechanism handles requests for operations on specific objects.

object's location. They merely send a request to the object and receive a response.

SELF-CONTAINED CREATURES

Some academics insist that we should avoid anthropomorphic analogies for describing software. Software, after all, has no resemblance to biological things. Dijkstra recommends that faculty members be fined $5 each time they use anthropomorphic terminology [2]. However, teaching without analogy is as sterile as making films without editing. Analogies based on nature can help beginners to grasp a strange-sounding subject. So here is an analogy that could give Dijkstra a heart attack.

Think of an object as a little creature that has only one purpose in life; to apply certain methods to a specified collection of data. The creature protects its data with a vengeance, not allowing anyone to access the data except with the creature's methods.

The creature only goes into action when it receives a correctly formatted message. The message tells it what operation to use and may specify parameters. The creature performs its function and sends a message back. In a complex system, many different creatures are all doing their own thing.

There are many different types of creatures. Several different types of creatures all share the properties of a higher-level type. There are subtle variations of types just as there are in a taxonomy of plants.

Some creatures work in the same computer, waiting their turn to be active. Some work in networked systems where a server creature can operate at the same time as client creatures in different machines. We are beginning to use parallel (concurrent) computers in which many creatures can be active on different processors simultaneously.

If we have vast numbers of these creatures, how do we organize them? In society, we have vast numbers of humans, and we devise ways of organizing them so that society can function—some are factory workers, some are decision makers, some are executives, and some are police. Just as we put humans into departments, so we can arrange our creatures into groups in which a collection of creatures together carry out a particular function. The group is a high-level class. Other creatures interact with this class as a whole, sending it messages and receiving messages. An enterprise has many departments. People outside of the enterprise do not know how it is structured; they request the enterprise as a whole to do something. The enterprise is complex, but outsiders can interact with it by using its catalog, placing orders, and so on.

Creatures are organized into groups, and groups are organized into entire applications. Each creature is self-contained. It executes its methods when asked without knowing why and without knowing the consequences.

As we design distributed computing, we ask: What creatures and groupings of creatures should work on what machine? When one object sends requests to another object, it does not know where that object is. It could be on the same machine or a different machine. We should usually not split a low-level object, so that its methods and data are on different machines. A high-level object may be composed of objects that *are* on different machines.

NATURE'S BUILDING BLOCKS
David Taylor points out that object-oriented design reflects the techniques of nature [3]. All living things are composed of cells. Cells are organized packages that—just as objects—combine related information and behavior. Information is contained in the DNA and protein molecules within the nucleus of the cell. The methods of the cell are carried out by structures outside the nucleus.

The cell is surrounded by a membrane that both protects and hides the internal workings of the cell from outside intrusion. Cells cannot read *each other's* protein molecules or control *each other's* structures; they can only read and control their own. Instead, they send chemical requests to one another. By packaging the information and behavior in this way, the cell is encapsulated.

Taylor comments: "This message-based communication greatly simplifies the way cells function . . . . The membrane hides the complexity of the cell and presents a relatively simple interface to the rest of the organism . . . . As you can see from the structure of the cell, *encapsulation* is an idea that's been around for a very long time."

Cells are a remarkably universal building block in nature. There are blood cells that transport chemicals, bone cells, brain cells, cells that make the eye retina work, and muscle cells that distort their shape to perform mechanical functions. The components of plants, insects, fish, and mammals are all built of cells that have a common structure and operate according to certain basic principles. All software could, in principle, be similarly built out of classes. Although cells are enormously diverse, many cells, like objects, are of similar types. One type of cell may operate in a way similar to another type, because both have inherited similar properties in evolution. Cells are grouped together into organs, such as muscles or toenails. Organs are grouped together into systems, such as the cardiovascular system.

An organism is composed of multiple systems. Although part of a complex organism, each cell acts on its own, like an object, without knowing the reason why a message was sent to it or the eventual consequences of its behavior.

The computerized enterprise is like an electronic organism. It will increasingly need complex software composed of vast numbers of objects. We need to analyze complex application areas in terms of the objects they employ and the behavior of object types.

In analyzing an enterprise, we create an *enterprise model*. At a high level, this model reflects the individual business areas. If the enterprise model is built with an object-oriented viewpoint, we ask what its object types are and specialize them into subtypes, sub-subtypes, and so on. Business rules are associated with the object types, expressing how we want the enterprise to behave.

The object types can be implemented as *classes*. Lower-level subclasses *inherit* behavior from higher-level classes. The classes *encapsulate* behavior, rather like biological cells encapsulating behavior. The electronic enterprise has many different encapsulated classes, linked with enterprisewide networks like a creature's nervous system.

We thus progress from a model of the enterprise with object types to a working software implementation of those object types. The classes representing object types are *active* and automatically execute their methods when requests are sent to them. Higher-level classes are composed of lower-level classes, just as the liver is composed of cells.

The world of the future will consist of millions of enterprises like electronic organisms, each with its nervous system linking thousands of computers with object-oriented databases and software that make objects respond to requests. The nervous system of one enterprise will interact directly with the nervous systems of many other enterprises with EDI (electronic data interchange) systems. EDI systems are evolving from batch interaction to real-time interaction.

Two trading partners both profit from real-time EDI interaction, so financial incentives will drive the rapid interlinking of corporate computer systems. The nervous systems are becoming worldwide, high-bandwidth, and intermeshed with one another.

In one way, objects are different from the creatures we describe or biological cells. They do not *each* contain their methods; the methods are kept centrally. There would be mass redundancy if each object contains its own methods, as cells do. The methods for the object are part of the *class*. We might regard the object as something we perceive—a virtual thing that packages data and methods. The actual implementation is different, because it avoids redundant storage of methods. But it is useful to think of objects as packages of behavior, like biological cells.

Such analogies break down when pushed too far. However, this somewhat cartoon-like description of object-oriented software enables us to discuss, in the next chapter, how its benefits will revolutionize the way we build systems.

REFERENCES

1. Cox, Brad J. and Andrew J. Novobilski, *Object-Oriented Programming: An Evolutionary Approach* (2nd edition), Addison-Wesley, Reading, MA, 1991.

2. Dijkstra, Edsger W., "On the Cruelty of Really Teaching Computing Science," *Communications of the ACM,* 32:12, December 1989, pp. 1398-1404.

3. Taylor, David A., *Object-Oriented Technology: A Manager's Guide,* Addison-Wesley, Reading, MA, 1991.

3 WHY OBJECT-ORIENTED?

Object-oriented techniques improve the capability of the computer professional in surprisingly diverse ways.

Recently, I conducted in-depth interviews on videotape with analysts and implementors who had become proficient with OO tools and techniques [4]. I asked all of them: "Why object-oriented?" "Why would you not consider going back to conventional techniques?" "Why should an enterprise go through the difficulties of changing to OO analysis and design?" Different professionals quoted completely different types of reasons why OO techniques made them more proficient. On the other hand, none of these professionals were achieving *all* of the major benefits. What made Mike so excited about object orientation had not been considered by Mary. What Chris said was the payoff was not on Karen's wishlist.

It is desirable to understand *all* of the potential benefits of OO techniques and attempt to achieve them *all* rather than just a subset. Driving for the entire family of benefits in this chapter is likely to change the way we manage development teams and I.S. organizations.

CHARACTERISTICS OF OO TECHNIQUES

OO analysis and design have several important characteristics:

1. They change the way we think about systems. The OO way of thinking is more natural for most people than the techniques of structured analysis and design. After all, the world consists of objects. We start to learn about them in infancy and discover that they have certain types of behavior. If we shake a rattle, it makes noise. From an early age we categorize objects as we discover their behavior. End users and business people think naturally in terms of objects, events, and triggers. We can create OO diagrams that business people can relate to, whereas they have difficulty with entity-relationship diagrams, structure charts, and data-flow diagrams.

2. Systems can often be built out of existing objects. This leads to a high degree of reusability, which saves money, shortens development time, and increases system reliability.
3. The complexity of the objects we can use continues to grow, because objects are built out of other objects. These in turn are built from objects, and so on.
4. OO techniques have a natural fit with CASE technology. Some elegant and powerful tools exist for OO implementation. Many other CASE tools need enhancing to support OO analysis and design.
5. The CASE repository should contain an ever-growing library of object types, some purchased and some built in-house. These object types are likely to become powerful as they grow in complexity. Most such object types will be designed so that they can be customized to the needs of different systems.
6. Creating systems that work correctly is easier with OO techniques. This is partly because of OO classes that are designed to be reused, and partly because classes are self-contained and neatly divided into methods. Each method is relatively easy to build, debug, and modify.
7. OO-CASE technology—with code generators that produce code for methods expressed through formal declaration—gives us the potential for engineering software of extremely high reliability.

SUMMARY OF THE BENEFITS OF OO TECHNOLOGY

Box 3.1 summarizes the many benefits of OO analysis and design.

BOX 3.1   Benefits of Object-Oriented Technology

Many of these benefits are realizable only when OO analysis and design are used with repository-based, OO-CASE tools that generate code.

- **Reusability.** Classes are designed so that they can be reused in many systems. To maximize reuse, classes can be built so that they can be customized. A repository should be populated with an ever-growing collection of reusable classes. Class libraries are likely to grow rapidly. A preeminent goal of OO techniques is achieving massive reusability in the building of software.
- **Stability.** Classes designed for repeated reuse become stable in the same way that microprocessors and other chips become stable. Applications are built from software chips where possible.
- **The designer thinks in terms of behavior of objects, not low-level detail.** Encapsulation hides the detail and makes complex classes easy to

BOX 3.1 *(Continued)*

use. Classes are like black boxes; the developer uses the black box and does not look inside it. He has to understand the behavior of the black box and how to communicate with it.

- **Objects of ever-growing complexity are built.** Objects are built out of objects, which in turn are built out of objects. Just as manufactured goods are constructed from a bill of materials of existing parts and subassemblies, so too is software created with a bill of materials of existing well-proven classes. This enables complex software components to be built which themselves become building blocks for more complex software.
- **Reliability.** Software built from well-proven stable classes is likely to have fewer bugs than software invented from scratch. Each method in a class is, by itself, relatively simple and can be designed to be reliable.
- **Verification of correctness.** OO design with formal techniques for the creation of methods can potentially generate software of high reliability. Techniques for verifying and guaranteeing the correct operation of a class are likely to emerge in a new generation of OO-CASE tools.
- **New software markets.** Software companies should provide libraries of classes for specific areas, easily adapted to the needs of the using organization. The era of monolithic packages is being replaced by software that incorporates classes and encapsulated packages from many different vendors.
- **Faster design.** Applications are created from preexisting components. Many components are built so that they can be customized for a particular design. The components can be seen, customized, and interlinked on the CASE tool screen.
- **Higher-quality design.** Designs are often of higher quality, because they are built from well-proven components which have been tested and polished repeatedly.
- **Integrity.** Data structures can be used only with specific methods. This is particularly important with client-server and distributed systems in which unknown users might try to access a system.
- **Easier programming.** Programs are built in small pieces each of which is generally easy to create. The programmer creates one method for one class at a time. The method changes the state of objects in ways that are usually simple when considered by themselves.
- **Easier maintenance.** The maintenance programmer usually changes one method of one class at a time. Each class performs its operations independently of other classes.

(Continued)

BOX 3.1 *(Continued)*

- **Inventability.** Implementors proficient with the most powerful OO-CASE tools, running on a workstation, find they can generate ideas rapidly. The tools encourage them to invent and rapidly implement their inventions. The brilliant individual can be much more creative.
- **Dynamic lifecycle.** The target of system development often changes during implementation. OO-CASE tools make midlifecycle changes easier. This enables implementors to meet end users better, adapt to changes in the business, refine goals as the system comes into sharper focus, and constantly improve the design during implementation.
- **Refinement during construction.** Creative people such as writers and playwrights constantly change the design of their work while implementing it. This leads to much better end results. The best creative works are refined over and over again. OO-CASE tools give software builders the capability to refine the design as they implement it.
- **More realistic modeling.** OO analysis models the enterprise or application area in a way that is closer to reality than conventional analysis. The analysis translates directly into design and implementation. In conventional techniques, the paradigm changes as we go from analysis to design and from design to programming. With OO techniques, analysis, design, and implementation use the same paradigm and successively refine it.
- **Better communication between I.S. professionals and business people.** Business people more easily understand the OO paradigm. They think in terms of events, objects, and business policies that describe the behavior of objects. OO methodologies encourage better understanding as the end users and developers share a common model.
- **Intelligent enterprise models.** Enterprise models should describe business rules with which executives want to run their business. These should be expressed in terms of events and how events change the state of business objects. Application designs should be derived with as much automation as possible from the business model.
- **Declarative specifications and design.** The specifications and design built with the formality of CASE tools should be declarative where possible—stating explicitly what is needed. This enables the designer to think like an end user rather than to think like a computer.
- **A user-seductive screen interface.** A graphic user interface should be used so that the user points at icons or pop-on menu items that relate to objects. Sometimes, the user can, in effect, see an object on the screen. To see and point is easier than to remember and type.

BOX 3.1 *(Continued)*

- **Images, video, and speech.** Binary large objects (BLOBs) are stored, representing images, video, speech, unformatted text, or other long bit streams. Methods such as compression or decompression, enciphering or deciphering, and presentation techniques are used with these objects.
- **Design independence.** Classes are designed to be independent of platforms, hardware, and software environments. They employ requests and responses of standard formats. This enables them to be used with multiple operating systems, database managers, network managers, graphic user interfaces, and so on. The software developer does not have to worry about the environment or wait until it is specified.
- **Interoperability.** Software from many different vendors can work together. One vendor uses classes from other vendors. A standard way exists of finding classes and interacting with classes. (The standards from the Object Management Group are discussed in Chapter 21.) Interoperability of software from many vendors is one of the most important goals of OO standards. Software developed independently in separate places should be able to work together and appear as a single unit to the user.
- **Client-server computing.** In client-server systems, classes in the client software should send requests to classes in the server software and receive responses. A server class may be used by many different clients. These clients can only access server data with the class methods. Hence, the data is protected from corruption.
- **Massively distributed computing.** Worldwide networks will employ software directories of accessible objects. Object-oriented design is the key to massively distributed computing. Classes in one machine will interact with classes elsewhere without knowing where the classes reside. They send and receive OO messages of standard format.
- **Parallel computing.** The speed of machines will be greatly enhanced by building parallel computers. Concurrent processing will take place on multiple processor chips simultaneously. (Eventually one chip will have many processors.) Objects on different processors will execute simultaneously, each acting independently. A standard Object Request Broker will enable classes on separate processors to send requests to one another.
- **A higher level of database automation.** The data structures in OO databases are linked to methods that take automatic actions. An OO database has intelligence built into it in the form of methods, whereas a basic relational database does not.

(Continued)

> **BOX 3.1** *(Continued)*
>
> - **Machine performance.** Object-oriented databases have demonstrated much higher performance than relational databases for certain applications with very complex data structures. This and concurrent computing with OO design jointly promise major leaps in machine performance. LAN-based client-server systems will employ server machines with concurrency and object-oriented databases.
> - **Migration.** Existing or non-OO applications can often be preserved by fitting them with an OO wrapper, so that communication with them is by standard OO messages.
> - **Better CASE tools.** CASE tools will use graphic techniques for designing classes and their interaction and for using existing objects adapted to new applications. The tools should facilitate modeling in terms of events, triggers, object states, and so on. OO-CASE tools should generate code as soon as classes are defined and allow the designer to use and test the methods created. The tools should be designed to encourage maximum creativity and continuous refinement of the design during construction.
> - **Industry class libraries.** Software companies sell libraries for different application areas. Application-independent class libraries are also important and these are best provided as a facility of CASE tools.
> - **Corporate class libraries.** Corporations should create their own libraries of classes that reflect their internal standards and application needs. The top-down identification of business objects is an important aspect of information engineering.

DIFFERENT BENEFITS

The benefits listed in Box 3.1 affect different types of developers in different ways. Let us examine the benefits as they might be perceived by five different types of I.S. professionals:

- A highly creative software inventor
- A software factory
- The corporate CIO
- An I.S. project team
- A systems integrator

A Highly Creative Software Inventor

Consider a brilliant, highly innovative, software builder. This person works alone at a powerful workstation using software creatively to solve problems. He would like a powerful toolset to help invent and generate code quickly. With an OO toolset, he can create object classes, add behavior, generate code immediately, and observe the application running. The application invention is constantly being modified. Object-oriented representation helps clarify the system being invented and makes it easy to modify or add.

If a professional programmer, the inventor might write code in C++ or Smalltalk. However, the most interesting software inventors should be people whose expertise lies in the application area rather than in professional programming. They do not want to code in C, C++, or languages of that detail. They want to create methods quickly with powerful techniques using pictures, tables, declarative statements, rules, and nonprocedural techniques. The code is created interpretively by the toolset as they add details to their application. Later, it is compiled for maximum speed. They want a rich set of classes that they can easily find and use, and customize when necessary. Some classes are application independent and many relate to the application area.

> The software inventor would like the OO-CASE toolset to generate code as fast as she can put ideas on the screen.

A Software Factory

A software factory is different from the lone inventor. The software factory requires teamwork and discipline. All the developers should share common I-CASE tools with a common repository. A powerful repository coordinator must enforce consistency with careful version control (see Chapter 18). The repository and its coordinator should be an object-oriented database.

The software factory needs to maximize reusability. It manages a library of reusable classes. Some developers create new classes, and they are measured on the reuse of what they build. Some developers employ classes, and they are measured on how they will reuse what exists. The software factory strives to make its reusable classes as stable as possible, so that bugs are rare and maintenance costs are minimized.

> To create rich and interesting products, the software factory needs to incorporate much software from other vendors into its designs.

The era of monolithic single-vendor software is coming to an end. Software builders should make use of existing software, where possible, standing on the shoulders of others. They would like this licensed software to be object-oriented and to obey standards (see Chapter 21). Standard requests and responses should be used for communication with classes.

The software factory should steadily increase the functionality of the classes it uses—building objects out of component objects. Stable classes of ever greater complexity are desirable and are built using both in-house components and those licensed from other companies. The software should be built independently of the environment—the operating system, LAN management, database management, user interface, and so on. It should be linkable to multiple environments by means of standard class requests and responses.

The Corporate CIO (Chief Information Officer)

The CIO's major concern is making the corporation more competitive by identifying ways to streamline and automate the corporation, cut costs, and improve customer service. Business windows of opportunity are shortening, and the CIO needs an environment in which new applications can be built and changed quickly.

The CIO uses information engineering to maintain a model of the enterprise [2]. Preferably, this would be an OO model that reflects the rules used to respond to events. The business area models are in an I-CASE repository (encyclopedia) used to help drive the design of systems. The OO approach makes the enterprise model understandable to business people and easy to modify when needed. OO diagrams facilitate more realistic modeling. Most corporations need re-engineering to be efficient with 1990s technology. A realistic OO enterprise model is needed to analyze and design the potential changes to the enterprise.

Most enterprises need redesign to make them more automated and competitive. This redesign needs a model of the enterprise that communicates as clearly as possible with the enterprise management.

The top-down approach of information engineering enables the identification of object classes that are reusable across the enterprise. Such classes are designed so that they can be adapted to specific needs. Systems are built with a RAD lifecycle by small teams with I-CASE tools linked to the corporate repository [3]. The teams employ reusable classes, either purchased or designed in the corporation.

> The goal is to assemble as many high-quality applications as possible from reusable parts and use a generator for all new code.

The CIO would like software companies to sell class libraries and application packages designed for OO usage, to reside in the corporate repository (encyclopedia).

To make the corporate systems as easy to use as possible the CIO would like a standard graphic user interface, such as the Macintosh, MOTIF, Windows, or IBM's graphical CUA. The screen icons and menu words should relate to objects in OO design.

An I.S. Project Team

An I.S. SWAT team is a small group that works and stays together, moving from one project to another [3]. It is highly skilled and has a repository-based, I-CASE toolset. Its goal is building very high-quality applications at high speed, constantly striving to improve its own measured performance. It can do this by growing its own collection of reusable classes and being skilled in using them.

A SWAT team using an OO-CASE toolset would like the up-front design thought out in terms of objects, methods, and events that trigger operations. (Many SWAT teams work today with non-OO-CASE tools and non-OO design.)

The SWAT team works with end users, showing them pieces of the application as it is built and making modifications if necessary.

> OO-CASE tools enable the SWAT team to continually adjust or redesign the application while it is being built to meet user needs as closely as possible.

The application should be delivered while the users are still excited about it, and there should be no surprises at cutover. The users know exactly what they are going to get.

A Systems Integrator

A systems integrator is concerned with building networked systems with machines and software from different vendors. A major problem is getting the software of different vendors to work together. Standards are now emerging for enabling the interoperation of classes from any vendor who conforms to the standards (see Chapter 21).

Object-oriented analysis and design are the best way to handle distributed computing for a variety of reasons. Separate machines should have separate objects and low-level objects should normally not be split between machines. A standard Object Request Broker [6] is desirable to interlink the classes—locating the classes and sending standard-format requests to them. Applications or software that are not object-oriented should have a wrapper put around them that makes them appear object-oriented to the Object Request Broker.

REUSABILITY

One of the most important benefits of OO is its high level of reusability.

One day we will have personal computers as powerful as HAL in Stanley Kubrick's movie 2001, but this will have little point if they run only spreadsheets. They will need software of immense functional richness. One day a hundred million lines of code will come with each personal computer. The cost of LOTUS 1-2-3 is currently close to $100 per line of code. A vital question for the software industry is: How do we create software of functional richness at a fraction of today's cost?

Software is expensive today because most programmers are reinventing something that has been invented a thousand times before. We must move to an era when developers design software in the way that electronic engineers design machines—from preexisting components some of which are very complex. It is appropriate to think about software "chips." Software components, like microchips, will be bought from other vendors. The software designer should have a large library of reusable components. The software you buy in ten years might, like your car, contain components from hundreds of vendors around the world.

> OO techniques enable us to achieve reusability in two ways. First, we build software out of components (classes) that already exist. Second, we create modified classes using inheritance which enables us to reuse the methods and data structures of high-level classes.

OO analysis, if done well, enables us to achieve a high degree of reuse. Several organizations have reported a level of reusability above 80 percent, using OO design and programming (i.e., less than 20 percent of the system code is new; the rest comes from reusable classes). The COOPERATION project in NCR attempted to push this number from 80 percent to 90 percent [1]. With careful management of the class library and good motivation by the developers with design reviews for reusability, 80 percent seems generally achievable. An overhead is required to achieve this level of reuse, but it results in faster, cheaper development and higher software quality.

Reusability is a management act. A development environment should be designed and tightly managed to achieve high reusability [4].

MORE LIKE HARDWARE ENGINEERING

OO techniques make software engineering more like hardware engineering in that software is built from existing components, where possible. Just as a hardware designer does not change a microchip, a software designer does not tamper with the software chips.

When people are first taught to program, their teacher usually tells them to think like a computer. This technique seemed to work when we learned programming, because we wrote very simple programs. However, loops and branches give us such a vast number of path combinations, that we cannot think like a computer about all of them. The operation of most real software depends on conditions that are not known until the software is running. With multiprocessing, the machinery is doing many things at once, and then to think like a computer becomes hopeless.

To help deal with the complexities, structured programming came into use. It reduced the spaghetti in code, but programming was still based on the expected sequence of executing instructions. The attempt to design and debug programs by thinking through the order in which the computer does things ultimately leads to software that nobody can fully understand. Thinking like a computer is well beyond our mental capabilities.

The world of object-oriented techniques carried out with repository-based CASE tools is different. The designer thinks in terms of objects and their behavior, and code is generated. The CASE tools and code generator must be bug free (so we have not eliminated all manual programming). However, most systems can be built without having to think about loops, branches, and program control structures. The system builder learns a different style of thinking. Events cause changes in the state of objects (as we will discuss later). Most of these state changes require small pieces of code, so coding is less error prone. Object types are built out of other object types. If an object type works well, the designer should treat it as a black box which he never looks inside (just as you never look inside your VCR). Software engineering then assumes more of the characteristics of hardware engineering.

ORDERLY BEHAVIOR

The problem with conventional programming is that it allows the programmer to do anything he wants. Data can assume any structure and processes can do anything to the data that the programmer desires. A branch instruction can link to far-away code and change variables. Any instruction in a computer can modify any location in the machine's memory. The number of path combinations exceeds any capability to test them all. The program becomes unpredictable and uncontrollable.

In object-oriented programming, each object is restricted to sending requests to other objects. An object receiving a request checks its validity and executes a method. Most methods are relatively simple and, by themselves, relatively easy to test.

To make the operation more reliable, we should create each method with techniques that help us to make it as trustworthy as possible. It should be created with a code generator, if possible, from declarative statements of rules, equations, database access, screen modification, report generation, and so on. The entire range of CASE code-generation techniques should be applied to creating methods (see Chapter 15).

Traditional engineering has enabled us to build machines of staggering complexity, such as jumbo jets, which are extremely trustworthy. This could only be done by building isolated components and then designing and testing each component thoroughly. Components are themselves built out of reliable components. If one component, such as the navigation system, had direct logical connections to another component, such as the landing gear, their unexpected interactions would probably cause undesirable effects. Each component must carry out its own tasks independently. It can then be tested and made trustworthy. Parts are separated to ensure that no unexpected interactions occur. Conventional programs, however, are rife with unexpected interactions that are difficult to trace and eliminate. OO techniques remove much of this problem.

The contrast between process orientation and object orientation can be summarized in the following way. Conventional data processing focuses on the types of processes that manipulate types of data. Object orientation focuses on the types of objects whose data structure can be manipulated only with the methods of the object class. Events occur that change the state of an object. Each state change is usually simple to program by itself, so we divide programming into relatively simple pieces. Each object, in effect, performs a specific function independently of other objects. It responds to requests, not knowing why the request was sent or what the consequences of its action will be. Because objects act individually, each class can be changed largely independently of other classes. This makes the class relatively easy to test and modify. Maintenance of object-oriented systems is much easier than maintenance of conventional systems.

The object-oriented world is more disciplined than that of conventional structured techniques. It leads to a world of reusable classes, where much of the software construction process will be the assembly of existing well-proven classes.

RELIABILITY NEEDS SIMPLICITY

One important way to achieve reliability is to pursue the utmost simplicity. Spaghetti code, convoluted designs, and clever deviations from basic structures almost always result in loss of reliability. Testing is difficult and subtle errors lurk in supposedly debugged code.

OO programming consists of *methods* each of which changes the state of one object type. Each *method*, by itself, is simple and easy to test, with some exceptions.

PROGRAM COMPLEXITY METRICS

Program complexity is a measure of program understandability. The more complex a program, the more difficult it is to understand. Program complexity is a function of the number of possible execution paths in a program and the difficulty of tracing paths. Avoiding unnecessary complexity improves program reliability and reduces the effort needed to develop and maintain a program.

The McCabe Cyclomatic Complexity Metric, named after its creator, is the most widely used measurement of complexity. It has measured programs written in languages such as FORTRAN, COBOL, PL/1, C, and Pascal. It has been automated by many re-engineering and CASE tools. Cyclomatic complexity is a graph-theoretic complexity measure that is based on counting the number of individual logic paths contained in the program. For example, the small program shown in Fig. 3.1 has three possible logic paths depending on the IF-statement conditions.

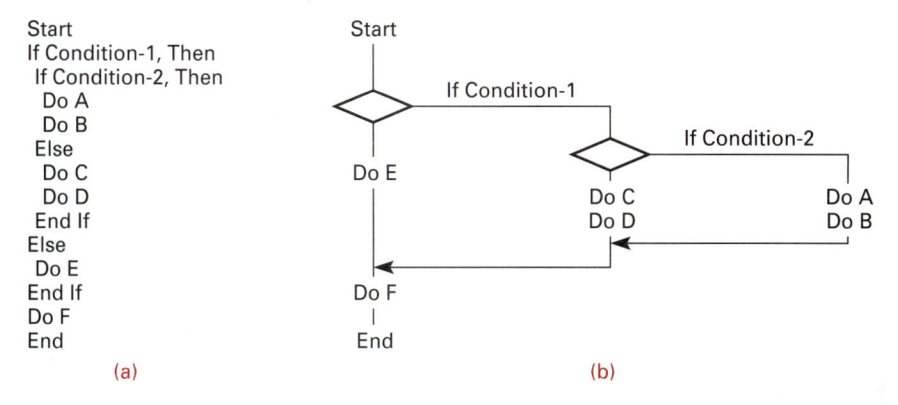

```
Start
If Condition-1, Then
  If Condition-2, Then
    Do A
    Do B
  Else
    Do C
    Do D
  End If
Else
  Do E
End If
Do F
End
    (a)
```

Figure 3.1 This simple program has a McCabe Cyclomatic Complexity Metric of 3, because there are 3 possible paths through the program. OO programming lowers the McCabe Cyclomatic Complexity Metric from figures typically in the range of 10 to 15, to an average often about 3.

Program analyzers that automatically measure the McCabe number reveal that many programs have a McCabe metric of 15. McCabe recommends that the number should not exceed 10. He found that modules, and indeed programs containing modules, whose cyclomatic complexity was greater than 10 were generally more troublesome and less reliable.

A study was conducted during the development of the AEGIS Naval Weapon System, which was composed of 276 modules with approximately half the modules at a complexity level above the threshold of 10. Those modules having a complexity above the recommended level had an error rate of 5.6 errors per 100 source statements. In contrast, those below 10 had an error rate of only 4.6 [5]. The error count increased significantly at the complexity level of 11.

OO design and programming give much lower McCabe metrics and, hence, make software much easier to debug and maintain. For example, the development of the COOPERATION software in NCR was a massive project done with OO techniques. The techniques resulted in a McCabe metric of 3 [1]. On previous non-OO software projects, NCR had a McCabe metric averaging above 10. The reason for the dramatically lower number is that each *method* is relatively simple and self contained. Other software organizations also report a McCabe metric of around 3 with OO techniques.

GREAT ROLLING SNOWBALLS OF CODE

Programs written with traditional techniques are often supplemented while being maintained by different programmers. Each addition increases the complexity of the already amorphous mass of code. The programs act like a snowball rolling down a hill, gathering code. They become unwieldy, fragile, and increasingly difficult to change.

OO techniques neatly subdivide the complexity. The code relates to defined objects and to methods that manipulate those objects. Each method is relatively simple and easy to change. As the richness and complexity of systems grow, much of the new functionality is added to existing classes. Classes are subtypes and inherit the methods of their parent. New methods are added in a discrete fashion, similar to adding a new word to a dictionary. The new methods do not accumulate in the existing code like sticks and slush adhering to a rolling snowball.

Traditional programs are a maintenance trap, steadily becoming more difficult to maintain because of the worsening collection of ill-structured patches. These programs, then, cost more to maintain than they cost to build. The goal of OO techniques is to retain the clear separation of methods, and encapsulation of classes as the system evolves with time and, hence, avoid the worsening difficulties of maintenance.

ENHANCED CREATIVITY

While reliability in software is vitally important, many developers emphasize a quite different advantage from using OO tools. The tools make them more creative.

Developers can create objects, add behavior to objects, make objects interact, and watch what happens. They can use powerful classes from the library to build interesting systems. Because the tools are interpretive, developers can quickly and repeatedly modify what they create and observe the result. Mike Williams of IntelliCorp described his use of ProKappa to be "more like a sculptor than a programmer.... The medium is fluid: you can constantly mould it to your needs, observe it, and change it until it looks right" [7].

By using a good class library, the builder can assemble complex software in this fluid way. He does not have to worry about the internals of a class, which may be complex; he merely uses the class and sometimes creates subtypes of it to modify its methods. He can build new classes out of existing classes and may build very complex classes that will themselves be reusable.

Good software can rarely be specified, then designed, then coded; the creative process requires trial and error and experimentation. OO tools encourage this. The lifecycle can more easily be dynamic and iterative. The tools encourage creative developers to invent and then rapidly implement and refine their inventions. The constant polishing and reiteration lead creative individuals or small teams to much better results. The most creative work is refined over and over again.

OO techniques enable us to build models, such as models of part of an enterprise, which can draw end users into the creative process. They can discuss how their business *ought* to work and what rules *ought* to govern various actions.

OO modeling is useful in the process of creatively redesigning an enterprise or business process. Its expression of events and the resulting operations, and of the rules which govern this, causes those rules to be constantly challenged.

IMMEDIATE FEEDBACK To make developers as creative as possible, they need immediate feedback. As soon as they change something, developers should be able to see it running. When they make an error, the error should be caught and pointed out to them immediately. They should be able to invoke powerful design constructs as they interact with the screen. As soon as they create something, they should be able to experiment with it and change it.

OO modeling and design need powerful OO-CASE tools that operate interpretively. Later, as the design is completed and debugged, the same design should be used with a compiler that provides good machine efficiency.

THE BAD NEWS Introducing OO technology can present problems, and some OO projects have failed. Like any other software technology, OO is not a panacea.

To use OO technology well, much careful training is needed. It takes time for computer professionals to think in terms of encapsulation, inheritance, and the diagrams of OO analysis and design. After an attempted switch to OO, traditional analysts may still tend to think in terms of structured decomposition, data-flow diagrams, and conventional database usage. They often think in terms of data independence rather than class encapsulation. C++ and other nonpure OO tools allow developers to use non-OO constructs, and some of them regress to non-OO design and programming.

Good use of inheritance and reusable classes requires cultural and organizational changes. The class library needs to be well managed. In most organizations, building up the library of classes needed to achieve a high level of reusability will take a long time.

Currently, OO tools, although exciting, suffer from immaturity compared with the well-established, traditional CASE tools. Some traditional tools have been given a flavor of OO but still require non-OO techniques.

When a traditional project gets in trouble, it can often be rescued with skilled people. When a project with new tools and techniques gets in trouble, the talent may not be available to rescue it.

Successful introduction of OO technology needs both good education for every developer and managers who know what they are doing. The support staff needs to be established. The developers who build classes are often separate from the developers who use classes. OO has succeeded spectacularly with individual developers and small skilled teams. However, introducing it to a large group of traditional developers is more difficult. The biggest payoff in OO technology comes when its use is widespread which maximizes reusability and minimizes maintenance costs.

There is little doubt that eventually OO techniques will pervade almost all software development. Only the most backward shops will be non-OO. The corporations that get there first will receive the benefits earliest. However, its acceptance will spread slowly, and many organizations will get into trouble because of inadequate education and lack of management expertise.

A CHANGE IN THE WAY WE THINK This chapter has described a rich set of benefits that derive from object-oriented technology. However, perhaps the most important benefit in the long run is a change in the way people think. I.S. professionals were all taught to think like a computer. This breaks down when the complexity level is high—particularly when computers use highly parallel processors. OO analysis resembles the way humans naturally categorize and comprehend their world. OO-CASE tools enable us to generate code based on this more human way of thinking.

> As computers become more complex, humans should not have to think like computers; instead, computers should be made to think like humans.

This fundamentally different idea about software and systems will enable us to build better systems and, particularly important, improve communication with end users. I.S. professionals and business people need to interact, together formulating enterprise models that reflect business policies. OO thinking will enable us to achieve more powerful automation of highly complex enterprises.

This change in the way we think about systems is so fundamental that it needs to be taught to I.S. professionals everywhere—in universities, technical schools, and business schools. In the long run, it will change the entire computer profession and the way in which end users interact with that profession.

REFERENCES

1. Hazeltine, Nelson, Director of Architecture and Systems Management, Cooperative Computing Systems Division, NCR, "Principles of Object-Oriented Technology," videotaped interview series, James Martin Insight, Naperville, IL, 1991.

2. Martin, James, *Information Engineering,* Prentice Hall, Englewood Cliffs, NJ, 1990.

3. Martin, James, *Rapid Application Development,* Macmillan, New York, 1991.

4. Martin, James, *Reusability,* videotaped training series, James Martin Insight, Naperville, IL, 1992.

5. McCabe, Thomas and Charles Butler, "Design Complexity Measurement and Testing," *Communications of the ACM,* 32:12, December 1989, pp. 1415-1425.

6. Soley, Richard Mark, ed., *Object Management Architecture Guide,* Object Management Group, Document 90.9.1, November 1, 1990.

7. Williams, Michael D. Interview in videotaped seminar *Object-Oriented Analysis and Design,* James Martin Insight, Naperville, IL, 1991.

PART II MODELS AND DIAGRAMS

4 BASIC GUIDELINES

Before beginning the tutorial on OO analysis and design, we should state some basic guidelines.

END USER INVOLVEMENT MUST BE ENHANCED

We cannot build good systems for business or engineering unless the end users are thoroughly involved. End users are the *customers* of the I.S. organization, and the I.S. goal should be to delight its customers. Developers make a fundamental mistake when they think they know better than users what the users need. The users have subtle knowledge about running the business that system developers lack.

The OO models must be built in conjunction with the end users. The users must understand the models at least at a high level, and there must be an ongoing creative dialog about how to improve models and resulting systems and, more fundamentally, how to improve the business procedures by using technology better. Some of this dialog should take place in a workshop environment (described in Chapter 14). OO modeling tools should be designed so that they give maximum assistance in such a facilitation workshop.

THE OO MODELS MUST BE EASY FOR END USERS TO UNDERSTAND

The OO models, and the diagrams used to represent them, must be as easy for business people to understand as possible. OO analysis gives us an opportunity to fundamentally improve communication between business people and developers. Model representations must be found that end users can comprehend and use to participate in the reinvention of business procedures.

Business people do not respond well to data-flow diagrams and structure charts, which are closer to the language of programming than to the language of business. However, business people do understand the event diagrams shown in Chapter 9 and the rule representations shown in Chapter 10. They can think of their world in terms of objects, methods, events, rules, and operations.

Many of the papers on OO formalism use representations that are obscure and inhibit rather than enhance communication with business people. Diagrams and tools must be created that fundamentally improve business communication.

OO DIAGRAMS SHOULD BE EXECUTABLE

When we say that a diagram is *executable,* we mean that code can be generated from it. For this to happen, the diagram must be rigorous and precise. Code should be generated as quickly as possible from OO diagrams and tested. This facilitates iterative redesign.

The diagrams for OO modeling should be *executable.* In contrast, data-flow diagrams, dependency diagrams, and many other diagrams from the past are not executable.

We are seeking diagram forms that both enhance communication with end users and are executable. With these properties, we should build models that help users visualize their enterprise. *Enterprise visualization* clarifies users' understanding about how the enterprise works. Users can experiment with the models and help improve the enterprise.

The linkage from high-level models to code generation should be as direct and automated as possible.

OO TECHNIQUES SHOULD FACILITATE ENTERPRISE REDESIGN

The more powerful information technology becomes, the more opportunities exist for re-engineering our enterprises. Most enterprises of more than 100 people now need redesigning to take advantage of worldwide networks, EDI (electronic data interchange, that is, the electronic transmission of data between enterprises), powerful workstations, client-server computing, LANs (local area networks), image processing, strategic partnerships, intercorporate computing, and so on. Large enterprises offer massive scope for streamlining and removing redundant or clumsy procedures. Enterprises can be made more competitive in numerous ways.

To redesign enterprise procedures at the department, division, and enterprise levels, we need to build models of the enterprise and experiment with changes in the models. Techniques for *enterprise visualization* are required. OO modeling techniques and OO software for executing procedures are helping some corporations reinvent themselves. The highly computerized corporation of the future will be very different from most corporations of today.

ENTERPRISE MODELS SHOULD BE "INTELLIGENT"

Many organizations have built enterprise models. This is part of the *information engineering* methodology. Most of these models, however, are simple. We can build a model airplane that looks nice but does nothing, or we could build one that flies. To build enterprise models that fly, and that can still simulate aspects of the enterprise, the models should reflect those policies wanted by end users to run their operations. The models should contain the rules of the business. They should help us to creatively challenge these rules.

OO methodologies progress from models of a system to code that makes the system work. The models should be built with diagrams that are *executable,* making the model executable. *Intelligent* models, reflecting the rules of operation, should be built both for systems with a narrow focus and for entire business areas.

OO TECHNIQUES SHOULD BE AS AUTOMATED AS POSSIBLE

The designer of a microchip would not dream of working without powerful computerized tools. Tools are similarly needed for the design of software. Some powerful CASE tools now exist that progress in a seamless fashion from the highest level of planning through analysis, design, code generation, and testing. The best of these tools generates 100 percent of the code—code with no syntax errors. If a syntax error or ABEND occurs, a bug exists in the code generator. Design errors still occur in the generated code: garbage-in garbage-out applies to code generators.

When methodologies are designed for this level of automation, they can be quite different from methodologies designed for plastic templates. A machine can do things that would be far too complex to do by hand. Computers can help synthesize our models and designs. They can apply complex checks on integrity and consistency and they can generate code. Computer systems can integrate the work of many developers. Computers can also aid our understanding of complex operations through animation or visualization techniques.

OO analysis, modeling, and design techniques should be designed to use the maximum level of automation.

THE EMPHASIS SHOULD BE ON OO-CASE TOOLS NOT OO PROGRAMMING LANGUAGES

Much of the work and writing done on OO techniques relates to OO programming languages and techniques—particularly C++ and Smalltalk. (See discussion of OO languages in Chapter 17.) Instead, the main thrust of the industry ought to be that OO-CASE tools will be used and code will be generated. Often the generated code will not be C++ or Smalltalk. The code should be compilable with the highest machine efficiency and should be portable.

The diagrams used for OO analysis, modeling, and design should be easy to build and maintain on the screen of CASE tools with multiple windows. The diagrams should be executable—code should be generated immediately from the diagrams.

This book is written with the assumption that when OO techniques are learned, most analysts will employ CASE tools sooner or later. The diagrams *can* be drawn by hand but benefit greatly from the discipline and power of automated tools.

The diagram types that are most effective on OO-CASE tools are different from the diagrams that work best on paper. The CASE tool can create an attractive overview of complex diagrams and can allow its users to examine different aspects of the design in windows. Computerized diagrams can be animated and actions followed one step at a time. The OO diagrams should take advantage of the power of the computer to help end-user communication, creativity, inventiveness, and, particularly important, should use computerized integrity controls wherever possible to produce higher quality systems.

OO DEVELOPMENT NEEDS DIAGRAMMING STANDARDS

Philosophers have described how our thinking depends upon our language. When mankind used only Roman numerals, ordinary people could not multiply or divide. Multiplication and division spread with the adoption of Arabic numerals. The OO diagrams described in this book are a form of language. With computers, we create processes more complex than those we perform manually. Appropriate diagrams help us to visualize and invent those processes.

Object-oriented analysis and design require precise diagrams. The diagrams should appear on the screen of OO-CASE tools. These tools should collect enough information to drive a code generator producing code that is free from syntax errors. The diagrams, therefore, must have an engineering-like precision.

If only one person is developing a system or program, the diagrams that person uses are an aid to clear thinking. A good choice of diagramming technique can speed up work, improve the results, and enhance creativity, while a poor choice can inhibit thinking.

When several people work on a system or program, the diagrams are an essential communications tool. A formal diagramming technique enables the developers to interchange ideas and make their separate components fit together precisely.

When systems are modified, clear diagrams simplify maintenance. With them, a new team can understand how the system works and can design changes. Such changes often affect other parts of the system. However, clear diagrams enable maintenance staff to understand the consequences of their changes. In debugging, clear diagrams are a valuable tool for understanding how the system ought to work and for tracking down what might be wrong.

Diagramming, then, is a language essential for clear thinking, human communication, and design precision. An enterprise needs standards for I.S. diagrams, just as it has standards for engineering drawings.

OO DIAGRAMMING STANDARDS MUST BE AS EASY TO LEARN AS POSSIBLE BY CONVENTIONAL SYSTEMS PEOPLE

Millions of I.S. professionals use pre-OO techniques. To help these I.S. professionals learn OO techniques, OO diagrams should be made as similar as possible to the diagrams that are already in use. Diagrams for conventional techniques are widely used on CASE tools and should be incorporated as far as possible by the diagrams for OO techniques.

Many widely used CASE tools employ the diagrams described in my book written at the start of the CASE era *Recommended Diagramming Standards for Analysts and Programmers* [1]. This book has been a "bible" for many CASE vendors. The OO diagrams used in the following chapters are an extension of the diagrams in *Recommended Diagramming Standards.* Builders of OO-CASE tools should use diagrams that are already widely understood instead of inventing incompatible diagrams. These cause confusion and make the techniques difficult to learn. (OO-CASE tools using strange diagrams are best avoided.)

The diagramming standards recommended for OO analysis and design are summarized in the Appendix.

A REPOSITORY IS NEEDED FOR OO ANALYSIS AND DESIGN

CASE tools need a repository (which some vendors call an *encyclopedia).* A repository stores details of the objects that are used in CASE development (see Chapter 18). Over time, the repository accumulates a vast amount of knowledge about the enterprise—its systems, plans, models, designs, and code.

With repository-based development, *paper is no longer the primary form of documentation.* The documentation in the repository is represented formally so that the software can validate and cross-check it. Paper documentation is printed from the repository if people request it.

The repository needs an information model—a model of the types of information stored in it. Both the DEC and IBM repositories, for example, have their own information model. The information model needs to contain the types of objects used for OO analysis and design. It must be able to store and cross-check the information represented by the OO diagramming tools.

Such models exist from various tool vendors. It is desirable that the computer industry develop a standard (or generally accepted) information model for OO-CASE.

The repository acts both as a facility for the OO-CASE tools and as a class library. Classes with wide reusability should be available as resources for developers.

THE PRINCIPLE OF OCCAM'S RAZOR SHOULD BE APPLIED TO OBJECT TYPES

William of Occam, the fourteenth-century philosopher, declared that when slicing the world into categories, thou shalt not multiply entities needlessly (the Principle of Occam's Razor). A similar principle applies to OO analysis: *Minimize the number of object types.* A small number of high-level object types have subtypes that inherit their parent's properties. Subtypes have *their* subtypes, and so on. If we model a corporation with the minimum number of object types and event types, we will end up with the minimum amount of code to generate and maintain.

One large bank had 1800 different transaction types. After OO analysis was done across the bank, 49 transaction types were found sufficient. All transactions could be handled as variations of the basic 49 transactions. The 1800 transactions had developed over 20 years, as analysts designed each new application from scratch. This was expensive—but worse, vast amounts of code resulted that was very expensive to maintain.

An application might cost $500,000 to create with traditional techniques, but the cost of maintaining it grows. After three years or so, maintenance typically costs 40 percent of the development cost *per year.* The more applications built like this, the greater the financial burden of maintenance. It resembles buying a large house with a low down payment and later being unable to afford the mortgage payments.

OO tools and techniques give us ways to minimize the code created. Following the Principle of Occam's Razor, we should strive to minimize the number of object types. In addition, we should use analysis and design techniques that will minimize future maintenance work.

SKILLED ANALYSIS IS ESSENTIAL

Much of the work already done on OO techniques relates to programming. Regrettably, much less attention has been paid to analysis. Most of the major benefits and financial payoff from OO techniques occurs when analysis is done really well.

Good analysis enables us to maximize reusability and hence minimize development costs. New systems can be built at high speed if they are built largely from reusable classes with a code generator.

Particularly important, maintenance costs can be minimized. Systems can be created that *evolve* easily as the business requirements evolve. A change in business policies can be reflected directly in the OO models and code generation.

Managers of large OO projects often comment that if the high-level object types are well thought out, the lower-level subtypes tend to work well. Where this analysis has not been done well, many of the benefits of OO techniques are lost.

In designing buildings, making television programs, and many other creative disciplines, careful thinking must go into the high-level architecture. The high-level architecture may be refined in many iterations. If it is done well, the lower-level designers can create a good product. Often, however, when an elaborate project is reaching completion, the creative designers say that the architecture needs improving. They could do a much better job if they started again.

The methods for high-level analysis are critical in OO projects. Clear OO modeling of a business area is needed before that business area can be designed effectively.

ENTERPRISEWIDE ANALYSIS IS NEEDED

The maximum benefits occur when analysis is done throughout the enterprise. This is done with OO information engineering (discussed in Chapter 16). A high-level overview model is created of the enterprise, more detailed models are built of business areas, and still more detailed models are built of individual systems. The more detailed models inherit properties of higher level objects.

Enterprisewide modeling has three benefits:

1. Enterprisewide modeling enables separately built systems to work together. A corporation has chains of processes that collectively create value (referred to as the *value chain*). The separate systems in the value chain should interact with one another electronically to achieve the maximum level of corporate automation.

2. Enterprisewide OO analysis produces a higher level of reusability than analysis by separate teams working on separate systems. Since objects are shared across the enterprise, the development and maintenance are faster and cheaper once the analysis is done.

3. Enterprisewide modeling is a vital tool in enterprise redesign. Great savings are occurring in some corporations from streamlining procedures, eliminating redundant procedures, changing the electronic flow of work, and redesigning the corporation so that it reacts faster and gives better customer service.

REFERENCE

1. Martin, James, *Recommended Diagramming Standards for Analysts and Programmers,* Prentice Hall, Englewood Cliffs, NJ, 1987.

5 OO MODELS

MODELS OF REALITY When we analyze systems, we create models of the application areas that interest us. A model might involve one system, such as a production-planning system, focus on one business area, or cover an entire enterprise. Enterprise modeling is important in planning enterprise automation.

The model represents an aspect of reality and is built in such a way that it helps us to understand reality. The model is much simpler than reality, just as a model airplane is simpler than a real airplane. Manipulating the model helps us to invent systems or redesign business areas.

With object-oriented analysis, the way we model reality differs from conventional analysis. We model the world in terms of object types and what happens to those object types. This also leads us to design and program systems in an object-oriented way, striving for the benefits summarized in Chapter 3.

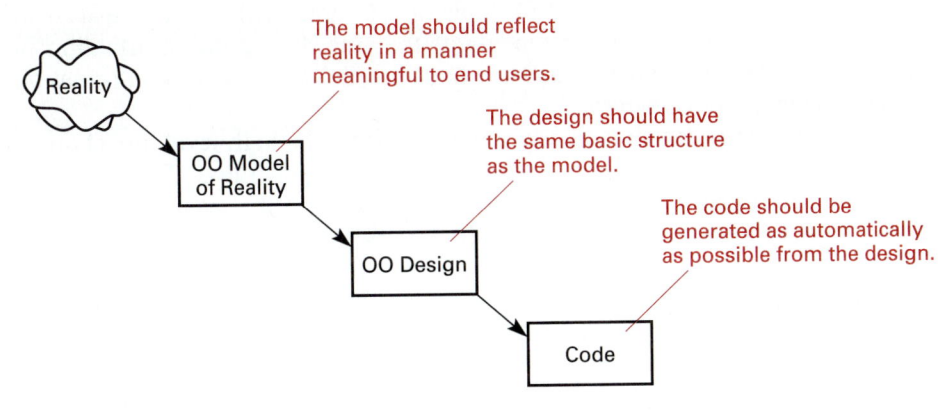

Figure 5.1 How to build a system.

Figure 5.1 illustrates how we build systems. The analyst creates a model of the area of interest. This model is converted into a design and then code. The model should represent how the end users perceive the area or what the users want the system to do. As far as possible, this model should be in a form that users can understand and helps them be creative about their needs. The implementor uses the model and creates a design from which code can be written or generated.

The models we build in OO analysis reflect reality more naturally than the models in traditional systems analysis. Reality, after all, consists of objects and events that change the state of those objects. Using OO techniques, we build software that more closely models the real world. When the real world changes, our software is easier to change. We would like to capture the end users' view of the world and translate it into software as automatically as possible. Then, when the users' needs change, the software adapts.

For example, business people have rules about business operations. These rules relate to objects, operations, and events that trigger operations. They have rules about backordering, rating bad payers, scheduling production, and selecting suppliers. With traditional systems, those rules are buried in multiple COBOL programs. When the business people change the rules, altering the programs is very difficult. With OO analysis and design, we want to express the business rules explicitly in our models and use them to create the design and code. When the rules change, we can change the design and code as automatically as possible.

The OO models encapsulate knowledge about how the business people want to run the business.

TOOLS
OO-CASE tools (see Chapter 18) help the analyst to create models of the area. Using the information in the models, a design is created and methods are built. All of this information resides in a common repository.

With OO tools, design naturally progresses from the high-level model down to a detailed model from which operational code is generated. These models relate to object types, the methods that objects use, and the events that trigger operations with the objects. The repository stores many classes and helps us to find those classes useful in the design.

Every time we tell an advanced CASE tool about classes, inheritance, and so on, it should generate code. Code in existing classes or methods is reused. Code for new methods may be generated from declarative statements, collections of rules, decision tables, SQL statements, logic represented on action diagrams, and other means. Systems of great complexity have been built without having to program in languages, such as COBOL, C, C++, and so on. Ideally, the code should be created *interpretively,* so that we can run it whenever we change the system, like running a spreadsheet as we grow it with a spreadsheet tool. Later, the code is *compiled* for machine efficiency.

TWO ASPECTS OF AN OO MODEL An OO model has two aspects that we can examine separately. The *first* is a representation of the object types and their structure and the *second,* a representation of what happens to the objects. We create a set of diagrams for each of these aspects: *object-structure diagrams* showing the objects and their interrelationships and *event diagrams* showing what happens to the objects.

Both OO analysis and design have these two aspects, illustrated in Fig. 5.2. The first aspect concerns object types, classes, relationships among objects, and inheritance, and is referred to as *Object Structure Analysis* (OSA) and corresponding *Class Structure Design.* The other aspect concerns the behavior of objects and what happens to them over time and is referred to as *Object Behavior Analysis* (OBA) and *Method Design.*

Chapters 6 and 7 discuss object structure; Chapters 8 through 15 discuss object behavior. These chapters show the diagrams that are used.

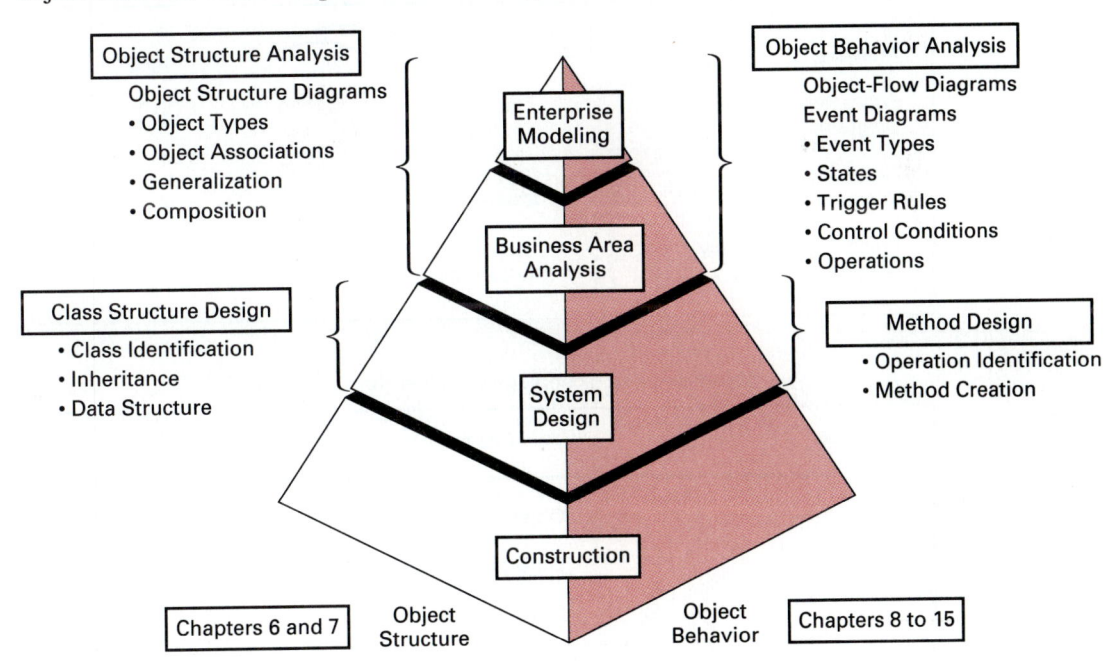

Figure 5.2 Analysis and design both divide into two parts—on the left is object structure representation and on the right is object behavior representation.

THE SIMILARITY OF ANALYSIS AND DESIGN

In traditional development methodologies, the conceptual models used for analysis differ from those used for design. Programming has yet a third view of the world. Analysts use entity-relationship models, functional decomposition, and matrices. Designers use data-flow diagrams, structure charts, and action diagrams. Programmers use the constructs of COBOL, FORTRAN, C, or Ada.

In OO techniques, analysts, designers, programmers, and, particularly important, end users all use the same conceptual model (see Fig. 5.3). They all think of object types, objects, and how the objects behave. They draw hierarchies of object types or classes in which the subtypes share the properties of their parent. They think about objects being composed of other objects and use generalization and encapsulation. They think about events changing the states of objects and triggering certain operations.

The transition from analysis to design is so natural, that specifying where analysis ends and design begins is sometimes difficult. This is especially so where an integrated CASE tool employs the same paradigm for analysis and design, and generates code.

In traditional methodologies, analysts, designers, and programmers have different conceptual models.

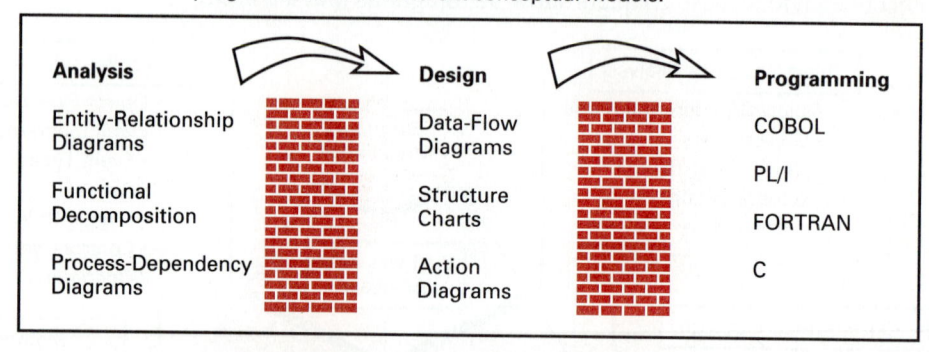

Analysis	Design	Programming
Entity-Relationship Diagrams	Data-Flow Diagrams	COBOL
Functional Decomposition	Structure Charts	PL/I
Process-Dependency Diagrams	Action Diagrams	FORTRAN
		C

Object-oriented technology uses one consistent model.

Analysis	Design	Programming

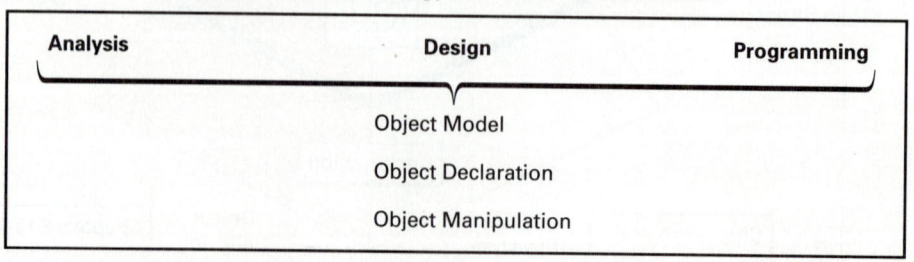

Object Model

Object Declaration

Object Manipulation

Figure 5.3 Since OO techniques use the same conceptual model for analysis, design, and programming, they tear down the conceptual walls between analysis, design, and programming (or code generation).

Chap. 5 OO Models 63

When traditional development crosses the walls shown in Fig. 5.3, information is often lost and misunderstandings occur. The transition is time consuming and often lowers the quality of the end product.

The employment of a single conceptual model with an integrated CASE tool for that model results in

- Higher productivity
- Fewer errors
- Better communication among users, analysts, designers, and implementors
- Better quality results
- More flexibility
- Greater inventability

Object Structure Analysis (OSA)

Concerned with Object Types and Their Associations

- Object Types and Associations
- Generalization Diagrams
- Object-Relationship Diagrams
- Composed-of Diagrams

Object Behavior Analysis (OBA)

Concerned with What Happens to the Objects over Time

- Object-Flow Diagrams
- Event Schemas
- Operation Diagrams Showing Operations and the Sequence in Which They Occur
- Object States and Object State Changes
- Trigger Rules that Link Cause and Effect

Class Structure Design (CSD)

Concerned with Classes, Methods, and Inheritance

- Classes
- Class Methods
- Class Hierarchies
- Inheritance
- Data Structures
- Database Design

Method Design (MD)

Concerned with the Design of Methods

- Methods and Operations
- Procedural Logic
- Nonprocedural Code
- Input to Code Generators
- Screen and Dialog Design
- Prototyping

Figure 5.4 The two halves of OO analysis and design.

Figure 5.4 shows what is of interest to the two sides of analysis and design.

Object Structure Analysis is concerned with defining the kinds of objects and the way in which we associate them. We ask: What types of objects exist? What are their relations and functions? What subtypes and supertypes are useful? Is a certain kind of object composed of other objects?

As this pushes into Class Structure Design, we identify classes (the implementation of object types). Superclasses and subclasses, their inheritance paths, and the methods they use are defined. Detailed design of the data structures or database is done.

Object Behavior Analysis is concerned with modeling what happens to the objects over time. We ask: What states can the object classes be in? What types of events change these states? What succession of events occurs? What operations result in these events, and how are they triggered? Particularly important—what rules govern the actions taken when events occur?

As this pushes into design, we become concerned with the detailed design of methods, either using procedural or nonprocedural techniques. The input to code generators is developed. Screen design is done, dialogs are designed and generated. Prototypes are built and evolved.

The CASE tool used should tightly integrate these aspects of analysis and design. Figure 5.5 shows how the two halves of OO analysis and design are described in the following chapters.

INFORMATION ENGINEERING

The modern enterprise needs to be highly automated. Many computerized systems need to work together as efficiently as possible. Many events happen between a customer taking an order and the finished goods being delivered. The separate systems supporting this chain of events need to fit together, so that the chain happens as effectively as possible, with minimum costs. To create this complex collection of systems, a model of the enterprise must be built: identifying the object types in the enterprise, how they interrelate, what events occur to change the state of objects, and what rules govern the responses to events. This model is extended in greater detail as business areas are analyzed. When separate systems are built, they relate to the same model and, hence, should work together efficiently.

This process of creating an enterprise model, extending it into business-area models, and building systems that relate to the models is called *information engineering* (see Fig. 5.6). The practice of information engineering has been evolving from entity models to object models. In the former, procedures are separated from the data. In the latter, procedures (i.e., methods) are packaged with the data to form classes.

Traditional information engineering has built detailed models of entity types, subtypes, and supertypes across the enterprise. In OO information engineering, these become object types. Object types are often composed of other

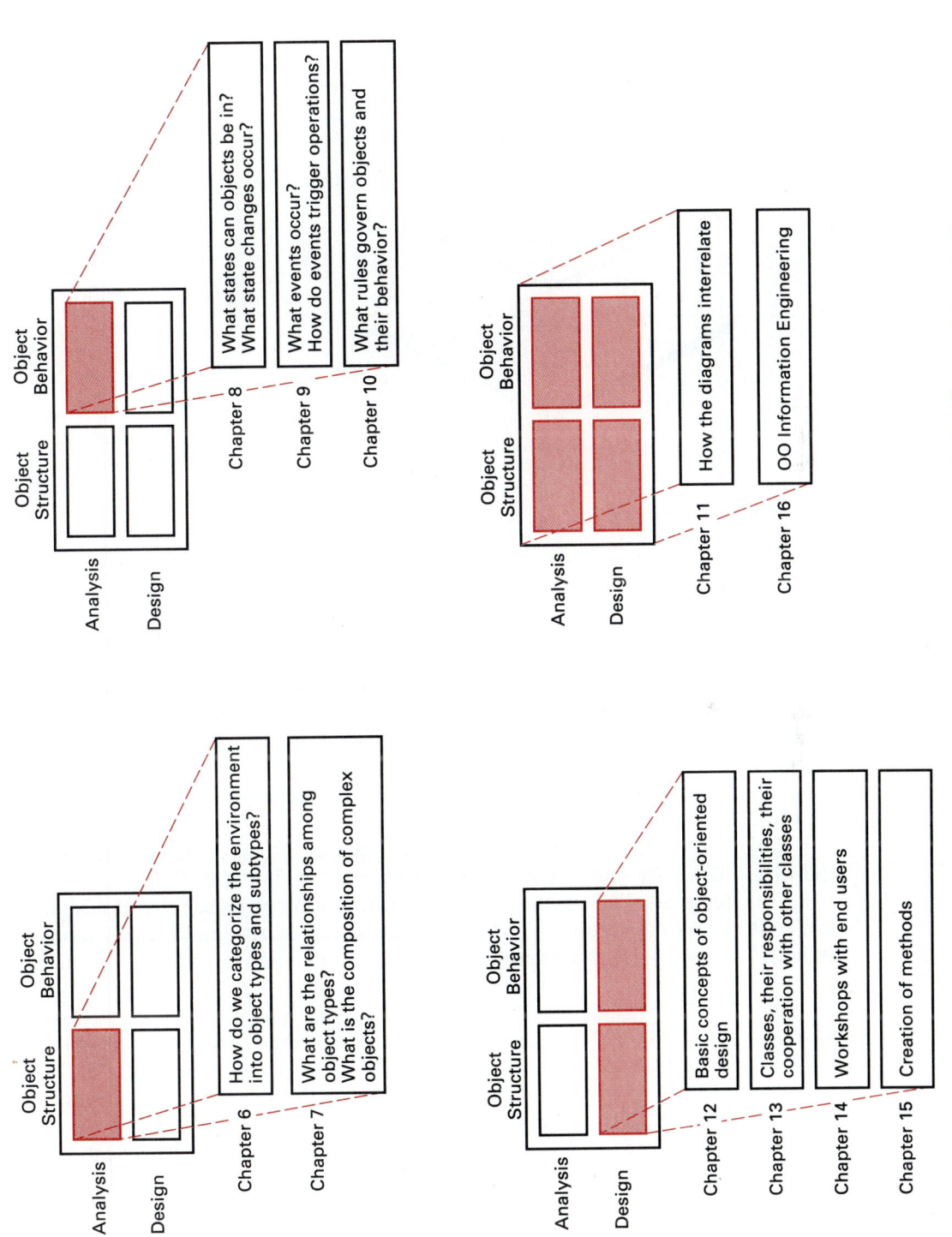

Figure 5.5 How the two halves of OO analysis and design are described in Chapters 6 through 16.

65

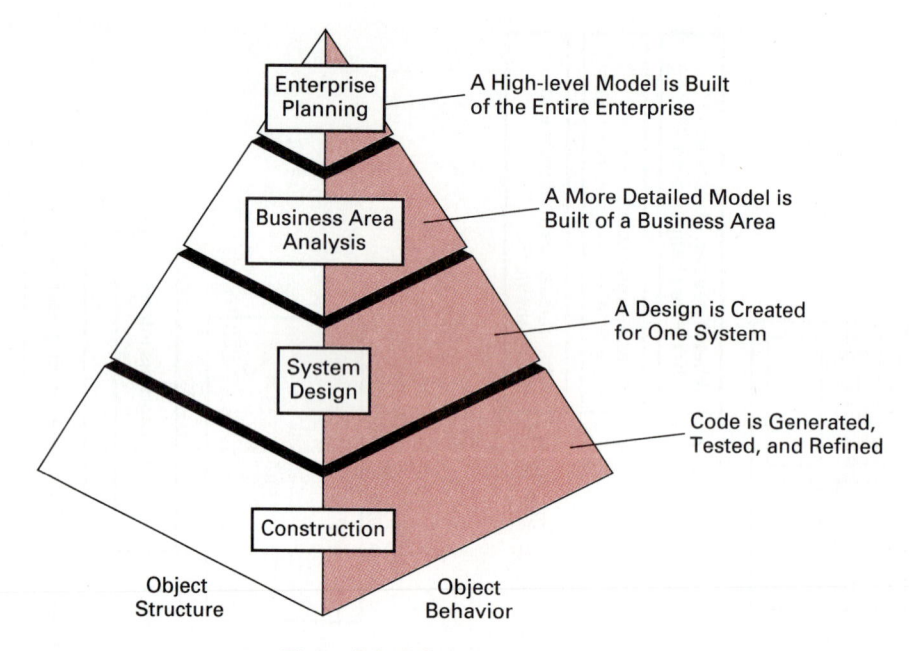

Figure 5.6 Information engineering.

object types, and the diagrams must show this. In traditional information engineering, a matrix diagram shows what processes occur and what entity types they relate to. In OO information engineering, the processes become methods packaged with the data structures. Traditional information engineering is enhanced by thinking about events. Operations cause events to occur, and rules govern actions taken when events occur. Event diagrams and rules reflecting business policies, then, enhance information engineering as it assumes the object-oriented view of the world.

Object-oriented information engineering applies Object Structure Analysis and Object Behavior Analysis at various levels as shown in Fig. 5.7.

A major goal of information engineering is to achieve reusability of design and code across the enterprise. This becomes easier to accomplish, and more effective, with the formal class structures of object-oriented analysis and design.

ACCOMMODATION OF OLD SYSTEMS

Since many applications already exist, the information engineer has to make a new world of clearly designed systems fit in with the old world. (Sometimes they are called *legacy applications,* as they are a legacy from the past.) Using OO techniques, we can often put a wrapper around the old applications that enables new classes to communicate with them using the standard messages of the OO world. An old application, for example, can have its terminal dialog

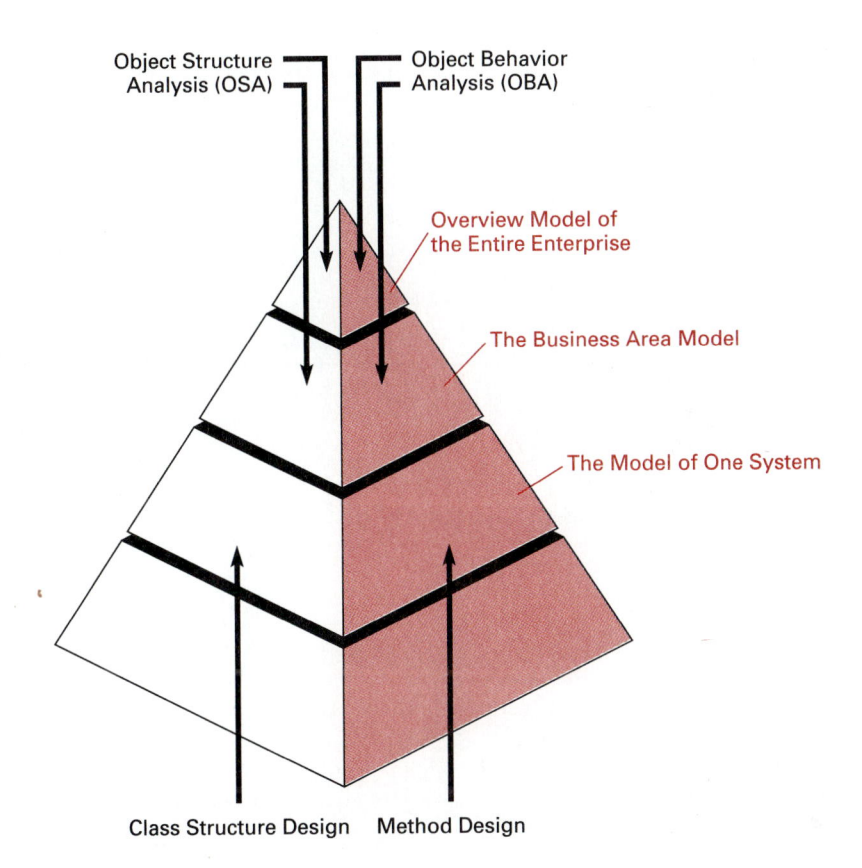

Figure 5.7 Object Structure Analysis (OSA) and Object Behavior Analysis (OBA) are used at the various levels of information engineering.

replaced with a graphical user interface. The user can then employ it along with new OO applications using the same style of PC interaction.

As we evolve to the new OO environment with all its benefits, we cannot scrap the old. For years, perhaps decades, new systems will have to coexist with past systems. Where the legacy systems are expensive to maintain, they will be steadily rebuilt with repository-based OO techniques.

6 CATEGORIZING OBJECTS

Since Aristotle, mankind has tried to categorize the objects in its world. For example, botanists create taxonomies of plants. Now systems analysts in an enterprise categorize those objects relevant to the software of that enterprise.

> An *object type* is a category of object.

Object types are important, because they create conceptual building blocks for designing systems. In object-oriented programming, these building blocks guide the designer in defining the classes and their data structures. In addition, object types provide an index for system operations. For instance, operations such as Hire, Promote, Retire, and Fire are intimately tied to the object type

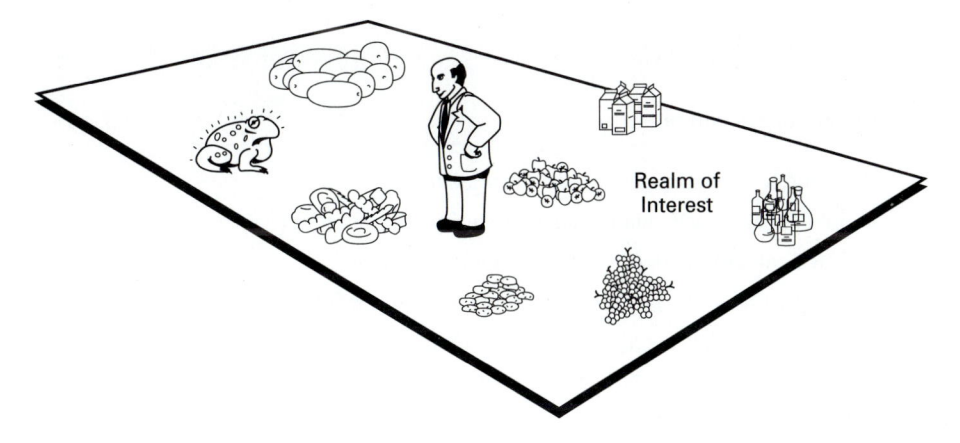

Figure 6.1 We choose how to categorize our world.

69

Employee, because they change the state of an employee. In other words, an object should only be manipulated via the operations associated with its type. Without object types, then, operations cannot be defined properly.

The object types we define and use can be varied, because we choose them based on how we understand our world (see Fig. 6.1).

While this may seem rather arbitrary, it is how our minds work. In fact, an object can be categorized in more than one way. For example, in Fig. 6.2 one person may regard the object Betty as a **Woman**. Her boss regards her as an **Employee**. The person who mows her lawn classifies her as an **Employer**. The local animal control agency licenses her as a **Pet Owner**. The credit bureau reports that Betty is an instance of the object type called **Good Credit Risk**—and so on.

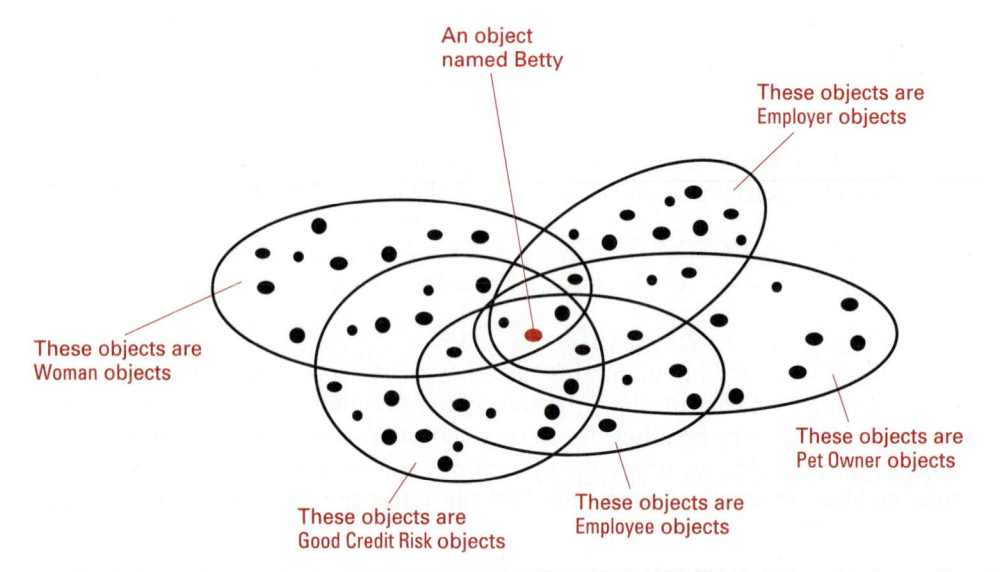

Figure 6.2 The same object can be categorized in many ways.

Object types can be

- concrete—person, pencil, car, machine tool
- intangible—time, quality, social security account, idea
- roles—doctor, patient, owner, data administrator
- judgments—high pay, good example, productive job
- relational—marriage, partnership, ownership
- events—sale, stock-falls-below-reorder-point, system crash
- displayable—string, integer, icon, image

GENERALIZATION HIERARCHIES

One of the common-sense ways in which humans organize their mass of knowledge is by arranging it into hierarchies from the general to the more specific. For example, Fig. 6.3 depicts a hierarchy with knowledge of the object type of Person at the top. This means that Person is a more general type of object than Employee and Student. Employee and Student are *subtypes* of Person, or conversely Person is a supertype of Employee and Student.

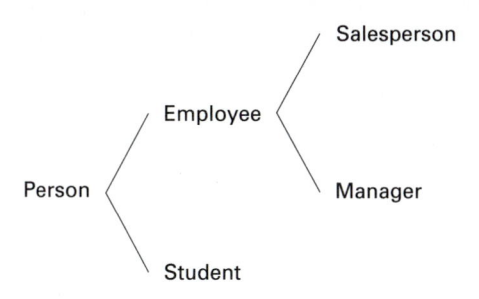

Figure 6.3 A generalization hierarchy of object types indicating that Person is a supertype of Employee and Student. In turn, Employee is a supertype of Salesperson and Manager.

All the properties of an object type also apply to its subtypes. For example, Sony makes many video cassette recorders (VCRs) of which one high-selling model is the AH-8500. VCR is an object type with certain features. AH-8500 is a subtype of VCR. Therefore, the AH-8500 has all the properties of a VCR and properties of its own. Additionally, Sony makes several models of the AH-8500. AH-8500-12 is one model. Therefore, all the properties of the AH-8500 apply to the AH-8500-12, while the AH-8500-12 also has some special properties.

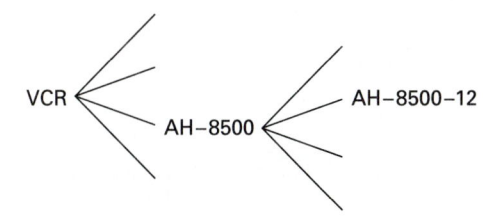

Generalization is the result (or act) of distinguishing an object type as being more general, or inclusive, than another. Everything that applies to an object type also applies to its subtypes. Every instance of an object type is also an instance of its supertypes.

An object type may have subtypes, sub-subtypes, and so on. For example, Acid is a subtype of Liquid, and Nitric Acid is a subtype of Acid. Product 739 is a subtype of Nitric Acid. This generalization hierarchy appears in Fig. 6.4.

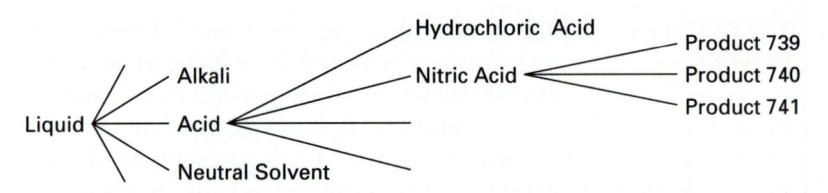

Figure 6.4 A generalization hierarchy indicating that all the properties of Nitric Acid apply to Product 739, Product 740, and Product 741, but each product has specialized properties of its own. Similarly, all the properties of Acid apply to Nitric Acid, Hydrochloric Acid, and so on.

A categorization of the techniques for controlling a network to which multiple machines have access is shown in Fig. 6.5.

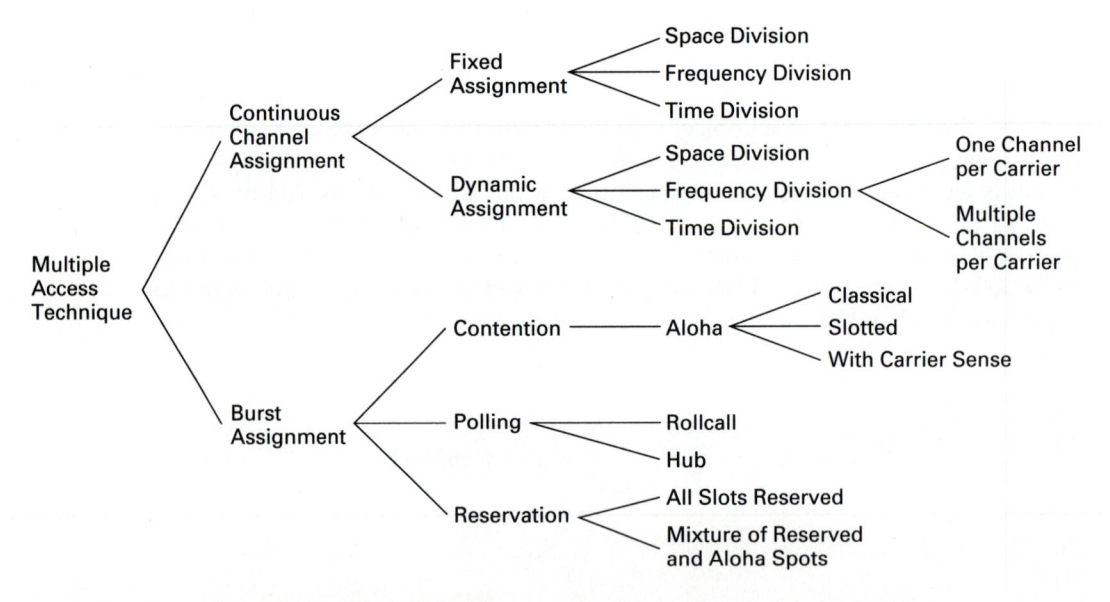

Figure 6.5 A categorization of the ways in which networks, for example local area networks, can be controlled. Each item has the properties of the parent item to its left but also has properties of its own.

FERN DIAGRAMS Generalization diagrams are sometimes network structures rather than tree structures, because a subtype can have more than one supertype. It can inherit properties from two or more parent objects.

The following is a tree structure:

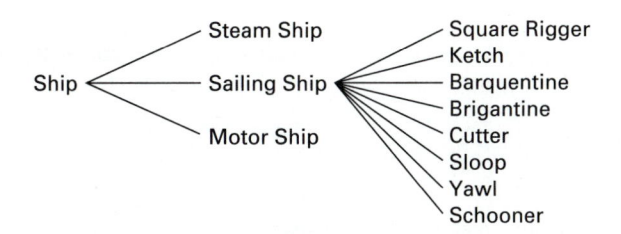

Chap. 6 Categorizing Objects 73

```
                  ┌─ Steam Ship      ┌─ Square Rigger
                  │                  ├─ Ketch
Ship ◄────────────┼─ Sailing Ship ◄──┼─ Barquentine
                  │                  ├─ Brigantine
                  └─ Motor Ship      ├─ Cutter
                                     ├─ Sloop
                                     ├─ Yawl
                                     └─ Schooner
```

The following is a network structure:

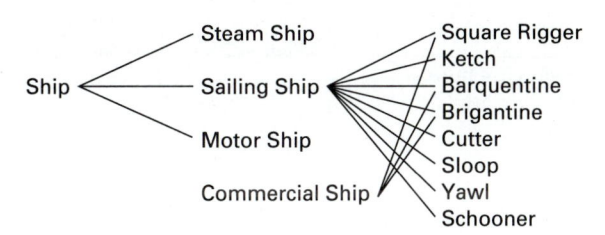

```
                  ┌─ Steam Ship      ┌─ Square Rigger
                  │                  ├─ Ketch
Ship ◄────────────┼─ Sailing Ship ◄──┼─ Barquentine
                  │                  ├─ Brigantine
                  └─ Motor Ship      ├─ Cutter
                                     ├─ Sloop
                    Commercial Ship  ├─ Yawl
                                     └─ Schooner
```

Here the object types **Square Rigger, Barquentine,** and **Brigantine** have two *supertypes*. A **Square Rigger** is an example of a **Sailing Ship** and also a **Commercial Ship**.

Diagrams such as these are referred to as *fern diagrams*. A fern diagram usually progresses from left to right and has no arrows on it. Inheritance is based on generalization. Object types on the fern diagram inherit the properties of the supertypes on their left. The fern diagram does not depict *what* is inherited.

BENEFITS OF FERN DIAGRAMS

Fern diagrams are useful for two reasons. First, they help us to think clearly about good categorization. Is Fig. 6.6, for example, the best categorization? Second, they show the inheritance paths that will be implemented in class hierarchies. Clear categorization and good design of the class hierarchies are essential to achieve the full benefits of OO development.

Fern diagrams sometimes become complex. (Glancing ahead, Fig. 12.5 shows a real-life one.) OO-CASE tools need to be able to show portions of large fern diagrams.

TYPES AND INSTANCES

Fern diagrams sometimes show *instances* of objects that are connected to their object with dashed lines. For example, a generalization of creatures is shown in Fig. 6.6. The creature **Bear** is a subtype of **Mammal**, while **Wilber, Edward,** and **Yogi** are instances of **Bear**, that is, they are specific bears.

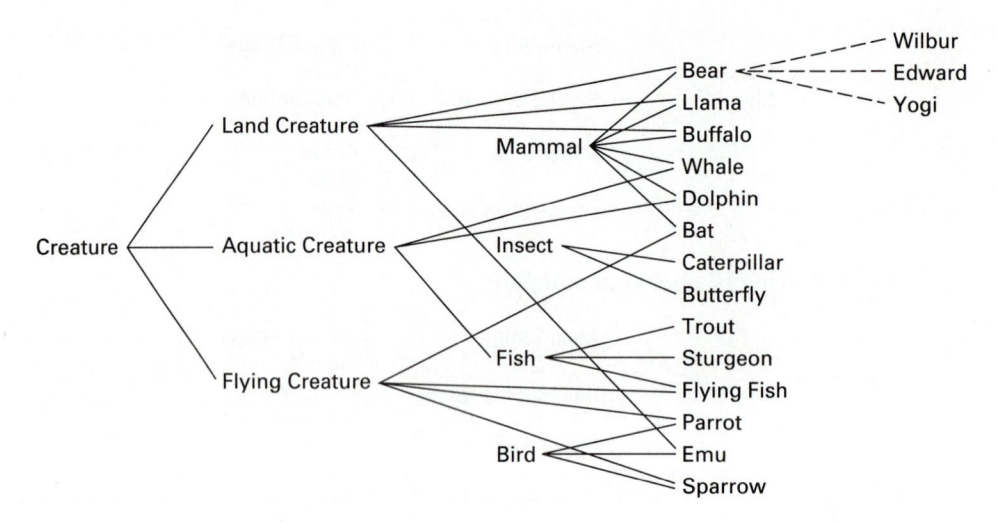

Figure 6.6 A fern diagram showing a categorization of creatures. Some creature types have multiple supertypes and inherit properties from these supertypes. For example, a **Whale** has properties of an **Aquatic Creature** and a **Mammal**. The diagram also shows three instances of **Bear** with dashed lines indicating that these are specific bears rather than an object type.

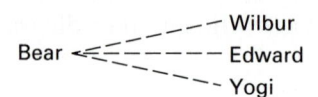

Showing instances, such as these, is often impractical, because they are too numerous—even a whole database full. However, when an object has a small number of instances that have particular meaning in the design, they may be shown.

BOX DIAGRAMS   An alternative way to show generalizations is with box diagrams—boxes within boxes. The same categorization with a fern diagram and a box diagram is shown in Fig. 6.7.

Fern diagrams are generally neater. Box diagrams should only be used with a small number of object types, since they become unwieldy for representing object types with multiple supertypes. Figure 6.6, for example, is neat as a fern diagram but clumsy and difficult to draw as a box diagram with intersecting boxes.

Box diagrams showing subtypes are useful as a component of other diagrams showing object relationships, as we shall see in Chapter 7.

Chap. 6 — Categorizing Objects — 75

```
                  ┌─ Steam Ship                    ┌─ Square Rigger
Ship ─────────────┼─ Sailing Ship ──────────────────┼─ Ketch
                  └─ Motor Ship                    ├─ Barquentine
                                                   └─ Brigantine
```

```
┌─────────────────────────────┐
│ Ship                        │
│  ┌───────────────────────┐  │
│  │ Steam Ship            │  │
│  └───────────────────────┘  │
│  ┌───────────────────────┐  │
│  │ Sailing Ship          │  │
│  │  ┌─────────────────┐  │  │
│  │  │ Square Rigger   │  │  │
│  │  └─────────────────┘  │  │
│  │  ┌─────────────────┐  │  │
│  │  │ Ketch           │  │  │
│  │  └─────────────────┘  │  │
│  │  ┌─────────────────┐  │  │
│  │  │ Barquentine     │  │  │
│  │  └─────────────────┘  │  │
│  └───────────────────────┘  │
│  ┌───────────────────────┐  │
│  │ Motor Ship            │  │
│  └───────────────────────┘  │
└─────────────────────────────┘
```

Fern Diagram   Box Diagram

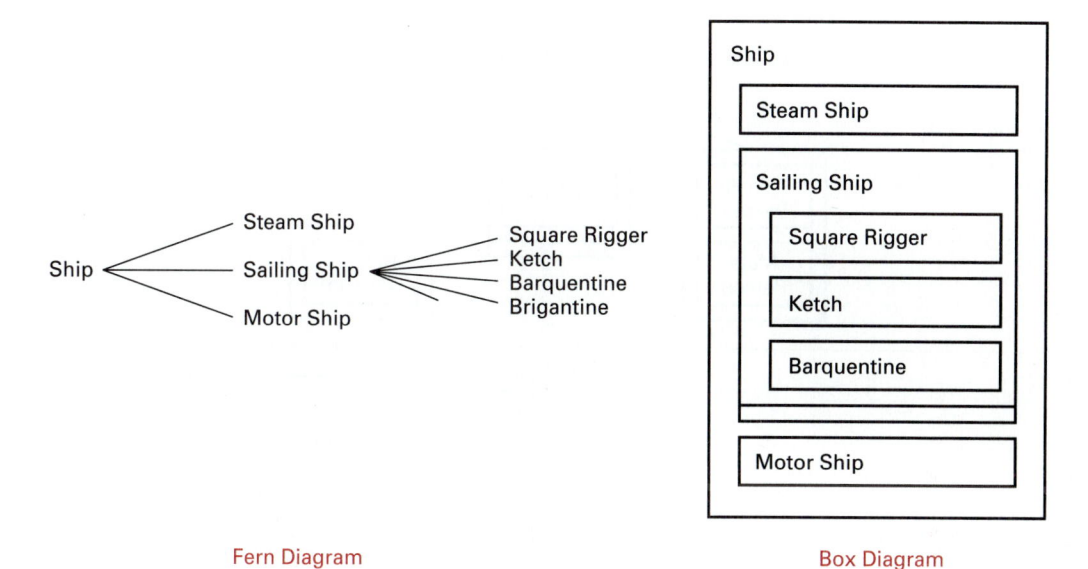

Figure 6.7 A fern diagram and a box diagram showing the same information. Fern diagrams are used for large categorizations (see Fig. 12.5). Box diagrams are used when subtyping in object-relationship diagrams (see Fig. 7.5).

COMPLETE AND INCOMPLETE SETS OF SUBTYPES

A set of subtypes indicated on a fern diagram or a box diagram might show all possible subtypes or it might show only some of the subtypes. A line at the bottom of a box with an empty area below it represents an incomplete set, as illustrated in Fig. 6.8.

Incomplete sets can also be indicated on a fern diagram by a line from a supertype that is not connected to anything:

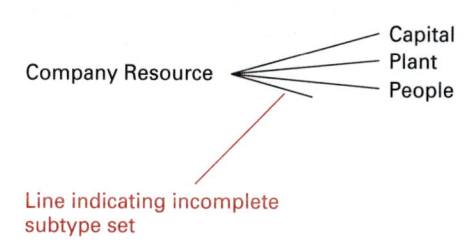

```
                          ┌─ Capital
Company Resource ─────────┼─ Plant
                          ├─ People
                          └─
```
Line indicating incomplete subtype set

AN OBJECT CAN BE AN INSTANCE OF MULTIPLE SUBTYPES

A box diagram can show that an object can be categorized in different ways at the same time. Consider the following diagram, for example:

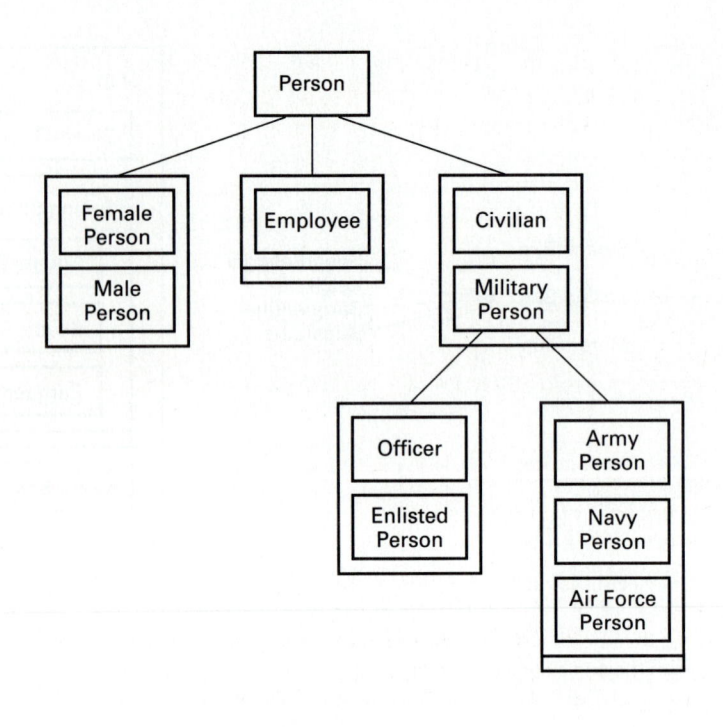

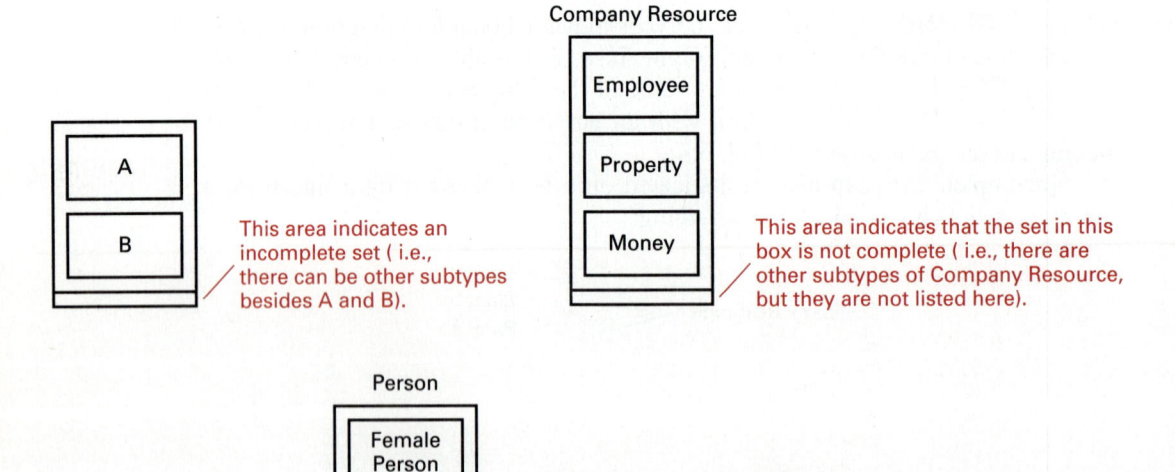

Figure 6.8 An empty area at the bottom of a box showing subtypes indicates that there may be other subtypes that are not shown.

76

A Person can be a Female Person, Employee, and Civilian at the same time. A Person can *not* be a Female Person and a Male Person at the same time. Similarly, a Military Person can be an Officer and an Army Person but has to be only one of Army Person, Navy Person, or Air Force Person.

OBJECTS CATEGORIZED IN VARIOUS WAYS   An object can be thought about in different ways. It can be a member of various subtypes—various forms of categorization.

For example, a satellite may be categorized as a low-orbit satellite or geosynchronous satellite. These two subtypes have different behaviors and properties, although both inherit the properties of Satellite. A satellite can also be categorized as military or civilian—inheriting properties of Satellite but having properties of its own.

We could draw this as follows:

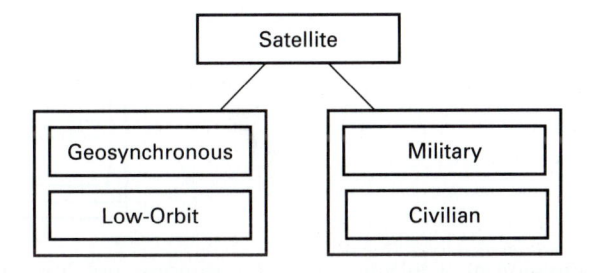

```
              Satellite
             /        \
    Geosynchronous    Military
    Low-Orbit         Civilian
```

This indicates that a satellite might be both Geosynchronous and Military; it could not be both Geosynchronous and Low-orbit or both Military and Civilian.

Which of these categorizations is the most important? If we think Low-orbit or Geosynchronous is the most important, we would draw the fern diagram indicating inheritance paths as follows:

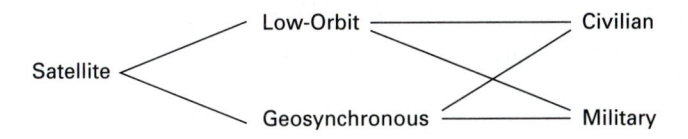

```
                    Low-Orbit  ─────  Civilian
Satellite  <                  ><
                    Geosynchronous ── Military
```

If the major difference lies between military and civilian satellites, we would draw categorization as follows:

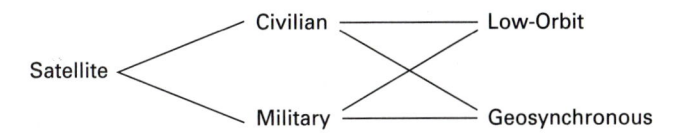

```
                    Civilian  ─────  Low-Orbit
Satellite  <                  ><
                    Military  ─────  Geosynchronous
```

In general, the analyst should choose the categorization levels so that the ones with the biggest differences are at the top of the hierarchy (that is, the left of the fern diagram).

Other categories of satellites include telecommunications satellite, solar observatory, missile-detection satellite, and so on as shown below:

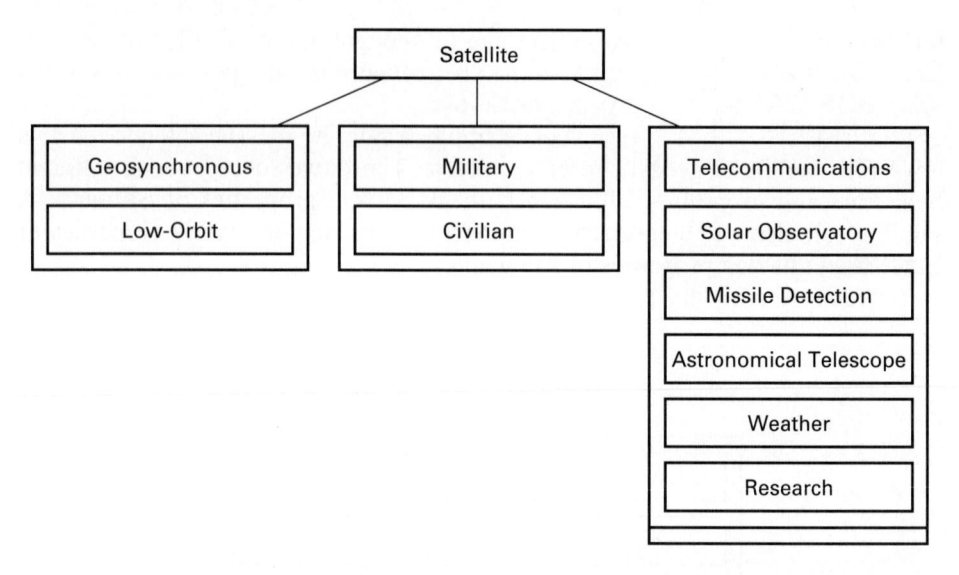

Telecommunications satellite is geosynchronous, not low orbit. A missile-detection satellite is military, not civilian. Therefore, the above fern diagram needs to be fully expanded.

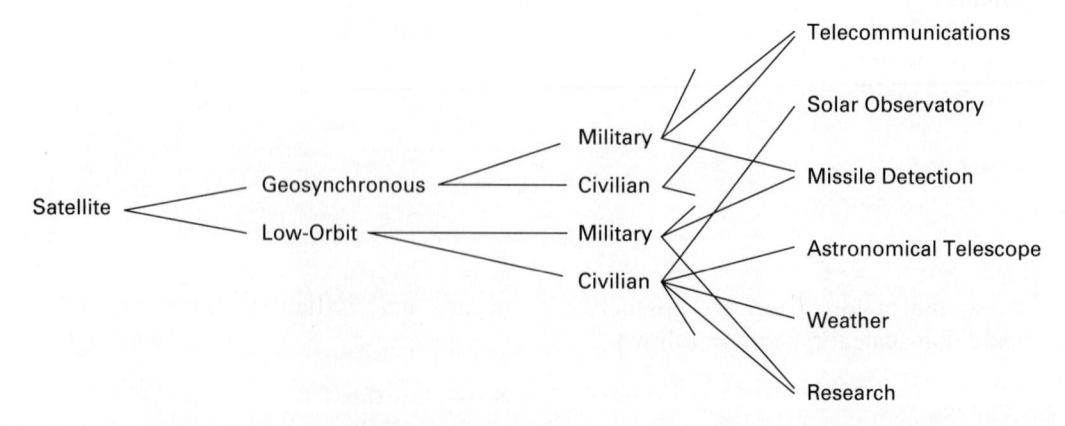

Careful thought is needed about categorization because the class hierarchies and their inheritance are designed from it. Good categorization leads to higher reusability and lower maintenance.

HOW TO DETERMINE WHAT SHOULD BE A SUBTYPE

Deciding what should be a subtype is sometimes confusing. Consider the case of a bureaucratic organization that has people with the following titles:

- official
- advisor
- subagent
- representative

Should each of these be a separate object type? And if so, which are subtypes of others?

To help clarify questions like these, a simple test can be applied. We ask: Is A a B? and Is B an A? The permissible answers are *always, sometimes,* and *never.* If both answers are *never,* we are not concerned with subtyping. If both answers are *always,* A and B are synonyms. If the answers are

Is A a B?—*always*

Is B an A?—*sometimes*

then, A is a subtype of B

The answers can be arranged in a table. The cells in the following table answer the question Is A a B?

		B: Official	Advisor	Subagent	Representative
A:	Official	—	Sometimes	Never	Always
	Advisor	Never	—	Never	Never
	Subagent	Never	Never	—	Always
	Representative	Sometimes	Never	Sometimes	—

We first look for the word *always.* An **Official** and a **Subagent** are *always* a **Representative** and, thus, are subtypes of the object type **Representative**. An **Official** is *never* a **Subagent** and vice versa, so they are mutually exclusive subtypes. Can there be representatives other than **Officials** and **Subagents**? *No.* Therefore we draw

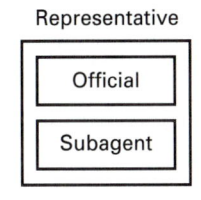

Representative
```
┌─────────────┐
│  Official   │
├─────────────┤
│  Subagent   │
└─────────────┘
```

79

An **Advisor** is *never* any of the others, so it is a separate object type.

```
    Representative          Advisor
   ┌──────────────┐      ┌──────────────┐
   │  Official    │      │              │
   ├──────────────┤      └──────────────┘
   │  Subagent    │
   └──────────────┘
```

Do we really need to regard **Official** and **Subagent** as subtypes of **Representative**, or should they merely be attributes of **Representative**? To answer this, we ask: Does their behavior differ from that of **Representative**? or Will they have different *methods* than **Representative**? We decide that they do! A **Subagent** is an external employee working for a separate **Corporation**, so different information will be kept about him. An **Official** supervises a **Subagent**. Both **Official** and **Subagent** are objects with their own behavior but are subtypes of **Representative**.

7 RELATIONSHIPS AMONG OBJECT TYPES

In the previous chapter, we were concerned with the categorization of objects. In this chapter, we are concerned with relationships among object types and will explore four major forms of them:

1. general relations
2. instantiation
3. subtypes and inheritance
4. composed-of relationships

ENTITIES AND OBJECTS
An entity is something about which we store data. When implemented, each entity is typically stored as a record. Entities of the same type, then, are stored as a collection of records known as a file or relation.

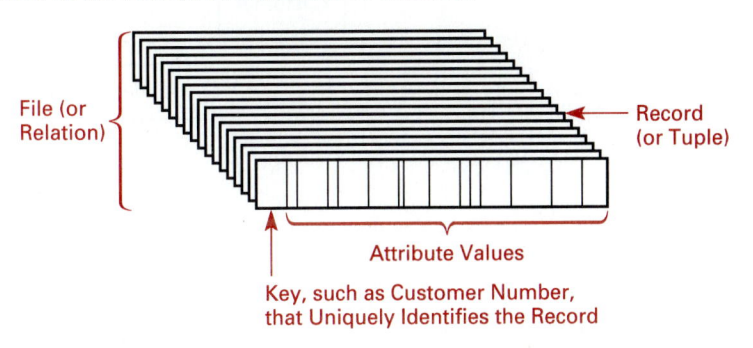

File (or Relation) — *Record (or Tuple)* — *Attribute Values* — *Key, such as Customer Number, that Uniquely Identifies the Record*

When data are well modeled, the records are normalized. *Normalization* is a precise, mathematically defined procedure by which data are decomposed into elementary record structures [1]. Each attribute in a record relates to the key of that record, the whole key, and nothing but the key.

Entities, then, are represented by elementary groupings of data items. An object type in OO design has a data structure that may be composed of many entity types.

An object type is thus fundamentally different from an entity type in three ways—*first*, in the packing and encapsulation of data and methods, *second*, in the use of data structures that may be complex, and *third,* in the emphasis on inheritance.

DATA MODELS

In conventional systems analysis, data models are created. Data models use an entity-relationship diagram that shows the relationships among entity types. Because the attributes of the entity types are precisely normalized, the overall data model can be constructed in a rigorous fashion [2]. The data model is implemented in a database management system and becomes a foundation on which many applications are built.

This book does not discuss the details of data modeling. However, data modeling is still important in OO analysis and design, because the objects need to use well designed data structures. Corporations that have built good corporate data models find it much easier and faster to build OO models.

OBJECT-RELATIONSHIP DIAGRAMS

An object-relationship diagram is similar to an entity-relationship diagram. It maps the relationships among object types. Since it is often built by analysts who are familiar with entity-relationship diagrams, the same diagramming conventions should be used. An object type is drawn as a square-cornered box. Object types have relationships with other object types. For example, an **Employee** works in a **Branch Office**, or a **Customer** places an **Order** for many **Products**. This can be drawn as follows:

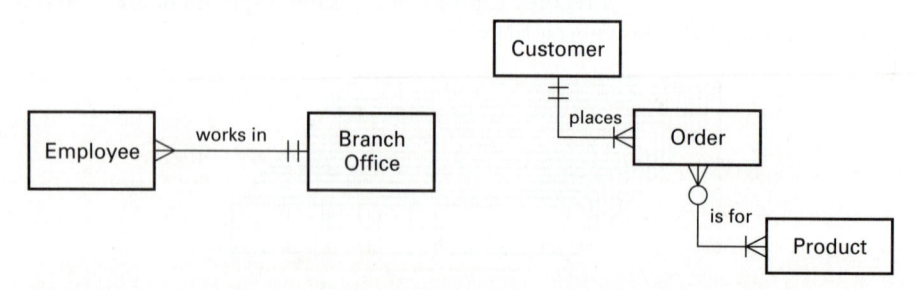

The boxes contain the names of objects. The lines linking the boxes are relationships. The word on the line is a verb describing the relationship. The object names and verbs form sentences:

Employee works in **Branch Office**.

Customer places **Order**.

Order is for **Product**.

ATTRIBUTES

The traditionally accepted view in data modeling is that an attribute is a descriptor associated with an object type. With a CASE tool, one can click on the object type and view details of its attributes. An alternate view states that every attribute is really an object. An integer, for example, is an object.

In OO modeling, it is not useful to *draw* every attribute as an object. The diagram becomes far too cluttered. In conventional data modeling, an entity is defined as *any* thing, real or abstract, about which we store data. This is a useful guideline in OO modeling—object-relationship diagrams are similar to entity-relationship diagrams.

All information modelers have encountered the dilemma of an attribute that becomes an entity type on further investigation. The difficulty is that the classification of a fact as an attribute or an object type is dependent on perspective. In one scenario, a given fact may be an attribute of an object type and in another, additional facts emerge about the concept and it becomes an object type in its own right.

If the discovery of additional facts happens during the analysis or design of a given system, then the reclassification can take place followed by an appropriate implementation.

INSTANCES

Instances may be associated with object types using dashed lines.

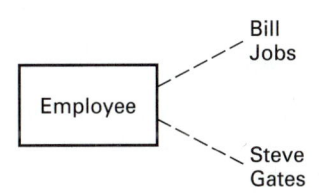

```
                      Bill
                    - Jobs
          ┌──────────┐
          │ Employee │
          └──────────┘
                    ╲ Steve
                      Gates
```

In addition to the dashed line, some diagramming approaches require a special symbol for objects as well, such as a dashed box.

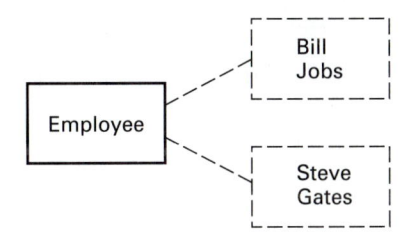

```
                    ┌──────┐
                    │ Bill │
                    │ Jobs │
          ┌──────────┐ └──────┘
          │ Employee │
          └──────────┘ ┌──────┐
                    │Steve │
                    │Gates │
                    └──────┘
```

CARDINALITY CONSTRAINTS

The term *cardinality constraint* refers to the restriction of how many of one item can be associated with another. For instance, a cardinality can be constrained

83

as one-with-one or one-with-many. Sometimes, numbers can be used to designate the upper and lower limits on cardinality.

Crow's Feet

A crow's foot connector from a line to a node is drawn like this:

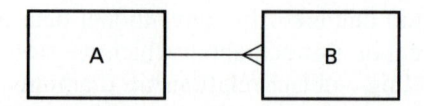

[A]———⊲[B]

It means that one or more instances of B can be associated with one instance of A. It is called a *one-with-many association.*

One-With-One Cardinality Constraints

On diagrams using cardinality constraints, one-with-one cardinality is drawn with a small bar across the line (looking like a "1" symbol):

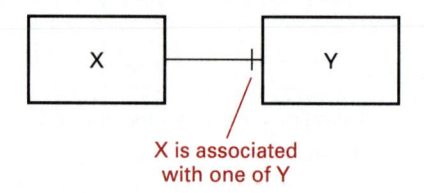

[X]———|[Y]

X is associated with one of Y

Zero Cardinality Constraints

A zero as part of the cardinality-constraint symbol means that an instance of one object type is not associated with any instances of another. In other words, an object of one type can have zero associations with the objects of another type:

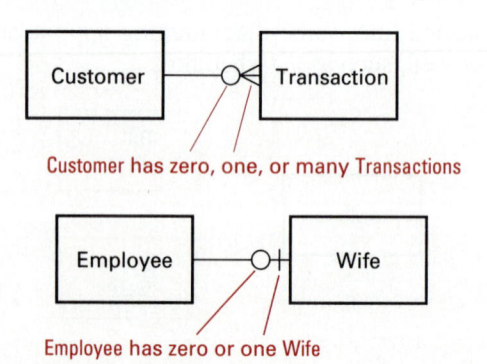

[Customer]——O⊲[Transaction]

Customer has zero, one, or many Transactions

[Employee]——O|[Wife]

Employee has zero or one Wife

The line linking object types should *always* have a cardinality-constraint symbol at both ends. Drawing a line to connect an object-type rectangle with no cardinality-constraint symbol is sloppy analysis.

Minimum and Maximum

The cardinality symbols express a maximum and minimum constraint:

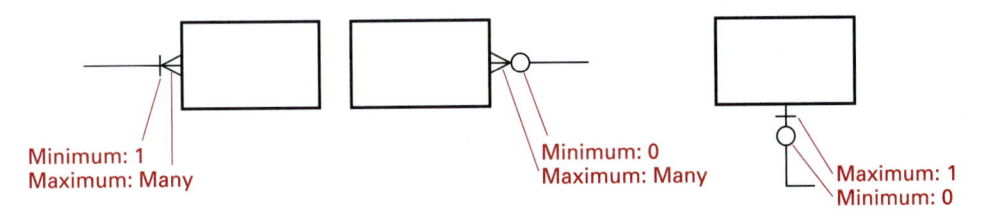

Minimum: 1
Maximum: Many

Minimum: 0
Maximum: Many

Maximum: 1
Minimum: 0

The maximum is always placed next to the box to which it refers. Where minimum and maximum are both 1, two 1-bars are placed on the line. The two bars mean "one and only one":

Husband ⊦⊦——⊦⊦ Wife

Customer ⊦⊦——○⊰ Order

The representation of minimum and maximum cardinality constraints is summarized in Fig. 7.1.

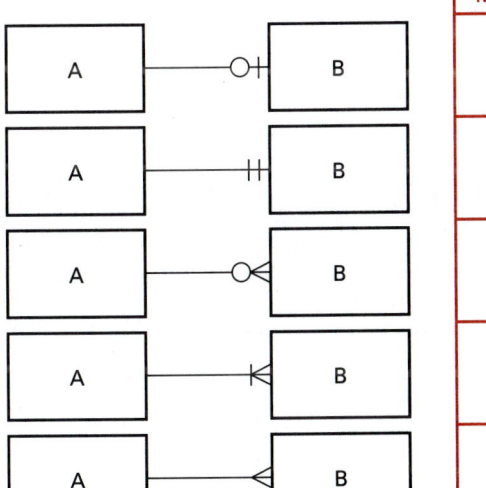

Diagram	Each Instance of A Is Associated with How Many Instances of B?	
	Minimum	Maximum
A ——○⊦—— B	0	1
A ——⊦⊦—— B	1	1
A ——○⊰—— B	0	More than 1
A ——⊦⊰—— B	1	More than 1
A ——⊰—— B	More than 1	More than 1

Figure 7.1 Cardinality-constraint symbols indicate minimum and maximum cardinality constraints.

Figure 7.2 depicts four object types with associations between the types. It is expressed in the same way as an entity-relationship diagram.

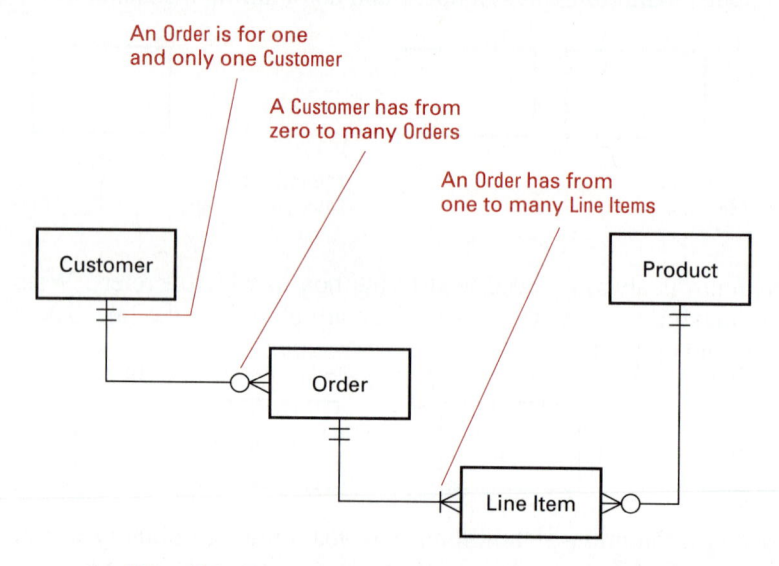

An Order is for one and only one Customer

A Customer has from zero to many Orders

An Order has from one to many Line Items

Figure 7.2 Four object classes with cardinality symbols.

Sometimes cardinality cannot be expressed in terms of zero, one, or many. For example, a **Meeting** requires at least two **Person**s. Here, the minimum cardinality is two. In addition, an organization can place a restriction that a meeting can have no more than 20 people attending it. This is expressed by enumerating the cardinality constraint:

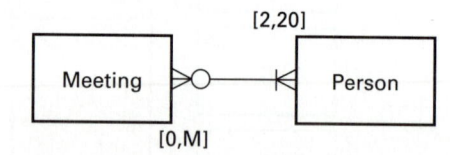

[2,20]

Meeting — Person

[0,M]

LABELING OF LINES Lines between object-type boxes can be read in either direction:

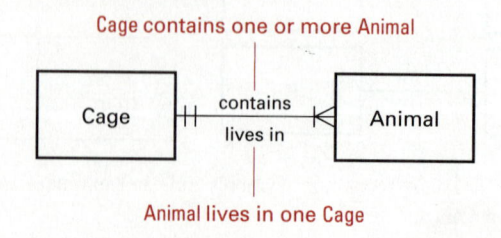

Cage contains one or more Animal

Cage — contains / lives in — Animal

Animal lives in one Cage

Some analysts label object-relationship lines in one direction only; others believe labeling lines in both directions is more thorough.

A label *above* a horizontal line is the name of the association when read from left to right. A label *below* a horizontal line is the name when read from right to left. As the line is rotated, the label remains on the same side of the line:

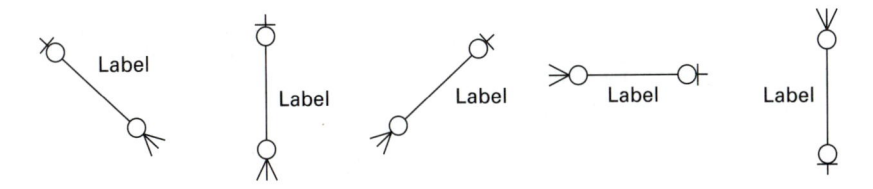

Thus, the label to the right of the vertical line is read when going *down* the line. The label on the left of a vertical line is read going *up* the line.

READING ASSOCIATIONS LIKE SENTENCES

Lines between object types give information about the association between the objects. This information should read like a sentence, for example:

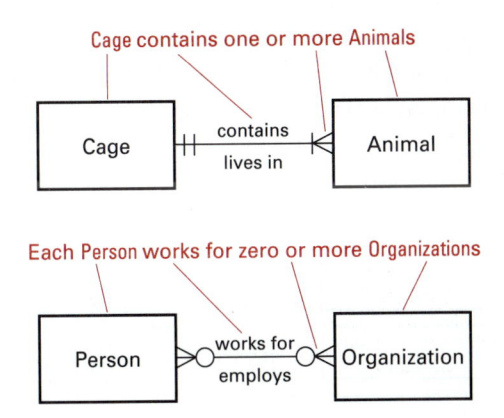

Cage contains one or more Animals

Each Person works for zero or more Organizations

Sometimes more than one relationship exists between two object types. Two (or more) lines are then drawn connecting those object types, each with its own wording.

SUBTYPES

As described earlier, object types can have more specialized types called *subtypes* and more general types called *supertypes*. Subtype hierarchies can be expressed as boxes within boxes:

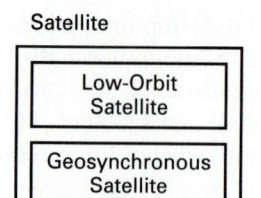

Satellite

```
┌─────────────────────┐
│  ┌───────────────┐  │
│  │  Low-Orbit    │  │
│  │  Satellite    │  │
│  └───────────────┘  │
│  ┌───────────────┐  │
│  │ Geosynchronous│  │
│  │  Satellite    │  │
│  └───────────────┘  │
└─────────────────────┘
```

Subtypes can be shown in this way on object-relationship diagrams. An alternate way of drawing subtypes is to place a box beneath the object type—decomposing it into subtypes:

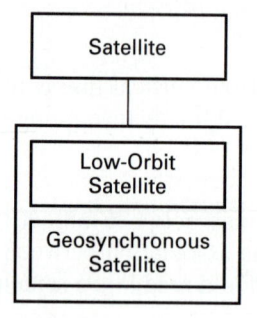

```
        ┌───────────┐
        │ Satellite │
        └─────┬─────┘
              │
    ┌─────────┴─────────┐
    │ ┌───────────────┐ │
    │ │  Low-Orbit    │ │
    │ │  Satellite    │ │
    │ └───────────────┘ │
    │ ┌───────────────┐ │
    │ │ Geosynchronous│ │
    │ │  Satellite    │ │
    │ └───────────────┘ │
    └───────────────────┘
```

The object subtypes may be linked to other object types. **Orbit Detail** is important for **Low-orbit Satellite**, but for **Geosynchronous Satellite** the position in the geosynchronous orbit is needed.

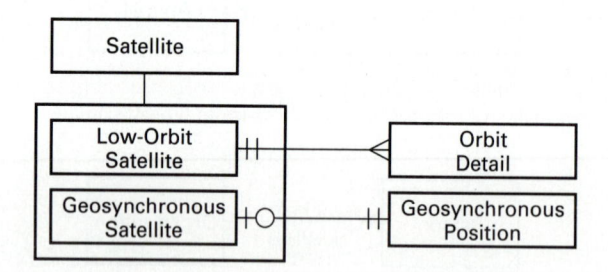

As described in the previous chapter, an object type may have more than one set of subtypes. Figure 7.3 shows multiple subtypes of **Satellite** and shows relationships between the subtypes and other object types.

ARROWS INDICATING SUBTYPES

Boxes within boxes are an intuitive way to show subtypes. Their meaning is easily understood. However, generalization diagrams can grow complex (for example, glance ahead to Fig. 12.5). They grow too com-

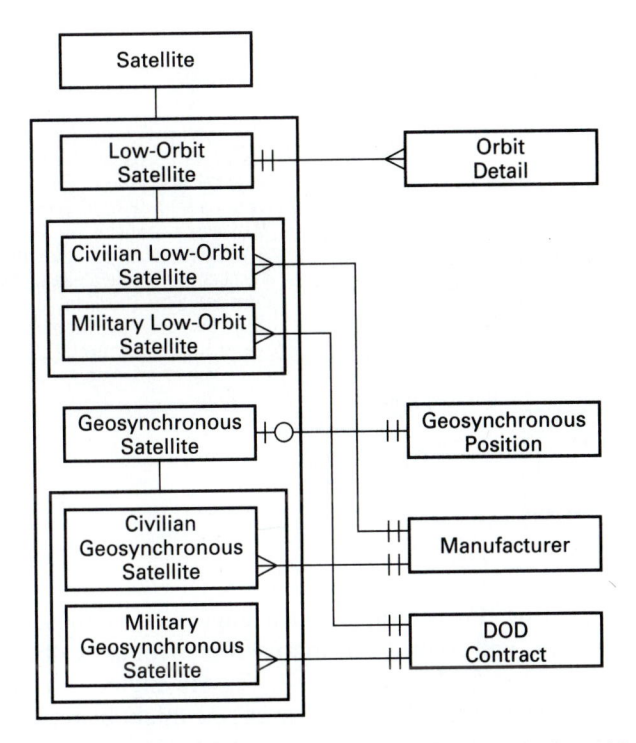

Figure 7.3 Multiple subtypes of Satellite and their association with other object types.

plex to show them as boxes within boxes, especially when we want to link them to other object types as in Fig. 7.3. Because of this, a line with a triangle arrow is used as an alternate notation to show subtyping:

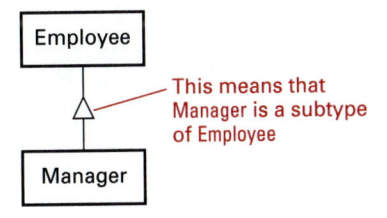

Figure 7.4 shows two levels of subtyping; Fig. 7.5 shows multiple levels. Other object types are associated with appropriate subtypes.

COMPOSED-OF DIAGRAMS

Part of the power of OO software comes from its ability to handle a complex object type that is, in fact, composed of many other objects. This is a normal

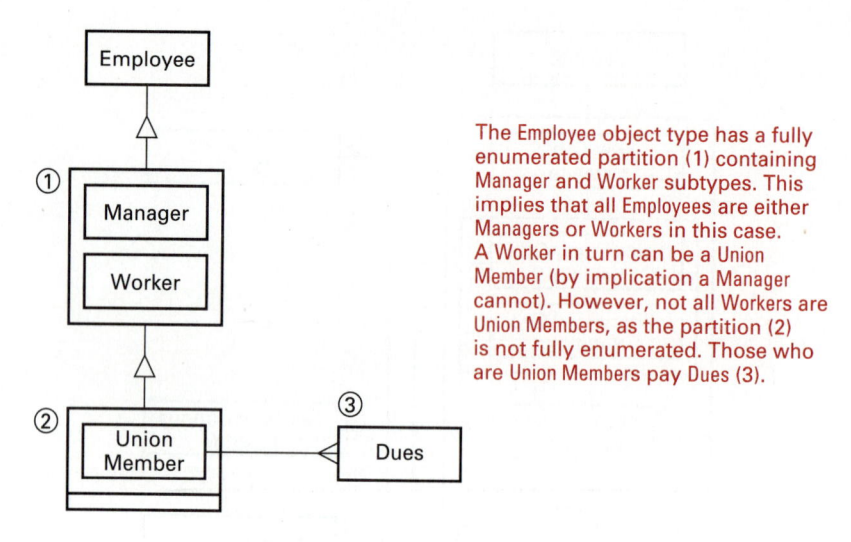

[Figure 7.4 diagram]

The Employee object type has a fully enumerated partition (1) containing Manager and Worker subtypes. This implies that all Employees are either Managers or Workers in this case. A Worker in turn can be a Union Member (by implication a Manager cannot). However, not all Workers are Union Members, as the partition (2) is not fully enumerated. Those who are Union Members pay Dues (3).

Figure 7.4 Two levels of subtyping.

practice in engineering. For example, a car engine is composed of an engine block, valves, pistons, and so on. A piston itself is a complex object made up of piston rings, a piston rod, and a piston head. Yet, the engine is handled and cataloged as one component. If it fails, the entire engine might be replaced.

A special form of relationship among object types is the *composed-of relationship*. This relationship could be drawn for a car engine as follows:

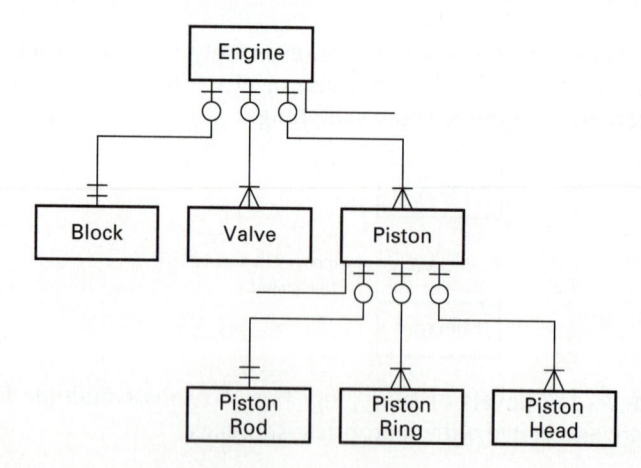

[Composed-of diagram: Engine composed of Block, Valve, Piston; Piston composed of Piston Rod, Piston Ring, Piston Head]

A composed-of relationship may appear on a composed-of diagram, such as that above, which only shows object composition. It may also appear on more general object-relationship diagrams. To distinguish it, a composed-of relationship is drawn with an easily recognizable symbol—an arrow drawn like a "C" for composition.

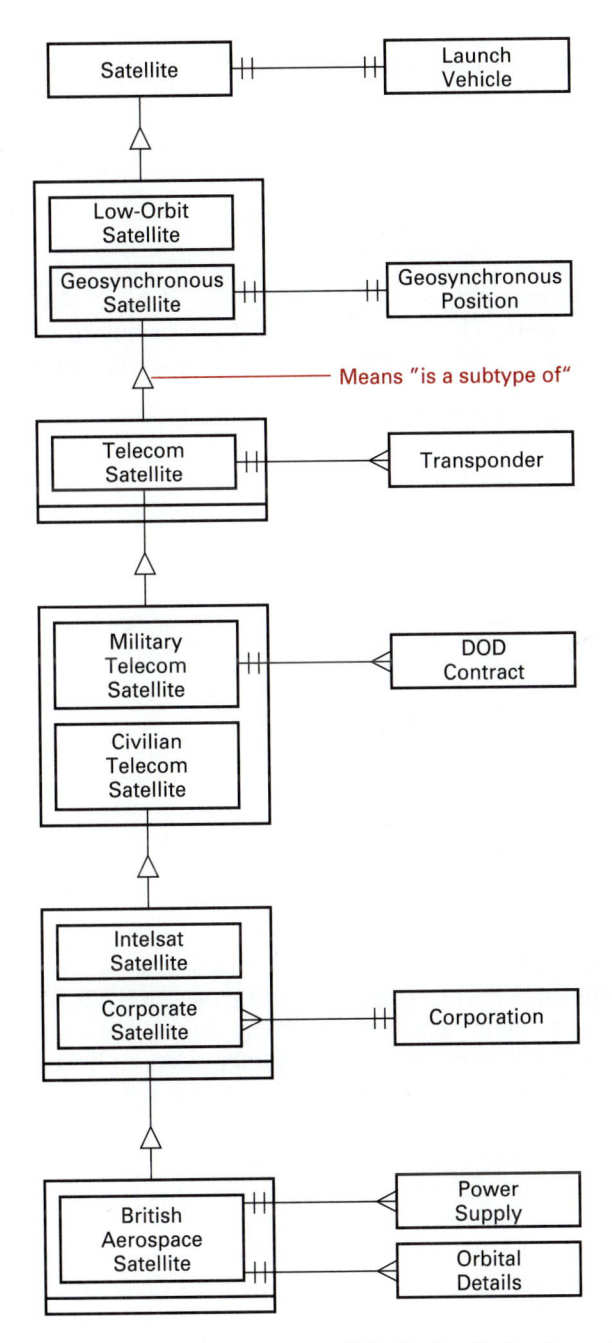

Figure 7.5 Triangle arrows showing multiple levels of subtyping and object types associated with appropriate levels.

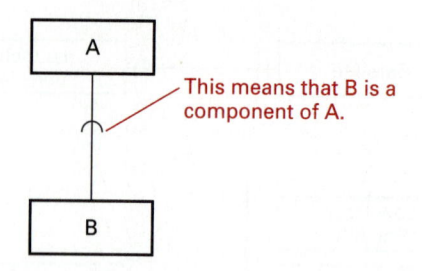

[Diagram: Box A above box B connected by a line with a "C"-shaped symbol whose arms point toward B. Annotation: "This means that B is a component of A."]

The symbol means *is a component of*. The arms of the "C" are directed toward the component. This shorthand avoids our having to write "is a component of" on many lines. For example, here is a diagram of a track-lighting unit:

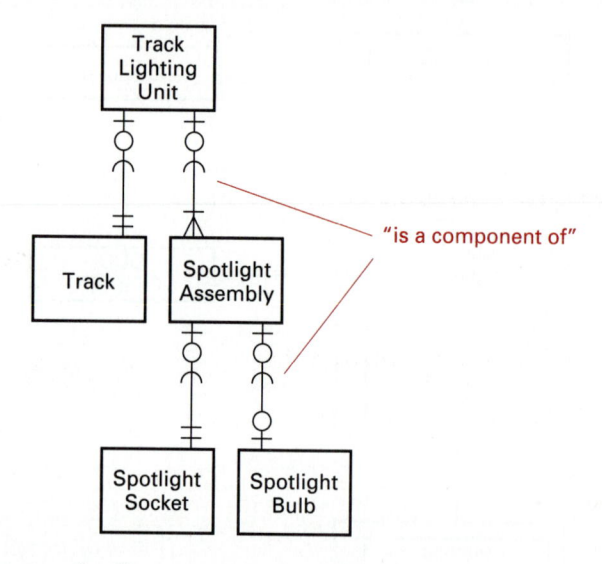

[Diagram: Track Lighting Unit at top, connected down to Track and Spotlight Assembly. Spotlight Assembly connects down to Spotlight Socket and Spotlight Bulb. Annotation points to the symbols: "is a component of"]

Expressing cardinality constraints on composition associations is important, because a composite object can consist of zero, one, or many objects of different types. For instance, while each Track Lighting Unit will always have one Track, it will also have one or more Spotlight Assembly objects. In addition, while each Spotlight Assembly always has one Spotlight Socket, it may or may not have a Spotlight Bulb in it.

In OO, object composition helps to describe that machines are made up of certain parts, jobs are composed of specific tasks, organizations consist of other organizations, and so on. In advanced office systems, the analyst will describe how an order can consist of not only line items but contain verbal instructions from the customer and a handwritten diagram as well. Orders of this kind are called *complex objects*. Each order can be manipulated as a single object consisting of other objects that, in turn, can be manipulated separately, if necessary.

SUBTYPING VERSUS COMPOSED-OF DIAGRAMS

Hierarchical diagrams can show *composed-of* relationships or *generalization* (subtyping, as described in the previous chapter). Subtyping relates to inheritance—a subtype inherits all the properties of its parent.

A generalization diagram might represent a class hierarchy. This is entirely different from a composed-of hierarchy. The lower-level items in a composed-of hierarchy do not inherit properties from the higher-level items.

To distinguish these meanings a "C" symbol is used for composed-of diagrams and a triangle arrow is used for generalization diagrams.

"is a component of"   "is a subtype of"

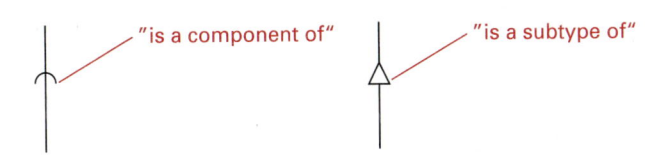

Figure 7.6 contrasts two similar looking diagrams that have quite different meanings.

A subtyping hierarchy is referred to as a *generalization hierarchy* or *generalization-specialization* diagram (*gen-spec*, for short). It could be referred to as an inheritance hierarchy or subtyping diagram. An inheritance mechanism is not always used in a program; a generalization hierarchy could be implemented with flags rather than inheritance.

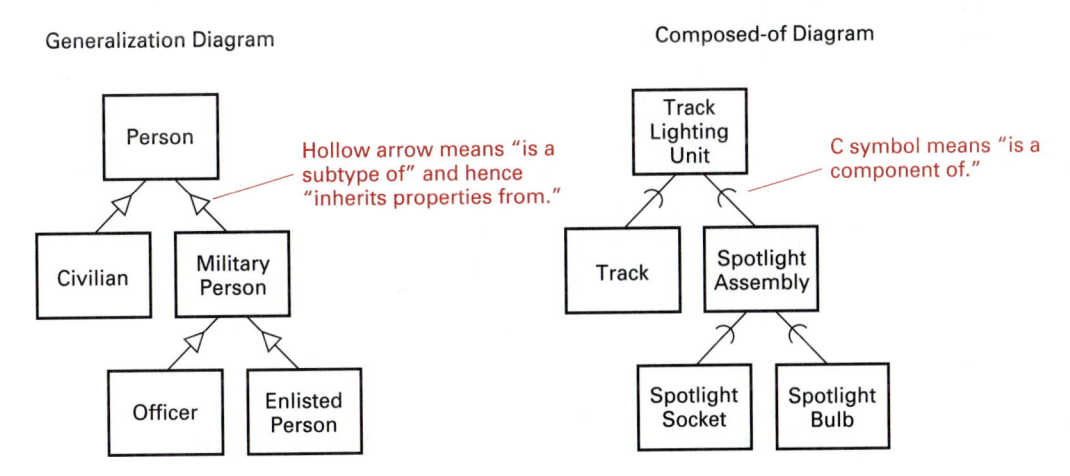

Figure 7.6 Triangle arrows (or no arrows on fern diagrams) are used on generalization (subtyping) diagrams; "C" symbols are used on composed-of diagrams.

SUBTYPING AND COMPOSITION ON THE SAME DIAGRAM

Sometimes, both subtyping and composition must be shown on the same diagram, as in the following:

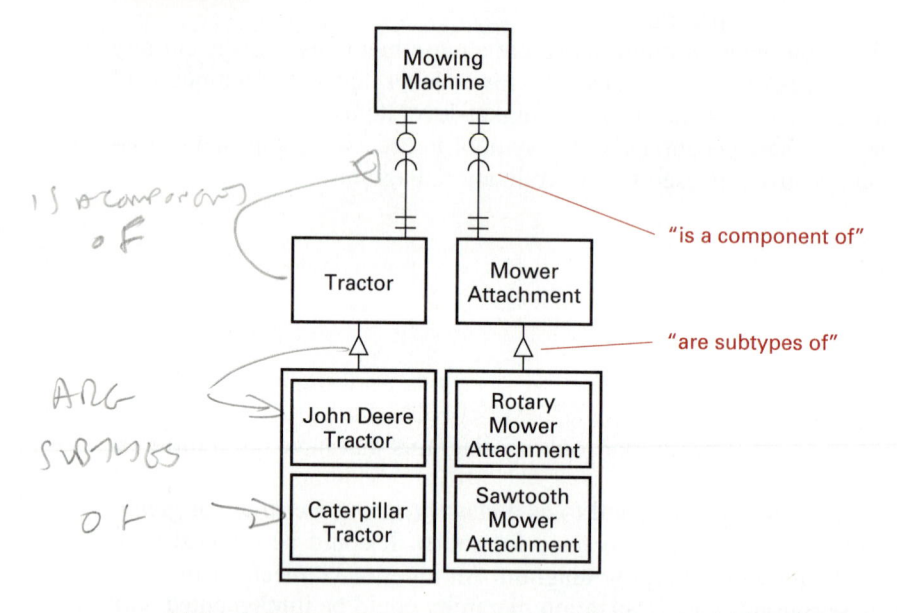

[Diagram: Mowing Machine composed of Tractor (subtypes: John Deere Tractor, Caterpillar Tractor) and Mower Attachment (subtypes: Rotary Mower Attachment, Sawtooth Mower Attachment). Annotations: "is a component of", "are subtypes of".]

This diagram indicates that the tractor in a mowing machine can be a John Deere, a Caterpillar, or some other tractor. The mower attachment can be either rotary or sawtooth.

A block showing what an object is composed of may contain an object-relationship diagram, as shown below:

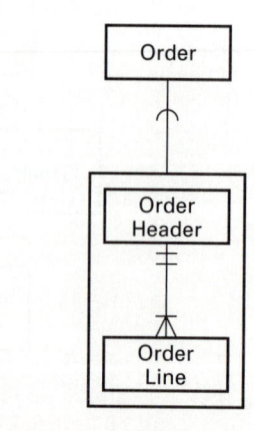

[Diagram: Order; Order Header composed of Order Line.]

Figure 7.7 shows other such examples.

94

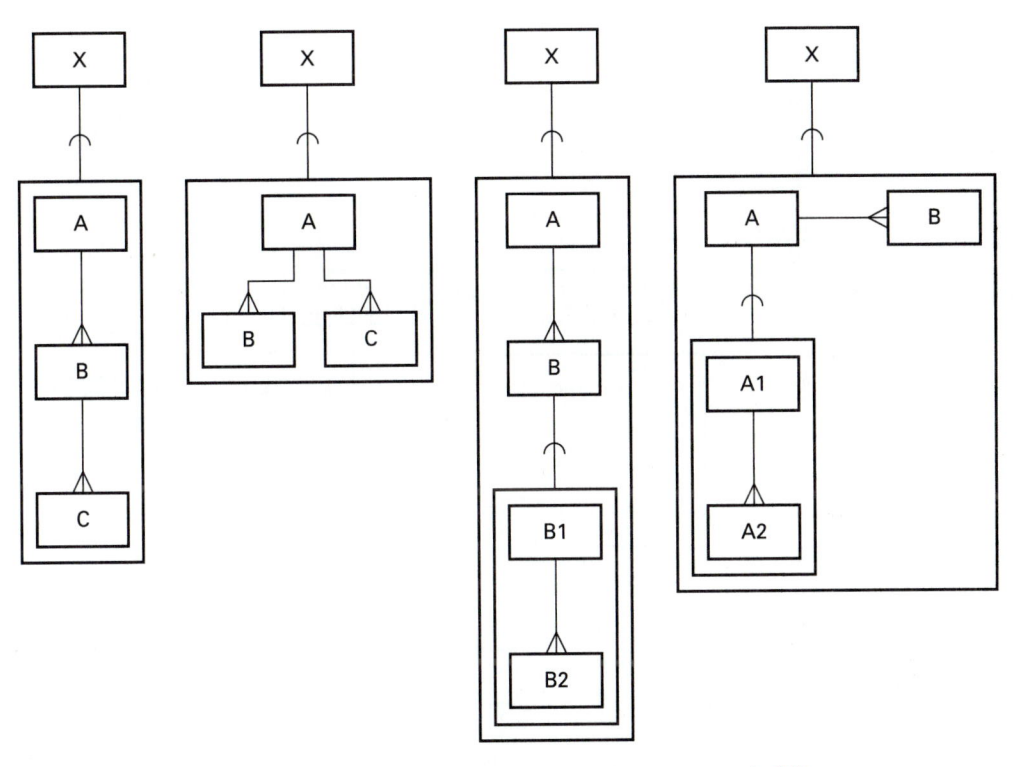

Figure 7.7 Object-relationship diagrams with blocks on composed-of diagrams.

Figures 7.8 and 7.9 each have general relationships, composed-of relationships, and subtyping on the same diagram.

OCCAM'S RAZOR AT WORK The analyst drawing an object-relationship diagram should be looking for commonality wherever possible—applying the Principle of Occam's Razor that two object types should not be used where one will suffice. For example, a diagram of object types on an invoice is shown in Fig. 7.10. It shows how the separate object types **Goods** and **Service** could be made subtypes of one object type **Product**.

The subtyping represented on the lower diagram means that **Goods** and **Service** inherit properties of **Product**. This leads to a high level of reusability. If the analyst does not identify the common supertype **Product**, he will probably design and code redundant attributes and operations.

We described earlier a bank that had 1800 transaction types that could be consolidated into 49—the result of overlooking commonality. For 20 years, each analyst built his own transactions when high-level OO modeling could have cre-

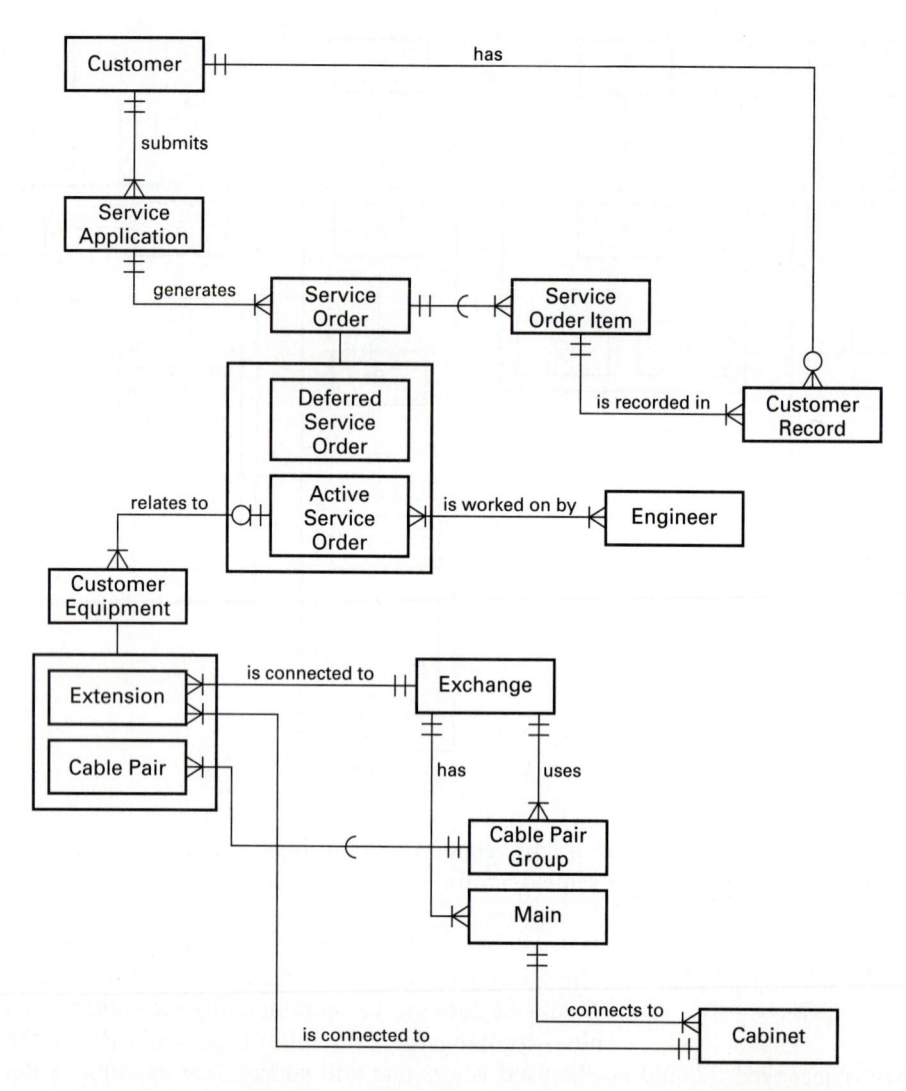

Figure 7.8 An object-relationship diagram for a telephone company. General relationships, composed-of relationships, and subtyping (with inheritance) all appear on this diagram.

ated commonality and inheritance. When the small example in Fig. 7.3 is multiplied by many analysts for many years, the results are high maintenance costs and less flexibility in changing the business systems.

OVERVIEW DIAGRAMS

Object-relationship diagrams grow large, especially when they describe an entire business area. To handle

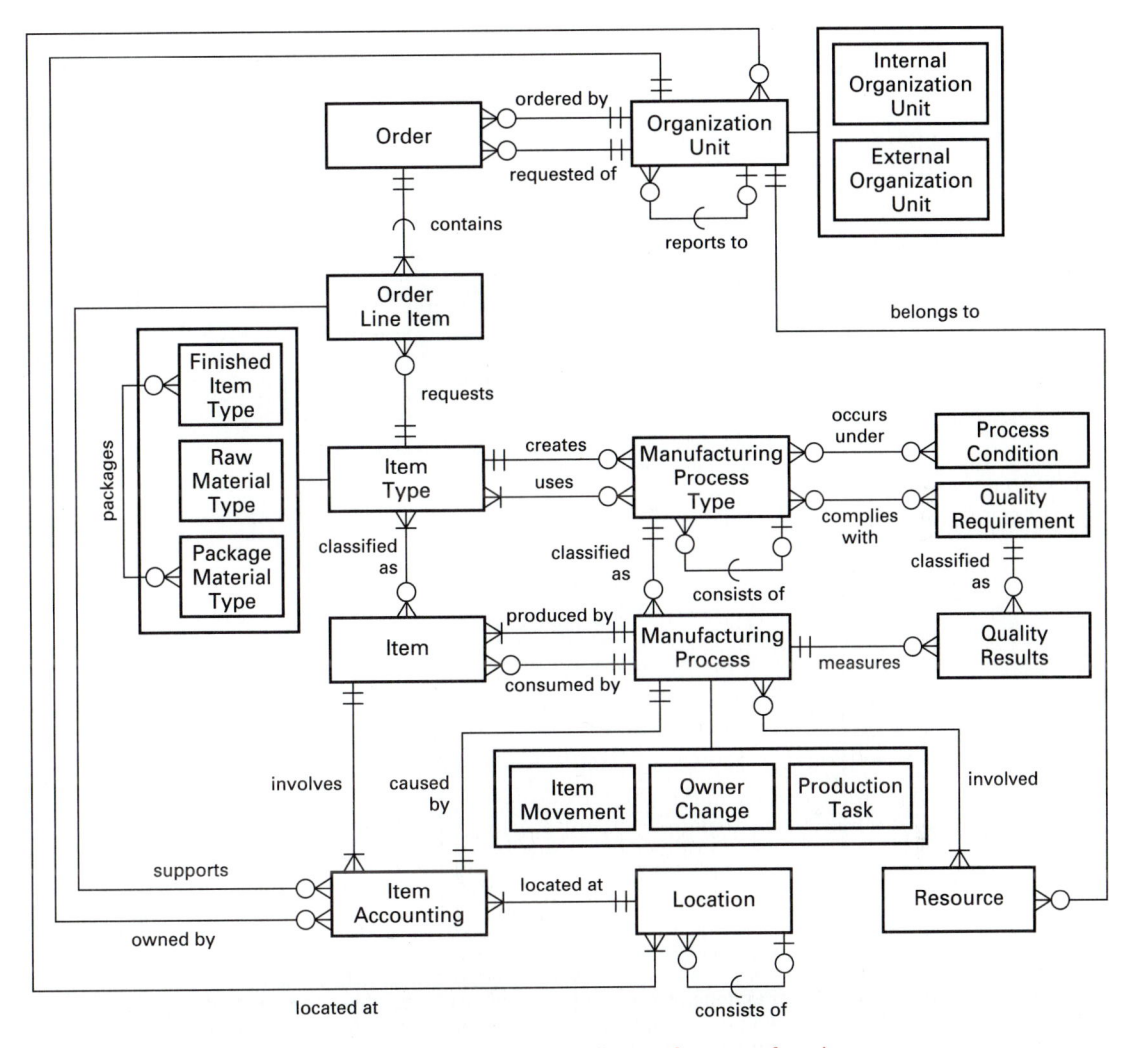

Figure 7.9 A sample object-relationship diagram for a manufacturing company.

such large diagrams, CASE tools employ a variety of techniques—scrolling, zooming, subsetting, the use of windows, and so on.

It is very helpful to produce an overview of a complex diagram. To make it easy to understand, the details are hidden or summarized. The diagram may indicate that more detail is viewable at the click of a mouse. Overview diagrams are particularly important to use in workshops with end users (discussed in Chapter 14). A CASE tool should be able to produce overview diagrams that maximize comprehensibility for end users. CASE tools are very effective at hiding details and displaying them when needed.

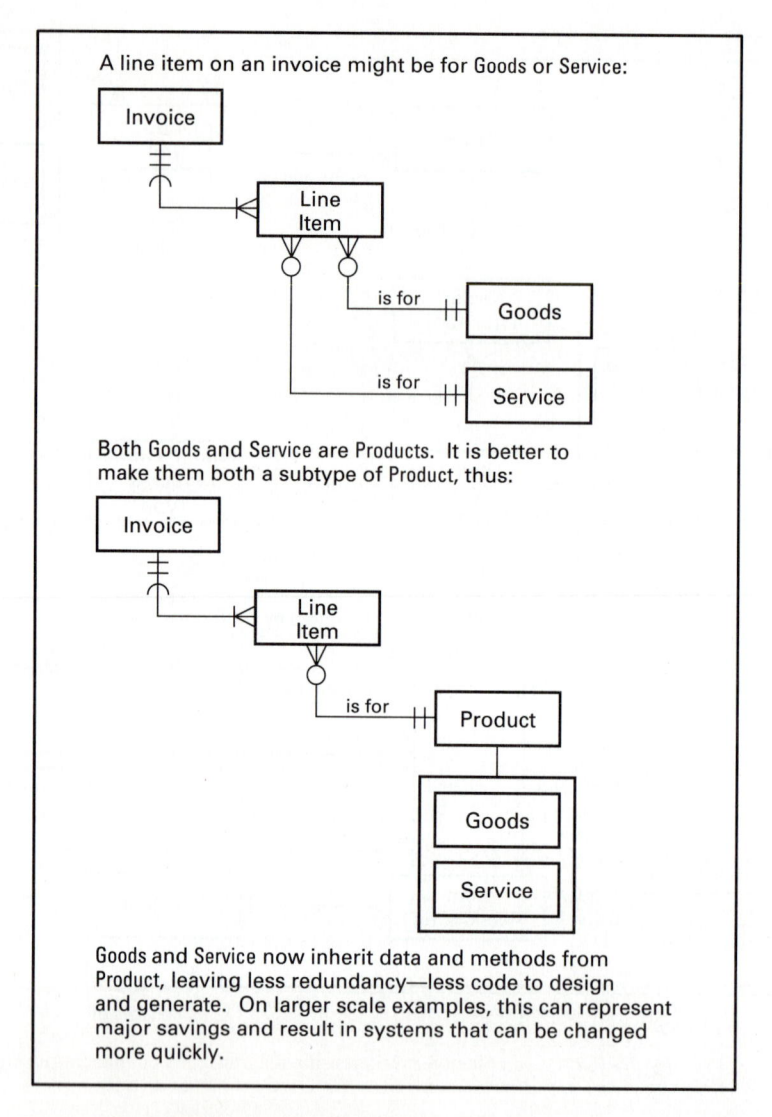

> A line item on an invoice might be for Goods or Service:
>
> [diagram: Invoice — Line Item, Line Item "is for" Goods, Line Item "is for" Service]
>
> Both Goods and Service are Products. It is better to make them both a subtype of Product, thus:
>
> [diagram: Invoice — Line Item, Line Item "is for" Product, with Goods and Service as subtypes of Product]
>
> Goods and Service now inherit data and methods from Product, leaving less redundancy—less code to design and generate. On larger scale examples, this can represent major savings and result in systems that can be changed more quickly.

Figure 7.10 Subtyping should be used wherever possible, because it results in less coding and maintenance.

To show that details are hidden, a "+" symbol is used on CASE diagrams. If the user mouse-clicks on the "+" symbol, the diagram expands or a window appears showing details. A "–" (minus) symbol may have the opposite effect—when the user clicks on it the diagram contracts. It is often possible to expand within expand within expand, or contract large diagrams into one block. Sometimes, an ellipsis (". . .") is used instead of a "+" symbol.

The expand symbol may indicate that different types of expansion can occur. For example, the user may expand in order to show subtypes or composition. The "+" may be beside a subtype symbol or a composition symbol:

On some tools, clicking on a block or symbol produces a menu of ways in which its contents can be displayed in more detail.

Figure 7.11 shows a detailed model being converted to an overview when the model contains both composition and subtyping.

This example illustrates another requirement when creating an overview—the associative relationship between object types must be abstracted. In the detailed model, there is an association between mail-order product and order line. At this level, it is a one to zero-or-many association. In the translation to the overview model, the internal structure within an order is recognized, and the association appears as a many to zero-or-many between **Product** and **Order**.

(a) Detailed View   (b) Overview

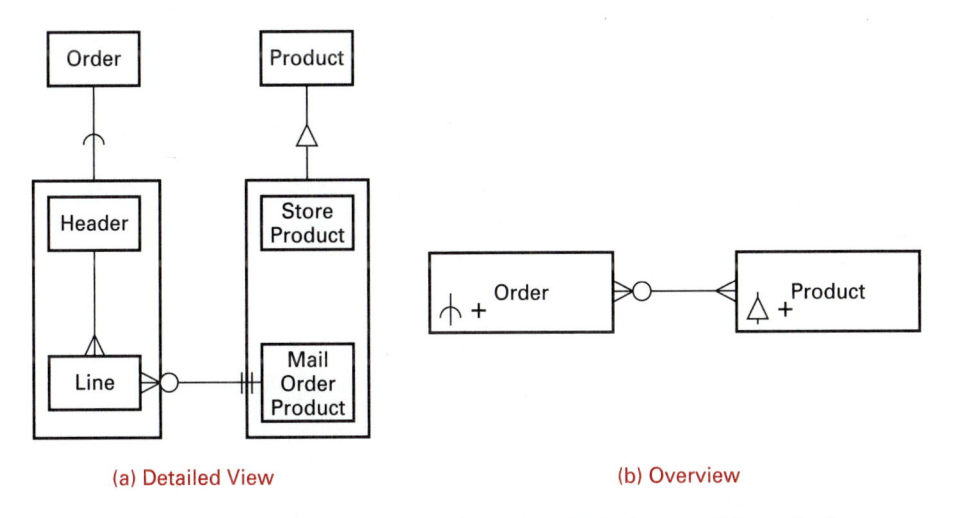

Figure 7.11 An overview created of a model with both composition and subtyping. An associative relationship appears in the overview.

Figure 7.12 illustrates a set of associations for a composition. The associations to A, B, C, and D are aggregated as the composition of **Order** is collapsed. In the case of A, B, and C, the relationships remain as in the detailed view; it is D that becomes a many to many in the overview.

It is not only cardinality that must be abstracted, the implications for optionality must also be considered. In Fig. 7.13, the associative relationship in the

(a) Detailed View *(b) Overview*

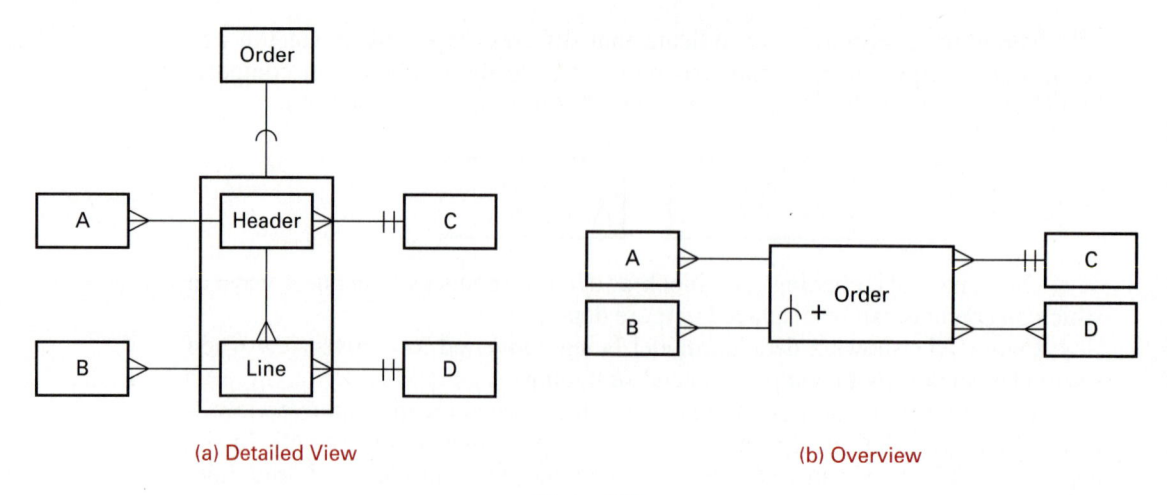

Figure 7.12

(a) Detailed View *(b) Overview*

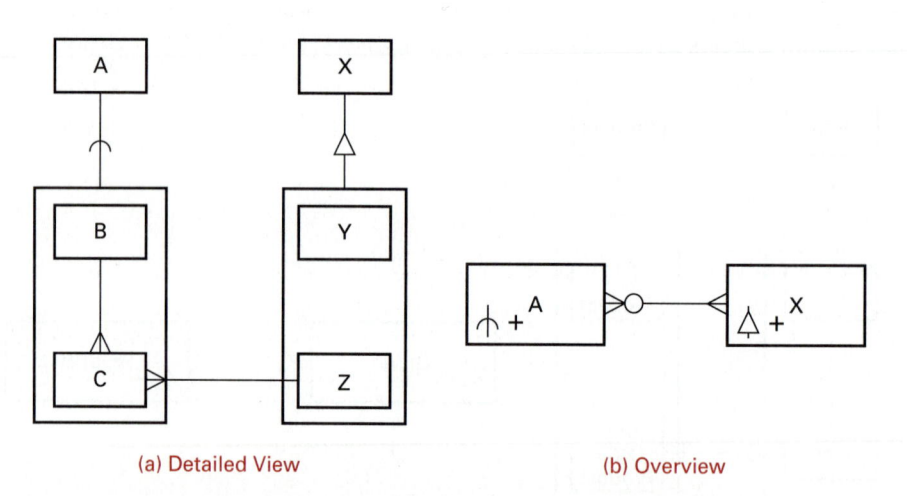

Figure 7.13

detailed model is fully mandatory. Due to the generalization, this cannot be the case in the overview model. In fact, wherever a generalization subtype is involved in a relationship, by definition all associative relationships become partially optional in an overview.

Automatically creating overviews of complex diagrams is very important, especially when the models are used to communicate with the business community or end users in general. OO modeling tools need to be designed so that they communicate as effectively as possible with the people who should use the models to reinvent business processes.

SUMMARY Three types of relationships exist among object types.

1. *General relationships.* These are shown, appropriately labeled, on an object-relationship diagram.
2. *Composed-of relationships.* This special type of general relationship may be indicated with a "C" symbol on the line:

"is a component of"

Composed-of diagrams show only this relationship.

3. *Subtypes and inheritance.* Object subtypes *inherit* the properties of their *parent.* This inheritance is indicated with a triangle arrow.

"is a subtype of"

It may also be indicated by boxes within boxes.

These three types of relationships sometimes appear on the same diagram. When this happens, it is usually best to draw the subtypes as boxes within boxes. Examples of these three types of relationships are shown in Figs. 7.5 and 7.6.

Although subtyping and composition might appear on general object-relationship diagrams, a CASE tool should be employed that can also display this information separately in generalization diagrams and composition diagrams.

REFERENCES

1. Codd, E. F., "Further Normalization of the Data Base Relational Model," *Courant Computer Science Symposium 6: Data Base Systems,* Courant Computer Science Symposium 6 (New York), Randall Rustin ed., Prentice Hall, Englewood Cliffs, NJ, 1972, pp. 33-64.
2. Martin, James, *Managing the Data Base Environment,* Prentice Hall, Englewood Cliffs, NJ, 1983.

8 STATE AND STATE CHANGES

An object can be in one of many states. For example, a traffic light can be in one of four states:

- green
- yellow
- red
- red and yellow

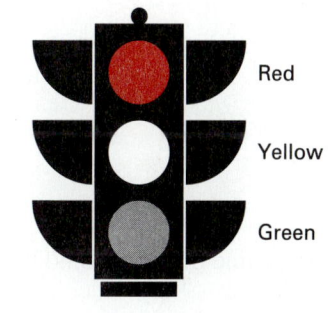

When its state changes, various actions take place.

A noteworthy state change is an *event*. For example, a traffic-light change is an event for motorists and pedestrians. A machine breaking down is an event as well as a change in the state of the machine. The receipt of a purchase order is an event and also a change in state of the **Purchase Order** object.

Object-behavior analysis is concerned with what events occur, the corresponding state changes, and the operations resulting from these state changes.

> State changes trigger operations.
> Operations result in state changes.

STATE LIFECYCLES An object can exist in one of many states. It can be thought of as having a lifecycle that is the sequence of states the object has in its lifetime. Sometimes, an object is created, passes through various states, and is then destroyed. For example, a job in a factory is started, progresses through various stages, and is then completed. Other objects cycle continuously through their states like a traffic light. In the language of OO, *requests* are sent and cause *methods* to be activated. The methods change the *state* of an object. The state is recorded in the object's data.

STATE-TRANSITION DIAGRAMS   The sequence of states are drawn on a *state-transition diagram.* Each state is drawn as follows:

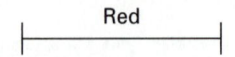

|—————— Red ——————|

Vertical lines show the transitions among states. For example, the lifecycle of a traffic light is as follows:

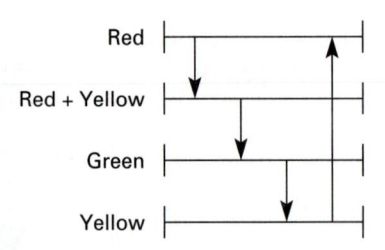

Red
Red + Yellow
Green
Yellow

An airline booking could be in one of the following states:

- Requested
- Waitlisted
- Denied
- Confirmed
- Modified
- Fulfilled
- Cancelled
- Archived

Figure 8.1 shows these states and some possible transitions among them.

Another example is a state-transition diagram to show the flow of a dialog on a screen. Each display can be in many different states. A screen dialog is represented in Fig. 8.2. This type of diagram is used in some CASE tools to show the interaction among the different displays. It illustrates the structure, or flow, of the dialog, that is, the dialog transitioning from one state to another. It is sometimes called a *dialog-flow diagram.*

Chap. 8 State and State Changes **105**

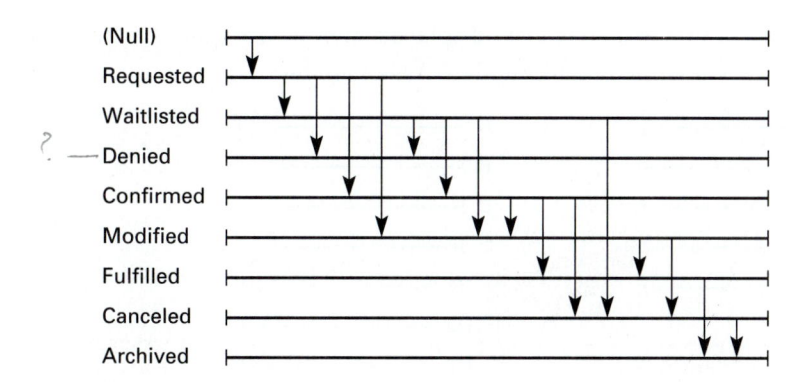

Figure 8.1 A state-transition diagram expressing some possible states of an Airline Booking object. The horizontal lines represent states, while the vertical lines represent transitions among states.

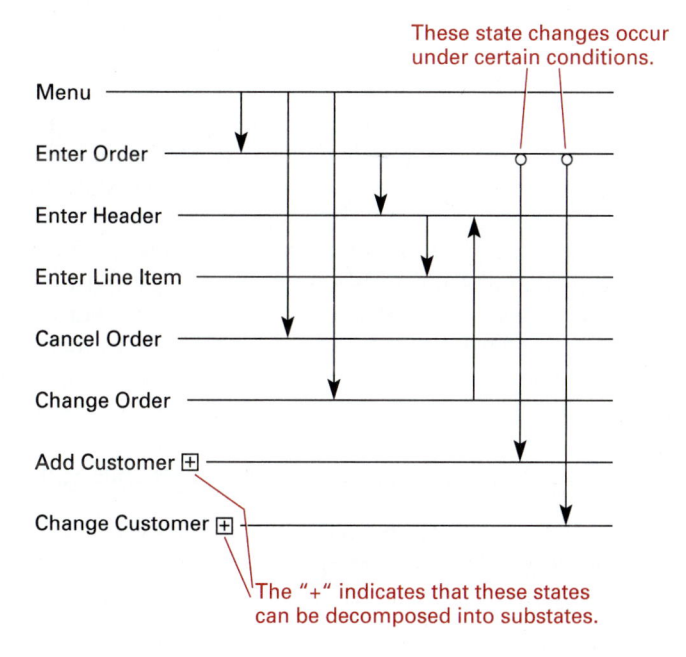

Figure 8.2 A state-transition diagram indicating that a Screen Dialog object can be in one of many states, each displaying a different panel. The horizontal lines represent states; the vertical lines show transitions between states.

SUBSTATES

An object can have many permissible states, which can be drawn more clearly by representing them as states and substates. When the substates of a particular state are not shown on a diagram, a "..." or "[+]" symbol is displayed next to the state. Clicking on this symbol causes the display of its substates (see Fig. 8.3).

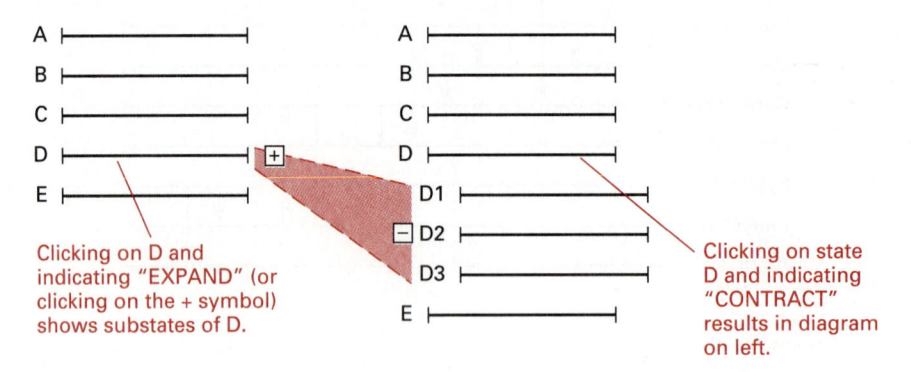

Clicking on D and indicating "EXPAND" (or clicking on the + symbol) shows substates of D.

Clicking on state D and indicating "CONTRACT" results in diagram on left.

Figure 8.3 There may be multiple levels of substates.

REUSABILITY IN STATE TRANSITIONS

Permissible states differ slightly, depending on the attributes of the object. For example, Fig. 8.4 shows five states that relate to objects of the type **Person** getting up in the morning. The state transitions are slightly different for a male person than for a female person.

In object-oriented analysis, recognizing opportunities for reusability is important. When diagramming object behavior, the analyst must consider which operations and object types can be reused and which cannot. For example, is the operation that makes a **Male Person** ambulatory the same as that for a **Female Person**? If so, the same behavior should be specified for both. Without this understanding, uncontrolled redundancy will run rampant. For instance, an order-processing system may have over a hundred different kinds of orders—each with its own lifecycle. By blindly analyzing each lifecycle separately, no opportunity

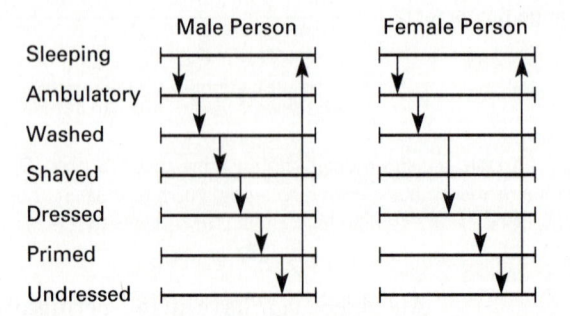

Figure 8.4 Personal-grooming related state changes can be slightly different for a male and female person.

for reusability will be discovered. A notation combining the generalizations and specializations on the same diagram can help remedy this.

COMPLEX STATE-TRANSITION DIAGRAMS

On a complex state-transition diagram, the lines representing states may not span the entire diagram, as in Fig. 8.1 and Fig. 8.4. For example, only two of the states span the entire diagram in Fig. 8.5.

FINITE-STATE MACHINES

Long before object-oriented design came into use, *finite-state machine* design was used. A finite-state machine is a hypothetical mechanism that can be in one of a discrete number of states. State changes occur at discrete points in time, instead of a slow, continuous change. Events represent an instantaneous change in the state of the finite-state machine. Certain complex software was designed as though it consisted of multiple finite-state machines. An input caused the finite-state machine to change state and produce an output. Figure 8.5 is one of many finite-state machines that defines the protocols of IBM's Systems Network Architecture (SNA).

Finite-state machines fit closely into the object-oriented view of the world. An object can be a finite-state machine. It is a black box. Send it an input and it behaves in a certain way. The finite-state machine is isolated from cause and effect and acts without knowing why an input was received or how its output will be used. Complex software may consist of many finite-state machines.

A class is a finite-state machine that is organized in a particular way—with methods, inheritance, and encapsulation.

MULTIPLE SIMULTANEOUS STATES

One object can have more than one set of states. For example, an airline booking could be in one each of the following two sets of states:

①

- Requested
- Denied
- Confirmed
- Waitlisted
- Modified
- Fulfilled
- Canceled

②

- Unpaid
- Deposit paid
- Fully paid
- In need of refund
- Refunded

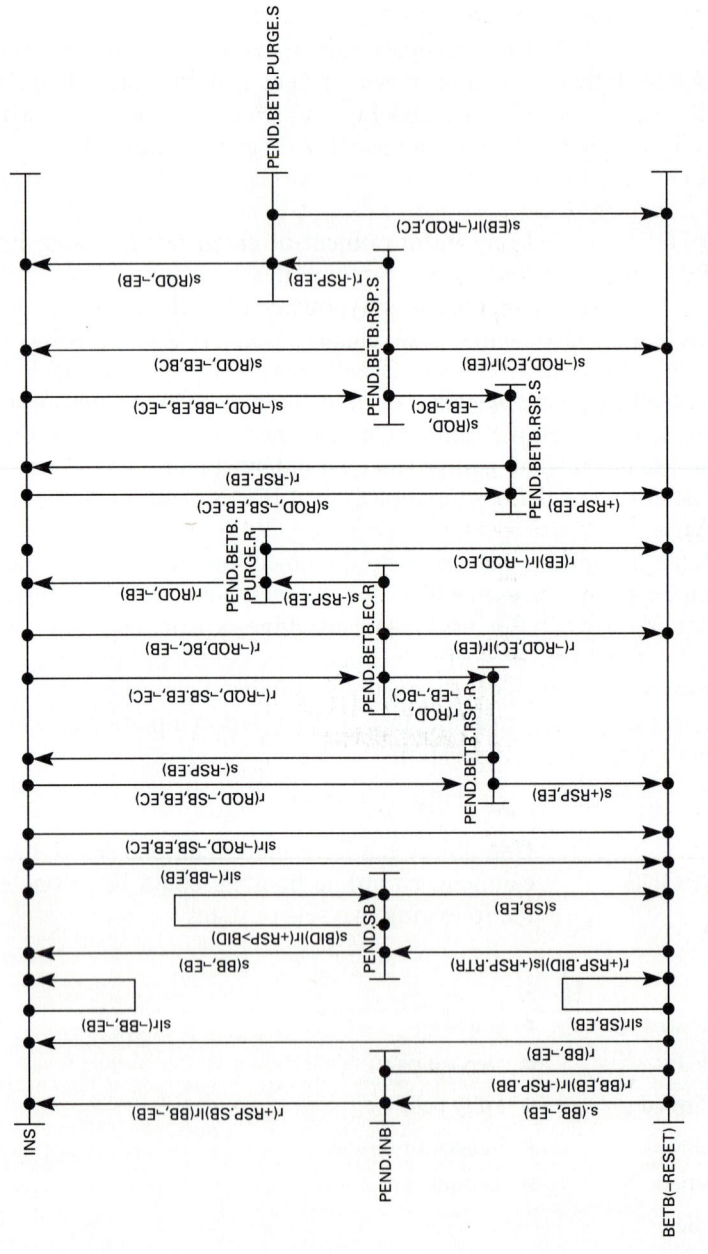

Figure 8.5 A complex state-transition diagram, one of many finite-state machines that defines the protocols of IBM's SNA (Systems Network Architecture) [1].

A separate state-transition diagram and separate object lifecycles could exist for each set.

The separate sets of states may not be entirely independent of one another. For example, an airline might have a rule that a booking state cannot change from **Requested** to **Confirmed** until the payment state is either **Deposit Paid** or **Fully Paid**. This is one of the types of *rules* expressing object behavior that should be explicit input to OO-CASE tools, discussed in Chapter 10.

Some objects can have many sets of states. The overall state of an object is the collection of states that it is in at one instant.

When implemented, the states are recorded in the data stored about the object. The overall state of the object is the collection of variables stored about the object. OO programmers sometimes define this by saying that the *state* of an object is the collection of associations the object has.

EVENTS

Our world is full of events. The cat has kittens. Aunt Agatha arrives unexpectedly. An airline customer requests a booking. A machine tool breaks down. A job is completed.

In object-oriented analysis, the world is described in terms of objects and their states, as well as events that change those states.

> An *event* is a noteworthy change in the state of an object.

For example, in Fig. 8.6 an object's state is changed from being a **Wait-listed Airline Booking** to a **Confirmed Airline Booking**.

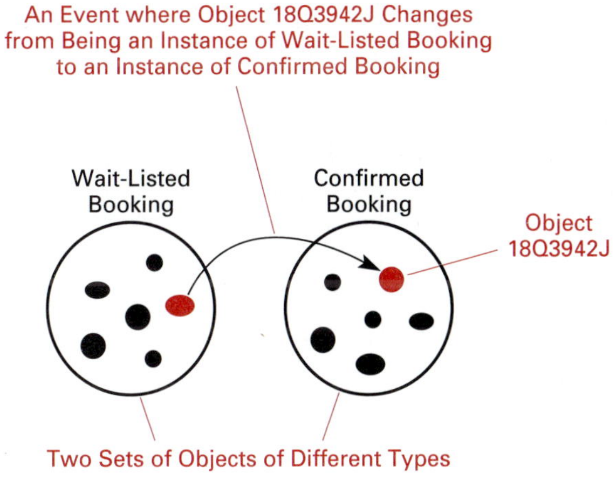

Figure 8.6 The state of an object changing from one object type to another.

The next chapter discusses *events* and *event diagrams.*

REFERENCE

1. IBM, *IBM Systems Network Architecture, Format and Protocol Reference Manual: Architecture Logic,* Manual Number SC 30-3112, IBM, White Plains, NY.

9 EVENTS, TRIGGERS, AND OPERATIONS

EVENTS

To model the behavior of object-oriented systems, we determine what *events* happen. Events cause the systems to take various actions. We map the events and corresponding actions with an *event diagram*. The following are examples of events.

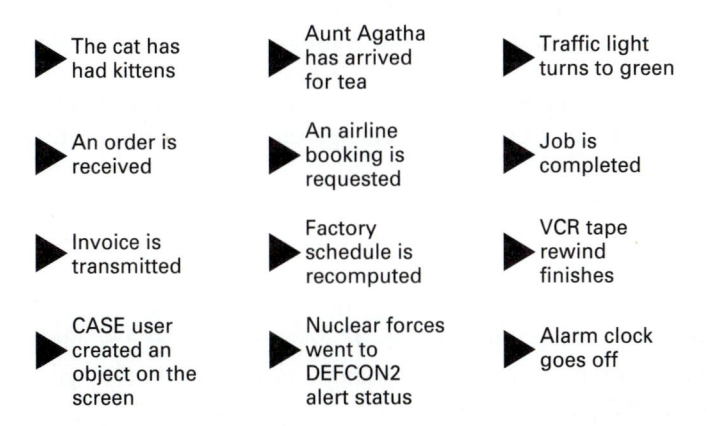

▶ The cat has had kittens
▶ Aunt Agatha has arrived for tea
▶ Traffic light turns to green

▶ An order is received
▶ An airline booking is requested
▶ Job is completed

▶ Invoice is transmitted
▶ Factory schedule is recomputed
▶ VCR tape rewind finishes

▶ CASE user created an object on the screen
▶ Nuclear forces went to DEFCON2 alert status
▶ Alarm clock goes off

The event diagram shows events and the operations triggered by events. End users tend to think intuitively about events and operations triggered by events. Instead, they should be taught how to read event diagrams and validate their correctness. The event diagram is a primary means of communicating OO behavior to end users.

A SEQUENCE OF OPERATIONS

An event diagram contains a sequence of operations. The operations are drawn with round-cornered boxes as in the following examples:

111

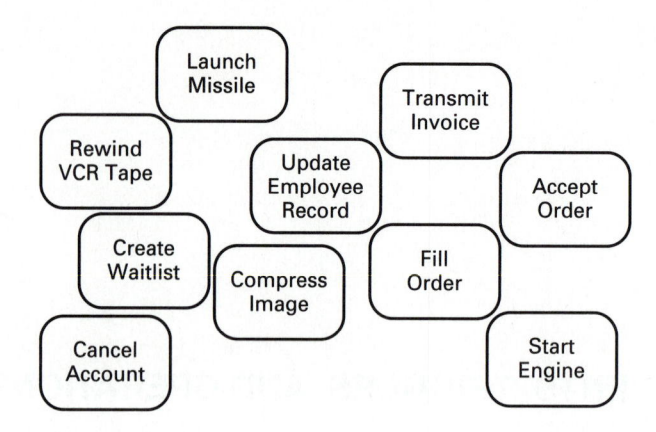

[Diagram of operation boxes: Launch Missile, Rewind VCR Tape, Update Employee Record, Transmit Invoice, Accept Order, Create Waitlist, Compress Image, Fill Order, Cancel Account, Start Engine]

Figure 9.1 tells a story: a driver runs a red light and is chased by the police. In such a diagram, the sequence of operations is self-explanatory and can be easily understood by end users. We need only add some detail to show events, trigger rules, and control conditions.

The term operation refers to a unit of processing that can be requested. The corresponding procedure is implemented with a *method. The method is the specification of how the operation is carried out: it is the script for the operation.* At the program level, the method is the code that implements the operation.

Operations are *invoked.* An *invoked operation* is an *instance* of an operation. An operation may or may not change the state of an object. If it does, an *event* occurs.

EVENTS AND OPERATIONS

While some events are external to the system, most occur within the system and result from an operation. Events are drawn as small solid triangles. When an event results from an operation, the triangle is attached to the operation box, as shown on the next page.

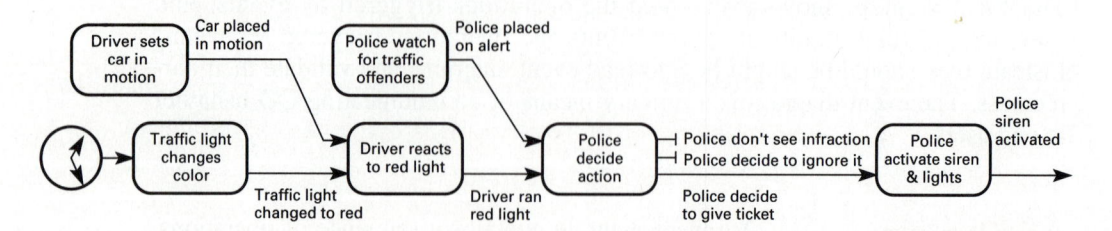

[Event diagram showing: Driver sets car in motion → Car placed in motion → Traffic light changes color → Traffic light changed to red → Driver reacts to red light → Driver ran red light → Police decide action → Police don't see infraction / Police decide to ignore it / Police decide to give ticket → Police activate siren & lights → Police siren activated. Also: Police watch for traffic offenders, Police placed on alert]

Figure 9.1 An event diagram for a car chase with all symbols and event subtype representation contracted.

Chap. 9   Events, Triggers, and Operations   **113**

Operation   *Event Type*

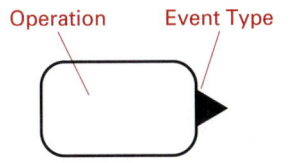

The event occurs at a point in time. The small triangle represents this point in time when the corresponding state change occurs.

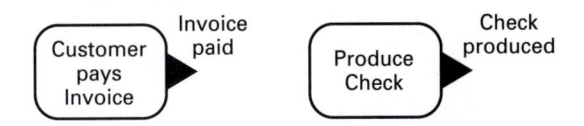

Customer pays Invoice → Invoice paid

Produce Check → Check produced

Sometimes, one operation results in multiple events:

Store Part in Bin →
- Bin Contents increased
- Part stored in Bin
- Inventory Storage Process completed

EVENTS AND STATE CHANGES

Events are, in effect, changes in the state of an object. **Traffic Light turns to Green** is a change in the state of the object **Traffic Light**. **Job is completed** is a change in the state of **Job**. An **Order is received** results in the creation of a new **Order** object. **Invoice is transmitted** is a change in the state of Invoice.

When the stock level of an item falls below its reorder point, this is a change in the state of a **Stock** object. Such an event also prompts us to act.

The process causing a state change may not be a part of the system we are building. However, the underlying object and its event may be important to the systems being specified.

An event is a noteworthy change in the state of an object. Because of this, event diagrams must be tightly linked to state-transition diagrams.

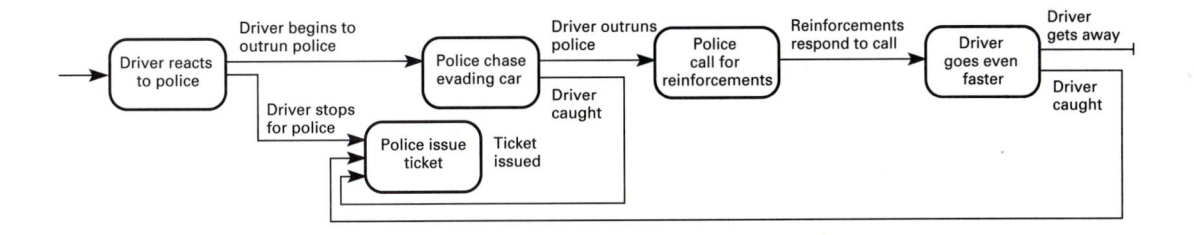

Driver reacts to police → Driver begins to outrun police → Police chase evading car → Driver outruns police → Police call for reinforcements → Reinforcements respond to call → Driver goes even faster → Driver gets away

Driver stops for police → Police issue ticket → Ticket issued

Driver caught

Driver caught

When we create diagrams showing events, we think about the equivalent diagrams showing objects and states. Event diagrams are linked to state-transition diagrams. On the screen of a CASE tool, a change to an event diagram is linked to the corresponding state-transition diagram that itself relates to the object-structure diagrams.

THE LINKING OF OPERATIONS

A model showing the behavior of an object-oriented system has many operations linked together, as shown in Fig. 9.2.

> Operations result in events.
> Events cause other operations to occur.

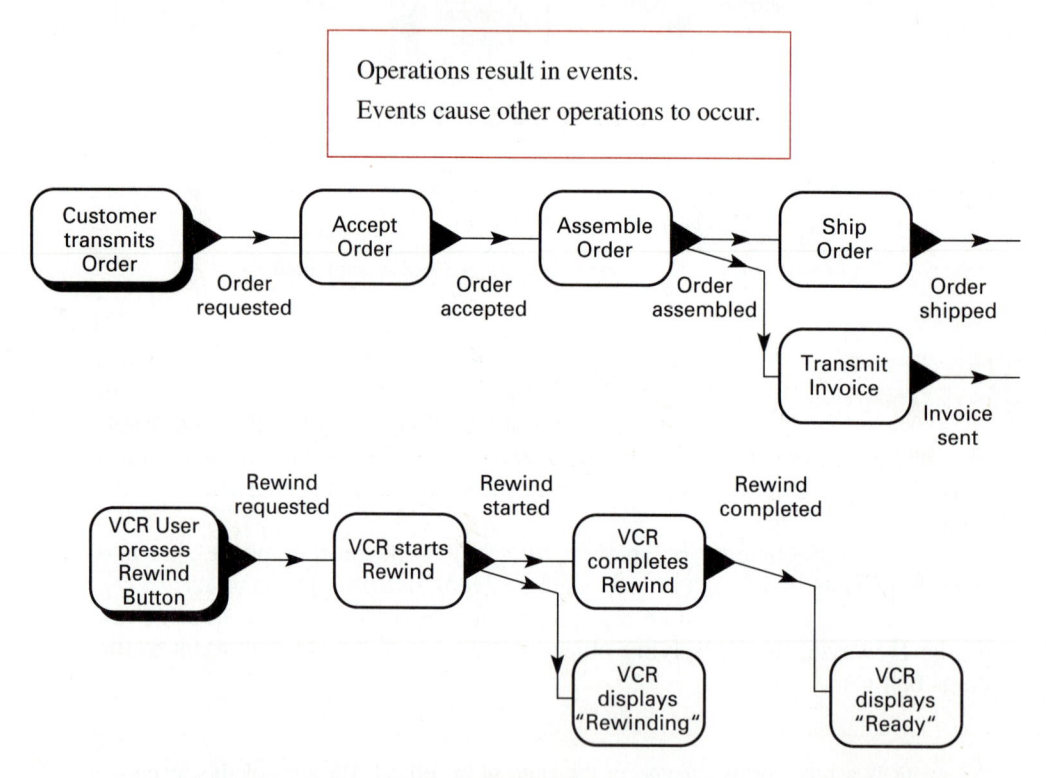

Figure 9.2

An operation may be performed by one *class*. The lines entering the operation often relate to the *requests* sent to that class. Sometimes, an operation is complex and needs expanding into more detailed event diagrams. At the lowest level of this expansion, *one* operation is usually performed by *one* class. One class has multiple methods that may be reflected by *multiple* operation blocks on event diagrams.

CAUSE-AND-EFFECT ISOLATION

Each operation carries out its task, regardless of what happens elsewhere. An operation is triggered by one or more events, executes its method, and is expected to change the state of one object. The operation has no knowledge of what event triggered it and why. Additionally, it does not know what operations are triggered from its event(s). In short, it does not recognize its cause and effect—only that it is invoked to produce a state change of a given object. This isolation from cause-and-effect considerations is necessary for the operation to be reusable in many different applications.

> An operation has no knowledge of what triggered it and why.
>
> An operation does not know what operations are triggered by *its* result.
>
> The operation is isolated from cause-and-effect considerations.
>
> This isolation makes it reusable in different applications.

PRECONDITIONS AND POSTCONDITIONS

An operation has a precondition and postcondition. Preconditions and postconditions are of vital importance in helping to ensure that a system operates correctly.

> *Preconditions* are those conditions that must be true before an operation can take place.
>
> *Postconditions* are those conditions that must hold when the operation is completed.

If the precondition is not satisfied when an operation is invoked, then the operation should not execute; it returns an error message. The postcondition describes the result; if it is not correct after execution then the operation did not execute correctly (see Fig. 9.3).

Because an operation should have no knowledge of what triggered it or what will be triggered by its result, it should also have a precondition and post-

Request → Operation → Result

Preconditions must apply before the operation is executed. If the precondition is not satisfied the operation will not execute; it returns an error message.

Postconditions must apply if the operation is executed correctly. Postconditions describe the correct behavior of the operation.

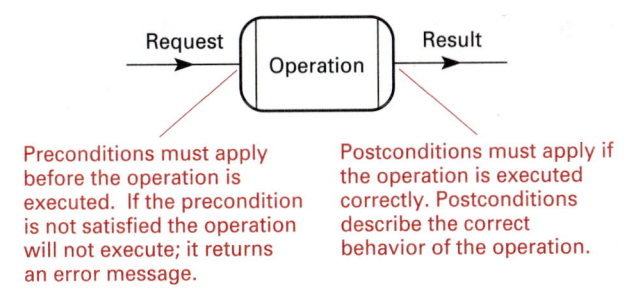

Figure 9.3 Preconditions and postconditions are independent of where the operation is executed.

condition that are independent of where it is used. The operation is implemented in software as a *method* in a *class*. The method may be invoked by different applications. It can provide a service to multiple *clients*. In effect it has a contract with its clients saying that if they send a request for which the precondition is satisfied, then the operation will execute so as to satisfy the postcondition.

> The presence of operation precondition and postcondition rules is, in effect, a contract that binds the operation. The operation says: "If you call me with the precondition satisfied, I promise to deliver a final state in which the postcondition is satisfied" [1].

A real-estate broker has a contract with its customers. The contract might have preconditions such as "I agree to pay the broker 6 percent of the purchase price if a property is purchased" and postconditions such as "A legal verification will have been made that the property has no encumbrances." This contract might be used by a broker for all of its clients, and the same contract might be used by many brokers.

In OO software design, a class, in effect, provides a contract to all potential users saying that if they invoke an operation with the correct precondition, it will provide a result satisfying the postcondition.

The existence of this contract simplifies programming. The program for the operation *is not required* to check the precondition. It can assume that the operation precondition rule is checked and is true before the operation executes.

Meyer comments:

> One of the main sources of complexity in programs is the constant need to check whether data passed to a processing element (routine) satisfy the requirements for correct processing. Where should these checks be performed: in the routine itself or in its callers? Unless module designers formally agree on a precise distribution of responsibilities, the checks end up not being done at all, a very unsafe situation or, out of concern for safety, being done several times.
>
> Redundant checking may seem harmless, but it is not. It hampers efficiency, of course; but even more important is the conceptual pollution that it brings to software systems. Complexity is probably the single most important enemy of software quality. The distribution of redundant checks all over a software system destroys the conceptual simplicity of the system, increases the risk for error, and hampers such qualities as extendibility, understandability, and maintainability.
>
> The recommended approach is to systematically use preconditions, and then allow module authors to assume, when writing the body of a routine, that the corresponding precondition is satisfied. The aim is to permit a simple style of programming, favoring readability, maintainability, and other associated qualities [1].

With an OO-CASE tool, it should be possible to point to an operation box and display its precondition and postcondition.

CLEAR MODULARIZATION

OO techniques provide two important ways to divide complex software into simple procedures. First, methods should result in a state change in one object. This state change, by itself, is usually simple and easy to program. Second, each operation is isolated from cause and effect. The operation can be reused on different software and on multiple interacting processors. The precondition and postcondition help to ensure its correct behavior.

OO techniques thus provide clear modularization that is simpler and more precise than that of conventional structured techniques. Objects of great complexity may be used with relatively simple requests, such as the use of a VCR. Complex objects can interact in one piece of software or on machines scattered across a network. Maintenance of software designed with OO techniques is easier than conventional software maintenance.

A world of difference exists between this clear modularization and the amorphous jelly-like nature of most non-OO software.

CLOCK EVENTS

A special type of event is a clock time being reached that triggers some operation. This type of event is drawn like a clock face:

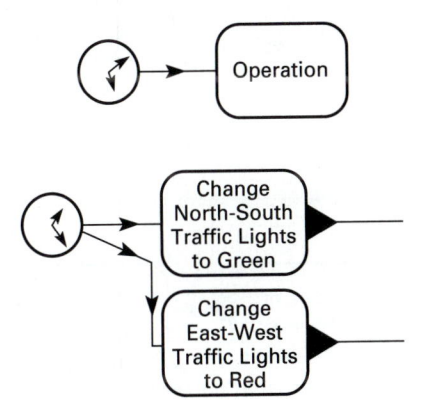

EXTERNAL SOURCES OF EVENTS

Events are state changes that a system must know about and react to in some way. Often, many of the operations that cause these events are *external* to the system. In these circumstances, the operation symbol is drawn as a shadowed box with round corners as illustrated in Fig. 9.4(a).

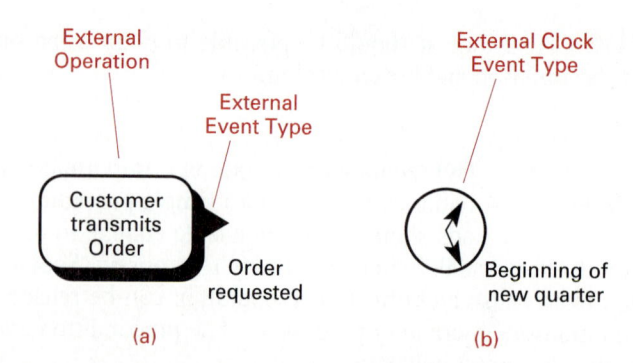

Figure 9.4 External operations are represented as round-cornered boxes with a shadow. When the event type is caused by an external clock, a clock face is used.

An *external clock* is a special form of external source. It indicates that an external process will emit clock ticks at some previously specified frequency, such as every second, the end of every day, the beginning of every month, or April 15th of every year. The event, then, is when the external clock tick occurs. External clocks are represented as clock faces.

Two external events resulting from an external operation can be seen in Fig. 9.5.

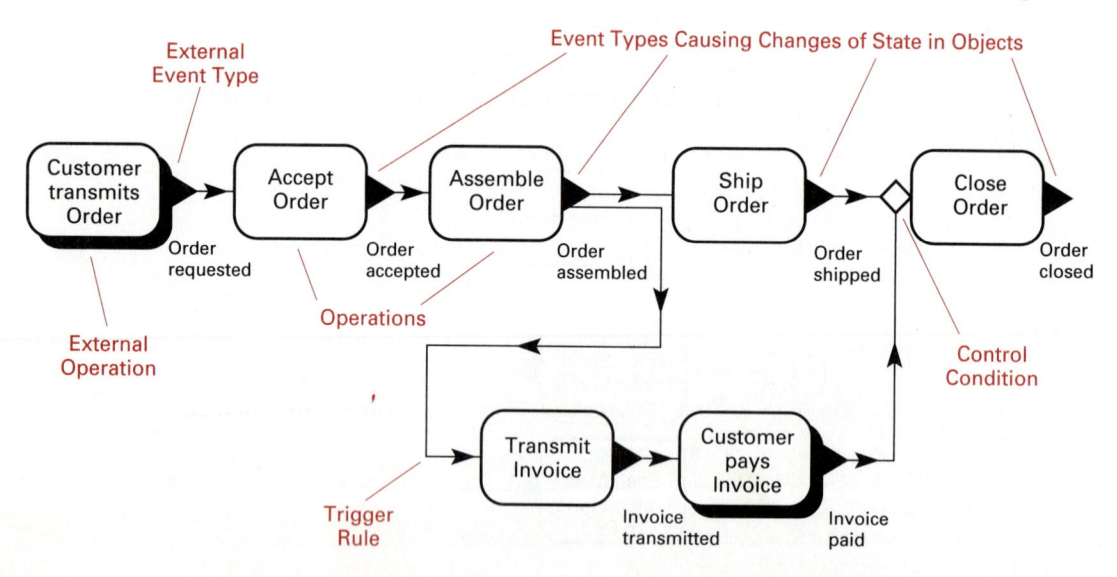

Figure 9.5 An event diagram showing operations and events that trigger operations. The events may relate to a corresponding state-transition diagram.

TYPES OF EVENTS

The OO analyst does not wish to know about every event that occurs in an organization—only the *types* of events. Just as we talk about object types and instances of object types, so we talk about event types and instances of event types. For example, the **Waitlisted Booking Confirmed** event type is the collection of those events in which an object changes from a **Waitlisted Booking** to a **Confirmed Booking**.

Event types indicate simple changes in object state, for example, when money is added to a bank account or an employee's salary is updated. Fundamentally, event types describe the following kinds of state changes:

- An object is *created*. For example, an airline booking is created.
- An object is *terminated*. For example, a product is destroyed or a contract is terminated.
- An object is *classified* as an instance of an object type. For example, a wife becomes a mother; a firm becomes a customer; an employee becomes a manager.
- An object is *declassified* as an instance of an object type. For example, a firm ceases to be a customer; a product is dropped from the sales catalog.
- An object *changes* classification. For example, a lawyer changes from associate to partner; an account changes from a normal account to an overdue account.
- An object's attribute is changed.

Events can associate one object with another. For example, in most organizations when an object is classified as an **Employee**, it must be associated with a **Department**. One event will classify the object as an **Employee**. A different event will create an association between the **Employee** object and a **Department** object. (Associations are objects like everything else. If named, this kind of association could be called the **Employee-Department Assignment** object type.) If the **Employee** changed **Department**, a new **Employee-Department Assignment** would be created and the old one terminated.

Updating an account balance is another example of an event. When $10 is added to account number 14274, an event associates the account with a different value.

Some events require other events to occur first. For example, before a **Department** can be closed, all of its **Employee**s must be allocated to a different **Department**, the **Office**s it occupied must be allocated to a different use, and so on.

Sometimes one event causes a chain reaction of other events. Changing a node on the screen of a CASE tool, for example, may require a set of changes to other objects in order to preserve integrity. Adding a circuit to the wiring of a jumbo jet may require mandatory changes to many objects.

TRIGGER RULES

When an event occurs, it usually triggers an operation, as in the above diagrams; it *may* trigger multiple operations. The line going from the event to the operation it triggers represents a *trigger rule*.

```
                    Trigger Rule
                         |
         ( )────▶( )
          |          |
      Event Type  Operation
```

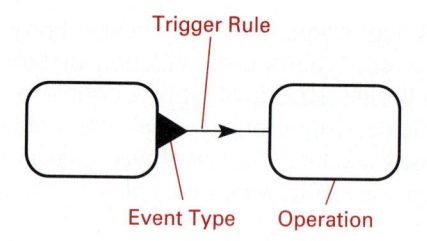

The *trigger rule* defines the causal relationship between event and operation. Whenever an event of a given type occurs, the trigger rule invokes a predefined operation. In the following diagram, the event type **Order Assembled** has two trigger rules—each of which triggers an operation:

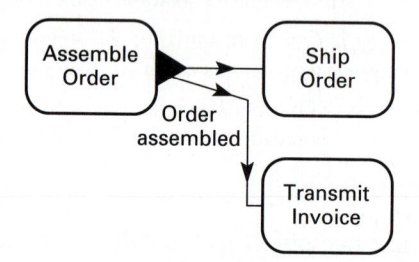

```
   Assemble ────▶ Ship
    Order          Order
         Order
       assembled
                ▶ Transmit
                   Invoice
```

An event type may have many trigger rules—each invoking its own operation *in parallel*. Parallel operations can result simultaneously in multiple state changes.

A trigger rule invokes an operation and defines the necessary objects to be supplied to that operation.

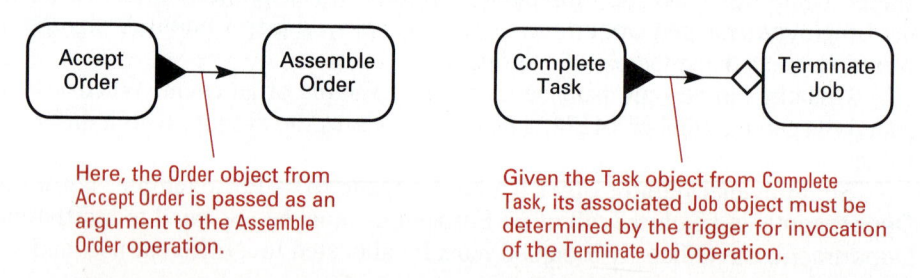

```
  Accept ────▶ Assemble         Complete ────▶◇ Terminate
  Order         Order             Task              Job
```

Here, the Order object from Accept Order is passed as an argument to the Assemble Order operation.

Given the Task object from Complete Task, its associated Job object must be determined by the trigger for invocation of the Terminate Job operation.

Trigger lines on an event diagram, then, indicate two things. First, they link the event to the operation that results from it. Second, they determine the objects required as arguments for the operation that the trigger invokes. These lines, therefore, define the rules for triggering an operation when a particular kind of event occurs. Because of that, they are called *trigger rules*.

MULTIPLE TRIGGERS

Sometimes an operation may be triggered in multiple ways. For example, **Produce Statement** may occur when a statement is requested or automatically at the end of the month:

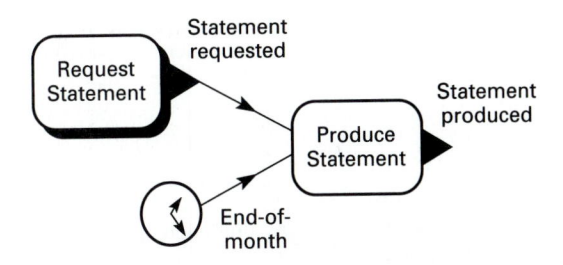

Chap. 9   Events, Triggers, and Operations   **121**

[Diagram: Request Statement —Statement requested→ Produce Statement —Statement produced→; End-of-month clock event also triggers Produce Statement]

In the following illustration, any one of the three events can trigger Estimate Modified Revenue.

[Diagram: Assess Monthly Sales, Adjust Price, Adjust Promotion Budget — any one triggers Estimate Modified Revenue]

Any one of these events may trigger Estimate Modified Revenue.

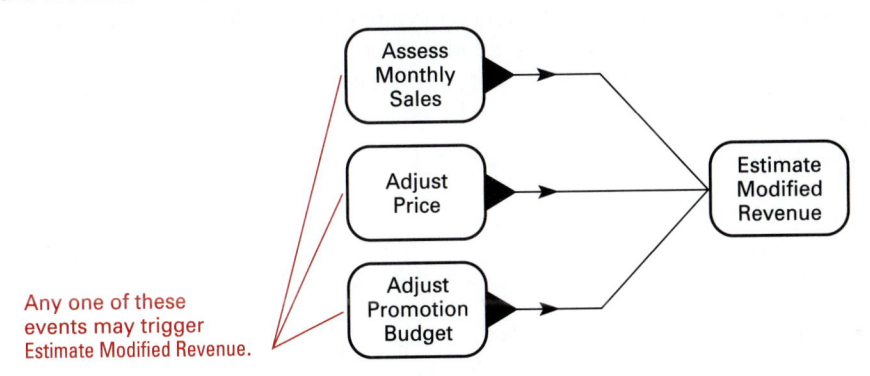

CONTROL CONDITIONS

The above operations are invoked by one trigger rule (one event). Often, an operation requires multiple triggers to invoke it. For example, the operation **Fire Missile** can occur only if multiple conditions are obeyed:

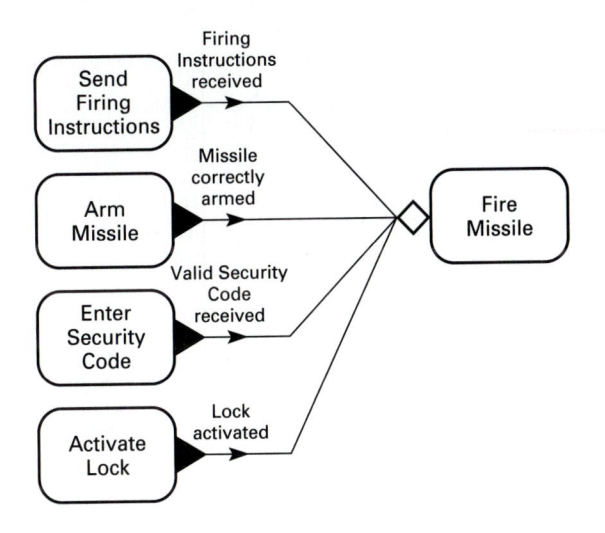

[Diagram: Send Firing Instructions (Firing Instructions received), Arm Missile (Missile correctly armed), Enter Security Code (Valid Security Code received), Activate Lock (Lock activated) — all four combine at an AND gate to trigger Fire Missile]

The diamond in front of the **Fire Missile** block is referred to as a *control condition*.

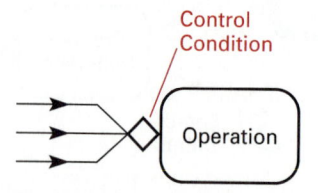

```
        Control
        Condition
          |
  ──▶
  ──▶◇──( Operation )
  ──▶
```

The control condition must be checked prior to invoking the operation. (The diamond shape is similar to the decision symbol used in flow charting.) The control condition can define a single condition or a complex collection of Boolean conditions. Control conditions are not necessarily just "and" conditions. They can involve elaborate conditions with "ands" and "ors":

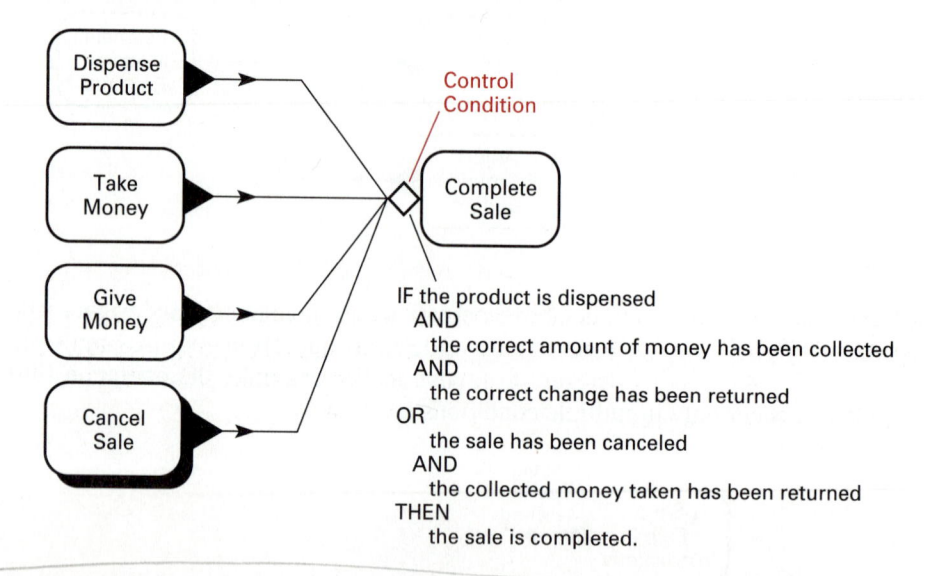

```
( Dispense )
(  Product )──▶╲
                ╲    Control
                 ╲   Condition
( Take   )        ╲    |
( Money  )──────▶──◇──( Complete )
                 ╱    (   Sale   )
( Give   )      ╱
( Money  )──▶──╱
              ╱
( Cancel )   ╱
(  Sale  )──╱
```

IF the product is dispensed
   AND
      the correct amount of money has been collected
   AND
      the correct change has been returned
OR
      the sale has been canceled
   AND
      the collected money taken has been returned
THEN
      the sale is completed.

THE BASIC CONSTRUCT OF

Event diagrams are thus constructed from operation blocks (see Fig. 9.6) and their connecting links as follows:

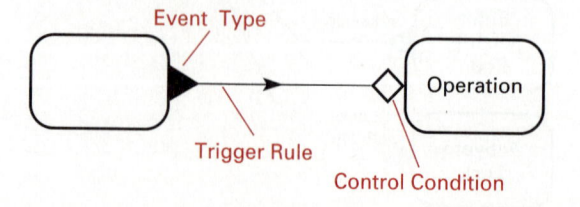

```
               Event Type
                   |
(       )▶────────▶◇──( Operation )
                   |         |
              Trigger Rule   |
                       Control Condition
```

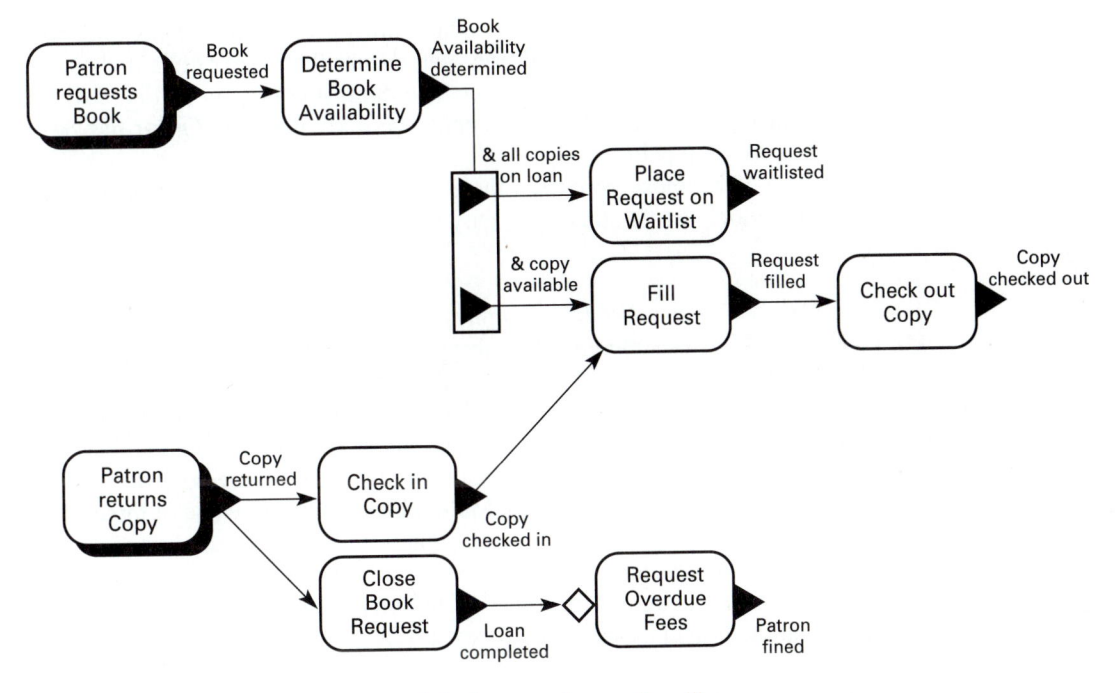

Figure 9.6 An event diagram for a library.

SIMULTANEOUS OPERATIONS

Event diagrams often indicate that multiple operations could be carried out at the same time. For example, in the following diagram **Ship Order** and **Send Invoice** could be done simultaneously.

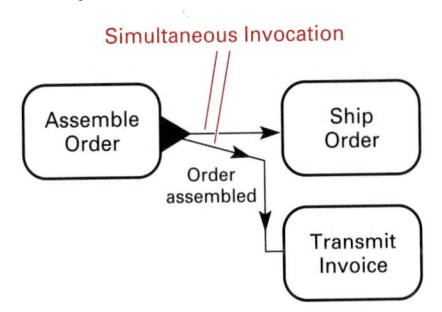

Simultaneous operations might be done on separate computers on a network. Much future computing will employ parallel (concurrent) processing. Design techniques are needed to indicate what processing can be done simultaneously on separate processors. Event diagrams indicate when processing can occur in parallel.

Control conditions can also act as synchronization points for parallel processing. In other words, control conditions can ensure that a set of events is complete before proceeding with an operation. The control condition in Fig. 9.4, for instance, might state that **Close Order** cannot be done until the **Order** has been shipped and its **Invoice** paid.

In models of business processes there are many operations that occur concurrently. The model should show how they interrelate.

OPERATION SUBTYPES AND SUPERTYPES

We have emphasized that objects and classes are subtyped. The subtype inherits the properties of its parent which leads to substantial reusability.

In a similar way, operations are subtyped. The analyst should search for similarities in operations, so that the classes that perform the operations can inherit the same data and methods where possible.

Suppose that the operation **Prepare Materials** is followed by one of three operations. The operations are mutually exclusive, that is, only one of them can occur.

Mutual exclusivity can be represented by a branching line with a filled-in circle at the branch. As shown in Fig. 9.7, the circle looks like an "o" for "or" and means that the branches are mutually exclusive.

Circle, like an "o" for "or" indicates that one and only one of the three operations follows.

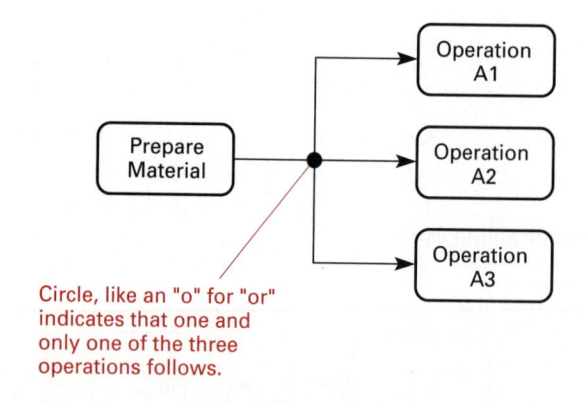

Figure 9.7

To represent this better, indicate that each of the three operations is a subtype of a general operation. In Fig. 9.8, they are shown in a partitioned box, as subtypes of **Operation A**.

Here, **Operation 1, Operation 2,** and **Operation 3** all inherit properties for **Operation A**. This form of representation encourages the analyst to think about inheritance and reusability. It resembles the subtyping of objects illustrated in Fig. 7.4. This can lead to less redundancy—less code to design and generate. On larger scale examples, this can represent major savings and result in systems that can be changed more quickly.

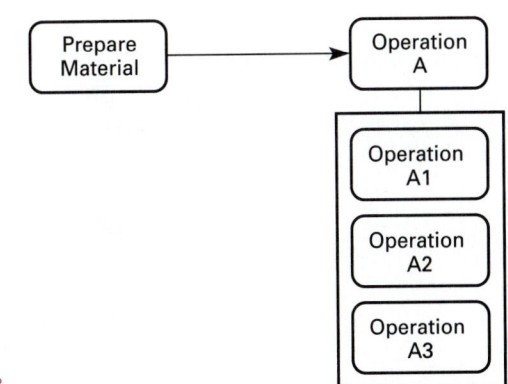

Figure 9.8

EVENT SUBTYPES AND SUPERTYPES

In a similar way, events are subtyped. This gives reusability of the trigger rules and control conditions.

The following diagram shows two events resulting from the **Review Task** operation.

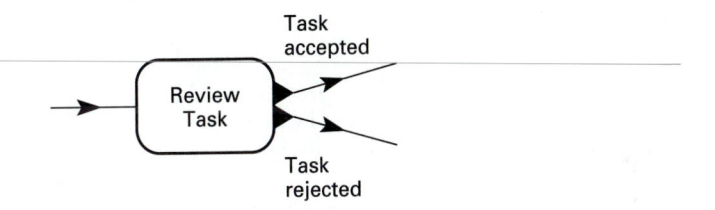

However, only one of the events can occur when a task is reviewed. The two event types are mutually exclusive. It is better, therefore, to show one event type **Task reviewed** with subtypes **Task accepted** and **Task rejected**.

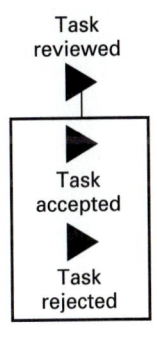

The resulting event diagram is as follows:

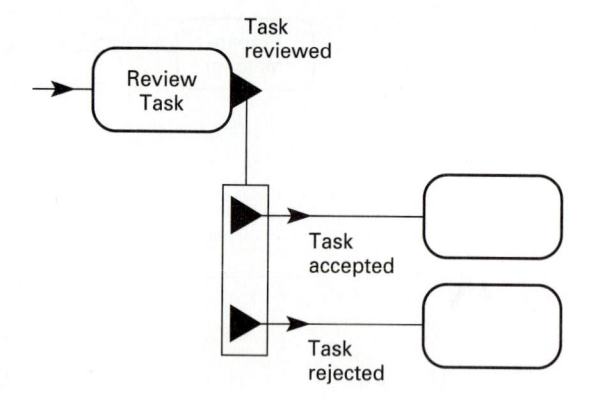

[Diagram: Review Task event with Task reviewed, branching via event-subtype box into Task accepted and Task rejected]

As with the object-subtype boxes (see Chapter 6), the above event-subtype box indicates that the events in it are mutually exclusive. An event-subtype box (such as the object-subtype boxes in Fig. 6.8) can also indicate that other event subtypes might occur.

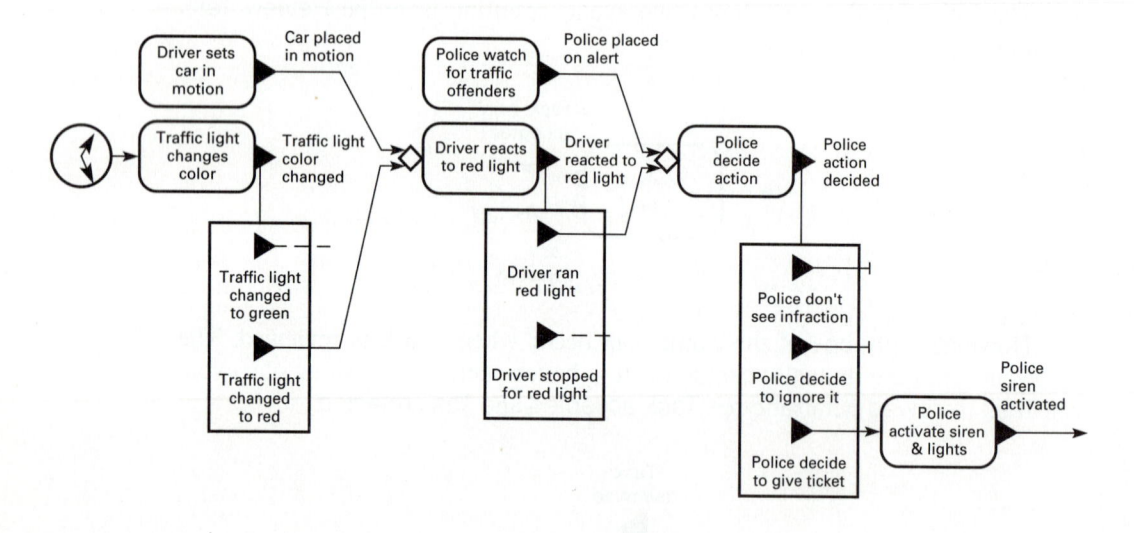

[Diagram: Event diagram for a car chase, showing events such as "Driver sets car in motion" (Car placed in motion), "Traffic light changes color" (Traffic light color changed) with subtypes "Traffic light changed to green" and "Traffic light changed to red"; "Police watch for traffic offenders" (Police placed on alert); "Driver reacts to red light" with subtypes "Driver ran red light" and "Driver stopped for red light" (Driver reacted to red light); "Police decide action" with subtypes "Police don't see infraction", "Police decide to ignore it", "Police decide to give ticket" (Police action decided); "Police activate siren & lights" (Police siren activated).]

Figure 9.9 An event diagram for a car chase with event and control-condition symbols and with expanded event subtypes.

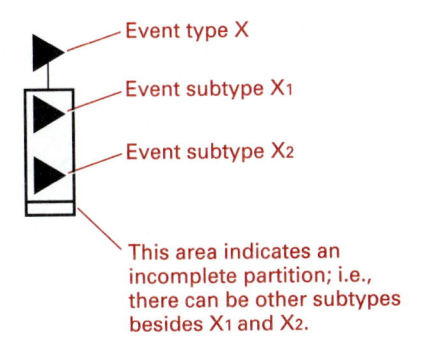

```
                    ◢  ─ Event type X

                  ◢    ─ Event subtype X₁

                ◢      ─ Event subtype X₂

                       ─ This area indicates an
                         incomplete partition; i.e.,
                         there can be other subtypes
                         besides X₁ and X₂.
```

The car chase of Fig. 9.1 is redrawn in Fig. 9.9 showing events and event subtypes.

HIERARCHICAL SCHEMAS

The operation that causes an event to happen may be complex. The operation that rewinds a VCR tape appears simple—the VCR user just presses one button. When the **Tape rewound** event occurs, the user receives a simple message when the rewind is complete. However, internally, the rewind operation involves a whole set of operations and events, as illustrated in Fig. 9.10.

Figure 9.10 illustrates a hierarchical decomposition of event schemas. Boundaries can be placed around a complex event schema and treated as one high-level operation. The lower-level event schema, then, becomes the *method for the operation it decomposes*.

The events and operations that occur when the morning alarm clock goes off and a person prepares for the day are shown in Fig. 9.11.

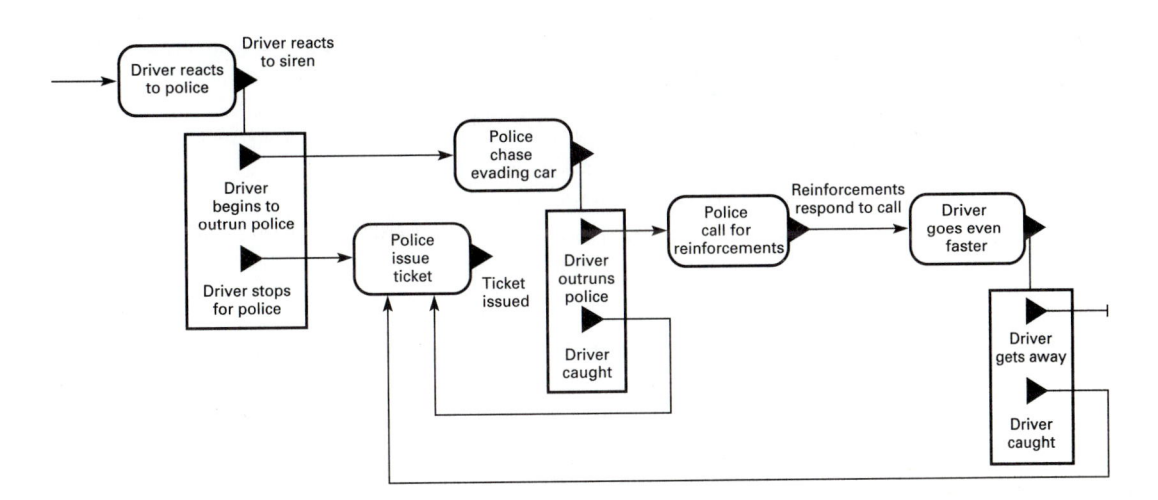

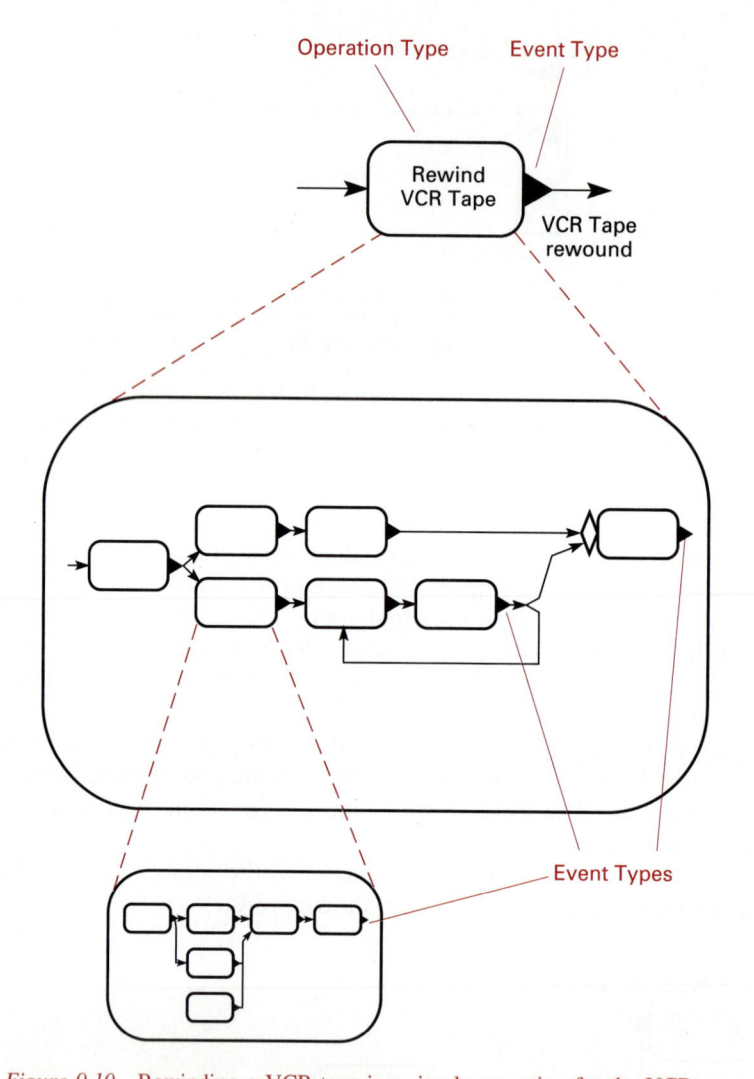

Figure 9.10 Rewinding a VCR tape is a simple operation for the VCR user. However, a complex set of operations and events have to occur inside the VCR in order for it to perform the rewind operation. They define the *method* for the rewind *operation*. Event diagrams may be decomposed hierarchically, like this, making a high-level operation appear simple.

OBJECT-FLOW DIAGRAMS

Event diagrams are appropriate for describing processes in terms of events, triggers, conditions, and operations. However, expressing large complicated processes in this way may not be appropriate. Often a system area is too vast or intricate to express the dynamics of events and triggers. Perhaps, in addition,

Chap. 9 Events, Triggers, and Operations **129**

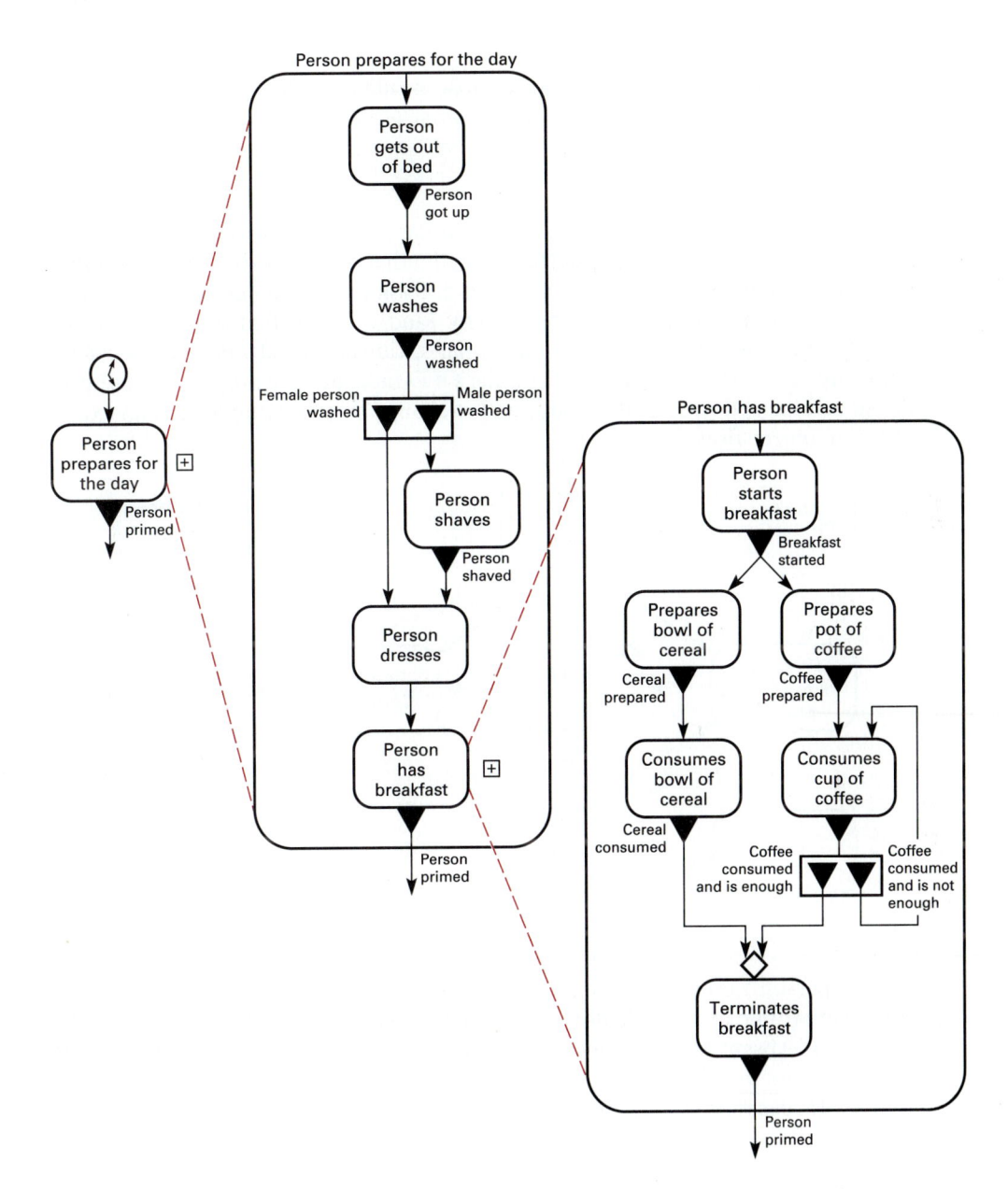

Figure 9.11 An operation for a person getting up in the morning. The window on the right shows the detail of the Person has Breakfast operation.

only a high level of understanding is necessary. This is particularly true of strategic-level planning. In situations such as these, an *object-flow diagram* is useful.

> It is generally true that the diagrams we draw should be designed so that code can be generated from them. An *object-flow diagram* is an exception to that. It is a useful overview diagram.

Object-flow diagrams (OFDs) are similar to data-flow diagrams (DFDs), because they depict activities interfacing with other activities. In DFDs, the interface passes data. In OO techniques, we do not want to be limited to data passing. Instead, the diagram should represent any kind of thing that passes from one activity to another: whether it be orders, parts, finished goods, designs, services, hardware, software—or data. In short, the OFD indicates the *objects* that are produced and the activities that produce and exchange them. Figure 9.12 is an example of an object-flow diagram.

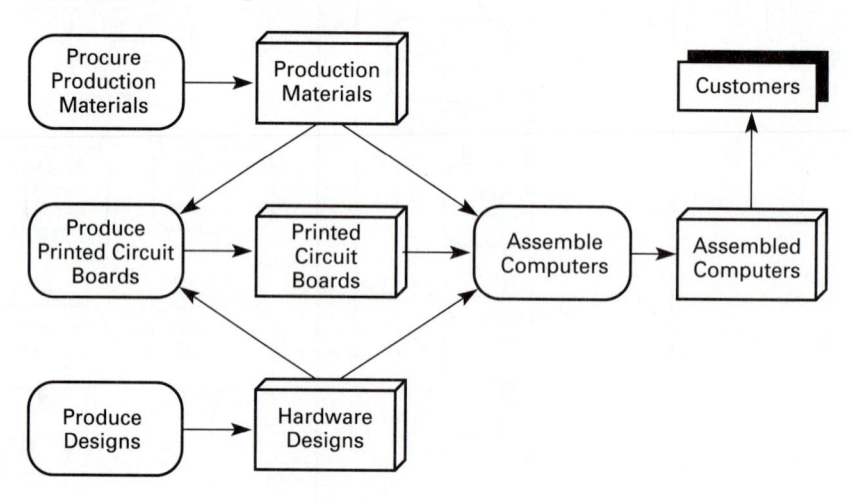

Figure 9.12 Object-flow diagram.

A person familiar with data-flow diagrams will recognize the round-cornered activity boxes, the shadowed, external-agent box, and the direction of the flow lines. Absent here, however, is the data-store symbol. A three-dimensional box is used to represent real-life objects that flow between activities.

OFDs describe objects and the way in which they are produced and consumed:

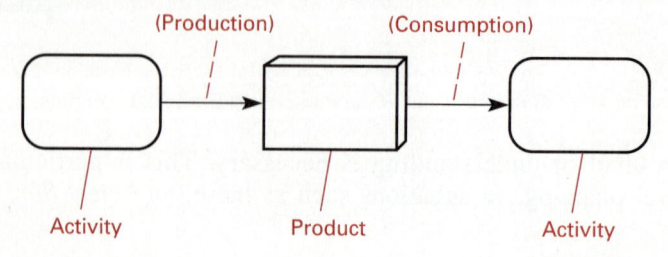

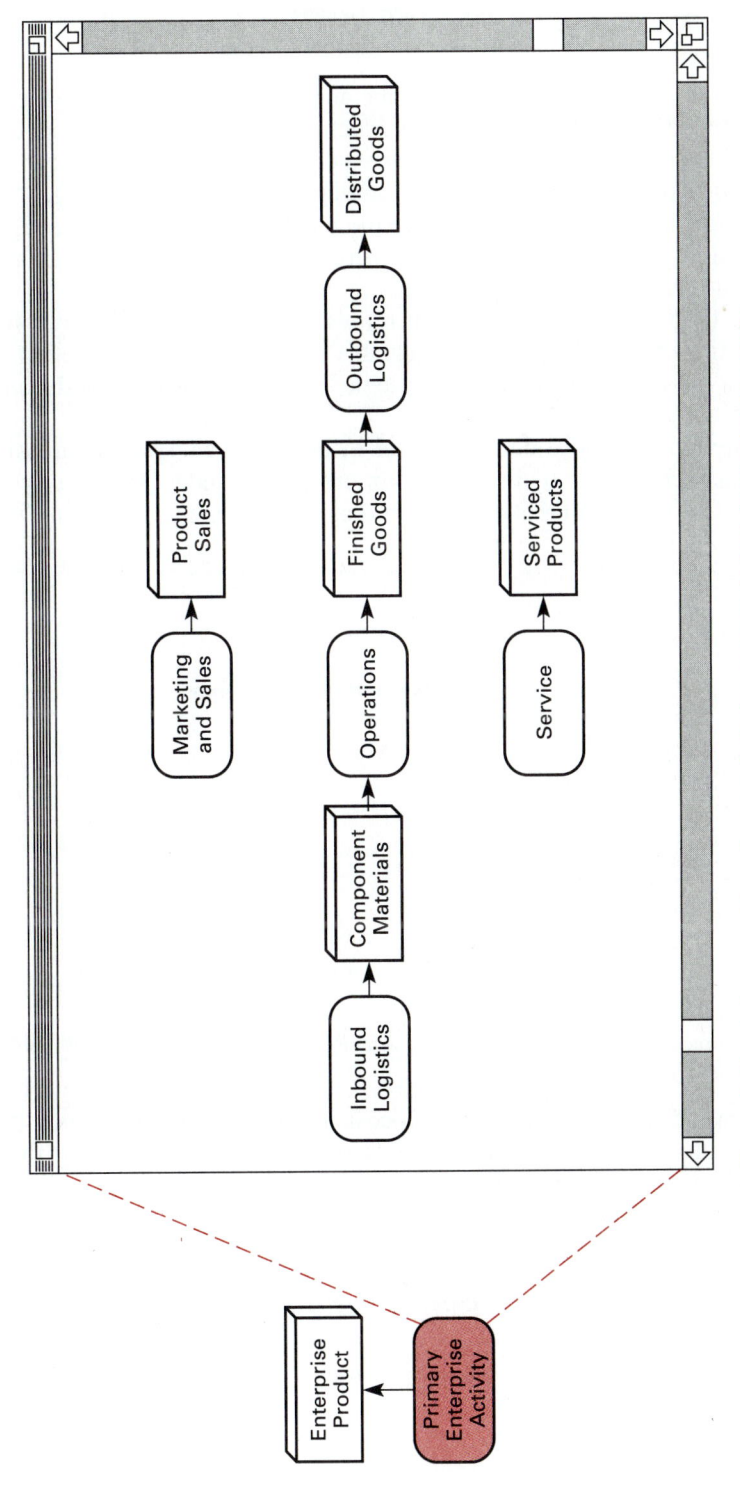

Figure 9.13 A decomposition of a manufacturing company's high-level primary activity.

The *product* is the end result that fulfills the purpose of the activity. Products move to other activities that add value to the product—to produce another more complex product. At every step, new qualities are created. In this way, the OFD can be used for strategic business planning as well as strategic information planning.

Any activity may be expanded into more detail. For example, the high-level primary activity of a manufacturing company could be represented in more detail as shown in Fig. 9.13.

Object-flow diagrams, then, can represent either top-down or bottom-up modeling. In particular, object-flow diagrams are very useful in modeling organizations in a top-down fashion at the strategic level. Activities can be decomposed into OFDs.

However, at a more detailed level in behavior analysis, expressing the dynamic aspects of event diagrams is more appropriate. An activity can be expressed in terms of an OFD or an event diagram, or both as shown in Fig. 9.14.

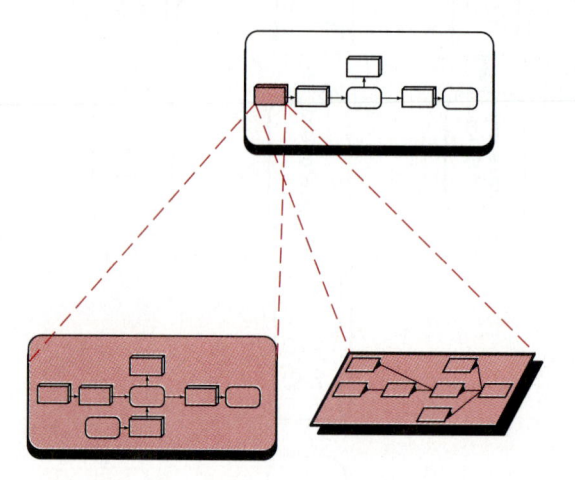

Figure 9.14 Each activity can be expressed as an object-flow diagram, an event schema, or both.

The event diagram expresses a process in a more rigorous fashion that can generate code. To represent basic control structures and processing flow, and when the dynamics of events and triggers are not yet comprehensible, the object-flow diagram is useful.

REFERENCE

1. Meyer, Bertrand, *Object-Oriented Software Construction,* Prentice Hall, Englewood Cliffs, NJ, 1988.

10 RULES

One goal of object-oriented development ought to be to avoid programming wherever possible.

> Wherever possible, the code for systems should be generated from models that are easy for end users to understand and experiment with.

The desired behavior of systems can be described with the help of *rules*. Business policies, for example, can be expressed in rules such as the following:

WHEN a customer has bought more than twice the average sales per customer
    for the previous 12 months
THEN it is categorized as a good customer

WHEN stock falls below reorder point for a product
THEN only good customers have their orders processed immediately

WHEN new stock arrives
IF orders are on hold
THEN orders are sorted by customer rating then earliest order date, and filled
    in that sequence

WHEN orders are filled
IF the customer is a bad payer
THEN the order is put on hold until the amount due is received
AND the customer is notified

RULES EXPRESSED IN ENGLISH

Rules need to be rigorous so that they form a basis for code generation. However, it is particularly important that rules are understandable by end users. End users must be able to check that the rules correctly represent business policies and desired system behavior. Rules should therefore be expressed in English (or the national language of the end users).

A typical rule expression in the language Prolog is as follows:

sister (x,y) : - female (x), parent (x,z), parent (y,z)

This is not likely to be understood by most end users. (It means x is the sister of y if x is female and if x has a parent, z, and y has the same parent, z.)

When we use rules in object-oriented modeling, the rules can be expressed in English but at the same time be rigorous. English-language rules can be built with a rule editor that is part of an OO-CASE toolset. At the same time that the English is created, code is generated so that the rule can be executed immediately. The resulting English may be clumsy and tedious for end users to comprehend. When this is so, the analyst should write a more elegantly phrased sentence expressing the same rule. We then have both formal and easy-to-read English in windows which are linked to an OO model that end users can understand and work with. Their business policies are expressed in such a model, and code is generated directly from the business policies. This is done, for example, with the OO-CASE tool OMW, Object Management Workbench, from Intellicorp.

DECLARATIVE VERSUS PROCEDURAL STATEMENTS

We can distinguish between *declarative* and *procedural* languages or statements.

Conventional programming languages are *procedural*. They give a set of instructions that a computer must execute in a specified sequence. The sequence may vary depending on conditions tested. Groups of instructions can be executed repetitively (loops).

Declarative languages declare a set of facts and rules. They do not specify the sequence of steps (procedure) for doing processing. The computer uses the facts to derive a program for a particular procedure. The facts may be expressed in various ways. They may, for example, be in the form of a record:

Book	Author	Publisher
Future Shock	Toffler	Random House

Facts may be values that populate a spreadsheet. They may be expressed with statements such as the following.

Pathogens associated with **Gastrointestinal Tract** include

- Enterococcus
- Clostridium Gangrene

- Bacteroids
- Klebsiella
- Pseudomonas
- E Coli
- Enterobacterium
- Proteus

Facts may also be expressed with equations, for example:

PRINCIPAL = INSTALLMENT X 100/INTEREST_RATE (1 −
(1 + INTEREST_RATE/100) * * − N) (1 + INTEREST_RATE/100)

If *any* three of the four variables in this financial equation are entered, the fourth will be calculated. *The user does not give the sequence of steps in doing the calculation.* Similarly, several simultaneous equations could be used.

End users, who generally have difficulty understanding programs and checking their correctness, can easily understand statements of facts and rules.

> Declarative statements are much easier to grasp and validate than procedural language.
>
> Where possible, we should build systems from declarative statements linked to OO diagrams that end users can understand.

To a large extent, but not completely, the design of an OO system can be created automatically from facts and rules of the type described in this chapter, and code can be automatically generated.

MAKING BUSINESS KNOWLEDGE EXPLICIT

The rules described in this chapter capture the know-how about how the business or system should operate.

> Rules are encapsulated business knowledge.

We need techniques with which business know-how can be captured, made explicit, made easy to read, and translated directly into executable code. With traditional structured techniques, business policies are not made explicit. They become buried in code written in COBOL or other languages. One rule is often reflected in multiple programs and may be virtually impossible to extract from those programs by examining the code. When the policy changes, it is difficult to change the code or even to know what code ought to be changed.

> We need to make business policies explicit and translate them directly into code. When the policies change, it should be possible to regenerate the code quickly.

Our challenge is to find diagrams that are meaningful to executives and business people, that enable such people to visualize how their enterprise operates and to help redesign it where necessary. An OO-CASE tool should enable its users to navigate through the diagrams and expand windows that show the rules.

> Collectively, the OO diagrams and rules should represent the laws about how the business is run.

With traditional structured techniques, there is a poor translation of business policies into programs. With OO techniques and rules, we want the most direct translation of business policies into generated code. When business policies are changed, we want that to be reflected quickly in regenerated code.

RULES LINKED TO DIAGRAMS

We have emphasized the value of OO-CASE tools for OO modeling, analysis, and design. CASE tools use the diagrams described in Chapters 6 to 13. Rules should be associated with these diagrams. The CASE tools may show them in windows linked to the blocks or symbols on the diagrams.

Some rules are associated with the diagrams used in Object Structure Analysis (described in Chapters 6 and 7):

- Inheritance and subtyping diagrams
- Object-relationship diagrams
- Composed-of diagrams
- Diagrams showing data structures

Other rules are associated with the diagrams used in Object Behavior Analysis (described in Chapters 8, 9, and 13):

- Event diagrams
- State-transition diagrams
- Diagrams showing methods

CATEGORIES OF RULES

Several different types of rules exist. Business rules can be classified as integrity rules, derivation rules, and behavior rules [2].

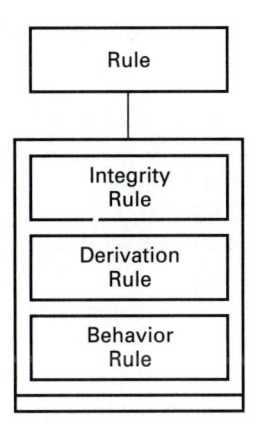

```
        ┌─────────────┐
        │    Rule     │
        └──────┬──────┘
               │
     ┌─────────┴─────────┐
     │  Integrity Rule   │
     ├───────────────────┤
     │  Derivation Rule  │
     ├───────────────────┤
     │  Behavior Rule    │
     └───────────────────┘
```

Integrity rules state that something must be true. For example, a value must be within a certain range, an object relationship must have a stated cardinality, a precondition must hold before an operation is executed, and so on. *Operation precondition rules* and *operation postcondition rules* are important special cases of integrity rules.

Integrity rules should start with the phrase "it should always hold that." Box 10.1 gives some examples of integrity rules.

Derivation rules state how a value or a set of values is computed. Box 10.2 gives examples of derivation rules.

Behavior rules describe dynamic aspects of behavior. They are commonly associated with event diagrams. They often express business rules that describe what conditions must be true for an operation to be triggered.

In some methodologies, cardinality constraints are referred to as "business rules" and are the only form of business rule. These should be referred to as "cardinality rules" to indicate that they are only one narrow type of business rule.

STIMULUS/RESPONSE RULES

Stimulus/response rules express triggering behavior and generally have the form

```
WHEN    <event>
IF      <condition to fulfill>
THEN    <operation>
```

In a business model this can be

BOX 10.1 Examples of integrity rules.

These are easy-to-read versions of rules, which are in more formal English when created by a CASE rule-builder. The same applies to Box 10.2.

IT MUST ALWAYS HOLD THAT
    The number of employees is less than 1,000

IT MUST ALWAYS HOLD THAT
    The number of employees who are managers and earning a salary greater than 100,000 is less than or equal to 3

IT MUST ALWAYS HOLD THAT
    The number of hotels (with the same hotel name and located in the same resort) is less than or equal to 1

IT MUST ALWAYS HOLD THAT
    A manager is not a secretary

IT MUST ALWAYS HOLD THAT
    IF an employee has a company car
    THEN this employee does not receive a monthly transport reimbursement

IT MUST ALWAYS HOLD THAT
    IF an employee works on a project
    THEN this employee works for a department

IT MUST ALWAYS HOLD THAT
    IF an employee has a marked parking slot
    THEN this employee has a company car and is a manager with a salary greater than 60,000

IT MUST ALWAYS HOLD THAT
    IF a flight is scheduled to depart from City C
    THEN this flight is not scheduled to arrive in City C

AFTER modify of salary of an Employee.E IT MUST HOLD THAT
    The new salary of Employee E is greater than the
    old salary of an Employee E

IT MUST ALWAYS HOLD THAT
    The age of an employee is less than 65

IT MUST ALWAYS HOLD THAT
    The sum of salaries of employees working for
    Department D is less than 0.6 * budget of Department D

BOX 10.2 Examples of derivation rules.

PRODUCT.NET_PRICE = PRODUCT.PRICE * (1 + TAX_PERCENTAGE/100)

DERIVE Employee reporting to Manager M
   as Employee working for Department managed by Manager M.

Invoice.Total = Sum of Invoice.Line_totals + Sale_tax + Service_charge

---

WHEN Invoice.Net_total > 0 and < 2500
   Taxes = Invoice.Net_total * 0.15

ELSEWHEN Invoice.Net_total >2500 and < 50000
   Taxes = (Invoice.Net_total - 2500) * 0.18 - 3750

ELSEWHEN Invoice.Net_total.> 50000 and < 75000
   Taxes= (Invoice.Net_total - 50000) * 0.30 - 8250

ELSEWHEN Invoice.Net_total > 75000 and < 100000
   Taxes= (Invoice.Net_total - 75000) * 0.40 - 15750

ELSEWHEN Invoice.Net_total.> 100000
   Taxes= (Invoice.Net_total - 100000) * 0.46 - 25750

IF Symptom_of_Problem is equal to "biscuits pale" or
   Symptom_of_Problem is equal to "biscuits not risen"

THEN set Hypothesis_of_Problem to "low temperature gases"

IF a customer has bought more than twice average sales per customer for the last 12 months

THEN classify customer as a "Good Customer"

WHEN immediate shipment cannot be accomplished for all batches

THEN give priority to batches containing items for a Good Customer

---

WHEN immediate shipment cannot be accomplished for all batches containing items for a Good Customer

THEN give priority to batches with nearby delivery requirements

WHEN   an event happens
IF   a condition is fulfilled
THEN   do something

In a technical system, it can be

ON   <stimulus>
IF   <condition>
THEN   <response>

In these expressions the IF clause is optional.

This form of expression relates to the basic construct of the event diagram:

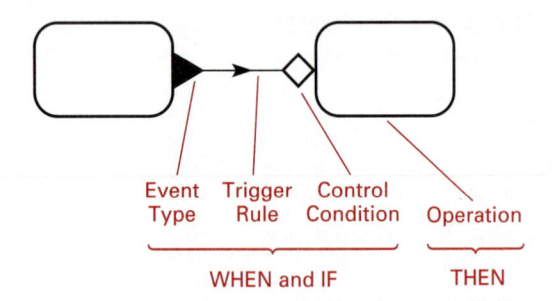

Event Type | Trigger Rule | Control Condition | Operation

WHEN and IF | THEN

Such stimulus/response rules can be expressed rigorously but can also be translated into an English statement that end users can validate. For example

WHEN Account is posted to Sales Ledger
IF Customer is of type D
  and Balance has been negative for 18 days
THEN set Status to Credit Stopped.

The THEN part of a rule is an operation. For example, set Status to Credit Stopped is an operation. Often, however, the THEN part of a rule invokes an operation by name. For example, when a stock item falls below the reorder point, send a request to Reorder the stock item.

OPERATION CONDITION RULES   As commented in the previous chapter, each operation has its own context-independent precondition and postcondition. Preconditions and postconditions should be expressed with rules that end users can understand and verify. These rules are of vital importance in helping to ensure that software operates correctly. Bertrand Meyer states that the presence of these rules in a routine should be viewed as a contract that binds the routine and its callers [1]. It is, in effect, a contract relating to software reliability.

Operation precondition rules express those constraints under which an operation will perform correctly. The operation cannot go ahead unless these constraints are satisfied. Operation precondition rules have the form

>Order a Product
>>ONLY IF there is an authorized Supplier offering this Product
>
>Promote Staff Employee to Manager
>>ONLY IF Employee has a Staff position
>>and Employee is not a Manager

In contrast, the *operation postcondition rule,* in effect, guarantees the results. It says that when the operation is executed, certain state changes will occur. Operation postcondition rules have the form

>Order Product from supplier IS CORRECTLY COMPLETED
>>ONLY IF the Product Order for supplier is created
>
>Promote Staff Employee to Manager IS CORRECTLY COMPLETED
>>ONLY IF Employee is not in a Staff position
>>and Employee is a Manager

Events are those state changes to which a system must react. Therefore, *events* (represented by a black triangle), reflect an aspect of an operation postcondition rule. When that aspect is true, the event occurs:

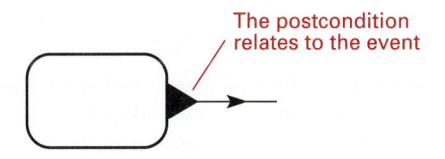

CONDITIONS FOR EXECUTING AN OPERATION

Before an operation can be executed, two things must be true: its precondition, which is *independent* of the particular application, and its control condition, which is *dependent* of the application. Both of these are expressed as rules.

The user of an OO-CASE tool should be able to point at the control condition diamond or at the operation box and display the control condition rules or the operation precondition rules.

Diagram: an operation symbol with labeled arrows — Postcondition, Trigger Rule, Operation Precondition, Control Condition.

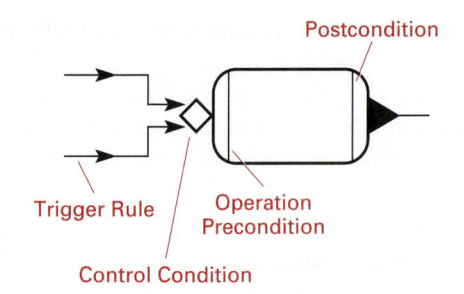

The control condition relates to the trigger rules and is often designed to achieve correctness of the precondition.

These rules, displayed in windows on the event diagram, should reflect how the business people want to run the business. Business policies are explicitly stated.

EXECUTABLE DIAGRAMS The event diagram, including statements of rules to express preconditions, triggers, control conditions, and the calculations or transformations done in an operation, is an executable diagram, that is, it can be converted to program code. The operation itself may be expressed declaratively or in a form that can drive a code generator.

> An event diagram with rules is executable.
>
> The diagrams of traditional structured analysis are not executable.

The most useful form of an OO-CASE tool is one that generates code immediately from diagrams that are executable. The code can be immediately executed to see whether it is doing what the designer intended—rather like a spreadsheet tool. When you create the columns, rows, and calculations of a spreadsheet, you can immediately run it, then quickly change it, and rerun it. You can experiment with it, adjusting its design.

An OO model is likely to be much more complex than a spreadsheet but the tool should make it equally interactive. You should be able to build it and immediately run it, add instances of class data, and observe its behavior, grow it, and change it quickly. You should be able to experiment with your design as you build it.

At first, the code will be generated interpretively and need not be machine-efficient. Later, when the design works well, it can be compiled and perhaps redesigned for maximum efficiency.

The ability to run the design immediately, experiment with it, and change it, greatly increases creativity. It expands our ability to invent interesting software.

RULES ATTACHED TO OTHER OO DIAGRAMS

Rules can be linked to other types of diagrams as well as event diagrams.

> Rules can be attached to any of the diagrams in the previous chapters.

Examples of rules associated with the diagrams of OO analysis are shown in Box 10.3.

Rules can be divided into two types—object-state rules and object-behavior rules. Object-state rules are identified in object-structure analysis. They are associated with diagrams, such as the data-structure diagram, object-relationship diagram, or composed-of diagram. Object-behavior rules are identified in object-behavior analysis. Most are associated with the event diagram; some are associated with the state-transition diagram.

Figure 10.1 shows a variety of OO diagrams with rules linked to them, as they should be in an OO-CASE tool. The rules may be expressed both in formal notation and easy-to-read English, so that either may be displayed.

Figure 10.2 shows a rule window linked to an event diagram in the IntelliCorp Object Management Workbench (OMW). A variety of such rule windows can be connected to the diagrams this tool uses. With a rule editor the analyst builds rules in English and at the same time generates executable code for the rules. The analyst can immediately run his model, animate it, and generate spreadsheets of values from it. He can thus immediately test and modify the model. The business people using the tool, possibly in facilitated workshops (discussed later), can try out different business policies and observe their effect. They can thus redesign business processes and observe the effects of the redesign.

THE PROGRAMMER AS LAWYER

The English expression of rules precise enough for code generation is formal and sometimes difficult for business people to read. The analyst should therefore translate the executable rules into easy-to-read English.

The bottom box of the Rule Editor Probe window in Fig. 10.2 contains the formal English. The box above, labeled "Meaning," contains the analyst's easy-to-read version of the same rule. The "Comment" box above this may contain comments about who wants the business policy that the rule represents, or why it is used.

Figure 10.3 shows three more rule windows that are linked to appropriate items in OO diagrams. The red item in each diagram is a rule in formal English that is created with the tool's rule-builder. As the Rule Editor assists the analyst in building the rule it simultaneously generates executable code. The analyst can compose an easy-to-read version of the rule in the box labeled "Meaning."

> **BOX 10.3 Examples of business rules associated with the diagrams for OO analysis.**
>
> **Object Structure Analysis**
>
> - *Rules associated with attributes,* such as
>   - A Customer is good if it has bought more than twice the average sales per customer for the last 12 months.
>   - When Employee has Salary > 150,000 it can have stock options.
> - *Rules associated with object-relationship diagrams,* such as
>   - A good Customer can place any number of Orders.
>   - A bad Customer can place no more than 10 Orders.
> - *Rules associated with composed-of diagrams,* such as
>   - A Lighting Track has a maximum of 12 spotlights.
>
> **Object Behavior Analysis**
>
> - *Rules associated with transitions,* such as
>   - When Salary is updated new value must exceed old value
> - *Rules associated with event diagrams*
>   - Trigger rules, such as
>   When Stock < Reorder Level then reorder
>   - Control condition, such as
>   If Security Code is correct then . . .
>   If time is between 9 AM and 5 PM . . .
>   If good Customer . . .
> - *Complex rules expressed with event diagrams,* such as
>   - When Immediate Shipment cannot be accomplished for all Batches, then give priority to Batches containing items for Good Customers.
>   - When Immediate Shipment cannot be accomplished for all Batches containing Items for Good Customers, then give priority to Batches with nearby Delivery Requirements.

From the model and its attached rules a spreadsheet is created automatically. The analyst can populate the spreadsheet with values and observe the effects of the rules. The operations on the event diagram may be resequenced, the business policies changed, and the spreadsheet changed accordingly. Graphics and charts can be generated from the spreadsheet. Business people can thus explore the behavior of the model, the effects of their policies, and the possibilities for business process redesign.

With this approach, business people can express their business policies in normal English. The analyst, rather like a lawyer, translates this into precise English and corresponding code. When the business people change a policy, this change can be translated directly and quickly into software that implements the new policy.

THE INFERENCE ENGINE

In the 1980s, artificial intelligence systems became highly fashionable. The primary mechanism of such systems built in the 1980s was an *inference engine*.

An inference engine uses a collection of facts and rules about a specific area of knowledge and makes deductions using the techniques of logical inference. It can respond to a request by selecting rules and firing them, effectively chaining the rules together to perform inferential reasoning. It may use forward chaining (input-directed reasoning), backward chaining (goal-directed reasoning), or both. It enables a computer to make complex deductions without programmers having to code an application.

The concept of the inference engine was used to build *expert systems.* Expert systems store knowledge culled for an expert in the form of facts and rules and make deductions by employing an inference engine. The goal is to make the computer give advice like a human expert in a specific narrow domain of knowledge.

The rules that an inference engine chains together to make deductions are called *production rules*. The rules referred to in this chapter are generally not production rules. They are rules that are linked to OO diagrams in order to generate meaningful models and code.

An inference engine, like any other computing technique, may be used to implement *methods* in a *class*. Usually, this requires a *small* collection of rules rather than the large rule collections that characterize some artificial-intelligence systems. Each method makes a relatively simple change to the data in the class. Because it uses a small collection of rules (usually fewer than 100), it can be relatively fast and efficient.

Some expert systems were built with a large number of rules. There was an ill-thought-out notion that if an inference engine could use a vast collection of rules, it could solve formidable problems. Some early expert systems used more than 10,000 rules. Large amorphous collections of rules present two problems. First, machine performance is bad. Inferencing algorithms do not scale up efficiently when there are thousands of rules. Second, it is difficult to tell what the inferencing system is doing and hence it is difficult to debug it. Changing the behavior of a rule-based system is very easy, in principle. One simply changes the rules—which is much easier than changing a COBOL program. However, its behavior is difficult to understand if the collections of rules are large and unstructured.

DATA STRUCTURE DIAGRAM

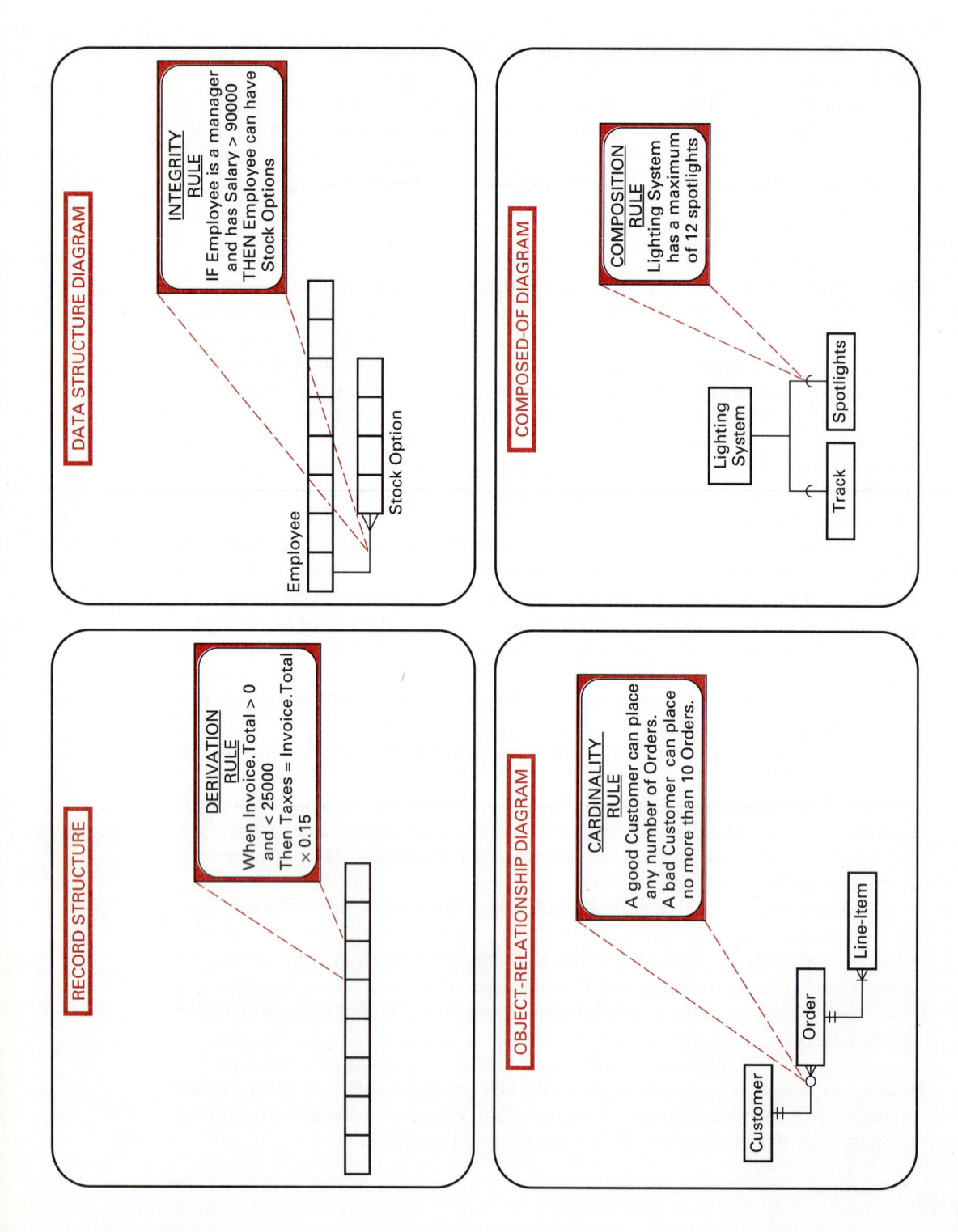

INTEGRITY RULE
IF Employee is a manager and has Salary > 90000 THEN Employee can have Stock Options

Employee
Stock Option

COMPOSED-OF DIAGRAM

COMPOSITION RULE
Lighting System has a maximum of 12 spotlights

Lighting System
Track
Spotlights

RECORD STRUCTURE

DERIVATION RULE
When Invoice.Total > 0 and < 25000
Then Taxes = Invoice.Total × 0.15

OBJECT-RELATIONSHIP DIAGRAM

CARDINALITY RULE
A good Customer can place any number of Orders.
A bad Customer can place no more than 10 Orders.

Customer
Order
Line-Item

146

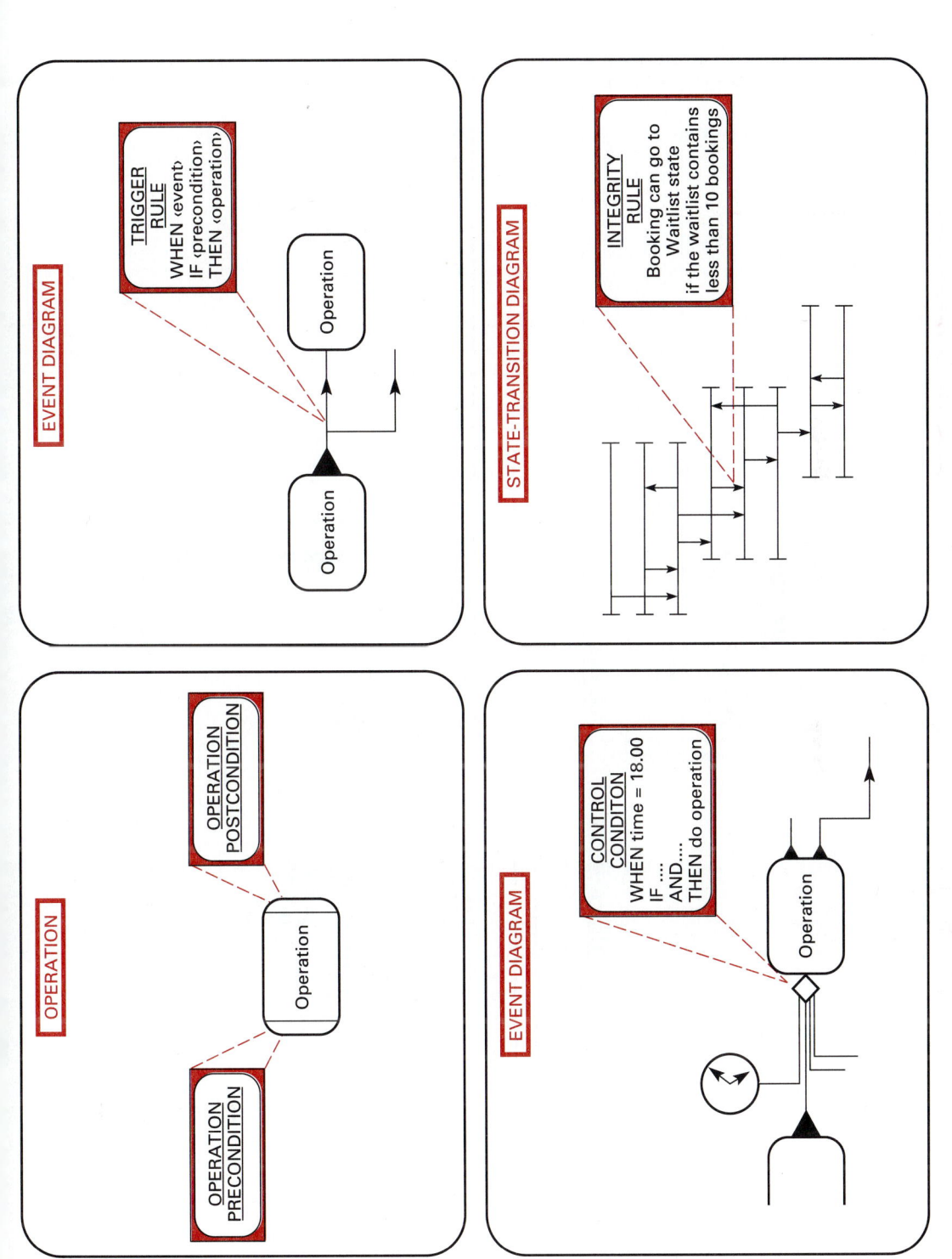

Figure 10.1 Rules linked to OO-CASE diagrams. The formal English which a CASE rule-builder creates is less easy to read than some of these illustrations. The analyst supplements the formal English with easy-to-read English to aid communication with business people.

147

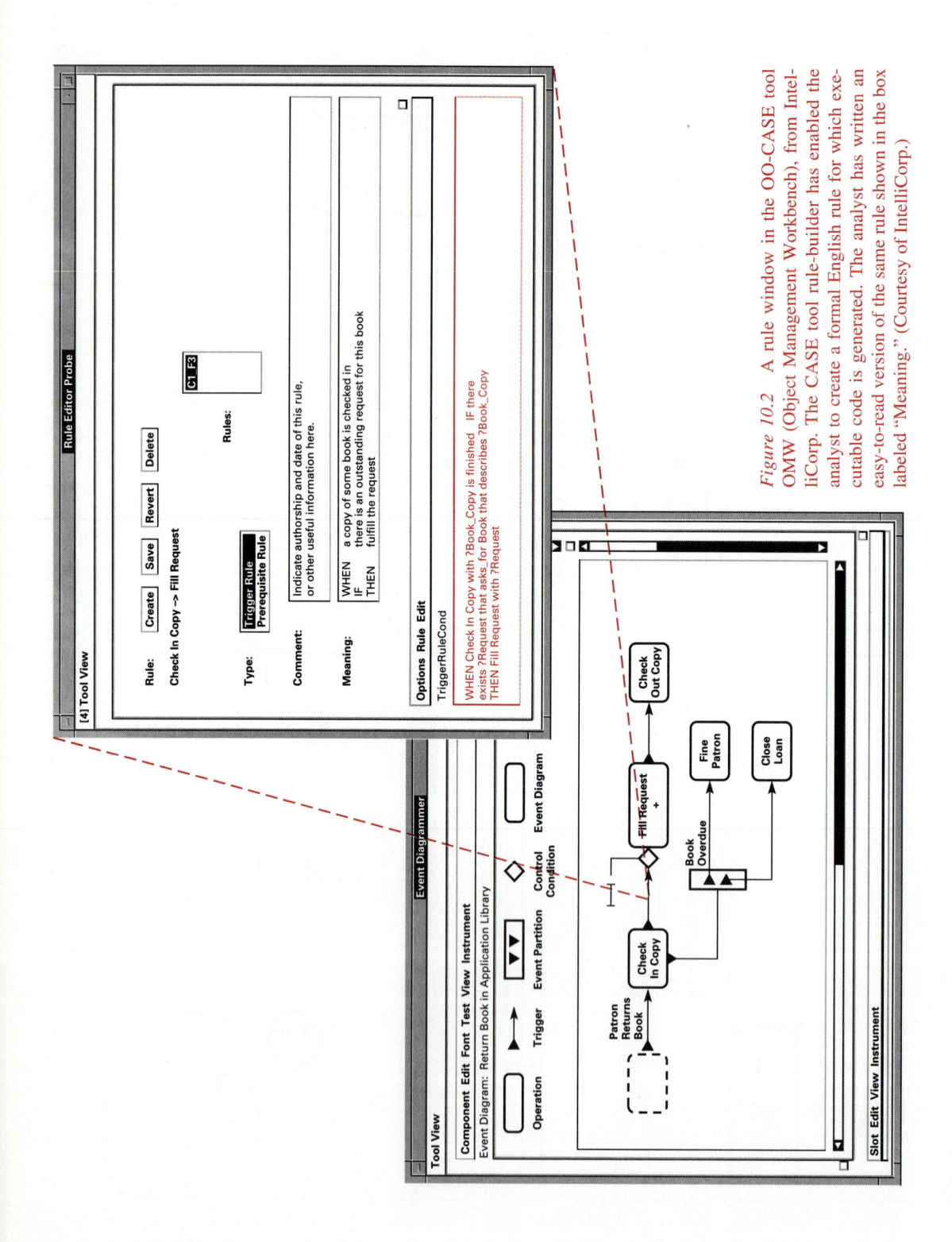

Figure 10.2 A rule window in the OO-CASE tool OMW (Object Management Workbench), from IntelliCorp. The CASE tool rule-builder has enabled the analyst to create a formal English rule for which executable code is generated. The analyst has written an easy-to-read version of the same rule shown in the box labeled "Meaning." (Courtesy of IntelliCorp.)

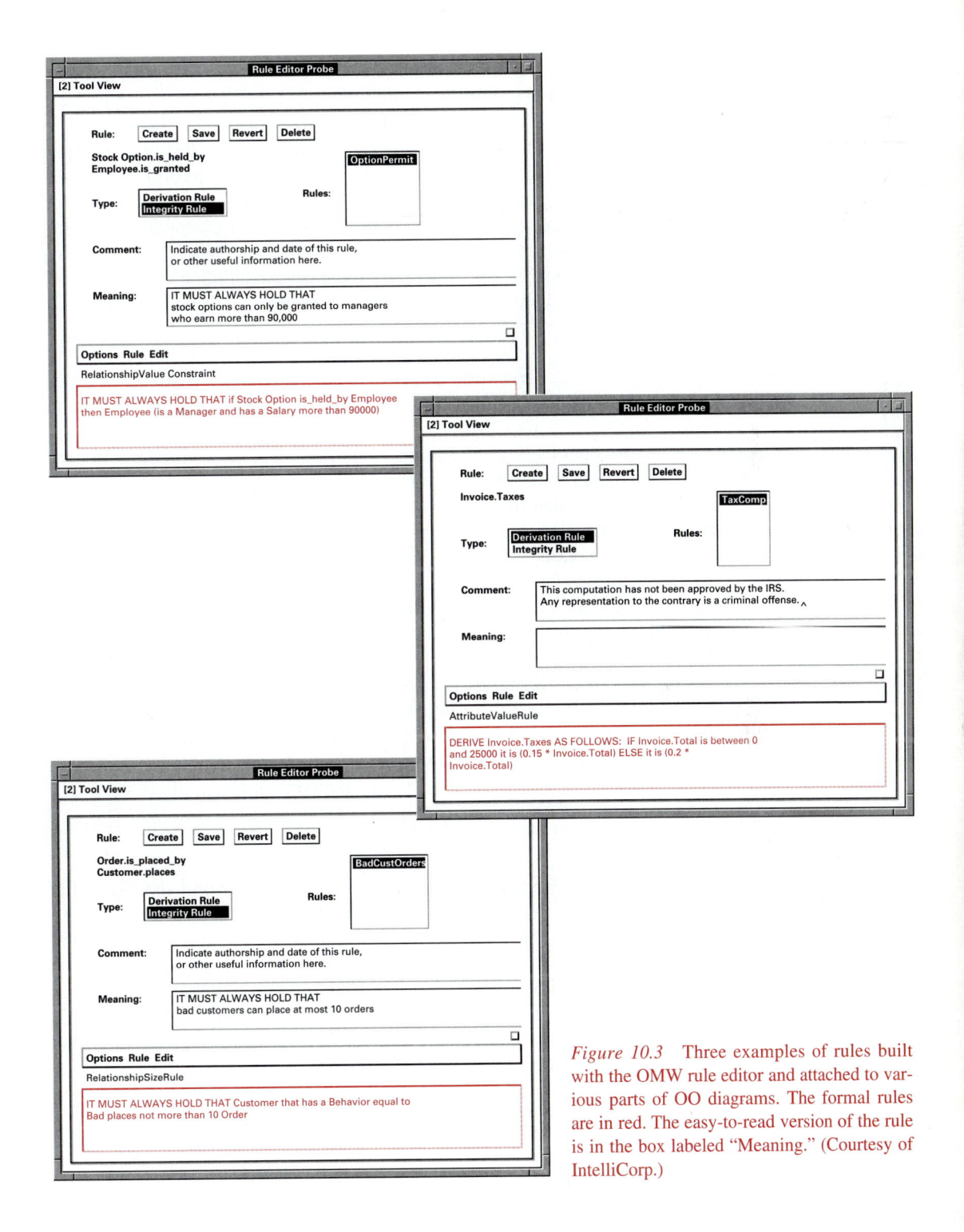

Figure 10.3 Three examples of rules built with the OMW rule editor and attached to various parts of OO diagrams. The formal rules are in red. The easy-to-read version of the rule is in the box labeled "Meaning." (Courtesy of IntelliCorp.)

Just as traditional programs, repeatedly added to, become great rolling snowballs of code, which are murder to maintain, so large expert systems grew into vast collections of rules that became difficult to understand. The answer to both situations is design in an object-oriented fashion where the classes have *methods* that are relatively simple and the overall model is easy to understand.

The artificial-intelligence community developed *frame-based* techniques for designing expert systems and representing knowledge. A *frame* is essentially an object. It has packets of rules associated with it that are used with an inference engine when a request is sent to the frame. Some frame-based software for building expert systems evolved into object-oriented toolkits with methods, inheritance, and encapsulation.

UNNECESSARY RULES

The early expert systems used a large bucket of rules in which the inference engine went fishing for rules to use. Most of the rules in these early systems are unnecessary when object-oriented design is done. They represent information that should be affiliated with OO diagrams, such as object-relationship diagrams, composed-of diagrams, state-transition diagrams, and event diagrams. For example, cardinality information on object-relationship diagrams and the information in normalized data models were represented as production rules. They should have been quite separate from the production rules.

To assume that *all* knowledge should be represented by production rules was a simplistic viewpoint that led to severe code inefficiencies and systems that were difficult to debug and evolve.

OO analysis has a different viewpoint. Rules and other declarative statements should be associated with OO diagrams so that the diagrams are executable. Most of these rules are not used by an inference engine. Sometimes, one *method* does employ an inference engine, just as a method could be implemented with any other computing technique. When this happens, it is usually done with a small number of rules (often less than 100) and so the inferencing is fast.

VISIBLE AND NONVISIBLE RULES

Some rules need to be visible to end users so that they may check them in a workshop (Chapter 14). These should be in English, perhaps with detailed comments.

Other rules are for I.S. professionals and need not be seen by end users. These include certain integrity rules and rules for technical design.

Yet other rules are internal to the OO-CASE tool and the facilities that ensure integrity and consistency in its repository. These rules are part of the basic tool design and need not be directly visible to I.S. users of the tool.

We should distinguish these three categories of rules (Box 10.4).

Box 10.5 gives other examples of rules which business people see as part of the OO enterprise model.

BOX 10.4 Categories of rules.

Nonvisible Rules

Rules internal to repository
Rules internal to OO-CASE toolset

Rules for I.S. Technicians

Rules for technical design
Integrity rules

Rules for End Users

Business policy rules
Derivation rules
Intelligent enterprise model

TRACEABILITY

Each business policy should be directly traceable from the business people who help establish the rules to the code that is generated from them.

Traceability may begin in an end-user workshop in which the policies are established or reviewed with the business people most familiar with the subject area. In such a workshop, each rule is expressed both in formal and easy-to-read English. Comments may be recorded about the rule to state why it is used, to establish its business context, or to indicate when it should be reexamined. A CASE tool for OO analysis ought to record *spoken* comments about rules. Spoken comments can indicate why the rule was established and who was responsible for it. At a later time, the spoken comments might be reviewed and some rules refined or replaced.

To trace the effect of rules, an interpretive code generator is useful that immediately generates code and allows tables to be populated with instances of the objects and their data. This allows an analyst to check with end users in a workshop that the system, or a piece of the system, is working as intended. The interpreted code grows and is refined. Eventually, it will be compiled for efficiency.

CHANGING HOW BUSINESSES ARE RUN

The ability to translate policies directly in executable code has the potential of changing the way businesses are run. Just as a plant controller can turn a valve and

BOX 10.5 Examples of visible rules.

Examples of rules that business people can validate and change. All such rules appear in windows on the OO-CASE diagrams. (From IntelliCorp's OMW.)

Banking

If LiquidityRatio < 1 then Liquidity is bad

LiquidityRatio = ShortTermAssets/ShortTermLiabilities

ShortTermAssets = CashinHand+AccountsReceivable

ShortTermLiabilities = BankLoans+AccountsPayable

When ReviewLoan is completed
    If MonthlyRepayment <= 10% of MaximumRepayment
    then GrantLoan

When ReviewLoan is completed
    If MonthlyRepayment > MaximumRepayment
    then RejectLoan

When ReviewLoan is completed
    If MonthlyRepayment > 50% and <= 100% of MaximumRepayment
    then SeekGuarantees

When ReviewLoan is completed
    If MonthlyRepayment > 10% and < 50% of MaximumRepayment
    then ReviewSituation

Car Rental

On CheckInCar
    MileageUsed = MilesReturned − MilesOut
    GasUsed = 1 − GasGaugeReading
    DateReturned = Today

When CheckInCar is completed then CalculateCharges

On CalculateCharges
    RateCharge = (HireRate)*(DateReturned − DateOut)
    GasCharge = GasUsed*ModelRefuelCharge
    TaxCharge = (RateCharge + GasCharge)*StateTax

BOX 10.5 (Continued)

It must hold that DateReturned >= DateRented

HireRate = ModelDailyRate if DateReturned − DateOut < 7

HireRate = ModelWeeklyRate if DateReturned − DateOut >= 7

Credit Card Application

ApplicationStatus = Rejected
    If MonthlyIncome < IncomeThreshold or
    If ApplicantAge < 18

When ReviewApplication is completed
    if ApplicationStatus is Rejected
    then ProcessRejection

When ReviewApplication is completed
    if ApplicationStatus is not Rejected
    then ReviewCreditworthiness

ApplicantPosition = MonthlyIncome − MonthlySpending

If ApplicantPosition is Negative
    then ApplicantCreditworthiness is bad

MonthlyIncome = MonthlySalary + OtherIncome

MonthlySpending = MonthlyHousingCost + OtherSpending

It must hold that an Applicant
    is a PersonalApplicant
    or a CorporateApplicant

When Today = ApplicationReceivedDate + 30 then ResponseOverdue

---

adjust a manufacturing process, so business people may in the future be able to modify rules of the business and make a direct change in the automated operation of the business. They will adjust and try to optimize how the business is conducted.

REFERENCES

1. Meyer, Bertrand, *Object-Oriented Software Construction,* Prentice Hall, New York, 1988.

2. Van Assche, Franz, *Rule-Based IEM,* James Martin and Co., internal paper, December, 1991.

11 HOW THE DIAGRAMS INTERRELATE

The diagrams of the previous chapters all relate to one another. Together they form a unified model that should reside in the repository of an OO-CASE tool. Each diagram is one view of a more complex and integrated whole. The diagrams enable us to explore the overall model by viewing it in digestable pieces and give us a tool for building and changing the model.

If the model changes, various different diagrams must change or they will not represent the model correctly. If we change one diagram and enter the change, other diagrams that relate to the same part of the model must change in a corresponding fashion.

> The diagrams on the screen of an integrated CASE tool are *active*, so that if one diagram is changed and that changes the repository contents, other diagrams must change automatically.

This chapter illustrates the relationships among the different diagrams. The diagrams in this chapter were created with the OO-CASE tool OMW (Object Management Workbench) from IntelliCorp.

An object-relationship diagram for a college, showing the staff, students, courses, and so on, is shown in Fig. 11.1. The same object types are shown on a fern diagram in Fig. 11.2. Instances of the object types **Administrator** and **Instructor** are shown on the fern diagram. (The college has two administrators and five instructors.)

The tool for building Figs. 11.1 and 11.2 allows *attributes* to be associated with these objects and may allow values to be assigned to some or all of these attributes.

Figure 11.3 shows a window in an OO-CASE tool for building the diagram in Fig. 11.1. The developer adds attributes to the object **Student**. Figure 11.4 shows a window with which the values of attributes can be entered. The developer creates just a few values as he builds his model, so that he can test the model.

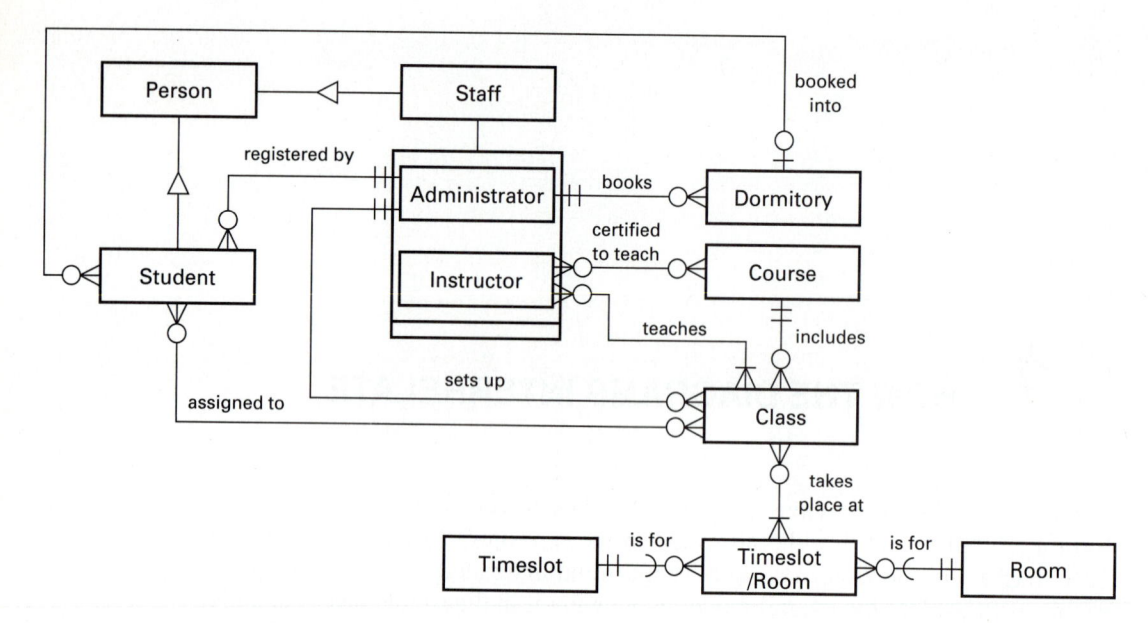

Figure 11.1 An object-relationship model for students and classes.

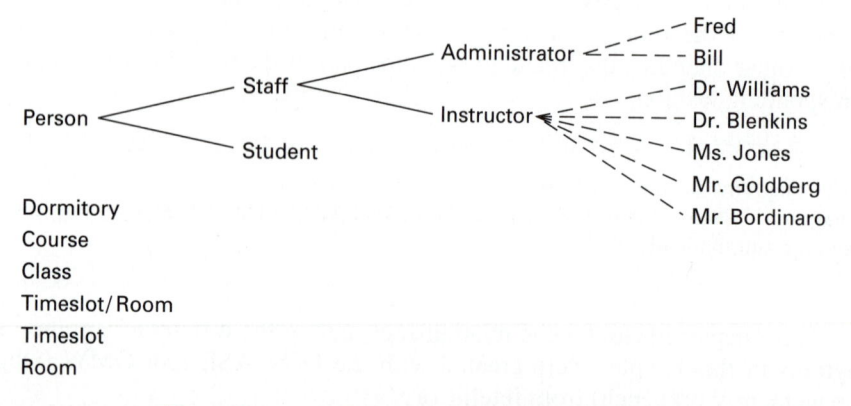

Figure 11.2 A fern diagram corresponding to Fig. 11.1.

Traditional CASE tools have allowed data models to be built but have not allowed the assignment of values to the data. We would like OO-CASE tools to be *instant* CASE, that is, the model can be run as soon as it is built. The model can then be tested as it is built, a step at a time.

> An *instant* CASE tool allows a model to be run immediately and, hence, tested while it is being built.

Chap. 11 How the Diagrams Interrelate 157

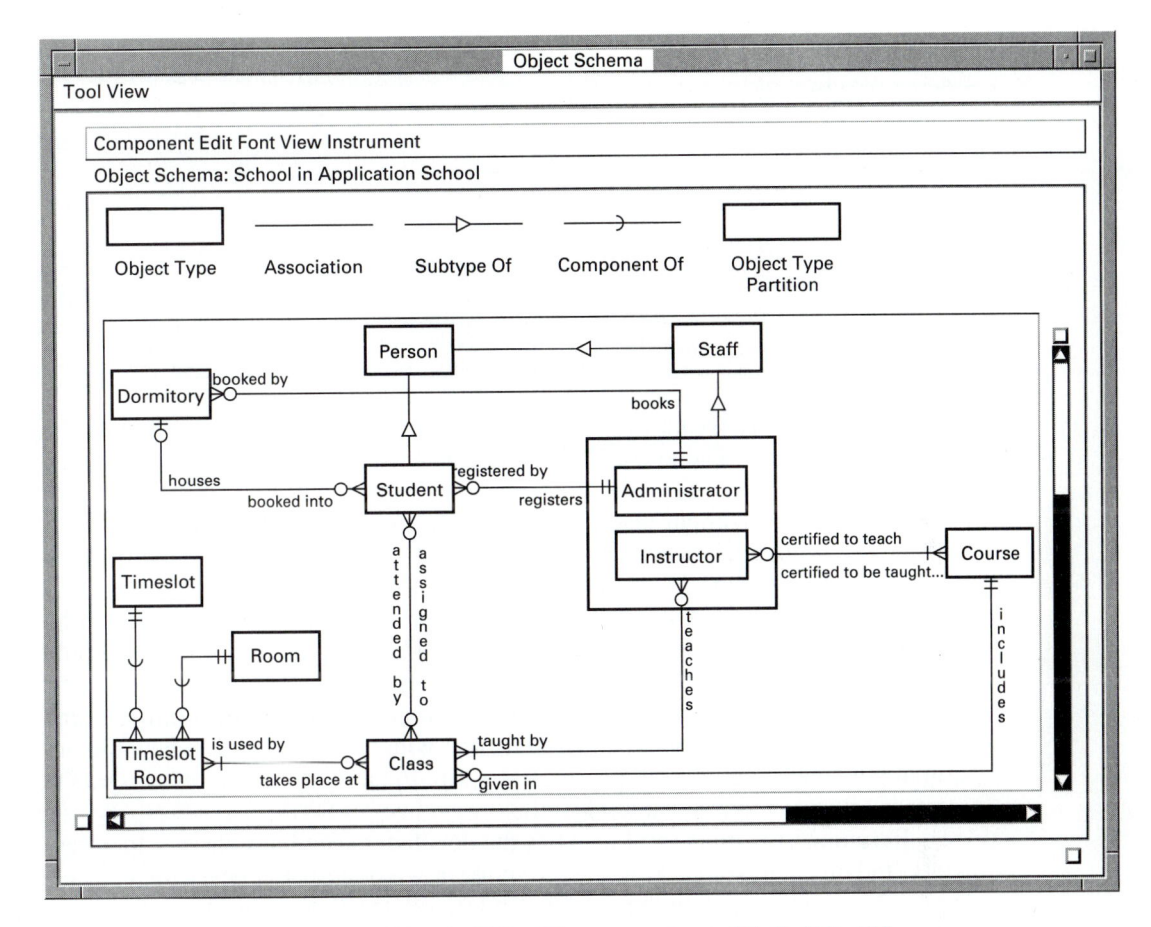

Figure 11.3 IntelliCorp's Object Diagrammer (part of their Object Management Workbench, OMW) being used to construct an object-relationship diagram. (Courtesy of IntelliCorp.)

As the model is built, some values should be allocated to the attributes. We can then immediately examine the spreadsheets and generate reports.

To generate spreadsheets or reports, it is necessary to focus on a portion of an object-relationship diagram. The top of Fig. 11.5 shows a portion of the object-relationship diagram in Fig. 11.1. The bottom of Fig. 11.5 shows a spreadsheet that relates to it, showing a timetable for the courses and their classes. From this spreadsheet, reports of various formats could be generated.

Once objects are selected from the object-relationship diagram, a variety of spreadsheets can be generated. One could be generated, for example, from the following objects, showing the student the time slots for which he has classes:

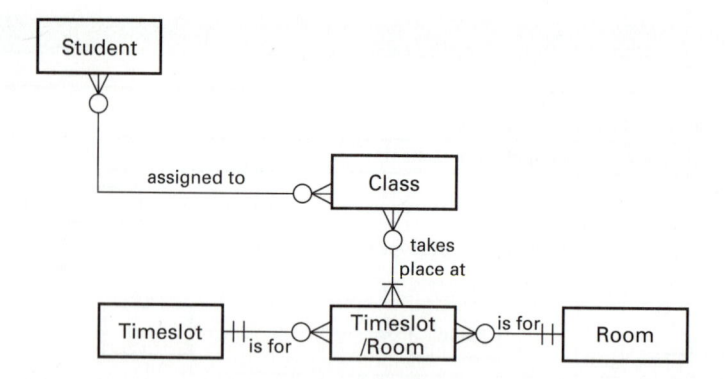

Fig. 11.6 shows an event diagram indicating events that happen with the objects in Fig. 11.1. The event **Room Scheduled** is subtyped into two events—one for scheduling a room in which machines are required and the other for scheduling a room without machines. Similarly, the **Student Registered** event is subtyped for situations in which the class is full or class is not full, and then for local students or nonlocal students (who need a dormitory room).

With an instant-CASE tool, when an event diagram is created it should be immediately possible to make the model active and run events. The model should be *animated,* so that different blocks and event subtypes light up as events and operations happen. The model can thus be immediately tested, modified, and experimented with. This immediate interaction with the model adds a new dimension of creativity to the developer. It allows him to be more inventive and quickly create innovative models that work well.

In running the model in Fig. 11.6, the developer schedules classes, then registers students, and so on. Figure 11.7 shows a window that appears for registering students. The information in the window relates to the data model with its attributes and values entered as in Figs. 11.3 and 11.4.

The tool may have access to a database that already contains details of students. The developers may enter the identifier of an item and the tool fills in attribute values from its database.

LINKING ACTIVITIES AND STATE CHANGES

We have commented that *an event is a change in state of an object.* It is therefore natural to link state-transition diagrams to event diagrams.

The state-transition diagram in Fig. 11.8 shows the changes of state in the event diagram of Fig. 11.9. Both describe the process of registering students which is part of Fig. 11.6.

Figure 11.9 shows the states which on Fig. 11.8 are drawn like this:

Accepted

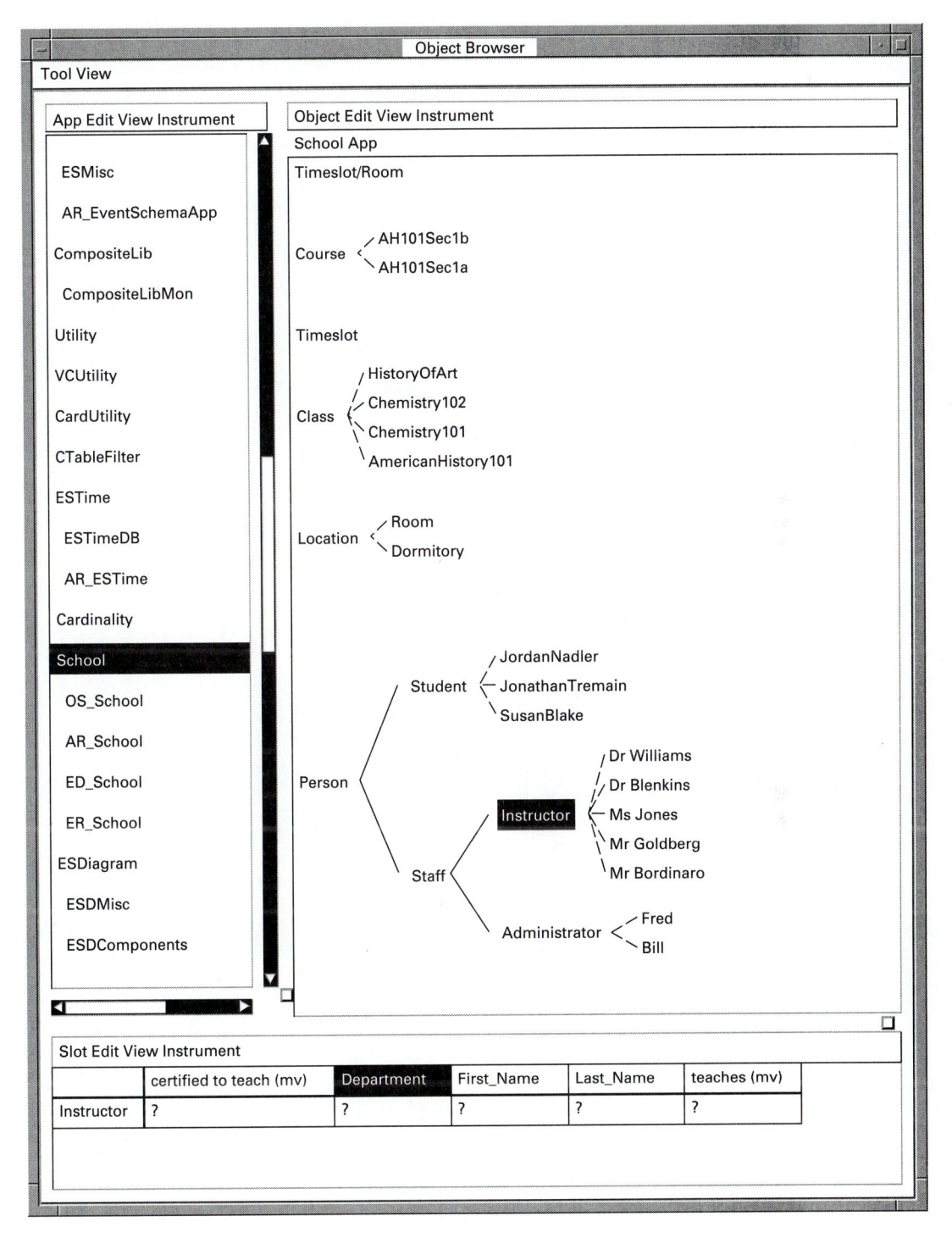

Figure 11.4 An Object Browser graph showing an object hierarchy resulting from building the object-relationship diagram with the OMW CASE tool in Figure 11.3. The designer has added instances of the objects. (Courtesy of IntelliCorp.)

(a)

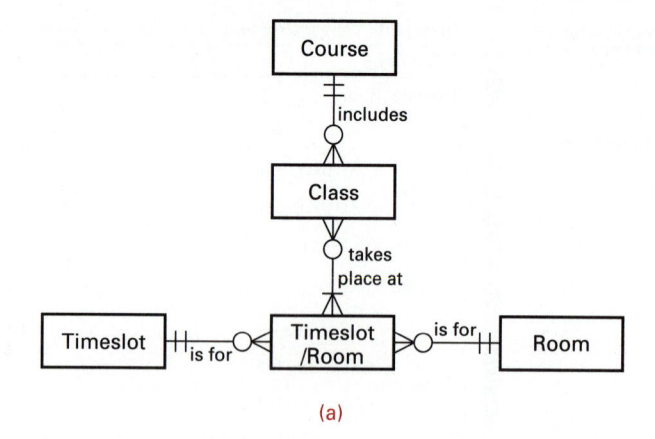

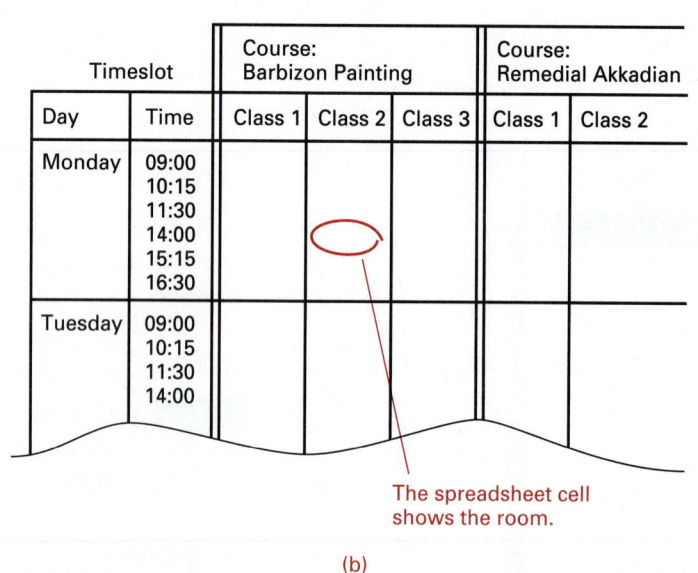

[Object-relationship diagram showing Course includes Class, Class takes place at Timeslot/Room, with Timeslot is for Timeslot/Room is for Room]

(b)

Timeslot		Course: Barbizon Painting			Course: Remedial Akkadian	
Day	Time	Class 1	Class 2	Class 3	Class 1	Class 2
Monday	09:00 10:15 11:30 14:00 15:15 16:30					
Tuesday	09:00 10:15 11:30 14:00					

The spreadsheet cell shows the room.

Figure 11.5 A portion of the object-relationship diagram in Fig. 11.1 and a related spreadsheet.

A state-transition diagram like Fig. 11.8 is useful to the analyst. He can examine it to see whether all appropriate states and state transitions are included. It thus acts as an integrity check on an event diagram such as Fig. 11.9. The analyst may draw a state-transition diagram before creating an event diagram to clarify his thinking about what happens to an object. He then builds the event diagram so that it includes all of the necessary state transitions.

The event diagram often includes state transitions for multiple objects. It relates to both the data model and state-transition diagrams. The OO-CASE tool should ensure that these representations are consistent.

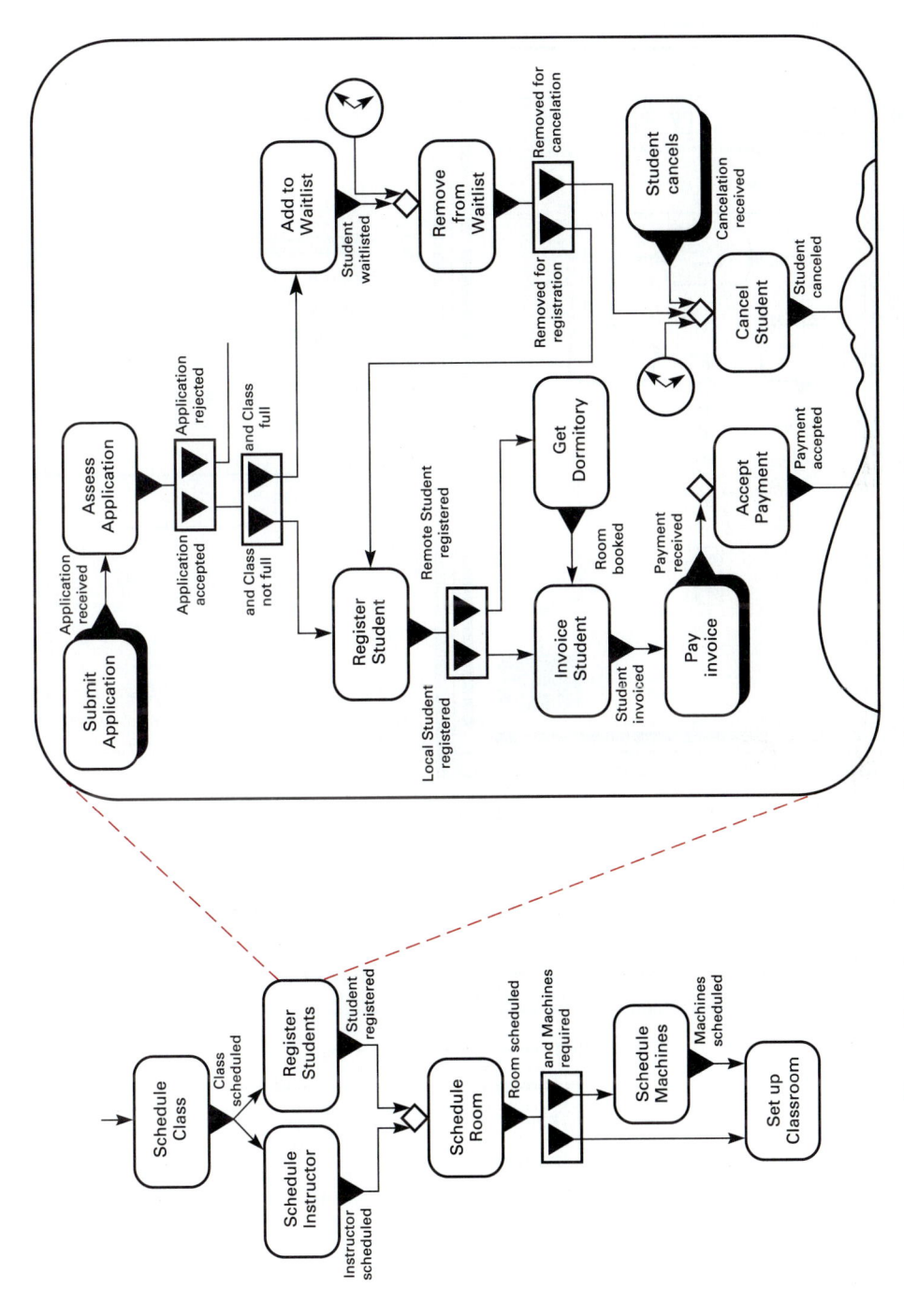

Figure 11.6 An event diagram for scheduling classes and registering students. The operation Register Students is expanded in a separate window.

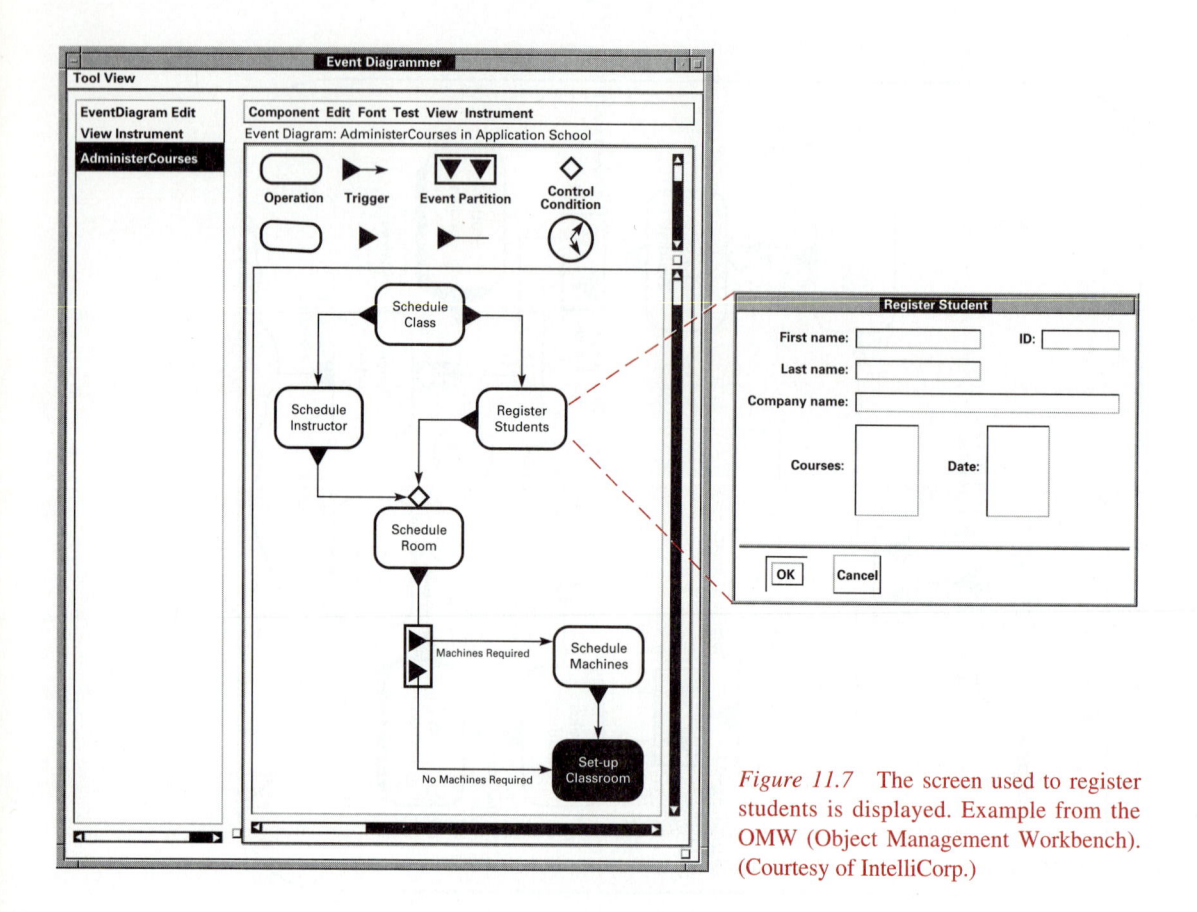

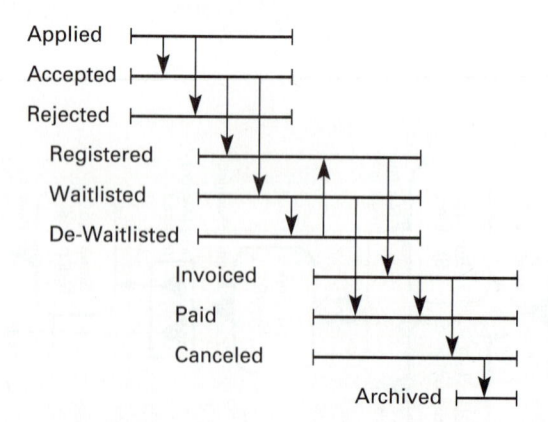

Figure 11.7 The screen used to register students is displayed. Example from the OMW (Object Management Workbench). (Courtesy of IntelliCorp.)

Figure 11.8 A state-transition diagram showing changes in state of the Student object during the registration process described by Fig. 11.9. The states on this diagram are shown on Fig. 11.9.

Chap. 11 How the Diagrams Interrelate 163

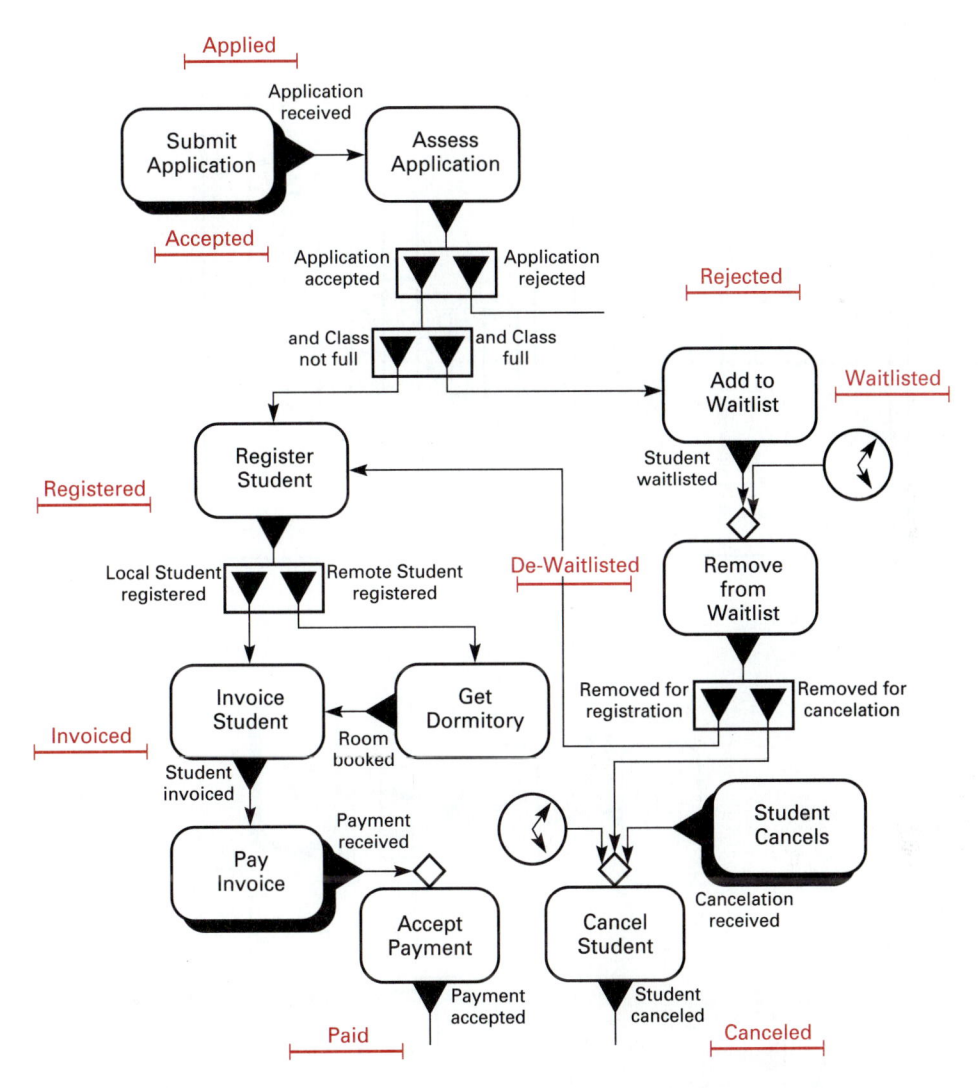

Figure 11.9 An event diagram for the process of registering students. The states of the **Student** object are shown on this diagram. Figure 11.8, showing the state changes in this diagram, can be generated automatically from this diagram.

State-transition diagrams may be shown as windows that are opened over event diagrams. Figure 11.10 shows two state-transition windows opened on the event diagram of Fig. 11.9, with color showing the state of the **Student** object type.

Conversely, Fig. 11.11 shows a state-transition diagram and a window containing an event diagram corresponding to one state transition.

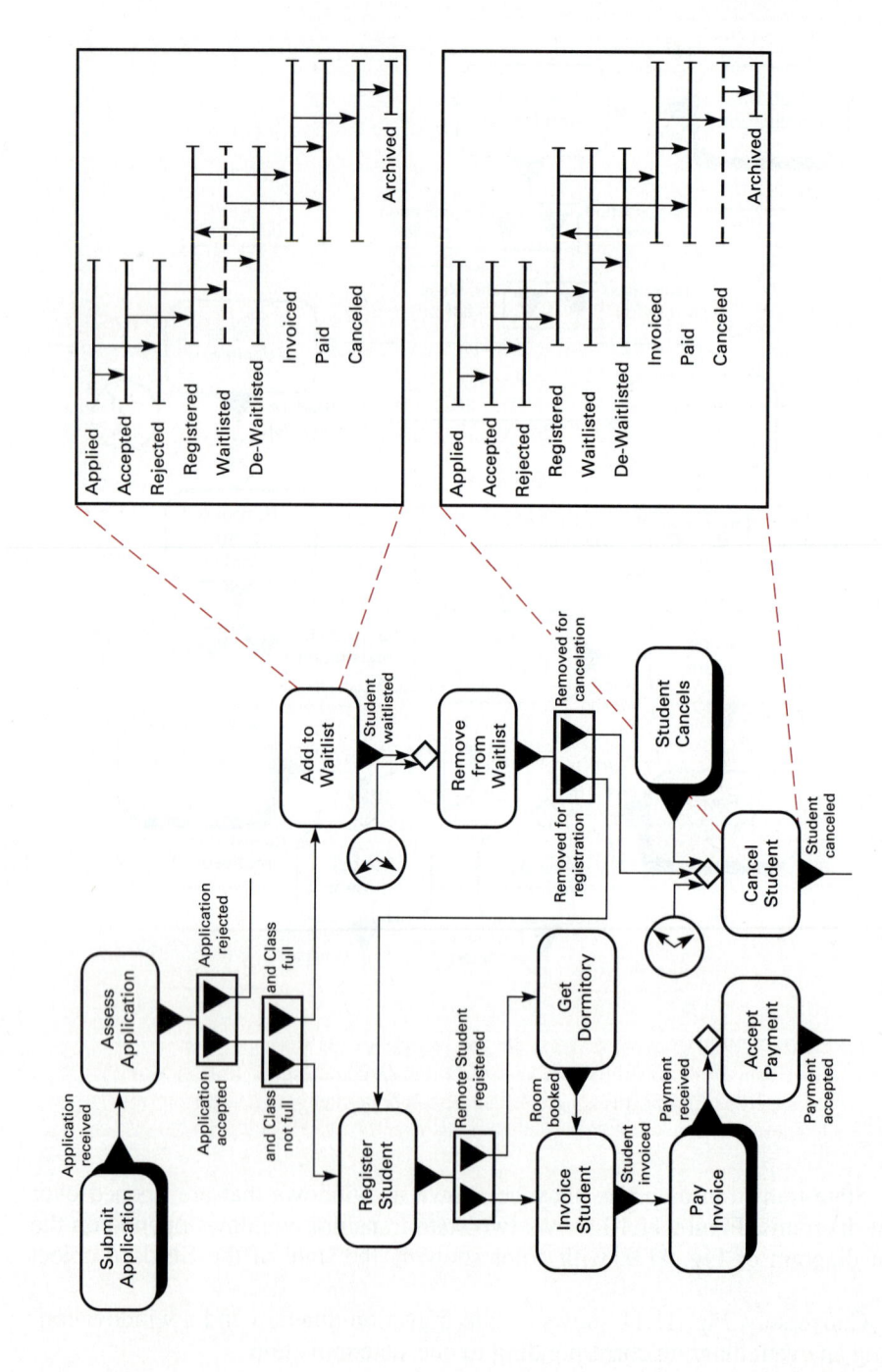

Figure 11.10 Two state-transition windows opened on the event diagram for registering students.

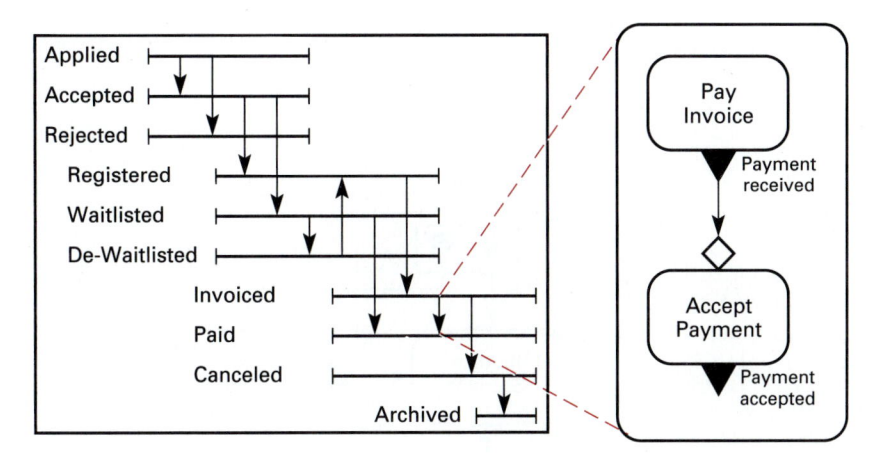

Figure 11.11 The operation that transforms the state of **Student** from Invoiced to Paid is expressed in the window on the right.

Operations could be represented on state-transition diagrams, as in Fig. 11.12. Conversely, states may be represented on event diagrams, as in Fig. 11.13.

Tying the behavioral aspects of modeling to the structural is very important. The resulting state of a **Person** object may have a corresponding object

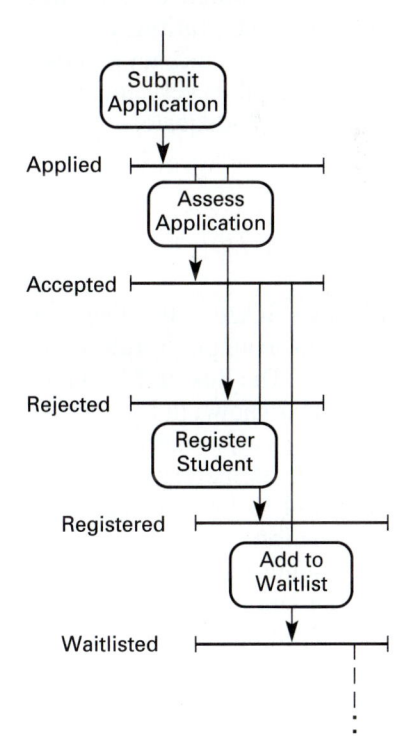

Figure 11.12 The operations that cause the state changes are represented on a state-transition diagram.

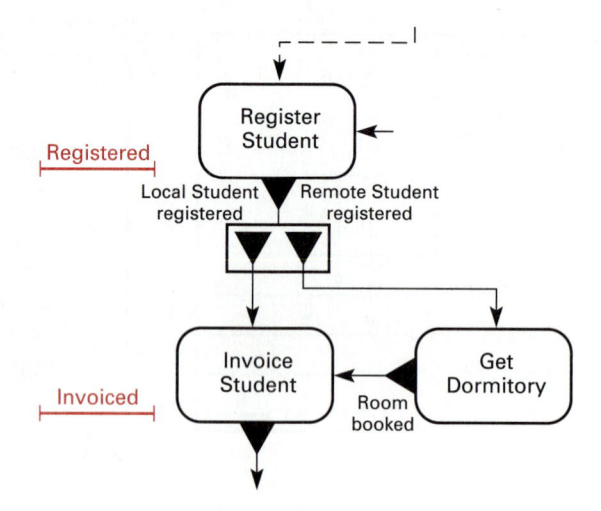

Figure 11.13 On an event diagram, the resulting state of the object **Person** can be depicted after each event type.

subtype in the object diagram. For instance, the result of a **Person dressed** event is a **Person** object that is an instance of **Dressed Person**. Without this modeling integration, object-oriented implementation with fully automated CASE tools would not be possible. Tying the behavioral aspects of modeling to the structural is very important. Without this modeling integration, OO-CASE tools are not adequate.

RULES LINKED TO DIAGRAMS

The importance of *rules* was emphasized in Chapter 10 which indicated that rules can be connected to any of the OO diagrams. The rules may be displayed in windows linked to the diagrams.

For example, a rule may be connected to a link on an object-relationship diagram. The link on Fig. 11.1 from **Instruct** to **Class** might have a rule connected to it, as shown in Fig. 11.14.

The rule window might be linked to comments giving the reason for the rule, its history, its creator, its politics, and so on. Additionally, it may be useful to have a digitized speech record giving comments or background information.

Similar windows may be associated with objects showing how attribute values are computed. This may be similar to the mechanisms in spreadsheets for computing the values in cells. A rule for computing student discount (shown in Fig. 11.15) is linked to the Student object type which contains the **Student Discount** property and is used to compute the student's bill.

Chap. 11   How the Diagrams Interrelate   **167**

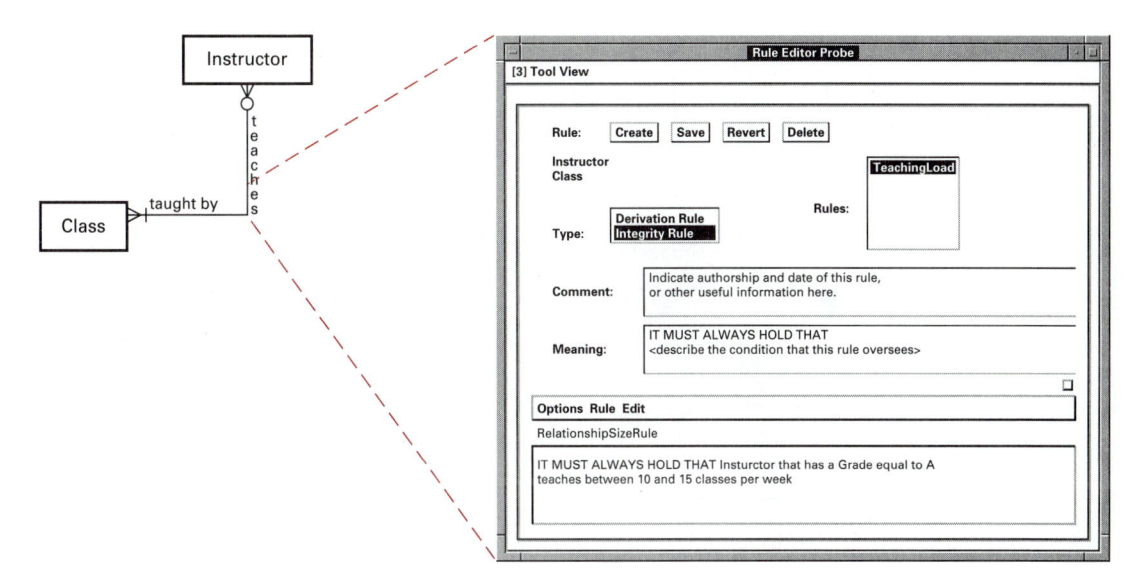

Figure 11.14 A rule editor window connected to a relationship on the object-relationship diagram of Fig. 11.3. Rules can be built with the rule editor and converted to code which is immediately run. The analyst may add an explanation of the rule in the window. Example from the OMW (Object Management Workbench). (Courtesy of IntelliCorp.)

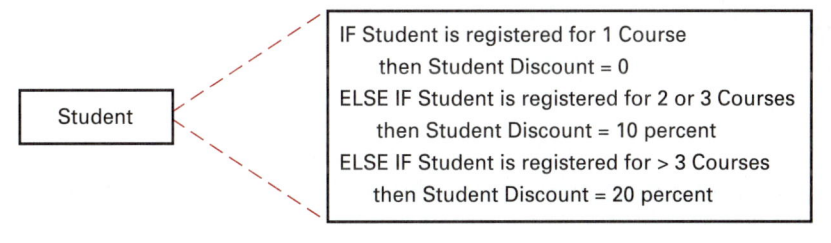

Figure 11.15 A rule for computing a data value connected to the object that contains that value.

Rules connected to event diagrams are particularly important. They can represent business policies and provide accuracy controls on the design where they can express preconditions and postconditions. A rule expressing a control condition (shown in Fig. 11.16) is part of the event diagram of Fig. 11.6.

As mentioned before, rules should be expressed in English so that they can be validated with end users and quickly changed when business policies change.

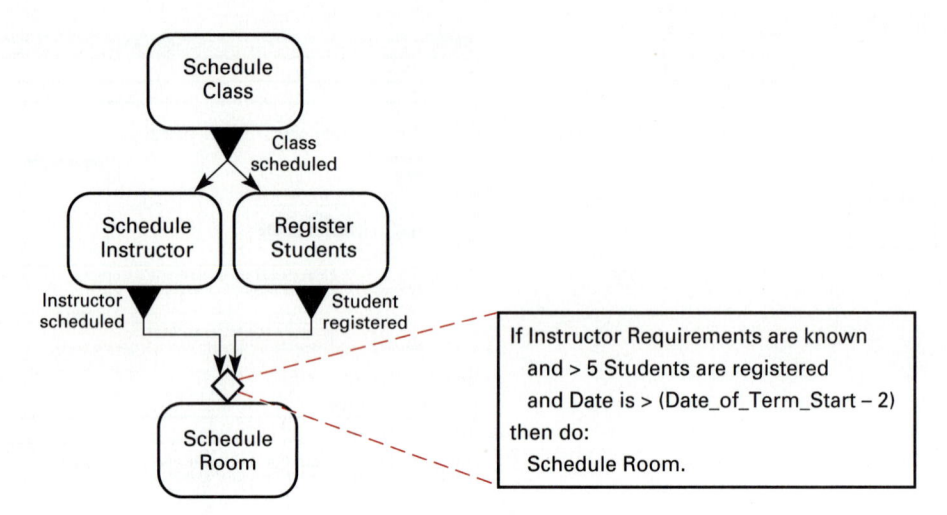

Figure 11.16 A rule connected to the event diagram of Fig. 11.6.

12 BASIC CONCEPTS OF OO DESIGN

As we progress from analysis to design, our model of the world stays essentially the same. OO technology removes the impedance mismatch between analysis and design (see Fig. 5.3).

- Object types are expressed in more detail as *classes.*
- Object-type generalization hierarchies become *class hierarchies,* with inheritance.
- Operations, along with their events, rules, and control conditions, become *methods.*
- Data models become the data structures used by classes.
- The user interface is designed and prototyped.

A code generator should be used so that code can be implemented directly and immediately from methods specification. Database description code is implemented directly from the data structure design. The user interface, preferably a graphic user interface (GUI) is generated and adjusted as prototyping is done. OO-CASE tools should be selected to accomplish code generation as automatically as possible (see Chapter 18).

Figure 12.1 shows the transition from analysis to design and implementation.

Analysis may apply to a whole business area; design applies to one system. For one system, the distinction between analysis and design may be blurred; analysis flows into design. Analysis is critically important because OO programming without good analysis achieves relatively few of the benefits of OO. Class Structure Design and Method Design tend to be intertwined and will be described together. Box 12.1 lists what is identified in OO design.

Models and Diagrams

Analysis	Object Types	Object Structures, Generalization	Data Models	Operations Events, Rules	
Design	Classes	Class Hierarchy (Inheritance)	Class Data Structure Design	Operations, Method Specification	GUI Design
Implementation			Database/File Implementation	Code	Code

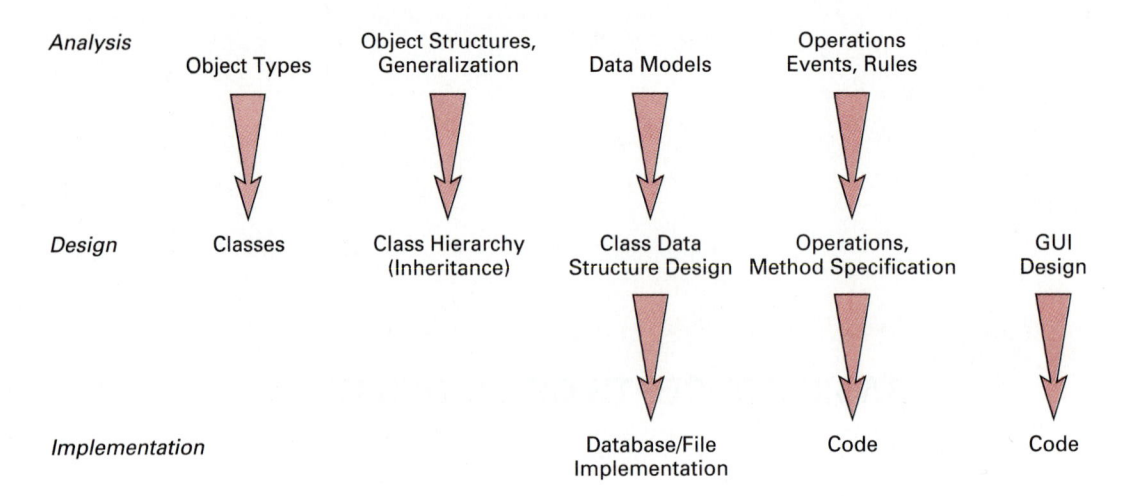

Figure 12.1 The transition from analysis to design and design to implementation.

BOX 12.1 The components of object-oriented design.

In object-oriented design, the following components are identified:

- What classes will be implemented? The object types from Object Structure Analysis will guide this decision.
- What data structure will each class employ? A diagram can be drawn to represent the data structure.
- What operations will each class offer and what will their methods be? The operations are listed and their methods are specified.
- How will class inheritance be implemented and how will it affect the data and methods? Class hierarchies are built.
- What user interface is needed? Screen design, GUI (graphic user interface) is done with code generators. Prototyping is employed with end users.
- What variants are there? Likely variants of classes are identified. ("Same-as, except..." applies to most reusable components.)

THE SELF-CONTAINED VIEWPOINT OF THE OBJECT

Often the most difficult problem in teaching OO design and programming is to make programmers adopt the simple viewpoint of the object. They must give up the *global* knowledge that they might have used with procedural programs and use only the local knowledge that the object has.

Kent Beck, an OO designer who used to work for Apple Computer Inc., wrote: "Novice designs are littered with regressions to global thinking: gratuitous global variables, unnecessary pointers, and inappropriate reliance on the implementation of other objects" [1].

He comments:

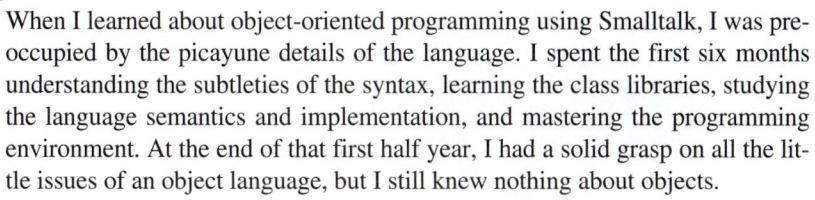

> When I learned about object-oriented programming using Smalltalk, I was preoccupied by the picayune details of the language. I spent the first six months understanding the subtleties of the syntax, learning the class libraries, studying the language semantics and implementation, and mastering the programming environment. At the end of that first half year, I had a solid grasp on all the little issues of an object language, but I still knew nothing about objects.
>
> I had been reimmersing myself in issues familiar to me from my days as a procedural programmer. I focused on the non-object-oriented aspects of my object-oriented language to avoid the uncomfortable feeling that I didn't know what was going on. By clinging to my old ways of thinking, like a nervous swimmer to the side of the pool, I was preventing myself from reinventing my perspective. It was only through patient and expert tutelage that I was able to break free of my old habits and begin to make use of the power in objects [2].

The problem that Beck describes exists with many traditional programmers now trying to do OO design. Programmers using C++ often have more difficulty than programmers using pure OO languages, such as Smalltalk, because C++ allows coding to be done in a traditional non-OO fashion if the programmer wishes.

Procedural programming encourages a global perspective. Any data is accessible and a link to any subroutine can be used. OO programming, on the other hand, has a strictly local perspective. The data and code for one class are encapsulated. It is essential to decide *what* classes have *what* responsibilities and then encapsulate those responsibilities. According to Beck, it is necessary to "think like an object" [2].

The following chapter discusses a technique for designing the classes and their responsibilities.

CLASS

In Object Structure Analysis, we identify object types. In design, we focus on the implementation of these object types.

> A *class* is an implementation of an object type. It specifies the data structure and the *methods* for implementing each operation.

Figure 12.2 illustrates a *class*.

A Class — Data Structure

Permissible Operations Whose Methods Allow Access to and Modification of the Data Structure

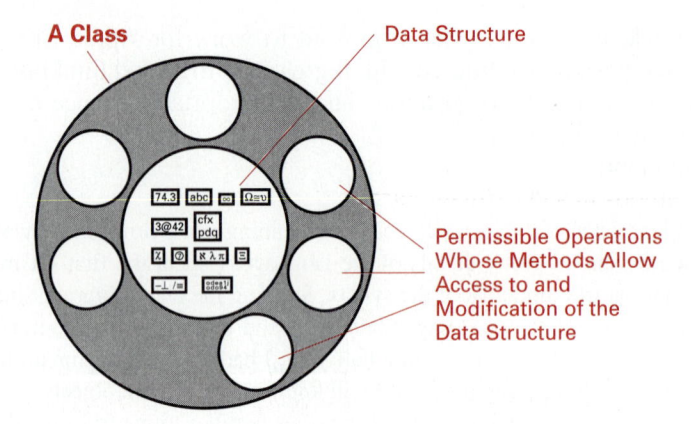

Figure 12.2 Each class specifies a data structure, operations, and methods used with those data.

Figure 12.3 illustrates an object that is an instance of the class in Fig. 12.2. The data and operations it encapsulates are specified by its class.

An Object — The data structure is specified by the class of which the object is an instance.

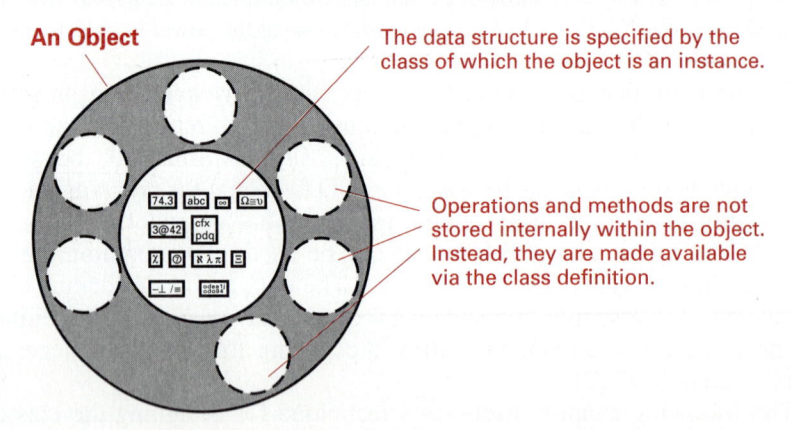

Operations and methods are not stored internally within the object. Instead, they are made available via the class definition.

Figure 12.3 The object's *data* are stored within the object and are accessed and modified *only* by permissible operations. This restriction to access is due to *encapsulation,* which protects the data from arbitrary and unintended use. Direct user access or update of an object's data would violate encapsulation. Users observe object "behavior" in terms of the operations that may be applied to objects and the results of such operations.

FROM OPERATIONS TO METHODS

Operations are processes that can be requested as units. *Methods* are procedural specifications of an operation within a class. In other words, the operation

Chap. 12 Basic Concepts of OO Design 173

is the kind of service requested, and the method is the specification of the programming code for it.

> An *operation* is a process that can be requested as a unit.
>
> A *method* is the specification of an operation.

The methods in a class manipulate *only* the data structure of that class. They cannot directly access the data structure of a different class. To use the data structures of a different class, they must send a request to that class. *Encapsulation* must be preserved in OO design.

The designer takes an operation on the event diagram and adds more detail to it in order to create a design. For example, a model produced in analysis may contain the operation Create Purchase Order:

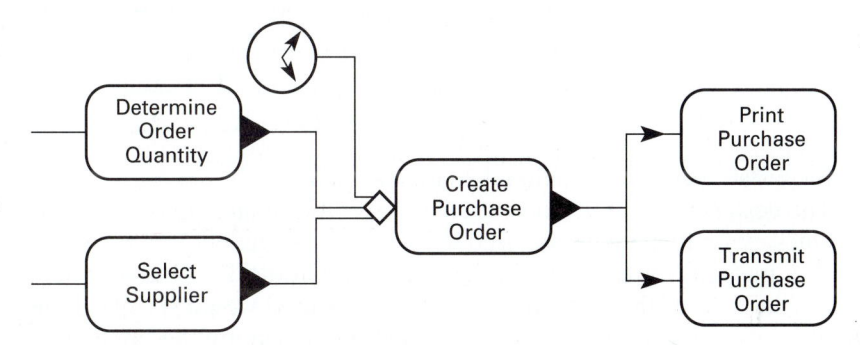

Along with this, Object Structure Analysis has identified object types, such as Supplier, Purchase Order, and Product.

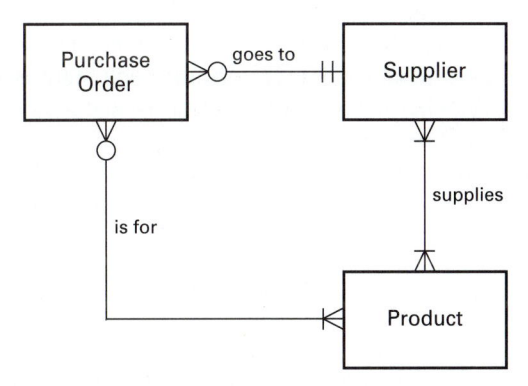

Data modeling has identified the attributes that are required for each of these objects. The attributes are associated with the object identifier in a correctly normalized manner. One object may have multiple normalized groups of attributes (i.e., it contains multiple entity types).

The designer might now take the operation **Create Purchase Order** and design it. The designer converts the object types into classes and the operations into methods. The object type **Purchase Order** becomes a class of the same name. The state transition diagram indicates that multiple operations are used with this object type and its corresponding class.

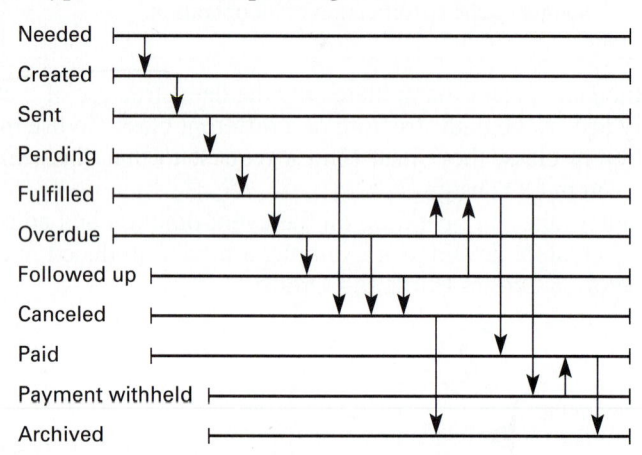

```
Needed          ├─────────────────────────────────────────┤
                         │
Created         ├───────┤│
                         │   │
Sent            ├───────────┤│
                             │   │
Pending         ├───────────────┤│
                                 │   │
Fulfilled       ├───────────────────┤│                  ▲       ▲
                                     │   │              │       │
Overdue         ├───────────────────────┤│              │       │
                                         │   │          │       │
Followed up     ├───────────────────────────┤│          │       │
                                             │   │      │       │
Canceled        ├───────────────────────────────┤ ▼   ▼ │       │
                                                                 │
Paid            ├───────────────────────────────────────┤│      │
                                                         │      │
Payment withheld├───────────────────────────────────────────────┤│
                                                                 │   │
Archived        ├───────────────────────────────────────────────────┤
```

Each state transition should relate to *one* operation.

The designer takes each operation and specifies a *method* or *methods* for it; sometimes multiple methods are used to create one operation.

One method, for example, in the operation **Create Purchase Order** might compute the total of the **Purchase Order**. The method would specify the way of computing the total. In doing so, the method might acquire the price of an item on the order by sending a request to a **Product** class which stores the data item **Price**. The method does this for each item on the **Purchase Order**.

In computing the total of the **Purchase Order**, the method might need to add the state purchase tax. To compute this, it needs the **State Tax Rate**. The designer needs to decide whether the tax rate for each state is stored in the **Purchase Order** class, or whether a separate class is needed, such as **State Tax**, which stores **State Tax Rate**.

In order to carry out a responsibility, a class often needs to send requests to other classes. Sometimes, a group of classes are clustered together to form a subsystem. The subsystem can be thought of as one object type that performs a given responsibility or set of responsibilities. This grouping of classes to implement one object type or subsystem is illustrated in the following chapter.

CLASS INHERITANCE

Generalization is a conceptual notion. *Class inheritance* (usually referred to simply as *inheritance*) is an implementation of generalization. Generalization states that the properties of an object-type apply to its subtypes. Class inheritance makes the data structure and operations of a class *physically available for reuse by its subclasses.* Inheriting the operations from a superclass enables code sharing—rather than code redefinition—among classes. Inheriting the data structure enables structure reuse.

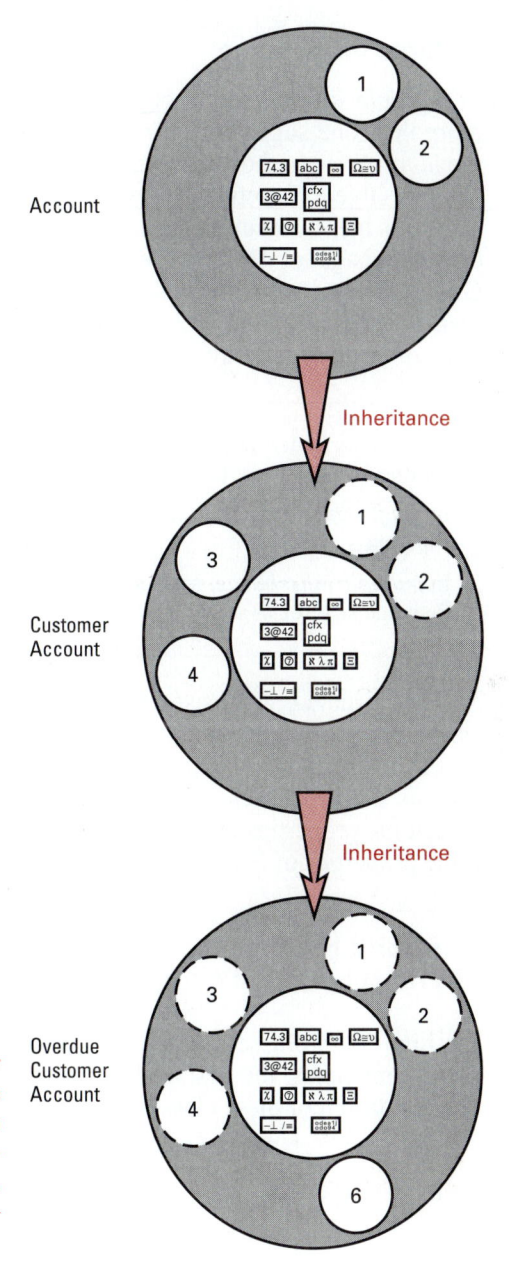

Figure 12.4 Inheritance. The class **Customer Account** inherits methods 1 and 2 from the class **Account**. **Customer Account** has two methods of its own: 3 and 4. The class **Overdue Customer Account** inherits methods 1, 2, 3, and 4 from the class **Customer Account**—while having its own method 6.

For example, in Fig. 12.4 **Customer Account** inherits operations 1 and 2 from **Account**. In addition to these, it has operations of its own—3 and 4. Overdue **Customer Account** also inherits operations 1, 2, 3, and 4 from **Customer Account**, as well as having 6 as its own.

Multiple Inheritance

In *multiple inheritance,* a class can inherit data structures and operations from more than one superclass. *Single inheritance* is shown in Fig. 12.4, while *multiple inheritance* is shown in Fig. 12.5.

In Object Structure Analysis, the analyst indicates that **Overdue Customer Account** has two supertypes—sharing a common **Account** supertype. In OO design, this generalization hierarchy is implemented using inheritance. **Overdue Customer Account** inherits the features from classes **Customer Account** and **Overdue Account**. Therefore, **Overdue Customer Account** has the following operations physically available for reuse—1, 2, 3, 4, 5, and 6.

> *Class inheritance* implements the generalization hierarchy by making it possible for one class to share the data structure and operations of another class.
>
> In *single inheritance,* a class can inherit the data structure and operations of one superclass.
>
> In *multiple inheritance,* a class can inherit the data structure and operations of more than one superclass.

Fern diagrams are used for showing multiple inheritance paths among classes. Figure 12.6 is such a diagram that shows some of the classes in the OO-CASE tool ProKappa. At the top of Fig. 12.6, for example, a **CoerceToSlotProbeHook** inherits the properties of **SelfCoercingProbeHooks**, **SelfCoercingProbeHooks** inherit the properties of **CoercingProbeHooks**, and **CoercingProbeHooks** inherit the properties of **ProbeHooks**.

CLASSES HIGH IN THE HIERARCHY   Classes high in the hierarchy (on the left of Fig. 12.6) need to be particularly well designed, because they are employed multiple times in multiple subtypes. If the high-level classes are poorly designed, their lower-level subtypes will be poor. Sometimes, the best designers are assigned to work on the high-level classes. The design of these classes should be reviewed carefully.

SELECTING A METHOD   When a request is sent to an object, the software selects the methods that will be used. We commented earlier that the method is not stored "in the object,"

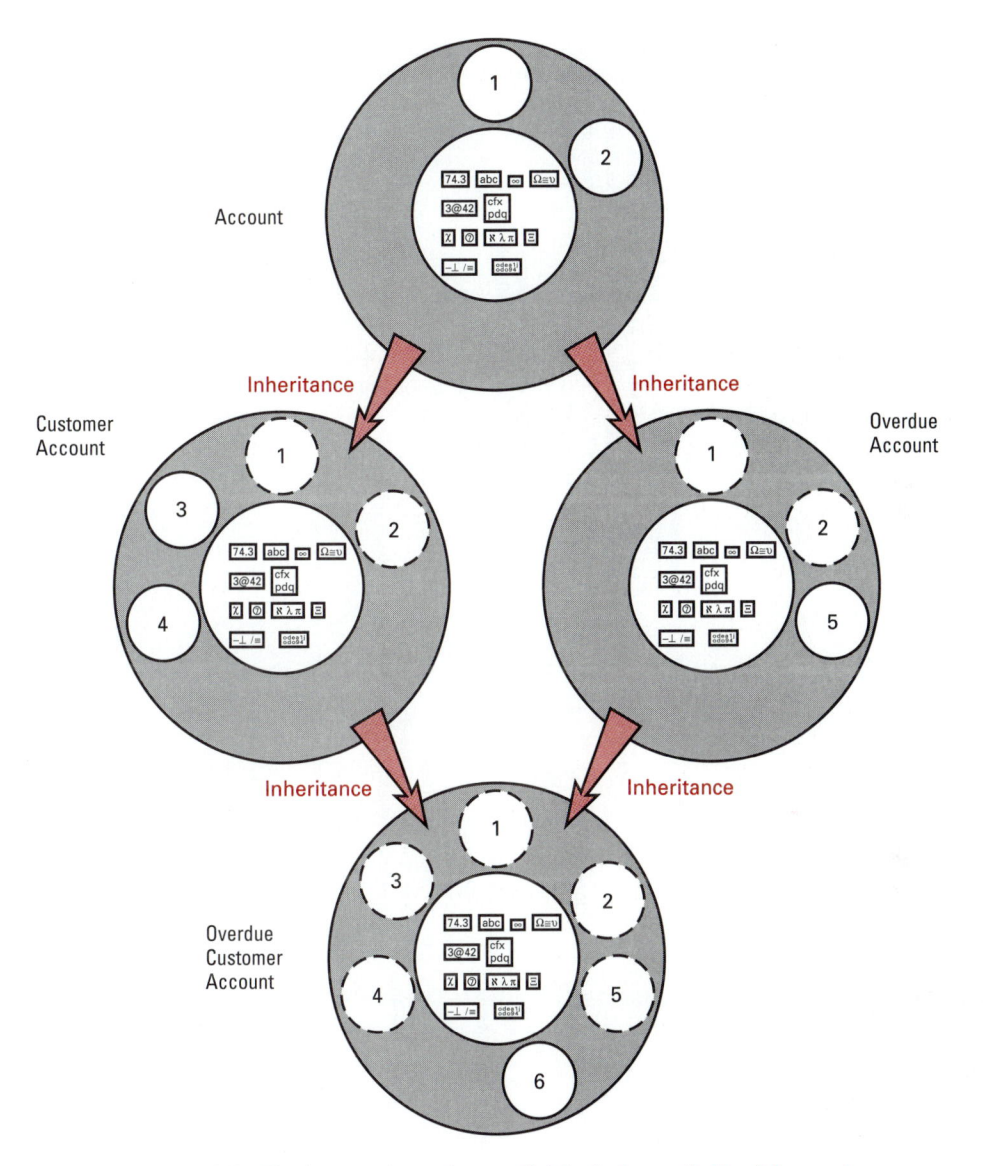

Figure 12.5 The bottom three classes all inherit the methods of **Account**. **Overdue Customer Account** inherits methods from both **Customer Account** and **Overdue Account**. (When operations with identical names are inherited from multiple superclasses, problems can arise.)

because this would cause multiple replication. Instead, the method is associated with the *class*. The method may not be in the class of which the object is an instance—but rather in a superclass. Figure 12.7 illustrates one way of thinking about this.

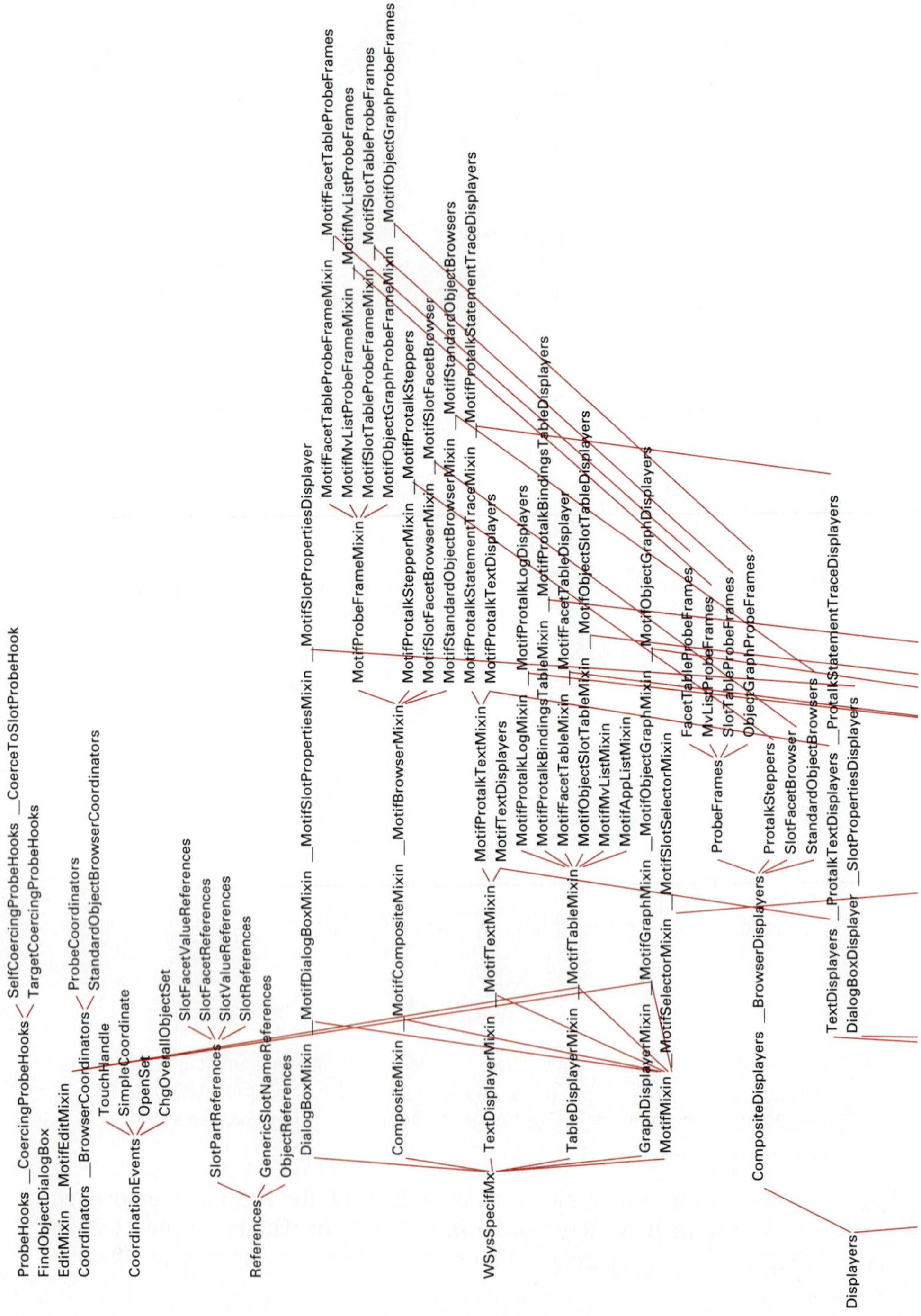
ProbeHooks
CoercingProbeHooks
SelfCoercingProbeHooks
CoerceToSlotProbeHook
TargetCoercingProbeHooks
FindObjectDialogBox
EditMixin
MotifEditMixin
Coordinators
BrowserCoordinators
ProbeCoordinators
StandardObjectBrowserCoordinators
CoordinationEvents
TouchHandle
SimpleCoordinate
OpenSet
ChgOverallObjectSet
References
SlotPartReferences
SlotFacetValueReferences
SlotFacetReferences
SlotValueReferences
SlotReferences
GenericSlotNameReferences
ObjectReferences
WSysSpecifMx
DialogBoxMixin
MotifDialogBoxMixin
MotifSlotPropertiesMixin
MotifSlotPropertiesDisplayer
MotifProbeFrameMixin
MotifFacetTableProbeFrameMixin
MotifFacetTableProbeFrames
MotifMvListProbeFrameMixin
MotifMvListProbeFrames
MotifSlotTableProbeFrameMixin
MotifSlotTableProbeFrames
MotifObjectGraphProbeFrameMixin
MotifObjectGraphProbeFrames
CompositeMixin
MotifCompositeMixin
MotifBrowserMixin
MotifProtalkStepperMixin
MotifProtalkSteppers
MotifSlotFacetBrowserMixin
MotifSlotFacetBrowser
MotifStandardObjectBrowserMixin
MotifStandardObjectBrowsers
MotifProtalkStatementTraceMixin
MotifProtalkStatementTraceDisplayers
TextDisplayerMixin
MotifTextMixin
MotifProtalkTextMixin
MotifProtalkTextDisplayers
MotifTextDisplayers
TableDisplayerMixin
MotifTableMixin
MotifProtalkLogMixin
MotifProtalkLogDisplayers
MotifProtalkBindingsTableMixin
MotifProtalkBindingsTableDisplayers
MotifFacetTableMixin
MotifFacetTableDisplayer
MotifObjectSlotTableMixin
MotifObjectSlotTableDisplayers
MotifMvListMixin
MotifAppListMixin
GraphDisplayerMixin
MotifGraphMixin
MotifObjectGraphMixin
MotifObjectGraphDisplayers
MotifSlotSelectorMixin
MotifMixin
MotifSelectorMixin
Displayers
CompositeDisplayers
BrowserDisplayers
ProbeFrames
FacetTableProbeFrames
MvListProbeFrames
SlotTableProbeFrames
ObjectGraphProbeFrames
ProtalkSteppers
SlotFacetBrowser
StandardObjectBrowsers
TextDisplayers
ProtalkTextDisplayers
ProtalkStatementTraceDisplayers
DialogBoxDisplayer
SlotPropertiesDisplayers

Figure 12.6 A portion of a fern diagram showing classes in the software of the OO-CASE tool ProKappa. Classes on the right inherit the data structures and methods of the classes on the left to which they are connected. (Courtesy of IntelliCorp, Inc.)

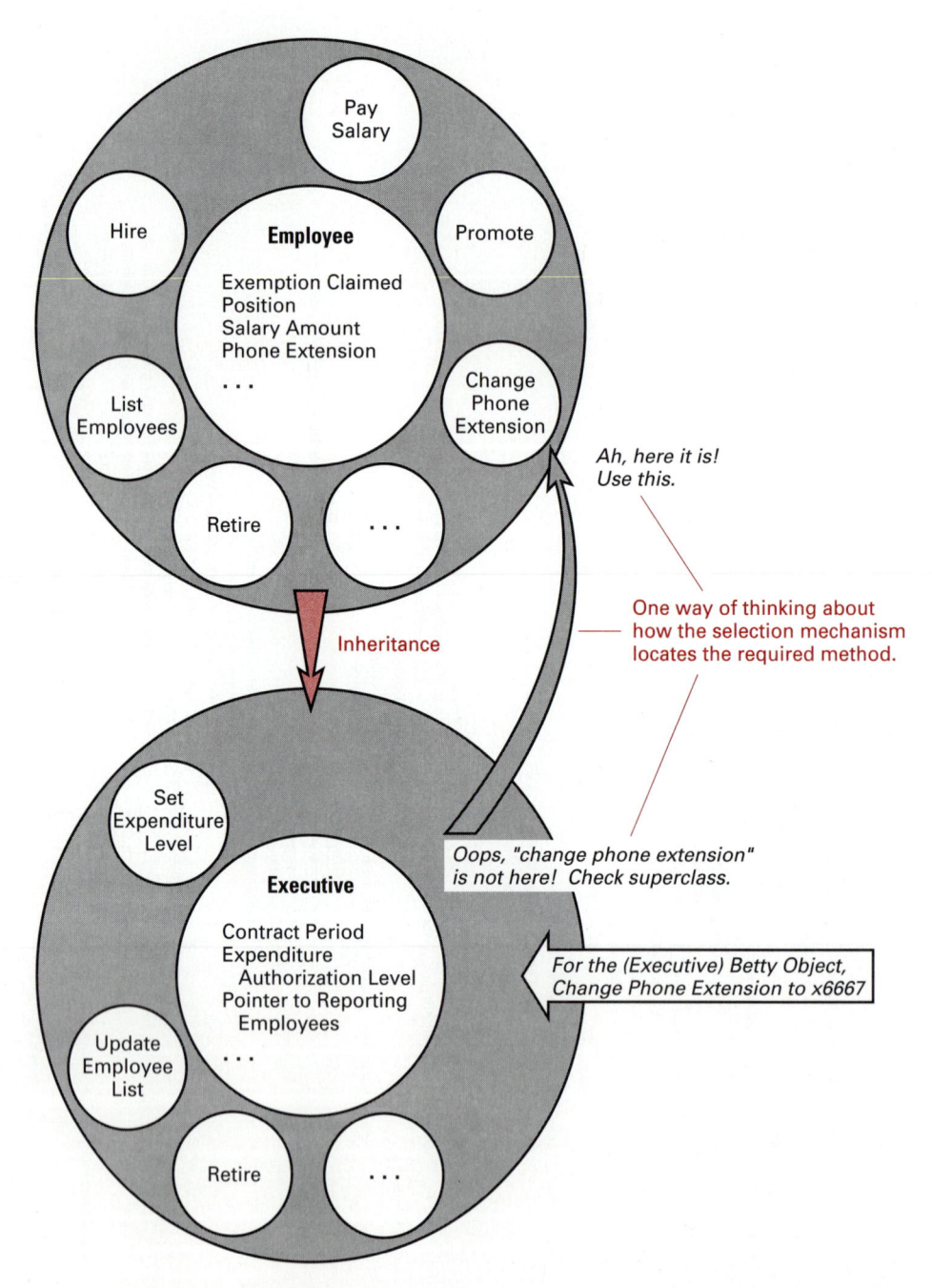

Figure 12.7 The OO *selection mechanism* locates the appropriate method for the requested operation.

Here, a request is sent to an **Executive** object named Betty to change her phone extension to x6667. The list of permissible operations within the **Executive** class is checked, and "change phone extension" is not there. The OO implementation then automatically checks the superclass of **Employee**. In this example, the "change phone extension" operation is found in **Employee** and selected to carry out the request. Should the operation not be found in that superclass, the inheritance selection mechanism would continue its search through all the object's superclasses, level-by-level. If found, the operation would be selected. If the operation is not found at any level of superclass, the source of the request would be regarded invalid. OO programming languages, such as Smalltalk, detect these invalid requests at runtime. OO programming languages, such as C++ or Objective C, resolve these requests at compile-time so that no invalid requests can occur.

Inheritance, then, allows a class to reuse the features of its superclasses. In this way, users need only specify what should be done—leaving the *selection mechanism* to determine how the operation is located and executed. The selection mechanism shifts the burden of locating the correct operation from the source of the request to the OO application.

POLYMORPHISM

Polymorphism means that the same request could be sent to different classes and they would implement it in a slightly different way. Polymorphism means *many forms*. For example, the request is made to print a document. There are different types of printers that need somewhat different software for controlling them. The user or object that sends the **Print-a-Document** request does not care about these detailed differences. It merely wants a good-looking document. The classes responsible for printing can therefore select the technique that gets the job done.

> *Polymorphism* is the ability for two or more classes to respond to the same request, each in its way.

In an analogy, the members of an orchestra create their own interpretation. Although each player has the same score and watches the same conductor, each interprets the score and the conductor according to the needs of his own instrument.

A **PRINT** request might go to classes that control different kinds of printers or different types of fonts. The same **PRINT** request might refer to text files, charts, line diagrams, or bit-mapped graphics. The responsible class finds the information that it must interpret in order to print the item correctly. It may direct the request to the printer with the shortest print queue. It may send a request to other classes to help it. The originator of the **PRINT** does not need to know how the printing is accomplished. Users are glad that they do not have to the learn details about controlling different types of printing.

In Fig. 12.8, the **Employee** class defines the method for the retire operation. In OO implementations, this method is automatically inherited by all the subclasses of **Employee**. However, an organization may have different methods for retiring an **Executive** than for retiring an **Employee**. In this situation, the method for retiring executives *overrides* the general method for retiring employees. Yet, even though these methods differ, they accomplish the same operational purpose. This retire operation is polymorphic, because the method of implementation depends on whether an object is an **Employee** or an **Executive**.

One strength of polymorphism is that a request for an operation can be made without knowing which method should be invoked. These implementation details are hidden from the user. Instead, the responsibility rests with the selection mechanism of the OO implementation.

"SAME AS, EXCEPT..." Most reusability in practice requires the implementor to modify the reusable component. A house architect takes a standard bathroom design and modifies it to include pink marble and a larger tub. A lawyer takes a prenuptial agreement from a repository and customizes it. (The lawyer charges 50 hours for only 2 hours of actual work.)

> The phrase "same as, except..." describes most reusability.

Object-oriented techniques should allow customization of classes. We do not want implementors to change the code of a class any more than we want them to change the circuit boards of their VCR. Classes become highly complex and, therefore, should be designed so that they can be customized easily on a CASE-tool screen. In good CASE tools, OO designs can be used from a repository and customized.

A simple illustration of customization is shown in Figs. 12.9 and 12.10. A class stored in the CASE repository is **Field**. Screens are built from **Fields** and **Field Groups**, while **Dialogs** are built from **Screens**.

The class **Field** has several attributes—row, column, color, and so on. The default value for color is "Green." This means that every instance of the class **Field** will be created with a color value of "Green"—unless the value is specifically changed by the user. This form of inheritance is called class-instance inheritance.

Various subclasses of **Field** that inherit the values of their parent unless the designer overrides a value are shown in Fig. 12.9. The designer makes the **Color** of input fields "White." **Customer Number** and **Customer Name** are both input fields, so they appear white on the screen.

Retire (Employee) Bob Object

Although the Retire operation is inherited from the Employee class, its method is overridden in the Executive class.

The Retire operation, therefore, is *polymorphic* because its method is dependent on the type of object.

Retire (Executive) Betty Object

Inheritance

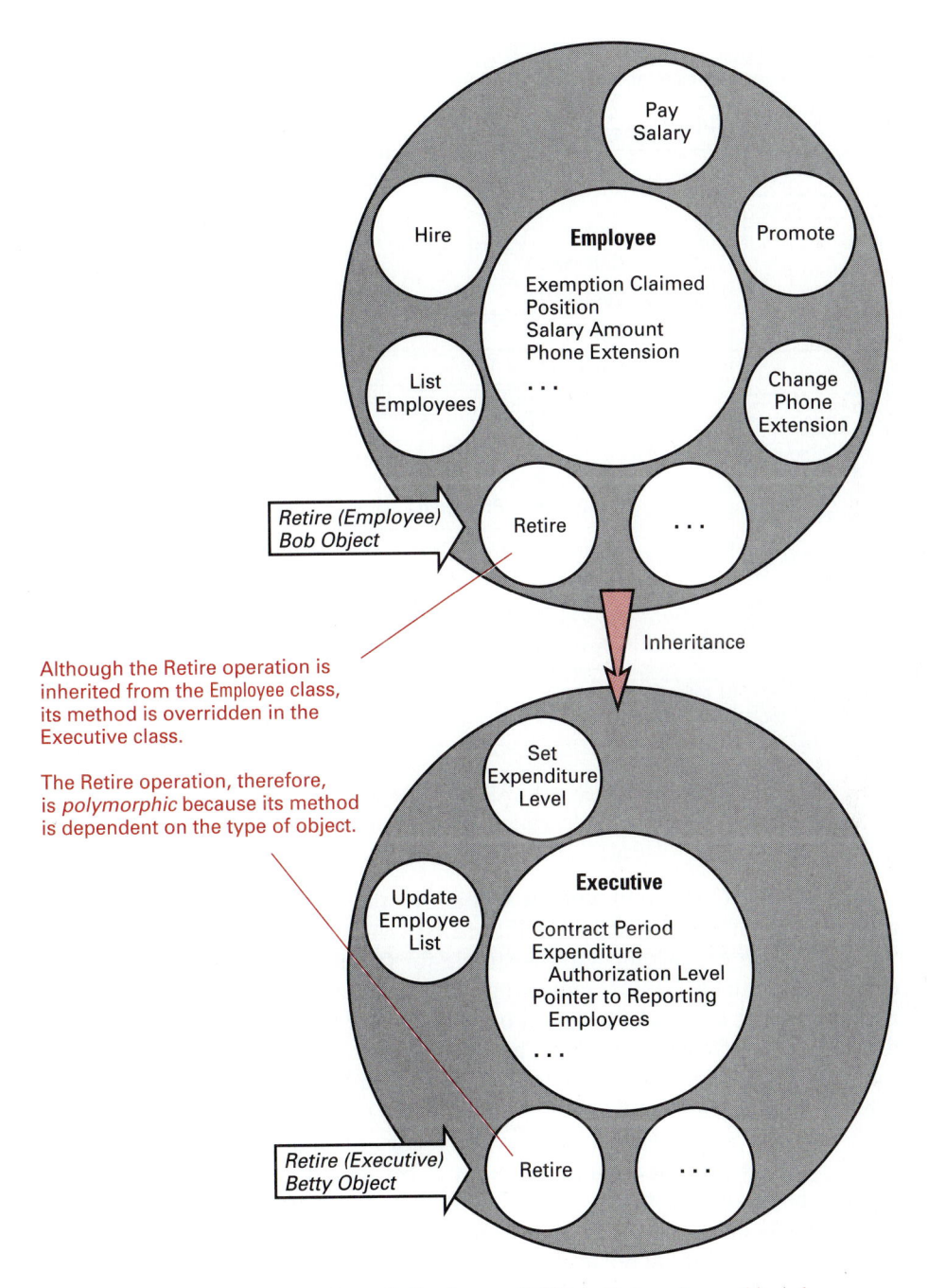

Employee
Exemption Claimed
Position
Salary Amount
Phone Extension
...

- Pay Salary
- Hire
- Promote
- List Employees
- Change Phone Extension
- Retire
- ...

Executive
Contract Period
Expenditure
 Authorization Level
Pointer to Reporting
 Employees
...

- Set Expenditure Level
- Update Employee List
- Retire
- ...

Figure 12.8 A method may be implemented differently in a class and its subclass. Subclasses can respond to the same request and implement the same operation with different methods. This is called *polymorphism*.

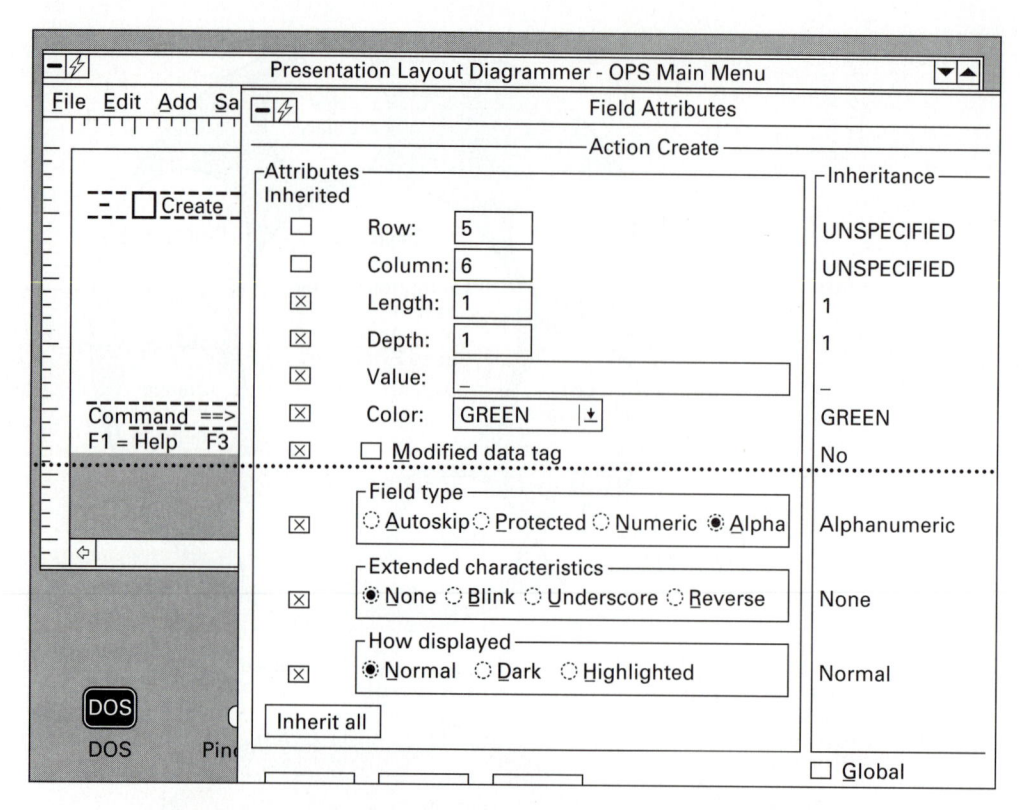

Figure 12.9 A window from an I-CASE tool that allows the designer to override inherited properties of the object class **Field**. (Courtesy of KnowledgeWare, Inc., Atlanta, GA.)

A type of CASE-tool window that allows the designer to override inherited properties of an object is shown in Fig. 12.10.

This type of customization is simple for the user. Customized applications can be built quickly without tampering with the code of a class. Designers should anticipate what aspects of a design users will want to modify and provide easy-to-use means of customization. This is an essential aspect of both OO-CASE tools and *methodologies* for systems development that use OO techniques to achieve high reusability.

The analyst or designer who creates a class should be asking the question, "How will this class be used in the future?" He should create the class in a way that can be easily adapted for future needs. In a well-managed OO environment, everything is either built out of existing classes or new classes are created for future reuse. Everything relates to past or future reusability.

Some corporations have achieved a high degree of reuse. Noma Industries, a large Canadian manufacturer, emphasized reusability across its 14 divisions. It succeeded in achieving such a level of reusability that only 3.8 percent of its code

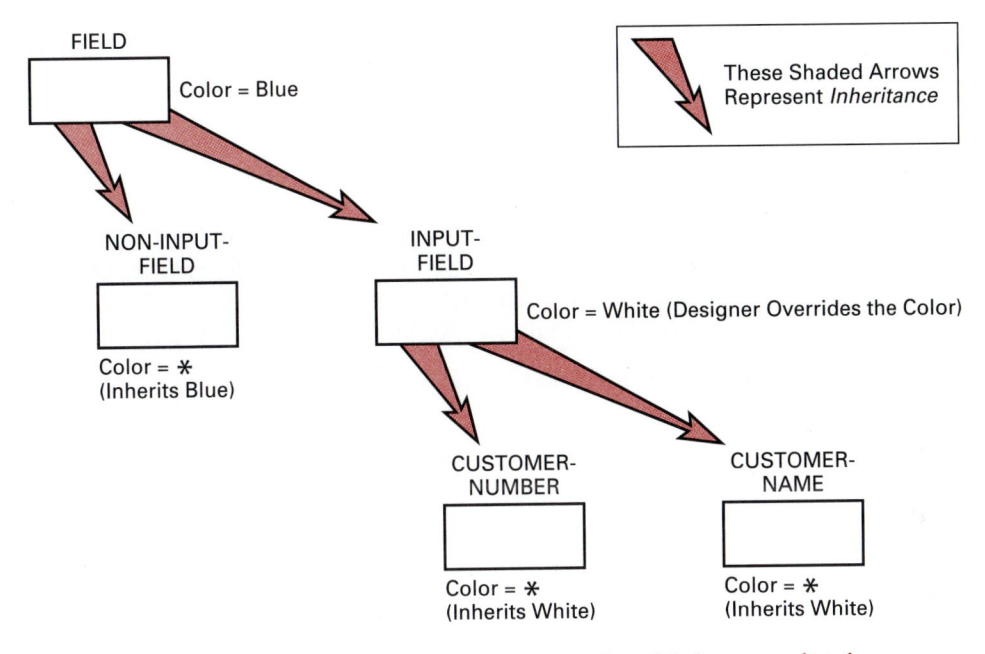

Figure 12.10 Subclasses of Field inherit the color of their parents, but the designer can override the color.

is custom built. Because of this high level of reuse, the code added or replaced per developer-person-day, with a code generator, averages about 1000 source lines of COBOL.

As OO-CASE tools spread, managing software development will provide challenges. The highest level of automation will be achieved by assembling applications from object classes and easily adapting the objects in a *same-as, except* fashion.

Reusability, one of the great potential benefits of OO techniques, is achieved in two ways, as we have commented earlier. First, low-level classes inherit data structures and methods from high-level classes. Second, the same classes are used in multiple different applications.

> The achievement of a high level of reuse in software building is a management act. It must be deliberately planned and carefully managed.

Human motivations and metrics are established which relate to software reuse.

To achieve a high level of reuse, modeling should be done across an entire enterprise (or at least a major section of the enterprise). This modeling should identify both reusable objects and generalizations that lead to inheritance. Classes should be designed so that they can be modified easily (the "same as, except . . ."

principle). Enterprisewide modeling, with the goal of maximum reusability is best done with OO information engineering techniques described in Chapter 16.

REFERENCES

1. Beck, Kent and Ward Cunningham, "A Laboratory for Teaching Object-Oriented Thinking," *Proceedings of the 1989 OOPSLA—Conference on Object-Oriented Programming Systems, Languages and Applications,* OOPSLA '89 (New Orleans), Norman Meyrowitz ed., ACM, New York, 1989, pp. 1-6.

2. Beck, Kent, "Think Like an Object," *Unix Reviews,* 9:10, 1991.

13 RESPONSIBILITY-DRIVEN DESIGN

The essence of object-oriented technology is that objects hide their internals through encapsulation. The internals can be changed without changing how one interacts with an object. In a similar way, the internals of a VCR can be redesigned without changing its user interface, because the user does not know what goes on inside a VCR.

RESPONSIBILITIES A class can be thought of as having responsibilities. It can respond to only a specific group of *requests* and must respond to each of those requests correctly.

OO design should identify the classes and their responsibilities before any work is done on designing the internals of the classes. This is sometimes referred to as *responsibility-driven design*.

The analyst should have already created OO models. In doing this, he should have categorized the object types in a business area and created event diagrams—showing what business events occur and how they trigger operations. In addition, he should have identified the business rules that relate to state changes, triggers, and control conditions. Now the software designer needs to determine what classes should exist and what their responsibilities should be. Only when the responsibilities are clear should the designer think about the details of *methods* that specify the code.

In the past, developers have argued about *data-oriented methodologies* versus *process-oriented methodologies*. In data-driven methodologies, the data are modelled first and then the procedures are created that use those data. In process-driven methodologies, the processes are decomposed hierarchically and then data structures are created to support those processes. In object-oriented design, the starting point is identifying classes and determining the responsibilities of those classes. This must be done well—before the internals of a class can be tackled.

Each class is then designed to meet its responsibilities in a self-contained fashion. Each class responds to requests without knowing what caused the requests to be sent or what effect its responses have.

> Each class is a self-contained unit that performs its responsibilities with no knowledge of cause and effect.

Once the responsibilities are clearly defined, creating the internals of the class is relatively straightforward. Each *method* for implementing a responsibility is relatively simple and is isolated from the world at large.

RESPONSIBILITIES AND COLLABORATORS

Kent Beck and Ward Cunningham devised techniques for identifying class responsibilities that they call CRC methods [1].

> CRC stands for
> - class
> - responsibility
> - collaborator

When a class has a responsibility for acting on a request, it may do so in one of two ways. It may either use a method of its own or transfer the task to another class—referred to as a *collaborator*. We need to draw diagrams of how classes interact with one another, and how they use collaborators.

CLASSES ARE ACTORS

Each class resembles an actor, who must be told what to do and is given certain responsibilities. He can accomplish some responsibilities on his own; for others, he must send requests to collaborators.

The designer is like a director, who must assign parts to the actors: he tells them their class, name, and description as well as their responsibilities. The director puts the actors to work and polishes their performances.

CRC CARDS

OO-CASE tools are powerful and invaluable in managing complex models, checking their consistency, and generating code. However, computers, while good at meticulous detail, do not replace human creativity. Ward Cunningham advocates a technique that enhances human interaction in OO design [1]. He uses 4-by-6 inch index cards—called CRC cards—to represent classes. On each class is written

- the *class* name
- the *responsibilities* of the class
- the *collaborators* that the class may use to achieve its responsibilities

A pile of CRC cards is used to represent all the classes in a design. People sitting around a table use the cards to discuss the classes, responsibilities, and collaborators. Different people may become actors and assume the roles of different classes. A person assuming the role of a class holds the card for that class and thinks about its responsibilities—whether the responsibilities are appropriate and what collaborators must be sent requests.

Each person playing the role of a class compiles a list of possible responsibilities and debates them with the group. Various situations or problems are discussed, and team members think through how their cards need to interact. Classes may be combined or subtyped and responsibilities moved from one class to another.

The cards have the following format:

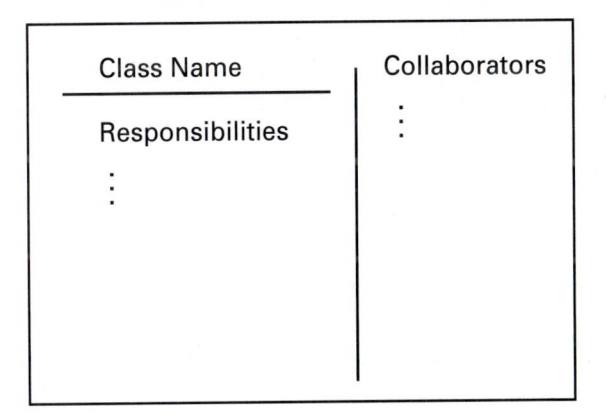

```
┌─────────────────────────────────────┐
│   Class Name         Collaborators  │
│   ──────────           ⋮            │
│   Responsibilities                  │
│     ⋮                               │
│                                     │
└─────────────────────────────────────┘
```

The class name is written at the top left, responsibilities are listed below the class name, and collaborators (if any) are noted on the right. A description of the class may be put on the back of the card.

THINKING LIKE AN OBJECT

Design with the cards, like other creative design, tends to progress from the known to the unknown. The cards representing classes are spread out on the table and arranged into groups. The owner of a class talks about what its responsibilities ought to be, and how it interacts with other classes. Details are steadily filled in and sometimes new cards are created. Cards are then arranged into piles that represent class supertypes and subtypes. Responsibilities moved to the supertypes should have indicators on the subtypes that these responsibilities are inherited.

The group simulates how the system will behave, with each card owner playing the role of its class and stating what requests that card sends to other cards. The group asks "what-if?" questions and the card owners go through their classes' behaviors. Members are encouraged to say, "OK. I'm this object. What do I do about so-and-so?" In the early stages, the situation sometimes calls for responsibilities that do not exist yet. The group discusses what class should have those responsibilities. If a class acquires too many responsibilities, some responsibilities may be moved to collaborators and sometimes a new class is created. Team members suggest scenarios aimed at suspected weaknesses or omissions. In the early stages, they frequently discover responsibilities that have been missed.

When members of the group pick up a card, they tend to identify with it—arguing its case and discussing its responsibilities. They must look at the rest of the design as the class would, knowing no more than the class does. They learn to think like an object. The team members change the position of the cards on the table—grouping related cards together and pointing from one card to another showing the messages that pass among them. The design becomes steadily refined. The members try to ensure that it works and should group the responsibilities and subclasses to maximize reusability.

CRC cards encourage group interaction. This human interaction tends to work more creatively than computerized techniques. At each stage, the process must be explained to make sure that all the participants understand. The process of explaining decisions helps to clarify the design and test it.

The participants should sit around a table small enough so that any participant can pick up any card or change the layout of the cards. The setup should encourage equal participation of all group members.

The participants should change roles occasionally and discuss the responsibilities of a different class. Sometimes, the cards may be shuffled to see whether new viewpoints emerge.

As cards become changed multiple times, they need to be rewritten. If a card becomes too full, that class probably has too many responsibilities and should be split into component classes. A card representing a class with components may be clipped to the cards for those components. In other words, a subsystem may be clipped together.

Designs reach closure when the participants run out of scenarios and "what if?" questions. The resulting CRC cards can be pinned on a cork board.

Beck and Cunningham have used sessions with CRC cards for training programmers to think in an OO fashion.

FINDING THE RIGHT WORDING

During the CRC session and later during implementation and maintenance, group interaction is greatly helped by having internally consistent names for classes and by using the best phrases to describe responsibilities.

Kent Beck says that he always has a dictionary and thesaurus handy to assist in naming classes. He comments

> When a group of designers has been struggling to find a word to describe an object or responsibility, the members will lean forward over the cards. When someone finally discovers just the right word, they collectively heave a sigh of relief and sit back, confident that the important concept they have all understood is now in the design. The words you use to describe your objects will live on for years in the lexicons of developers, maintainers, and even users. Poorly chosen words can hinder the acceptance and understanding of a product, while the right words can make your design much easier to explain [1].

Words such as manager, object, and thing should be eliminated from class names. Related metaphors can sometimes be appropriate. Responsibilities should be defined with a short phrase using active, not passive, verbs such as

- display the source menu
- compute net asset value
- prompt user for destination
- transmit invoice
- tell cancel key to reset
- update source data

An effective description can identify a problem that must be solved when many variants of the solution are possible. The right phrase is needed to ensure that potential solutions are discussed.

CONTRACTS

Some of the responsibilities of the class can be grouped together. This grouping of responsibilities implies a grouping of *requests*.

The group of requests may be thought of as moving from a *client* class to a *server* class that has the group of responsibilities. The group of responsibilities defines a service that the server provides to the client. The group of requests asking for this service is referred to as a *contract* [4].

> A *contract* defines a set of requests that a client can make of a server. The server must respond to those requests.

Contracts can be drawn as a semicircle (like a reversed "C" for contract) on the edge of a class box [4].

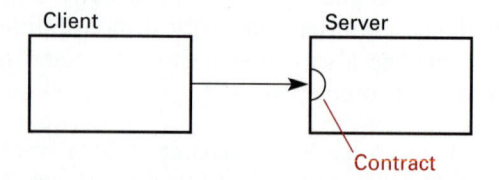

Client → Server (Contract)

A responsibility is something one object does for other objects by executing a method. A contract defines a cohesive set of responsibilities as well as a cohesive set of requests that a client can use to ask for those responsibilities. The contract could relate only one request and corresponding responsibility. More than one client may have the same contract.

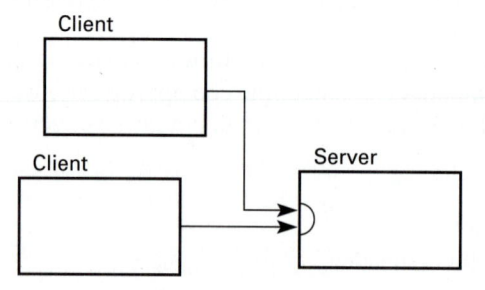

A class can support any number of contracts.

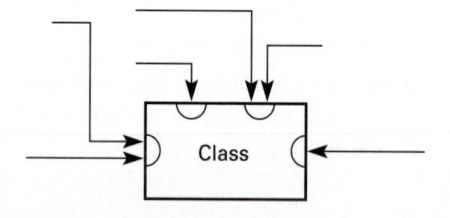

A class can act as both a client and a server. In other words, a class can have responsibilities that can be requested by clients and it can also make requests of other classes:

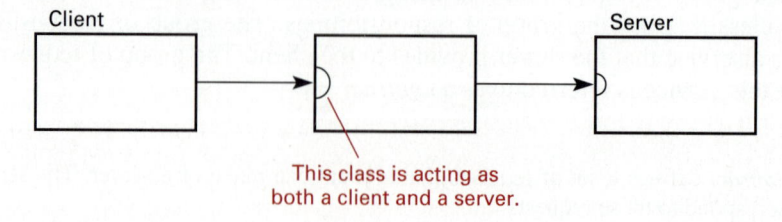

This class is acting as both a client and a server.

PUBLIC AND PRIVATE RESPONSIBILITIES

A *public* responsibility is one that can be requested by other objects. It is part of a contract (and might be the entire contract).

A *private* responsibility is one that cannot be requested by other objects. It is part of the internal workings of the class. Private responsibilities cannot be part of a contract. Examples of private responsibilities are

- update a database
- check a security code
- prompt user for a password
- eject a bank card (in an automated teller machine)
- log an audit trail

A goal of object design is to make the object as automatic and self-managing as possible and to make the interface to the object as simple as possible. Objects should hide their internal processes. A **Purchase** object, for example, should conduct its responsibilities without outside intervention—placing orders and periodically following up on the orders, determining the payment date, issuing a check, keeping a log, and updating records. *Requests* from the outside tell it to make a purchase, suspend a purchase, and report its current state.

In order to do these operations, the class has some internal, private responsibilities that are not reflected directly in its external interface.

SUBTYPES

A card for a class may be paper-clipped to cards representing its subtypes. For example, a **Printer** might have subtypes **Laser Printer** and **Dot Matrix Printer**:

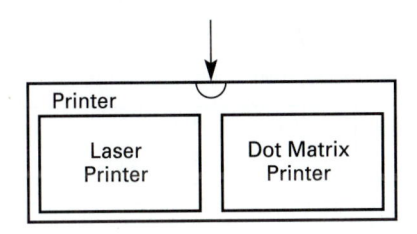

```
       ↓
┌─────────────────────────────┐
│ Printer                     │
│  ┌──────────┐ ┌──────────┐  │
│  │  Laser   │ │Dot Matrix│  │
│  │ Printer  │ │ Printer  │  │
│  └──────────┘ └──────────┘  │
└─────────────────────────────┘
```

OBJECTS COMPOSED OF OBJECTS

Objects are often composed of other objects. The composed-of diagrams illustrated in Chapter 7 show this:

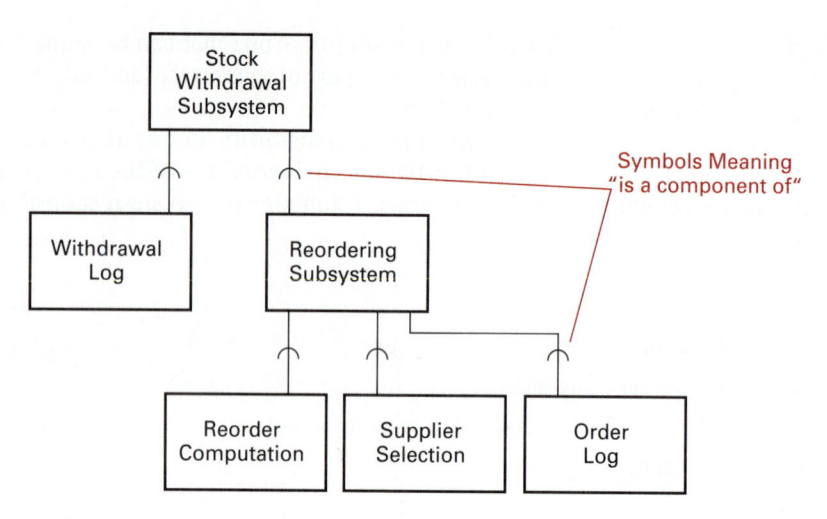

```
                    Stock
                  Withdrawal
                  Subsystem
                                        Symbols Meaning
                                        "is a component of"
       Withdrawal      Reordering
          Log          Subsystem


    Reorder       Supplier      Order
  Computation    Selection       Log
```

As discussed earlier, composed-of hierarchies are entirely different from generalization hierarchies that show subtyping. The latter are drawn with a triangle arrow as in Fig. 7.3.

Just as objects are composed of other objects, subsystems can be composed of classes—as well as other subsystems. Subsystems, then, act like container classes. Any request sent to the subsystem is delegated to the class that actually supports the request. Therefore, from the outside, each subsystem appears to be a class with its own distinct supported contracts. Other classes communicate with it, but have no knowledge of its internals. From the inside, subsystems can be complex structures and are drawn as round-cornered boxes. We can draw the **Stock Withdrawal Subsystem** as follows:

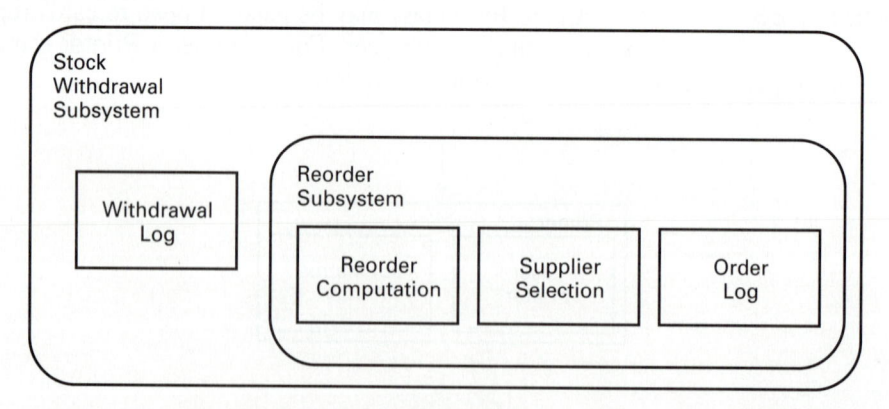

```
  Stock
  Withdrawal
  Subsystem
                    Reorder
                    Subsystem
     Withdrawal
        Log         Reorder      Supplier     Order
                   Computation   Selection     Log
```

The **Stock Withdrawal Subsystem** appears as a class that supports specific contracts. The **Withdrawal Log** and **Reordering Subsystem** classes are totally separate—each with its own class definition but related to the **Stock Withdrawal Subsystem**. Similarly, the **Reordering Subsystem** is a class composed of a data structure and methods and is related to the **Reorder Computation, Supplier Selection,** and **Order Log** classes. Classes are not *composed of* other classes, otherwise the principle of OO modularity would be lost. A class that is a subsystem *cooperates* with other classes that enable the subsystem behavior to be executed.

The subsystem class, like any other class, can have one or more contracts. It is independent of cause and effect. This subsystem class does not know what clients use its services or what effect its behavior will have on other classes.

A class can honor its contract by sending a request to one or more different classes.

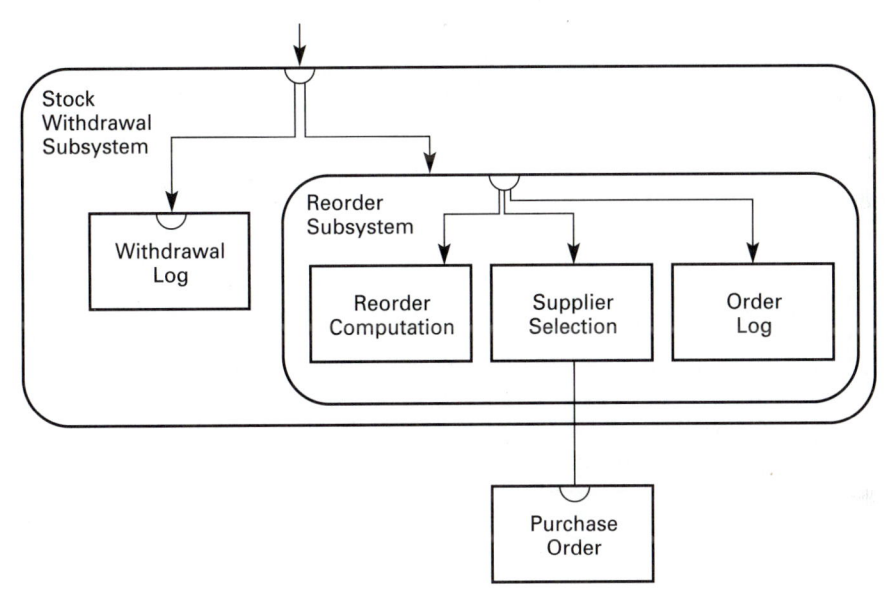

Subsystems are groupings of classes that fulfill a common overall purpose. They provide a natural way to divide responsibilities among *groups* of classes.

> Subsystems are identified by finding a group of classes, each of which fulfills different responsibilities, such that each collaborates closely with other classes in the group in order to cumulatively fulfill a greater responsibility. Such responsibilities appear, from outside the system, as discrete contracts. If the group of classes collaborates to fulfill a common overarching purpose, it forms a subsystem [4].

CLASS-COMMUNICATION DIAGRAMS

Diagrams showing the communication among classes are called *class-communication diagrams.* A class-communication diagram could show subsystems *com-*

posed of other subsystems (shown in Fig. 13.1) or could show requests passing among separate classes.

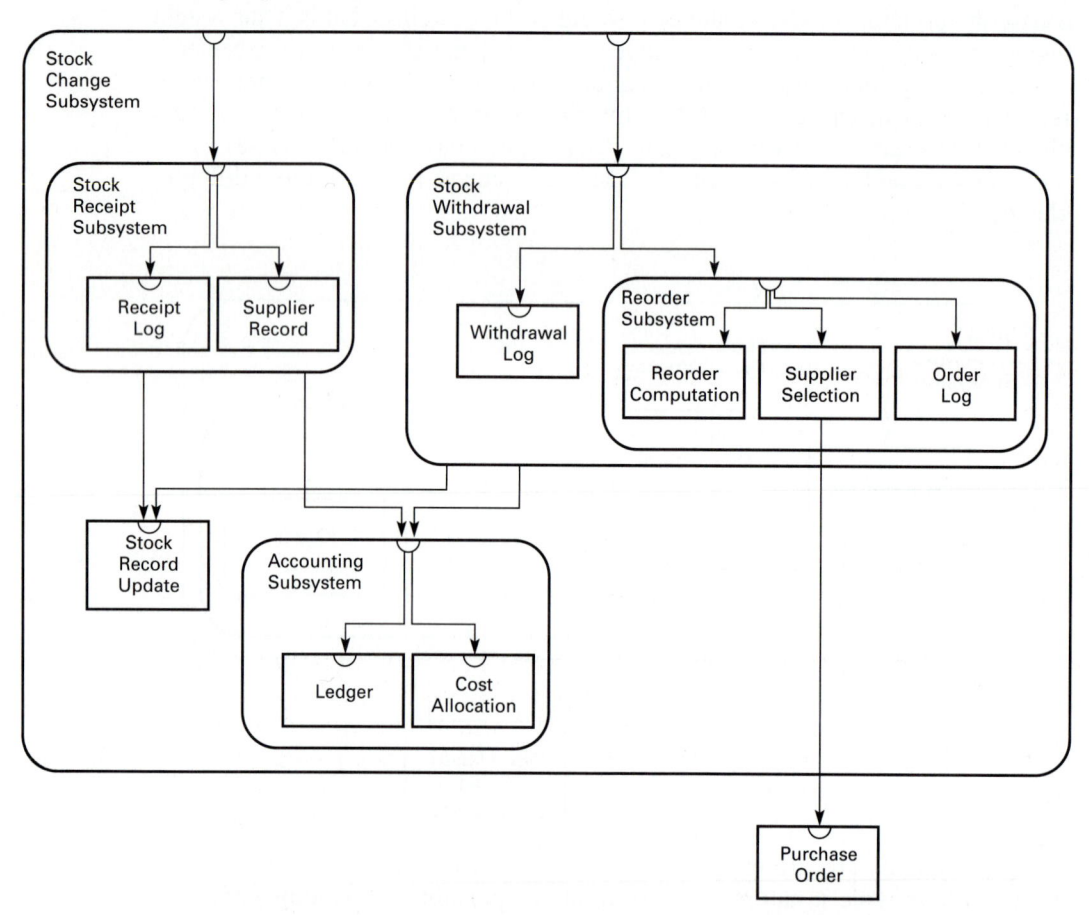

Figure 13.1 A **Stock-Change Subsystem** that is composed of other classes. This *composed-of diagram* is a form of *class-communication diagram.*

    In a CRC card session, the responsibilities should be grouped in contracts. Classes may be grouped into subsystems, and the class cards of one subsystem clipped together. Contracts (groups of responsibilities) should be identified by examining those responsibilities in the group that provide services to objects outside the subsystem. Cards will be reshuffled frequently as subsystems are formed, improved, and adjusted to minimize redundancies. If a class outside the subsystem collaborates with a class inside it, this is changed to collaborating with the subsystem as a whole. A subsystem is not just any collection of cards clipped together; it is a group united to fulfill a specific contract (or more than one contract with a cohesive purpose). **Stock Receipt** or **Stock Withdrawal** are good examples of subsystems that can be united into a **Stock Change Subsystem**.

> From the outside world, there is no difference between a class, a subsystem, or even an entire application. All are encapsulated objects that have contracts to provide a given service.

An advantage of encapsulating a subsystem is that it can be changed without affecting the outside world that uses it.

LEGACY APPLICATIONS An existing application that was built in a non-OO fashion will often be preserved and made to look like a class. It will have one or more contracts. Defined requests can be sent to it and it will perform its contractual services. Old systems, which might have been preserved in this way, are called *legacy systems*.

Legacy systems may have to be subdivided in order to make them behave like classes. Sometimes, the user interface must be separated from the rest of the code. This can be easy to do if the user interface was designed as a largely independent subsystem; if not, it will require work. If today's staff are still building applications in a non-OO fashion (which is happening in most I.S. organizations), they should be instructed to design the user interface, as well as other interfaces to the outside world, in an independent fashion. The code should be designed so that it can be shrink-wrapped and perform like an OO subsystem when OO techniques eventually take over.

CLASS RESPONSIBILTY COLABORATE.

COMBINING CARDS AND CASE CRC cards encourage human debate and creativity and help developers to find problems in designs. They facilitate designs that meet the needs of the end users better, especially when the end users participate in the CRC card sessions. However, OO-CASE tools should never be far in the background.

The repository contains valuable knowledge from analysis and modeling and may contain details of systems to which the current system must connect. The repository often contains both reusable designs of classes that should be incorporated in the current system as well as designs of similar applications.

When decisions are made in a CRC card session, these decisions should be entered into an OO-CASE tool immediately. The tool can help check the design and quickly generate information structures on the screen which enable instances of the design to be entered and validated.

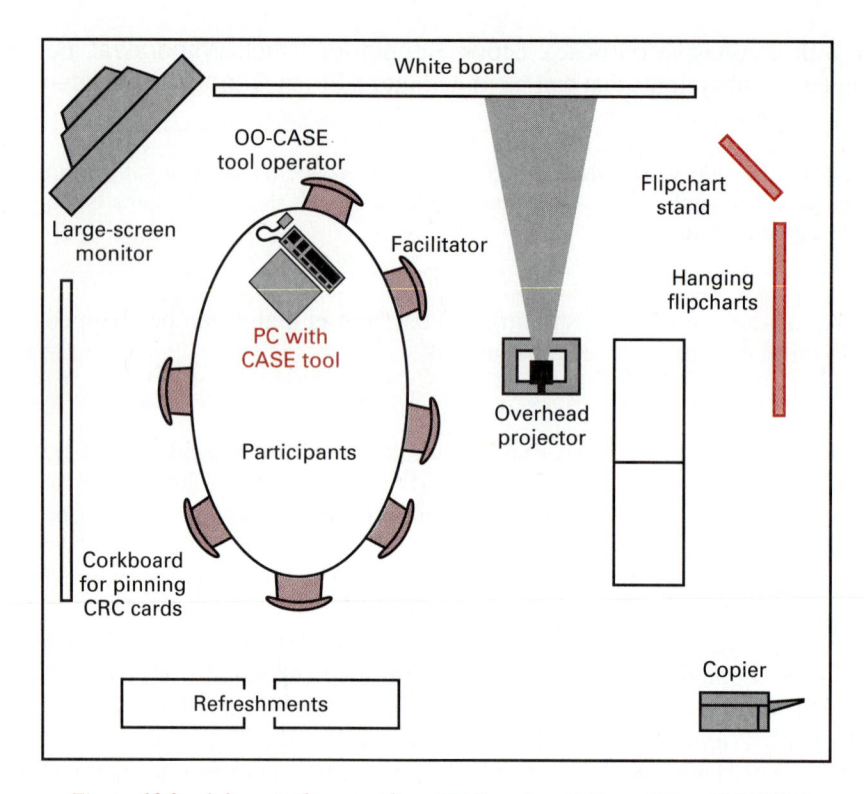

Figure 13.2 A layout of a room for a CRC card workshop with an OO-CASE tool operator and a large screen monitor.

A CRC card session can be conducted in a room (see Fig. 13.2) that is equipped with a large-screen monitor so that card holders can see the information that is in the OO-CASE repository. An OO-CASE tool operator may be able to quickly enter details of classes, rules, responsibilities, contracts, and links between classes. He can display the evolving design and the analysis models to which the design relates.

The responsibility-driven approach should not be thought of as a complete system specification technique and it should not replace proper analysis and design. It is a component of, rather than a self-sufficient, a specification technique.

The CRC techniques

- can only handle small systems
- do not define data structures
- are not rigorous enough to generate code

The CRC techniques are, however, very useful for teaching OO thinking, for showing programmers how to think like an object, and for involving end users in OO design in a creative way. A good design process integrates techniques for human creativity with techniques that have rigor and can handle large systems. CRC card sessions are good for encouraging human creativity and refinement of ideas.

REFERENCES

1. Beck, Kent and Ward Cunningham, "A Laboratory for Teaching Object-Oriented Thinking," *Proceedings of the 1989 OOPSLA—Conference on Object-Oriented Programming Systems, Languages and Applications,* OOPSLA '89 (New Orleans), Norman Meyrowitz ed., ACM, New York, 1989, pp. 1-6.

2. Budd, Timothy, *An Introduction to Object-Oriented Programming,* Addison-Wesley, Reading, MA, 1991.

3. Wirfs-Brock, Rebecca and Brian Wilkerson, "Object-Oriented Design: A Responsibility-Driven Approach," *Proceedings of the 1989 OOPSLA—Conference on Object-Oriented Programming Systems, Languages and Applications,* OOPSLA '89 (New Orleans), Norman Meyrowitz ed., ACM, New York, 1989, pp. 71-76.

4. Wirfs-Brock, Rebecca, Brian Wilkerson, and Lauren Wiener, *Designing Object-Oriented Software,* Prentice Hall, Englewood Cliffs, NJ, 1990.

14 OO WORKSHOPS WITH END USERS

A major goal of I.S. today ought to be getting business people involved in all aspects of business system design. We cannot redesign businesses effectively without their thorough involvement. Consequently, we need enterprise models that reflect business policies. Making these models easy for business people to understand should be a major goal of OO-CASE tools. We must be able to translate those models quickly into working software. The changes that occur constantly in a business and its rules must be reflected quickly in the working systems. The era when computerized systems put business in a straitjacket must end.

To involve the end users in OO analysis and design, a workshop technique is employed. Key end users participate in a workshop that progresses through a structured set of steps for reviewing models, planning systems, or designing systems. The users or business people are encouraged to do most of the talking, but an I.S. workshop leader, *facilitator,* guides the session—moving it toward the goal of a model, specification, prototype, or design represented in an OO-CASE repository. The users understand and debate the evolving models and designs. Often these workshops are highly creative and enjoyable. They have been taking place successfully for years in non-OO requirements planning and design and can be more effective with OO techniques.

Three types of workshops are called JEM, JRP (pronounced "jerp"), and JAD:

- JEM—Joint-enterprise modeling
- JRP—Joint-requirements planning
- JAD—Joint-application design

They are sometimes collectively referred to as facilitated workshops, meaning workshops organized, controlled, and moderated by a professional facilitator.

JAD was the first of these to become popular. JAD has progressed through four generations, as indicated in Fig. 14.1. The early workshops were done with no computerized tools [1]. The second generation of workshops used either prototyping tools or CASE diagramming or both but did not use integrated CASE. The third generation used integrated CASE tools with which code could be generated directly from the design that is built in a repository. In this third generation, JRP and JAD were an integral part of a repository-based lifecycle. The term RAD (rapid-application development) was used for this lifecycle that had the goals of high quality, high speed, and lower cost [4, 5].

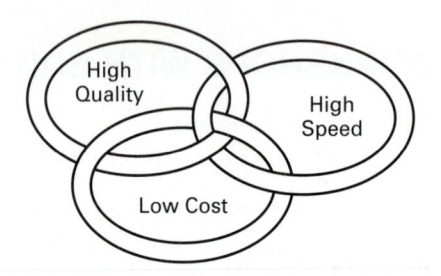

The fourth generation uses the OO techniques described in previous chapters. JRP and JAD should both use the knowledge established in joint-enterprise modeling with business rules and usually help add to these models. CRC cards can be used to encourage debate about the responsibilities of objects. Particularly important, the JEM, JRP, and JAD workshops should use the same OO-CASE tool, and this tool should generate code.

THE BEST OF COMPUTERS AND PEOPLE

The goal of such workshops is to encourage human creativity and link it to the power and rigor of repository-based tools.

> We need to create the maximum synergy between human creativity and the power of computerized tools.

To aid human creativity, the diagrams must help the users to visualize the complex operations of the enterprise. A major goal of OO-CASE is designing diagrams that effectively communicate with business people. These diagrams help to represent a growing body of knowledge that resides in the CASE repository.

The JEM workshop should help executives to think creatively about how their enterprises can be streamlined, made more competitive, or made to function better. The workshop causes an examination of the goals, problems, critical success factors, and strategic opportunities, possibly analyzed in a separate study [3]. It should use OO models of the activities in an enterprise and attempt to eliminate

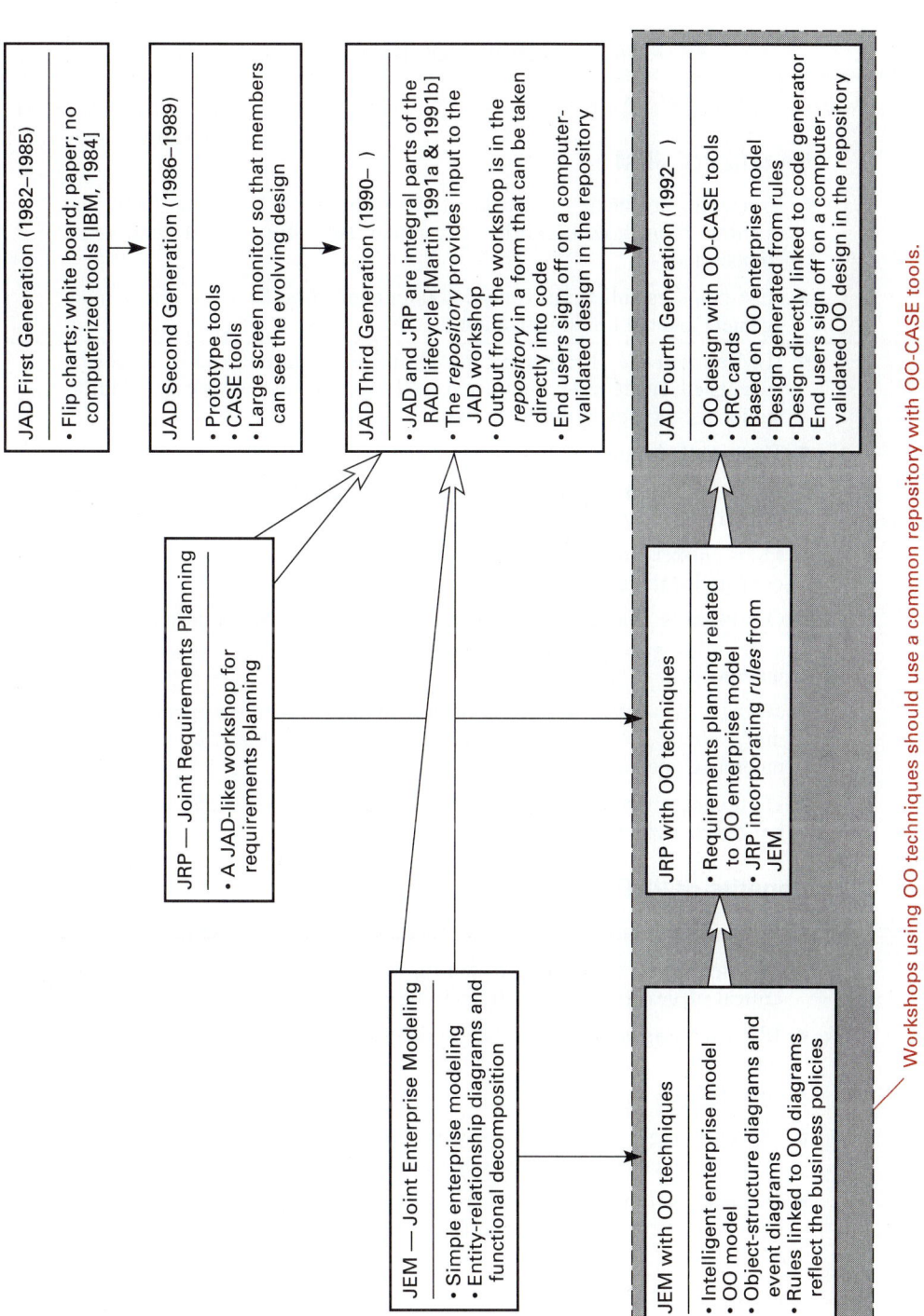

```
┌─────────────────────┐     ┌─────────────────────┐     ┌─────────────────────┐     ┌─────────────────────────────┐
│ JAD First Generation│     │ JAD Second Generation│    │ JAD Third Generation│     │ JAD Fourth Generation       │
│ (1982–1985)         │ ──▶ │ (1986–1989)         │ ──▶ │ (1990– )            │ ──▶ │ (1992– )                    │
│                     │     │                     │     │                     │     │                             │
│ • Flip charts; white│     │ • Prototype tools   │     │ • JAD and JRP are   │     │ • OO design with OO-CASE    │
│   board; paper; no  │     │ • CASE tools        │     │   integral parts of │     │   tools                     │
│   computerized tools│     │ • Large screen      │     │   the RAD lifecycle │     │ • CRC cards                 │
│   [IBM, 1984]       │     │   monitor so that   │     │   [Martin 1991a &   │     │ • Based on OO enterprise    │
│                     │     │   members can see   │     │   1991b]            │     │   model                     │
│                     │     │   the evolving      │     │ • The repository    │     │ • Design generated from     │
│                     │     │   design            │     │   provides input to │     │   rules                     │
│                     │     │                     │     │   the JAD workshop  │     │ • Design directly linked to │
│                     │     │                     │     │ • Output from the   │     │   code generator            │
│                     │     │                     │     │   workshop is in the│     │ • End users sign off on a   │
│                     │     │                     │     │   repository in a   │     │   computer-validated OO     │
│                     │     │                     │     │   form that can be  │     │   design in the repository  │
│                     │     │                     │     │   taken directly    │     │                             │
│                     │     │                     │     │   into code         │     │                             │
│                     │     │                     │     │ • End users sign off│     │                             │
│                     │     │                     │     │   on a computer-    │     │                             │
│                     │     │                     │     │   validated design  │     │                             │
│                     │     │                     │     │   in the repository │     │                             │
└─────────────────────┘     └─────────────────────┘     └─────────────────────┘     └─────────────────────────────┘
```

Figure 14.1 The evolution of JAD and end-user workshops.

BOX 14.1 Benefits of JEM, JRP, and JAD.

Benefits of JEM

- Executives are made to visualize their enterprise in ways that help them to think about how it can be redesigned, streamlined, and made more competitive.
- JEM helps establish much-needed communication between senior management and the I.S. organization.
- JEM encourages brainstorming about how the enterprise might be redesigned, made more automated, and made to take advantage of information technology in different ways.
- The potential impact of emerging technologies should be examined.
- JEM encourages business people to think creatively about the policies and rules for running the business.
- I.S. is unlikely to devise the best set of rules for running the business without detailed dialog with the business people.
- OO models that evolve with the help of JEM workshops become a valuable resource in constantly improving and streamlining the enterprise.
- JEM focuses attention on the need to eliminate certain operations and unify others. JEM can put the Principle of Occam's Razor to work on the enterprise operations.
- High executives are made to understand the business value of building better I.S. architectures.

Benefits of JRP

- JRP harnesses business executives to the system-planning process.
- JRP links system planning to the top-level analysis of goals, problems, critical success factors, and strategic systems opportunities [3].
- JRP encourages brainstorming to determine the most valuable system functions.
- JRP eliminates functions of questionable value.
- JRP encourages creative business executives to consider how information systems can enhance business opportunities.
- JRP helps get the requirements right the first time. Changing them after a system has been designed or implemented is expensive and harmful.

BOX 14.1 *(Continued)*

Benefits of JAD

- With JAD sessions, the specification and design of systems take a much shorter elapsed time than with traditional system analysis.
- JAD substantially improves productivity of the development process.
- JAD harnesses the end users to the design process and helps avoid dissatisfaction.
- JAD replaces voluminous paper specifications with live screen designs, report designs, prototypes, concise structures, and design diagrams that are easily edited. When created with rigorous design tools, these greatly help programmers or system implementors.
- JAD results in systems that often are higher quality and have greater business value.
- JAD helps increase the computer literary of a user community. Users often become more imaginative and inventive about creating better procedures.
- JAD saves money by avoiding the need to preprogram or to modify inadequately designed systems. Maintenance expenses are reduced.
- JAD helps integrate and unify the needs of different parts of the organization.
- JAD relieves the I.S. analyst from having to resolve political conflicts between end users, who can work out potential differences in a JAD workshop.
- JAD results in user satisfaction. Because users design the system, they take an interest in it, feel ownership, and help in the construction phase.
- JAD is done with a toolset, so the design uses classes, rules, and enterprise models already in the repository. The toolset enforces consistency and rigor in the design and can link precisely to other systems designed with the toolset.
- RAD JAD produces a computerized design that directly feeds into the construction phase. The implementation then employs the JAD output directly.
- JAD helps get the design right the first time. Changing the design after a system is built is expensive and harmful. Design errors caught early lower the cost.

activities that do not add value. It may interlink activities in different functional areas to make the enterprise achieve its goals more effectively. The JRP workshop focuses on the requirements of a specific system. Business executives and end users brainstorm the possible functions of the system, identify the most useful functions, and eliminate or defer those of questionable value. The JAD workshop helps to ensure that a system fully meets the needs of its users and that the design will work well. It is also concerned with producing low-cost systems that can be modified and maintained inexpensively.

Box 14.1 lists the benefits of JEM, JRP, and JAD.

The advantages of these workshops with computer users and business people are so great in corporations that conduct them well, that it would be unthinkable to build systems without them. Surprisingly, many I.S. organizations do not yet use such workshops, and consequently they experience higher costs, longer development times, lower quality, fewer business improvements, and less-happy users. Some I.S. organizations have used JAD, JRP, and JEM workshops for many years, steadily learning how to do them better. This experience is shown in detail in the author's videotapes on user workshops [6].

Currently, most of these workshops do not use OO techniques; they use conventional data modeling, process modeling, and structured techniques. OO techniques have the advantages we have described and are slowly being adopted. OO models are more intuitive to most business people than conventional structured techniques. Facilitators using OO techniques report that they obtain high-quality results, often with a higher level of creative debate about the redesign of processes or business areas.

REPOSITORY, NOT PAPER

The workshops should not generate much paperwork; they generate a computerized model or design. When designing a system, the users sign off on a design *in a repository* that can be used directly with a code generator. RAD lifecycles often have a *requirements-planning phase* using a JRP workshop, separate from a *user-design phase* using one or more JAD workshops. For systems where the requirements are already well known or obvious, JRP and JAD may be combined into one workshop. The lifecycle for one system can be faster and better if enterprise modeling has already been done with the help of JEM (joint-enterprise modeling) workshops.

All these workshops should use the same repository. The *object categorizations* (see Chapter 6), *object-structure diagrams* (see Chapter 7), *state-transition diagrams* (see Chapter 8), *diagrams of events and operations* (see Chapter 9), and *business rules* (see Chapter 10) should all be part of the enterprise model (or business-area model) and should directly aid the requirements planning and design of many systems. At the planning and design level, *responsibilities* are identified (see Chapter 13), *CRC cards* may be used in the JRP or JAD workshops (see Chapter 13), then *methods* are created (see Chapter 14). All of this should fit into an information-engineering framework (see Chapter 16)—creating a growing set of knowledge that resides in the repository.

THE EXECUTIVE SPONSOR

When systems are built, a high-level user executive should be the owner of the system. Though sometimes called the *executive sponsor,* the term *executive owner* might be preferable. It emphasizes that the executive's budget pays for the system. Establishment of this end-user executive, who is at a suitably high level and *committed* to the system, is an essential prerequisite to the workshop activity.

Because this executive is financially committed, he is entitled to kill the system after the JRP workshop if the planning does not indicate that the system will meet his needs with a high enough return on investment.

The executive sponsor should ensure that the right people attend the workshops and should motivate the participants appropriately. When disputes or political arguments occur, the executive sponsor should resolve them, off-line. The executive sponsor should open the workshops and review their conclusions but usually not be present during the body of the workshop.

THE FACILITATOR

Particularly critical to the success of these workshops are the skills of the person, referred to as the *facilitator*, who organizes and oversees them. Being a facilitator should be regarded as a profession, needing professional skills that require time to develop. The facilitator should stay in that job full time until he is promoted or moves, and then a new facilitator should work with him early enough to learn the skills. Large I.S. organizations have a Facilitator Department with skilled facilitators who are allocated to one project after another.

A facilitator is not likely to do a perfect job in the first session. After the third or fourth, confidence and skill increase to make the activity as effective as possible. When JEM, JRP, or JAD fails, the facilitator is usually at fault—more skilled leadership could have made it work. Appointing different facilitators for each project team often results in unskilled leadership and inadequate results. The most successful use of JAD is generally in organizations that have a full-time facilitator doing one project after another. Often this person conducts a JRP workshop and continues with a JAD for the same system.

The facilitator should be chosen primarily for skills in communication along with the additional characteristics listed in Box 14.2. The facilitator needs to be diplomatic and not associated with any politics that might affect the session. Above all, the facilitator must appear to be *impartial.* The job includes preparing and orchestrating the session, making discussions occur within a structured framework, and having the session move reasonably quickly to the required conclusions. The facilitator acts as the focal point for tying together the views of management, end users, and I.S. professionals (see Fig. 14.2).

BOX 14.2 Characteristics of a good workshop facilitator.

- Excellent human communication skills
- Impartial, unbiased, neutral
- Good negotiating skills, sensitive to corporate politics, diplomatic
- Good at conducting a meeting
    — has leadership qualities similar to those of a good board chairman
    — makes the meeting move quickly to conclusions and avoids tangents
    — can turn a floundering meeting into a productive session
    — can summarize what has been said
- Understands group dynamics and can excite the participants, getting them to work hard on items that need detailing
- Something of a "ham" in front of an audience
- Capable of organizing the research, documents, and people
- Not an expert on the applications but capable of researching and learning quickly
- Fully familiar with the diagramming techniques used in the workshop and familiar with OO modeling
- A professional facilitator who has become skilled at the job by practice

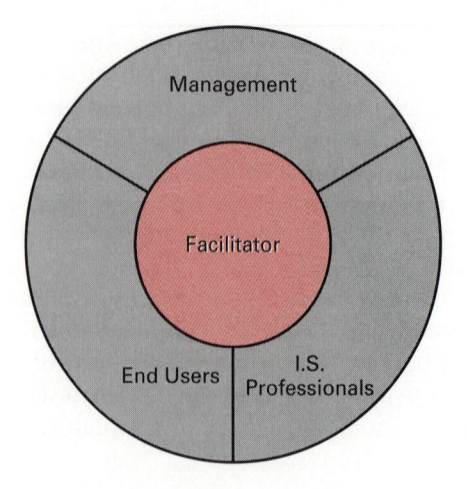

Figure 14.2 JEM, JRP, and JAD sessions need the commitment of management and the partnership of management, end users, and I.S. professionals. Their cooperation is facilitated and coordinated by an impartial session leader who needs the skills listed in Box 14.2.

Thorough preparation is extremely important. The facilitator needs to research and prepare the meeting well, providing the participants with a suitable level of printed detail.

The facilitator needs to be comfortable standing in front of a group of people—confident in the task and capable of directing discussion and fact-finding activities. The respect of all parties at the session is essential. This can be gained by being well prepared, knowledgeable about the business area, and competent in the techniques used. The ability to control controversies and stay flexible is important.

A good facilitator can eliminate the effects of politics, power struggles, and communication gaps. He puts I.S. and end users on equal terms and establishes them as partners. He assumes the role of a referee at times—arbitrating debates. He should constantly elicit questions. He should encourage the quieter members to participate, ask questions, and respond when the more aggressive members take a position. He needs to prevent domineering participants from overpowering the meeting and to draw out shy participants. He needs to redirect participants who have a hidden agenda. He should have his own agenda well thought out and should stick to it.

A good facilitator knows that certain goals must be accomplished by a given time. He moves the session forward until the requisite designs are completed, along with screens, reports, and, possibly, prototypes. He obtains concurrence of the users on these designs. The goal is to discuss the ideas fully and reach agreement as a group without too much delay or haggling. The facilitator must be enthusiastic about the session and convey this excitement to the participants about how well it can work.

THE SCRIBE

The user workshop needs a professional who is highly skilled with the CASE tool that is used. The medieval word *scribe* is often used to describe this person, because in the earliest JAD workshops the scribe wrote down what was said and produced paper documentation. Today, the scribe builds the CASE representation of the models, plans, and designs, updates the repository, and uses the tools to ensure integrity and consistency in the repository information. The scribe must be able to operate the CASE tool quickly and accurately. The scribe may create prototypes during a JAD workshop.

Some documentation at high-level workshops may be done by the scribe without a CASE tool, but usually there are major advantages to having documentation in the repository.

A good integrated-CASE toolset correlates the information entered with knowledge already in the repository, indicating any flaws or inconsistencies. Because of this, the scribe may interrupt the meeting frequently and indicate whether what has just been said is consistent with previous decisions or already in the repository. The scribe is thus an active, not a passive, participant.

The facilitator is highly dependent on the scribe. It helps if the same facilitator and scribe continually work together as a team, understanding and enhancing each other's capabilities.

FACILITATOR TRAINING

An organization that incorporates JEM, JRP, and JAD into its development methodology should train one or more facilitators and make this their job for two years or more. Experience increases the facilitators' skill.

The facilitator should be trained in areas listed in Box 14.1. He should have had on-the-job training in other workshops. A mock-up session should put him in a variety of problematical situations that are videotaped and then critiqued. He should have thorough knowledge of the automated tools used. The facilitator should have management skills, business savvy, and a good reputation, because credibility will make the job of working with a variety of end users, executives, and I.S. staff much easier.

A facilitator should be regarded as a trainee until his fourth workshop. In the first, as an apprentice working with and helping an experienced facilitator, he observes the initiation, research, and preparation, as well as the final workshop. In the second and third, he co-leads with an experienced facilitator to build skill and confidence. In the fourth, he is on his own. If a corporation is doing its first workshops, it may employ an outside consulting firm to run them until its own facilitator becomes experienced.

WHO ATTENDS THE JRP WORKSHOP?

Selecting the best user participants is very important. The participants should have the right mix of knowledge about the business and have the authority to make decisions about the design. All should communicate well. Often, one or more key people are critical for creating the design and having it accepted. *If these key players are not available, the workshop should not be run.*

Workshops are particularly valuable for projects that span user organizations or for applications that affect multiple locations or disciplines. The workshops are useful for resolving operational, organizational, or procedural differences. The end users or managers in the workshop confront each other under the guidance of a facilitator trained in negotiating skills and must sign off on a design that both sides accept. Systems analysts are not to be trapped in the middle of political conflicts. Conflicts are brought into the open in a constructive planning or design session.

Often, contentious political issues are known before the workshop. They should be dealt with by identifying the *sponsoring executive* and having him meet with the parties in question, seeking consensus on the issues, or motivating the parties to achieve consensus during the workshop. The workshops attempt to achieve consensus among participants with different experiences, needs, or visions.

A goal of a JRP or JAD workshop is to get the planning or design *right the first time* or, at least, as close as possible to the final system. It is expensive and time consuming to change the requirements of the system after it has been designed or to change the design after it has been constructed. To get it right at the workshop, those end users and managers who really understand the requirements *must* be present.

Increasingly today, electronic document interchange (EDI) systems are being built that transmit data electronically among enterprises. Corporations are placing workstations on the locations of agents, wholesalers, retailers, buyers, suppliers, or dealers. Online cooperation between organizations is important for minimizing inventory costs and improving service. Because of this some corporations include customers or suppliers in their JRP or JAD sessions. It can be essential to include representatives of the external organization and achieve intercorporate consensus.

A GELLED TEAM

Teams play an important part in the lifecycle. A team has to gel. Team members must develop respect for one another, know each other's talents, and like to call on each other's talents to address a situation collectively. The members of a gelled team need to have a common goal. A task of the facilitator is to establish that goal with clarity and make sure that all team members are motivated to drive hard for the same goal. Any hidden agendas of the participants should be temporarily set aside. When a team of talented people are hell-bent to achieve a single, clear goal, they can do so with great energy and find the experience rewarding.

An important principle is that all members of the team are equal for the duration of the workshop. However, various individuals in the team may provide leadership, taking charge temporarily when dealing with subjects relating to their expertise. Except for the facilitator, no individual should dominate for more than periodic bursts, or the contributions of the others may be lost. The facilitator must preserve the right balance.

A gelled team usually has fun. It enjoys its ability to address problems in concert, with different team members peeling off periodically to prepare a presentation, invent a chart, or create a segment of a design. In some cases, such teams have a wonderful time working on tasks that could otherwise be dull. The skilled facilitator knows how to help the team and build up momentum so that it attacks problems like a cavalry charge.

It usually takes two days for the team to gel. Teams spend much of the first two days becoming comfortable with one another. If the first workshop lasts five days, the real work is usually done on the last three days.

WORKSHOP DURATION

JAD workshops typically last three to five days. It usually takes a day for the team to become comfortable with one another and gel.

JRP workshops vary in length depending on the complexity or newness of the requirements. They typically range from one to three days.

Workshops with top management are shorter than workshops with lower-level users. High management has less available time, more impatience and outside pressures, and often a lower attention span.

Corporations conducting facilitated workshops for several years often state that the workshops have become shorter as experience and skills have increased. Good OO modeling often requires multiple short JEM workshops interspersed with periods of detailed work. The workshops help to validate the models and deal with many questions raised in the modeling process.

GROUP DYNAMICS

Workshop sessions work because of the group dynamics. The facilitator needs to know how to use group dynamics constructively. The participants are shut away in a workshop knowing that they have a given task to accomplish by a given time, with a given agenda. This task-oriented environment helps participants concentrate on sharing ideas and achieving the established goals. It helps to ensure that the information provided is complete. When appropriately motivated, such groups tend to police themselves and avoid the bickering and pettiness of politics.

The facilitator may follow the agenda by asking questions of the users at each state:

- What business rules apply here?
- What are the responsibilities of this object?
- What information is needed to improve decisions?
- What other control conditions could affect this operation?
- Could this operation be eliminated?
- Could this step be delegated to another object?
- Should this decision be made in a different place?

The answers and discussions should be made tangible by displaying screens that users could employ. As new flows or structures are designed, they should be printed by the design tool so that session members can study and make notes on them.

The main participants of the workshop must attend *full time*. If they miss a day, they cannot contribute fully, and others waste time updating them. They may also cause earlier decisions to be reexamined which wastes time. Each day in a workshop builds upon the previous day. Participants must be there today to understand what will happen tomorrow. Each person is dependent on what others contribute, so part-time attendance should be banned.

Some JRP and JAD workshops have observers who come in to see what is happening. This practice should be discouraged. If it is impractical to keep out observers, they should be kept quiet and not allowed to interrupt the meeting. The group dynamics depend upon intense, full-time participation.

The number of participants varies from one system to another. The session should not be too big. Large groups tend to argue too much or waste participants' time. The most effective sessions usually have fewer than nine people plus the facilitator and scribe.

The group should follow a structure with agreed-upon stages, goals, and deliverables. In this way time-wasting, ad-hoc debate is avoided.

OPEN ISSUES

The workshop should move along at a rapid pace. When an issue comes up that cannot be resolved, the meeting should not become bogged down in discussion. After declaring the problem an open issue, the scribe should note the following:

- issue number
- issue name
- person assigned to resolve the issue
- date for resolution
- description

The scribe may have forms or computer screens for recording open issues.

THE FIVE-MINUTE RULE

When arguments threaten to slow down the progress, the facilitator should stop them and declare them an open issue. Some facilitators impose a five-minute rule: *no argument is allowed to go on for longer than five minutes*. If it cannot be resolved within five minutes, it is declared an open issue.

Open issues are reexamined at the end of the day. If an issue still cannot be resolved, the person to whom the issue has been assigned must try to produce a solution. Major disagreements among participants should be taken to the *executive sponsor* for resolution.

THE WORKSHOP ROOM

The workshops need an appropriately equipped room. Facilities in such a room are listed in Box 14.3 and its typical layout is shown in Fig. 14.3. This layout may

BOX 14.3 Facilities in the workshop room.

- Large white board with colored pens
- Flip-chart board, colored pens, and space to display multiple flip charts
- Overhead projector and screen, with both prepared and blank transparencies, colored pens
- Possibly a magnetic or felt board with a kit for building diagrams
- Small round table if CRC cards are used
- PC or workstation
- Large-screen monitor or projector so that all participants can see and discuss what is on the screen of the prototyping and OO-CASE toolset
- Printer so that designs can be printed for the participants
- Photocopier so that all participants can be given copies of information created
- Polaroid camera to record white-board drawings or wall charts
- Slide projector if the facilitator has prepared slides
- Videotape player and television monitor if the facilitator has planned to use videotapes
- Coffee and refreshments
- Name cards and stationery for participants
- *No telephone!*

be varied. For example, when CRC cards are used, a small, round table is needed (see Fig. 13.2).

OO-CASE and prototyping tools should be used by the scribe in the workshop. The participants should be able to see, periodically, what is on the toolset screen and discuss it. The personal computer should, therefore, have a large-screen monitor or projector. This is not permanently switched on, because the scribe wants to build the design in private much of the time.

The projector is used with a white board so that participants can scribble on the design. The workbench tool has a printer so that parts of the design, specifications, agenda, and so on can be printed and distributed to users.

Large white boards used to create sketches and lists, as well as flip charts, should remain visible throughout the session. An overhead projector is used to make prepared presentations and sketch diagrams during the session. A slide projector or videotape player may also be included. The facilitator may arrange for

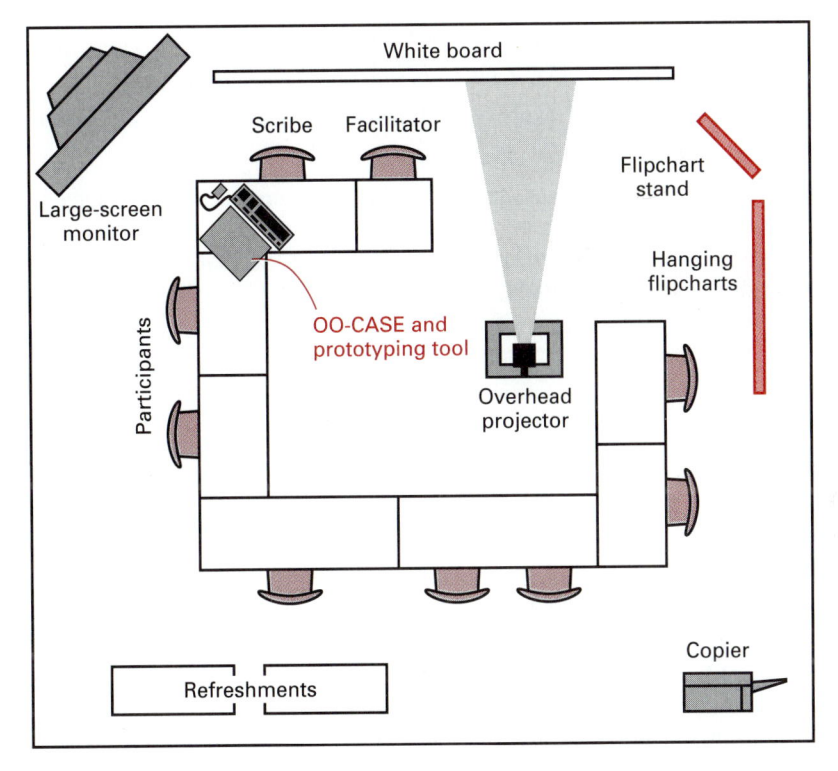

Figure 14.3 Layout of a room for JEM, JRP, and JAD. A small round table should be used when CRC cards are employed. There should be no telephone.

slides or videotapes to be available of the processes that need automating. A PC printer and a copying machine should be available.

The room has refreshments but no telephone. An important aspect of the workshop is its isolation from the interruptions of daily business.

A permanently established JAD room may be designed to serve other functions also, such as other meetings, training, demonstrations, and sales presentations.

TRAINING THE PARTICIPANTS

Non-I.S. people participating in workshops may need some training prior to the workshop, since they must be able to read and think constructively about the types of diagrams used.

A criterion for tool selection is that the diagrams should be easy for non-I.S. people to use. Complex details should be displayable in windows so that they do not clutter the main diagrams. The diagrams used should be

- object-categorization diagrams (see Chapter 6)
- object-relationship and composed-of diagrams (see Chapter 7)
- event diagrams (see Chapter 9) with windows displaying rules (see Chapter 10)
- state-transition diagrams (see Chapter 8)
- diagrams showing requests, responsibilities, and contracts (see Chapter 13)

End users can be taught to read these diagrams, so that they can use them as a basis for discussion in a four-hour training class. They may then do some studying of relevant diagrams prior to the workshop.

WALL CHARTING

Groups discussing complex subjects commonly use wall charts. Participants stand in front of white boards or pin flip charts to the wall. Kits especially designed for wall charting are available. Blocks of different shapes can be written on with an erasable pen and stuck to the wall to create a chart, such as an object-relationship or *composed-of* diagram, event diagram, class-hierarchy diagram, or class-communication diagram. With some kits, the blocks are stuck on a metal board with magnets; with others, pieces of cardboard are stuck to a wall with a gummy adhesive. The workshop room should have a wall-charting facility which makes charts easy to change.

Sometimes large event diagrams are drawn, showing many activities. They may be drawn in a summary fashion, without showing event triangles or control conditions (as in Fig. 9.1). Pieces of string may be stretched across the diagram showing how the operations could be interlinked in different ways, or how a value stream might be reorganized to eliminate work or give faster responses to customers.

When viewed from a distance, a large wall chart gives an overview of the subject. When viewed up close, it gives detail. The scribe or facilitator may have a Polaroid camera so that temporary wall charts can be recorded. The scribe enters information from the wall-chart discussions into the OO-CASE tool (see Fig. 14.4).

SUMMARY

JEM, JRP, and JAD are three similar techniques for achieving creative end-user participation in OO-modeling, planning, and design and combining this with the power and rigor of CASE and prototyping tools. They are referred to as *facilitated workshops*. Corporations that have used them well have found them to be extremely effective and in some cases will not build any system without facilitated workshops that include end users [6].

JRP and JAD are discussed in more detail in the author's book *Rapid Application Development* [4].

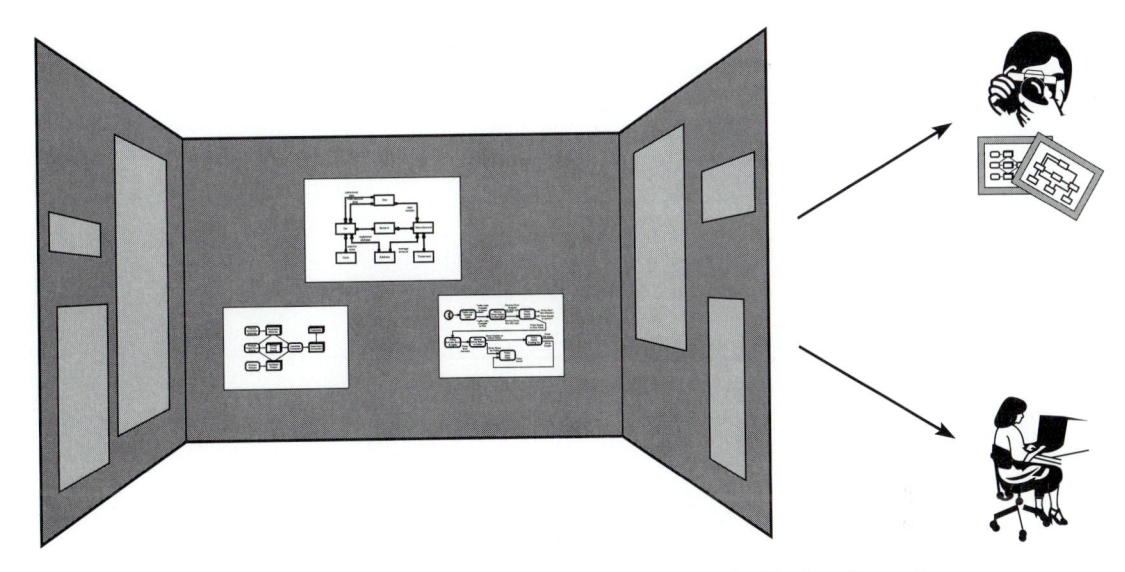

Figure 14.4 Information on wall charts, flip charts, and white boards may be photographed with a Polaroid camera. The scribe enters this information into the OO-CASE tool. The tool detects inconsistencies and helps build a design with overall integrity.

REFERENCES

1. IBM Overview Pamphlet, *JAD: Joint Application Development,* IBM, White Plains, NY, 1984.

2. JM&C, *RAD Expert,* a methodology in hyperdocument form adaptable to different toolsets, available from James Martin and Company, Reston, VA, 1991.

3. Martin, James, *Information Engineering,* Book II, Prentice-Hall, Englewood Cliffs, NJ, 1990.

4. Martin, James, *Rapid Application Development,* Macmillan, New York, 1991.

5. Martin, James, *Rapid Application Development,* a series of videotapes, James Martin Insight, Naperville, IL, 1991.

6. Martin, James, *Workshops with End Users (JAD, JRP and JEM),* a series of videotapes, James Martin Insight, Naperville, IL, 1992.

15 METHODS CREATION

When a system is being designed with CASE tools, JAD, and CRC sessions, we want to be able to build the system quickly. We need to create the *methods* and produce code as rapidly as possible.

> To build the system as quickly as possible, we should avoid manual programming, where possible.

Many OO systems have been programmed with C++. However, C++ should generally be avoided for commercial and administrative systems, because it is difficult to learn and commercial programmers know languages such as COBOL. C++ (and COBOL) are low-level languages, so that coding and debugging are time consuming. (OO programming languages are discussed in Chapter 17.)

Wherever possible, code should be generated or reusable building blocks employed. *Methods,* then, should be designed with techniques that feed some form of code generator.

In a well thought-out OO design, most methods do something relatively simple and self-contained. They are therefore easier to create and debug than code designed with conventional techniques. Furthermore, many classes inherit methods so that they are not recoded for each class. Good design tools provide reusable designs with menus or fill-in-the-blank screens for customizing the design, as illustrated in Fig. 15.1.

INCREASING THE POWER OF LANGUAGES

OO-CASE tools with code generators represent a search for simplicity. We have emphasized that each *method,* by itself, is relatively simple. We must find

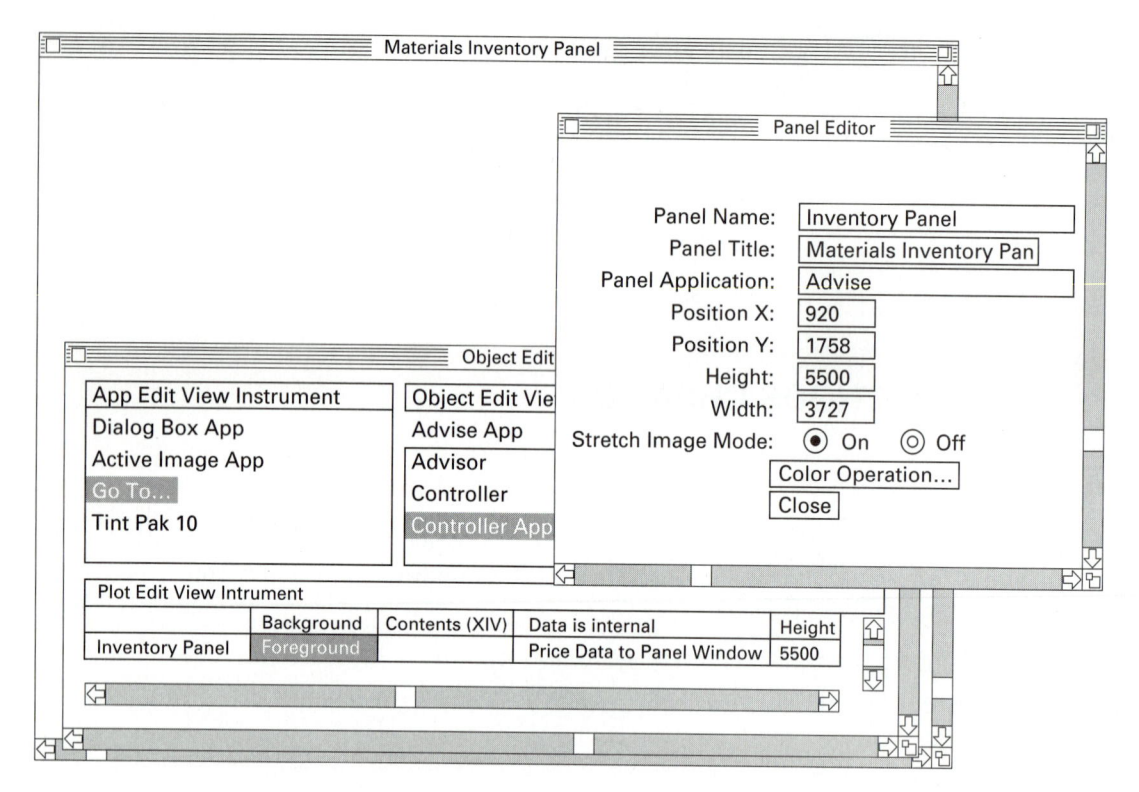

Figure 15.1 A panel-editor, dialog box from ProKappa. (Courtesy of Intelli-Corp.)

easy ways to generate code for these methods. In the 1960s and 1970s, we made computing too difficult. It was the province of highly specialized technicians who learned complex forms of encoding. Like ancient scribes with hieroglyphics and medieval monks with Latin, they enjoyed their closed intellectual world, which the layman could not penetrate.

The computer world is full of programming masochists. They have learned to program machines the hard way and resist the idea that it can be made easy. One of the most famous computer-science professors described graphics editors designed to make programming easier as "an idea which any serious computer scientist is only too anxious to ignore" [private memo].

The earliest computers had no interpreter or compiler to translate the language into a different form. Early computers were programmed with a binary notation. For example

011011 000000 000000 000001 110101

might mean "clear the accumulator and add the content of storage location 117 to it."

Using this way to program computers—without errors—was very difficult. The situation was improved slightly by using mnemonic codes to represent operations. Our sample instruction might then be

>CLA 000000 000000 000001 110101

Some of the most distinguished computer authorities of that time vigorously resisted this new use of mnemonic codes—after all, they could not be set with binary switches.

In Russia, the early COBOL compilers were copied from the West. Because of this, DP programmers wrote their code in English-language COBOL for several years. Eventually, a Russian-language COBOL computer became available, but most professional COBOL programmers continued to use the English-language version. They made new entrants to their profession pay their dues by learning the English version, although English is a difficult language for most Russians. Somehow, the foreign-language version seemed more professional, just as writing prescriptions in Latin seemed more professional to doctors until recently. We should not use C++ just because it seems more professional.

Removing unnecessary acronyms and complexity is very important because it allows the user to spend mental effort on what really matters—the purpose of the application. Alfred North Whitehead commented about mathematical notations: "By relieving the brain of all unnecessary work, a good notation sets it free to concentrate on more advanced problems, and in effect increases the mental power of the race" [1]. Before the introduction of Arabic notation for representing numbers, multiplication was difficult, and long division was almost impossible. Whitehead commented

> Probably nothing in the modern world would have more astonished a Greek mathematician than to learn that a large proportion of the population of Western Europe could perform the operation of division for the largest numbers. This fact would have seemed to him a sheer impossibility. [1]

We must find OO-CASE techniques that increase the mental power of their users.

PROCEDURAL VERSUS NONPROCEDURAL TECHNIQUES

We can categorize the techniques for representing methods as procedural and nonprocedural.

> *Procedural* techniques specify *how* something is accomplished.
>
> *Nonprocedural* techniques specify *what* is accomplished without describing how.

Traditional programming languages, such as COBOL, PL/I, FORTRAN, PASCAL, and C, are procedural. Their programmers give precisely detailed instructions for how each action should be accomplished. With nonprocedural languages the user says *what* is to be done and is not concerned with the detailed procedure for *how* it is done. Most query languages, report generators, graphics packages, and application generators are nonprocedural.

COBOL, PL/I, FORTRAN, and so on are referred to as third-generation languages. Fourth-generation languages (4GLs) became popular in the 1980s [2]. Among the better known ones were FOCUS, RAMIS, NOMAD, NATURAL, IDEAL, and MANTIS. These languages simplified procedural coding and introduced a variety of nonprocedural capabilities.

NOMAD, for example, is a high-level language with which some end users obtain fast results from a computer. Most professionals would call it a programming language because it has IF statements and DO loops. However, results can be obtained with brief nonprocedural statements, such as

LIST BY CUSTOMER AVERAGE (INVOICE TOTAL)

This is a complete program. It leaves the software to decide how the list should be formatted, when to skip pages, how to number pages, how to sort into CUSTOMER sequence, and how to compute an average.

Similarly,

PLOT REVENUE, EXPENSES, MARK-UP, EMPLOYEE BY MONTH

is a complete program. It does not say what type of plot is needed. The software may be capable of many different types of plotting. It decides the best form of plot from the statement and nature of the variables. It may select colors, determine an appropriate scale, label the plot, and print a color key. The user may be able to click on chart samples in a "gallery" of charts, and see what his data looks like when plotted with the charts he selects.

The following is another example:

GENERATE A MONTHLY PLOT
TITLE "SALES VOLUME BY DISTRICT"
X AXIS LABEL "MONTHS OF 1982"
Y AXIS LABEL "MILLIONS"
INPUT DATA

```
"WEST"
SELECT QUANTITY FROM SALES
WHERE DISTRICT = WEST
AND YEAR = 1982
"EAST"
SELECT QUANTITY FROM SALES
WHERE DISTRICT = EAST
AND YEAR = 1982
GO
```

Many nonprocedural tools have evolved away from "languages" to forms of GUI interaction in which the user points to areas of spreadsheets or text with a mouse and clicks on pull-down menus or icons. The user sees displays on a screen and can fill them in, point to them, and manipulate them. The result is a statement of requirement that the software can translate into executable code. A picture can be worth a thousand words and graphics representations of requirements or logic can be made easy to use and manipulate.

Many nonprocedural languages can handle only limited types of applications, such as query languages or report generators. A few, however, can handle general applications with highly complex logic. While some languages are purely procedural or purely nonprocedural, others combine both of these types of statement. This is generally desirable because nonprocedural operation speeds up and simplifies the use of the language, whereas procedural code extends the range of applications that can be tackled, giving more flexibility of logical manipulation. Tools for implementing OO methods should employ both procedural and nonprocedural techniques.

We can use the analogy of giving instructions to a taxi driver. With a *procedural* language, you give detailed instructions: "Drive 500 yards. Turn left. Drive 380 yards. Turn right. Drive to the traffic lights. If the lights are green . . . ." With a *nonprocedural* language, you simply state the goal: "Take me to the Criterion Cinema on Main Street."

We will see nonprocedural languages of greater power emerge. A more powerful semantics for instructing the taxi driver would be: "Take me to *Alien VII*." The taxi driver must then solve the problem, finding out where *Alien VII* is playing and taking you there.

Fourth-generation languages should now be reexamined. Their most powerful techniques for creating methods need to be set into the framework generated with an OO-CASE tool.

PROCEDURAL TECHNIQUES

Procedural techniques enable the structure of a program to be specified—loops, conditions, alternate-choice structures, and nested routines.

Fourth-generation languages enable procedural code to be written with fewer instructions and in a neater way than with COBOL or other third-generation languages. Here, for example, are some illustrations of code in IDEAL from Computer Associates.

```
SELECT ACCT-PERIOD
  WHEN 'MONTH'
    DO MONTH-END
  WHEN 'QUARTER'
    DO QUARTER-END
  WHEN 'YEAR'
    DO YEAR-END
WHEN OTHER
  DO DISPLAY-MSG
ENDSELECT
IF ACTIVITY-CODE = 'A'
  IF ACTIVITY-STATUS = 'S'
       SET W-TAG = 'SALARIED'
  ELSE
       SET W-TAG = 'HOURLY'
  ENDIF
ELSE
  SET W-TAG = 'INACTIVE'
ENDIF
```

The following code selects all the employees who are engineers (JOB = 3). For each selected **Employee** record it reads all the **Projrate** records for that employee and calculates an average value for all the **Rating** fields in those **Projrate** records. If an employee's average rating is greater than 6, it updates that employee's **Salary** field by adding 1000 to it.

```
FOR EACH EMPLOYEE
   WHERE JOB = 3
      SET W-TOTAL-RATING = 0
      <<PROJ-RECS>> FOR EACH PROJRATE
         WHERE PROJ-EMP-NO = EMPLOYEE.EMP-NO
         ADD RATING TO W-TOTAL-RATING
      ENDFOR
      SET W-AVG-RATING = W-TOTAL-RATING / $COUNT (PROJ-RECS)
      IF W-AVG-RATING > 6
         ADD 1000 TO EMPLOYEE.SALARY
      ENDIF
ENDFOR
```

Selecting the program-structure commands from a menu is preferable to typing them. This helps ensure against spelling mistakes, missing ENDs, missing ELSE statements in a condition, and so on. The menu has items such as the following:

PERFORM (subroutine)
Simple action
IF...
Multiway choice
DO WHILE
DO UNTIL
FOR... (relating to variables)
FOR EACH (relating to records)
ESCAPE (leave a construct with an orderly closedown)

ACTION DIAGRAMS   Action diagrams use brackets to draw the components of procedural code, as shown in Fig. 15.2 [3]. Programs consist of nested brackets as shown in Figs. 15.3, 15.4, and 15.5. The brackets may be selected by mouse as a program is built on the screen.

Brackets for code executed once:
- ENTER
- EXIT

- IF...
- ELSE...
- ENDIF

- IF...
- ELSEIF...
- ELSEIF...
- ENDIF

Brackets for code executed multiple times:
- LOOP WHILE...
- ENDLOOP

- LOOP WHILE...
- UNTIL...
- ENDLOOP

- FOR ALL...
- ENDFOR

Terminations:
- ESCAPE
- ESCAPE
- NEXT

Transfer control to the end of this bracket with an orderly closedown.

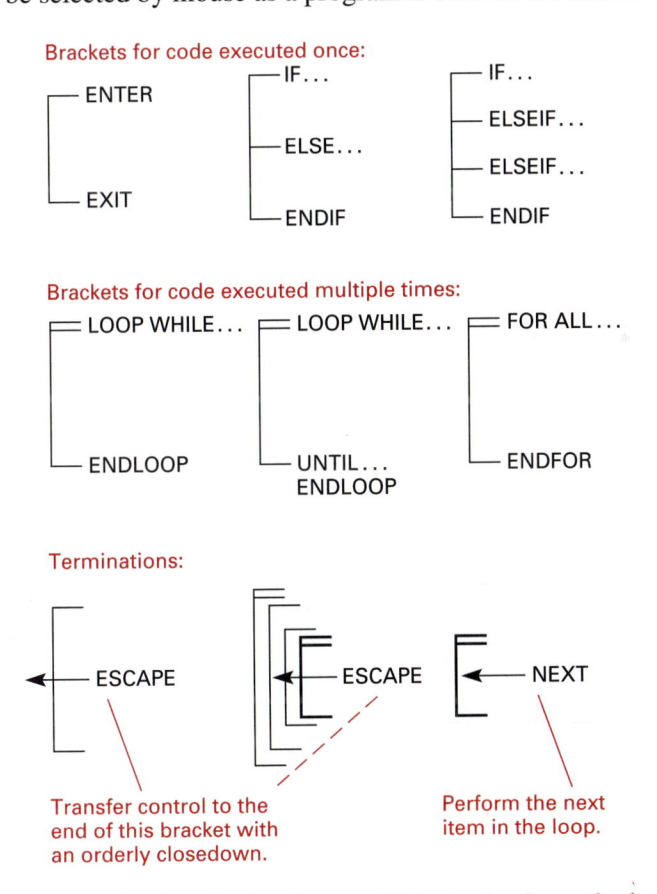

Perform the next item in the loop.

Figure 15.2   The bracket of action diagrams. Fully structured procedural code is built with nested brackets as in Fig. 15.3.

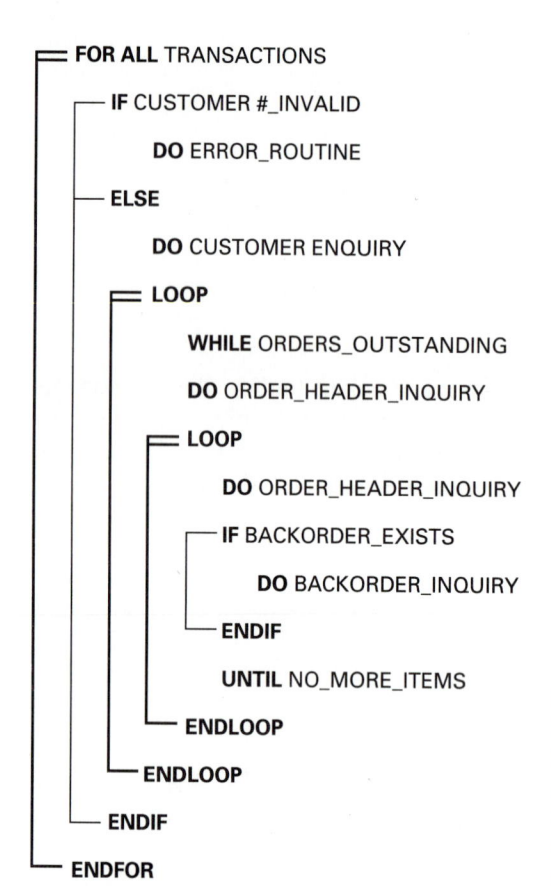

```
┌─ FOR ALL TRANSACTIONS
│   ┌─ IF CUSTOMER #_INVALID
│   │      DO ERROR_ROUTINE
│   ├─ ELSE
│   │      DO CUSTOMER ENQUIRY
│   │   ┌═ LOOP
│   │   │     WHILE ORDERS_OUTSTANDING
│   │   │     DO ORDER_HEADER_INQUIRY
│   │   │  ┌═ LOOP
│   │   │  │     DO ORDER_HEADER_INQUIRY
│   │   │  │  ┌─ IF BACKORDER_EXISTS
│   │   │  │  │     DO BACKORDER_INQUIRY
│   │   │  │  └─ ENDIF
│   │   │  │     UNTIL NO_MORE_ITEMS
│   │   │  └─ ENDLOOP
│   │   └─ ENDLOOP
│   └─ ENDIF
└─ ENDFOR
```

Figure 15.3 Action diagrams can be labeled with the control statement of the language used. This example uses statements from the language IDEAL from Computer Associates. The **bold** words are control words of the language. The bracket should be mouse selected from a menu.

The principles of structural programming should be adhered to when OO methods are created with procedural techniques. GO TO commands that encourage spaghetti code should be avoided. Action diagrams are a visual representation of fully structured procedural code.

The brackets of action diagrams can be expanded and contracted on the screen. The user can *contract* within *contract* within *contract*, and similarly expand multiple brackets with one mouse click. This enables the user to hide detail and navigate through a complex routine.

CODE GENERATION WITH ACTION DIAGRAMS

Some of the best CASE code generators help the designer build action diagrams using English words and generate executable code from the action diagrams. Figure 15.6 shows code specification built in action-diagram form with the IEF CASE tool from Texas Instruments. This generates 100 percent of the code in COBOL or C with no syntax errors.

```
$ /$ Executable Section $/
  Switch (adtab[curline].action){
    case ACT_JUNK:
    case ACT_CASE:
    case ACT_EXIT:
      itfrst = curline;
      itnext = curline + 1;
      break;

    case ACT_BEGL:
    case ACT_BEGB:
      adlevel = 1;
      itfrst = curline;
      for (itnext = curline+1; itnext <= numadtab & adlevel >0 itnext++){
        switch (adtab[itnext].action){
          case ACT_BEGL:
          case ACT_BEGB:
            adlevel++;
            break;
          case ACT_END:
            adlevel--;
          }
        }
      if (adlevel > 0)
        aborts ("ad: ? no matching end ??");

      break;

    default:
      itfirst = numadtab;
      itnext = numadtab;
      beep();
      }
    itdel = itnext - itfirst;
    for (itab = itfirst: itab < numadtab; itab++) {
      adtab[itab].action = adtab[itab+itdel].action;
      adtab[itab].count  = adtab[itab+itdel].count;
      adtab[itab]. text  = adtab[itab+itdel].text;
      }
    numadtab -= itdel;
    if (curline > numadtab)
      curline = numtab;

    showbuffer ():
```

Figure 15.4 Nested brackets, of which two are case structures and two are repetition brackets, are part of a program written in the language C.

To help eliminate input errors, the developer should type as little as possible. The program constructs and operators should be mouse selected. Operators are mouse selected from a set that fits the context. The variable names should also be mouse selected from a data model. Procedure names are entered once only. No syntax and naming errors can then occur, because only

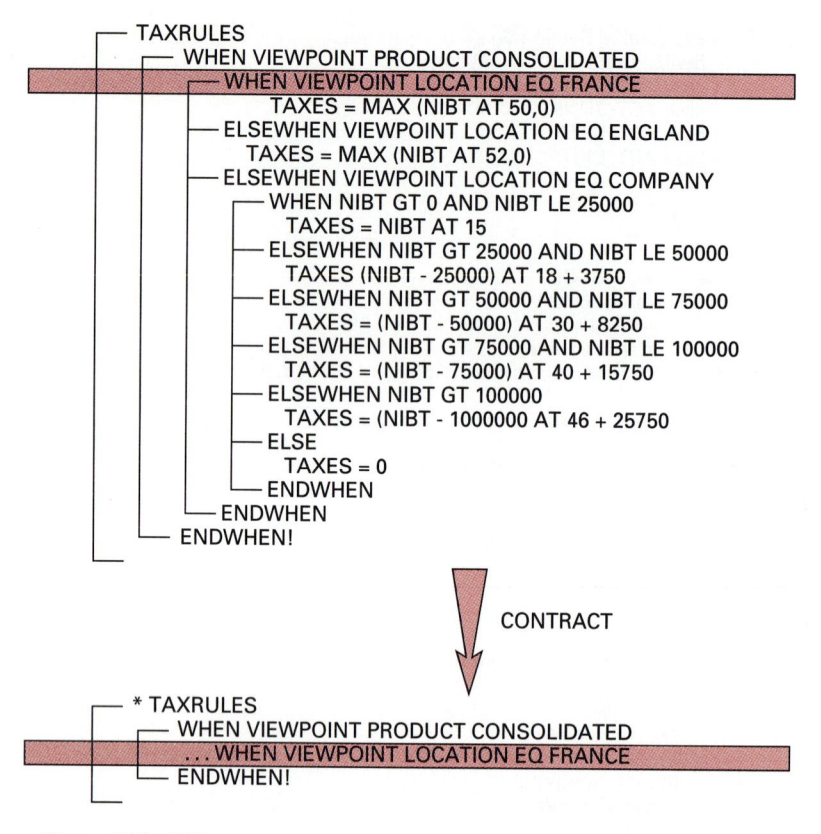

```
┌─ TAXRULES
│  ┌─ WHEN VIEWPOINT PRODUCT CONSOLIDATED
│  │  ┌─ WHEN VIEWPOINT LOCATION EQ FRANCE
│  │  │     TAXES = MAX (NIBT AT 50,0)
│  │  ├─ ELSEWHEN VIEWPOINT LOCATION EQ ENGLAND
│  │  │     TAXES = MAX (NIBT AT 52,0)
│  │  ├─ ELSEWHEN VIEWPOINT LOCATION EQ COMPANY
│  │  │  ┌─ WHEN NIBT GT 0 AND NIBT LE 25000
│  │  │  │     TAXES = NIBT AT 15
│  │  │  ├─ ELSEWHEN NIBT GT 25000 AND NIBT LE 50000
│  │  │  │     TAXES (NIBT - 25000) AT 18 + 3750
│  │  │  ├─ ELSEWHEN NIBT GT 50000 AND NIBT LE 75000
│  │  │  │     TAXES = (NIBT - 50000) AT 30 + 8250
│  │  │  ├─ ELSEWHEN NIBT GT 75000 AND NIBT LE 100000
│  │  │  │     TAXES = (NIBT - 75000) AT 40 + 15750
│  │  │  ├─ ELSEWHEN NIBT GT 100000
│  │  │  │     TAXES = (NIBT - 1000000 AT 46 + 25750)
│  │  │  ├─ ELSE
│  │  │  │     TAXES = 0
│  │  │  └─ ENDWHEN
│  │  └─ ENDWHEN
│  └─ ENDWHEN!
```

▼ CONTRACT

```
┌─ * TAXRULES
│  ┌─ WHEN VIEWPOINT PRODUCT CONSOLIDATED
│  │  ... WHEN VIEWPOINT LOCATION EQ FRANCE
│  └─ ENDWHEN!
```

Figure 15.5 This tax computation, which might be a *method* in an OO class, was condensed from an example in which the actual code was 20 pages long and written in the decision-support language System W. Brackets can be either contracted, as illustrated here, or expanded. We can *contract* within *contract* within *contract*. The symbol "..." or "+" indicates that a line can be expanded.

valid options are available for selection. The designer can, of course, still make mistakes by entering wrong conditions or wrong calculations, so each *method* should be tested as soon as it is built. The tool can help generate test data for this purpose.

The developers should not have to inspect or change the generated code. The *method* is tested like a black box. If it has an error or needs modifying, this is done by modifying the generator input and code is immediately regenerated and tested. The cycle of design should quickly generate, test, redesign, and so on to aid human creativity.

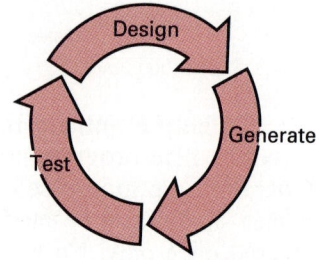

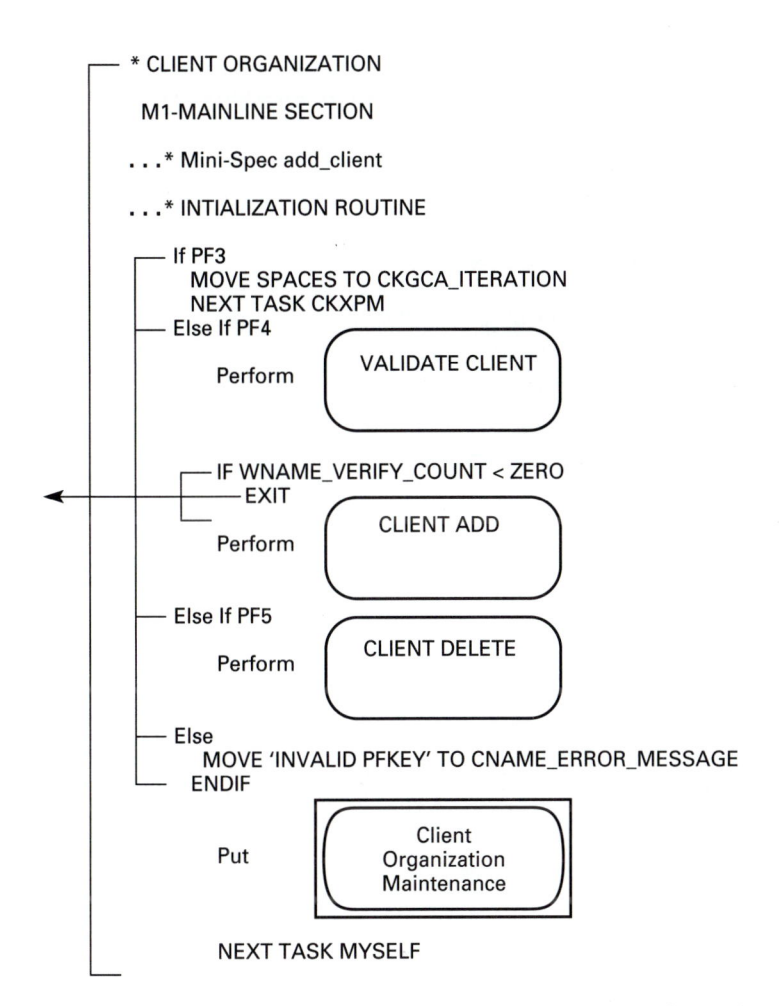

```
— * CLIENT ORGANIZATION

  M1-MAINLINE SECTION

  ...* Mini-Spec add_client

  ...* INTIALIZATION ROUTINE

  — If PF3
      MOVE SPACES TO CKGCA_ITERATION
      NEXT TASK CKXPM
  — Else If PF4

      Perform     VALIDATE CLIENT


     ┌── IF WNAME_VERIFY_COUNT < ZERO
     └── EXIT

      Perform     CLIENT ADD

  — Else If PF5

      Perform     CLIENT DELETE

  — Else
      MOVE 'INVALID PFKEY' TO CNAME_ERROR_MESSAGE
  — ENDIF

      Put         Client
                  Organization
                  Maintenance

  NEXT TASK MYSELF
```

Figure 15.6 Code specification built in action diagrams. (Courtesy of KnowledgeWare Inc., Atlanta, GA.)

AVOIDANCE OF PROCEDURAL DESIGN

Procedural design can be neatly diagrammed, and code free from syntax errors can be generated directly from these diagrams. Nevertheless, we should create methods with nonprocedural techniques where possible, because these are more powerful, easier to change, and more easily understood by end users. Not all code can be generated nonprocedurally, but certainly most of it can. It is an interesting challenge to see how completely procedural design can be avoided.

Box 15.1 lists techniques for generating code nonprocedurally and for representing methods without low-level programming.

BOX 15.1 Techniques for representing methods without low-level coding. Appropriate combinations of these techniques are needed.

Procedural Techniques

- Fourth-generation language constructs
- Action diagrams
- Procedural-code generators

Nonprocedural techniques

- Report generators
- Screen painters
- GUI interface builders
- Dialog generators
- English statements
- Intelligent defaults
- Declarative languages
- Rule processing
- Inference engine
- Event diagrams link to rules
- Equations
- Spreadsheet tools
- Declarative tables
- Decision tables/decision trees
- State-transition diagrams

Class Libraries

- Application-independent classes, such as print, plot, transmit, display, dialog, and so on
- Application-dependent classes with application templates that can be customized
- Problem solvers, such as nonlinear-equation problem solvers

REPORT GENERATORS Many tools contain techniques for generating reports. A COBOL program for producing a report is shown in Fig. 15.7 alongside IDEAL code which produces the same result.

Generating reports and charts is still easier with techniques that are used in some spreadsheet tools. Here, the user enters the relevant calculations and selects the cells to be printed or charted. The user can generate a specimen of the report or chart format and then use it multiple times.

SCREEN AND DIALOG PAINTERS A screen can be painted with a mouse, the requisite variables being positioned as needed. Screens can be linked together to create a dialog.

Interaction by means of a graphic user interface (GUI) is desirable. Some CASE products have elegant tools for building a GUI dialog. Programming GUI dialogs is difficult—generators are almost essential.

DEFAULT OPTIONS Generators should use *default options* wherever possible. If a user has a choice of options and does not exercise this choice, the software makes the selection. The software's choice is called a *default option,* or simply a *default.* The user is trusting the software to make a good selection.

The use of default options is important because it can enable results to be obtained quickly. The application builder does not have to spell out every detail. The more the software makes its own choices, the less the effort required to obtain results. We therefore want the software to exercise intelligent choices wherever it can.

At one extreme, the software may select formats, screen layouts, access mechanisms, and so on without giving the user a choice. This is fast but inflexible. At the other extreme, the user has to tell the software everything, as in a typical COBOL program. This is flexible but slow. We can achieve both speed and flexibility if the software makes choices but allows the user to override them. The range of possibilities with selectable options is illustrated in Fig. 15.8.

DECLARATIVE LANGUAGE A declarative language enables its user to state a set of facts, equations, or rules, and then generates code from these. For example, a user may enter a collection of equations. To solve a problem or do a computation, the software scans the equations and puts them into a sequence. The software can solve the equations for a specific variable.

A report written in COBOL:

```
100-INV-LIST SECTION.
  PERFORM 700-INITIALIZE.
  PERFORM 200-LIST-INVENTORY-ITEMS
        UNTIL END-OF-FILE.
  PERFORM 400-PRINT-SUMMARY.
199-EXIT.
  EXIT.
200-LIST-INVENTORY-ITEMS SECTION.
  IF (UNIT-PRICE < 5 AND QTY-ON-HAND > 1000)
  THEN
    NEXT SENTENCE
  ELSE
    PERFORM 500-READ-INVENTORY-ITEM
    GO TO 299-EXIT
  COMPUTE VALUE-ON-HAND = QTY-ON-HAND * UNIT-PRICE
  MOVE ITEM-NO         TO PRINT-ITEM-NO.
  MOVE ITEM-DESC       TO PRINT-ITEM-DESC.
  MOVE UNIT-PRICE      TO PRINT-PRICE.
  MOVE QTY-ON-HAND     TO PRINT-ON-HAND.
  MOVE VALUE-ON-HAND   TO PRINT-VALUE.
  MOVE INVENTORY-DETAIL TO PRINT-LINE.
  PERFORM 300-PRINT-DETAIL-LINE.
  ADD +1              TO ITEM-COUNT.
  ADD UNIT-PRICE      TO AVERAGE-PRICE.
  ADD VALUE-ON-HAND   TO AVERAGE-VALUE.
  PERFORM 500-READ-INVENTORY-ITEM.
299-EXIT.
  EXIT.
300-PRINT-DETAIL-LINE SECTION.
  IF END-OF-PAGE
  THEN
    PERFORM 600-PRINT-HEADING
    MOVE 'N' TO END-OF-PAGE-SWITCH.
  PRINT PRINT-LINE.
  IF PAGE-OVERFLOW
  THEN
    MOVE 'Y' TO END-OF-PAGE-SWITCH.
399-EXIT.
  EXIT.
400-PRINT-SUMMARY SECTION.
  IF ITEM-COUNT = 0
  THEN
    NEXT SENTENCE
  ELSE
    COMPUTE AVERAGE-PRICE = AVERAGE-PRICE/ITEM-COUNT.
    COMPUTE AVERAGE-VALUE = AVERAGE-VALUE/ITEM-COUNT.
  MOVE AVERAGE-PRICE TO PRINT-AVERAGE-PRICE.
  MOVE AVERAGE-VALUE TO PRINT-AVERAGE-VALUE.
  MOVE SUMMARY-LINE TO PRINT-LINE.
  PERFORM 300-PRINT-DETAIL-LINE.
499-EXIT.
  EXIT.
500-READ-INVENTORY-ITEM SECTION.
  READ INVENTORY-ITEM.
  IF END-OF-FILE
  THEN
    MOVE 'Y'TO END-OF-FILE-SWITCH.
599-EXIT.
  EXIT.
600-PRINT-HEADING SECTION.
  ADD +1 TO PAGE NUMBER.
  MOVE TOP-OF-PAGE TO CONTROL-CHARACTER.
  PRINT HEADING-LINE.
  MOVE SPACE TO CONTROL-CHARACTER.
699-EXIT.
  EXIT.
700-INITIALIZE SECTION.
  MOVE 0  TO PAGE-NUMBER
          ITEM-COUNT
          AVERAGE-PRICE
          AVERAGE-VALUE.
  MOVE 'Y' TO END-OF-PAGE-SWITCH.
  PERFORM 500-READ-INVENTORY-ITEM.
799-EXIT.
  EXIT.
```

The same report program in IDEAL:

```
<<INV-LIST>>PROCEDURE
  FOR EACH INVENTORY-ITEM
      WHERE(UNIT-PRICE < 5 AND QTY-ON-HAND > 1000)
      SET VALUE-ON-HAND = QTY-ON-HAND * UNIT-PRICE
      PRODUCE INV-RPT
  ENDFOR
ENDPROCEDURE
```

Figure 15.7 A COBOL program for generating a report is abominably clumsy compared with report generators.

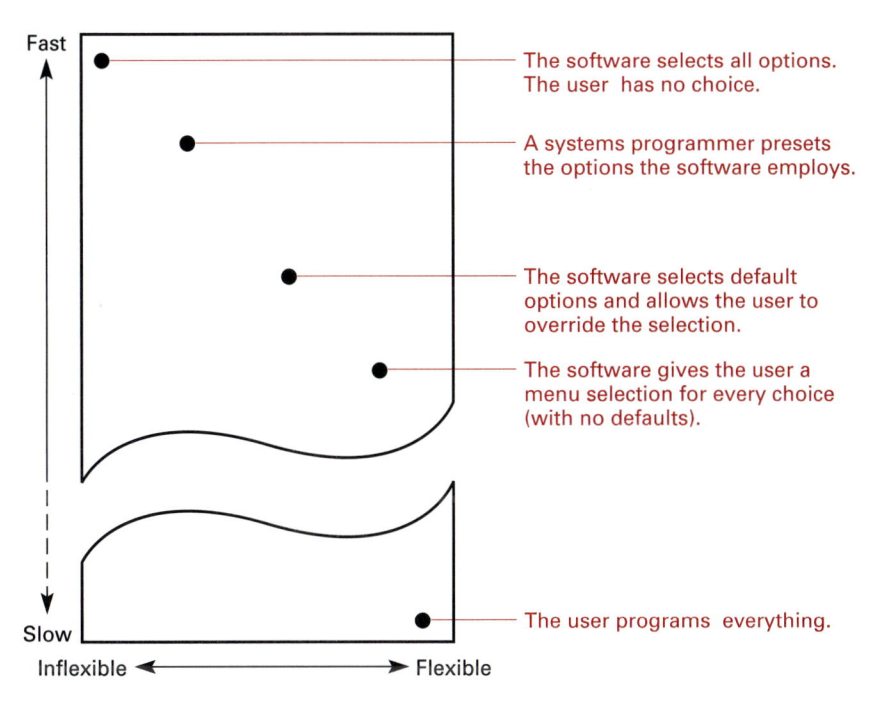

Fast
— The software selects all options. The user has no choice.

— A systems programmer presets the options the software employs.

— The software selects default options and allows the user to override the selection.

— The software gives the user a menu selection for every choice (with no defaults).

— The user programs everything.

Slow

Inflexible ←——→ Flexible

Figure 15.8 Selectable options and default options.

Making *declarative* statements is easier than *procedural* statements and end users or business people can check them.

RULES

Rules are a particularly valuable form of declarative statement. The rules described in Chapter 10 are both statements that business people can check and statements from which much of the code can be generated. When connected to OO-CASE diagrams such as those in Fig. 10.1, they provide a powerful means of generating code and immediately instantiating and running an OO model. They enable us to represent business policies in a model which business people can understand, and then animate the model, produce spreadsheets, and adjust the model, simulating redesigned business processes.

Sometimes a business rule is not worded with sufficient precision to generate code from it. The implementor of the method needs more precise wording, naming data items selected from the data model. For this purpose an editor is needed to build the formal rule representation with accuracy. C code generated from rules is illustrated in Fig. 15.9 and an example of forward chaining of rules is illustrated in Fig. 15.10.

```
forule ColorChange in ChemicalRules
{
  if:
    ?complaint.Problem == ColorChange:
    ?complaint,Product.MiddleLayer != DPL18:
  then:
    ?complaint.Advice = MoreUVResistance:
    ?complaint.AffectedLayer = MiddleLayer:
    ?complaint.NewMaterial = DPL18:
}

forule BleedingInkI in RepairRules
{
  if:
    ?complaint.Problem == BleedingInk
  then:
    ?complaint.Advice = LessPermeability:
    ?complaint.AffectedLayer = MiddleLayer:
}

forule BleedingInkII in RepairRules
{
  if:
    ?complaint.Advice == LessPermeability:
    ?old_material == ?complaint.Product.Middlelayer:
    ?old_class == direct classof ?old_material:
    Print(?old_class, "Is the parent class of the problem material."):
    ?new_material == instanceof ?old_class:
    Print("\n", ?new_material, "is a material in the same class,"):
    ?new_material != ?old_material:
    Print("and it is different,"):
    ?new_material,Permeability < ?old_material,Permeability:
    Print("and it is less permeable,"):
    ?new_material,CostPerLb <= 1,2 * ?old_material,CostPerLb:
    Print("and its cost is acceptable.\n"):
    Print(?new_material, "is a possible new material."):
  then:
    ?complaint.NewMaterial +== ?new_material:
}

/* Establishing a ruleset hierarchy: RepairRules--ChemicalRules */

ruleset ChemicalRules (RepairRules)

/***********************************************************
 *              Addition to be made by student             *
 ***********************************************************
ginger//tmp_int/net/nill/users/trainee/tutorial/ch8(23):
```

Figure 15.9 Example of C code generated from rules. (Courtesy of Intelli-Corp.)

Chap. 15　　　　　　　　　Methods Creation　　　　　　　　　　**235**

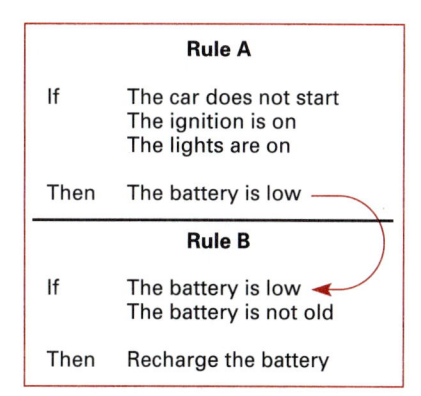

```
┌─────────────────────────────────────┐
│              Rule A                 │
│  If      The car does not start     │
│          The ignition is on         │
│          The lights are on          │
│                                     │
│  Then    The battery is low ──┐     │
│ ─────────────────────────────  │    │
│              Rule B            │    │
│  If      The battery is low ◄──┘    │
│          The battery is not old     │
│                                     │
│  Then    Recharge the battery       │
└─────────────────────────────────────┘
```

Figure 15.10　Example of forward chaining of rules.

INFERENCE ENGINE　Sometimes methods use an inference engine to scan a collection of rules and facts and deduce a procedure that achieves a specific result.

EVENT DIAGRAMS　The diagrams of the previous chapters are associated with various aspects of code generation. Object-structure diagrams and categorization diagrams generate code for the representation of objects. Inheritance diagrams generate code for data structure and methods that are inherited. State-transition diagrams are linked to operations in event diagrams to establish how operations change the state of objects.

　　Particularly important are event diagrams that show the preconditions and postconditions for operations. The rules used in conjunction with event diagrams translate into segments of code, as shown in Fig. 15.11.

　　The programming of methods is needed to fill in the overall code representation.

DECISION TREES AND TABLES　Decision trees and decision tables are a useful way to represent certain types of detailed logic. A decision tree for computer **Order Discount Percentage** is shown in Fig. 15.12. Sometimes, a decision table is used for showing information like that in Fig. 15.12.

　　A decision tree or table can be converted *automatically* into program code and be a useful component of a toolkit for creating *methods*.

DECLARATIVE TABLES　Various other types of tables are useful for declarative representation of computations. Spreadsheets, for example, can be built and tested quickly and can con-

```
/* ----- TOKEN::declassify ===== */
ObjectState *TOKEN::declassify_TOKEN (Boolean reclassifyFlag) {
  PtechObject *ptechObj:
  Boolean saveFlag:
  /* is the object currently classified as a TOKEN. */
  if (!TOKEN::isCurrent())
    return this:

  saveFlag = inferrDeclassify:
  InferrDeclassify = TRUE:
  ptechObj = ObjectOf():

  /* Mark object declasified so removeValue() won't recurse, */
  currentState = FALSE:

  /* Declassify object as direct subtype trough partitions. */
  if(isClassified(NICKEL_Tag))
    NICKEL_of(this)->declassify_NICKEL():

  if(isClassified(DIME_Tag))
    DIME_Of(this)->declassify_DIME():

  if(isClassified(QUARTER_Tag))
    QUARTER_Of(this)->declassify_QUARTER():

  if(isClassified(SLUG_Tag))
    SLUG_Of(this)->declassify_SLUG():

  /* Invoke destructor to delete C++ object. */
  deleteObject(TRUE):

  InterDeclassify = saveFlag:

  /* If the ptechObject has no other active states return 0 */
  /* to show object was terminated, else return ptechObject. */
  if (!reclassifyFlag && (ptechObj->countStates() == 1)) {
    ptechObj->deleteObject(TRUE):
    return (ObjectState *)0:
  }
  else {
    ptechObj->removeStaeAS(TOKEN_Tag):
    return (ObjectState *)ptechObj->getAnyState():
  }
}
```

Figure 15.11 Example of C++ generated from an event diagram of a vending machine. (Courtesy of Ptech, Westborough, MA.)

tain complex computations. The computations represented by spreadsheets can be translated into the code for specific methods.

Sets of equations may be represented as declarative specifications or may be a component of spreadsheets used for code generation.

Some spreadsheet tools provide the capability to generate elegant looking charts. The user can quickly explore a gallery of chart representations to see

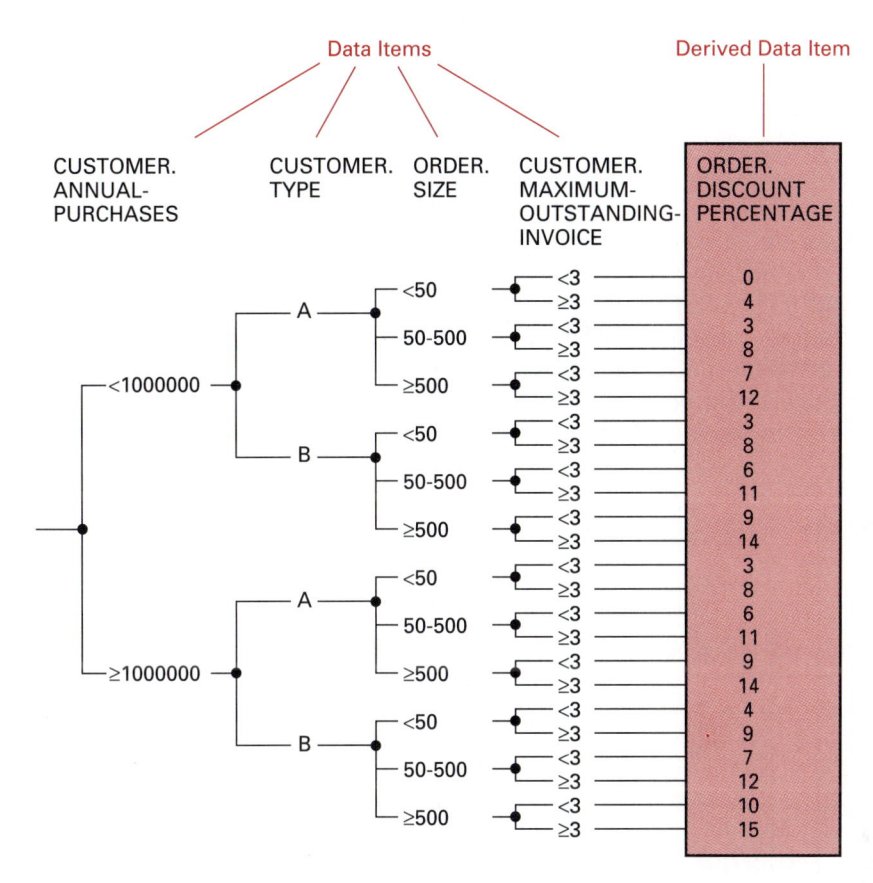

Figure 15.12 Decision tree for computing Order.Discount Percentage. Decision trees and tables can be converted directly into code to become a component of a method.

which enable the data to be visualized most effectively. This capability may also be used for *methods* generation.

ENGLISH

Various tools have enabled end users to express their needs in English. English has been used as a source of code generation. RAMIS ENGLISH, for example, allows the users to enter a string of sentences similar to the following:

```
LET REVENUE = UNIT × LISTPRICE.
SHOW ME TOTAL REVENUES FOR TERMINALS.
SORT ON PRODUCT NUMBER AND INCLUDE THE NAME.
NAME MEANS PRODUCT NAME.
```

English is useful for simple queries but not for most *methods* unless it is linked to a means of representing procedures.

English abounds in ambiguities, such as "You wouldn't recognize Mary now. She's grown another foot." A notice in a government office once read, "during the present fuel shortage please take advantage of your secretary between the hours of 12 and 2." A colleague described his son reading that a certain airplane was used for liaison duties. The youngster looked up liaison in the dictionary and found it defined as "an illicit sexual adventure." In the Anglican communion service, the priest offers a chalice of wine and says, "Drink ye all of this." He would be surprised if a communicant drank it all, not knowing that the word *all* referred to the communicants rather than the wine.

English can be used with precision in computing if relatively simple sentences are linked to action diagrams, as in Fig. 15.13.

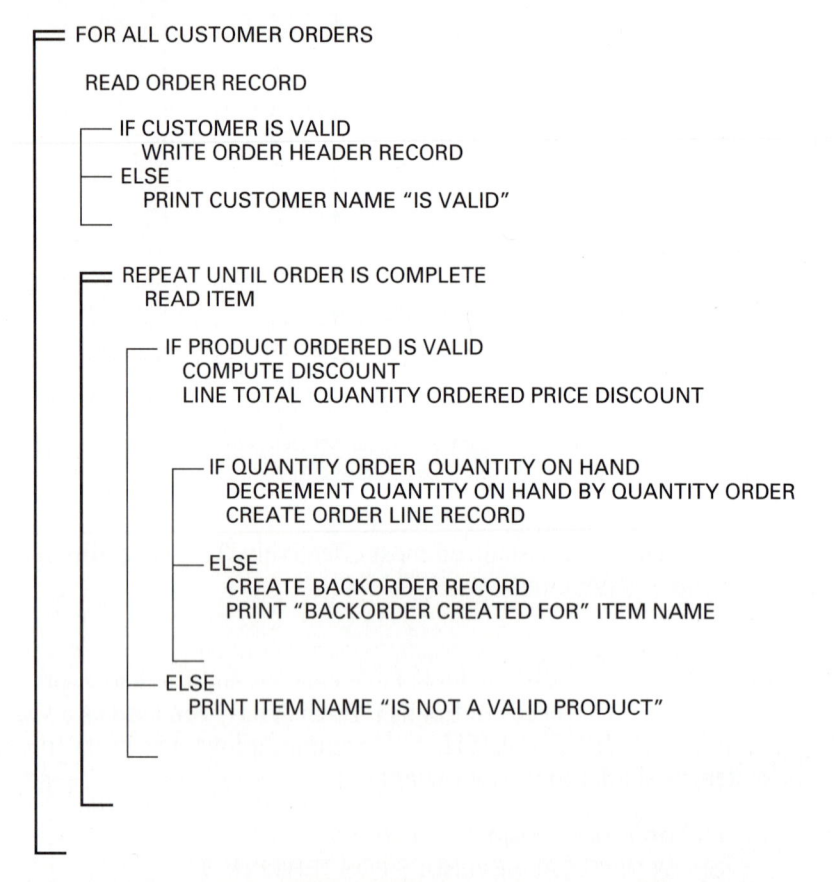

```
FOR ALL CUSTOMER ORDERS
    READ ORDER RECORD
        IF CUSTOMER IS VALID
            WRITE ORDER HEADER RECORD
        ELSE
            PRINT CUSTOMER NAME "IS VALID"

    REPEAT UNTIL ORDER IS COMPLETE
        READ ITEM
            IF PRODUCT ORDERED IS VALID
                COMPUTE DISCOUNT
                LINE TOTAL  QUANTITY ORDERED PRICE DISCOUNT

                IF QUANTITY ORDER  QUANTITY ON HAND
                    DECREMENT QUANTITY ON HAND BY QUANTITY ORDER
                    CREATE ORDER LINE RECORD
                ELSE
                    CREATE BACKORDER RECORD
                    PRINT "BACKORDER CREATED FOR" ITEM NAME
            ELSE
                PRINT ITEM NAME "IS NOT A VALID PRODUCT"
```

Figure 15.13 An action diagram with statements in natural English similar to the statements that are input to INTELLECT or RAMIS ENGLISH. English linked to precise structures can be input to a code generator.

The computer should check each English phrase to determine whether ambiguity is possible and, if so, conduct a dialog with the developer to remove the ambiguity.

CLASS LIBRARIES

A particularly important way to avoid programming is to employ reusable classes. Increasingly, class librar-ies for different purposes are likely to be sold in the OO world.

Some classes are application independent. They provide valuable functions, such as printing, displaying, compression of images or speech, secure transmission, and so on. They should provide the complex management controls needed on transaction processing systems to prevent transaction loss, double updating of files during recovery, and so on. A rich set of application-independent classes is needed that can greatly speed up development.

Other classes are templates for specific applications. Complex applications may be designed in an OO fashion, so that parameters can be selected for pre-planned variations, and classes can be subtypes and added to for non-preplanned variations. A major promise of OO development is the growth of libraries of classes that facilitate maximum reusability of classes and inheritance of methods.

SUMMARY

A large and diverse set of techniques exist for generating the code for *methods* without manual programming in languages such as C++. The modularity of OO design enhances the ability to use nonprocedural specification of methods. Box 15.1 lists a collection of nonprocedural techniques.

OO-CASE tools should generate 100 percent of the code for methods so that the analyst can quickly run his models and designs, without needing to be a C, C++, or COBOL programmer.

REFERENCES

1. Whitehead, A. N., *An Introduction to Mathematics,* Oxford University Press, Oxford, 1911.

2. Martin, James, *Fourth-Generation Languages,* Prentice Hall, Englewood Cliffs, NJ, 1985.

3. Martin, James and Carma McClure, *Action Diagrams* (2nd edition), Prentice Hall, Englewood Cliffs, NJ, 1989.

16 OBJECT-ORIENTED INFORMATION ENGINEERING

Building a space shuttle would be unthinkable without an overall plan. Once the overall plan exists, however, separate teams can work on the components. Corporate information systems development is scarcely less complex than building a space shuttle. Yet, most corporations do it without an overall plan of sufficient detail to make the components fit together.

The overall architect of the shuttle cannot conceivably specify the detailed design of the rockets, electronics, or other subsystems. These subsystems must be developed by different teams working autonomously. Imagine, however, what would happen if these teams enthusiastically created their own subsystems without any coordination from the top. The data-processing world is full of inspired subsystem builders who want to be left alone. Their numbers are rapidly increasing as small computers proliferate and end users learn to acquire their own facilities. A corporation with computing that fits into an overall architecture differs greatly from a corporation with incompatible systems. Systems must be integrated throughout the value chain in an enterprise.

INFORMATION ENGINEERING Software engineering applies structured techniques to one project. Information engineering applies structured or OO techniques to the enterprise as a whole or to a large sector of the enterprise.

> *Information engineering* (IE) is the application of an interlocking set of techniques for the planning, analysis, design, construction, and maintenance of information systems *for a whole enterprise* or across a major sector of the enterprise.

Just as different organizations vary their practice of software engineering, so there are variations on the theme of information engineering. Information engineering should not be regarded as one rigid methodology but rather as a generic class of methodologies. The object-oriented approach described in this book is probably the most effective variant of IE. All variants of IE should have the characteristics listed in Box 16.1.

BOX 16.1 Characteristics of information engineering that apply to both traditional and OO information engineering.

- IE applies modeling techniques to either the entire enterprise or a large sector of it, rather than on a projectwide basis.
- IE provides a variety of development paths or task structures—each generally progressing from planning, through analysis, design, and construction to cutover, with reiteration to earlier stages to reflect knowledge gained during later stages.
- As it progresses through these stages, IE steadily populates a repository (encyclopedia) with knowledge about the enterprise, its system designs, and their implementation.
- IE models cross-functional streams of operations (for example, OO event diagrams) and provides the capability to redesign these streams.
- IE creates a framework for developing a computerized enterprise. Separately developed systems fit into this framework. Within the framework, systems can be built and modified quickly.
- There is no attempt to achieve central control of application development, but rather to facilitate faster development by decentralized groups who understand their own application needs. The separately developed systems use resources such as networks, data models, and class libraries which are supported centrally.
- The enterprisewide approach makes it possible to achieve coordination among separately built systems and facilitates the maximum use of shared data and reusable designs, models, and classes.
- IE involves end users strongly at each of the stages by facilitated workshop techniques (Chapter 14) and RAD (Rapid Application Development).
- IE facilitates the long-term evolution of systems.
- IE identifies how computing can best aid the strategic goals of the enterprise.
- IE helps in redesigning the enterprise, business areas, or processes, to remove redundant or unnecessary operations and to take maximum advantage of networks, databases, and automation.

In traditional data processing, separate systems are built independently. Systems are usually incompatible with one another, have incompatible data, and are difficult to link together. These systems are often unnecessarily redundant and expensive, and the information needed for overall management control cannot be extracted from them. OO techniques without information engineering similarly lead to a proliferation of unnecessarily redundant and incompatible systems—a Tower of Babel.

Most large enterprises have an unnecessary proliferation of separately coded systems which are separately maintained at great cost. A thousand transaction types can be found where a hundred would suffice. Object-oriented IE applies the Principle of Occam's Razor to the whole enterprise—minimizing the unnecessary duplication and drastically reducing the total maintenance effort.

> An objective of OO information engineering is to identify common object types across the entire enterprise and, consequently, to minimize redundant system development work and maintenance.

With information engineering, high-level plans and models are created, and separately built systems link into these plans and models. Strategic planning is applied to the whole enterprise. More detailed analysis is applied to separate business areas within the enterprise, or streams of related activities which span the enterprise. Design and construction techniques are applied to individual systems.

The same I-CASE (integrated CASE) toolset and repository are used for all of the IE stages. The repository stores detailed information about the enterprise strategy and the business area analysis. The latter uses detailed data models and process models. Different teams of system developers, in different places and at different times, will build systems that link into the computerized framework. Their personal computers and I-CASE tools will be on line to the shared repository, sometimes via telephone lines.

Prior to the 1990s, IE used traditional structured techniques rather than OO techniques: indeed, some of the IE toolsets are still oriented to traditional structured techniques. OO techniques are much more powerful for modeling an enterprise, reflecting the policies that business people want to use in running the enterprise, and building systems that implement these policies. Particularly important, OO models using event diagrams work well in facilitated workshops for redesigning the business processes. They help in achieving cross-functional redesign, which can have a major payoff in reduced costs and faster responsiveness.

The IE Pyramid

The pyramid, used to represent information engineering, indicates that it progresses steadily into more detail—from enterprisewide planning to business area

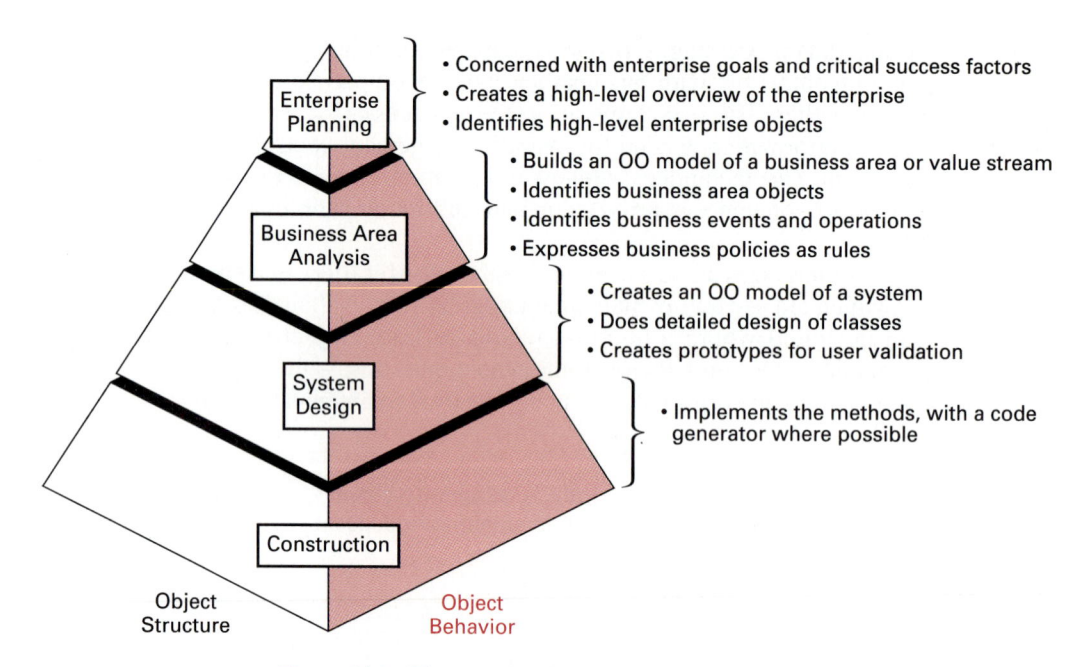

Figure 16.1 The pyramid of OO information engineering.

Enterprise Planning
- Concerned with enterprise goals and critical success factors
- Creates a high-level overview of the enterprise
- Identifies high-level enterprise objects

Business Area Analysis
- Builds an OO model of a business area or value stream
- Identifies business area objects
- Identifies business events and operations
- Expresses business policies as rules

System Design
- Creates an OO model of a system
- Does detailed design of classes
- Creates prototypes for user validation

Construction
- Implements the methods, with a code generator where possible

Object Structure | Object Behavior

analysis, system design, and then construction. Figure 16.1 gives the version of this pyramid for OO IE.

At the top level an overview model is built. Part of this is expanded into more detail at the level of business area analysis. Part of this model is expanded into yet more detail at the level of system design. The system is then constructed with OO classes and methods. The same repository is used at all levels and is successively filled with more detail.

The left-hand side of the pyramid is concerned with object-structure analysis (see Chapters 6 and 7); the right-hand side is concerned with object-behavior analysis (see Chapters 8 through 15). Enterprisewide, high-level object types are identified at the top of the pyramid. These are subtyped into more detail at the business area analysis level. These may be further subtyped at the system design level.

At the highest level, the planning of I.S. should relate strongly to the strategic planning of the business. At the top, management must be aware of what strategic opportunities would make the enterprise more competitive. A strategy must be developed relating future technology to its effect on the business, its products or services, or its goals and critical success factors. This is important, because technology is changing so fast. No enterprise is untouched by the growing power of technology; some organizations and industries will be changed drastically by it.

The top-level planning needs to guide and prioritize the expenditures on computing, so that the I.S. department can contribute to the corporate objectives as effectively as possible. The high-level enterprise model should help top management and the CIO (chief information officer) to understand how the enterprise might be restructured.

The second level relates to a business area or stream of related activities. Whereas the top level relates to the enterprise as a whole (or to a major portion of the enterprise), the second level relates to a specific area of the enterprise (or to a clustered group of functions and data subjects). A model is built of the object types, events, and operations in the business area. The business policies are expressed in rules, as discussed in Chapter 10. The model can focus attention on the redesign of the business area. Sometimes a stream of activities which spans functional areas is modeled and redesigned.

The third layer narrows the focus further to a specific system. It defines how a particular portion of the business area analysis (BAA) model will be implemented.

The bottom layer includes the implementation of the designed system. This includes both the construction and cutover phases.

OO models are successively expanded into more detail as IE progresses down the stages (see Fig. 16.2).

Information engineering itself needs to fit into a high-level framework that involves the strategic planning for technology networks and how they could affect the business.

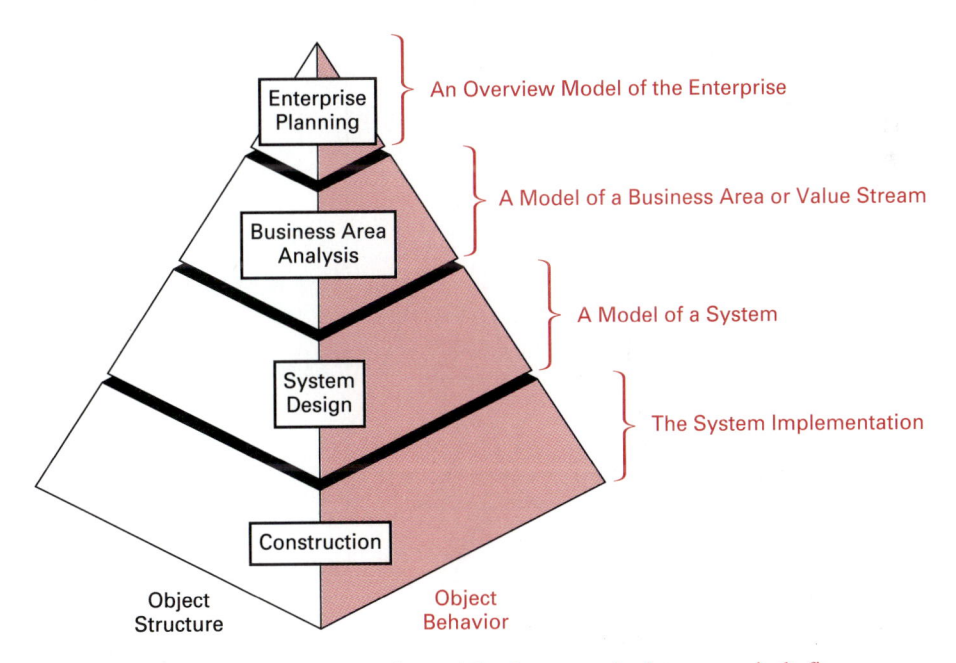

Figure 16.2 Models are used at each level, progressing into successively finer detail.

Information engineering applies an engineering-like discipline to all facets and levels of the pyramid, resulting in timely implementation of high-quality systems grounded in the business plans of the enterprise. An engineering-like discipline needs formal techniques. These are implemented with computerized tools that guide and help the planners, analysts, and implementors. While the tools impose formality on all stages, they should be designed to maximize the speed with which systems can be built and the ease with which they can be modified.

DIVIDE AND CONQUER

Rebuilding all of the data-processing resources required by an enterprise is an exceedingly complex undertaking. An objective of information engineering is to make the separate systems relate to one another in an adequate fashion. This does not happen when the separate development activities are not coordinated. Information engineering, therefore, starts with a top management view of the enterprise and progresses downward into greater detail. The Development Coordination function manages the architectures and in particular the system boundaries.

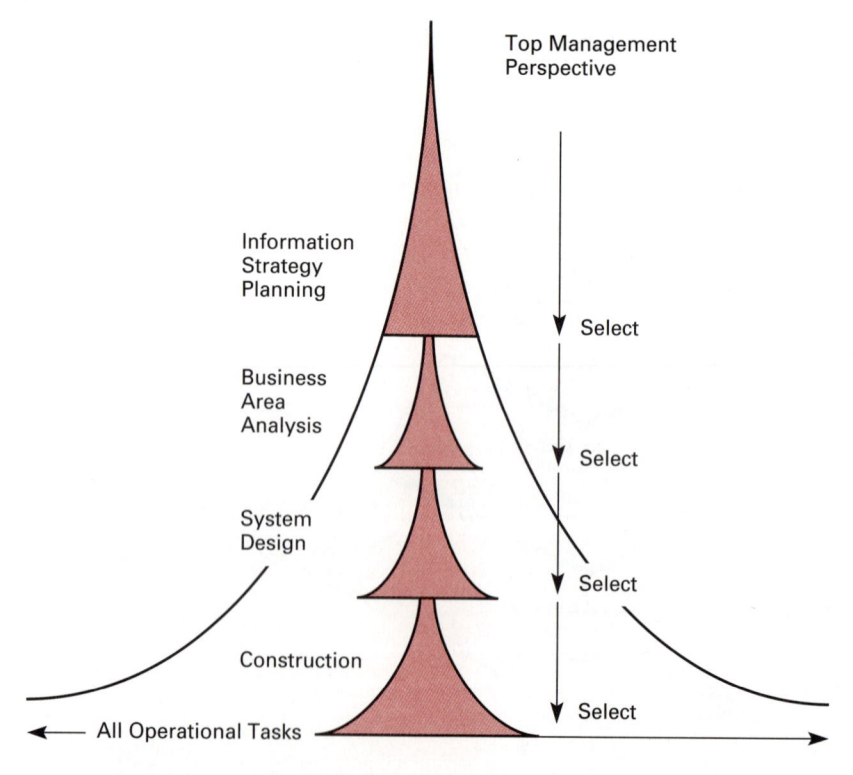

Figure 16.3 Divide-and-conquer approach to system development.

As the progression into detail occurs, selections must be made concerning which business areas should be analyzed and which systems should be designed. A divide-and-conquer approach is used, as illustrated in Fig. 16.3.

Information engineering, at its best, begins at the top of an enterprise by conducting an information strategy plan. From this plan, a business area is selected for analysis. A portion of the business area is selected for detailed system design. If the system is complex, its detailed system design is divided into subsystems, each of which can be built by a construction team.

GOALS OF INFORMATION ENGINEERING

When practiced well, IE has given massive advantages. It has provided somewhat different advantages in different corporations. If the goals of information engineering (listed in Box 16.2) are achieved, the benefit is great.

The most important goals cannot be achieved without top management involvement. In some enterprises top management are involved; in others a major communication barrier exists between the I.S. management who understand IE and the business management who could reap long-term benefits.

Every top executive today must build a computerized enterprise, and a computerized enterprise cannot be created effectively without information engineering.

To succeed fully, information engineering needs the commitment of top management; it is a corporatewide activity that needs firm direction from the top. The methodology relates to top management planning. When taken to its logical conclusion, it almost always results in the redesign of an enterprise—to streamline it, remove redundancy, enable employees to add more value, and make it most cost competitive.

In some corporations, the primary focus of IE has been on development coordination—how to make separately developed systems work together. In corporations, a chain of processes add value, and the software for these processes should work together like the gears of a well-oiled machine. Separate systems in the value chain are developed by different people in different places at different times. Coordination can only be successful if these separate teams use a common repository. The information in the repository is created by higher level modeling.

In broad terms we can categorize the corporations practicing IE as having three primary goals:

1. Coordination of separately developed systems
2. Maximizing reusability
3. Redesigning the enterprise or business area

The highest payoff from these is likely to be that of redesigning the enterprise. This, however, is not likely to succeed without top management involve-

BOX 16.2 Goals of information engineering (which can be better achieved with OO techniques).

Improve the Enterprise
- Focus I.S. on the goals of the business
- Create models that help top management visualize how the enterprise could be streamlined, restructured, or reinvented
- Link I.S. expenditure to enterprise critical success factors
- Achieve the maximum level of enterprise automation

Redesign Business Areas
- Streamline the enterprise procedures, eliminate unnecessary procedures
- Take maximum advantage of new technology, rethink the entire business area
- Facilitate the redesign of business processes
- Facilitate the redesign of cross-functional streams of activities

Coordinate the Development of Separate Systems
- Create an architectural framework within which separate systems are built
- Achieve integration of systems across the value chain
- Establish an enterprise repository for system development

Maximize Reusability
- Apply the Principle of Occam's Razor to system design across the enterprise
- Establish a high level of reusable design
- Reduce the proliferation of transaction types
- Drastically reduce what has to be maintained

Speed Up Development
- Apply RAD (rapid application development) techniques with repository-based development
- Speed up development by building systems out of existing classes
- Design systems for high-speed maintenance
- Achieve rapid evolution of systems

> **BOX 16.2** *(Continued)*
>
> **Meet User Needs Better**
> - Express business policies in clear rules that are used to generate systems
> - Regenerate systems when business rules change
> - Facilitate fast change of systems
> - Involve end users thoroughly in system planning and design
> - Assist employees in redesigning their business processes, using facilitated workshops

ment. The modeling techniques used must be meaningful to top management. We must enable top management to visualize their enterprise with models that facilitate redesign of the enterprise. This requires good communication and trust between top management and the IE leaders. Many corporations have failed to achieve this goal of IE, and many have not seriously tried to achieve it.

The second highest payoff of the above three goals is that of maximizing reusability. When we build products from reusable, previously tested components, it can be done quickly. A high-quality corporate library of reusable classes evolves slowly and eventually has a high payoff in fast design and low maintenance cost. The mess of the past with massive unnecessary proliferation of separate systems is avoided, or slowly cleaned up.

Reusability is a management act. It requires strong coordination from the top, high-quality design of reusable components, and the overcoming of parochial "not-invented-here" attitudes. Many corporations that have successfully used IE to speed up and coordinate application development have not attempted to achieve design reusability.

Like enterprise modeling, reusability works best with OO techniques.

ENTERPRISE PLANNING

The planning at the top layer of the pyramid takes an enterprisewide viewpoint. Top management should be directly interested in and involved in this level. It should identify the goals and critical success factors. It should indicate how technology can be used as a weapon against competition. It should identify problems and possible solutions.

Enterprise planning creates diagrammed representations of the enterprise that challenge management to think about its structure and how it might be streamlined or changed to better meet its challenges. It takes a corporatewide viewpoint of systems and determines what technology is needed to seize new business opportunities more quickly.

It focuses on how systems will be integrated corporatewide. For example.

- How will they be integrated along the value chain so that information can pass from the sales planning and order-entry systems to the production planning and control systems; to the inventory control and purchasing systems; to the delivery and billing systems; and to the financial control systems?
- How will systems be integrated vertically so that information passes from the low-level operational systems up to the tactical planning systems and up to the executive information systems?

The strategy level is concerned with creating a systems architecture so that changes in procedures can be designed and implemented quickly while preserving the integration along the value chain. In organizations following an object-oriented path, object-structure diagrams and object-flow diagrams model this architecture, as shown in Fig. 16.4.

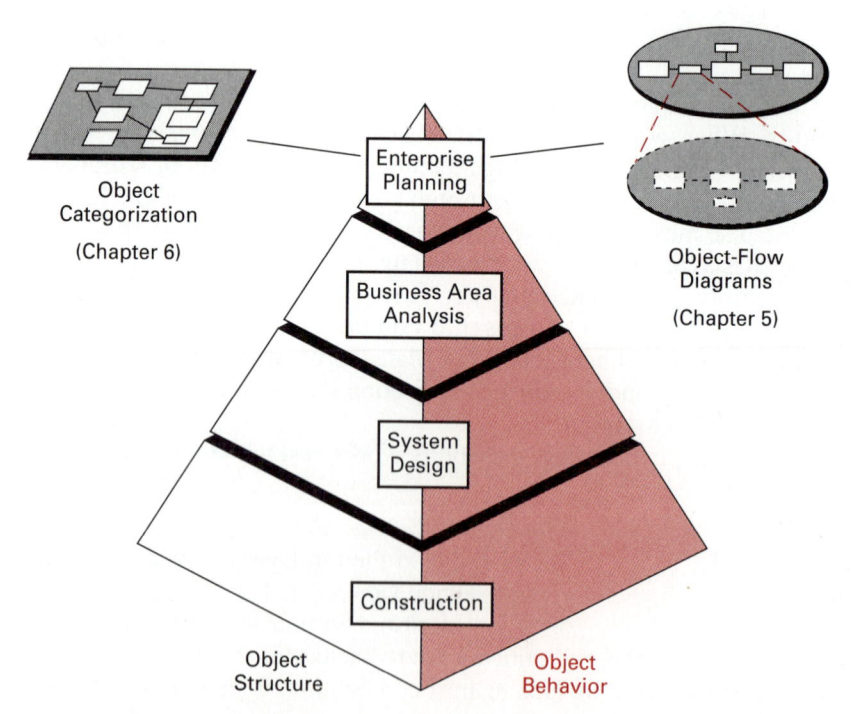

Figure 16.4 The enterprise planning level categorizes objects and uses object-flow diagrams.

BUSINESS AREA ANALYSIS

Business area analysis is done separately for each business area. The results are integrated into the overall repository. High-level object types identified at the enterprise planning level are subtyped into more specialized object types at the business area level. The repository coordinator of the CASE toolset should help to integrate the models created for separate business areas.

A typical business area analysis takes from one to six months, depending on the breadth of the area selected and the speed at which the analysts can operate. Several such studies for different business areas may be done by different teams simultaneously.

Business area analysis does not attempt to design systems; it merely attempts to understand and model the processes and objects required to run the business area. In organizations following an object-oriented path, object-structure diagrams and event diagrams are used to model business areas, as shown in Fig. 16.5.

Business area analysis should also be independent of current systems. The old systems in use in an enterprise often constrain it to continue inefficient procedures with batch processing, dumb terminals, unnecessary keypunching, redundancy, too much paperwork, and the bureaucracy that goes with paperwork. Entirely different procedures may be designed if every knowledge-worker's desk can have a personal computer—online to databases anywhere in the enterprise. A fundamental analysis of what processes are needed often causes a fundamental rethinking of the best way to implement them.

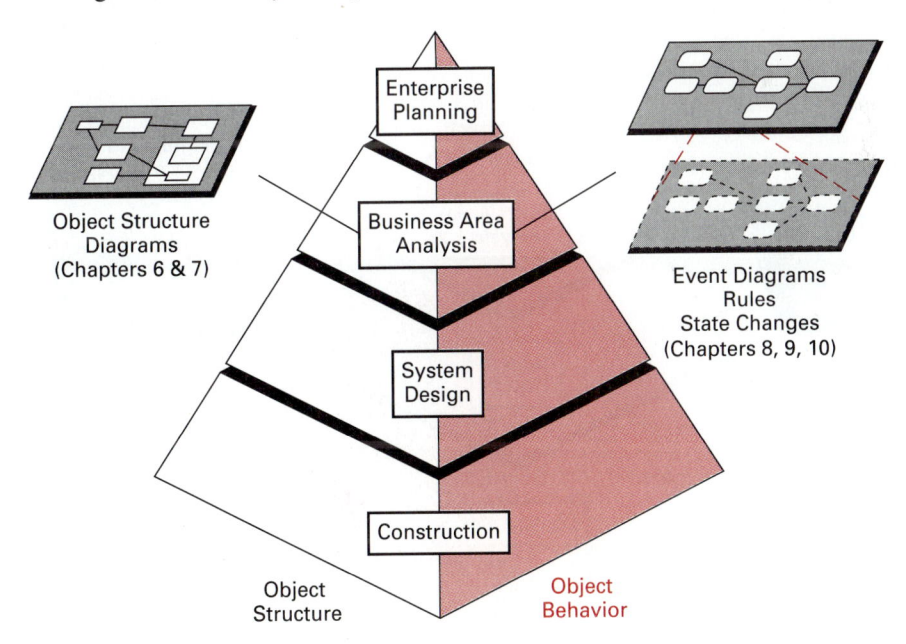

Figure 16.5 Object-oriented BAA uses object schemas and event schemas.

Business area analysis (BAA) has particular characteristics:

- It is conducted separately for each business area with boundary issues handled through the Development Coordination function.
- It creates detailed models of the objects and events in the business area.
- The results are recorded and maintained in the repository.
- It requires intensive user involvement.
- It remains independent of implementation technology.
- It remains independent of current systems and procedures.
- It often causes a rethinking of systems and procedures.
- It identifies areas for system design.

SYSTEM DESIGN   At the third level, OO techniques are used to design the classes and methods for a system (see Fig. 16.6). Object types identified in business area analysis are used to design the classes. Responsibility-driven design (as discussed in Chapter 13) may be used to analyze in detail the behavior of the classes.

User workshops should be used for joint requirements planning (JRP) and joint application design (JAD) as described in Chapter 14. Prototyping tools

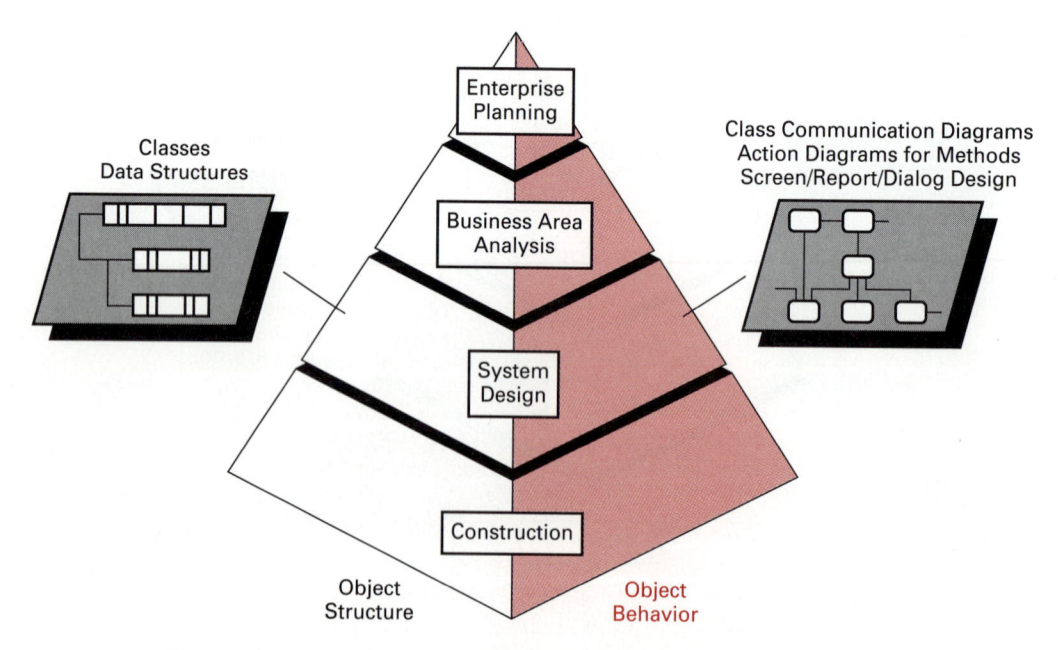

Figure 16.6 System design specifies the classes, their data structure and methods.

should be used for quickly demonstrating the system to users and obtaining their feedback.

CONSTRUCTION

At the construction stage, a code generator should be used, where possible.

The RAD (rapid application development) lifecycle links design and construction, and uses four stages:

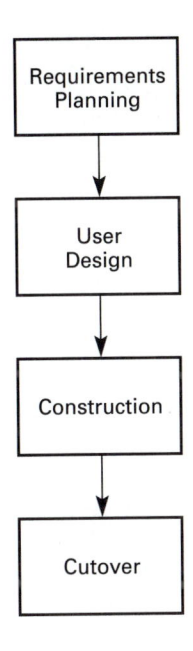

```
Requirements
Planning
    ↓
User
Design
    ↓
Construction
    ↓
Cutover
```

A RAD lifecycle should fit into the framework of enterprise planning and business-area analysis. The better the enterprise models in the repository, the faster the RAD lifecycle is likely to be. The RAD lifecycle should employ reusable classes to the maximum extent.

ANALYSIS FOR REUSABILITY

We have emphasized that one of the most powerful properties of IE is the construction of systems from existing components. A system may be constructed from reusable building blocks, or an existing design may be modified to create a new application.

To maximize the value of reusability, large-scale planning is needed. Reusable design should be a major goal of information engineering. In most large enterprises, many systems exist that do almost the same functions. There are multiple order-entry systems, multiple inventory-control systems, and so on. These systems have been separately designed and coded, as well as, separately maintained—which is expensive.

Analysis for reusability establishes the common procedures and subprocedures that are needed across an enterprise. An attempt is made to create these from a single set of basic designs rather than from multiple sets of designs. The basic designs are kept in an I-CASE repository and can be easily adapted to the needs of separate systems.

Object-Oriented Analysis

Object-oriented analysis identifies the object types in an enterprise, as well as their properties. Object subtypes *inherit* the properties of their parents. Behavior is associated with object types. Therefore, the object will exhibit that behavior regardless of the specific application.

Instead of being associated with one object type, some processing routines are associated with a relationship between two or more object types (e.g., when a **Customer** places an **Order**, when a **Passenger** makes or changes a **Reservation**, or when a **Warehouse** ships a **Delivery**). Certain reports must be printed, certain information must be filed, or a given user dialog must occur. Particular validation checks must be applied, and an audit trail must be maintained, regardless of the location, department, type of warehouse, or type of application. Procedures should be designed and programmed that are reusable across the enterprise (rather than being designed and programmed uniquely for each project).

OO modeling makes it clear that the same object types are used in numerous applications. Whenever they are used, certain routines may be invoked, such as computing derived attributes, applying integrity checks, or creating summary data. A corporation may have many factories that, to a large extent, have the same object types.

Many of the data-processing procedures may be the same from one factory to another; some will be entirely different. The accounting and reporting should be the same in each factory, so that higher-level management can make comparisons. Dialogs programmed for data entry, updating, reporting, and so on should be common across applications and locations. HELP panels should be common. Certain screen designs, user dialogs, validation routines, and so on may be needed whenever an object type is employed. OO templates of business operation may be used in multiple factories or locations. When a better way of doing business is designed in one location it should be transferred to other locations and modified as appropriate. OO models, as well as classes, are reusable.

Often, the processing done on an object or the dialog used is not identical from one process to another, but is sufficiently close that the same code or dialog can be used after minor modifications. The end user would like the different application to look similar and have a common dialog style in order to increase familiarity and minimize the training needs. *Similar* processes should be identified in order to minimize the subsequent design, coding, and training requirements.

Modeling must be applied to one business area or value stream at a time, or models become unwieldy and the team bogs down. Nevertheless, some object types and their operations will be used outside that business area. The *enterprisewide* object types are discovered (at a summary level) during the top-level study and are recorded in the repository. During business area analysis, the object types and operations having applicability beyond that business area should be marked in the repository. When other business areas are analyzed, the common object types and operations will be identified in detail, so that procedures can be designed to span business areas.

ENTERPRISEWIDE IMPLEMENTATION

The most spectacular examples of reusable design and code are generally found in corporations that have done information engineering with a repository-based, I-CASE toolset.

One large organization, confronted with new types of competition, set out to rebuild its collection of core I.S. systems over a five-year period. Its business goals were to

- Create an environment that would enable it to generate new services or respond to new business opportunities significantly faster than its competition.
- Undercut its competition by being able to build new services at a lower cost.
- Streamline its operations, making them less expensive.
- Provide better service to customers by giving, for example, customized services as opposed to off-the-shelf packages.

Top management endorsed these business goals fully. To achieve them, more technical goals were added:

- Maximize reusability of design throughout the entire enterprise by building a library of reusable classes.
- Generate code for all new applications using CASE tools.
- Drastically reduce the proliferation of separate applications that need separate, expensive maintenance.

At the enterprise planning level, the enterprise identified the highest-level object types. Each of these, such as **Customer**, **Account**, and **Employee**, was placed at the top of a generalization hierarchy. All lower-level object types were subtypes of these.

At the BAA (business area analysis) level, the enterprise identified *business conceptual objects*—the next level below the top. These were further decomposed into objects that were variants of the business conceptual objects.

Prior to this OO analysis of the corporation, the enterprise had nearly 2000 transaction codes, each with its own separate program. Maintaining this large collection of programs was expensive. The programs could be replaced with a relatively small number of classes, each with its own methods and subclasses with some new methods.

This analysis was done with a CASE toolset that was also used for designing the methods. Code for the methods was generated with a code generator. While neither of these tools was designed for object-oriented development, both could be adapted to support the OO paradigm. Indeed, development would be smoother if an integrated OO toolset were used.

When the enterprise had established its class library, with some application classes developed in-house and other application-independent classes coming from a software vendor, it could assemble new applications at high speed.

A lesson learned from this experience was that the planning and modeling take a long time. It is essential to drive downward from the models to some live working systems as quickly as possible. This provides a reality test of the process and provides some early financial benefits, which give the process credibility with higher management.

HUMAN COORDINATION

As reusability becomes a way of life in an enterprise, more applications can be built from reusable components. A system designer requiring a class must first find out whether a similar class exists that he can use or adapt. If so, he uses it; if not, he creates a class in such a way that it might be reused in the future by some other analyst. Similarly, models or templates of business operations are reused, to transfer good designs and minimize the modeling effort. All development, thus, relates to reuse of existing classes or models or the design of classes or models with future reuse potential.

After this pattern of development has been in place for some years, a high level of reusability is achieved. One characteristic of reusability is that the facilities for reusability take time to build up, but they eventually enable an enterprise to create most applications rapidly. OO-CASE companies ought to sell classes that handle most of the application-independent operations associated with screens, reports, and databases.

Human coordination of the reusable components stored in the repository is necessary. A development team might create new classes or improve upon an existing class. The reusability coordinator must decide whether to make the new class generally available in the repository. It is important that the central repository of reusable classes does not become a mess. The classes should be carefully cataloged. A knowledgeable human decision is needed regarding when to store a new version of a class and whether the old version must be retained.

A class that is reused hundreds of times needs to be very carefully designed and debugged. The higher the class in the class hierarchy, the more it is reused. Therefore, the best analysts and designers ought to work on the classes highest in the hierarchy.

Some I.S. organizations have divided the staff into people who build classes for the class library and people who build applications by employing classes from the class library. The former group are measured by the degree to which their classes are reused, the latter in terms of how rapidly they can build applications by using or modifying existing classes.

All Levels of the Pyramid

At all levels of the information-engineering pyramid, there should be a search for commonality. Commonality of object types is usually obvious in building the object-structure diagrams. Common objects should be identified at the *planning* level, common processes at the *analysis* level, and common procedures, screens, dialogs, and methods at the *design* level.

In order to find commonality, a central repository is essential. Analysts in different places use a shared repository that steadily accumulates knowledge of the enterprise. When an analyst is planning a procedure that uses an object type, the repository will inform him what other procedures use that object type, so that he can employ common modules where possible. Usually, a central group reporting to a chief information engineer (or equivalent) helps ensure that common modules are used where possible.

When a code generator is driven from a design workbench, the primary reusability emphasis may be on reusable design. Classes that are reusable are stored in the repository and modified, if necessary, before code is generated.

An advantage of information engineering done with object-oriented techniques is that the conceptual model is the same at each of the four levels of the pyramid. Analysis, design, programming, database definition, and access all use essentially the same conceptual model (see Fig. 5.3). The enterprise model at the ISP and BAA levels should be as meaningful as possible to business people. They can think of their world in terms of business objects, the events that occur, and the business rules that ought to control those events. The high-level models are expanded into detail as we progress lower in the pyramid but have the same conceptual framework. The high-level analyst establishes an overview with high-level objects, and the lower-level designer adds detail to those objects.

The object types in the enterprise model become active objects when they are implemented. If implemented with OO databases, they retain essentially the same form they have in the model.

REFERENCES

1. Bassett, Paul, Communication from Paul Bassett, Vice President, Netron Inc., Downsview, Ontario, 1990.

2. Martin, James, *Information Engineering,* Prentice-Hall, Englewood Cliffs, NJ, 1990.

3. Martin, James, *Rapid Application Development,* Macmillan, New York, 1991.

PART III TOOLS

17 OBJECT-ORIENTED PROGRAMMING LANGUAGES

THE GENESIS OF OO TECHNOLOGY

The genesis of the technology now called *object-oriented* dates back to the early 1960s. It arose from the need to describe and simulate a variety of phenomena such as nerve networks, communications systems, traffic flow, production systems, administrative systems, and even social systems. In the spring of 1961, Kristen Nygaard originated the ideas for a language that would serve the dual purpose of system description and simulation programming. Together with Ole-Johan Dahl, Nygaard developed the simulation language now known as Simula I. The first Simula-based application package was implemented for the simulation of logic circuits. However, operations research applications were the most popular usage. For example, in 1965 a large and complex job shop simulation was programmed in less than four weeks—with an execution efficiency at least four times higher than that of available technology [4,10].

Simula was intended to be a system description and simulation programming language. However, its users quickly discovered that Simula also provided new and powerful facilities when used for purposes *other than* simulation, such as prototyping and application development. In September 1965, the possibilities of a "new, improved Simula" as a general purpose language were being planned. By December 1966, the necessary foundation for the new, general programming language, called Simula 67, was defined.

SMALLTALK

In the late 1960s, another development of OO technology was under way, guided by research at the University of Utah and by the central ideas of Simula. Alan Kay envisioned that by the 1980s

[B]oth adults and children will be able to have as a personal possession a computer about the size of a notebook with the power to handle virtually all their information-related needs. . . . Ideally the personal computer will be designed in such a way that all ages and walks of life can mold and channel its power to their own needs [7].

Early in the 1970s, Alan Kay went to Xerox and formed the Learning Research Group. Xerox was responsible for producing the interim model for the personal computer, called Dynabook. The group was engaged to produce the software, called Smalltalk. They quickly realized that one of the major design problems involved expressive communication—particularly when children were seriously considered as users. For this reason, the group invited some 250 children (aged six to fifteen) and 50 adults to try versions of Smalltalk and suggest ways of improving it. In order to test the usability of Smalltalk, they started with simple situations that embodied a *concept* and gradually increased the complexity of the examples. A major goal of Smalltalk was providing a single name (or symbol) for a complex collection of ideas. Later, these ideas could be invoked and manipulated through the name. They found that children by the age of six were able to do this.

While the Dynabook project did not realize its goal, Smalltalk evolved into an important OO language. Alan Kay foresaw the need to characterize and communicate application *concepts* in developing computer programs. Smalltalk provides the means to write programs in a style that brings our concepts to life. The term *object-oriented* originated during the development of Smalltalk [1, 6].

THE EVOLUTION FROM UNTYPED TO TYPED LANGUAGES

The kinds, or *types*, of data on which a program can operate need to be organized. Initially, only one data type described the universe of bit strings in a computer memory—the data type Word. Words are bit strings of fixed size that can be used as units of information.

The need for data types arises whenever data must be categorized for a particular usage. As early as 1954, FORTRAN distinguished between Integer and Floating-point types of data. Later, Algol 60 incorporated data types for Integer, Real, and Boolean. Still later, languages included additional data types, such as the Character, String, Bit, Byte, Array, Pointer, Record, File, and Procedure.

A *data type* describes a certain kind of data—its representation and the set of valid operations that access and maintain that data. In this way, each data type is a known commodity, protected from unintended use. For example, the data type Character describes the kind of data that is displayable by a program. Furthermore, a set of operations is provided for creating, destroying, examining, and manipulating Character data. Since arithmetic operations such as add and subtract are not defined for Character data, computational requests are not permitted [9].

USER-DEFINED TYPES (UDTs)

Prior to the early 1970s, a programmer could reference only those data types built into a programming language compiler. As a result, even often-used types such as **Month, Date, Time, Coefficient, Tree,** and **Stack** were not explicitly accessible. These ideas had to be implicitly embedded somewhere in the programmer's code. An additional limiting characteristic of built-in types was their definition by the way in which the information was physically stored. They had little useful relationship to the real-world objects that the application was trying to implement.

Eventually, the computer industry felt pressured to provide programmers with a facility for expressing their own typing needs. The first languages to offer *user-defined types* (UDTs) were Pascal and Algol 68. In Pascal, for example, a programmer could write

> type month = (January, February, March, April, May, June, July, August, September, October, November, December);

This expression defines the UDT **Month** as being the set of twelve literals. The developer could define relational operations to compare two given **Month** variables for less than, equal to, and so on. Other operations could include computing the preceding or succeeding month when supplied with a **Month** variable.

The *types* of Pascal and the *nodes* of Algol 68 were an important step forward. They permitted the programmer to go from manufacturer-imposed types to user-imposed types. UDTs raised the expressive power of programming languages. More importantly, they encouraged systems developers to translate the real-world types of the system application into coded data types.

ABSTRACT DATA TYPES (ADTs)

The *abstract data type* (ADT) extends the notion of the *user-defined type* (UDT) by adding encapsulation.

The ADT contains the representation and the operations of a data type. The *encapsulation* feature of the ADT not only hides the data type's implementation but provides a protective wall that shields its objects from improper use. All interfacing occurs through named *operations* defined within the ADT. The operations, then, provide a well-defined means for accessing the objects of a data type. In short, ADTs give objects a *public* interface through its permitted operations. However, the representations and executable code, or *method,* for each operation are *private*.

The ADT facility first appeared in Simula 67. Its implementation is called a *class*. Modula refers to its ADT implementation as a *module,* while Ada uses the word *package*. In all cases, the ADT provides a way for the systems developer to identify real-world data types and package them in a more convenient and compact form. In this way, ADTs can be defined for things such as **Dates, Screen Panels, Customer Orders,** and **Part Requisitions**. Once defined, the developer can address the ADTs directly in future operations.

Figure 17.1 illustrates an example of the ADT named **Employee**. At its heart, the ADT is defined by its data structure representation. For **Employee**, this includes data about exemptions, position, salary amount, phone extension, and so on. The ADT is also defined by a set of permissible operations. These operations—such as hire, promote, and change phone extension—provide a suit of armor that protects the underlying **Employee** structure from arbitrary and unintended use. In other words, the **Employee** operations provide the only method of accessing and maintaining the data of an **Employee**.

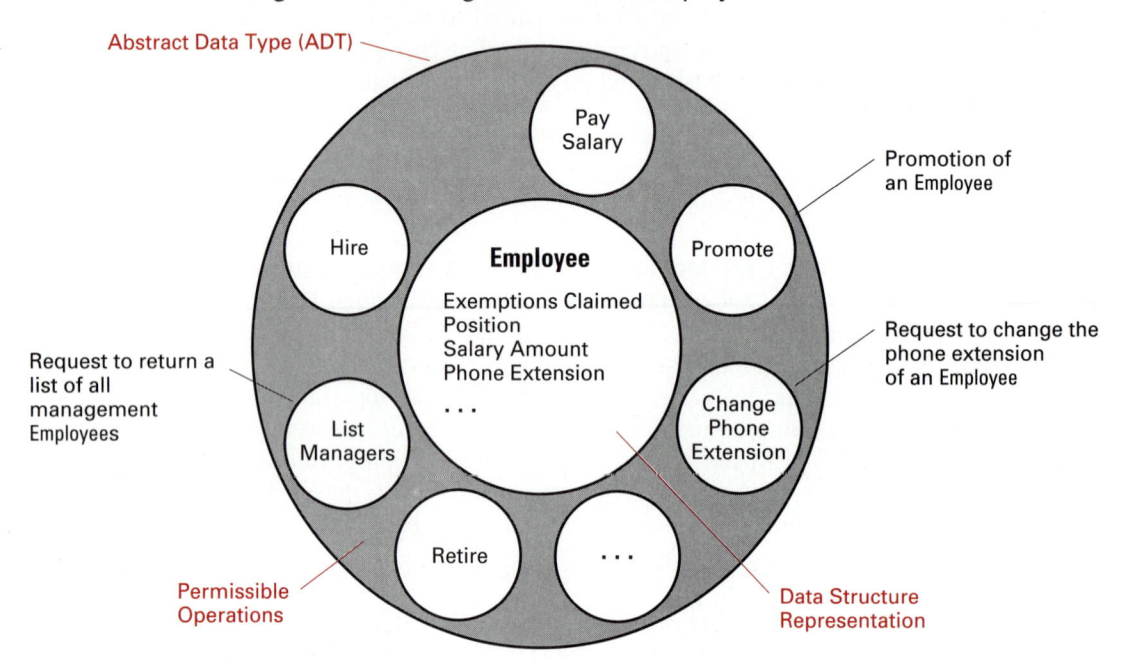

Figure 17.1 Objects are accessible only by named operations; all else is hidden.

Additionally, each *method* or processing algorithm, employed to carry out an operation, is hidden from its users. What the user must provide is an appropriate object to *request* the operation along with any applicable supporting parameters. For example, Fig. 17.2 depicts three instances, or *objects,* of **Employee**. In order to give Bob a promotion, the request must specify Bob, the promote operation, and the salary grade of his promotion. In its abbreviated form, this request could be written: Bob, promote, director.

Objects as Encapsulations

Figure 17.2 depicts three **Employee** objects as specific representations of the **Employee** ADT. In this way, an object can be regarded as any instance of an abstract data type—each encapsulating its own private data and its own permissi-

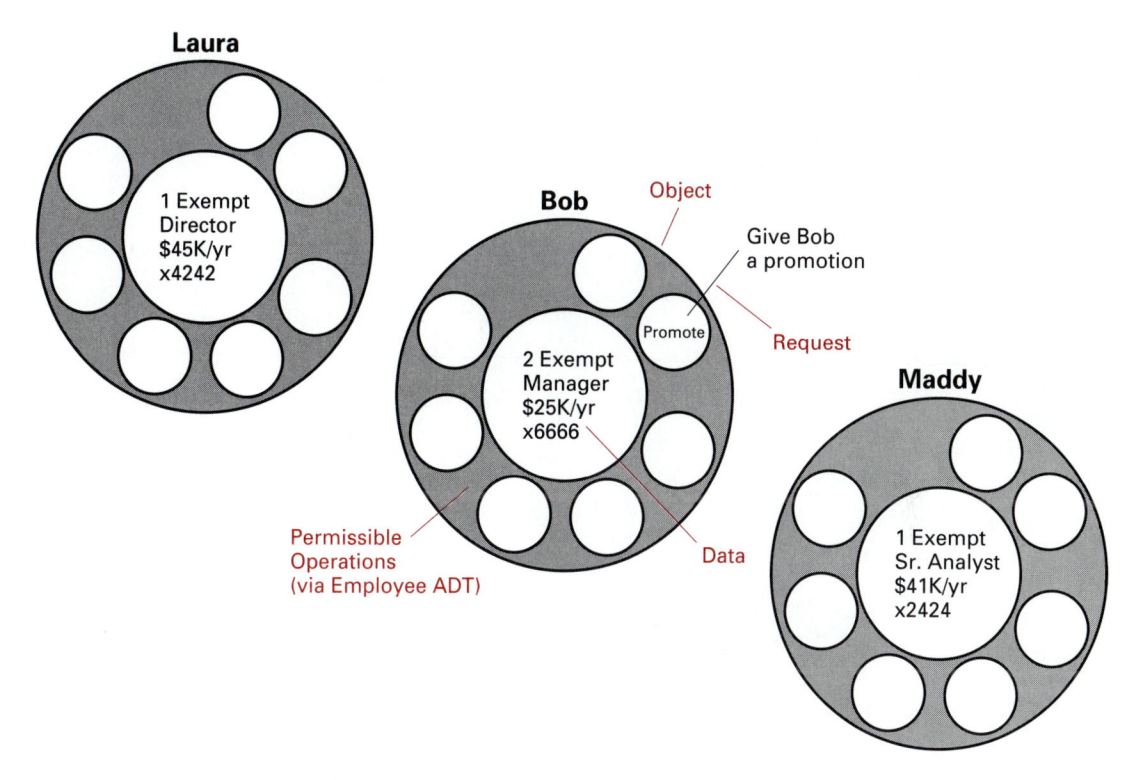

Figure 17.2 An object's permissible operations are defined by its ADT.

ble operations. Each object can be considered as a thing in its own right, with its own behavior. While each object should encapsulate a physical record of its own data, encapsulating a physical copy of each operational method is unnecessary and wasteful. Since the same coding is contained within each ADT, an ADT's operations need only be *virtually* available to an object. In other words, all operations that apply to a particular ADT also apply to the instances of that ADT. As illustrated in Fig. 17.3, since Bob is an instance of the **Employee** ADT, all **Employee** operations (such as promote) also apply to Bob—without the object having to contain them physically. When an object is an instance of an ADT, this linkage is established. Most ADT-oriented languages accomplish this with a physical pointer mechanism.

OBJECTS AND REQUESTS

With encapsulation, each object need only know *what* it can request of another object, because operations are the *public* interface for all objects. All the specifics of *how* its structure is stored and *how* its operations are coded are tucked neatly out of sight. This not only protects each object, it simplifies the

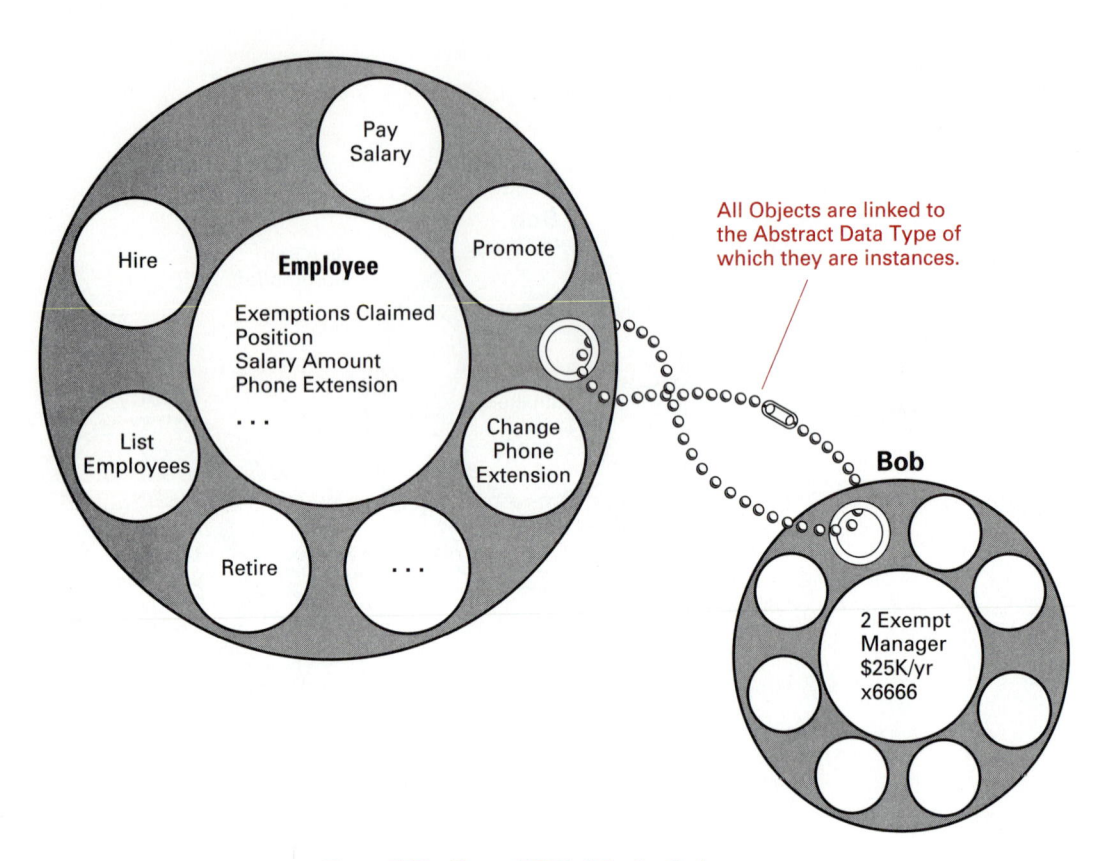

Figure 17.3 Every ADT is linked to its instances.

interactions among objects. Most OO languages call these interactions *messages*. For instance, a **Customer** object can send a message to an **Order** object to add a product to its already existing line items. The **Order** object, in turn, may send a message to a **Customer Account** object with a request to update the amount due for the customer.

The standard term emerging for a message is a *request* (Fig. 17.4). A request is a more general notion, because more than one object can participate in a request. For instance, to which object is a message sent so that a **Part** can be placed in a **Bin**: the **Part** or the **Bin**? A request involves both by specifying the **Part** and **Bin** objects as parameters along with the operation name. It then lets the method selection mechanism locate the appropriate method for placing inventory. In short, requests expand the notion of message by indicating: With *these* objects, do this.

INHERITANCE AND POLYMORPHISM

Inheritance is an important feature of OO design. While different OO programming languages have different inheritance mechanisms, we can think about

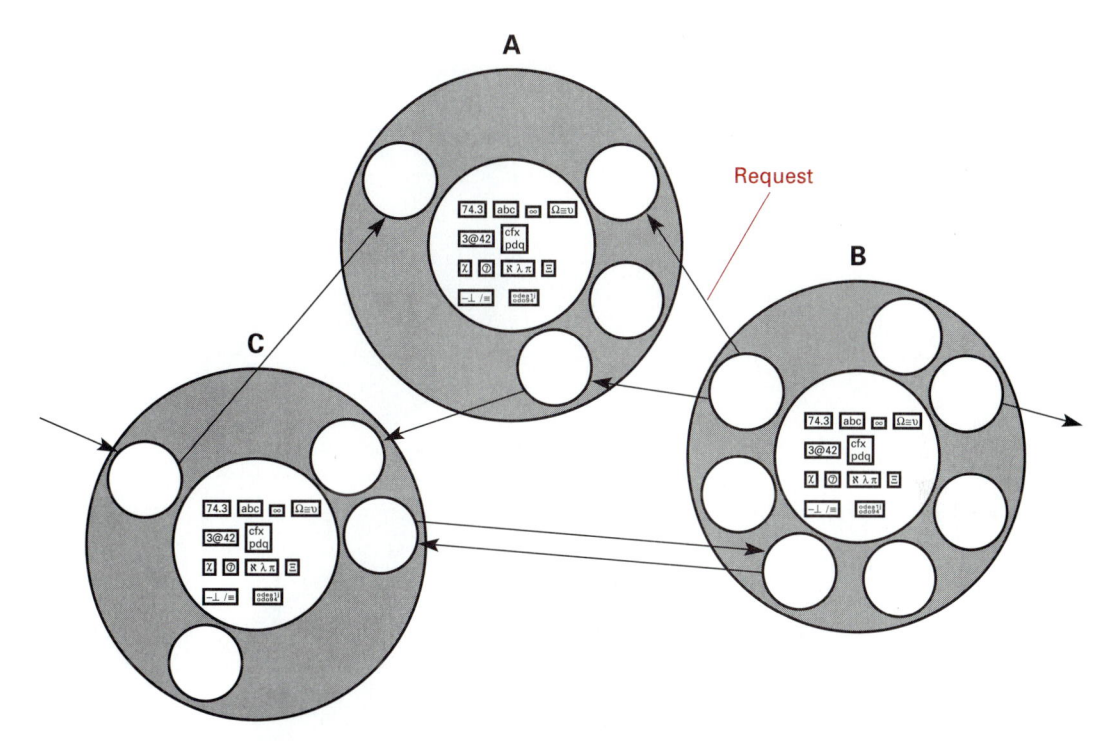

Figure 17.4 The operation of one object *requests* the operation of another.

them in the following way. When a request for an operation goes to a subclass, the list of permissible operations of that class is checked. If the operation is found on the list, it is invoked; if not, the parent classes are examined to locate the operation.

An important feature of inheritance is the ability of a class to *override* inherited features. Here, the processing algorithm, or *method,* of an inherited operation can be redefined at the subtype level. The example in Fig. 17.5 illustrates three classes. The most general, **Polygon**, contains the data structure and permissible operations for polygons. Because every instance of a **Rectangle** is also an instance of a **Polygon**, the **Rectangle** subtype need not repeat those features it inherits from **Polygon**. However, while all **Polygon** operations apply to subtypes, the *method* of operation may be different. For example, the method of rotating a **Polygon** is the same as rotating a **Rectangle**. However, the method of computing perimeters may differ. The perimeter of a **Polygon** is the sum of all its sides; the perimeter of a **Rectangle** is the sum of two of its adjacent sides multiplied by two. The **Square** perimeter differs again as the product of multiplying four times the length of any one side.

Whenever a request is made for an operation on an object, the method selected depends on whether or not the inheritance hierarchy has been overrid-

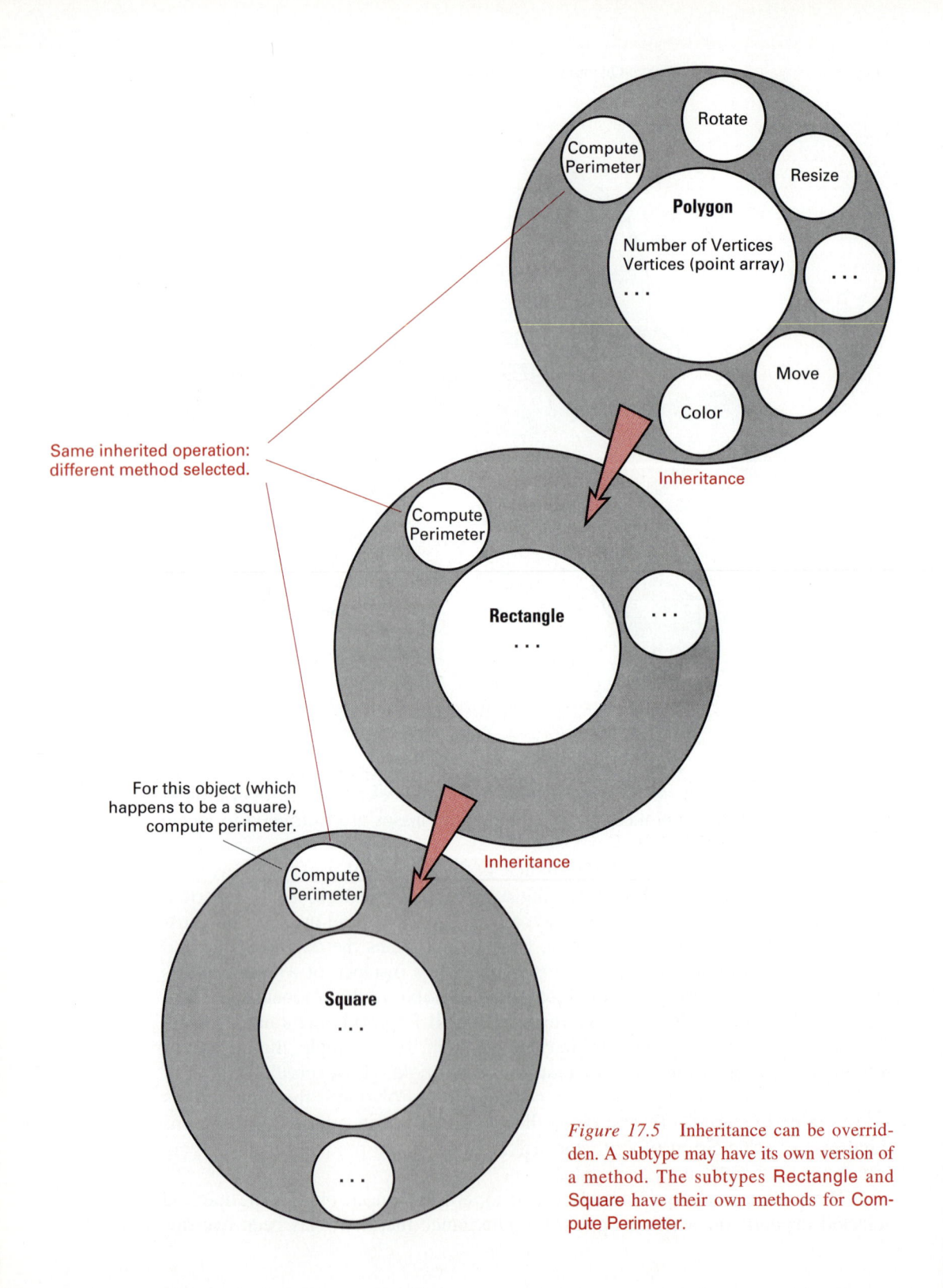

Figure 17.5 Inheritance can be overridden. A subtype may have its own version of a method. The subtypes Rectangle and Square have their own methods for Compute Perimeter.

den. The method for moving a **Square** three centimeters to the right is selected from **Polygon**. However, even though the *operation* for compute perimeter is inherited from the **Polygon**, the *method* selected for a **Square** is located in the **Square** class. This approach to overriding inheritance properties through redefinition is often referred to as a category of *polymorphism* known as *parametric polymorphism* [2]. An *operation,* then, is the kind of process being requested. Its *method* is the specification of how to carry out the operation.

CANCELING INHERITED FEATURES   Some expert systems in AI allow some inherited features to be canceled. For example, one of the features of **Birds** includes flying. However, this feature does not apply to **Penguin**s and **Ostrich**es. Therefore, this feature can be canceled. The arbitrary overriding and canceling of inherited features is a questionable practice. Logically it is incorrect, because, by definition, all features of a type apply to its subtypes. Therefore, to rectify the problem of **Birds** flying and **Penguins** not, the subtyping hierarchy needs to be changed. To solve this, **Bird** can be specialized into two subtypes: **Flying Bird** and **Nonflying Bird**. Following this, all the data structures and operations relating to flying should be shifted from **Bird** to **Flying Bird**. Types such as **Penguin** and **Ostrich** should then be realigned as subtypes of **Nonflying Bird**. This would correct the logical inconsistency. However, *physically* it might create an intolerable system overhead. For this reason, some languages allow the programmer to deviate from what is logically correct—for the sake of performance.

CHARACTERISTICS OF OO LANGUAGES   To be described as an OO programming language, a language must support

- *Classes and encapsulation.* Each class has certain kinds of data. Each class protects its data from improper use by offering a number of permissible operations. To accomplish this, both the data representation and its permissible operations are veiled with a protective covering that hides the details of its implementation.

- *Method selection.* With method selection, the user need only specify which operation should be applied to an object (or in more expanded languages, one or more objects). The system will then choose the method appropriate for the specified parameters. In other words, the user only needs to specify what is to be done, and the method selector determines how it is to be applied. Polymorphism is one of the common applications of method selection.

- *Inheritance.* Classes inherit the data types and methods of higher level classes. Inheritance allows systems to be constructed from existing class hierarchies. It provides mechanisms for both construction and reuse of software. In this way, we do not have to reinvent the wheel—only the portion of it that is different. Inheritance imposes a mechanism on classes that greatly reduces the complexity of the resulting systems.

Some OO languages support multiple inheritance; others support inheritance from only one parent class.

PURE VERSUS HYBRID OO LANGUAGES

Some OO languages have been designed specifically for OO programming with objects, encapsulation, method selection, and inheritance. Smalltalk was the first language developed purely for OO programming. Following Smalltalk, Actor and Eiffel evolved as *pure* OO languages.

Other languages used for OO programming are traditional languages that have had the capability added to them to handle objects, method selection, and inheritance. These are referred to as *hybrid* languages. The preeminent hybrid language C++, an extension of C, is currently the most commonly used language for OO programming. C++ uses a preprocessor that converts C++ code into C code, ready for compilation.

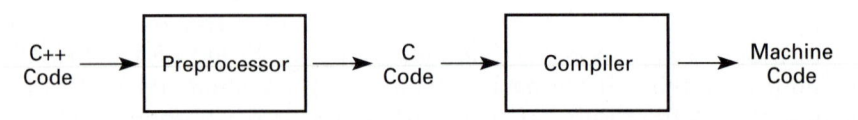

C++ Code → Preprocessor → C Code → Compiler → Machine Code

Following the lead of C++, various traditional languages have been adapted for OO programming. Object PASCAL evolved from PASCAL, CLOS from LISP, Objective-C from C, and Object COBOL from COBOL. This evolution of languages is shown in Fig. 17.6.

Traditional compilers can be used with hybrid languages by means of a preprocessor:

OO Language → Preprocessor → Traditional Language → Compiler → Machine Code

An advantage of adding OO capability to an existing language is that the users of that language learn an extension of what they already know, rather than a completely new language.

This evolutionary learning path, however, has a severe disadvantage. OO thinking is very different from traditional structured thinking, and hybrid languages encourage programmers to think in the way they are used to thinking. The programmers then tend to do traditional functional decomposition and use structure charts rather than think in terms of classes and inheritance. They tend to think in terms of data-flow diagrams rather than event diagrams. Many C++ programmers are using procedural code instead of OO methods, requests, and inheritance. They do not convert fully to the OO mindset.

Often, the best way to make a C programmer learn to use C++ in an OO fashion is to make him program in Smalltalk for six months. The problem with

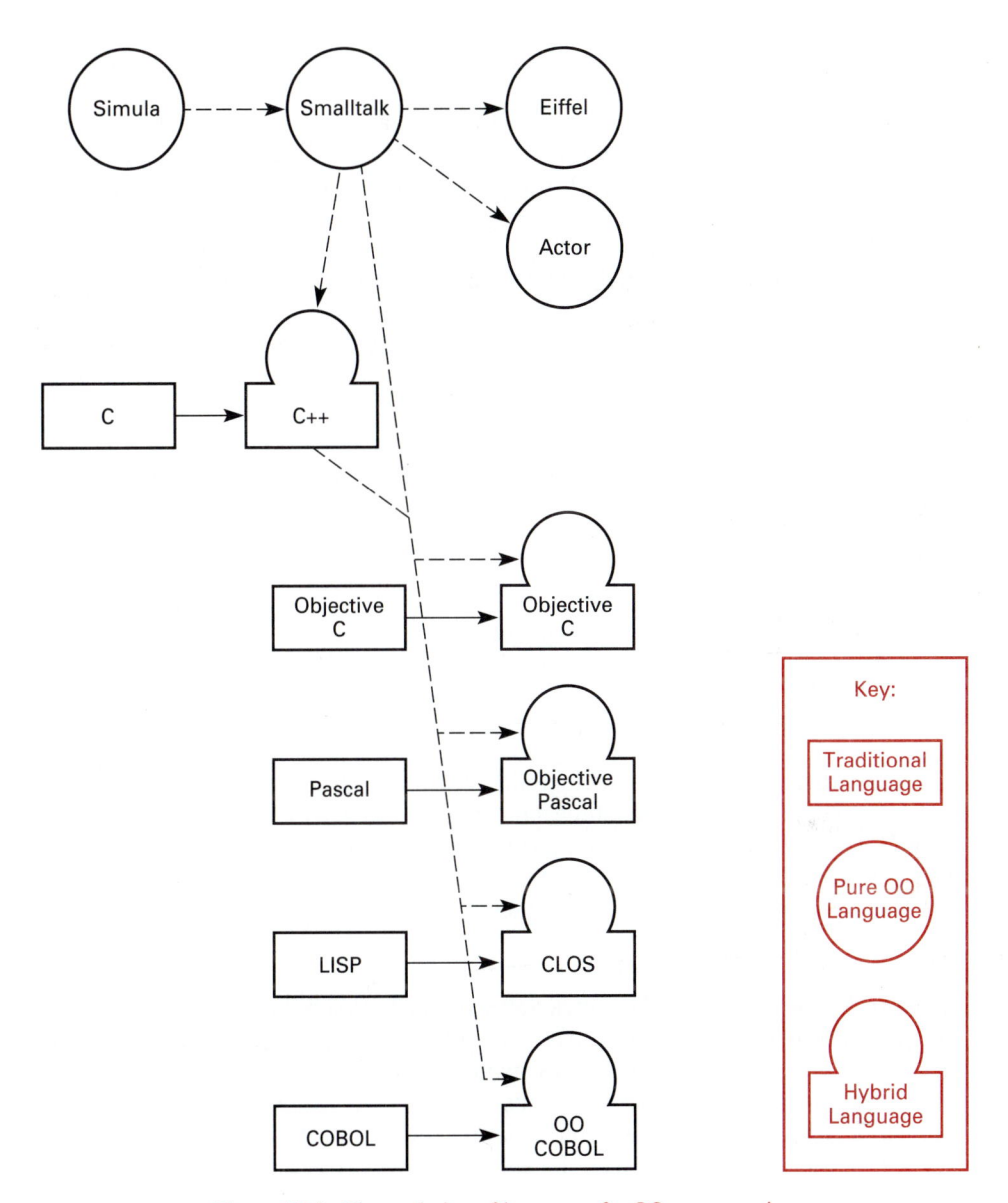

Figure 17.6 The evolution of languages for OO programming.

this is that he might not want to leave Smalltalk, which often stimulates creativity better than C++.

C++ has been referred to as a horseless carriage. The first automobiles were called horseless carriages because they looked like traditional carriages with the horse removed and a motor added. Because hybrid OO languages look like traditional languages, they tend to encourage traditional thinking—which is difficult to unlearn.

For a *new* programmer, the pure OO languages are easier to learn than the hybrid languages. Smalltalk is fairly simple and uses English-like constructs. New programmers tend to learn it quickly. However, C++ is particularly difficult to learn because it requires two stages of learning. The programmer must first learn C, which is a low-level language originally created for programming operating systems, and then the OO additions to C, which are unnecessarily difficult.

Pure OO languages, used well, have several advantages over traditional programming:

- easier learning
- reduction of complexity (a McCabe metric of 3 rather than 10)
- easier debugging
- reusable classes
- reusability from inheritance
- complexities hidden by encapsulation
- easier to make changes
- hence greater creativity

This increased power and flexibility for the programmer has a price. Pure OO languages often give machine performance lower than hybrid languages. Like C, C++ is a fast, compact language, finely tuned for high-speed execution. The performance disadvantage is steadily being overcome with better design of optimizing compilers for pure OO languages.

ENFORCEMENT OF DISCIPLINE OO advantages are achieved because of the discipline associated with encapsulation and inheritance. Hybrid languages make it only too easy to avoid this discipline. Programmers often bypass encapsulation in favor of a quick solution. This can cause debugging problems and make it much more difficult to make subsequent modifications to programs. It generally lowers the quality and reusability of the code.

> Enforcement of OO principles, with their substantial benefits, is an argument for using *pure*, rather than hybrid, OO languages. Similarly, at a higher level, it is an argument for using pure, rather than hybrid CASE tools.

INTERPRETERS VERSUS COMPILERS

An OO language should be interpretive, which enables the programmer to run the code as soon as he creates it. As he makes minor changes, he can immediately run them without waiting for the entire program to be relinked. This immediate running of changes enables the programmer to be more creative—quickly catching errors and observing the effect of changes.

Imagine a sculptor not being able to see changes he makes to his sculpture until some time later in the day when it is "compiled." This would drastically reduce the sculptor's ability to be creative. In a similar way, we want to increase the ability of the programmer to be creative.

A problem with interpreters is that they generally give worse machine performance than compilers. Optimizing compilers take multiple passes through the code linking it in such a way as to achieve the best machine performance. However, languages using conventional compilers limit creativity, because each small change requires relinking the whole program which takes from minutes to hours.

Some OO languages solve this problem by means of a *dynamic compiler*. This compiles a *method* (rather than compiling entire programs) whenever the method is encountered. It keeps a pool of recently compiled methods in the main memory to avoid recompilation whenever possible. This is a compromise between traditional interpreters and compilers. The programmer can run changes when he makes them, and the efficiency of runtime execution is high (Fig. 17.7).

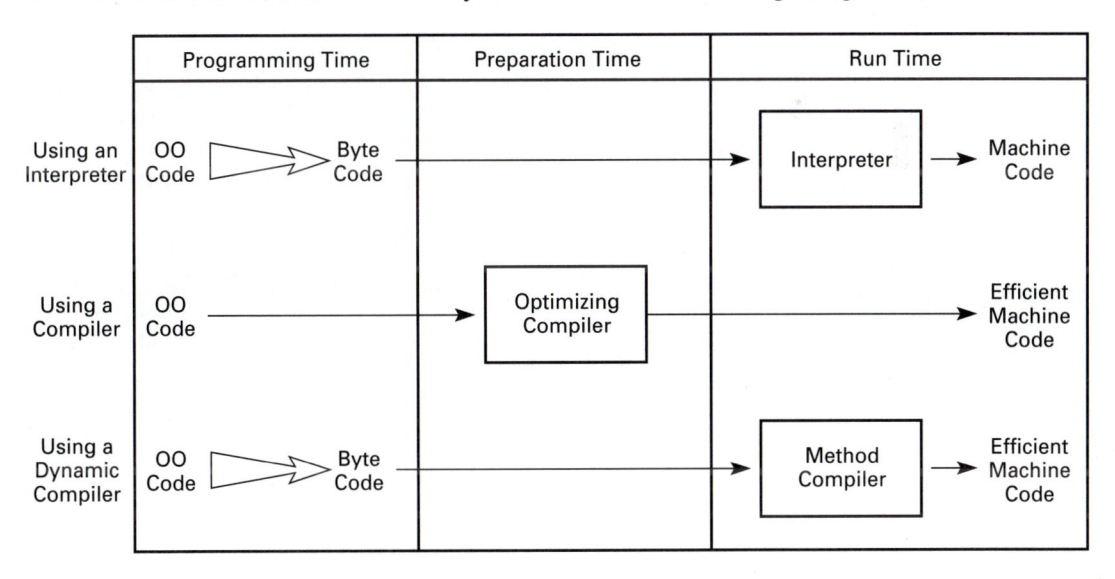

Figure 17.7 To maximize programmer creativity, the programmer should be able to execute changes as soon as he makes them—with no delay between programming time and runtime. This is achieved by using an interpreter or dynamic compiler.

To allow the programmer to interact immediately with evolving code and to achieve the best machine performance, a language should have both an interpreter for use during development and a compiler for use when the program is run (Fig. 17.8).

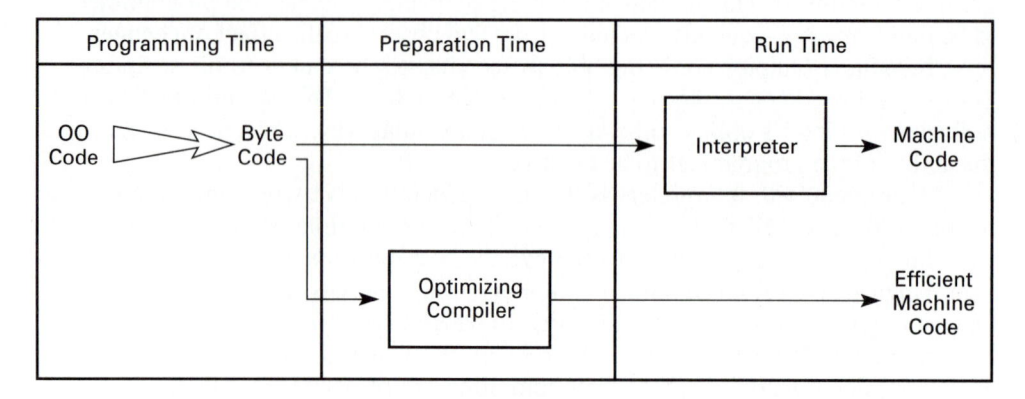

Figure 17.8 To maximize programmer productivity and machine performance, an OO language may have both an interpreter and an optimizing compiler.

POINTERS

OO software uses many pointers. Each object is linked to its class with a pointer mechanism. Finding the right method in a class hierarchy needs pointers. When an object sends requests to other objects, pointers are used.

The *fields* in an object may contain pointers to other objects. In order to point to an object, each object must be uniquely identifiable.

Figure 17.9 shows two **Musical Composition** objects. Each contains a pointer to a **Composer** object, Beethoven in this case. The **Musical Composition** objects have attributes to which it also points, such as *opus number* and *composition name;* the **Composer** object has attributes, such as *composer name, year of birth,* and *year of death.*

An OO language must provide a good pointer mechanism. This employs unique object identifiers (IDs). The object IDs should be automatically assigned and maintained by the system; the system ensures that they are unique. The pointer links are built by the software either at compilation time or runtime.

Object IDs have important advantages. They are small and require minimal storage. They are much smaller than human-readable names or references based on content. The pointer to the object can be followed quickly. The object can be located with tables, regardless of where it is stored. The ID is independent of the object content. Every variable in the object can be changed and the pointer still points to the correct object.

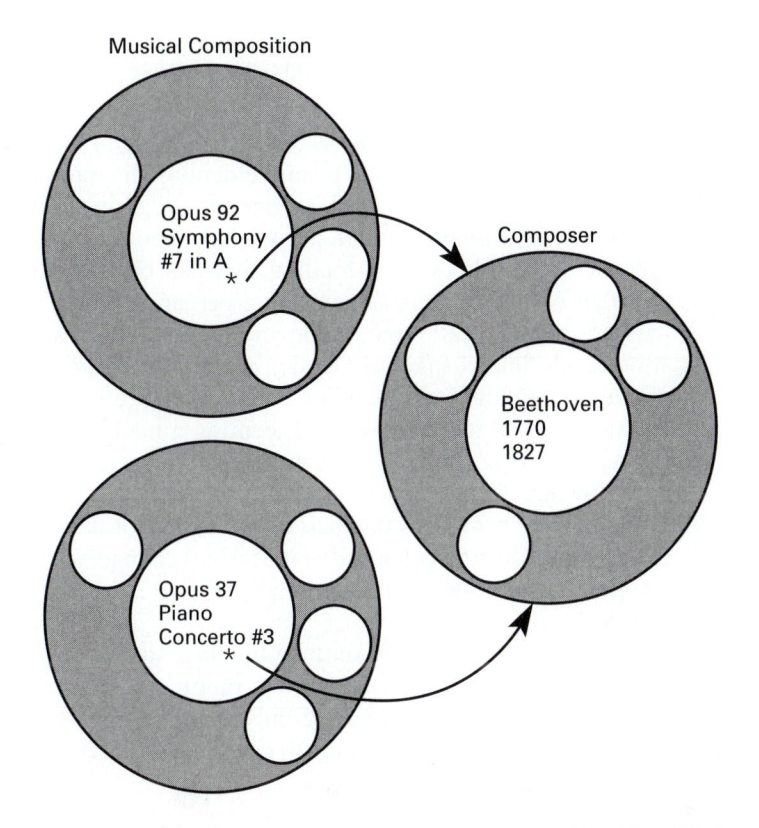

Chap. 17　　　　　　　Object-Oriented Programming Languages　　　　　　　**275**

Figure 17.9 Objects are automatically allocated unique identifiers (IDs) so that points can link to them.

STATIC VERSUS DYNAMIC BINDING

Pointers are essential to OO operation. The process of determining the item that is pointed to is called *binding*. Binding identifies the receiver of a request and can be done when either the program is compiled or the program is run. The two categories of binding can be elaborated:

Binding done when the program is compiled is called	*Binding done when the program is run* is called
• compiletime binding,	• runtime binding,
• early binding, or	• late binding, or
• static binding.	• dynamic binding.

Runtime, or dynamic, binding requires somewhat more overhead when the program runs, but it makes *polymorphism* possible. Because of this, some authorities regard it as an essential component of OO systems.

An object may send a request to another object telling it to do something. The receiving object may have its own way of implementing the method requested. It may use a method that did not exist at the time the program was compiled. For example, it might print a chart, but the printer has been changed. It might compute the value of a portfolio with a method that has been modified. The request might go to an object in a distant machine, perhaps even in a different corporation. It may not be practical to recompile all the linkages between objects in different locations each time changes are made, so runtime (or dynamic) binding is used. This gives a high level of flexibility.

Each object knows about its own way of executing a method, but different objects may execute that method in different ways. This is *polymorphism*. The request to **Compute Invoice Total** might be done differently in different locations because of particular discount schemes or sales, but a request of the same format is sent to all locations. The discounts and sales incentives change so often that it would not be practical to compile all linkages whenever a change occurs. So, runtime binding is used.

Because overhead is associated with runtime binding, some languages automatically use compile-time (or static) binding unless runtime binding is specified. Some versions of C++ permit runtime binding only within one class hierarchy, because polymorphism can usually be confined to one class hierarchy.

AVOIDANCE OF CASE STATEMENTS

Procedural languages have statements (called CASE statements) that allow multiple options. For example

IF PRINTER IS TYPE-A DO
- - - - - - -
IF PRINTER IS TYPE-B DO
- - - - - - -
IF PRINTER IS TYPE-C DO
- - - - - - -
IF PRINTER IF TYPE-D DO
- - - - - - -

CASE statements such as these can usually be replaced by one statement: PRINT. PRINT refers to a method that will be implemented differently in different objects depending on the type of printer used. A new type of printer can then be added and the same request remains valid.

Sometimes CASE statements are lengthy because many possible options are specified, for example a different option for each type of customer. The CASE statement may be repeated in many programs. All options are *hardcoded* into the program. To add a new option or delete an old one, a change has to be made wherever the CASE statement occurs. A large system may have thousands of CASE statements, hardcoding decisions into its programs. Changing the CASE options requires all the programs to be changed and tested. In OO systems, the hardcoding of options can often be avoided. Each object receiving a request has its own method of implementing that request. New objects with different variations on the theme can be added without changing a request or the code that sends it. This flexible use of methods and polymorphism makes systems much easier to change.

The more complex the system, and the more frequently changes are desired, the greater the advantage of not hardcoding options into the programs. The maintenance of commercial systems would be much easier if they had been built with OO techniques. New objects or new options could be added easily when needed without changing existing objects. This increased flexibility will likely lead to a much higher rate of change in commercial systems.

LANGUAGES AND ENVIRONMENTS   Some OO languages have merely a compiler or interpreter (or both), others have a language development environment, and yet others have a CASE environment (discussed in the following chapter). These facilities are summarized in Fig. 17.10.

REFERENCES

1. Budd, Timothy, *A Little Smalltalk,* Addison-Wesley, Reading, MA, 1987.

2. Cardelli, Luca and Peter Wegner, "On Understanding Types, Data Abstraction, and Polymorphism," *ACM Computing Surveys,* 17:4, December 1985, pp. 471-522.

3. Cox, Brad J. and Andrew J. Novobilski, *Object-Oriented Programming: An Evolutionary Approach,* (2nd edition), Addison-Wesley, Reading, MA, 1991.

4. Dahl, Ole-Johan and Kristen Nygaard, "SIMULA - An Algol-based Simulation Language," *Communications of the ACM,* 9:9, Sept. 1966, pp. 671-678.

5. Horowitz, Ellis, *Fundamentals of Programming Languages* (2nd edition), W. H. Freeman, New York, 1984.

6. Goldberg, Adele and David Robson, *Smalltalk-80: The Language and its Implementation,* Addison-Wesley, Reading, MA, 1983.

7. Kay, Alan C., "Microelectronics and the Personal Computer," *Scientific American,* September 1977, pp. 231-244.

Language

- Pure OO
- Hybrid
- High-level; easy to learn and use

Interpreter/compiler interpreter

- Interpreter ⎱ It is desirable to have both
- Compiler ⎰
- Dynamic compiler

Inheritance

- Single
- Multiple

Binding

- Static (compiletime)
- Dynamic (compiletime)
- Dynamic only within a class hierarchy

Development Environment

- Editor
- Debugger
- Browser
- Windows

CASE Environment

- Analysis and modeling tools
- Design tools
- Prototyping tools
- GUI builder
- Code generator
- Visualization/animation tools
- Repository
- Repository coordinator

Class Library

- For basic development
- Application-independent mechanisms (such as for LAN transaction processing)
- For application areas

Figure 17.10 Characteristics of OO languages and development environments.

8. Khoshafian, Setrag and Razmik Abnous, *Object Orientation: Concepts, Languages, Databases, User Interfaces,* John Wiley & Sons, New York, 1990.

9. Liskov, Barbara and John Guttag, *Abstraction and Specification in Program Development,* MIT Press, Cambridge, MA, 1986.

10. Nygaard, Kristen and Ole-Johan Dahl, "The Development of the Simula Language," *History of Programming Languages,* ACM SIGPLAN History of Programming Languages Conference (Los Angeles), Richard L. Wexelblat ed., Academic Press, New York, 1981, pp. 439-493.

11. Soley, Richard Mark, ed., *Object Management Architecture Guide,* Object Management Group, Document 90.17.1, November 1, 1990, Framingham, MA.

12. Taylor, David A., *Object-Oriented Technology: A Manager's Guide,* Addison-Wesley, Reading, MA, 1992.

18 OO-CASE TOOLS

Object-oriented techniques and CASE technology fit naturally together. While the OO world initially emphasized OO programming, the emphasis, today, should be on repository-based development with integrated CASE tools and a powerful code generator.

OO is much more than a computer language or design technique: it is a way of thinking. CASE tools oriented to this way of thinking help the I.S. professional, as well as the business person, engineer, or end user, to visualize automation in terms of OO models and specifications.

Some non-OO CASE tools have impressive code generators which generate 100 percent of the code with no syntax errors. (There are often design errors; garbage-in-garbage-out applies to code generators) [3]. Code generators of equivalent quality ought to become the predominant way of creating OO applications, along with a CASE repository of reusable classes. With OO-CASE tools the main emphasis of system building will be modeling and design, rather than OO programming.

Several OO analysis methods already exist in the data-processing industry. However, most are based on the structure of object-oriented programming languages—rather than its fundamental principles. They begin by defining classes and superclasses and continue by specifying the data structure of the classes. Next, the operations associated with each class are identified. Since these operations must connect in some way, their interfaces or *request* structures are defined. Finally, the methods for each operation are specified. Most methodologies do not identify events, triggers, rules, and state changes (as described in Part II). These are important and should be an essential part of analysis and design methodologies.

> OO analysis methods should not be tied to OO languages and their support facilities.

Since technology for development is changing rapidly, we should analyze our systems *independently* of the programming tools used. Programming techniques should not drive the way we understand and communicate about our organizations.

A VARIETY OF TOOLS

Various tools have been created to help make I.S. development faster, cheaper, and higher quality. Some tools are simple, others are complex. Simple tools should be reserved for simple systems, where a complex tool might slow down development. Certain needs require only a report generator or a spreadsheet tool.

In the early 1980s, fourth-generation languages (4GLs) were invented [2]. Some 4GLs use nonprocedural languages that offer ways to express *what* result is required—not *how* to achieve it. SQL became a standard and provided a nonprocedural way to access relational databases. Other, more user-friendly, query languages and report-generation languages proliferated.

Most fourth-generation languages were invented before object-oriented techniques were well understood. Today, we need better end-user languages that incorporate OO techniques. Objects that have complex behavior may be shown on the screen as an icon. The end user can link many such icons together on a PC screen to build applications. This is done in some process-control software (e.g., from Gensym Inc.) and some decision-support software (e.g., from Metaphor Inc.).

Prototyping tools are important, enabling developers to build prototypes quickly and see how end users react to them. Prototyping languages gave rise to iterative development in which a prototype was successively refined.

CASE (Computer-Aided Systems Engineering) tools provided graphically oriented ways of expressing plans, models, and designs [4]. Code generators were created that could generate COBOL or other languages from high-level constructs [1].

As CASE tools became more powerful, much of the design could be synthesized rather than built from scratch. The design tools were linked to a repository containing information used in building the design. The repository stored the information involved in planning, analysis, design, and code generation. The repository contained templates and reusable constructs that could be customized for the system being built. It might contain specimen applications that could be modified. Particularly important now, the repository should contain reusable OO classes, designed to be incorporated in applications.

The tools really started to look powerful when these facilities were integrated. CASE tools for planning, for data and process modeling, and for creating designs were integrated with code generators. Prototyping capability was linked into the design tools. Nonprocedural languages, including SQL and report generators, were integrated into the CASE environment. The term I-CASE describes integrated CASE products. Most important in I-CASE is the ability to generate code directly from the CASE design tool. An I-CASE repository contains design components in the form of reusable classes.

PURE OO AND HYBRID CASE

Like programming languages, CASE tools can be divided into three categories:

- non-OO
- pure OO
- hybrid

The CASE industry grew up in the late 1980s building non-OO tools. Because of this, OO enthusiasts have poured scorn on CASE tools [6] despite their clear success in facilitating faster development and maintenance.

As OO techniques became better understood, some CASE vendors added OO concepts to their toolsets. Their repositories made available design objects, such as screens, dialogs, reports, tables, procedures, database-access mechanisms, transaction controls, and so on. Subtyping and inheritance made it possible to use these design objects in a flexible way. The objects could be modified by users to incorporate into a particular application, as in Figs. 12.8 and 12.9.

While design objects were used and helped with prototyping and code generation, the basic CASE diagrams generally remained the same. They supported traditional structured techniques with functional decomposition, structure charts, and data-flow diagrams, rather than class hierarchies, subtyping, event diagrams, and the OO diagrams in general. The tools had a flavor of OO, but their basic core did not reflect the paradigm shift from structured techniques to OO techniques.

More recently, pure OO-CASE tools evolved. These support all or most of the techniques described in Part II of this book and they generate code. Some of these evolved on one workstation, able to support one developer rather than teams of developers.

Integrated OO-CASE tools are urgently needed. They enable development teams to share a repository, so that development can progress from intelligent enterprise models to efficient system generation.

CATEGORIES OF CASE TOOLS

CASE tools can be categorized as *I-CASE* (supporting the whole lifecycle with a single logically consistent repository) and *fragment CASE* (supporting only a portion of the lifecycle). Fragment CASE tools include front-end tools (the analysis part of the lifecycle) and back-end tools (code generation). Some CASE tools support information engineering (see Chapter 16) and help their users to build a model of the enterprise and analyze business areas. We thus have IE-CASE (for complete information engineering), I-CASE (integrated CASE that is not necessarily information engineering), and fragment CASE. Any of these can be non-OO, traditional but with an OO flavor, pure OO, or can support *both* traditional techniques and OO techniques. This categorization is shown in Fig. 18.1.

		Non-OO	Traditional with an OO flavor	Both OO and non-OO	Pure OO
Fragmented CASE	Front-end tools				
	Back-end tools				
Integrated CASE (but not IE)					
IE CASE (Complete Information Engineering)					

	Non-OO	Traditional with an OO flavor	Both OO and non-OO	Pure OO
Diagrams for traditional structured techniques	3	3	3	
Diagrams for OO techniques			3	3
Design objects with inheritance		3	3	3

Figure 18.1 Categories of CASE tools

INSIGHTFUL MODELS

Figure 18.2 repeats Fig. 5.1 and shows how we model and design systems. The capabilities in this figure should be those of a CASE toolset. The methodology supported by the toolset should ensure that the modeling leads directly to design as automatically as possible and that code is generated immediately from the design.

The model of reality should be as meaningful as possible to end users. In corporate I.S. we build a model of the enterprise. This should reflect the way the business people want to run the enterprise and facilitate discussion of how the enterprise procedures should be changed.

The early CASE tools modeled the enterprise with functional decomposition, entity-relationship diagrams, and matrices mapping entity types against functions. This modeling did not reflect how the enterprise operated and was not very meaningful to business people. OO modeling is more effective, because we identify events and the operations triggered by events. Event diagrams show streams of operations and allow us to reorganize the stream and redesign the busi-

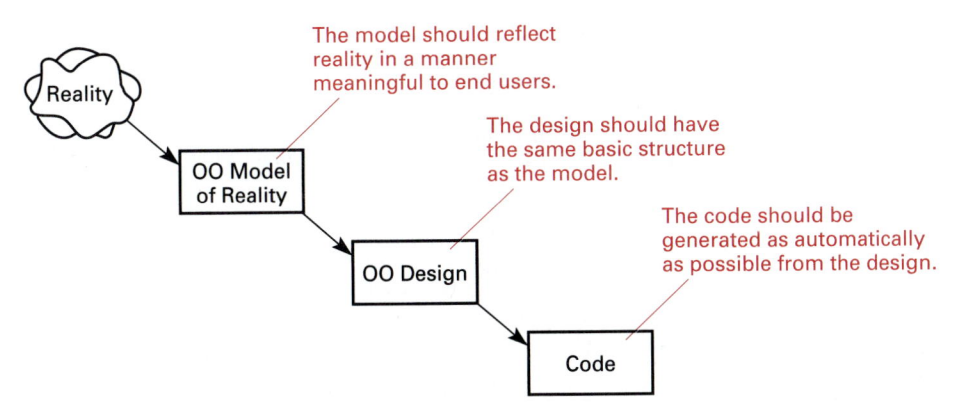

Figure 18.2 CASE tools should enable us to model reality in a manner as insightful as possible to end users and to translate those models as automatically as possible into the systems the users need.

ness process. The value added by each operation may be analyzed and operations of low value eliminated. Various business rules state how the business should react to events, such as what to do about late payers, what factors have priority in shop-floor scheduling, and so on. These rules relate to business objects. We identify the business objects, operations that change their states, and the rules that should govern these operations.

> The challenge of CASE tools today is modeling reality in a manner as insightful as possible to end users and translating the models as automatically as possible into the required systems. OO techniques help us to do that.

DESIGN SYNTHESIS AND CODE GENERATION

The most powerful I-CASE tools allow as much design as possible to be *synthesized* from high-level constructs in the repository. The designer assembles the design and creates its detailed logic. Some design may be generated from high-level behavioral and structural statements such as state-transition diagrams, rules, decision trees, event diagrams, and object schemas [4].

The design feeds a code generator that creates 100 percent of the code with zero programming errors. The generated code should never have an ABEND. The testing process is geared more for catching the *design* errors than catching detailed coding bugs.

The combination of *design synthesis* and *code generation*, shown in Fig. 18.3, enables high-quality applications to be built quickly. A world of difference exists between the modern development lifecycle using the tools in Fig. 18.3 and

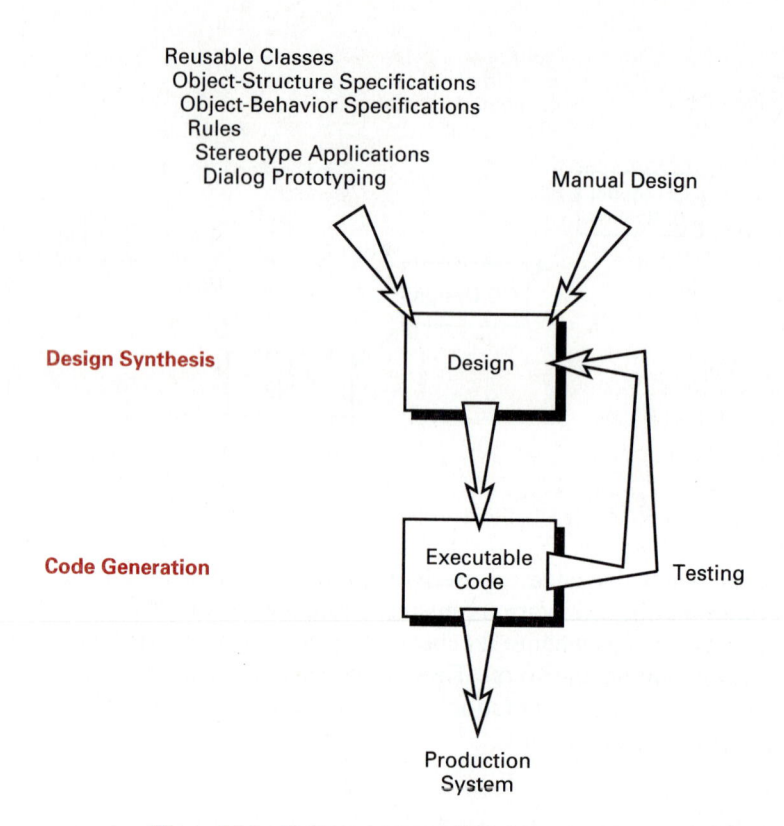

Figure 18.3 Design synthesis and code generation.

the traditional building of systems with plastic templates and line-by-line COBOL coding.

As far as possible, the design should be synthesized from

- Object-structure diagrams and specifications
- Object-behavior diagrams and specifications
- Rules
- Application-independent classes
- Classes for specific applications
- Entire applications, designed for customization
- Designs that can be customized
- Declarative tables (e.g., decision tables, event-condition-action tables)
- A report generator
- A screen painter
- A dialog prototyping tool (GUI)

CODE GENERATORS

Pure OO-CASE tools need not necessarily use OO programming languages. They can generate code in languages such as COBOL or C—both of which are efficient and portable and have highly efficient optimizing compilers.

A problem with COBOL and C compilers is that they do not provide dynamic (runtime) binding which has the advantages described in the previous chapter. Some OO-CASE tools generate C++ which provides dynamic binding as a requestable option but only for classes that belong to the same superclass.

A principle of integrated CASE is that debugging does not involve changing instructions at the code level, but rather changing the design that drives the interpreter or code generator. The interpreter or generator creates code with no syntax errors—this code can be tested like a black box and the source changed when necessary. This is particularly important if the tool generates a traditional language, such as COBOL or C, at the code level.

We will refer to this immediate instantiation as *instant CASE*. It helps the designer to be highly creative, observing his creation as he builds it, like a sculptor, and modifying it as it evolves. Developers find instant CASE far more satisfying than traditional CASE tools which require a long wait for code generation and compilation. With the latter, it takes too long to modify and improve what is being built.

INSTANT CASE

Building systems with an interpreter is highly desirable so that the developer can immediately run what he creates and repeatedly modify and evolve it. As with programming languages, a CASE toolset should have both an interpreter and an optimizing compiler.

With OO tools, as soon as an object type is described to the tool, it can create tables that allow instances of the object to be created. A description of its data can be built and tables of instances filled in. The designer can create subtypes, composed-of hierarchies, and object-relationship diagrams and immediately fill in details of instances. Methods can be created and the behavior of the objects observed, tested, and adjusted.

As soon as the designer describes object types to the tool, the objects *are there* and can be experimented with. This resembles a spreadsheet tool in which the designer can add columns and rows, specify computations, and immediately add values and run the spreadsheet, generating and modifying charts. This ability of spreadsheet tools to create *instant* results should be emulated with OO-CASE. As soon as object types and methods are created, they can be observed in action. The designer can build up structures far more complex than spreadsheets in an interactive manner, can experiment with them, and test them, as a spreadsheet designer does.

PRECISION IN DIAGRAMMING

An article in *Fortune* [5] attempts to describe why software is so difficult to create:

> Software is "pure thought stuff," so conceptual that designers cannot draw explicit, detailed diagrams and schematics—as creators of electronic circuits can—to guide programmers in their work. Consequently, routine communication among programmers, managers and the ordinary people who use software is a chore in itself.

This popular wisdom is *wrong* today. With the I-CASE tools, explicit, detailed diagrams and schematics are drawn, analogous to those used by electronic circuit designers, and code is generated from them. Much testing can be done at the diagram level. These diagrams are very effective for routine communications among programmers, analysts, managers, and end users. Just as other engineering disciplines have precision represented in formal diagrams, so computer system developers also need formality and precision—in this case, enforced by the computer.

Given appropriate diagramming techniques, describing complex activities and procedures is easier through diagrams than text. A picture can be much better than a thousand words, because it is concise, precise, and clear. Computerized diagrams do not allow the sloppiness and woolly thinking common in textual specifications. Engineers of different types use formal diagrams that are precise in meaning—mechanical drawings, architectural drawings, circuit diagrams, microelectronics designs, and so on. The diagrams become the documentation for systems (along with the additional information collected in the repository when the diagrams are drawn).

A good CASE tool employs diagram types that are precise and can be checked by computer. Large, complex diagrams can be handled by means of zooming, nesting, windowing, and other computer techniques. The computer quickly catches errors and inconsistencies even in very large sets of diagrams. Business, government, and the military need highly complex, integrated computer applications. The size and complexity of these applications require accurate diagramming using computers.

The *meaning* represented by the diagram is more valuable than its graphic image. A good CASE tool stores that meaning in a computer-processable form. The tool helps build up a design, a data model, or some other deliverable segment of the development process, so that it can be validated and used in a subsequent development stage.

The evolution of OO-CASE technology represents an evolution of application development from being a *craft* to being an *engineering discipline*.

DIAGRAMS FOR OO DEVELOPMENT

For OO analysis and development, CASE tools should enable their users to build the diagram types listed in Box 18.1. Many of these diagrams are the same as those for non-OO development:

- Data structure diagrams (showing records, their fields, keys, and interrelations)
- Action diagrams (showing the structure of procedural code)
- Declarative tables (e.g., decision tables or event-condition-action tables)
- Tools for designing the graphic user interface
- State-change diagrams (showing the state changes of an object)

Some of the diagrams are essentially the same as those used in conventional data-centered development but with an OO flavor:

BOX 18.1

CASE tools for OO analysis and design should enable their users to build the following types of diagrams and generate code from them:

For Object Structures:

- Data-structure diagrams
- Object generalization diagrams
- Object-relationship diagrams
- Object composed-of diagrams

For Object Behavior:

- Class-communication diagrams
- Representations of methods
    — Action diagrams
    — Declarative tables
- State-change diagrams
- Event diagrams
- Rules, linked to event diagrams
- Tools for designing the graphical user interface

- Object-inheritance diagrams (which are broadly similar to entity diagrams showing subtypes and supertypes)
- Object-relationship diagrams (similar to entity-relationship diagrams)
- Object composed-of diagrams (similar to diagrams showing hierarchical decomposition)

One important type of diagram is not supported by non-OO tools. This is the event diagram (discussed in Chapter 9) which should be linked to *rules* (discussed in Chapter 10).

REPOSITORY

A computer can be extremely effective at accumulating and storing in an organized fashion a large amount of knowledge, added to at different times, by different people, in different places. An I-CASE repository is designed for this purpose.

The best way we know of organizing the I-CASE repository is using object-oriented techniques. The repository stores and catalogs the reusable OO classes.

A repository is the heart of a CASE environment. It stores all the information about systems, designs, and code in a basically nonredundant fashion. It is used by all developers. Using powerful tools, the developers employ the information in the repository and create new information that, in turn, is placed in the repository. The repository and its affiliated system check and correlate all the information stored to ensure its consistency and integrity. The repository should contain reusable classes that enable the developers to build systems quickly.

As the repository is the heart of the CASE environment, it should also be the heart of the methodology employed for building systems. The developers create designs with the help of information from the repository. They progressively build their designs in the repository and generate code from them.

MORE THAN A DICTIONARY

It is important to understand that a CASE repository is more than a dictionary.

- A *dictionary* contains names and descriptions of data items, processes, variables, and so on.
- A *repository* contains a complete coded representation of the objects used in planning, analysis, design, and code generation. Object-oriented methods are used to ensure consistency and integrity of this knowledge. Many rules are used, with rule-based processing, to help achieve accuracy, integrity, and completeness of the plans, models, and designs. The repository stores the meaning repre-

sented in CASE diagrams and enforces consistency within this representation. The repository thus *understands* the design whereas a simple dictionary does not. Particularly important, the repository drives a code generator. The developer should not have to code languages with an arcane syntax, such as COBOL, C, or C++. The best code generators in use today produce 100 percent of the code for the production system.

The diagrams that appear on the screen of the CASE tools are created in real time from the repository. Different diagram types can be derived from the same information, representing different ways of visualizing the integrated body of knowledge in the repository (see Fig. 18.4).

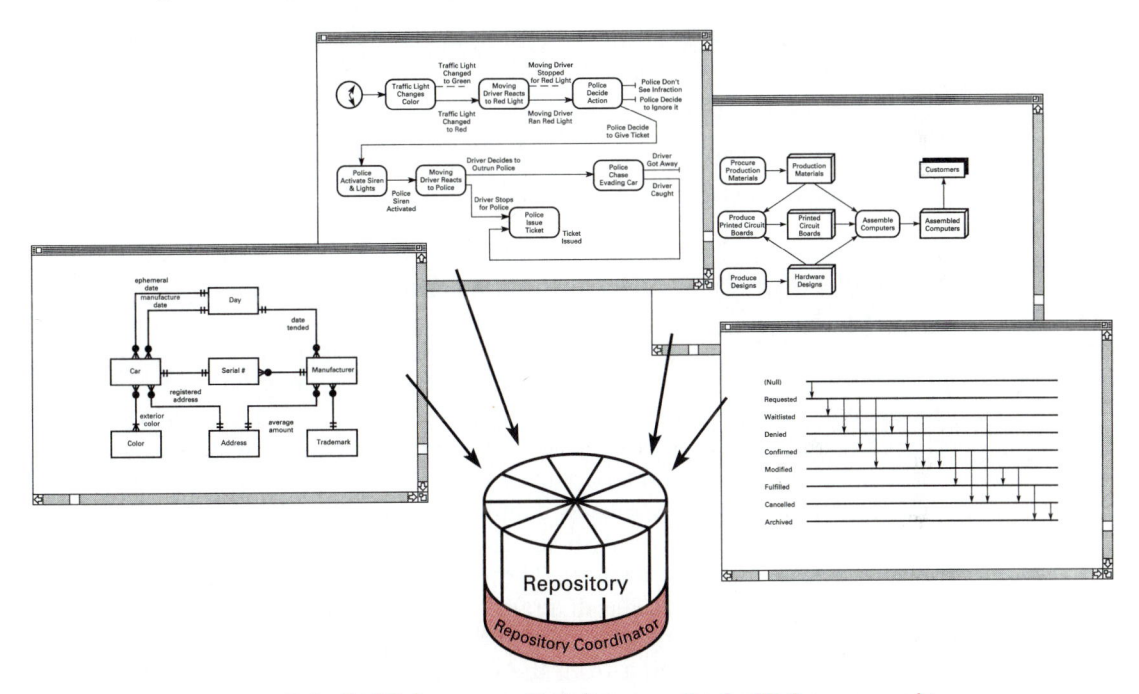

Figure 18.4 CASE diagrams, and windows associated with them, are used to communicate information to the repository. The repository stores the meaning represented in the diagrams. Diagrams are generated from the repository. The repository stores more detail than the diagrams contain. Additional detail can be obtained by pointing to an object on the diagram. Details will appear in another window. CASE tools use the objects in the repository to help synthesize designs.

The repository views the world as a collection of objects—appearing on the CASE screens as boxes, lines, or other elements of diagrams. The repository stores object types such as

- Object types themselves
- Relationships among object types
- Classes
- Event types
- Trigger rules
- Control conditions
- Operations
- Action diagrams showing *method* procedures
- Detailed components of action diagrams
- Declarative statement
- Data types
- Records in a database
- Screen designs
- Report designs

INTELLIGENCE IN THE REPOSITORY

The repository stores many types of objects. In order to handle them correctly, the repository requires its own set of classes and associated methods. These methods may be expressed as collections of rules or may be algorithms that process the information stored in the repository. The repository that contains rules can employ rule processing to help achieve accuracy, integrity, and completeness of the plans, models, and designs. Thus, the repository both stores development information and helps control its accuracy and validity.

Any one diagram on a CASE screen is a facet of a broader set of knowledge that may reside in the repository. The repository normally contains far more detail than is contained in the diagram. Any portion of this detail can be displayed in other windows by using a mouse.

The knowledge coming from the CASE diagrams must be coordinated to ensure that it fits together logically and consistently. IBM refers to this capability as *repository services*. KnowledgeWare Inc. calls it the *knowledge coordinator*. We will refer to it as the *repository coordinator*. A good repository coordinator is highly complex—capable of handling repositories with thousands of rules.

DOCUMENTATION

With repository-based development, the detailed documentation is in the repository—not on the paper. While paper documentation can be printed from the repository, this is secondary to the repository contents. This is important because the repository and repository coordinator enforce a level of precision that is almost always missing when paper is the primary documentation.

Many examples exist of paper-based specifications and design being transferred to repository-based tools. In such cases, the tools and repository coordinator catch many errors in the paper documentation. The big binders of paper documentation are generally full of errors, omissions, and inconsistencies that good CASE tools catch.

CONSISTENCY AMONG DIAGRAMS Different types of diagrams show different manifestations of the same information. These diagrams are logically interlinked in the computer. Data can be entered in one type of diagram and displayed with a different type of diagram. The repository tools ensure that the different diagrams reflect a consistent meaning.

Sometimes, analysts have two windows on the screen with different diagram types containing the same information. When they change one diagram, the change needed to ensure consistency should appear automatically on the other diagram. Object-structure diagrams and object-behavior diagrams must be consistent.

For example, knowledge *X* may be best entered into the repository by Mr. Jones via an *event diagram*. Ms. Smith then requests the same information from the repository, reinterpreted automatically, as a *state-transition diagram*. Mr. Epstein expresses business *rules* that link to the *event diagram*. Outlines of *methods* are created from the event diagram and its rules. This logically interconnected family of diagrams constitutes an integrated set of knowledge that the developers can explore via the screens of the I-CASE toolset.

CONSISTENCY AMONG DIFFERENT PROJECTS A computerized corporation has many different databases and systems. Consistency among different systems must be achieved, because they interact with one another in complex ways. Systems in different plants and locations transmit information to one another. Data are often extracted from multiple systems and aggregated for business management. Different locations need commonality of management measurements. Sometimes, the term *corporate transparency* is used to mean that detailed information in all locations is accessible in a computerized form by a central management group for decision support and control.

CASE tools make it practical to achieve consistency among multiple projects. Designs for different systems are derived from a common collection of reusable classes—available to implementors from the repository, that is accessible from all locations.

The term I-CASE (Integrated CASE) refers to a toolset utilizing a single, logically consistent repository. Complete I-CASE toolsets today have tools for planning, analysis, design, prototyping, full code generation, and testing. Maintenance is done by modifying the design diagrams and regenerating the code. Efficient development employs an I-CASE toolset and an I-CASE methodology (sometimes referred to as an ICM). OO-CASE refers to an object-oriented CASE toolset that also should be fully integrated. OOCM refers to an object-oriented CASE methodology that should take full advantage of an OO-CASE toolset (see Fig. 18.5).

I-CASE (Integrated CASE)

A CASE toolset that supports all lifecycle stages including complete code generation, with a single logically consistent repository.

ICM (I-CASE Methodology)

A methodology designed to take full advantage of an I-CASE toolset.

OO-CASE (Object-Oriented CASE)

An I-CASE toolset that supports object-oriented analysis and design.

OOCM (Object-Oriented CASE Methodology)

A methodology for object-oriented analysis and design that takes full advantage of an OO-CASE toolset.

Figure 18.5 Integrated CASE and object-oriented CASE.

MAXIMUM REUSABILITY Perhaps the single most important thrust in software development in the years ahead is achieving the highest level of reusability. Software should be built by assembling and customizing existing components with repository-based tools. Today, nearly every programmer is reinventing something that has been built, debugged, and painfully improved—a thousand times before.

Box 18.2 lists desirable properties of reusable components. The best way to achieve a high degree of reusability is with object-oriented techniques. The

BOX 18.2 Desirable properties of reusable components.

I-CASE workbenches should employ the techniques of object-oriented design to maximize reusability.

- *Formal semantic basis.* A formalism should be used that precisely describes the component.
- *Expressiveness.* The formalism should express all possible kinds of components.
- *Easy to understand.*
- *Easy to customize in an unplanned way.* Customizing the components should be easier than rewriting them from scratch.
- *Easy to add or delete details.*
- *Designed for graphics workbench.* In order to satisfy the above three properties, the design should be represented with the graphics capability of an I-CASE toolset that integrates multiple diagrammatic representations.
- *Clear, simple, precise interfaces.* The formalism should precisely define the interfaces between components.
- *Self-contained.* The components should be self-contained and have predictable behavior.
- *Cause-and-effect isolation.* The component should execute its behavior independently of preceding causes or subsequent effects.
- *Self-organizing.* The components should know which other components they need, so that the programmer does not have to remember or search for them.
- *Verifiable.* Techniques for verifying the behavior of components should be used where practical.
- *Flexible without compromising efficiency.* It should be possible to use standard components without suffering performance problems.
- *Independent of programming language.* The formalism should be independent of programming languages.
- *Application standards.* Standards should be used as fully as possible for the interface to networks, interface to database, interface to operating systems, end-user dialog, client-server operation, and so on.
- *Electronic document standards.* Standards for electronically represented documents should be used—for example, the ANSI X.12/ISO, Edifact EDI standards.
- *Defined protocols.* Protocols should exist for the use of components, so that a software builder can employ components licensed from many companies.

CASE repository should be populated with a library of reusable classes that enable development to be done rapidly and with high quality. In hardware engineering, the change from transistor-by-transistor design to chip-by-chip design gave orders-of-magnitude improvements in productivity. Design by a much wider range of people was made practical. The change from line-at-a-time programming to design using software chips will be similarly effective.

If you request an architect to build a house for you, he will usually not design the house from scratch. He may start with a preexisting design and modify it or assemble a design from separate, preexisting drawings. He has reusable plans, configurable in many ways. Details can be pulled from a large number of standard components—doors, windows, plumbing, fittings, electrical components, heating units, lights, and so on. These are listed in numerous catalogs of off-the-shelf components. Most components have standard plugs, sockets, or measurements so that they fit together.

The building of data-processing applications will one day be similar, shown in Fig. 18.6. The designer should start with preexisting plans that can be reconfigured in many ways, then use a repository of designs and components, and finally use tools for adapting these to the system in question. There should be catalogs of many reusable classes that can be purchased and loaded into the repository.

The designer may employ an expert system to help find the most useful classes. The house architect works with standard designs and components in order to minimize the amount of custom work. This reduces the time and cost of the project. Similarly, if the components are accessible, the system designer can minimize the amount of custom work for the same reason.

In the future, a major sector of the software industry will develop that sells reusable designs and classes. These classes will be easily found, understood, modified, and interlinked.

A House Builder Uses	A Software Builder Should Use
• Reusable plans that can be configured in many ways • Standard, well-proven designs and components • Off-the-shelf units • Catalogs of many components • Good knowledge of what components are available • Standard plugs and sockets	• Reusable plans that can be configured in many ways • Standard, well-proven designs and components • Off-the-shelf classes that are easy to modify • Catalogs of many classes • Good knowledge of what classes are available • Standard interfaces

Figure 18.6 Comparison of a house builder and a software builder. The software builder should use many of the techniques of the house builder.

THREE SOURCES OF REUSABLE COMPONENTS

When a developer builds an application from existing classes, these classes come from three different sources, shown in Fig. 18.7:

- tool vendors
- software companies that sell object-oriented applications
- internal development

To make its tools as useful as possible, a CASE tool vendor should package class libraries with the tools. Some classes are application independent, including screens, dialogs, LAN management, a database server, management controls for transaction processing, and so on. Other classes relate to specific applications and would include such items as order entry, general accounting, bill of materials, and so on. A successful tool vendor can resell classes developed by customers, consultants, or software entrepreneurs.

Application packages have been sold by software companies since the days of vacuum tubes. Many of these packages are ill-structured and difficult to modify but nevertheless need adapting to their users' procedures.

Some software companies are now selling applications in I-CASE format that are easy to modify with I-CASE tools. Some are selling object-oriented classes that can be used with multiple applications. A software industry will like-

I-CASE Tool Vendor

The tool vendor builds generic classes into the tool to facilitate rapid development. (Screens, dialogs, LAN management, database server, management controls for transaction processing, etc.)

Software Companies

Software companies build reusable object-oriented classes which can be used with multiple applications, and package these for use with multiple I-CASE tools.

In-House Development

Object-oriented analysis and design is done throughout a corporation by its I.S. organization, to identify and build those classes that can be used in many applications. This is done with information engineering techniques.

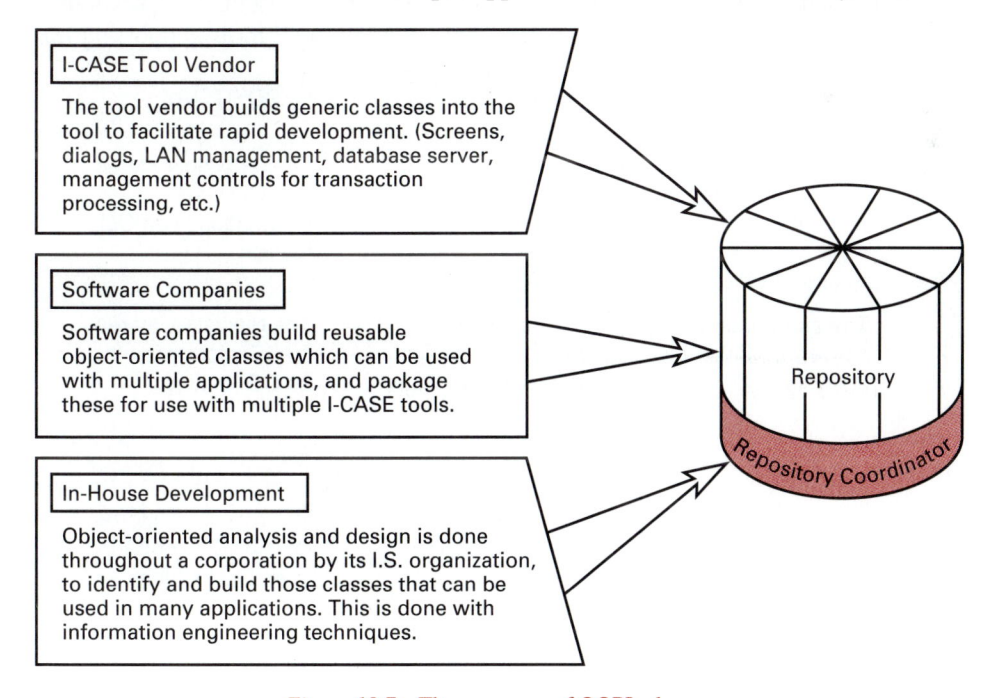

Figure 18.7 Three sources of OOPL classes.

ly grow selling libraries of reusable classes designed for standard repositories. Versions of such libraries may be created for all the leading I-CASE vendors.

Buying reusable classes is cheaper than building them (just as most manufacturers buy components). Where appropriate classes do not exist, they are sometimes designed by an I.S. organization for its own use. Some corporations have done top-down analysis and design with information engineering techniques. These organizations have identified and built reusable classes that apply to many applications, such as account, customer, part, and so on. This has enabled them to achieve such a level of software reusability that only a small proportion of lines of code for new applications are custom generated. They can quickly create most new applications by reusing available classes. Equally important, it enables them to modify (maintain) applications quickly and easily.

THE FUTURE OF CASE

Most application development will eventually be repository based with integrated CASE tools that generate code. The most powerful and flexible of such tools will be fully object oriented supporting OO diagrams. Instant CASE using OO techniques enables the developer to be highly creative and to build complex systems fast.

The dominant CASE vendors today make tools for traditional development, not OO development. The repository is generally object oriented even when it supports non-OO development (see Fig. 18.8). Some CASE tools supporting tra-

	ANALYSIS	DESIGN	REPOSITORY
1	The analyst uses conventional non-OO analysis.	The designer uses conventional non-OO analysis.	The repository stores non-OO CASE information in an OO fashion.
2	The analyst uses conventional non-OO analysis.	The designer uses design objects such as screens, dialogs, fields, reports, templates.	The repository stores CASE information in an OO fashion.
3	Analysis and design are fully OO and use object schemas, event schemas, and design objects.		The repository stores OO CASE information in an OO fashion.

Figure 18.8 The repository uses and operates in an OO fashion even if the analysts or designers do not.

ditional methods have introduced design objects with inheritance to increase reusability in design.

It is interesting to speculate whether the future vendors of the most powerful tools will be those who lead the CASE industry today. Today's vendors of tools for traditional development may be so weighted down by the pre-OO paradigm that they will fail to build tools that take full advantage of OO techniques with event diagrams, rules, multiple inheritance, dynamic binding, and powerful class libraries. On the other hand, today's OO language vendors seem to be ignoring the power of CASE and code generators. Instant CASE tools using power OO techniques may come from new corporations seizing the opportunity to build the world's most powerful development tools.

REFERENCES

1. Martin, James, *Principles of CASE,* a videotape series, James Martin Insight Inc., Naperville, IL, 1992.

2. Martin, James, *Fourth-Generation Languages,* Vol. I, Prentice Hall, Englewood Cliffs, NJ, 1985.

3. Martin, James, *I-CASE,* a videotaped series of seminars, James Martin Insight Inc., Naperville, IL, 1992.

4. Martin, James and Carma McClure, *Structured Techniques: A Basis for CASE,* Prentice Hall, Englewood Cliffs, NJ, 1988.

5. Schlender, Brenton R., "How to Break the Software Logjam," *Fortune,* 120:7, Sept 25, 1989, pp. 100ff.

6. Taylor, David A., *Object-Oriented Technology: A Managers' Guide,* Addison-Wesley, Reading, MA, 1992.

19 OBJECT-ORIENTED DATABASES*

A traditional database stores just data—with no procedures. It attempts to make the data independent from the procedures. The data are accessible by diverse users for diverse purposes. In contrast, an object-oriented database stores objects. The data are stored along with the *methods* that process those data.

After traditional databases had been in use for some time, a need arose to associate certain procedures with the data and activate them when the data were accessed. Such procedures were used to help control the integrity of the data or their security. Sometimes, a value was computed rather than stored—a procedure referred to as putting *intelligence* in the database. Intelligent database techniques were useful for controlling integrity in a client-server environment, because the identity of a client accessing a database server was never certain.

Object-oriented databases take the idea of intelligent databases to its logical conclusion. *No* data are accessed except with the methods stored in the database. These methods are ready to take action the moment they receive a request. The data of all objects are thus *encapsulated*. The data are generally *active* rather than *passive*.

We described the enterprise of the future as similar to an electronic organism. The corporate functions are carried out with object-oriented processing. Low-level objects, rather like cells in the body, are grouped into higher-level objects that carry out the functions useful to business people. The corporate network plays a role rather like the human nervous system, enabling fast interaction among the active collections of objects. Unlike the human nervous system, the network may be worldwide. The corporation will be like a worldwide electronic creature interacting electronically with other such creatures—its trading partners. The world patterns of commerce will change rapidly as these networked electronic organisms interact with one another using advanced forms of EDI (electronic data interchange). Many corporations that do not have this fast-reacting electronic infrastructure will be unable to compete effectively.

Object-oriented databases will become a very important corporate technology. There are complex questions about how such databases should be structured.

---

* Sometimes referred to as simply object databases

Should they be extensions of today's relational databases, or should they have entirely different structures?

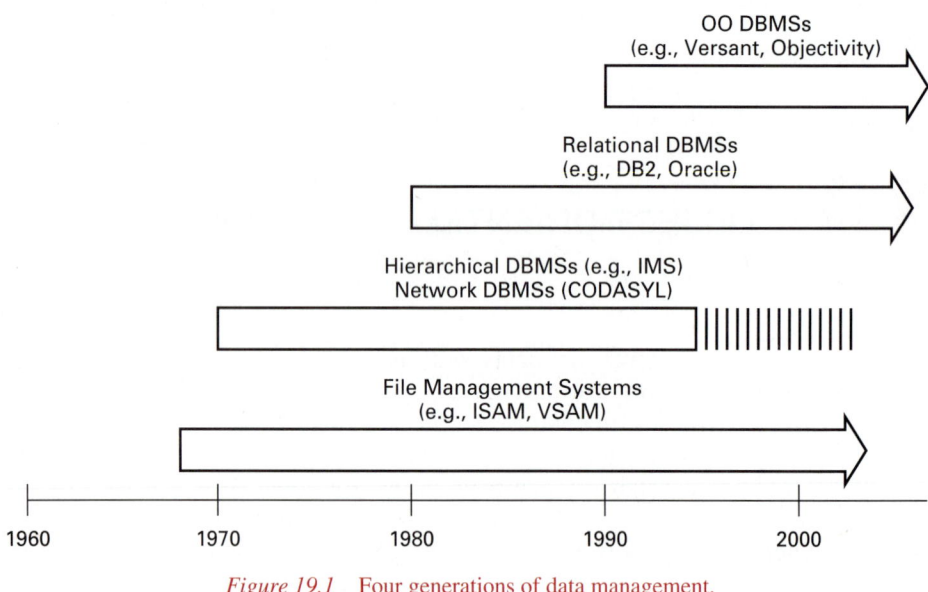

Figure 19.1 Four generations of data management.

A Brief History of Database Development

As Fig. 19.1 illustrates, four generations of systems have managed the storage of computer data.

In the beginning, languages and the machine instructions were very similar, resulting in a process-oriented programming model. For example, programs for addition were organized around the machine process of addition—loading registers with numbers, executing the add instruction, and dealing with overflow and underflow. Few results were stored for later use. Programmers soon realized the value of recording results. Recording program results greatly increased with the advent of rotating magnetic disk storage, which provided random-access capability for large amounts of storage.

File Systems

Eventually most programs made use of this new disk storage. However, the data on rotating media quickly became difficult to organize and man-

A Brief History of Database Development   *(Continued)*

age. This situation led developers to create packages of programs to ease the manipulation of disk storage. File management systems were born. With them, programmers could create files, store data, and read them back later for analysis or presentation. Programs were still generally organized around the process-oriented model, and availability of higher-level languages, especially COBOL, led to the development of large business programs. These programs viewed the data in files by their business purposes, typically sorted by categories or indexed by some logical key, for example, Order Number. The notion of a record and of a file as a group of records was developed. Each record represented an instance of some business concept, such as a Line Item in an Order.

While these early file systems aided the programmer, the data access methods were still primitive. Random access required the application program to know the physical placement of data on the disk. Computing these unique addresses required *hashing* algorithms. Developing hashing algorithms with a good, even distribution was an important skill—especially when different disk drives needed different algorithms. This prompted the first major *implementation-independent* aid—the indexed file. Instead of requiring an application to furnish the exact location of a piece of recorded data, only a symbolic key was needed. The index-enhanced file system, then, was necessary in order to compute and assign the data's physical location. Among the most widely used were (and, in many cases, still are) the ISAM (Indexed Sequential Access Method) and VSAM (Virtual Sequential Access Method) systems running on IBM mainframes.

The First DBMSs

The ever increasing demand for more capability from computer applications continued, and researchers realized that even indexed file systems were crude instruments. Order processing applications in particular tended to impose a hierarchical model on their data that corresponded to the hierarchical nature of an Order containing many Line Items and to Products described via hierarchical assembly structures. These pressures prompted the creation of the first systems that were layered on top of the file system and became known as database management systems (DBMSs). The most well known hierarchical DBMS was IMS (Information Management System) from IBM.

(Continued)

A Brief History of Database Development   (Continued)

The notion of a DBMS combined several ideas into a single system. DBMSs were based on a model of data, independent of any particular application. This step in implementation independence allowed application developers more time to concentrate on their application architecture. It also gave the DBMS a wide range of implementation freedom. With a DBMS, data design became the most important activity, causing a fundamental shift in paradigm to a *data-oriented* model of application development. This shift to a data-oriented model also led to the development of groups of related applications into business systems all running against a common DBMS. From this phenomenon, other needs arose, such as having multiple applications interact simultaneously with the DBMS and creating independent utility applications to manage the DBMS. Thus were born the notions of concurrency control and most of the activities known as database administration—backup, recovery, resource allocation, security, and so on.

The restrictions of the hierarchical data model imposed by IMS soon became apparent. Hierarchies provided a good model for many common business problems. However, developers began to realize that the world was not inherently hierarchical, and that nonhierarchical models were awkward to implement using a system like IMS. For instance, an inventory-control system needs to model the relationship between parts in an inventory and suppliers of those parts. This relationship is a lattice instead of a hierarchy, since most parts can be obtained from more than one supplier and most suppliers handle multiple parts. Lattice relationships were such a common problem that new DBMSs were developed that supported both set-based models and hierarchical models. Eventually, a standard model known as CODASYL was developed with several DBMSs providing implementations. A data definition language (DDL) was developed to describe a particular business model, along with a data manipulation language (DML) that created and processed data in a particular database. The DDL and DML could be used to completely specify and build applications or used in conjunction with other programming languages, such as COBOL. Finally, a set of ancillary functions administered physical storage of the DBMS, security, and other services not covered by the DDL and DML.

As systems built on top of DBMSs grew, so did the problems—centering around reorganization and navigation. Reorganization was the biggest problem, because the conceptual model and the physical

A Brief History of Database Development   (Continued)

implementation were so closely associated. Hierarchical and set-oriented relationships were typically implemented by placing the physical disk address of one record into another. The DML then compiled a data field for this address into an application. Unfortunately, this implied that any change to the DBMS record layout required, at a minimum, recompilation of all programs. Worse yet, if the physical address of a record changed, all references to it had to be found, so that the correct new location could be inserted. As these DBMSs had contributed to the processing and storage of large amounts of data, the physical reorganization could become untenable. During reorganization, large databases were typically unavailable for days at a time.

Navigation, the second problem, refers to the way that applications are bound to the DBMS. Applications use the DML to find a record, then use the DML to find related records. For example, in a hierarchical model one might find an Order and, then, find all Line Items of that Order stored as *child* records. In this way, applications could navigate between records in the database. This means the application had incorporated within it knowledge of the relationships in the model, which was fine. However, since the logical description of the relationships and their physical implementation were close, the application also contained implicit knowledge of the implementation. This was potentially confusing. Any change or extension to the model invalidated many applications, and recompilation would no longer cure the problem. The application had to be rewritten to accommodate the new model. With the current size of systems and the centrality of the DBMS to the business, change to and evolution of the model were inevitable. Large applications were rewritten many times at ever increasing expense. Maintenance activities began to dominate new development, and the time required to develop new applications became prohibitive. Like dinosaurs struggling in the ancient tar pits, systems became mired in ever-more expensive maintenance activities.

The Relational Database

During this period, E. F. Codd wrote his seminal paper on the relational data model, and several implementations of relational databases (RDBs) began to appear. RDBs had several important characteristics

(Continued)

A Brief History of Database Development   (Continued)

that solved many of the problems discussed above. In brief, the relational model was not based on any particular data structuring paradigm but rather a mathematical foundation. The resulting model could express a nonredundant description of data and a set of fixed operators from which the data could be formally derived. The relational model could be represented by a simple tabular structure, providing a useful visual format for displaying information contained in the database.

The relational data model moved the focal point of the system development process away from data structures and computer implementations toward modeling the business application realm. This was its most important aspect. The entire process moved to a higher level as the important questions focused on the central tenets of the business model, rather than the most convenient implementation vehicle for a particular application or set of applications. RDBs represented the first systems that provided an application interface for which implementation issues were removed from the process. A major goal of database technology was achieved—the data were independent of the processes.

The relational data model defines three data types: the table (relation), the row (tuple), and the column (attribute). The model specifies three operators on tables: select, project, and join. *Select* applies a Boolean operator to each row of a table and returns a new table containing only those rows for which the Boolean operator returns true. *Project* specifies a subset of the columns defined in a table. It returns a new table containing all of the original rows along with those rows that correspond to the column values specified by the project. The *join* operator combines the two tables and produces a single table. This table represents the Cartesian product of all the tables from which the join is formed. Then, a Boolean operator compares one column from each original table, and the join result is a new table containing those rows for which the Boolean operator returns true.

The relational data model provides several significant advantages' over its predecessors:

- **Data independence.** The data representation on the computer is independent of the interface to the application. The most significant advantage of this over earlier systems is that the physical representation can be modified without affecting applications. The database can be completely reorganized at the physical level without recompiling programs or schema. Performance features such as indexes can be added or removed dynamically, tables can be parti-

A Brief History of Database Development (Continued)

tioned across disk drives or compressed to reclaim unused space, and so on. None of this affects the applications developed. Thus, the investment in the application is maintained more easily—a major advantage over prior systems.

- **Declarative manipulation.** An international-standard language, SQL (Structured Query Language) is used to express the relational model is SQL. SQL is a declarative, nonprocedural language that expresses the kind of data desired—not the way to get it. SQL is generally a simpler mechanism for manipulating a database than using a typical programming language. SQL embodies the philosophy of data independence. It allows the database system to chose from alternative mechanisms and to obtain the desired results from the physical realization of the database. The database management system can dynamically optimize the way queries are executed, freeing the application programmer from this task.

- **Removing redundancy.** When relational data are designed, the process of normalization can be applied. Fully normalizing a data model produces a database in which data redundancy has been eliminated. This has two advantages over prior systems. First, it removes the possibility that portions of the database are out of sync due to redundant storage. This was a problem with both hierarchical and network databases, where redundant data were common. Second, it usually minimizes the amount of data stored, reducing the overall size of the database and saving disk space.

- **Simplicity.** The relational model has three basic types and three operations—an improvement over the programming languages that had to be mastered. Whether programmers or not, most people are already familiar with the basic concepts, since they have worked with tables, rows, and columns. The relational model is easier to learn and use.

- **Tables as presentation vehicles.** The result of all relational operators is a table, which often is the required application solution. Previous data models required extracting the appropriate information and then translating it into some desired result format—usually a table. RDBs eliminate this last step since the result is already in table form.

All of the above characteristics enable faster application development and easier application maintenance—hence, the current popularity of RDBs. A further reason is the modern application development environments spawned by RDBs, especially to fourth-generation languages (4GLs). Fourth-generation languages are characterized, in general, by a language with built-in database operators and, perhaps, report formatting. This again simplifies the application development process and reduces the time needed to complete a new application.

ACTIVE DATABASES The classic relational database is passive. It merely stores data in a data-independent way. An *active* database will take certain actions *automatically* when an attempt is made to read or update the data. This is referred to as putting *intelligence* into the database.

The basic structure of the relational database could be the same, but the database management system was changed so that it applied security controls, integrity controls, or automatic computations. This was done in Sybase, for example, and was particularly useful for a database on a client-server system where the clients were unknown.

KNOWLEDGEBASES The so-called artificial intelligence world brought another form of active database. It was desirable to store *knowledge*. Knowledge was regarded as being active, whereas data or information were passive. Knowledge was thought to consist of facts and rules that a computer could employ. For example, with expert systems appropriate rules were identified and chained using an inference engine to reason about a problem. The inference engine used forward chaining or backward chaining—or both. This powerful concept was applied successfully to some highly complex problems. This type of computing needed a *knowledgebase* that stored both data and rules, and employed an inference engine to search for rules and perform automatic reasoning. Knowledgebase systems were built by artificial intelligence companies which created software for expert systems.

OBJECT-ORIENTED DATABASES Object-oriented databases (OODBs) first evolved from a need to support object-oriented programming. Smalltalk and C++ programmers needed a store for what they called *persistent* data, that is, data that remain after a process is terminated. OODBs become important for certain types of applications with complex data, such as CAD (computer-aided design) and CAE (computer-aided engineering). They also became important for handling BLOBs (binary large objects) such as images, sound, video, and unformatted text. Applications, such as newspaper layout and video retrieval in advertising agencies, used OODBs with BLOBs. OODBs supported diverse data types rather than only the simple tables, columns, and rows of relational databases.

Users steadily realized the value of object-oriented techniques. OO techniques are good for both specialized systems, such as CAD, and for computing in general. An enterprise model should be a model describing business object types, subtypes, their behavior, the relationships among objects, object states, events that are changes in state, business rules, and so on. The enterprise model should be translatable directly in software that makes the enterprise function. This requires databases that store the objects and bring the associated methods into operation.

Various needs not met by traditional relational databases converged to form a new generation of database management systems. *Active* databases are best implemented with OO techniques. Knowledgebases became *frame*-oriented where a frame is an object having a collection of rules associated with it. Richly diverse abstract data types (user-defined data types) needed support, (including speech, image, and video). Complex data required access techniques that improved performance over relational databases. As shown in Fig. 19.2, these needs converged into OODBs.

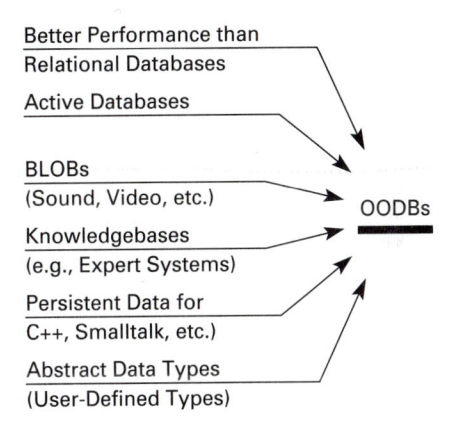

Figure 19.2 A variety of needs converged into OODB technology.

A UNIFIED CONCEPTUAL MODEL

In traditional computing, the conceptual models for analysis, the models for design, and the models for database definition and access are all different. In contrast, OO techniques use the same conceptual models for analysis, design, and construction as described in Chapters 5 through 15 (see Fig. 5.3). OODB technology gives a further stage of unification, illustrated in Fig. 19.3. The OO database conceptual model is the same as the rest of the OO world, rather than separate relational tables and SQL.

Using the same conceptual model for all aspects of development simplifies development, especially with OO CASE tools, improves communication among users, analysts, and programmers, and lessens the likelihood of errors.

Traditional *analysis* uses entity-relationship models and functional decomposition, and analysts develop matrices mapping functions and entity types. Traditional *design* uses a different view of the world—data-flow diagrams, structure charts, and action diagrams. *Programming* uses another different conceptual model—programmers do not think in terms of data-flow diagrams. Relational database technology uses yet another conceptual model employing tables, with the need to JOIN and PROJECT tables. The conceptual model of SQL is quite different from the conceptual models of entity-relationship diagrams, functional decomposition, data-flow diagrams, structure

Traditional development has four conceptual models.

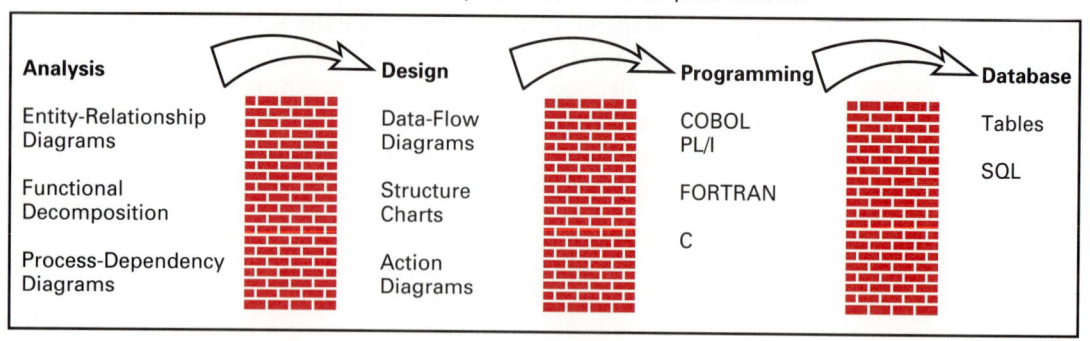

Analysis	Design	Programming	Database
Entity-Relationship Diagrams	Data-Flow Diagrams	COBOL PL/I	Tables
Functional Decomposition	Structure Charts	FORTRAN	SQL
Process-Dependency Diagrams	Action Diagrams	C	

Object-oriented technology uses one consistent model.

Analysis	Design	Programming	OODB

Object Model
Object Declaration
Object Manipulation

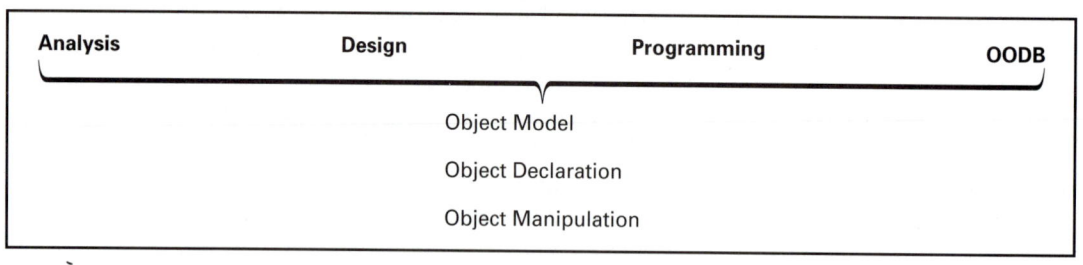

Figure 19.3 OODB uses the same conceptual model as OO analysis, design, and programming. OO techniques tear down the conceptual walls between analysis, design, programming (or code generation), and database definition and access.

charts, action diagrams, or COBOL. Figure 19.3 illustrates these four conceptual models.

By contrast, OODBs were designed to be well integrated with OO programming languages, such as C++ and Smalltalk. They use the same object model. A database language that is different from the programming language is unnecessary. For example, with some OODB products C++ is used for all database definitions and manipulation. The same object model is also used for analysis and design. The analyst may determine high-level objects and high-level behavior. The designer pushes this down to low-level objects that inherit properties and behavior from the higher-level objects. With good OO-CASE tools, as soon as the objects are specified on the screen, code can be interpretively generated for them.

Relational database design is quite separate from program design. The database is a separate space from the program space. The programmer has to figure out how to extract data from the tables and put data into the tables. With OODBs, the programmer deals with transient and *persistent* objects in a uniform way. The *persistent* objects are in the OODB, and thus the conceptual walls between programming and database are removed. Analysis, design, code generation, and database generation can be done iteratively by one person using a unified conceptual model. This can greatly increase the rate at which a creative person invents and refines systems.

As commented earlier, the employment of a unified conceptual model for analysis, design, programming, and database results in

- Higher productivity. The work of translating between paradigms is avoided.
- Fewer errors. Errors in translation between the paradigms are avoided.
- Better communication among users, analysts, and implementors
- Better quality
- More flexibility
- Greater inventability

The world is not a collection of tables. One common model of the world is the assembly hierarchy found in manufactured items. Here, a **Part** is decomposed into its constituent **Subparts**, that are, in turn, decomposed into additional subparts. These are difficult to represent and manipulate using tables. In fact, by using a standard SQL, all the **Subparts** of given **Part** cannot typically be determined with one query statement. In contrast, an OODB supports both the ability of objects to refer directly to each other and the computational facility of OO languages to process objects.

OO DATABASE ARCHITECTURE

In the late 1980s, the first OODBs appeared. Some of the main OODB products and their vendors are listed in Fig. 19.4. The early ones were designed as an extension of OO programming languages, such as Smalltalk and C++. The DML (data manipulation language) and DDL (data description language) were a common OO language. The design of current OODBs should take full advantage of CASE and incorporate methods created with any powerful technique, including declarative statements, code generators, and rule-based inferencing.

Product	Vendor
Gemstone	Servio Corporation, Alameda, CA
Itasca	Itasca Systems Inc., Minneapolis, MN
Objectivity	Objectivity, Menlo Park, CA
Object Store	Object Design Inc., Burlington, MA
Ontos	ONTOS Inc., Bellerica, MA
Versant	Versant Object Technology, Menlo Park, CA

Figure 19.4 Six OODB products and their vendors.

Many facilities of conventional database management are important in OODBs. These include locking for concurrent update controls, recovery, two-phase commits, security, data integrity, data distribution, and database tools.

Some features are independent of the fundamental architecture of an OODB but are common to most OODBs:

- **Versions.** Most database systems allow only one representation of a database entity to exist in the database. Versions allow alternative representation to exist simultaneously. This is useful in many application areas where a design is evolving and different strategies are being explored concurrently. For example, designers of a circuit may want to try different component layouts to maximize chip density, or software developers may have several versions of a particular subsystem using different algorithms to examine the effect that each has on overall system performance.

- **Shared Transactions.** Transactions typically isolate an individual's actions from the database until the transaction is committed to the database. Only then does it become globally visible. Shared transactions support groups of workstation users who want to coordinate their efforts in real time. In this way, users can share intermediate database results. The shared transaction allows several people to participate in a single transaction. This is useful in such applications as electronic conferences and document editing where several parties work on the document concurrently.

DEVELOPMENT WITH OODB

OODBs are developed by first describing the important object types of the application realm and the behaviors associated with those object types. These object types determine the classes that will form the definition of the OODB. For example, a database designed to store the geometry of mechanical parts would include classes such as **Cylinder**, **Sphere**, and **Cube**. The behavior of a **Cylinder** might include information about its dimensions, volume, and surface area:

```
class Cylinder {
        float height ();
        float radius ();
        float volume ();
        float surfaceArea ();
};
```

Similar definitions would be developed for **Cube** and **Sphere**. In the above definition, height (), radius (), volume (), and surfaceArea () represent the messages that can be sent to a **Cylinder** object. Note the absence of implementation details, including whether the information is stored or computed. The implementation is accomplished in the same language by writing functions corresponding to the OO requests:

```
Cylinder::height () {return Cylinder_Height;}
Cylinder::volume () {return PI * radius () * radius ()* height ();}
```

In this case, the height of the Cylinder is stored as a data element, while the volume is computed by the appropriate formula. Note that the internal implementation of volume uses requests to get height and radius. However, the most important aspect is the simplicity and uniformity that users of Cylinder experience. They just need to know how to send a request and what requests are available. The entire application can be written in one uniform style. Separating the programming language and DML is no longer necessary.

This approach also gives the OODB flexibility. Since the entire application is written by sending requests, implementations can be altered to any degree without affecting applications. Consequently, the application is simpler and much easier to maintain and enhance. In this sense, OODBs provide even greater separation between system specification and its implementation.

THREE APPROACHES TO BUILDING OODBs

OODBs can be built using three approaches. The first uses an existing conventional database management system and adds a layer for processing OO requests and storing methods. The DBMS is not changed. This approach has one merit: the highly complex code of today's database management system can be used, so that an OODB can be implemented faster than starting from scratch.

The second approach adds OO functionality to a relational DBMS. The tools, techniques, and vast experience of relational technology can then be used to build a new DBMS. Pointers may be added to relational tables linking them to large binary objects. Several existing RDB vendors advocate this approach.

The third approach rethinks the architecture of database systems and produces a new architecture optimized to meet the needs of OO technology. The OODB companies listed in Fig. 19.4 have all taken this approach, largely because they can achieve much better performance than by extending relational technology. Vendors taking this approach claim that relational technology is a subset of a more generalized capability. Relational data structures might be used where appropriate, but other data structures are usually better for complex objects and enable the data for a complex object to be accessed without moving the access mechanism. The OODB vendors quote cases involving complex objects in which nonrelational OODBs are roughly two orders of magnitude faster than relational databases for storing and retrieving complex information [8]. They are therefore essential in applications such as CAD (computer-aided design) and CAE (computer-aided engineering) and would enable a CASE repository to be a real-time facility rather than a batch facility (as it is with IBM's DB2). A CASE repository ought to be an OODB.

DATA INDEPENDENCE VERSUS ENCAPSULATION

A major goal of traditional database technology is *data independence*. Data structures should be independent of the processes that use data. The data, then, can be employed in any way the user wants.

In contrast, a major goal of object-oriented technology is *encapsulation*. This means that the data can *only* be employed with the methods that are part of a class. Object-oriented classes are intended to be reusable. Therefore, another goal of OO technology is achieving maximum reusability. Because of this, the class should be bug-free and should only be modified if absolutely necessary. Traditional database technology is designed to support processes that are subject to endless modification. Therefore, data independence is necessary. The OODB supports classes, some of which rarely change. Change comes from interlinking classes in diverse ways. The data structures in the OODB should be tightly optimized to support the class in which they are encapsulated. The goals, then, in relational databases and object-oriented databases are fundamentally different.

OODB WILL NOT COMPLETELY REPLACE RDB

The goal of relational databases, that of making the data independent of the application, will remain important for much data. We will always need to set up databases that can be used in unpredictable ways. In contrast, OODB establishes data that are used *only with defined methods*. RDB and OODB, then, meet different needs—both of which are important.

> In the foreseeable future, OO database technology will not replace relational database technology but will coexist with it.

COMPLEXITY OF DATA STRUCTURE

Objects are composed of objects that in turn are composed of objects and so on. Because of this, the data structures for one object sometimes become highly complex. When an object is used, its data should be readable without having to move the disk-access mechanism. The data for each object should be clustered together. This may not be the case if a relational database is used. The object may employ data from multiple relations and hence require multiple movements of the access mechanism.

OODB systems, such as those in Fig. 19.4, have deliberately avoided the relational model in order to improve machine performance. They allow the data for one class to be interlinked efficiently, often resorting to the pointer structure that relational databases tried to avoid.

If a class uses certain methods frequently, it makes sense to optimize the data structure to obtain good machine performance with these methods.

PERFORMANCE

OODBs greatly outperform RDBs for applications with lots of data connectivity. This is one of the primary reasons that applications sharing this characteristic currently use OODBs.

- OODBs allow objects to refer directly to one another using *soft pointers*. This makes OODBs much faster in getting from object A to object B than RDBs, which must use joins to accomplish this. Even an optimized join is typically much slower than an object traversal. Thus, even without any special tuning, an OODB is usually faster at these pointer-chasing mechanics.

- OODBs make physical clustering more effective. Most database systems allow the developer to place related structures close to each other in disk storage. This dramatically reduces retrieval time for the related data, since all data are read with one, instead of several, disk reads. However, in an RDB, implementation objects get translated into tabular representations and typically get spread out over multiple tables. Thus, in an RDB, these related rows must be clustered together, so that the whole object can be retrieved with one disk read. In an OODB, this is automatic. Furthermore, clustering related objects, such as all subparts of an assembly, can dramatically affect the overall performance of an application. This is relatively straightforward in an OODB, since this represents the first level of clustering. In contrast, physical clustering is typically impossible in an RDB, because it requires a second level of clustering—one level to cluster the rows representing individual objects and a second for the groups of rows that represent related objects.

- OODBs use diverse storage structures. In an RDB, data that cannot be easily expressed in tabular form is difficult to store and access efficiently. For example, multimedia applications require the storage of large data streams representing digitized video and audio data. CAD applications often require the storage of large numbers of very small objects, such as the points defining the geometry of a mechanical part. Neither is well-suited to representation in a table. Therefore, RDBs cannot provide efficient storage management for these application areas. The storage model for OODBs is unlimited, since the system is by nature extensible. OODBs can provide different storage mechanisms for different kinds of data. As a result, they have proven very effective in supporting both multimedia and CAD applications.

AVOIDING REDUNDANCY

With RDBs, data are normalized to help avoid redundancy [3, 6] and anomalies caused by data redundancy. This addresses redundancy in data but not redundancy in application code.

OO technology uses *inheritance* to lessen redundant development of *methods*. It also creates classes designed to be reused in many applications. Encapsulation and inheritance thus lower the amount of redundant *code*, as well as redundant data, in two ways—by inheritance and by reuse of classes. This lowers the cost of development and maintenance.

With traditional database technology, what ought to be common processing gets replicated and usually redesigned for many different applications, causing lower productivity and increased maintenance costs. More recently, RDBs have introduced the notion of triggers or procedures that can be executed by the database. Using these capabilities to place common processing into the database is an improvement. However, it still separates the processing from those entities naturally associated with the processing. For instance, one could write a trigger enforcing the behavior that a terminated employee's salary must be $0. However, the termination process cannot be associated with the Employee table. In an OODB, this process is straightforward, as the Employee class would define the terminate request and enforce the $0 salary constraint.

DIFFERENCES BETWEEN RDB AND OODB

Object-oriented and relational databases have some fundamentally different goals and characteristics. In some computing environments, the goals of classic relational databases predominate. In other computing environments, RDBs do not adequately meet the needs and OODBs have major advantages. It is not likely that one database management system will ever meet all types of computing needs.

Insight into the advantages of one database technology over another requires some understanding of the application development process. This development process is not completely general. One database technology cannot satisfy all application domains, and the requirements of applications must be considered when analyzing the advantages of one database technology over another.

Box 19.1 summarizes the differences between RDBs and OODBs.

A primary goal of relational databases is *data independence*. Data are separated from processing and normalized. Thus, they can be used for different applications, many of which may be unanticipated when the data are designed.

A primary goal of the OODB is *encapsulation*. The data are associated with a specific class that uses specific methods. The database stores that data plus the methods. The data and methods are inseparable. The data are not designed for any type of use but for use by the class. The class will be used in many different applications, many of which are not yet anticipated. We have *class independence* not merely *data independence*.

Relational databases and OO databases will coexist. Relational databases have the goal of *data independence*. Data is normalized so that it can be used by numerous unanticipated processes.

OO databases have the goal of supporting classes, with encapsulation, in which the data are used with specific methods. They have *class independence*, not data independence.

BOX 19.1   A summary of the differences between relational and object-oriented databases.

Relational Databases

Primary goal: data independence

Data only. The database generally stores data only.

Data sharing. Data can be shared by any processes. Data are designed for any type of use.

Passive data. Data are passive. Certain limited operations may be automatically triggered when the data are used.

Constant change. Processes using data constantly change.

Data independence. Data can be physically reorganized without affecting how they are used.

Simplicity. Users perceive the data as columns, rows, and tables.

Separate tables. Each relation (table) is separate. JOIN commands relate data in separate tables.

Nonredundant data. Normalization of data is done to help eliminate redundancy in data. (It does nothing to help redundancy in application development.)

Object-oriented Databases

Primary goals: encapsulation; class independence

Data plus methods. The database stores data plus methods.

Encapsulation. Data can be used only by the methods of classes. Data are designed for use by specific methods only.

Active objects. Objects are active. Requests cause objects to execute their methods. Some methods may be highly complex, for example those using rules and an inference engine.

Classes designed for reuse. Classes designed for high reusability rarely change.

Class independence. Classes can be reorganized without affecting how they are used.

Complexity. Data structures may be complex. Users are unaware of the complexity because of encapsulation.

Interlinked data. Data may be interlinked so that class methods achieve good performance. Tables are one of many data structures that may be used. BLOBs (binary large objects) are used for sound, images, video, and large unstructured bit streams.

Nonredundant methods. Nonredundant data and methods are achieved with encapsulation and inheritance. Inheritance helps to lower redundancy in methods, and class reuse helps to lower overall redundancy in development.

(Continued)

BOX 19.1 *(Continued)*

SQL. The SQL language is used for the manipulation of tables.

Performance. Performance is a concern with highly complex data structures.

Different conceptual model. The model of data structure and access represented by tables and JOINs is different from that in analysis, design, and programming. Design must be translated into relational tables, and SQL-style access.

OO requests. Requests cause the execution of methods. Diverse methods can be used.

Class optimization. The data for one object can be interlinked and stored together, so that they can be accessed from one position of the access mechanism. OODBs give much higher performance than relational DBs for certain applications with complex data.

Consistent conceptual model. The models used for analysis, design, programming, and database access and structure are similar. Application concepts are directly represented by classes in the OODB. The more complex the application and its data structures the more this saves time and money in application development.

With an RDB, the data can be physically reorganized without changing application programs that use the data. With an OODB, the class can be reorganized without disrupting systems that use the class.

OODBs support *active* objects, whereas traditional databases store passive data. As the world of computing progresses, more and more systems will be built with active objects.

The OODB supports complex data structures and does not break them down into tables. Complex data structures are encapsulated in the classes, just as DNA is encapsulated in biological cells. To take highly complex data structures and decompose them into tables every time you store them has been likened to decomposing your car into its components every time you put it in the garage. The more complex the data structure, the greater the advantage of the OODB.

The cells in your body would be very inefficient if their DNA was stored in relational form and accessed with SQL.

SUMMARY

OODBs represent the next step in database evolution, supporting OO analysis, design, and programming. OODBs allow complex applications to be developed and maintained at significantly lower cost. They enable the same conceptual model to be applied to analysis, design, programming, and database definition and access. This reduces the developer's burden of translating between different models throughout the lifecycle. The conceptual model should be the basis of fully integrated OO-CASE tools which help generate the data structures and methods (see Fig. 19.5).

OODBs give much better machine performance than relational databases for applications with complex data structures or classes with complex data structures. However, OODBs will coexist with relational databases for the foreseeable future, because relational databases can be used in unpredictable ways. In many situations, *data independence* is more important than *encapsulation*. A relational model will often be used as one form of data structure in an OODB.

A corporation tends to become locked into its form of database management system. When many applications share a corporate database, changing it is difficult and expensive. Future OODBs may have to incorporate the relational model in order to facilitate migration. OO systems can be, and are being, built with traditional databases. To do this, though, may preserve existing investments at the expense of efficiency.

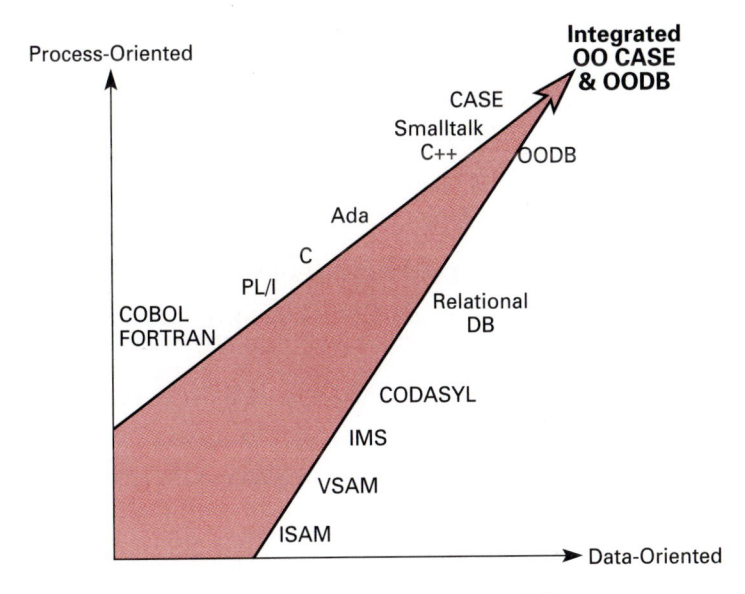

Figure 19.5 Languages and data management are evolving to a common conceptual model with integrated data structures and methods. This requires integrated OO-CASE and OODB tools.

Particularly important is that OO databases will be active, rather than passive, collections of data. As we commented earlier, the corporation of the future will be like an electronic organism with objects making requests of other objects, where these objects reside on databases. The OO databases of the future will directly reflect the OO model of the enterprise.

REFERENCES

1. Andrews, Timothy *et al.*, *The ONTOS Object Database,* Ontos, Inc., Technical Report, 1990.

2. Codd, E. F., "A Relational Model of Data for Large Shared Data Banks," *Communications of the ACM,* 13:6, June 1970, pp. 377-387.

3. Codd, E. F., "Further Normalization of the Data Base Relational Model," *Courant Computer Science Symposium 6: Data Base Systems,* Courant Computer Science Symposium 6 (New York), Randall Rustin ed., Prentice-Hall, Englewood Cliffs, NJ, 1972, pp. 33-64.

4. Date, C. J., *An Introduction to Database Systems* (4th edition), Addison-Wesley, Reading, MA, 1986.

5. Loomis, Mary, "Technical Q&A: Ask Mary," *ObjecToday,* 1:4, April 1991, pp. 2-3.

6. Martin, James, *Managing the Data-Base Environment,* Prentice-Hall, Englewood Cliffs, NJ, 1983.

7. Rosen, Steven and Dennis Shasha, "Using a Relational System on Wall Street: The Good, The Bad, The Ugly, and The Ideal," *Communications of the ACM,* 12:4, August 1989, pp. 365-381.

8. Versant, *Product Profile,* Versant Object Technology, Menlo Park, CA, 1991.

9. Wagner, R. E., "Indexing Design Considerations," *IBM Systems Journal,* 12:4, December 1973, pp. 351-367.

10. Wiederhold, Gio, *Database Design,* McGraw-Hill, New York, 1983.

11. Zdnonik, Stanley B. and David Maier, eds., *Readings on Object-Oriented Database Systems,* Morgan Kaufmann, San Mateo, CA, 1990.

20 FUTURE TOOLS FOR RELIABLE SOFTWARE

Society with its growing density of air traffic, electronic funds transfer, nuclear power stations, and so on is increasingly vulnerable to catastrophes caused by software failures. In one hospital the wrong patient was operated on because of a software error. We *must* learn how to engineer software with the utmost reliability.

> The opportunity exists today to create a new breed of OO tools for software development, where the goal is to produce ultrareliable software.

As we now move rapidly into a world of vast networks and client-server computing, guaranteed integrity of software will become more and more important. The software industry should develop growing libraries of classes whose operation is *certifiably* correct. These should be used with OO databases which ensure the integrity of data. With EDI (electronic data interchange) technology, the computers in one corporation will increasingly be *online* to the computers in other corporations. Software written by one team will interact in real time with software written by many other teams. *Server* software, accessed by many *clients*, should be able to guarantee that it correctly handles the requests it receives—either rejecting them with a clear error message or processing them correctly.

TRUE ENGINEERING OF SOFTWARE The state of the art of most software engineering lags far behind that of other areas of engineering. When most engineers complete their work and it is sold, we expect that it will work correctly. We do not expect jet engines to explode or buildings to collapse, but we are not too surprised if software does something weird.

> Most hardware products come with a warranty; most software products carry a disclaimer of warranty.

Software is sold, not when it is bug-free, but when bugs occur with suitably low frequency. When my spreadsheet tool goes berserk, I reflect that it has only 400,000 lines of code. Soon, we will use software with 40 million lines of code. Furthermore, my spreadsheet tool runs on a simple PC; we are now building software to run on parallel processors and networks with many computers running simultaneously. My spreadsheet tool has millions of users and has been tested endlessly. Compare that with the next generation of air traffic control software coming into use for the overcrowded skies.

To engineer software of true reliability, we need to combine three disciplines—those of the object-oriented world, the CASE world, and the world of formal methods with mathematical proofs of correctness. These disciplines should fit together with a synergy that creates a new era of software engineering.

Unfortunately, the practitioners of the three disciplines are barely on speaking terms. The OO gurus pour scorn on CASE [24]. The dominant CASE toolsets have been built with no knowledge of OO techniques—like their mass-market customers they support structure charts, data-flow diagrams, and so on. The relational database gurus attack object-oriented databases [4]. Almost no authorities in software practice understand mathematically formal methods, and the pioneers of formal methods, such as Dijkstra and Hoare, reject the notion that diagrams, such as those on a CASE tool screen, can be useful. Hoare in a beautifully written paper entitled "The Mathematics of Programming" states that structured diagrams

> actually inhibit the use of mathematics in programming, and I do not approve of them. They may be useful in first presenting a new idea, and in committing it to memory. Their role is similar to that of a picture of an apple or a zebra in a child's alphabet book. But reliance on pictures continued into later life would not be regarded as a good qualification for one seeking a career as a professional author. It is equally inappropriate for a professional programmer. [14]

In reality, diagrams that have semantic content and engineering-like precision are as important in systems engineering as they are in other engineering disciplines. (They are useful for professional authors also!) OO diagrams, such as those in this book, are essential for OO modeling. They can be linked to precise statements about preconditions and postconditions of operations, and mathematically precise specifications of those operations.

In Chapter 1 we described specialist gurus as resembling horses wearing blinders, each unable to see the value of a different specialization. To achieve ultrareliable software, the specialists in OO, CASE, and formal methods need to integrate their work.

> The integration of OO technology, CASE, and formal methods has immense potential and will lead to a new era of true software engineering.

MATHEMATICS AND PROGRAMMING

Tony Hoare, perhaps the most influential of the pioneers of formal methods, emphasizes in all of his work that *programs are mathematical expressions*. "They describe with unprecedented precision and in every minutest detail the behaviour, intended or unintended, of the computer on which they are executed." [14]

Unfortunately, programs have become so complicated that it has been entirely impractical to reason mathematically about their behavior. The only way to find out what they do is by experiment. Hoare comments:

> Such experiments are certainly not mathematics. Unfortunately, they are not even science, because it is impossible to generalize from their results or to publish them for the benefit of other scientists. [14]

To make it possible to apply mathematics to programming, we must break programs into components that are sufficiently small and disciplined. OO *methods* are generally small and carry out one tightly focused operation. They are candidates for the application of mathematical techniques.

When OO technology matures, application developers will build applications from libraries of classes, using generators to customize screens, reports, calculations, and rules, such as those discussed in Chapter 10. The classes in the library should be as reliable as possible and created in a mathematically verifiable fashion, where possible. If the developer builds from ultrareliable classes and cannot tamper with the internals of these classes, we can then raise the quality (and speed) of software development.

The developer should be able to express most of his design in terms of declarative statements and rules as well as existing classes. A (trustworthy) code generator is needed that can check the validity of declarative statements and generate code from them. The developer should never need to do procedural programming; he may use powerful nonprocedural statements to express *methods* or customize classes.

Mathematical proofs of program correctness, pioneered by Dijkstra, Hoare, and others, have led to mathematically-based specification languages, such as Z [23] and VDM [16]. The use of formal methods with these languages is steadily becoming more practical and its acceptance is slowly growing. Proofs of correctness are too difficult to achieve in large amorphous programs. The best hope for provably correct programs may be the building of OO *methods* with formal specification techniques that drive a code generator. Where each *method* is relatively small, this is achievable. Formal specification with languages such as Z has been applied both to data structures [17] and the *methods* that manipulate those structures [21].

Hoare comments that if only we could get the mathematics right, programming ought to be more reliable than other engineering disciplines. Programs have no components, such as O-rings, that can break up—programming is pure logic.

> We do not have to worry about problems of faulty castings, defective components, careless labourers, storms, earthquakes or other natural hazards; we are not concerned with friction or wear or metal fatigue. Our only problems are those we make for ourselves and our colleagues by our over-ambition or carelessness, by our failure to recognize the mathematical and theoretical foundations of programming, and our failure to base our professional practice upon them. [14]

On the other hand, failure to produce correct programs has proved disastrous. The *Mariner 1* shot to Venus plunged into space and was lost forever because a programmer had an undeclared variable. Today, Cruise missiles intended to carry hydrogen bombs are being programmed with a language that does not force its programmers to declare variables.

Hoare comments

> Our present failure to recognize and use mathematics as the basis for a discipline of programming has a number of notorious consequences. They are the same consequences as would result from a similar neglect of mathematics in the drawing of maps, marine navigation, bridge building, air traffic control, or the exploration of space. [14]

Ever since Dijkstra's early writing about a programming calculus [6, 7], a small number of researchers have attempted to apply mathematics to programming to produce provably correct code. A variety of different approaches have been used to derive correctness proofs [2, 3, 5, 6, 7, 8, 9, 10, 11, 15, 18, 19, 20, 25].

Mathematical techniques have been applied to proving programs correct and to creating specification techniques for verifiable programs. These techniques have worked with certain fairly small programs. A variety of approaches have been used, and Berg has summarized them concisely [1].

With a few rare exceptions, no programmer has used such techniques in practice for two reasons. *First,* they require a high level of mathematical sophistication. Even for simple programs, a level of mathematical maturity is needed far beyond that of ordinary I.S. analysts and programmers. The mathematical proofs involved are often several times longer than the program derived. So the whole subject has tended to be relegated to the world of exotic research with almost no attention being paid to it by I.S. executives and staff.

It is inconceivable that ordinary I.S. developers will acquire the mathematical skills to verify the correctness of their designs. Because of this, we need

CASE tools that enable their users to assemble designs from provably correct constructs and make it quite clear under what circumstances they may be correctly used. The mathematics is vital but must be hidden from the I.S. developers. The CASE tools, with diagrams, windows and prompts, must make the design techniques easy to use.

The second reason mathematical techniques have rarely been used is that most real-life programs have been too complex and unruly. This may be overcome by breaking the programs into fragments, that is, OO classes to which the techniques can be applied.

Conventional structured design seeks to lessen the number of unique paths that have to be tested. It does this by making the modules small (modular design), keeping the interfaces between modules simple, and limiting the control structures to those easier to test. Nontrivial programs, however, still have too many paths for complete testing. Furthermore, changes to the program—often necessary—cause unpredictable effects. Complex programs remain a minefield in which we can never be sure that all the mines have been removed.

Mathematically provable design takes a different approach. It limits the designer to the use of constructs that are provably correct. The use of hierarchies of such constructs permits the building of highly complex systems that are logically correct. Because mere humans cannot be trusted to follow the rules, each step in the design should be meticulously checked with software. Wherever possible in the future, *classes* should be built from provably correct constructs. OO-CASE tools should enforce, where possible, the correct use of those classes.

When we say "provably correct code," we do not mean that the program is necessarily without fault. We can still tell the computer to do things that are stupid. If we create a forecasting program based on the phases of the moon and the behavior of groundhogs, no mathematics will help. Provably correct code will not improve my stockbroker's predictions. However, the majority of bugs in programs today are caused by the mechanics of programming, inconsistent data, sequence errors, and so on. These can be eliminated.

We need to replace the ad hoc coding process that is so vulnerable to the frailties of the human coder. This is how the computer world *must* progress. Program coding as we know it today *must* disappear, because it is too error-prone and expensive and its results are too difficult to modify. It is an inhuman use of human beings because it asks them to do something beyond their capabilities—to produce perfect, intricate, complex logic that can be easily understood and modified.

> As automation of programming matures, the specification tools and languages that predominate will differ from those of today. They must be able to translate broad human thinking about requirements into a computable form and successively refine it until needed resources can be automatically allocated and provably correct machine code generated.

UP-FRONT VERIFICATION

In the early years of compiler design, a principle was established for ALGOL 60:

> Every syntactically incorrect program should be rejected by the compiler, and every syntactically correct program should give a result or an error message that is predictable and comprehensible *in terms of the source-language program itself.* Thus no core dumps should ever be necessary. [13]

OO-CASE tools, in effect, give us a higher-level source language. The same principle applies. Every syntactically incorrect *method* should be rejected and every syntactically correct *method* should give a result or an error message that is predictable and comprehensible *in terms of the source CASE-tool representation.* If the code generator produces COBOL, C++, or any other low-level language, inspection of this code should never be necessary.

Each *method* should be simple, if possible, and generated from the highest-level representation that enables the most complete verification.

The code generators and compilers need to be of the highest quality to ensure that they both catch errors and do not introduce errors of their own. Although rarely done today, formal, mathematically-based methods should be used for verifying the correctness of the code generator and compiler.

PRECONDITIONS AND POSTCONDITIONS

When a *request* is passed to a *method,* certain preconditions must apply if the method is to execute the request correctly, as discussed in Chapters 9 and 10.

The method should always check that these preconditions apply. If the preconditions are not satisfied, an error message should be returned. If the preconditions are satisfied, a result should be returned. The result may have to obey certain postconditions. These may be checked to ensure that the method has executed correctly.

Request → Method → Result

Preconditions must apply before the method is executed.

Preconditions must apply if the method is executed correctly.

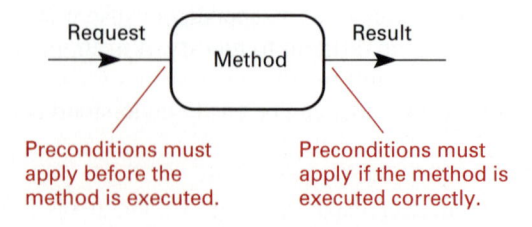

The operation, in effect, has a contract with its users that says "If you make a request that satisfies certain preconditions, I will return a result that satisfies certain postconditions."

ILLEGAL TO BYPASS THE CONTROLS

Where controls can be built into software to ensure reliability, bypassing them should be forbidden. The CASE tools, repository, code generator, and compiler should all enforce the safety controls. Tampering with generated code should be forbidden. Any patch or change to the generated COBOL, C, C++, and so on renders the safety controls meaningless.

Hoare comments that "in any respectable branch of engineering, failure to observe such elementary precautions would have long been against the law." [13]

In the Chernobyl nuclear power station, the operators switching off the safety controls led to the disaster.

Some OO tools are *pure* OO; others allow non-OO techniques to be used. C++, for example, can be used like C, as a general programming language, as well as in an OO fashion. Smalltalk, on the other hand, is pure OO. To be fully effective such a language needs compile-time enforcement of OO discipline. Tools for ensuring high reliability need to be *pure* and to actively prevent the bypassing of class encapsulation and the integrity controls built into methods. This should apply both to runtime facilities and OO databases.

IMMEDIATE FEEDBACK

The software creator needs to know immediately when he makes errors. This immediate feedback enables him to correct the error quickly and helps reinforce a learning process that may cause him to avoid making similar errors.

OO-CASE tools should therefore be interpretive. The developer should be able to instantiate objects when he specifies object types on the screen and to run methods when he designs them. The interpreter should check that the code meets its preconditions. Where possible the code should be constructed automatically (or semi-automatically) from the postconditions, so that it is not proved, nor even written, by the human system designer.

Although an interpreter should be used when building a system, an optimizing compiler is desirable to achieve maximum machine efficiency. The system should be built interpretively, then compiled. Every OO-CASE tool needs both an interpreter and compiler. It is important to ensure rigorously, in the future, that the interpreter and compiler give exactly the same result.

THE PROBLEM WITH PROGRAMMING LANGUAGES

Today's programming languages permit all manner of constructs that defy mathematical verification. They were not designed with mathematical verification in mind. Hoare comments

> Valiant research has been directed to formulate mathematical definitions of these standard languages. But the size and complexity of the definitions make

it impractical to derive useful theorems, or to prove relevant properties of programs in practice. [14]

Because of this, to build provably correct software, we should work with constructs that *are* mathematically verifiable—rather than the constructs of today's programming languages. We should employ only constructs that are built with mathematical axioms and proofs of correctness. The user does not perform the mathematical verification but the tools enforce correct usage. A library of provably correct *operations* should be built. These operations should manipulate precisely defined *data types* by means of provably correct *control structures*. As the collection of provably correct control structure grows, a library of classes is built in which the correct behavior of each class is guaranteed.

The control structures or classes need to be implemented in code in today's languages. We are ultimately dependent on this translation being correct. The code generator and compiler must be error-free. The best of today's code generators and compilers seem to have become trustworthy and may improve in the future as they are built with formal methods.

Good CASE tools completely hide the programming language from the developers. Because of this, new programming languages may come into use that are designed to facilitate mathematical proofs of correctness. Furthermore, the language may then be the basis of the microprocessor that executes the language.

The language OCCAM was designed to fill this role [22]. Hoare writes, "OCCAM is the first practical programming language which fulfills its role as a mathematical theory, giving practical assistance to programmers in writing provably correct programs" [14]. OCCAM was designed by INMOS, the microprocessor company. Because it is designed for parallel computers with many processor chips, it includes operators specifying concurrent execution of commands or processors. The language was the basis of the design of the *transputer,* a microprocessor intended for concurrent computing.

FROM MODEL TO CHIPS

We need a chain of resources for implementing reliable systems, illustrated in Fig. 20.1. At the top is an OO model designed to facilitate understanding of the process and its environment. This should be as easy to understand as possible by the end users and should help to reinvent procedures or design their business area.

The second block relates to prototyping. The designers should be able to assemble prototypes rapidly and use them to ensure that the designers really understand the user needs and that the human factoring works as well as possible.

The prototypes should evolve into a system design. The application should be built rapidly from provably correct constructs or classes.

```
┌──────────┐  Goal: Optimize understanding and inventiveness
│ OO Model │         of the end users.
└────┬─────┘
     ▼
┌──────────┐  Goal: Build the application rapidly from
│  System  │         provably correct constructs or classes.
│  Design  │
└────┬─────┘
     ▼
┌──────────┐  Goal: Ensure that the application meets the
│Prototypes│         user's needs and is well human-factored.
└────┬─────┘
     ▼
┌──────────┐  Goal: Generate a language that facilitates
│   Code   │         mathematical verification.
│Generation│         Generate code for concurrent processors.
└────┬─────┘
     ▼
┌──────────┐  Goal: Run on a machine with multiple micro-
│Execution │         processors, each designed to correctly
│          │         execute the mathematically based language.
└──────────┘
```

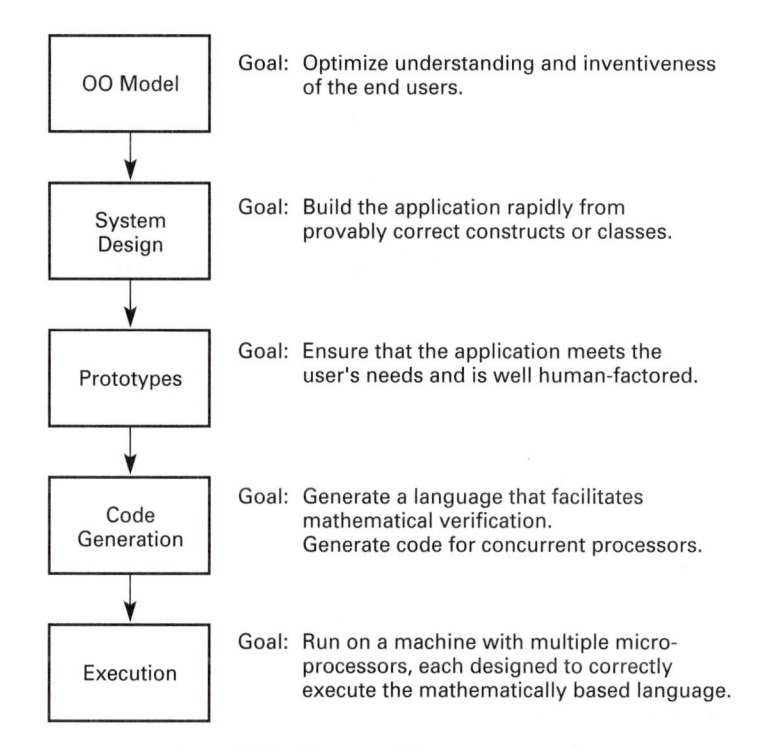

Figure 20.1 From model to system execution.

The design should drive a code generator. Concurrent (parallel) machines will increasingly be used so that the application is run on multiple processor chips simultaneously. The design and code generator should facilitate optimal multiprocessing. The language generated should be one (such as OCCAM) with a secure mathematical basis, which permits proof of correctness of the compiler and other transformation and checking tools.

The chips should correctly execute the mathematically-based language with parallel operation, like the transputer.

The machine will often employ a database. This should be an object-oriented database designed to extend the application integrity into database operation and ensure the protection of the data which are stored. OO databases can be made very fast with parallel processor operation.

A programming language that is designed to be generated, not hand coded, can be very different from COBOL, ADA, or C++. It should be much simpler, mathematically verifiable, designed for concurrent processing and designed to be the basis of the microprocessors that execute it. Design of the code generator, language, and microprocessor needs to be integrated. When this is done, the application developers will not see the language, only the CASE tools that provide input to the code generator.

> When we separate the application developers from the programming language, we can fundamentally change the nature of the programming language. This is one of the potential changes that will result from CASE technology.

A COMBINATION OF DISCIPLINES

Future tools for high-reliability software building should combine the capabilities of

- OO modeling and design
- CASE tools with code generation
- Declarative representations of OO *methods*
- OO databases
- An OO repository (which uses an OO database)
- A rigorous repository coordinator (see Chapter 18)
- Formal mathematically-based specification linked to a code generator
- Formal proofs of software correctness
- Classes of certified reliability (guaranteed to either reject a request with a clear error message or process it correctly)

Such tools should possibly contain

- A new programming language based, like OCCAM, on mathematical principles but which are higher level than OCCAM and have OO capabilites
- Microprocessors for executing the mathematically-based language with concurrent processing, like the transputer
- Design integration of code generator, programming language, and chip design

It will take years to achieve this combination of disciplines and create the new tools that we need. Most of the components already exist, so it need not take *many* years. However, it is a fundamental change in development culture, and this culture change will probably be a greater delaying factor than the technical difficulties. Many programmers will reject it because it seems alien to the God-given order. Many executives will be unaware of it because they are too busy putting out fires caused by the use of inadequate methodologies.

Fundamental changes in technology meet great emotional resistance. For example, Napoleon refused to believe in steam ships 20 years after the first one was working, even though he could have left Nelson's fleet standing on a windless day. Steam engine designers kept on building more elaborately tuned and complex mechanisms 30 years after the electric motor was in common use.

Many government departments are still issuing application development directives that lock their vast organizations into techniques from the past which prevent rigorous methods, modern requirements planning, and a higher level of automation. Most of this bureaucratization of inadequate techniques is accompanied by high-sounding phrases. A paper about the Department of Defense programming directives states, typically: "The theme pervading all of these steps is to elevate software policy, practices, procedure and technology from an artistic discipline to a true engineering discipline." The directives referred to *prevent* the use of rigorous engineering-like methods.

Next time you are in a new-technology jet approaching a big airport in a zero-visibility blizzard with computers operating the controls of the plane automatically and a complex air-traffic control system trying to prevent collisions, think about the need for technology that makes software ultrareliable.

REFERENCES

1. Berg, H. K., Boebert, W. E., Franta, W. R., and Moher, T. G., *Formal Methods of Program Verification and Specification,* Prentice Hall, Englewood Cliffs, NJ, 1982.

2. Blikle, A., and Mazurkiewicz, A., *An Algebraic Approach to the Theory of Programs, Algorithms, Languages and Recursiveness.* Mathematical Foundations of Computer Science, Warsaw, Poland, 1972.

3. Church, A., "The Calculi of Lambda-Conversion," *Annals of Mathematical Studies,* vol. 6, Princeton University Press, Princeton, NJ, 1951.

4. Codd, E. F., lecture at "The 3 Rs of CASE" conference chaired by Carma McClure, Chicago, June 1991.

5. Darringer, J. A. and King, J. C., "Application of Symbolic Execution to Program Testing," *Computer,* 11:4, 1978.

6. Dijkstra, E. W., "The Humble Programmer," *Communications of the ACM,* vol. 15, October 1972.

7. Dijkstra, E. W., *A Discipline of Programming,* Prentice Hall, Englewood Cliffs, NJ, 1976.

8. Flon, L., "On the Design and Verification of Operating Systems," Ph.D. Thesis, Department of Computer Science, Carnegie-Mellon University, 1977.

9. Gries, D., "An Introduction to Current Ideas on the Derivation of Correctness Proofs and Correct Programs," *IEEE Transactions on Software Engineering,* 2:4, 1976.

10. Hamilton, M. and Zeldin, S., "The Relationship between Design and Verification," *Journal of Systems and Software,* vol. 1, 1979. pp. 29-56.

11. Hoare, C. A. R., "An Axiomatic Approach to Computer Programming," *Communications of the ACM,* 12:10, 1969.

12. Hoare, C. A. R., "The Engineering of Software: A Startling Contradiction," *Computer Bulletin,* December, 1975.

13. Hoare, C. A. R., "The Emperor's Old Clothes," *Communications of the ACM,* 24:2, February 1981.

14. Hoare, C. A. R., *The Mathematics of Programming,* an inaugural lecture delivered before Oxford University, Oxford University Press, Oxford, 1986.

15. Howden, W.E., "Methodology for Generation of Program Test Data," *IEEE Transactions on Software Engineering,* 2:3, 1976.

16. Jones, D. B., *Systems Software Development Using VDM,* Prentice-Hall, Englewood Cliffs, NJ, 1986.

17. Josephs, M. B. and Redmond-Pyle, D., *Entity-Relationship Models Expressed in Z,* Oxford University Computing Laboratory Technical Report, PRG-TR-20-91, 1991.

18. Manna, Z., "The Correctness of Programs," *Journal of Computer and System Sciences,* 3:2, 1969.

19. Owicki, S., "Axiomatic Proof Techniques for Parallel Programs," Ph.D. Thesis, Department of Computer Science, Cornell University, 1975.

20. Owicki, S. and Gries, D., "Verifying Properties of Parallel Programs: An Axiomatic Approach," *Communications of the ACM,* 19:5, 1976.

21. *Proceedings of the Z User Workshop,* Oxford 1989, Springer-Verlag, Berlin, 1990.

22. Roscoe, A. W. and Hoare, C. A. R., *Laws of OCCAM Programming.* Monograph PRG-53, Oxford University Computing Laboratory, Programming Research Group, February 1986.

23. Spivey, J. M., *The Z Notation: A Reference Manual,* Prentice Hall, Englewood Cliffs, NJ, 1989.

24. Taylor, David A., *Object-Oriented Technology: A Managers' Guide,* Addison-Wesley, Reading, MA, 1992.

25. Wegbreit, B., "Constructive Methods in Program Verification," *IEEE Transactions on Software Engineering,* 3:2, 1977.

21 STANDARDS FOR OBJECT INTERACTION

Object-oriented technology cannot begin to reach its potential until there are industry standards that enable classes from one vendor to interact with classes from other vendors. The classes can execute on networked machines, from different manufacturers, with different operating systems, database systems, and user interfaces. Software vendors creating new classes are likely to do so by employing existing software from other vendors. International standards enabling classes to intercommunicate are as important as international *open* standards for networks.

CASE tools for OO design and code generation should help to enforce the standards, generating requests of standard format, and employing standard classes from a repository for object services and common facilities.

THE OBJECT MANAGEMENT GROUP

The organization primarily concerned with establishing industry standards is the Object Management Group (OMG). The OMG is a nonprofit, international, trade association, funded by about 200 computer and software companies. Its mission is stated as follows [3]:

- The Object Management Group is dedicated to maximizing the portability, reusability, and interoperability of software. The OMG is the leading worldwide organization dedicated to producing a framework and specifications for commercially available object-oriented environments.

- The Object Management Group provides a reference architecture with terms and definitions upon which all specifications are based. Implementations of these specifications will be made available under fair and equitable terms and conditions. The OMG will create industry standards for commercially available object-oriented systems by focusing on remote object network access, encapsulation of existing applications, and object database interfaces.

- The OMG provides an open forum for industry discussion, education, and promotion of OMG endorsed object technology. The OMG coordinates its activities with related organizations and acts as a technology/marketing center for object-oriented software.

The members of the Object Management Group, Inc. (OMG) have a shared goal of developing and using integrated software systems. These systems should be built using a methodology that supports modular production of software; encourages reuse of code; allows useful integration across lines of developers, operating systems, and hardware; and enhances long-range maintenance of that code. Members of the OMG believe that the object-oriented approach to software construction best supports their goals.

To achieve an industrial revolution in software the world needs many software factories all using off-the-shelf software components from many vendors to create new software which is reliable and inexpensive. We need an end to the age of monolithic software in which software vendors write all their own code.

> When you buy software in the future, it will be like buying a car; it will consist of components from many vendors, worldwide. To achieve this, we need standards for the interfaces to objects so that all vendors can use objects from other vendors.

We need standard mechanisms by which objects transparently make requests and receive responses: this interoperability needs to function over networks between different machines and different environments.

THE OMG OBJECT MODEL

The OMG has a generally agreed-upon model of object types, their properties, and operations (described in Chapter 5).

> The goal of the Object Model Task Force is "to facilitate portability of applications, reusability of object-type libraries, and interoperability of software components in a distributed heterogenous environment" [2].

A goal is that the OO products now evolving, such as OO database management systems, OO-CASE tools, OO preprocessors, and OO-GUI (graphic user interface) tools, should employ the model definitions. The OMG acknowledges that programming languages, at least those with ANSI or ISO standardization, "will be slower to evolve than some of the other system software products not so constrained."

OBJECT MANAGEMENT ARCHITECTURE

The OMG has a Reference Model for an *Object Management Architecture* [3]. The goal of the architecture is to enable different software from different vendors to work together. It is intended to influence the design of components only to the extent of achieving interoperability. Diverse design solutions can be accommodated.

The Reference Model addresses

- How objects make and receive requests and responses
- The basic operations that must be provided for every object
- Object interfaces that provide common facilities useful in many applications

The Object Management Architecture consists of four major parts as illustrated in Fig. 21.1.

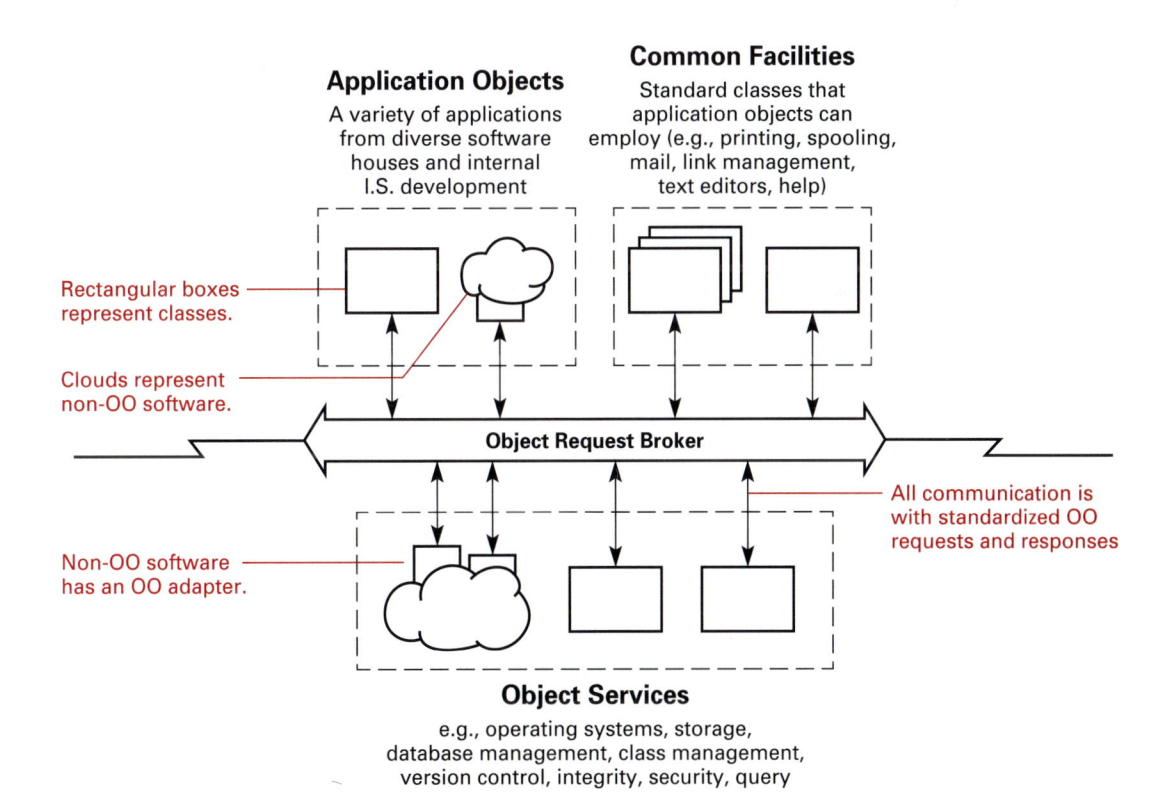

Figure 21.1 The OMG's Object Management Architecture is attempting to achieve industry standardization for OO interoperability.

Application Objects (AO)

Application Objects are end-use applications that may be built by diverse vendors or by in-house I.S. organizations.

Common Facilities (CF)

Common Facilities are objects and classes providing general purpose capabilities useful in many applications. It is a shared library of commonly used functions. It includes functions that were once in applications and are now migrating into operating systems or systems software. Various application objects may become common functions (CF) when they become popular enough to become de facto standards. This could include such things as 3-D graphic routines, spelling checkers, and hypertext. Types of facilities that are candidates for CF include

- Cataloging and browsing of classes and objects
- Link management
- Reusable user interfaces (e.g., text editors)
- Printing and spooling
- Error reporting
- Help facility
- Electronic mail facility
- Tutorials and computer-based training
- Common access to remote information repositories
- Agent (intelligent macro) facilities
- Interfaces to external systems
- Object querying facilities
- User preferences and profiles

Object Services (OS)

Object Services is a collection of services that provides basic functions for creating, storing, maintaining, subtyping, and managing objects. They include file or database management systems, transaction managers, directory services, and so on. OMG lists examples of the operations that Object Services can provide:

- *Class management.* The ability to create, modify, delete, copy, distribute, describe, and control the definitions of classes, the interfaces to classes, and the relationships between class definitions.
- *Instance management.* The ability to create, modify, delete, copy, move, invoke, and control objects and the relationships between objects.

- *Storage.* The provision of permanent or transient storage for large and small objects, including their state and methods.
- *Integrity.* The ability to ensure the consistency and integrity of object states both within single objects (e.g., through locks) and among objects (e.g., through transactions).
- *Security.* The ability to provide (define and enforce) access constraints at an appropriate level of granularity on objects and their components.
- *Query.* The ability to select objects or classes from implicitly or explicitly identified collections based on a specified predicate.
- *Versions.* The ability to store, correlate, and manage variants of objects.

THE OBJECT REQUEST BROKER (ORB)

The Object Request Broker is the heart of the Object Management Architecture (shown in Fig. 21.1). It allows objects to communicate independently of specific platforms and techniques. The goal of the Object Request Broker is to guarantee that objects can interoperate with one another, whether they are on the same machines, different machines, or diverse networks of heterogeneous systems.

An object makes a request in a standard fashion, and the Object Request Broker arranges for the request to be processed. The Object Request Broker causes some *method* to be invoked and conveys the results to the requester.

The ORB supports the view that objects of diverse types should be able to communicate but not reveal their insides. The objects may be relatively simple, such as print mechanisms, or highly complex, such as production scheduling systems. They may communicate within the same computer, across LANs, across corporate networks, or across multinetwork systems spanning corporations. The communicating objects may be implemented in different languages, on different vendors' hardware, with different operating systems.

The Object Management Group states

> The ORB is responsible for all mechanisms required to find the object implementation for the *request,* to prepare the object implementation to receive the *request,* and to communicate the data making up the request. The interface the client [requestor] sees is completely independent of where the object is located, what programming language it is implemented in, or any other aspect which is not reflected in the object's interface [1].

Most software systems are not designed to work in an all-encompassing environment; ORB systems are designed to span diverse environments and hide the implementation details of these environments. It is as though mechanisms were encapsulated, thus extending the benefits of OO across diverse platforms and networks.

The ORB standards say nothing about the network mechanisms over which the requests and responses are delivered. Networks are defined in different standards.

The ORB has to find the objects to which a *request* refers. In order to do this, there must be standard formats for requests and responses. In this way, ORB systems are rather like electronic mail systems in which messages travel over diverse networks between diverse computers. The difference is that OO systems make sure that the mail is read.

Box 21.1 lists functions that the Object Request Broker must address, at least to some degree.

In the world of large-scale networks, the need for a global naming and directory service was discovered, and this led to the widespread adoption of the CCITT X.500 standard. The ORB needs something equivalent to X.500. The ORB need not itself have all the information required to locate objects. It may use a directory or a service that can search for objects based on attributes, including changeable attributes such as *not-busy* or *within 200 feet*. It may use a service similar to the telephone yellow pages or call on a runtime library.

DIVERSE ORB IMPLEMENTATIONS

There are likely to be diverse types of implementations of ORB from different vendors. An ORB could be designed to operate in one machine, on a LAN-based system, on one vendor's network systems, or on far-flung multinetwork systems linking diverse environments. It could be seen as a normal program by the operating system, or it could be built into the operating system as an underlying service which could enhance security, robustness, and performance. It may be linked to an OO database management system or a class library system. It may be an integral part of software for distributed operations or system management. It could be built into system software such as OSF's DCE (Distributed Computing Environment).

The different ORB implementations will have to intercommunicate. Like objects, their internal mechanisms can assume any form, but the requests and responses they transmit must be of standard format. The OMG *Common Object Request Broker Architecture* (CORBA) assumes that the *Core Model* of the ORB will be implemented in fundamentally different ways, but there are certain components above the Core Model that provide common interfaces. The common interfaces hide the differences in ORB Core Models, and so the architecture gives the maximum freedom in ORB implementation.

> The OMG architecture thinks in terms of *client* and *server* objects. A *client* object requests services of a server object. A *server* object accepts the request and performs the service. The client and server could be on the same machine or on separate machines.

BOX 21.1 Functions of the Object Request Broker.

- **Name Services.** Object name mapping services map object names in the naming domain of the requestor into equivalent names in the domain of the method to be executed, and vice versa. The OMG Object Model does not require object names to be unique or universal. Object location services use the object names in the request to locate the method to perform the requested operation. Object location services may involve simple attribute lookups on objects. In practice, different object systems or domains will have locally preferred object naming schemes.

- **Request Dispatch.** This function determines which method to invoke. The OMG Object Model does not require a request to be delivered to any particular object. As far as the requestor is concerned, it does not matter whether the request first goes to a method that then operates on the state variables of objects passed as parameters, or whether it goes to any particular object in the parameter list.

- **Parameter Encoding.** These facilities convey the local representation of parameter values in the requestor's environment to equivalent representations in the recipient's environment. To accomplish this, parameter encodings may employ standards or de facto standards.

- **Delivery.** Requests and results must be delivered to the proper location as characterized by a particular node, address, space, thread, or entry point. These facilities may use standard transport protocols.

- **Synchronization.** Synchronization primarily deals with handling the parallelism of the objects making and processing a request and the rendezvous between the requestor and the response to the request. Possible synchronization models include: asynchronous (request with no response), synchronous (request; await reply), and deferred synchronous (proceed after sending request; claim reply later).

- **Activation.** Activation is the housekeeping processing necessary before a method can be invoked. Activation and deactivation of persistent objects is needed to obtain the object state for use when the object is accessed, and save the state when it no longer needs to be accessed. For objects that hold persistent information in nonobject storage facilities (e.g., files and databases), explicit requests can be made to objects to activate and deactivate themselves.

- **Exception Handling.** Various failures in the process of object location and attempted request delivery must be reported to requestor and/or recipient in ways that distinguish them from other errors. Actions are needed to recover session resources and resynchronize requestor and recipient. The ORB coordinates recovery housekeeping activities.

(Continued)

BOX 21.1   *(Continued)*

> - **Security Mechanisms.** The ORB provides security enforcement mechanisms that support high-level security control and policies. These mechanisms ensure the secure conveyance of requests among objects. Authentication mechanisms ensure the identities of requesting and receiving objects, threads, address spaces, nodes, and communication routes. Protection mechanisms assure the integrity of data being conveyed and assure that the data being communicated and the fact of communication are accessible only to authorized parties. Access enforcement mechanisms enforce access and licensing policies.

When a client issues a *request,* it names an object, an *operation* of that object, and zero, one, or multiple parameters for that operation. The input parameters are passed to the operation and output parameters and return values are passed back to the client object (unless the request is invalid or cannot be processed, in which case an exception message and parameters are sent back to the client).

The format of the request and response needs to be standardized. Objects can then communicate even though they may be implemented in different languages, on different platforms, by different vendors.

The request may be sent to the Object Request Broker, which arranges for the request to be processed and conveys the results to the requestor. This may be a simple operation. However, the Object Request Broker sometimes has to contact Object Services in order to find the class and operation that is requested. The Object Services may include a class dictionary service or might search runtime operation libraries.

OMG gives an example [3]:

> Consider the request "print layout_312 laser_plotter." This could be sent to the object "layout_312" whose "print" method would then print it on "laser_plotter." Or the request could be sent to "laser_plotter" whose "print" method would access "layout_312". Or the request could be sent to the generalized "print" routine that would figure out a good way to arrange the printing, based on some attributes of these two objects. Or, instead of relying on a generalized "print" routine, the Name Service in the ORB could determine an appropriate method jointly owned by the (the classes of) "layout_312" and "laser_plotter".

Clients can create objects by issuing requests. The response is then an object reference that identifies the new object. Similarly, objects can be destroyed.

OPERATIONS

Each operation has an *operation identifier*. If may be referred to with an *operation name*. The operation might be implemented in different ways in different objects.

An operation has a *signature* that describes legitimate values of request parameters and returned results. The signature consists of

- a specification of the parameters required in requests
- a specification of the return results
- a specification of the error messages (exceptions) that may be raised and the types of parameters accompanying them
- a specification of additional contextual information that may affect the performance of the request
- an indication of the execution semantics—for example, the execution can be
  - *at-most-once:* it returns a successful result once only or else an error message
  - *best effort:* the server does its best to perform the request but cannot return any results; the requestor never synchronizes with the completion, if any

OBJECT INTERFACES

An *interface* to an object type is the set of possible operations that a client may request of the object type.

A client knows only the logical structure of a server object as defined by its interface. The server object might provide its service by itself acting as a client to other objects.

INTERFACE DEFINITION LANGUAGE

Interfaces are specified in IDL, the interface definition language. This language defines the object type in terms of the operations that may be performed on it and the parameters to those operations. IDL fully defines the interface between client object and the server objects.

The programmer of a client object may write an IDL stub. The stub is used by the ORB which finds the required server object, relays the *request* to it, and returns the results. The stub should work with multiple ORBs which may be implemented differently. Clients are maximally portable. They can work without source changes with any server object that implements the desired interface and any ORB that supports the IDL. Clients have no knowledge of the implementation of the server object or the implementation of the ORB or the mechanism, networks, and so on which the ORB uses to locate the server object.

IDL is the means by which a particular object implementation tells its potential clients what operations it makes available and how they should be invoked. The IDL definitions may reside in a *runtime repository* which is part of the ORB.

IDL is a declarative language. It does not include any algorithmic structures or variables. IDL grammar is a subset of ANSI C++ with additional constructs to support mechanisms for invoking remote operations. Because most analysts and programmers are unfamiliar with C++, it is desirable that IDL should be generated by OO-CASE tools.

IDL supports inheritance. An interface can be a subtype of another interface, inheriting all of its characteristics and adding characteristics of its own.

THE ORB REPOSITORIES

The ORB needs a database, or persistent store, of information that enables it to function. The *Interface Repository* stores IDL representations and makes them available to the ORB at runtime, so that they may be used by the ORB to perform requests.

The Implementation Repository contains information that allows the ORB to locate objects and activate them.

Other information may be in the Implementation Repository, for example, information which aids in maintaining security, resource allocation, and possibly charging for the use of objects.

ORBs AND OODB

ORBs are likely to use OO databases. There is a strong argument for integration of an OODBMS and ORB.

The ORB should use an OODBMS both as part of Object Services and for its Interface Repository and Implementation Repository. The act of registering an object in the OODBMS should simultaneously register it with the ORB and vice versa. The capabilities of the ORB enhance those of the OODBMS by adding distribution capability, and the OODBMS helps implement the ORB by assisting with versions, naming, location, security, and so on. The language for accessing objects in the OODBMS should be the same as that in the ORB. There seems no point in having separate languages for the ORB and OODBMS.

MULTIPLE ORBs

Complex systems are likely to use multiple ORBs. These ORBs may be implemented by different vendors in different ways.

Classes are built in an ORB-independent way and use an IDL (interface definition language) defined in an ORB-independent way. Because of this, requests and responses can pass through multiple different ORBs and preserve the semantics necessary for client objects to interact with target objects.

Figure 21.2 shows various possibilities. The first two diagrams relate to OO software with no ORB. Classes interact with other classes directly without the overhead of an ORB. Most software packages or modules will be built so that the

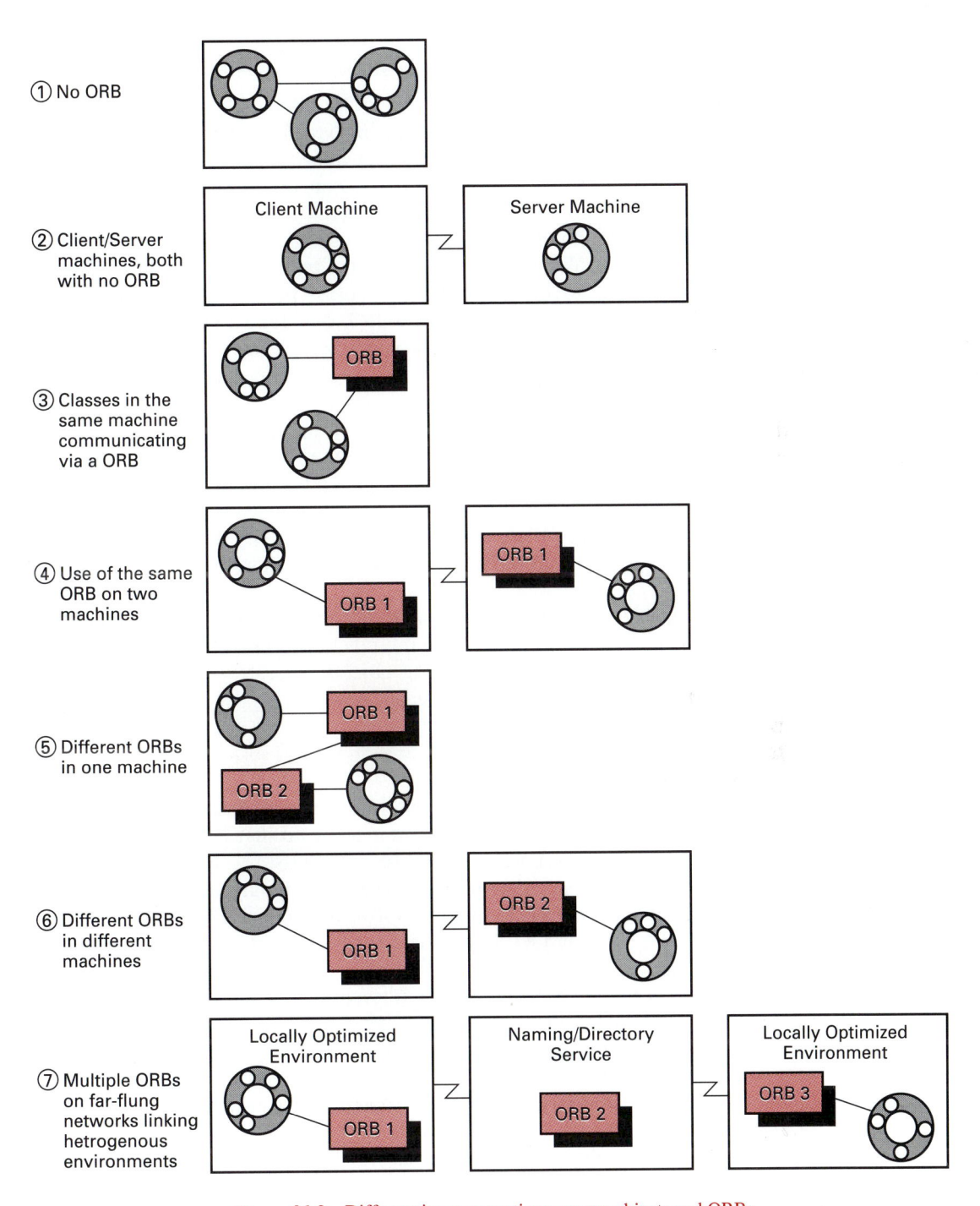

Figure 21.2 Different interconnections among objects and ORBs.

classes interact directly; only when they interact with a different package or service will an ORB be used.

The third diagram of Fig. 21.2 shows classes interacting via an ORB in one machine. The fourth shows classes interacting via the same ORB in different machines. Here, both implementations use the same object references and communication mechanism. An object reference can be passed freely from one machine to the other—no transformation is needed.

The fifth picture shows two ORBs. Some objects are implemented by ORB 1 and some by ORB 2. When an object connected to one ORB invokes an object connected to the other ORB, the object reference is passed as a parameter from one ORB to the other. Each ORB must be able to distinguish its own object references from those of other ORBs and be able to pass object reference parameters of other ORBs. The sixth diagram is similar to the fifth except that the ORBs communicate between separate machines.

The seventh diagram might relate to the far-flung network. ORB 1 and ORB 2 might each operate on an environment that is optimized locally, but objects on ORB 1's environment need to make requests of objects on ORB 3's environment. To find the requisite object, another ORB, ORB 2 provides a networkwide naming/directory service. The ORBs may have no commonality. It may be necessary to have gateways to translate object references and requests used in one ORB to those understood by another.

In ways such as these, ORBs from different vendors may intercommunicate. A class implicitly chooses an ORB when it binds to that ORB's object adapter.

The use of separate ORBs managing objects separately avoids the need to unify and optimize on a global scale. Instead, it allows locally optimized systems to be interlinked.

INTERFACE TO NON-OO SOFTWARE

If OO software is to have widespread use, it must interact with other software that is not OO in nature.

A vast amount of non-OO software exists, including basic software such as operating systems, database management systems, network software, and so on. Object-oriented software will ease its way steadily into a world that is largely non-OO. It will be a long time before all of the software that needs to interact is object-oriented.

The *Application Objects* and *Object Services* of Fig. 21.1 will often be non-OO. In order to connect to the Object Management Architecture, they must have an OO interface, sometimes called an *adapter* or *wrapper*, which accepts OO requests in their standard format and translates them to whatever form the non-OO software uses. Similarly, the wrapper translates the responses into standard OO responses.

Figure 21.1 draws non-OO software as clouds and shows it having a square-cornered OO interface. Providing software has an OMA-compliant interface, it can participate in the Object Management Architecture.

The Object Management Architecture does not define the screen interface for the end user. A variety of graphic, or other, user interfaces could be employed. These are the subject of standardization efforts outside the OMG. The user interface must interact with the Object Request Broker using standard requests and responses. Eventually, Common Facilities may provide standard user interface classes.

> Basically, the goal of the OMG is providing the "glue" that enables classes from all vendors to interoperate. Standards for this glue are needed quickly and need to have the widest industry support, so that the object-oriented revolution can gain maximum momentum.

REFERENCES

1. OMG, *Common Object Request Broker Architecture and Specification,* Object Management Group, Document 91.8.1, August 1991.

2. OMG, *The OMG Object Model,* Object Management Group, Document 91.9.1, September 1991.

3. Soley, Richard Mark, ed., *Object Management Architecture Guide,* Object Management Group, Document 90.9.1, November 1, 1990.

PART IV EPILOGUE

22 THE FUTURE OF SOFTWARE

INTRODUCTION   The human brain is good at some tasks and bad at others, while the computer is good at certain tasks that the brain does badly. The challenge of computing is to forge a creative partnership using the best of both.

The electronic machine is fast and absolutely precise. It executes its instructions unerringly. Our meat machine of a brain is slow and usually imprecise. It cannot do long, meticulous operations of logic without making mistakes. Fortunately, it has some remarkable properties. It can invent, conceptualize, demand improvements, and create visions. Humans can write music, start wars, build cities, create art, fall in love, dream of colonizing the solar system but cannot write bug-free COBOL.

The future challenge in most human endeavors will be merging human and machine capabilities—to achieve the best synergy between people and machines. This synergy will evolve rapidly, because machines are becoming more powerful and networks are growing at a furious rate.

The computers of the future will be nothing like the robots we see in the movies. They will not have the human abilities of an automated Schwarzenegger. In many ways, they will be more interesting, because they will use worldwide networks of immense bandwidth and have access to vast amounts of data and vast libraries of complex object-oriented software that are absolutely precise in their operation.

Today's software is relatively trivial. To make computers into synergistic partners for humans, they need complex software. Software of the necessary complexity probably cannot be built using traditional structured techniques alone. In the mid-1980s, authorities of structured techniques claimed that building the proposed systems of 50 million lines of code was impossible [4]. Our future requires software in which systems of 50 million lines of code will be commonplace. Object-oriented techniques with encapsulation, polymorphism, repository-based development, design automation, and code generators are essential for this.

OPTICAL DISKS

In the near future, desktop machines will have optical disks capable of holding hundreds of millions of lines of code. Billion line-of-code disks will eventually be commonplace. Software will probably be sold on optical disks, with one disk containing multiple related products—for example, a general office worker's set of tools or an I.S. professional's set of tools. If a COBOL programmer had been coding at today's average rate since the time of Christ, all the object code he produced would not fill one CD-ROM.

Future developers will have CD-ROMs containing libraries of applications and objects designed for reusability These libraries will appear in I-CASE format, so that their design can be displayed on the screen, modified, and linked to other system components. Mainframe and LAN server repositories will contain much larger libraries. The tools will need search mechanisms and expert systems to help the developers find the reusable components most appropriate to their needs. Computer users will also have CD-ROMs full of software. More than 100 million lines of object code can reside on one CD-ROM. Disks will be sold with many applications and tools integrated together. Cars, tanks, planes, robots, building controllers, household machines, security devices—machines of many types will have their own optical disks of software.

THE NEED FOR POWER TOOLS

We could not build today's cities, microchips, or jet aircraft without power tools. Our civilization depends on power tools. Yet, the application of computing power to corporate systems is often done by hand methods. Design of the interlocking computer applications of a modern enterprise is no less complex than the design of a microchip or a jet aircraft. To attempt this design using hand methods is ridiculous.

Power tools change the methods of construction. Object-oriented modeling and design change the basic way we think about systems. Now that such tools exist, the entire application development process should be reexamined and improved. Advanced power tools give rise to the need for an engineering-like discipline. OO techniques are the foundation for this discipline.

Important from the business point of view is that power tools for software change *what can be constructed,* just as power tools for building enable us to create skyscrapers. These changes need to be understood by management at every level. Making the changes is a critical success factor for business. Top management needs to ensure that its I.S. organization is adopting the new solutions as quickly as possible.

> Power tools change what is possible. They enable far more complex software to be built. This will lead to much higher levels of enterprise automation.

EVOLUTION OF SOFTWARE PRODUCTION

Since the industrial revolution, manufacturing techniques have evolved in an extraordinary way—from hand tools to power tools, from mass production to flexible robotic factories. Software building will also evolve from hand methods; the evolution will be very much faster. In manufacturing there have been four phases. Software building may evolve through four similar phases.

Phase 1: A Craft Industry

Most software today is designed and coded with manual techniques; each program is a unique piece of craftsmanship, rather like the making of clothes in cottages before the industrial revolution or the building of guns by individual gunsmiths in the eighteenth century.

Phase 2: Power Tools and Engineering Methods

I-CASE represents the coming of power tools to software building. Designs are synthesized with the help of a computer, and code with no coding errors is generated from the designs. The tools enforce structured techniques and apply rigorous checks to the design, bringing a much needed engineering-like discipline to the building of software.

Phase 3: Mass Production

In the early use of I-CASE tools, each program is still designed on a one-off basis. Later, repositories become populated with reusable classes, and libraries of reusable classes evolve. Applications are built by assembling preexisting building blocks.

Phase 4: Robot Production

As object-oriented design matures, classes of great complexity are created. Vast libraries of reusable classes are built. Tools assist the developer in specifying requirements and then automatically select and assemble the classes and class methods that can meet the requirements. The toolset carries on a dialog with the designer, enabling him to modify the design, selecting parameters and options.

This evolution could be compared to four generations of a family business making furniture. In the first generation, each piece of furniture is built by hand.

In the second generation, lathes, drills, and power tools become available (like I-CASE tools), but craftsmen still build each piece on a one-off basis. In the third generation, an inventory is built of reusable parts—table tops, legs, chair seats, and so on. Furniture is now assembled from reusable parts with minor custom work. Orders can be filled quickly. The capital required is higher, but the manufacturing cost is lower. Similarly, I-CASE tools will be used with a repository of reusable classes and minor custom work. In the fourth generation, robotic factories assemble the components and allow great variability in what can be built from the components. This is like software tools automatically synthesizing much of the design to meet high-level statements of requirements.

Software tools have not yet evolved to this fourth phase. It could be accomplished by combining object-oriented techniques with

- a standard repository capable of storing many thousands of classes
- classes of extreme reliability built with mathematically-based techniques
- a powerful repository coordinator
- intelligent enterprise models that express business rules
- expert system techniques for guiding the developer in stating requirements and translating them into design

INHUMAN USE OF HUMAN BEINGS

Norbert Wiener, the great pioneer of computers, wrote a book with the memorable title *The Human Use of Human Beings* [7]. In his view, jobs that are inhuman because of drudgery should be done by machines—not people. However, among these jobs, he omitted that of the COBOL programmer.

In a sense, the programmer's job is inhuman, because programmers are required to write large amounts of complex code without errors. To build the strategic and competitive systems that business needs, we want complex new procedures programmed in three months. This is beyond the capability of COBOL programmers.

Many of the tasks that I.S. professionals do are unsuited to our meat-machine brain. They need the precision of an electronic machine. Humans create program specifications that are full of inconsistencies and vagueness. Computers should help humans create specifications and check them at each step for consistency. Humans should not write programs from specifications, because they cannot do that well. A computer should generate the code needed. When humans want to make changes—a frequent occurrence—they have real problems changing the code. Seemingly innocent changes have unperceived ramifications that can cause a chain reaction of errors.

If the programs needed are *large,* we are in even worse trouble, because many people work together on them. When humans try to interact at the needed level of meticulous detail, communication errors abound. When one human makes a change, it affects the work of others. Often, however, the subtle interconnection is not perceived. Meat machines do not communicate with precision.

The end user perceives problems of the I.S. department but does not know how to solve them. A major part of the problem is that humans are so slow; they often take two years to produce results, and they are delayed by the backlog. It is rather like communicating with a development team in another solar system where the signals take years to get there and back.

Error-free coding is not natural for our animal-like brains. We cannot handle the meticulous detail and the vast numbers of combinatorial paths. Furthermore, if we want thousands of lines of code produced per day, then the job is even more inhuman. It is a job for machines. Only recently have we begun to understand how to make machines do it.

The era of code generators, specification tools, mathematically-based design, and software design automation is just at its primitive beginnings. The era of artificial intelligence is also young—with machines that can reason automatically using large numbers of rules. As these capabilities mature, machines will become vastly more powerful.

CHAIN REACTION

> The automation of software development is the beginning of a chain reaction.

When developers build software out of building blocks, they can create more complex building blocks (whether this is done with object-oriented design or other techniques). High-level constructs can be built out of primitive constructs. Still higher level ones can be built out of these and so on. Highly powerful constructs will evolve for different system types and application areas.

Essential in this is the rigor of the mechanism that enforces correct interfacing among the modules. This rigor allows pyramiding, so that modules can be built out of other modules. The rigor may be achieved by using rules and rule-based processing to enforce integrity in the designs and ensure consistency when separate components are linked. It may be achieved using mathematically-based constructs of provable correctness, using design techniques that scale up to large systems. As designers of rule-based, I-CASE tools have discovered, a large number of rules are needed to enforce consistency and integrity.

Essential to the chain reaction is an intelligent repository that stores a large quantity of reusable designs from which procedures can be built. Many developers will use large central repositories as well as desktop repositories.

As the software pyramids grow, software must be made as easy to use as possible. The complexity of software will become formidable but must be hidden from the users just as the complexity of the telephone network is hidden from telephone customers. Higher-level semantics will be needed for instructing computers to do complex tasks. Decision-support dialogs will help complex decision making. Each category of professional will employ an appropriate computer dialog. Click-and-point, object-oriented dialogs using icons will be employed. Speech input and output will mature. The pyramiding of complex software will evolve along with the human-interface tools for making the software easy to use.

Libraries of constructs need to be built for different classes of applications. Some examples of application classes that need their own libraries of operations and control structures are

- commercial procedures
- financial application
- design of operating systems
- automatic database navigation
- query languages
- design of circuits with NOR, NAND gates, and so on
- control of robots
- cryptanalysis
- missile control
- building architecture
- design graphics
- network design
- avionics
- CAD/CAM, computer-aided design and manufacturing
- production control
- project management
- decision-support graphics

The list is endless.

REPOSITORY STANDARDS

At the heart of CASE tools is the repository—providing libraries of reusable classes and facilitating reusable design. The repository should be an object-oriented database, storing information about the objects that appear on the screens of I-CASE tools and using methods to validate integrity and coordinate the knowledge in the repository. The repository, containing many objects and rules, is very complex.

It is essential for the future of software that standards exist for the repository. Having no *open* standard for the repository and its tool interfaces would be like having no standard for music CDs. Sony CDs would not play on Philips equipment, and so on. An open standard for the I-CASE repository and its interfaces is as important to the future of software development as the CD standard is to the music industry.

Open standards should incorporate the following:

- *A repository* with a standard means of accessing and using the information it stores
- *Repository model* that defines the classes stored in the repository, their methods, and the relationships among classes
- *Repository services* that use precisely defined methods for checking the consistency and integrity of information stored in the repository
- *Version control* for managing the separate versions of objects that are stored
- *Tool services* defining the objects that are created or modified by the tools and then stored in the repository
- *Standards formats* for object requests and responses. Standard techniques for object interoperability (such as the OMG Object Request Broker)
- *A standard GUI (graphic user interface)* to make CASE tools and their diagrams look and feel similar and easy to use
- *Workstation services* for enabling desktop computers to interact with the repository on a LAN server or mainframe
- Full use of existing open systems standards

Development tools will evolve and change. Diverse tools will be built by many corporations, often small, inventive corporations. The repositories ought to be usable with all these tools. Corporate repositories are already growing to a formidable size and are becoming a vital strategic resource, in some cases helping the corporation stay ahead of its competition. Repositories of reusable components will also contain a large quantity of knowledge—sometimes sold as CD-ROMs. If these repositories follow a standard format, they can be used with many different design tools.

PACKAGED SOFTWARE

Object-oriented techniques in combination with standard I-CASE repositories will have a major impact on the packaged software industry. A problem with mainframe application packages is that I.S. organizations buying them often have to modify the package to adapt it to their needs. These packages are difficult and expensive to modify. One survey by EDS showed that modification and maintenance of mainframe package software averaged six times the original cost of the software. To overcome this problem, packaged software should be sold in OO-CASE form, so that its design can be adapted and modified easily and code generated from that design. Having an open standard for the repository will facilitate this greatly.

A problem with the PC software industry is that low prices are dictated by the shops and organizations that distribute software. Creating complex and interesting new software at these low prices is difficult. Only a few items like word processors and spreadsheet tools can generate enough sales to pay for a 100-person-year development effort. Many PC software companies are embroidering their own products with features of questionable value, rather than striking out for a new 100-person-year innovation. They are stuck on a sandbar related to the cost structure of the industry. This dilemma can be resolved by assembling innovative products from licensable object-oriented components.

Recognizing this, Patriot Partners (originally formed by IBM and Metaphor, Inc.) envisioned a new software marketplace. In this vision, many companies create software units that become components of packages that can be used by many vendors on multiple platforms using multiple operating systems, LAN managers, network architectures, graphic user interfaces (GUIs), and so on. A vendor creating a new software product incorporates components from many other vendors. Some of these components may, themselves, represent 100-person-year development efforts. The initial effort of the partnership is called the Constellation project. The goal of Constellation is building a framework to provide interfaces between platforms, networks, operating systems, and GUIs. These interfaces will shield developers from spending their time on these issues.

> We are at the end of the era of single-vendor software. Software of the future will contain components from hundreds of vendors.

Patriot Partners visualized a world in which developers build software from many licensed components, rather than creating a monolithic application in-house. They described the following needs:

1. The data will include all kinds of text, numbers, and graphics, even video and sound, and will most likely reside in many different locations. The new breed of user will demand comprehensive and transparent access to all these data sources, as well as means to easily organize, analyze, and synthesize the information in persuasive new contexts.

2. Users need entire suites of software tools, able to span broad-ranging, variable tasks. These tools must be built on conceptual models that match the nature of the tasks and designed so that users do not face the disruptive transitions common today when moving from one software environment to another.

3. Users can create their own high-value application, intuitively and without coding. Business professionals are constantly confronted with context-specific tasks that can-

not be satisfied by generic applications. A task may be vital one week and all but forgotten the next. We must give those users the tools to fulfill computing needs as they arise, to attack this week's or this afternoon's new problem [2].

The vision of Patriot Partners looked promising, and IBM bought Metaphor in July 1991. The Patriot Partners brochure commented:

> The industry's challenge, then, is no less than redefining what an application is, how it is developed, how it gets distributed and how it is used by a new kind of user. If this challenge seems risky, remember that the low-hanging fruit has been picked; there are no more easy million-seller generic applications out there. The greater risk lies in taking today's products from the Baroque to the Rococo, trying to grow by shaving away at competitors' market shares with feature-laden products that add marginal real value at best.

The Patriot Partners' vision is in many ways similar to that of the OMG with its Object Management Architecture. The OMG is creating an open architecture, whereas an IBM-based initiative may lead to a proprietary architecture. OMG's Object Request Broker is a vital resource for linking the software components of many vendors and facilitating client-server interaction among objects.

REUSABILITY

The future of software depends upon being able to build it from reusable components. The best way to achieve reusability is probably with OO components designed to be used with OO-CASE tools. The potential value of reusable object-oriented designs is immense. Applications may one day be built largely with off-the-shelf components that can be assembled and modified very quickly. This opportunity presents a great challenge to the packaged software industry.

Reusable components should be designed to be modified. The dictum "SAME AS, EXCEPT..." applies to reusability.

Conversion of the software industry to OO-CASE design will not happen overnight. The investment tied up in existing software is large, and the resistance of major software companies to new methods is high. Perhaps relatively small or new corporations will sell reusable OO-CASE designs first. Patriot Partners gave two scenarios for software built from complex OO components with precisely defined protocols for interlinking the components [2]:

Scenario 1: An engineer working on a jet aircraft design uses his AeroCAD package's drafting assistant, dimension engine and parametric modeling component tools. To get a 3-D rendering, he pulls in the rendering component from another favorite application, Stanford Graphics. To complete the drawing, he calls up the blend tool in Stucco Illustrator to realistically shade the aircraft skin. Since all three applications use component-and-protocol architecture, the tools interact quickly and cooperatively, without forcing the engineer to load different programs, exit applications, or import and export files.

Scenario 2: A project team has a problem. The company's best seller bleach bottle is too heavy for the new molding machines and needs redesign. Manufacturing designs a bottle that meets requirements and creates wireframe and 3-D views of it. Packaging uses those images to figure how many will fit on store shelves, how they look side-by-side, and whether labels need changing. Advertising evaluates how the new design will work in ad layouts and point-of-sale displays. Finance analyzes manufacturing costs and the need for larger boxes to ship the new bottles. The brand manager reports the results of the project to management, relying on a database containing bottle images, dimensions, financials, and consumer responses. Because all project team members use component-based software, they easily share information over their network, manipulating images and data to contribute to the complete solution without recreating or reentering any material.

Box 22.1 describes desirable characteristics of future software development.

FORMAL METHODS Today's research on formal (mathematically-based) methods has led to a few impressive results. Building software with these techniques has been extremely difficult, so we need powerful tools that hide the difficulties. Software should be created from provably correct constructs. Designers should assemble building blocks, each of which is known to be correct, with tools that ensure that the interfaces among the building blocks are correct.

When CASE tools generate code that is untouched by human hand, the language the code runs in need not be COBOL, PL/I, or C; it could be a language designed to facilitate mathematical provability and parallel processing (such as OCCAM [5], discussed in Chapter 20). Chips may be designed to execute such a language (like the transputer). Specification languages may also be designed mathematically (such as Z [6], discussed in Chapter 20). It is desirable to have a design chain that progresses from the easiest and most powerful visualization of systems to mathematically formal specifications, to automatic generation of provable code, and to chips that correctly execute such code.

Probably the best way to put provable constructs to use is with OO techniques. Classes may be guaranteed correct and designed to check the preconditions and postconditions of every *method* executed.

BOX 22.1 Desirable characteristics of future software development.

In the near future, desktop machines will have optical disks capable of holding hundreds of millions of lines of code. Software of far greater complexity than today's is needed and will probably be sold on optical disks. Software components from many companies will be interlinked and cross-licensed. In such a world, the following characteristics are desirable:

- *Software is built out of components from many companies.* No one company is likely to build monolithic software of the complexity required. Instead, software companies will create new applications that are assembled from existing components and some new code.
- *Components have OO design with encapsulation and polymorphism.* Components should not only be reusable but easily maintained and extendable.
- *Many OO components are designed to be modified.* The dictum "SAME AS, EXCEPT. . ." applies. Modification is sometimes achieved with parameters or menus, sometimes by subtyping.
- *OO components are licensed with well-structured and controllable licensing terms.* Many corporations should sell reusable classes that other corporations can use in their software.
- *Open standards* should exist to allow objects to intercommunicate.
- *Components should reside on a standard repository.* In the absence of international open standards for software repositories, de facto standards from large vendors or industry consortia will define the repository meta-model and user interfaces.
- *A repository coordinator checks the integrity of the repository contents.* Thousands of rules are used with OO methods and inferential reasoning to ensure that the repository contents fit together with integrity (as with today's major I-CASE repositories encyclopedias).
- *All development is repository-based.* Integrated CASE tools facilitate the analysis and design of software and the linkage of repository components.
- *Licensed software components have OO descriptions (in the repository) that developers use when building applications.* Components are designed to work with OO I-CASE tools. All development is done with such tools.

(Continued)

BOX 22.1 *(Continued)*

- *Software design is generated, where possible, from classes, templates, OO models, rules, declarative statements, and menus.* CASE tools should provide the maximum design automation.
- *Code is generated where possible, not hand programmed.* CASE tools should provide the most powerful code-generation capabilities.
- *Design is independent of the platform on which the code runs.* Code can be generated from the design for many major platforms.
- *Specified interfaces make platform independence possible.* Specified and standard interfaces should enable software to run with
   — multiple host machines
   — multiple operating systems
   — multiple storage subsystems
   — multiple database management systems
   — multiple network architectures
   — multiple LAN managers
   — multiple GUIs (graphic user interfaces)
- *Specified protocols allow objects to work together.* Specified and standardized protocols should exist for both static and dynamic schema linkages.
- *Specified protocols allow interprocess, interhost, and networked interaction.* The same classes may be linked within one machine, within a client-server system, or across an enterprise.
- *Specified protocols allow portability.* There should be smooth portability from small machines to large machines, and from stand-alone systems to enterprisewide systems and interenterprise systems.
- *Software is designed for multimedia platforms.* Multimedia will include text, graphics, images, animation, sound, and video. Many objects will use images, animation, sound, and video.
- *Software is designed for maximum ease of use with a GUI.* Software should be designed for a graphic user interface and be able to work with the different dominant graphic user interfaces.
- *Software is designed for highly parallel processors.* An OO event diagram may be used to design how operations execute on different processors simultaneously. Parallel processors should be used for specialized functions such as database management, searching, and display generation.
- *Software is built where possible from executable specifications.* Specifications should be precise enough that code can be generated from them.

BOX 22.1 *(Continued)*

They should be built with OO I-CASE tools using graphics as well as rule-based and mathematical techniques.

- *Specification techniques provide a way to think about systems that improve conceptual clarity.* The techniques should be easy to use and learn. At higher levels, they should be employed by end users.
- *Formal (mathematically-based) techniques should be used to prove the correctness of software, where practical.* Provable code may be generated in languages that are themselves mathematically based (such as OCCAM).
- *Mathematically-based techniques for ensuring correctness should be made easy to use.* I-CASE tools should employ an easy-to-use, user interface that invokes mathematically-based techniques to achieve maximum precision in specification. Code should be generatable from this specification for different platforms.
- *System design and program design use visual techniques.* CASE users should be given maximum help in visualizing and automating designs.
- *Fast iterative prototyping is used.* CASE tools should give the fastest, smoothest prototyping capability. They should allow the system developer to progress as rapidly as possible through the following stages:

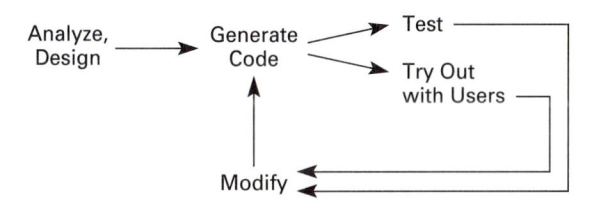

```
Analyze,  →  Generate  →  Test ─────┐
Design       Code      ↘             │
              ↑          Try Out ────┤
              │          with Users  │
              └── Modify ◄───────────┘
```

- *Expert systems help developers use libraries of components.* Developers should have access to vast libraries of components and have an expert system help them to locate the most appropriate components and use them correctly.
- *A comprehensive cataloging scheme is used for software components.* A scheme, perhaps like the Library of Congress classification for books, is needed for cataloging classes that form licensable software components.
- *Developers are able to locate and obtain software components they need via networks.* Software development and cross licensing will be a worldwide industry using worldwide networks.

(Continued)

BOX 22.1 *(Continued)*

- *Enterprise models are built with OO techniques.* Enterprisewide information engineering should employ OO modeling. Business people should be able to understand the business models and request changes when needed.
- *The enterprise models form input into a design generator that employs a code generator.* Enterprisewide information engineering should have a high-level OO enterprise model driving OO business area models. These business area models are input to OO system design, where the design tools link to a code generator.
- *A seamless and automated progression moves from high-level specification to design and code.* All stages in the progression update the knowledge in a single repository.
- *End users can validate and help create the high-level specifications.* Specifications should include business policies and rules expressed in English (or other human language), equations, professional drawings, or, in general, the language of the end user. Specifications should show event diagrams that users can understand.

As such controls to aid software validation are created and improved, it should be made illegal to bypass them. The controls should be applied automatically. The repository coordinator should enforce consistency. To tamper with generated code should be forbidden. Software builders left to their own devices find reasons to bypass controls and this results in loss of reliability and problems in maintenance, mysterious bugs, and much greater costs in the long run. Reliable software needs *pure* OO tools in which encapsulation cannot be bypassed. The integrity controls should be applied by runtime facilities and OO databases.

> Far more emphasis is needed on formal methods, provable correctness, and enforcement of integrity controls.

PARALLELISM The PC or LAN server of the future will have many processors. Processor chips of the future will be mass produced in vast quantities. When many millions of one processor chip are made, that processor can be very low in cost. Japan has plans to flood the world with low-cost processor chips. In the future, powerful computers should be built out of many small computers that yield to the economics of mass production. Examples of highly parallel machines have existed for some time, but designing software for applications that run efficiently on them has been very difficult.

The search for ways to introduce a high degree of parallelism into computing is an important one. A million-dollar computer should not be doing one thing at a time; it should be doing ten thousand things at a time. The Connection Machine, from Thinking Machines, Inc., has 65,536 small processors operating in parallel. Other machines with different architecture will be built from mass-produced wafers, each with many chips.

> The first four decades of computing was the evolution of single-processor machines.
>
> The second four decades of computing is the evolution of multiprocessor machines.

Software for highly parallel machines will necessarily be intricate. However, analysts do not think naturally in terms of parallel processes. The culture of computing and algorithm theory relates to sequential operations, not parallel ones. To bridge the gap between how analysts think and how parallel computers should be used, we need modeling techniques, design tools, and nonprocedural languages, such as SQL and PROLOG, that can be translated by generators into parallel processing. Some types of formal decomposition indicate clearly what steps in complex procedures can take place in parallel [1]. Some processes need parallel machines to be efficient, for example, searching large databases, high-throughput transaction processing, database machines (like Teradata), image generators, compression and decompression of digitized television signals, and possibly human speech processing.

Event diagrams indicate how different operations can function in parallel (i.e., simultaneously) on the same or different processors. A challenge of the OO-CASE industry today is to evolve CASE tools that help to visualize how multi-processor machines can be used, or to take specifications and implement them with different OO classes running on different machines. We need to evolve techniques that make it practical to use microelectronic wafers or boards containing many advanced RISC processors.

NETWORKS AND DISTRIBUTION OF OBJECTS

The first attempts at interaction between humans and computers were crude. They employed dumb terminals, slow transmission lines, and cumbersome mainframes. The personal computer brought a new world of interaction between humans and machines. The Macintosh demonstrated that computers could be made easy to use. However, personal computers had limited power. The desktop machine was needed, making use of more powerful machines. The desktop machine needed high-bandwidth links to powerful servers.

LAN technology provided the high-bandwidth link—initially, 10 million bits per second; as optical LANs spread, 100 million bits per second; and in the future, a billion or so bits per second. LANs have created islands of computing. If, instead of accessing a machine on the LAN, the user accesses a machine miles away, the transmission speed drops to low figures. A bit-mapped screen can no longer be painted with an interactive response time; thought processes dependent on subsecond interaction with the server can no longer occur. The telecommunications companies of the world are installing optical-fiber trunks. One trunk cable contains a large number of fibers, and each fiber transmits more than half a billion bits per second. A major market for fiber-based telecommunications will be the accessing of servers, previously only accessed with a LAN. Vast networks of optical fibers will be woven around the earth, linking a billion computers—the farthest one only 68 milliseconds away.

OO classes in one machine will interact with classes in many other machines. Object-oriented analysis and design is an appropriate way to think about distributed computing. A class will not necessarily know where a request comes from. Each class performs its own methods and is unaware of the effect it may have on other operations that follow. It must, however, protect its own data types.

In conventional distributed systems, data can be accessed in ad hoc ways. There may be little or no assurance of who is doing what to the data via the network. With object-oriented systems, the data is *encapsulated,* as it is in biological cells, and is not available for random manipulation. To build distributed systems open to masses of users, without encapsulation, is dangerous. Encapsulation seems essential to protect the integrity of data.

INTERCORPORATE COMPUTER INTERACTION

Networks have created many new business opportunities. Corporations have streamlined their procedures as it became possible to transmit any information to any location.

Initially, computer network applications were built within one corporation. Then, it became clear that major business advantages could accrue from intercorporate networks. Airlines built networks linking travel-agent PCs directly into airline reservation computers. Corporations put software in their customer locations enabling customers to reorder automatically. Supermarket computers transmitted market research information direct to their suppliers. Computers in one corporation became linked to computers in other corporations.

Commercial data processing is evolving through the following stages:

1. *Stand-alone batch processing.* Stand-alone machines process batches of work.
2. *Off-line telecommunications.* Batches are transmitted off line. Orders are sent by fax.
3. *Online transaction processing.* Terminals for handling transactions are linked directly to computer centers.
4. *Distributed network processing.* Localized processing environments, including client-server systems, are linked to computer centers in the same corporation.

5. *Simple EDI (electronic data interchange).* A corporate computer center is linked directly to the terminals or PCs of customers or suppliers.
6. *EDI networks.* Corporate computers can be connected online to computers in many suppliers, outlets, customers, and trading partners.
7. *Intercorporate computer interaction.* Computers in one corporation interact directly with computers in other corporations.

To achieve intercorporate computer interaction, standards are vital. The world of the future will be one of open systems and standards. Single-vendor, proprietary, vanity architectures will give way to architectures designed for open connectivity, portability, and worldwide access to databases.

Standards for electronic documents will be important, so that machines in one corporation can send electronic purchase orders, invoices, receipts, and so on, to the computers in other corporations. Where such standards are not yet adequate, corporations make contractual agreements about the format of electronically exchanged data.

SPEED OF INTERACTION

As we progress from the era of stand-alone batch processing through the above stages, business interactions tend to speed up. With online systems, events happen more quickly than with batch systems. With networks, information can flow immediately from where it originates to where it is used in decision making. With EDI, information passes between corporations quickly, facilitating just-in-time inventory control and continuous flow planning in manufacturing. Money passes around the world almost instantly with electronic transfer of funds.

> We are progressing to a world in which the computers in one corporation interact directly with the computers of its customers, suppliers, and service providers.

A manufacturer's purchasing application scans the possible supplier computers to find goods of the best price and delivery schedule. Computers in hospitals and clinics automatically reorder supplies by transmission to supplier computers (such as the pioneering system at American Hospital Supply—bought by Baxter). Travel-agent computers are online to airline computers, and soon, a secretary's computer will be able to do everything that a travel-agent's computer does. While travel agents' or secretaries' computers search for low fares, airline computers, in turn, adjust seat fares and bargain flights in an attempt to maximize the load factors on planes.

Trading rooms in stock markets and futures markets become automated, so that traders worldwide can make deals. Brokers worldwide can make trades, and often the public can buy stocks online, bypassing brokers and their commissions.

Bar scanners inform computers in stores what goods are selling, and stores adjust their prices constantly in an attempt to maximize profit. Computers in stores send details of sales to manufacturers' computers, bypassing traditional market research. Buyers' computers search for deals, and sellers' computers constantly adjust prices and terms. Both sets of machines try to maximize profits or provide the best service. When computers in one corporation interact directly with computers in another corporation, middlemen can be bypassed. Business transactions happen instantly. The windows of opportunity are much shorter. Prices, set by computers, change constantly. Complexity increases because the interacting machines can handle complex airline fares, price structures, manufacturing schedules, and so on.

An order placed in Ireland with an order-entry computer in Germany triggers a manufacturing planning system in New York to place items into a manufacturing schedule in Dallas that requires chips from Japan built into circuit boards in Taiwan for final assembly in the robotic factory in Dallas and shipment from a warehouse in England.

Society will be laced with networks for computer-to-computer interaction among separate enterprises—worldwide. These networks will decrease reaction times, decrease inventories and buffers, bypass middlemen and bureaucrats, and increase complexity as the machines handle ever more elaborate schemes to try to maximize profit. Small corporations will plug into the networks of computers that offer specialized goods or services at competitive prices.

In this world of interacting computers, software reliability and security will be vitally important. OO encapsulation will be essential.

THE NEED FOR FAST DEVELOPMENT

As commerce speeds up because of automated systems interacting worldwide, many new competitive opportunities emerge. An era of rapid change is always an era filled with new opportunities. Slow-moving corporations are bypassed. Entrepreneurs and inventive I.S. professionals will invent new systems with new ways to compete.

New competitive systems are needed. These systems need to be flexible, built quickly, and controlled by business people or end users. Avoiding the straightjacket of traditional mainframe development with its multiyear backlog and maintenance problems is vital.

To achieve fast development, new systems, as far as possible, should be built out of classes that already exist and can be adapted to circumstances. Repository-based development is needed—with automated tools. The tools should make it quick and easy to customize a standard graphic user interface. Systems should be built so that they can be changed quickly and easily, without the maintenance problems of the past.

The methodology for RAD (Rapid Application Development) is very different from traditional methodologies [3]. It should be designed to maximize the efficiency of OO repository-based techniques.

> RAD methodologies will be increasingly essential for business survival.

INTERNATIONAL STANDARDS FOR REUSABLE CLASSES

Large enterprises will have hundreds of thousands of computers, with many millions of MIPS (million instructions per second) worldwide. Managements that fail to build an efficiently functioning organism with this power will not survive. The efficient corporate organism will have repositories storing large amounts of knowledge about the enterprise, its classes, methods, and business values. The classes and operations will be designed for reusability across the enterprise. Commercial paperwork will be replaced by electronic documents in the format of international (or de facto) standards, because computers everywhere will exchange such documents with other computers.

Today, standards for EDI (electronic data interchange) are evolving rapidly. In some cases, standards committees are starting to define documents in object-oriented terms. ODA (the Office Document Architecture) from ISO (the International Standards Organization) defines MO:DCA—the *Mixed Object Document Content Architecture.* This includes an Object Contents Architecture defining image formats, graphics, fonts, and so on, and an Object Method Architecture, defining methods for employing fonts, images, and so on.

As Stage 7 of the above seven stages becomes widespread, changing the world's patterns of commerce, standards should be established for many of the reusable classes used in commerce—customers, accounts, orders, parts, locations, and so on. Millions of transactions will pass between corporations every second. Corporations whose computers interact need not have common classes. This commonality could come from mutual agreements or from large vendors such as IBM, DEC, or possibly large telephone companies. International standards for the major classes of commerce will become increasingly desirable.

CODE GENERATION FROM THE ENTERPRISE MODEL

Executable program code should be generated from the highest-level specification possible. A major evolution in OO-CASE tools will be the generation of code from higher level specifications. If the enterprise model contains rules expressing how the enterprise functions, code can be generated directly from the enterprise model. The enterprise model should be understood by the business managers. It should clarify thinking about how they want the enterprise to operate. A precise expression of how the enterprise operates should reside in the repository and should be discussed in workshop sessions. Code should be generated directly from this. A change in business procedures should then be directly translated into the code for implementing the procedures.

The term Code Generation from the Enterprise Model (CGEM) has been used to describe this higher-level code generation. It requires object-oriented modeling and design.

> The design chain should progress as automatically as possible from intelligent enterprise modeling and visualization, which is understood by the business managers, to the generation of bug-free code.

Events, objects, and business rules provide a way of describing the enterprise that business managers and staff can understand.

> We have stressed that object-oriented techniques provide *a way to think about systems*—a way to think about a business. As such, the subject ought to be taught in business schools and management training courses, as well as in computer science schools and system analyst courses.

At its different levels, it can be understood by both business people and computer professionals. It provides a vital way to bridge the gap between these two cultures.

Business schools should teach how businesses work with diagrams showing object types, operations, event types, and trigger rules. The courses should use CASE tools for planning and analysis. New types of charts will probably be devised that help human communication. To become a basis for system specification, they should be designed so that they have the precision that enables repository-based tools to check their integrity and their consistency with other diagrams.

As we acquire the capability to generate code from the enterprise model or business area model, the development lifecycle will become faster. The libraries of reusable classes will become more mature and enterprise models will evolve—representing business rules more comprehensively. Much development will consist of the successive refinement of existing applications, rather than the creation of entirely new applications.

THE EVOLUTION OF PROGRAMMING TECHNIQUES

Generating code from the enterprise model is one example of programming techniques reflecting *the way users think* rather than the way *the machinery works*.

In the beginning, humans had to program using the computer's instruction set. When computer programs changed from switches to languages, the new programs were organized around the machine instruction set. Therefore, the first languages and machine instructions were very similar. A process-oriented programming model was the result. For example, programs for addition were organized around the machine process of addition: loading registers with numbers, executing the add instruction, and dealing with overflow and underflow. As shown in Fig. 22.1, the programming technique steadily became more remote from the way the hardware operates. It moved closer to human language, to the way humans solve problems, and to human professional disciplines. As this happened, programming became more dependent on interpreters, compilers, and then code generators and CASE tools.

Meanwhile, the machinery evolved away from an instruction set that was good for humans to technology that was as fast and cost effective as possible. We had generations of RISC (Reduced Instruction Set Computing) chips and then concurrent computers with many processors. RISC chips will drift far from what humans could have programmed easily without software translation. Concurrent computers will carry the trend further. It would be difficult for humans to write code that executed on multiple independent processors simultaneously. We have a tradition of *sequential*—not parallel—logic, mathematics, algorithms, and languages. Processor chips of the future may be designed to execute mathematically-based languages to enhance verifiably correct behavior in software. CASE tools can generate code for such chips.

Object-oriented analysis and design help users to think about their world in terms that can be represented naturally on the CASE screen and help code generators to produce code for concurrent computers, leading eventually to massively parallel machines with large numbers of cheap processor chips. An object-oriented database engine may be one way to take advantage of parallelism. Corporations of the future may be run with vast networks of object-oriented database engines.

As users become familiar with using the icons, windows and fill-in panels on the computer screen, using computers and building applications becomes easier. The users should model their world in an OO fashion with tools that allow models to be expanded into detail and made to run actively. In this way, the distinction between modeling and executable systems blurs.

> At the same time that system building techniques become closer to human thinking, the code generators should become more rigorous and based on formal (mathematical) techniques. The language that the processor chips execute, in the future, may be a mathematically-based language that facilitates proofs of correctness and for which system builders never normally write code.

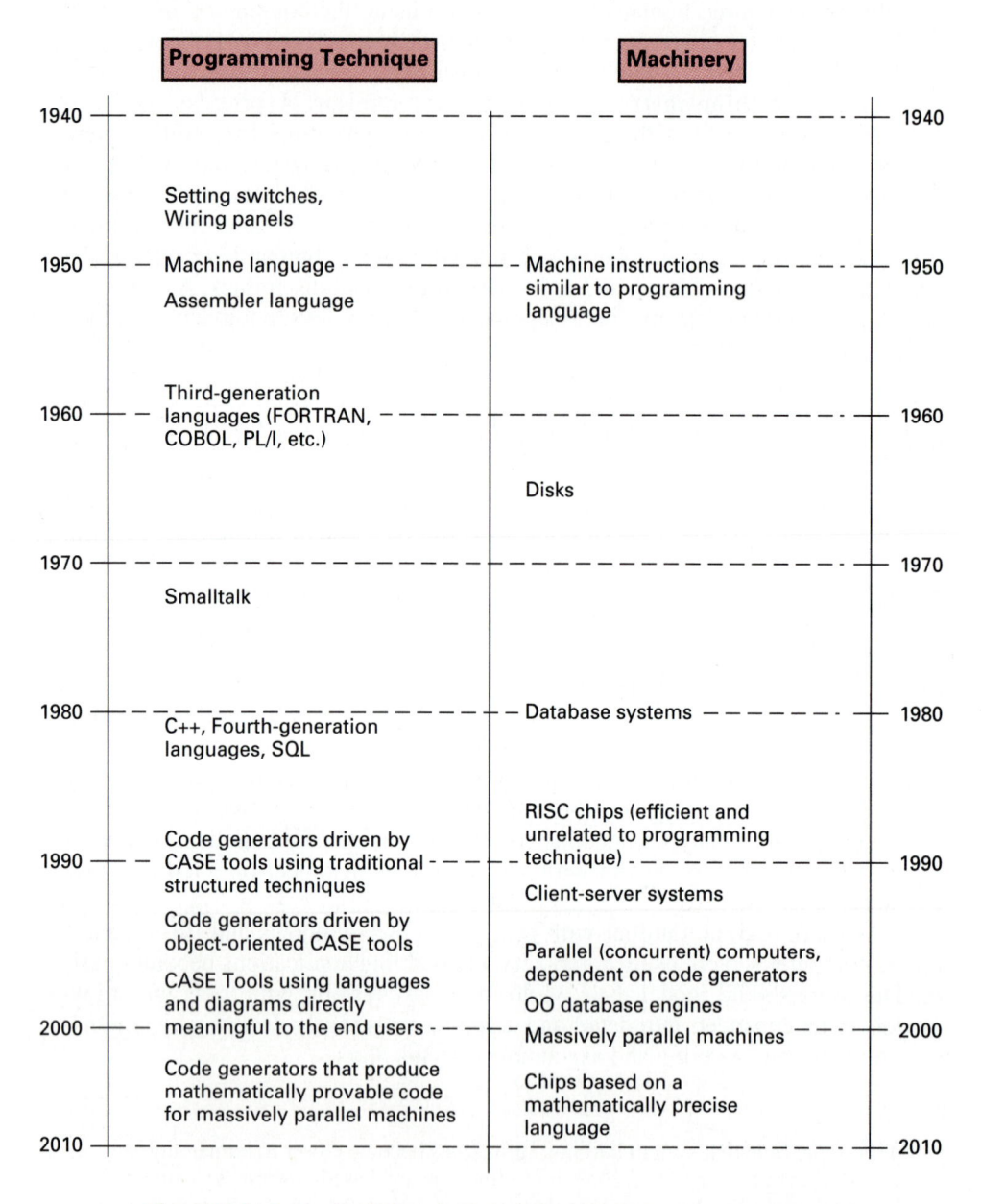

Year	Programming Technique	Machinery	Year
1940			1940
	Setting switches, Wiring panels		
1950	Machine language	Machine instructions similar to programming language	1950
	Assembler language		
1960	Third-generation languages (FORTRAN, COBOL, PL/I, etc.)		1960
		Disks	
1970			1970
	Smalltalk		
1980		Database systems	1980
	C++, Fourth-generation languages, SQL		
1990	Code generators driven by CASE tools using traditional structured techniques	RISC chips (efficient and unrelated to programming technique)	1990
		Client-server systems	
	Code generators driven by object-oriented CASE tools	Parallel (concurrent) computers, dependent on code generators	
	CASE Tools using languages and diagrams directly	OO database engines	
2000	meaningful to the end users	Massively parallel machines	2000
	Code generators that produce mathematically provable code for massively parallel machines	Chips based on a mathematically precise language	
2010			2010

Figure 22.1 In the beginning, humans had to program using the machine's instruction set. The programming technique and the machine steadily diverged, the hardware becoming more cost efficient and the programming methods becoming closer to the way users think about their world.

PYRAMIDS OF COMPLEXITY

The complexity of living things, built by nature, is awesome to a computer professional. The brain is so intricate that it cannot be mapped, imitated, or understood in detail. It is rich in diversity—yet, self-protecting and self-renewing. The things of nature are complex, because they are grown using organic components. Similarly, we can develop software and information system components and grow complex automated systems. However, we need disciplines and tools that facilitate and enable us to manage such growth.

> The designers of the future must stand on the shoulders of the designers of the present.

As the pyramids of complexity grow, we will reach very high-level OO constructs, often designed for parallel RISC engines. Vast libraries of such constructs will exist. Sophisticated tools and languages will enable developers to employ the constructs they need. Many millions of computers linked by worldwide data networks will exchange constructs from these libraries. Knowledge-based systems will acquire ever more knowledge and become self-feeding. Intelligent network directories will allow machines and users to find the resources they need.

The programmer of handmade COBOL with his ad hoc designs will become part of the romantic past of computer history like the weavers in their cottages when the industrial revolution began.

REFERENCES

1. Hamilton, M. and S. Zeldin, "Higher Order Software: A Methodology for Defining Software," *IEEE Transactions on Software Engineering,* 2:3, March 1976, pp. 25-32.

2. Liddle, David E., *Patriot Partners: A Vision of a New Software Marketplace,* brochure from Patriot Partners, Mountain View, CA, 1991.

3. Martin, James, *Rapid Application Development,* Macmillan, New York, 1991.

4. Parnas, David L., "Software Aspects of Strategic Defense Systems," *Communications of the ACM,* 28:12, December 1985, pp. 1326-1335.

5. Roscoe, A. W. and Hoare, C. A. R., *Laws of OCCAM Programming.* Monograph PRG-53, Oxford University Computing Laboratory, Programming Research Group, February 1986.

6. Spivey, J. M., *The Z Notation: A Reference Manual,* Prentice Hall, Englewood Cliffs, NJ, 1989.

7. Wiener, Norbert, *The Human Use of Human Beings: Cybernetics and Society,* Da Capo Press, New York, 1954 (reprinted Avon Books, 1979).

PART V APPENDIX

Appendix A

RECOMMENDED DIAGRAMMING STANDARDS*

We have emphasized that object-oriented analysis and design require precise diagrams which should appear on the screens of OO-CASE tools. These tools should collect enough information to drive a code generator producing code that is free from syntax errors. The diagrams, therefore, must have an engineering-like precision.

Diagramming is a language essential both for clear thinking and for human communication. An enterprise needs standards for I.S. diagrams, just as it has standards for engineering drawings.

The set of diagramming standards described in this chapter are employed throughout the book. Most I.S. professionals learning OO techniques are likely to have existing knowledge of conventional techniques. Diagrams for conventional techniques are widely used on CASE tools. As far as possible, the diagrams for OO techniques should incorporate those for conventional techniques.

Many widely used CASE tools employ the diagrams described in the author's book written at the start of the CASE era: *Recommended Diagramming Standards for Analysts and Programmers* [1]. This book has been a "bible" for many CASE vendors. The OO diagrams used in the current book are an extension of the diagrams in the earlier book. We recommend that builders of OO-CASE tools use diagrams that are already widely understood and avoid inventing incompatible diagrams. These would cause confusion and make the techniques difficult to learn. (OO-CASE tools using strange diagrams are best avoided.)

A NATURAL WAY TO THINK ABOUT SYSTEMS

We have emphasized that OO techniques give us a more natural way to think about our complex world than the techniques used for conventional program-

---

* In describing diagramming standards, this appendix repeats some material from the body of the book.

ming and analysis. Business people can easily visualize the procedures that need automating in terms of objects, events, event rules, and triggers, whereas they find it more difficult to relate to structure charts and data-flow diagrams. A vital challenge in I.S. today is improved communications for I.S. professionals and business people. I.S. professionals must understand the business and invent how it should change. Business people must think more clearly about systems and automation.

We ought to be building a generation of CASE tools that represent systems in a form that business people relate to easily and drive this representation into code. OO techniques are desirable for this.

When a CASE tool is used, the computer deciphers the *meaning* of the diagrams. The computer should help the designer to think clearly and help represent the procedures and generate code automatically.

The diagrams and their manipulation by computer are a form of *thought* processing. The analyst, designer, programmer, user, and executive need a family of diagram types that help them to think clearly. These diagram types should be as clear and simple as possible. Although there are many types of diagrams, the number of icons should be limited and their meaning should be relatively obvious.

The diagrams must be sufficiently complete and rigorous to serve as a basis for code generation and for automatic conversion from one type of diagram into another. The diagrams become the documentation for systems (along with a *repository* that stores the meaning of the diagrams and additional information collected when they were drawn). When changes are made to a system, the diagrams will be changed on the screen and the code regenerated. The design documentation does not slip out of date as changes are made.

The diagrams for designing systems are a language of communication. Good CASE tools enforce precision in this language. As with other languages, *standards* must apply to it so that diverse parties can communicate. Developers should be prevented from inventing their own forms of diagramming. Researchers should use existing diagramming techniques where they are applicable. Incompatible diagramming is a barrier to communication.

Above all, the diagrams need to be standardized throughout the corporation, so that all persons involved with computers have a common powerful language and can discuss one another's plans, specifications, designs, and programs.

CONVENTIONAL DIAGRAMS

Figure A.1 summarizes the symbols commonly used on diagrams with CASE tools employing conventional techniques. These symbols are used in many different types of diagrams, including entity-relationship diagrams, decomposition diagrams, dependency diagrams, data-flow diagrams, decision trees, state-transition diagrams, dialog-design diagrams, data-analysis diagrams, and action diagrams.

OBJECT-ORIENTED DIAGRAMS

The symbols used for OO analysis and design are summarized in Fig. A.2 which extends the set of symbols in Fig. A.1.

SQUARE-CORNERED AND ROUND-CORNERED BOXES

Recommended Diagramming Standards suggests that nodes representing data be drawn with square-cornered rectangles (fields, record layouts, entity types, and so on) and boxes representing activities be drawn with round corners (procedures, processes, program modules, and so on). These are widely accepted conventions.

Similarly, we recommend that object types and classes be drawn with square-cornered boxes and activities with round-cornered boxes. This makes some complex diagrams easier to interpret.

An entity type is drawn as a rectangle:

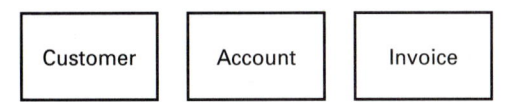

[Customer]   [Account]   [Invoice]

An object, like an entity, is a thing—real or abstract. We, therefore, use a rectangle for drawing object types:

[Product]   [Account]   [Invoice]

An object may be an instance of an entity type, but often object types incorporate *many* entity types.

Activities such as processes or operations are drawn with round-cornered boxes (sometimes called soft boxes):

(Update Employee Record)   (Transmit Invoice)   (Rewind VCR Tape)   (Launch Missile)

REALITY AND INFORMATION ABOUT REALITY

Most of the blocks on CASE diagrams represent how the computer reflects reality. These are drawn with two-dimensional boxes or symbols. However, some blocks on the CASE diagrams represent reality itself. They might, for example, represent a physical object moving from one process to another. These are drawn with three-dimensional boxes or other three-dimensional pictures.

DATA
Square-cornered boxes represent data (entity types, entity subtypes, records, datasets)

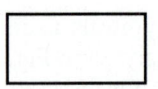

INTERSECTION DATA
An intersection record used to resolve many-to-many relationships.

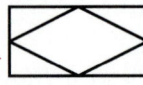

CARDINALITY
This is often drawn as a single bar

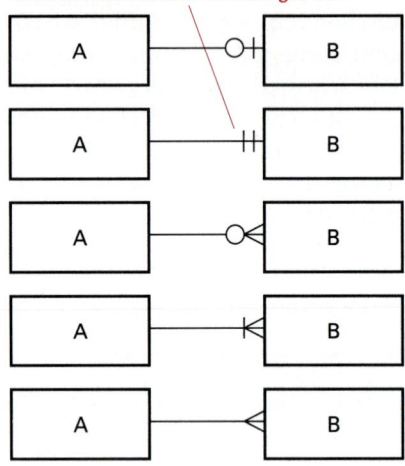

A	──O┤──	B
A	──┤┤──	B
A	──O⤜──	B
A	──⤜──	B
A	──⊲──	B

MUTUAL EXCLUSIVITY
One and only one of the branches is taken:

A is associated with X, Y, or Z

A → • → X / Y / Z

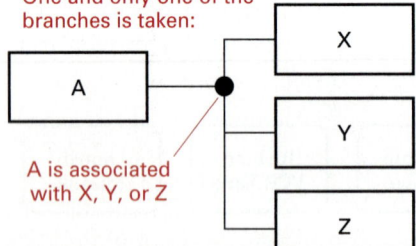

CONSTRUCTS ON ACTION DIAGRAMS, FOR REPRESENTING PROCEDURAL LOGIC

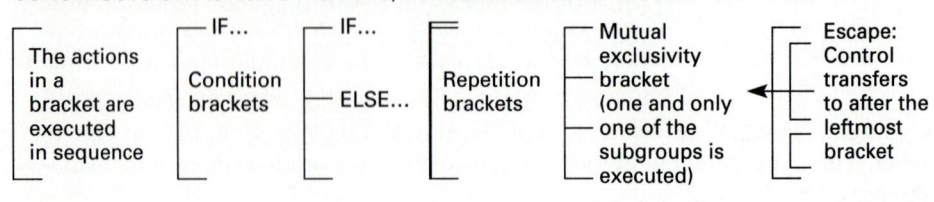

- The actions in a bracket are executed in sequence
- IF... Condition brackets
- IF... ELSE...
- Repetition brackets
- Mutual exclusivity bracket (one and only one of the subgroups is executed)
- Escape: Control transfers to after the leftmost bracket

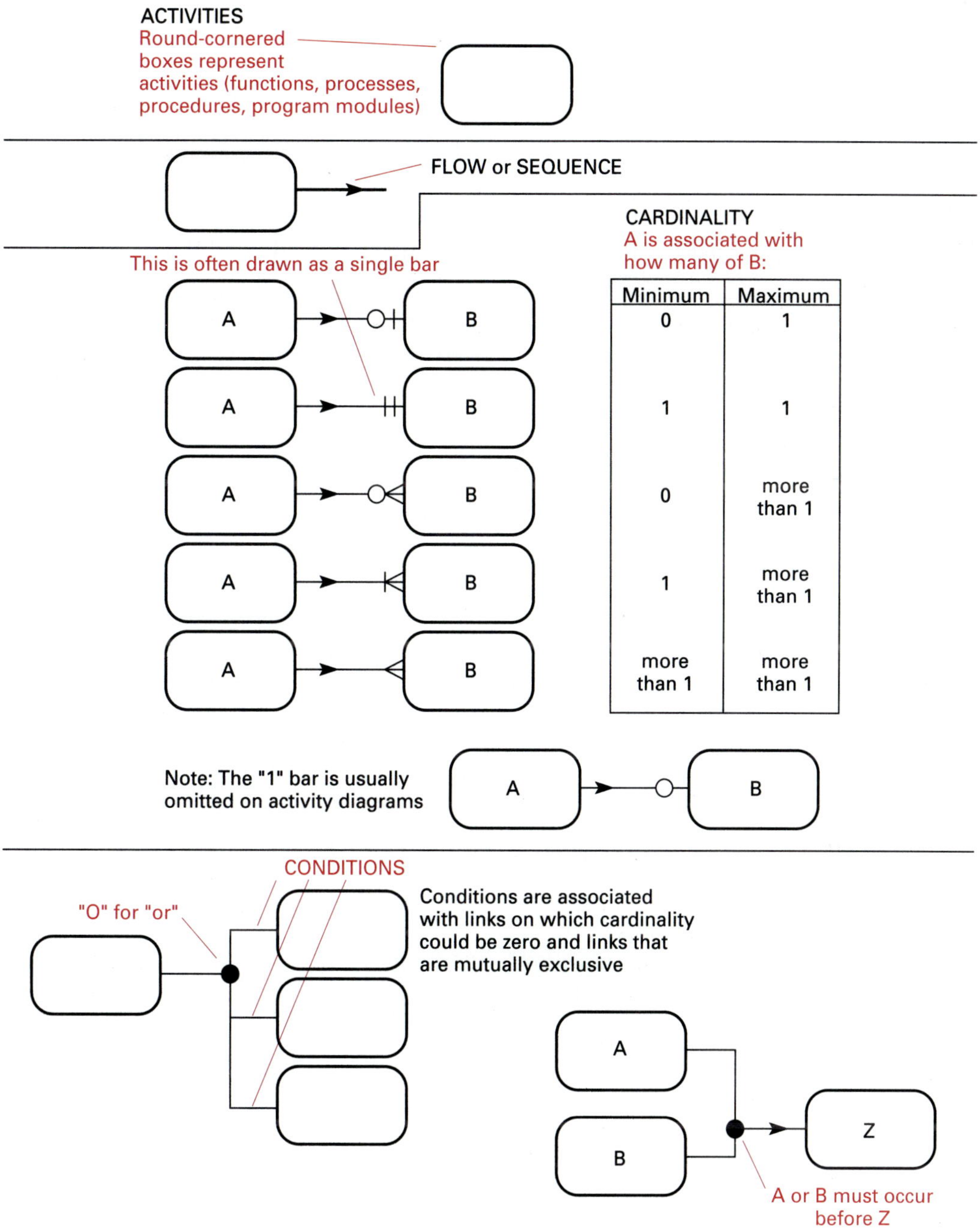

ACTIVITIES
Round-cornered boxes represent activities (functions, processes, procedures, program modules)

FLOW or SEQUENCE

CARDINALITY
A is associated with how many of B:

This is often drawn as a single bar

Minimum	Maximum
0	1
1	1
0	more than 1
1	more than 1
more than 1	more than 1

Note: The "1" bar is usually omitted on activity diagrams

CONDITIONS
"O" for "or"

Conditions are associated with links on which cardinality could be zero and links that are mutually exclusive

A or B must occur before Z

Figure A.1 Symbols used on diagrams with CASE tools employing conventional techniques.

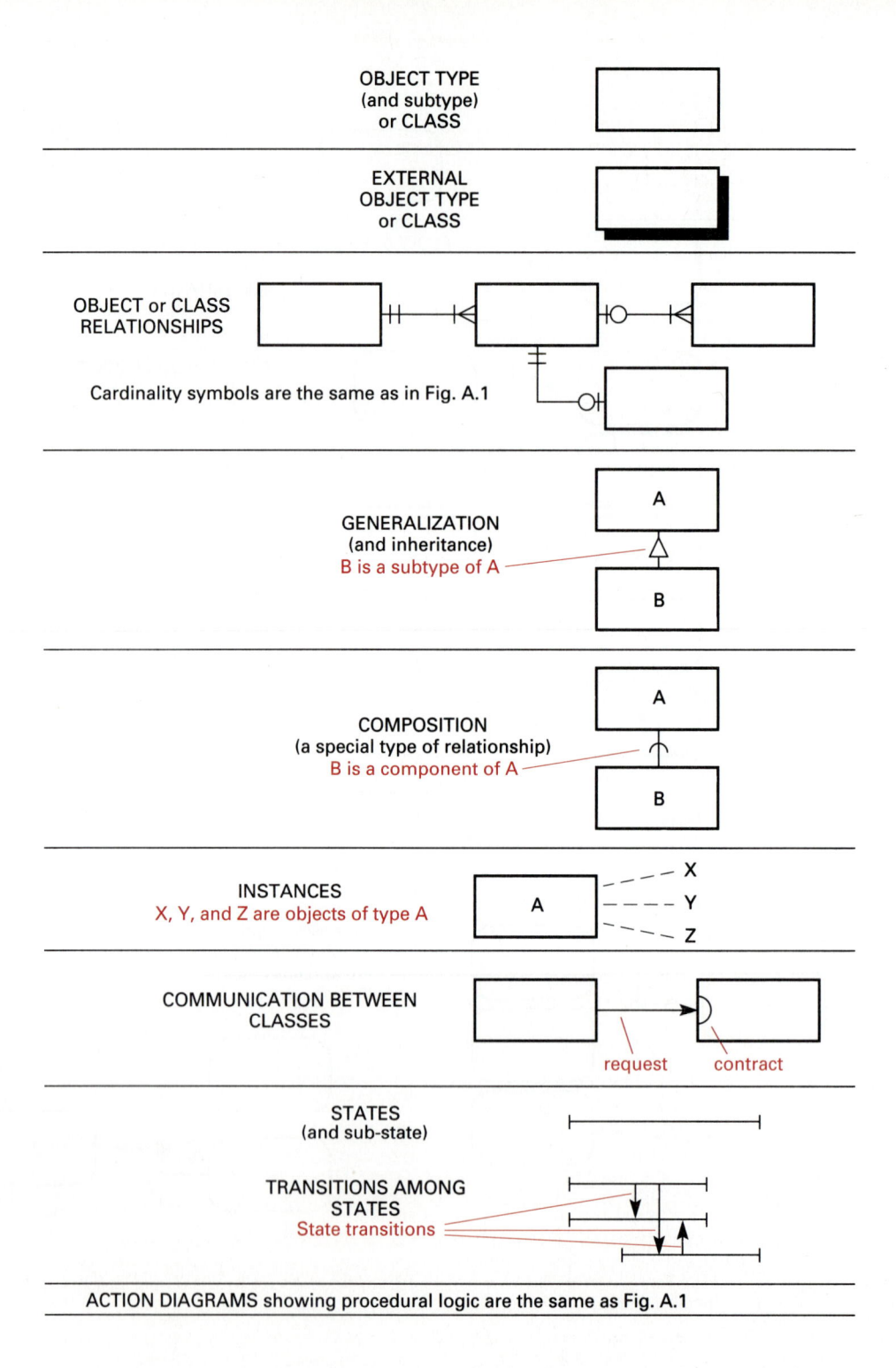

OBJECT TYPE (and subtype) or CLASS	
EXTERNAL OBJECT TYPE or CLASS	
OBJECT or CLASS RELATIONSHIPS Cardinality symbols are the same as in Fig. A.1	
GENERALIZATION (and inheritance) B is a subtype of A	A / B
COMPOSITION (a special type of relationship) B is a component of A	A / B
INSTANCES X, Y, and Z are objects of type A	A → X, Y, Z
COMMUNICATION BETWEEN CLASSES	request — contract
STATES (and sub-state)	
TRANSITIONS AMONG STATES State transitions	

ACTION DIAGRAMS showing procedural logic are the same as Fig. A.1

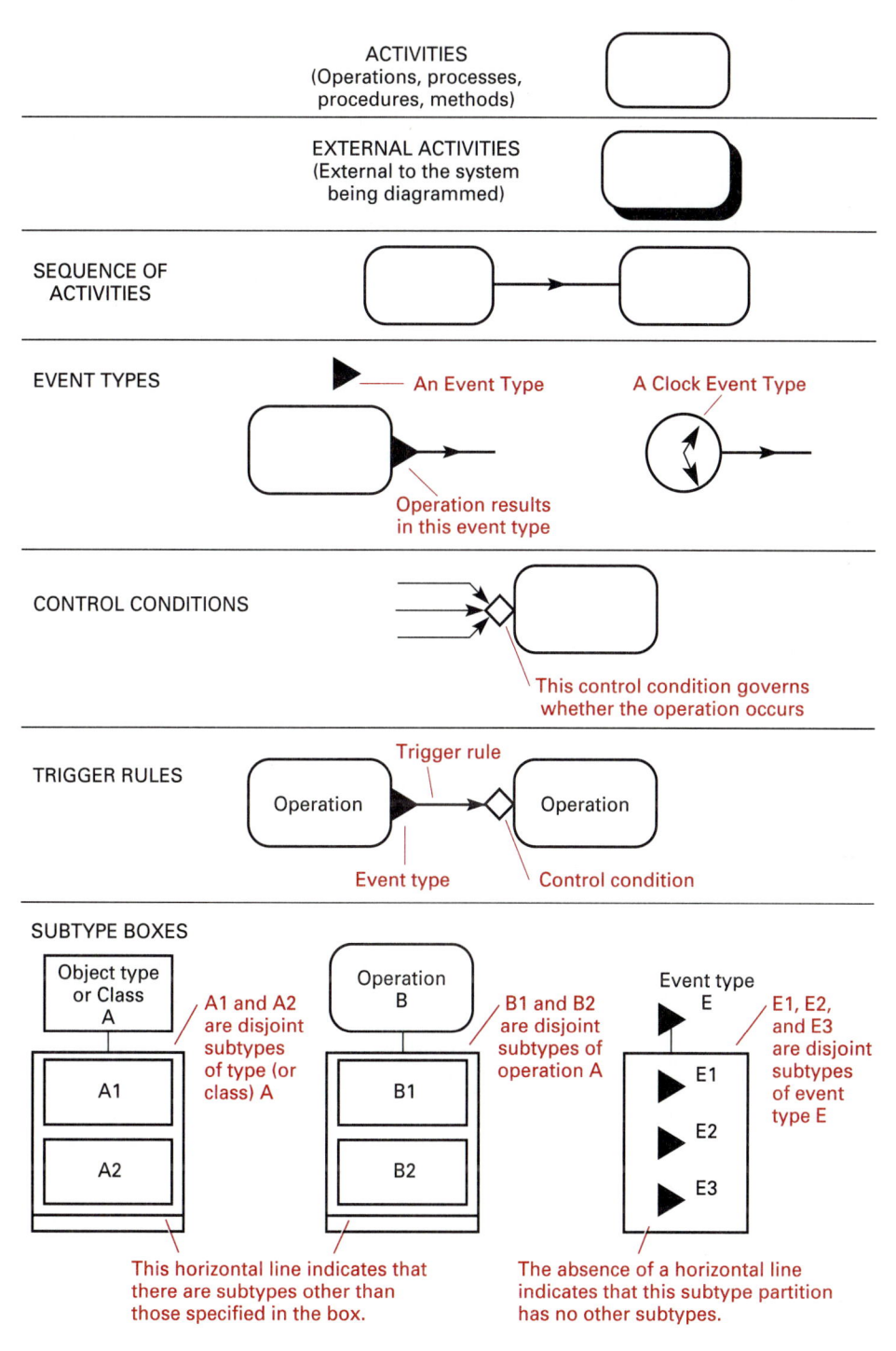

Figure A.2 Symbols recommended for OO-CASE tools. These should be a natural extension of the symbols in widespread use for conventional techniques (shown in Fig. A.1).

An object type, or an instance of an object type stored in the computer, is drawn with a rectangle. However on *object-flow diagrams,* shown in Chapter 5, the object is a physical thing, such as a product, rather than a symbolic representation in a computer. The physical object may be drawn as a three-dimensional box:

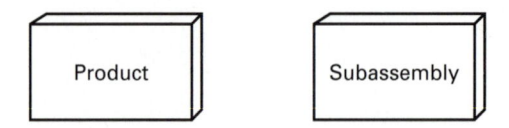

Product   Subassembly

Other three-dimensional pictures of objects are sometimes used:

EXTERNAL OBJECTS AND OPERATIONS

The diagrams represent mostly what goes on in a system or collection of systems. Sometimes, an object or an operation is external to the system but affects the system.

External objects and operations are drawn as boxes with shadows:

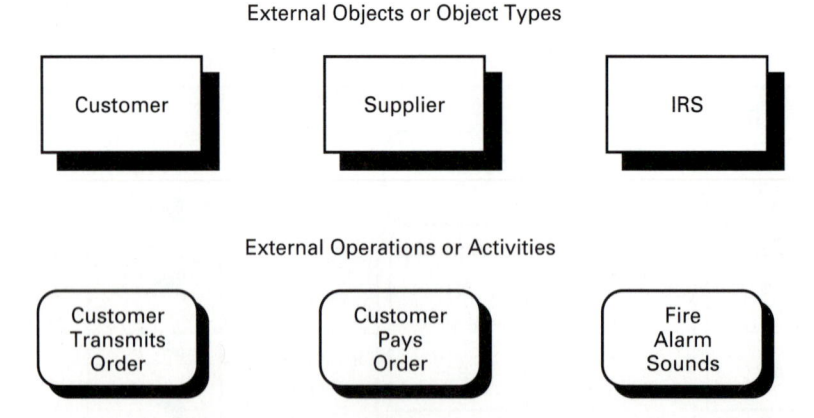

External Objects or Object Types

Customer   Supplier   IRS

External Operations or Activities

Customer Transmits Order   Customer Pays Order   Fire Alarm Sounds

An object-flow diagram can show operations, reality objects (three-dimensional), and external objects on the same diagram:

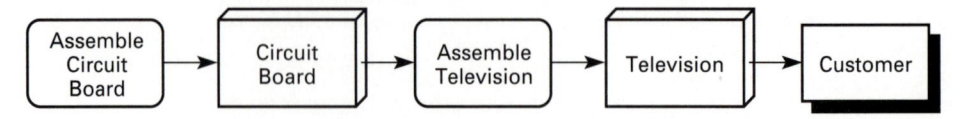

Assemble Circuit Board → Circuit Board → Assemble Television → Television → Customer

LINES AND ARROWS

Most diagrams have lines interconnecting the nodes. The line can represent such notions as associations, decomposition, flow, time dependencies, and trigger rules.

Sometimes, the lines connecting nodes have arrows on them to indicate the processing direction. For example, an event diagram indicates that one operation must occur *before* another. A trigger-rule line indicates that the occurrence of an event comes before an operation and causes the invocation of an operation. Depending on the context, one indicates only precedence, the other causality:

Precedence   Causality

Sometimes, the end of a line has cardinality symbols. In this case, the arrow should be placed in the middle of the line (or some distance from the ends).

CLASS COMMUNICATION DIAGRAM

An object or class has responsibilities (see Chapter 13). To fulfill a responsibility, it may send a *request* to another object or class. The receiving object or class, in effect, has a contract to fulfill a responsibility and respond to the request. The contract may relate to a set of different types of request. The contract is represented with a semicircle (like a reversed "C" for contract) in the box representing the object or class:

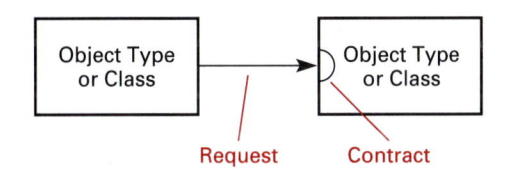

Object Type or Class → Object Type or Class
Request   Contract

Class-communication diagrams show multiple classes and the requests that pass among them, as in Fig. A.3.

CARDINALITY CONSTRAINTS

The term *cardinality constraint* refers to the restriction of how many of one item can be associated with another. For instance, a cardinality can be constrained as one-with-one or one-with-many cardinality. Sometimes, numbers can be used to designate the upper and lower limits on cardinality.

Crow's Feet

A crow's foot connector from a line to a node is drawn like this:

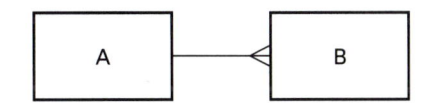

A ─────< B

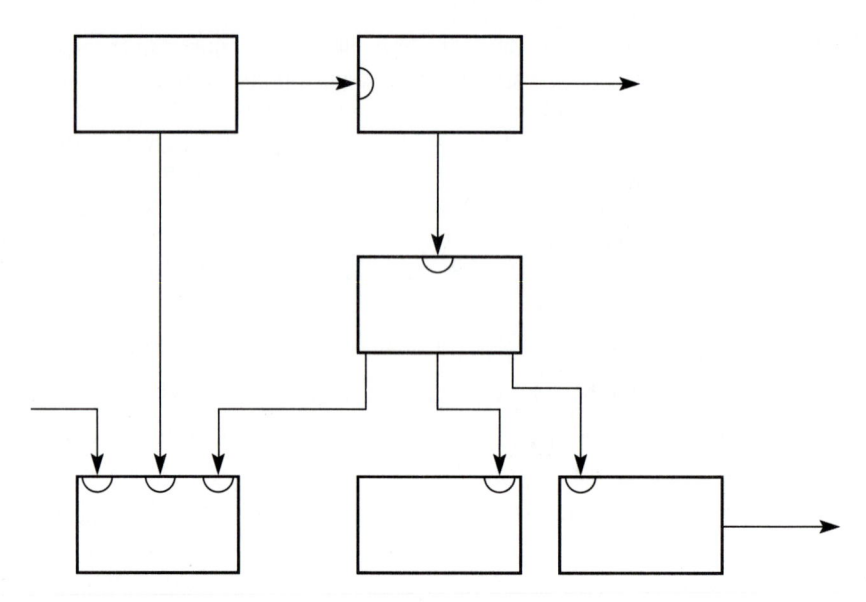

Figure A.3 A class-communication diagram shows classes and the requests that pass among them.

It means that one or more instances of B can be associated with one instance of A. It is called a *one-with-many association*.

One-with-one Cardinality Constraints

On diagrams using cardinality constraints, one-with-one cardinality is drawn with a small bar across the line (looking like a "1" symbol):

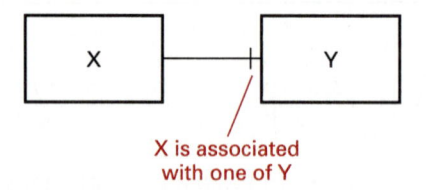

X is associated with one of Y

Zero Cardinality Constraints

A zero as part of the cardinality-constraint symbol means that an instance of one object type is not associated with any instances of another. In other words, an object of one type can have zero associations with the objects of another type:

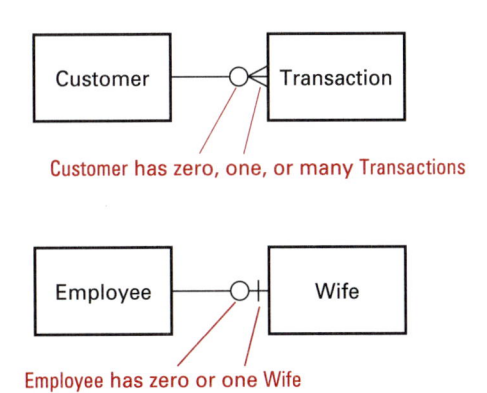

Appendix A   Recommended Diagramming Standards   **385**

[Customer]——o⊲[Transaction]
Customer has zero, one, or many Transactions

[Employee]——o|[Wife]
Employee has zero or one Wife

On object-relationship diagrams, however, a line representing an association between object types should *always* have a cardinality-constraint symbol on both ends. It is sloppy analysis to draw a line connecting an object-type rectangle with no cardinality-constraint symbol.

Minimum and Maximum Constraints

The cardinality symbols express a maximum and minimum constraint:

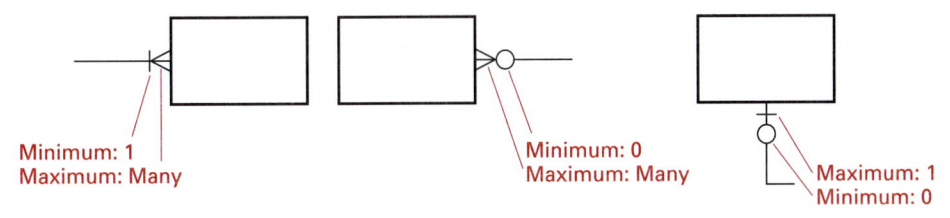

Minimum: 1
Maximum: Many

Minimum: 0
Maximum: Many

Maximum: 1
Minimum: 0

The maximum is always placed next to the box it refers to. Where minimum and maximum are both 1, two 1 bars are placed on the line. The two bars mean "one and only one":

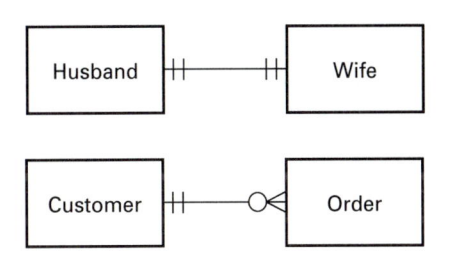

[Husband]|+——+|[Wife]

[Customer]|+——o⊲[Order]

Figure A.4 summarizes the representation of minimum and maximum cardinality constraints.

Figure A.5 depicts four object types with associations between the types. Its expression resembles an entity-relationship diagram.

	Each Instance of A Is Associated with How Many Instances of B:	
	Minimum	Maximum
A —O⊦— B	0	1
A —⊦⊦— B	1	1
A —O<— B	0	More than 1
A —⊦<— B	1	More than 1
A —<— B	More than 1	More than 1

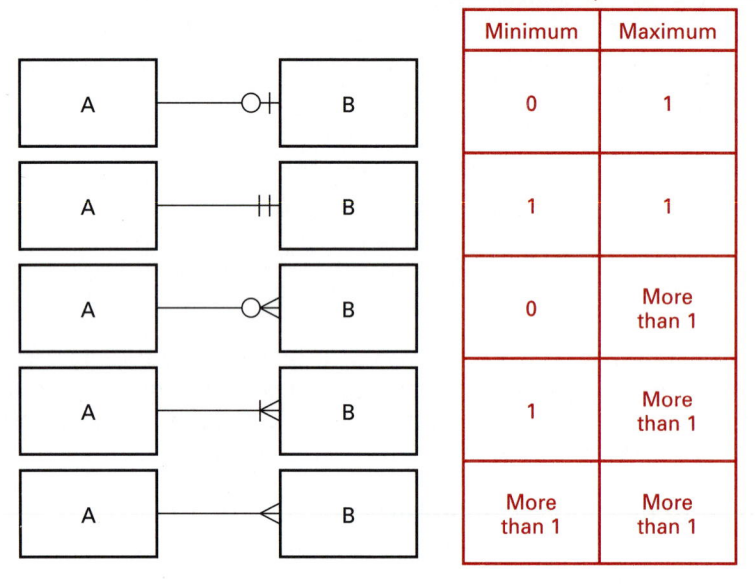

Figure A.4 Cardinality-constraint symbols indicate minimum and maximum cardinality constraints.

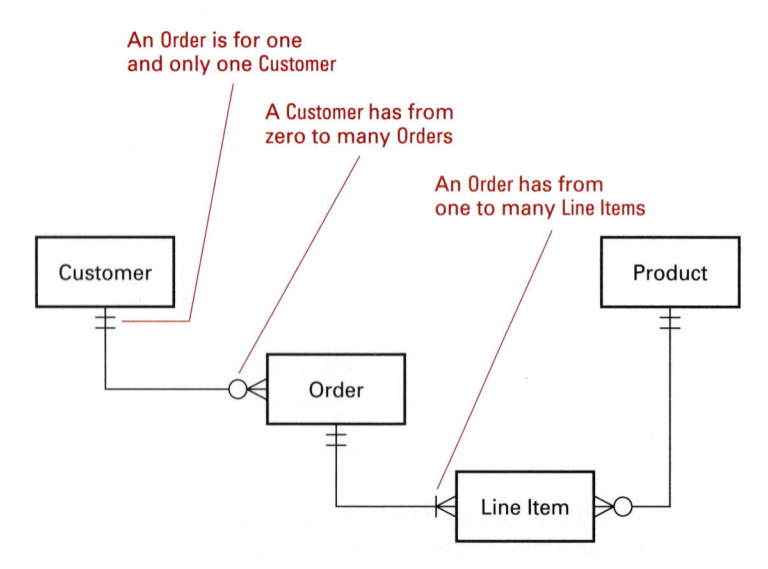

Figure A.5 Four object classes with cardinality symbols.

- An Order is for one and only one Customer
- A Customer has from zero to many Orders
- An Order has from one to many Line Items

Sometimes cardinality cannot be expressed in terms of zero, one, or many. For example, a **Meeting** requires at least two **Person**s and has a minimum cardinality of two. In addition, an organization can place a restriction that a meeting can have no more than 20 people attending it. This is expressed by enumerating the cardinality constraint:

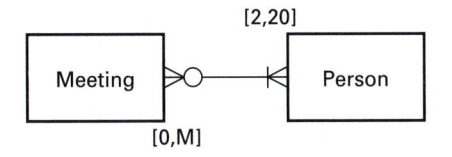

LABELING OF LINES

On some types of diagrams, the lines connecting nodes should be labeled. Lines between event types and operations are unidirectional. Lines between object-type boxes, on the other hand, are usually bidirectional. The line can be read in either direction:

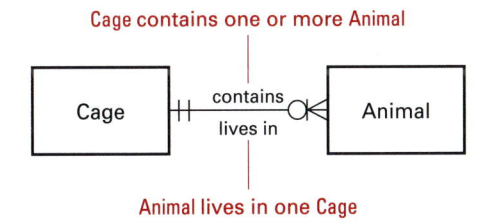

Only labeling lines in one direction is necessary, though labeling all associations between object types is recommended.

A label *above* a horizontal line is the name of the association when read from left to right. A label *below* a horizontal line is the name when read from right to left. As the line is rotated, the label remains on the same side of the line:

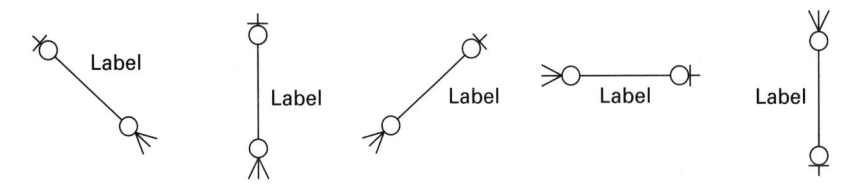

Thus, the label to the right of the vertical line is read when going *down* the line. The label on the left of a vertical line is read going *up* the line.

OBJECT-RELATIONSHIP DIAGRAMS

Entity-relationship diagrams are in common use in non-OO analysis and are similar to object-relationship diagrams (see Chapter 7). They show that one object type is associated with other object types. For example, an **Employee** works at a location; a **Customer** places **Orders**; an **Order** is for certain **Products**.

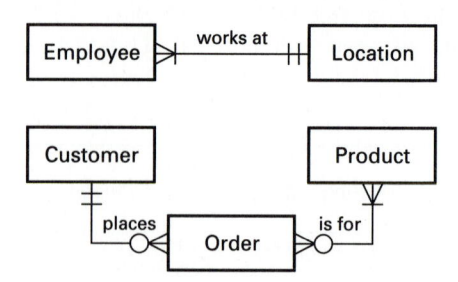

Cardinality-constraint symbols are used on object-relationship diagrams.

Reading Associations Like Sentences

Lines between object types give information about the relationship between the objects. This information ought to read like a sentence, for example:

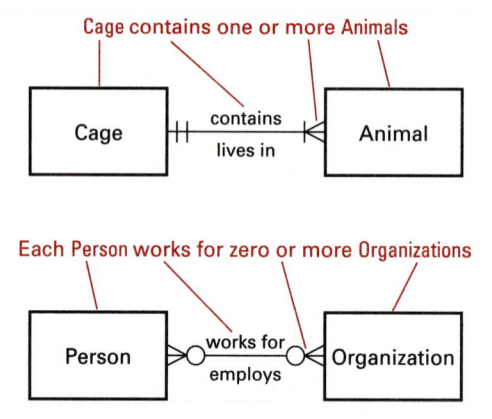

Cage contains one or more Animals

Each Person works for zero or more Organizations

COMPOSED-OF DIAGRAMS

A special type of relationship among object types or classes is one which could read "is composed of."

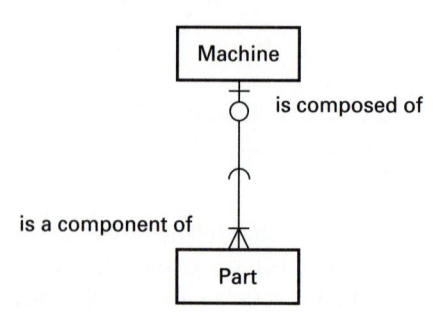

Appendix A   Recommended Diagramming Standards   **389**

Hierarchical diagrams are used to show that an object type (or class) is composed of other object types (or classes). To avoid labeling every line on a composed-of diagram, a ─∈─ ("C" for "composed-of") is used that means "is a component of."

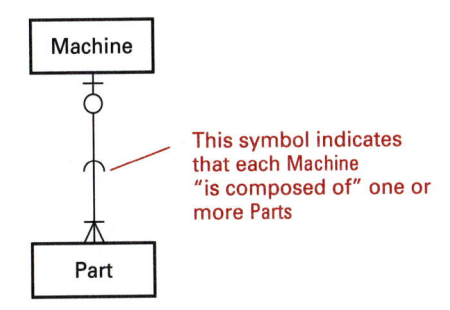

This symbol indicates that each Machine "is composed of" one or more Parts

Expressing cardinality constraints on composition associations is important, because a composite object can consist of zero, one, or many objects of different types. For instance, while each **Track Lighting Unit** will always have one **Track**, it will also have one or more **Spotlight Assembly** objects. In addition, while each **Spotlight Assembly** always has a **Spotlight Socket**, it may or may not have a **Spotlight Bulb** in it:

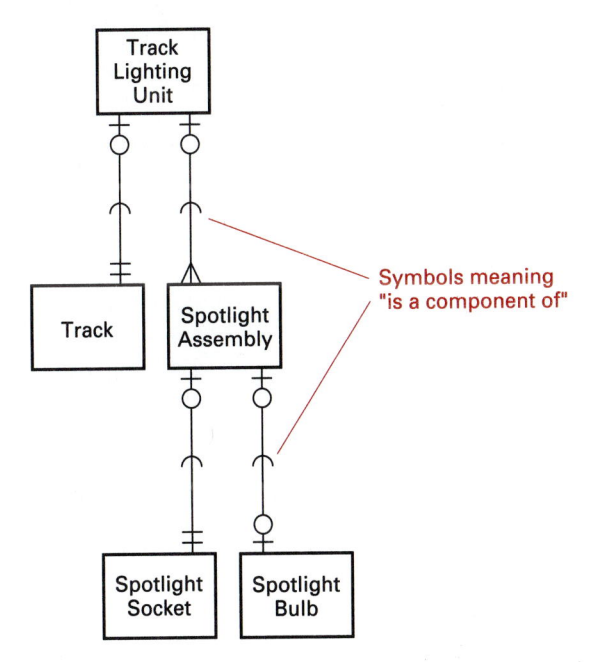

Symbols meaning "is a component of"

SUBTYPES AND SUPERTYPES

Object types or classes can have more specialized types called *subtypes* and more general types called *supertypes*. For instance, **Creature** is a supertype of **Aquatic Creature**, which is a supertype of **Fish**. **Fish**, in turn, has its own subtypes. Generalization hierarchies can be expressed as boxes within boxes:

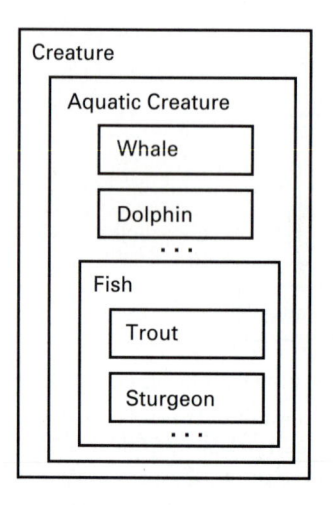

```
┌─────────────────────────────┐
│ Creature                    │
│  ┌────────────────────────┐ │
│  │ Aquatic Creature       │ │
│  │  ┌──────────────────┐  │ │
│  │  │ Whale            │  │ │
│  │  └──────────────────┘  │ │
│  │  ┌──────────────────┐  │ │
│  │  │ Dolphin          │  │ │
│  │  └──────────────────┘  │ │
│  │         ...            │ │
│  │  ┌──────────────────┐  │ │
│  │  │ Fish             │  │ │
│  │  │  ┌────────────┐  │  │ │
│  │  │  │ Trout      │  │  │ │
│  │  │  └────────────┘  │  │ │
│  │  │  ┌────────────┐  │  │ │
│  │  │  │ Sturgeon   │  │  │ │
│  │  │  └────────────┘  │  │ │
│  │  │      ...       │  │  │ │
│  │  └──────────────────┘  │ │
│  └────────────────────────┘ │
└─────────────────────────────┘
```

FERN DIAGRAMS Generalization is commonly represented with a fern diagram as in Fig. A.6. The fern diagram progresses from left to right and usually has no arrows on it. Since inheritance is based on

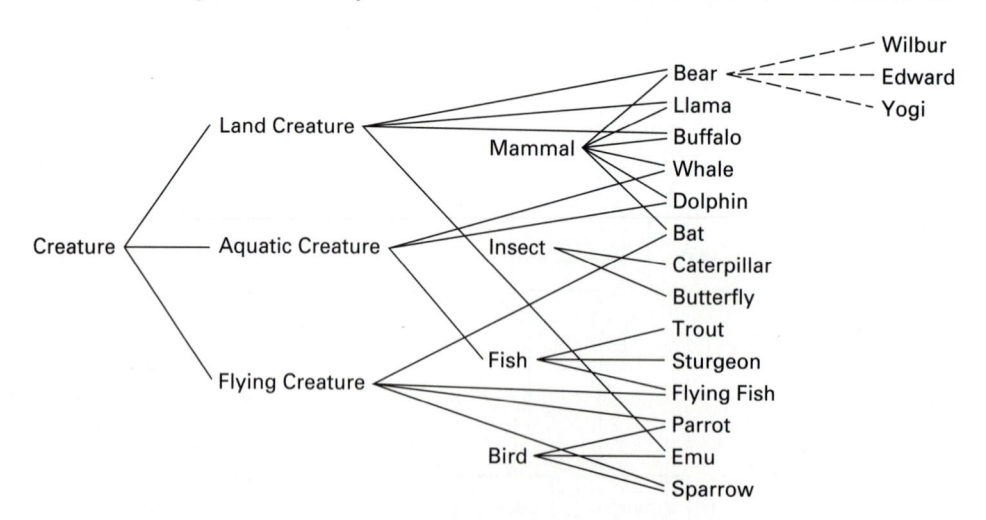

Figure A.6 A fern diagram showing a categorization of creatures. Some creature types have multiple supertypes and inherit properties from them. For example, a **Whale** has properties of an **Aquatic Creature** and **Mammal**. The diagram shows three instances of **Bear**. The dashed lines indicate that these are instances of bears rather than an object type.

generalization, diagrams are useful because they indicate the *direction* of inheritance. They do not, however, depict what is being inherited or how the inheritance mechanism works.

TYPES AND INSTANCES

A fern diagram sometimes shows instances of objects. Instances are connected to their object type with dashed lines. For example, **Bear** in Fig. A.6 is a subtype of **Mammal**, while **Wilber**, **Edward**, and **Yogi** are instances of **Bears**—that is, they are specific bears:

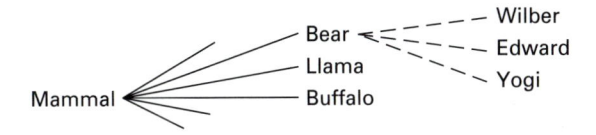

Fern diagrams sometimes become large. A CASE tool should be able to show a portion of the diagram when required, for example:

Sometimes, subtyping is shown on object-relationship or composed-of diagrams, as illustrated in Fig. A.7.

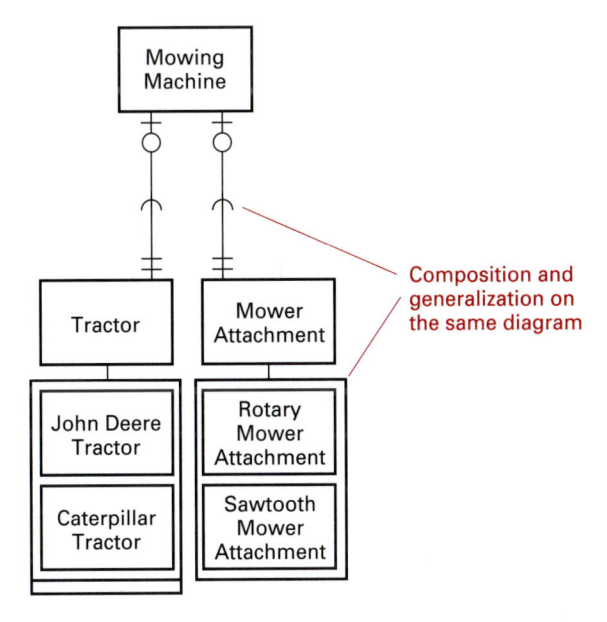

Figure A.7

Diagrams associating object types can show three types of information:

- Generalization or subtyping (which implies inheritance)
- Relationships
- Composition (which is a type of relationship)

It is possible to put all three types of information on one diagram, though often separate diagrams are used to show composed-of information and generalization or subtyping.

TRIANGLE ARROWS FOR SUBTYPING

When a diagram shows generalization or subtyping, triangle arrows are sometimes used to indicate the direction of generalization:

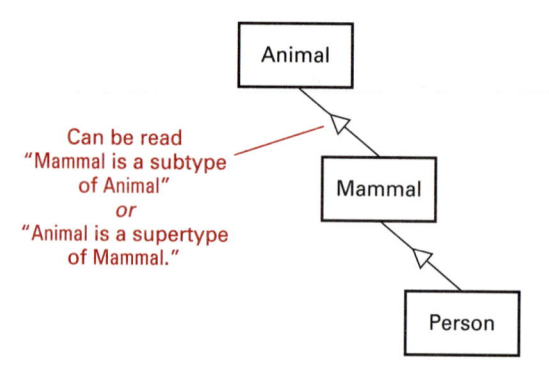

Can be read
"Mammal is a subtype of Animal"
or
"Animal is a supertype of Mammal."

Triangles are not necessary on a diagram that shows only generalization or subtyping. Generalization is represented from top to bottom or from left to right. Triangles for subtyping are used when the diagram also shows relationships.

The use of arrows on both generalization or subtyping diagrams and composed-of diagrams is contrasted in Fig. A.8.

EVENTS

An event is drawn as a small, filled-in triangle: ▶

An event occurs at a point in time, and the small triangle represents that point in time. An event usually causes an operation to occur. A line leads from the event triangle to that operation:

Appendix A — Recommended Diagramming Standards

Generalization (or Inheritance) Diagram:

Triangle arrow means "is a subtype of"

Composed-of Diagram:

C-shaped symbol means "is composed of"

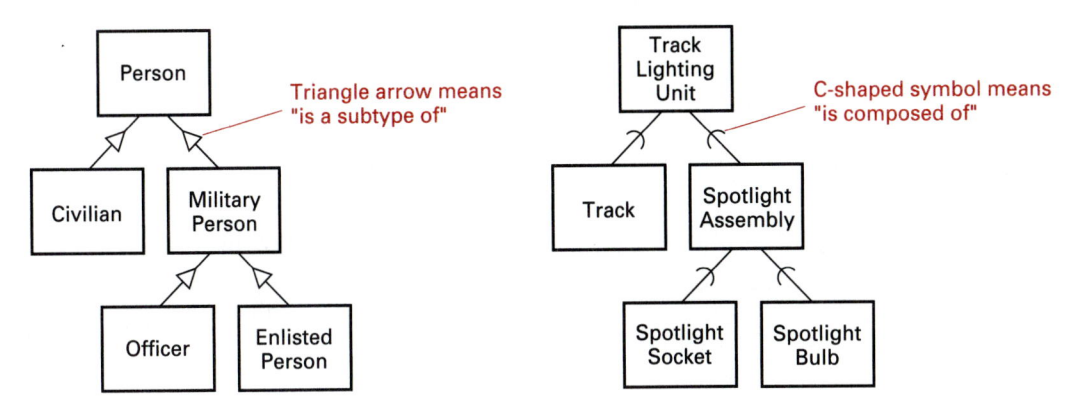

Figure A.8 —⊂— symbols are used to mean "is composed of." Triangle arrows are used to indicate subtypes (and, hence, inheritance). On a diagram that shows *only* generalization or subtyping, such as a fern diagram, no arrows are needed.

Operations are processes that can be requested as units. When operations are successful, events occur. Operations and events are thus closely connected. Event triangles may be attached to the box representing the operation that causes these events.

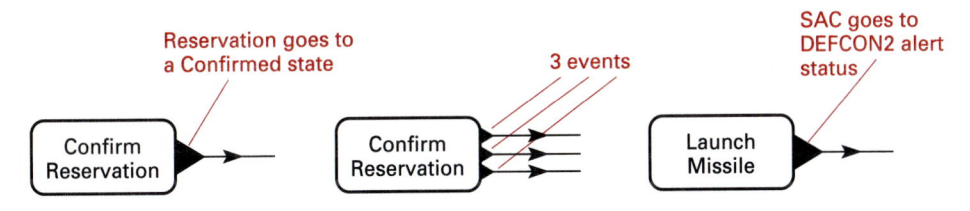

Reservation goes to a Confirmed state — Confirm Reservation

3 events — Confirm Reservation

SAC goes to DEFCON2 alert status — Launch Missile

An event diagram shows a string of events and operations:

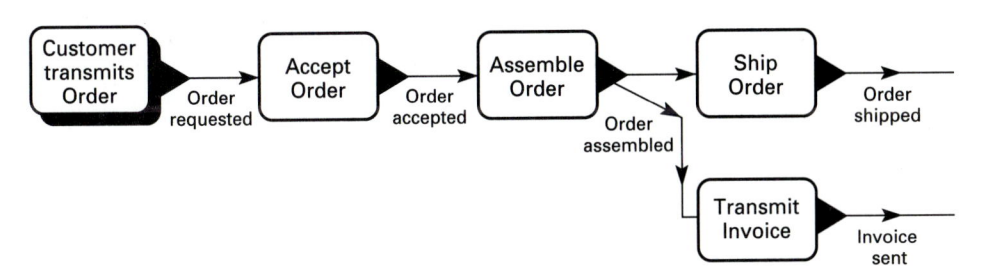

Customer transmits Order → Order requested → Accept Order → Order accepted → Assemble Order → Order assembled → Ship Order → Order shipped

Order assembled → Transmit Invoice → Invoice sent

An event represents a change in state of an object. A mouse-click on the event triangle should enable the tool user to examine the state change.

CLOCK EVENTS

A special type of event is a clock time being reached that triggers some operation. This type of event is drawn like a clock face:

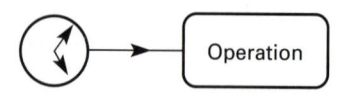

CONTROL CONDITIONS

Some operations can only take place when certain conditions apply. These are called *control conditions*. Control conditions are shown with a small diamond at the front of an operation box:

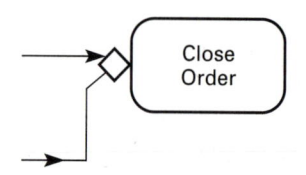

The diamond shape is similar to the decision symbol used in flow charting.

The control-condition diamond can define a single condition or a complex collection of Boolean conditions. The CASE-tool user should be able to mouse-click on the control-condition diamond and display a window showing the conditions.

TRIGGERS

A line going to an operation box indicates that the operation is triggered by the occurrence of a preceding event. The trigger may have a rule associated with it.

An event can trigger multiple instances of the same operation. A one-with-many crow's-foot notation can be used to indicate this:

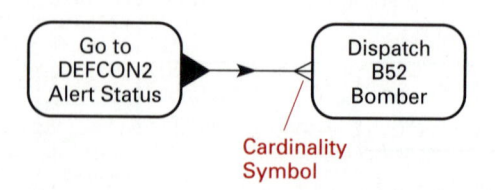

Cardinality Symbol

The trigger-rule line indicates the association of an event type to the operation invoked. Additionally, it can indicate the way in which the necessary objects are supplied to the operation it invokes. In this way, the trigger rule defines a causal relation between event and operation—as well as a form of "data flow."

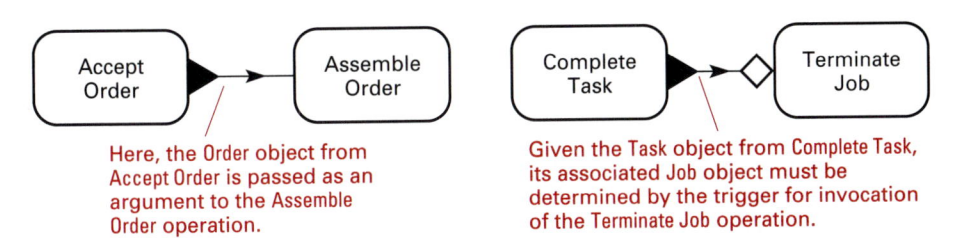

Appendix A Recommended Diagramming Standards **395**

Here, the Order object from Accept Order is passed as an argument to the Assemble Order operation.

Given the Task object from Complete Task, its associated Job object must be determined by the trigger for invocation of the Terminate Job operation.

Trigger lines, then, indicate two things. First, they link cause (the event) and effect (the operation). In other words, when an event occurs, a trigger invokes an operation. Second, they determine the objects required as arguments for the operation that the trigger invokes. These lines, therefore, define the rules for triggering an operation when a particular kind of event occurs. In this way, they are called *trigger rules*.

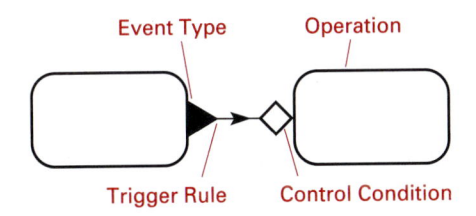

Operations may be triggered by one of many events occurring:

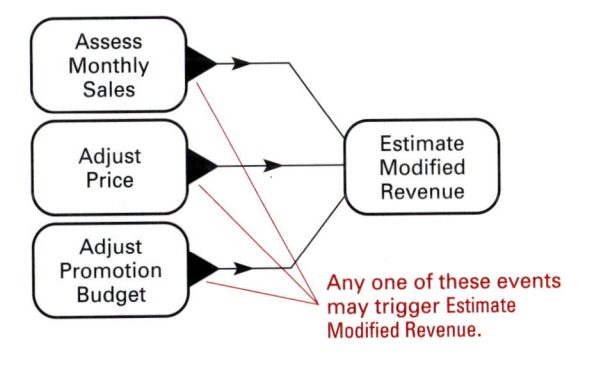

Any one of these events may trigger Estimate Modified Revenue.

This diagram indicates that only one of the three events must occur to trigger the **Estimate Modified Revenue** operation. In other words, the operation is triggered each time one of the three indicated events occurs. However, if a combination of conditions is necessary, a control condition is necessary. *Each* time a control condition is triggered, it checks whether a given condition is true or not. If true, its event occurs. Control conditions are not necessarily just "and" conditions. They can involve elaborate conditions with "ands" and "ors" as shown in Fig. A.9.

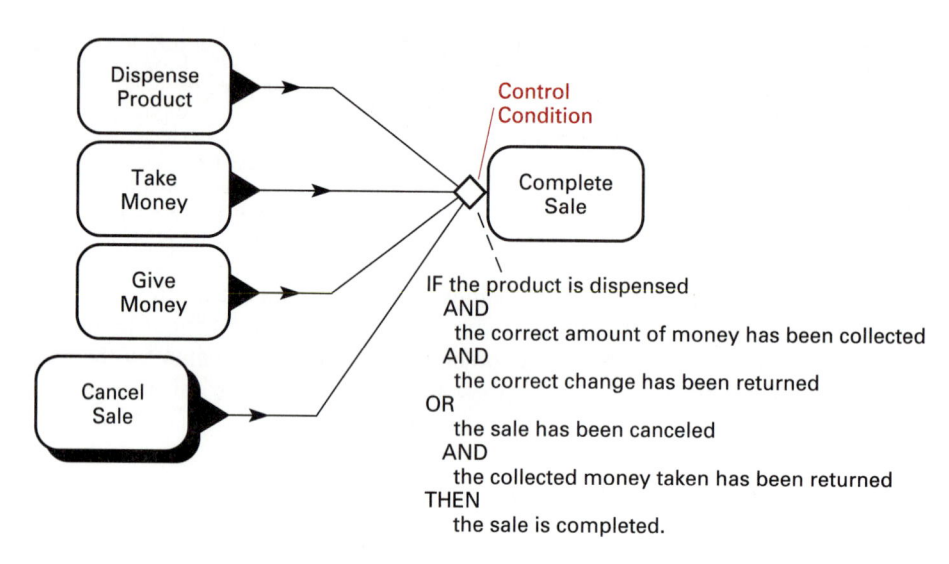

Figure A.9

```
[Dispense Product] ──▶ ◇ ──▶ [Complete Sale]
[Take Money]      ──▶ ↑ Control Condition
[Give Money]      ──▶
[Cancel Sale]     ──▶
```

IF the product is dispensed
  AND
    the correct amount of money has been collected
  AND
    the correct change has been returned
OR
  the sale has been canceled
  AND
    the collected money taken has been returned
THEN
  the sale is completed.

Operations, once triggered, are always expected to complete an event. When control conditions are specified, the operation may not be invoked unless its control conditions are true.

PARALLEL PROCESSING

Specifying parallel processing requirements is important in those environments having distributed processing requirements or using massively parallel computers. Event diagrams can indicate when processing can occur in parallel:

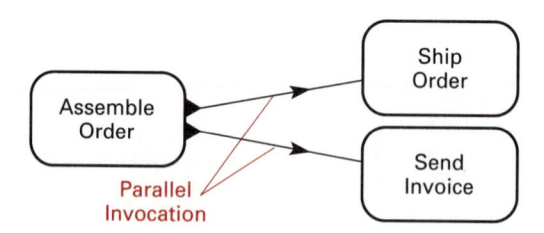

```
[Assemble Order] ──▶ [Ship Order]
                 ──▶ [Send Invoice]
     Parallel Invocation
```

OMITTING EVENTS AND CONTROL CONDITIONS

The lines between the operations on an event diagram indicate that operations result in events that trigger other operations. Because this is always the case, the event triangle is often omitted. Similarly, the control-condition diamond is often omitted, because all operations have these conditions (even if they are trivial). The CASE-tool user should be able to display the event or the control conditions with a mouse-click. All operations boxes have a set of control conditions and event types. An event diagram with the triangles and dia-

Appendix A   Recommended Diagramming Standards   397

(a)

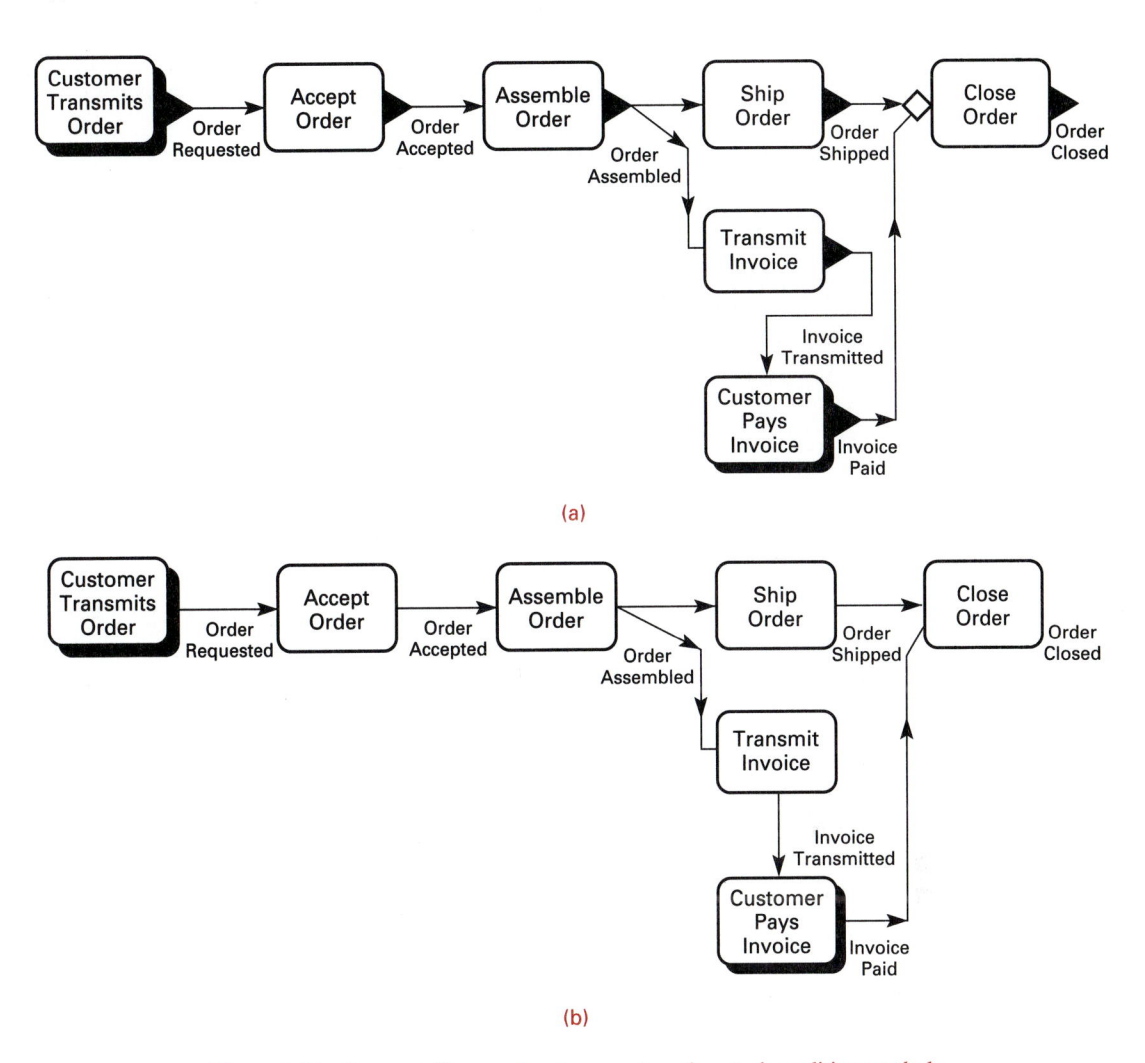

(b)

Figure A.10 An event diagram showing events and control-condition symbols (a) and the same diagram with the symbols omitted (b).

monds omitted is shown in Fig. A.10. With a CASE tool, it is better to have these symbols. They increase clarity, remind the user of their existence and fundamental importance, and the user can mouse-click on them to examine details.

STATES

An object can be in many states, where each state is drawn with the following symbol:

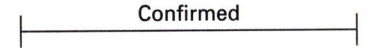

Confirmed

States are most commonly represented on state-transition diagrams. The transitions are represented as vertical lines connecting the states, as illustrated in Fig. A.11.

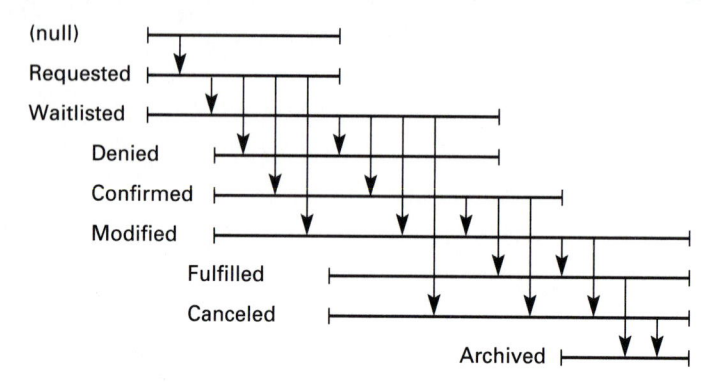

Figure A.11

Permissible states differ slightly, depending on the attributes of the object. For example, Fig. A.12 shows five states that relate to objects of the type **Person** getting up in the morning. The state transitions are slightly different for a male person than for a female person.

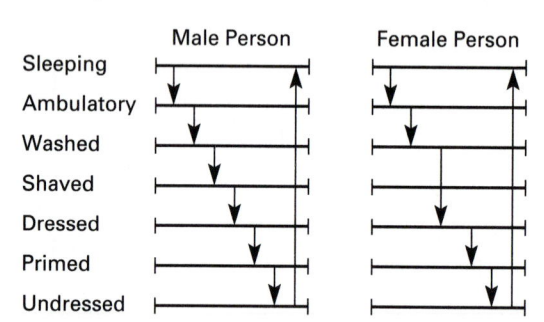

Figure A.12 State changes can differ slightly between male and female persons preparing for the day.

In object-oriented analysis, recognizing opportunities for reusability is important. When diagramming object behavior, the analyst must consider which operations and object types can be reused and which cannot. For example, is the operation that makes a **Male Person** ambulatory the same as that for a **Female Person**? If so, the same behavior should be specified for both. Without this understanding, uncontrolled redundancy will run rampant. For instance, an order-processing system may have over a hundred different kinds of orders—each with its own lifecycle. By blindly analyzing each lifecycle separately, no opportunity for reusability will be discovered. A notation combining the generalizations and specializations on the same diagram can help remedy this.

MUTUAL EXCLUSIVITY

Sometimes a block on a diagram is associated with *one and only one* of a group of blocks. They are mutually exclusive. For example, a **Product** is *either* **Goods** or a **Service**. The process **Prepare Material** may be followed by *either* **Operation A1** or **Operation A2** or **Operation A3**.

Mutual exclusivity can be represented by a branching line with a filled-in circle at the branch. The circle looks like an "o" for "or" and means that the branches are mutually exclusive as shown in Fig. A.13.

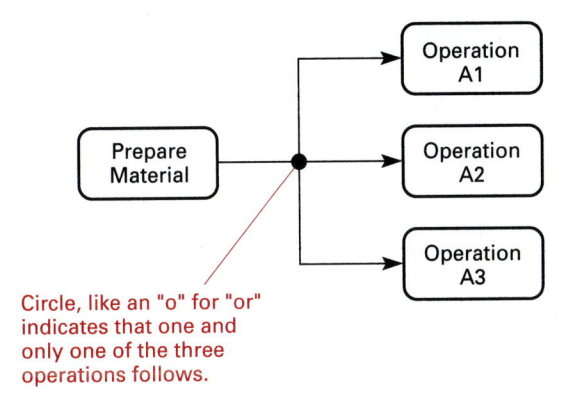

Figure A.13

SUBTYPE BOXES

Figure A.14 shows mutual exclusivity represented with a subtype box.

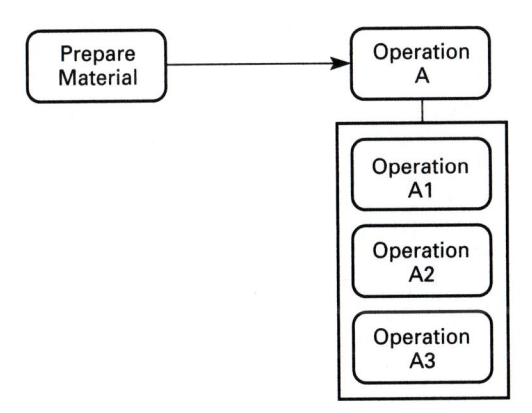

Figure A.14

Here, **Operation A1** or **Operation A2** or **Operation A3** are all mutually exclusive subtypes of **Operation A**.

While the mutual exclusivity ("or") circle is handy to use, using a subtype box to represent exclusive associations encourages the analyst to capitalize on a major feature in the OO approach—generalization. Without generalization, there would be no class inheritance. In the example, placing **Goods** and **Service** in a subtype box indicates that they both can have common attributes and operations. For instance, all **Products** have a unique **Product ID** and participate in order-processing operations. By not identifying a common supertype, the analyst runs the risk of defining redundant attributes and operations.

A subtype box, such as that above, can be used to show subtypes of operations, objects or classes, and events (see Fig. A.15).

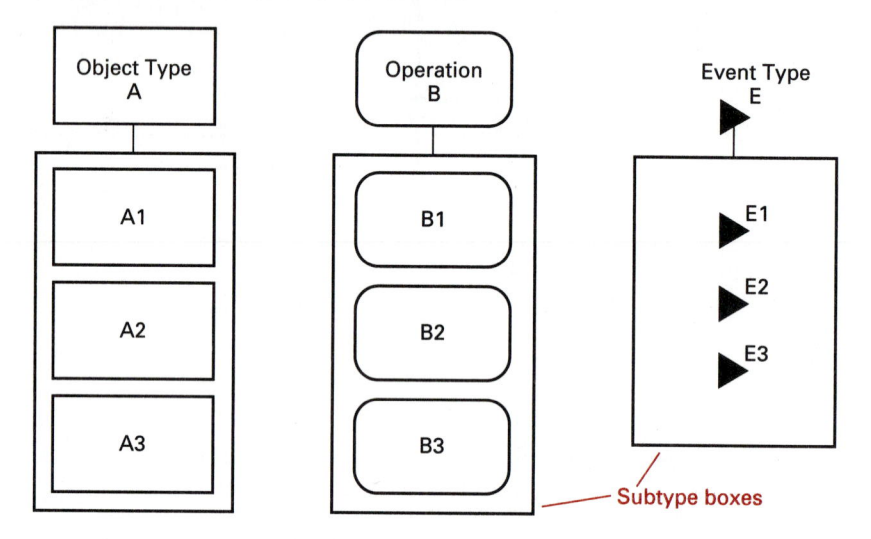

Figure A.15 Subtype boxes are used to show subtypes of operations, object types, classes, or events.

NONMUTUALLY EXCLUSIVE SUBTYPES

The subtypes in Fig. A.15 are mutually exclusive sets. For example, Event E must be either Event E1, E2, or E3. The subtypes in Fig. A.16 are not mutually exclusive. When a traffic light changes, for example, it could change to yellow, not merely to red or green. The empty partition at the bottom of the subtype box indicates that other subtypes could exist.

MULTIPLE SETS OF SUBTYPES

An object type may have many different subtypes. For example, a **Person** might be a **Male** or **Female**, Civilian or Military, and various subtypes of **Military**. These different subtypes may be drawn as shown in Fig. A.17.

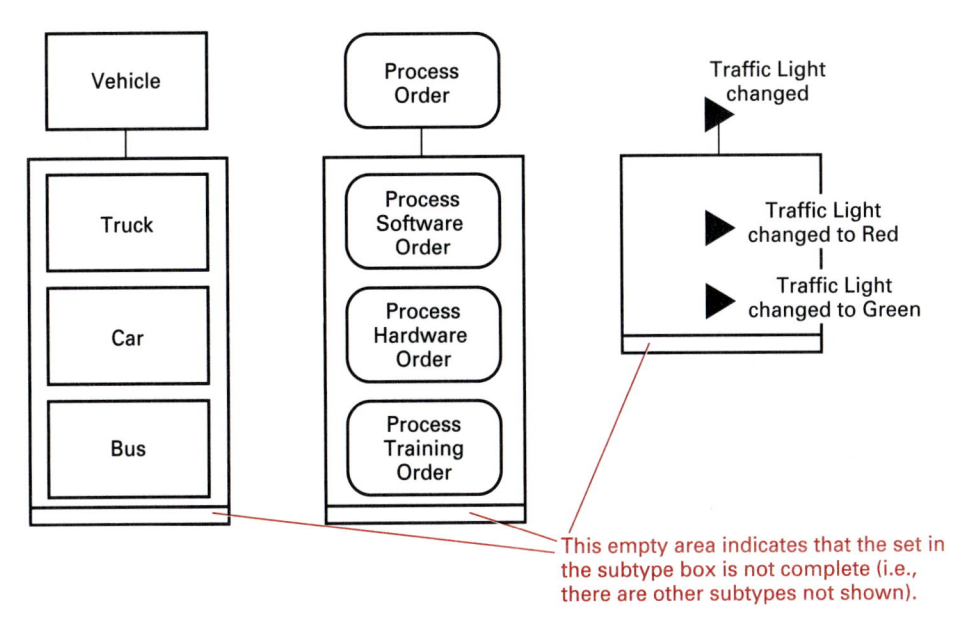

Figure A.16 An empty partition at the bottom of a subtype box means that more subtypes than those shown can exist, as in this figure. In Fig. A.15, there are no empty partitions indicating that the subtypes in Fig. A.15 are mutually exclusive.

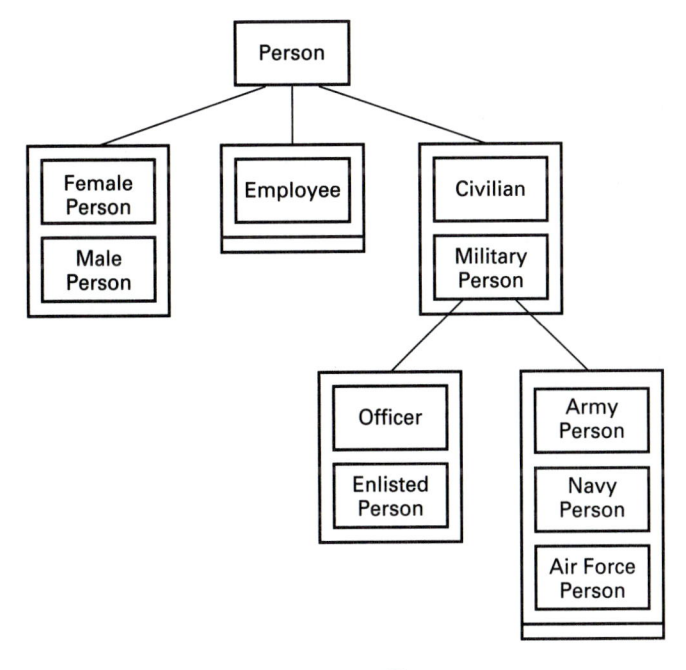

Figure A.17

401

EXPANSION AND CONTRACTION

Object-oriented diagrams become large. Scrolling and zooming techniques are used to inspect large diagrams on the screen. Particularly important, diagrams

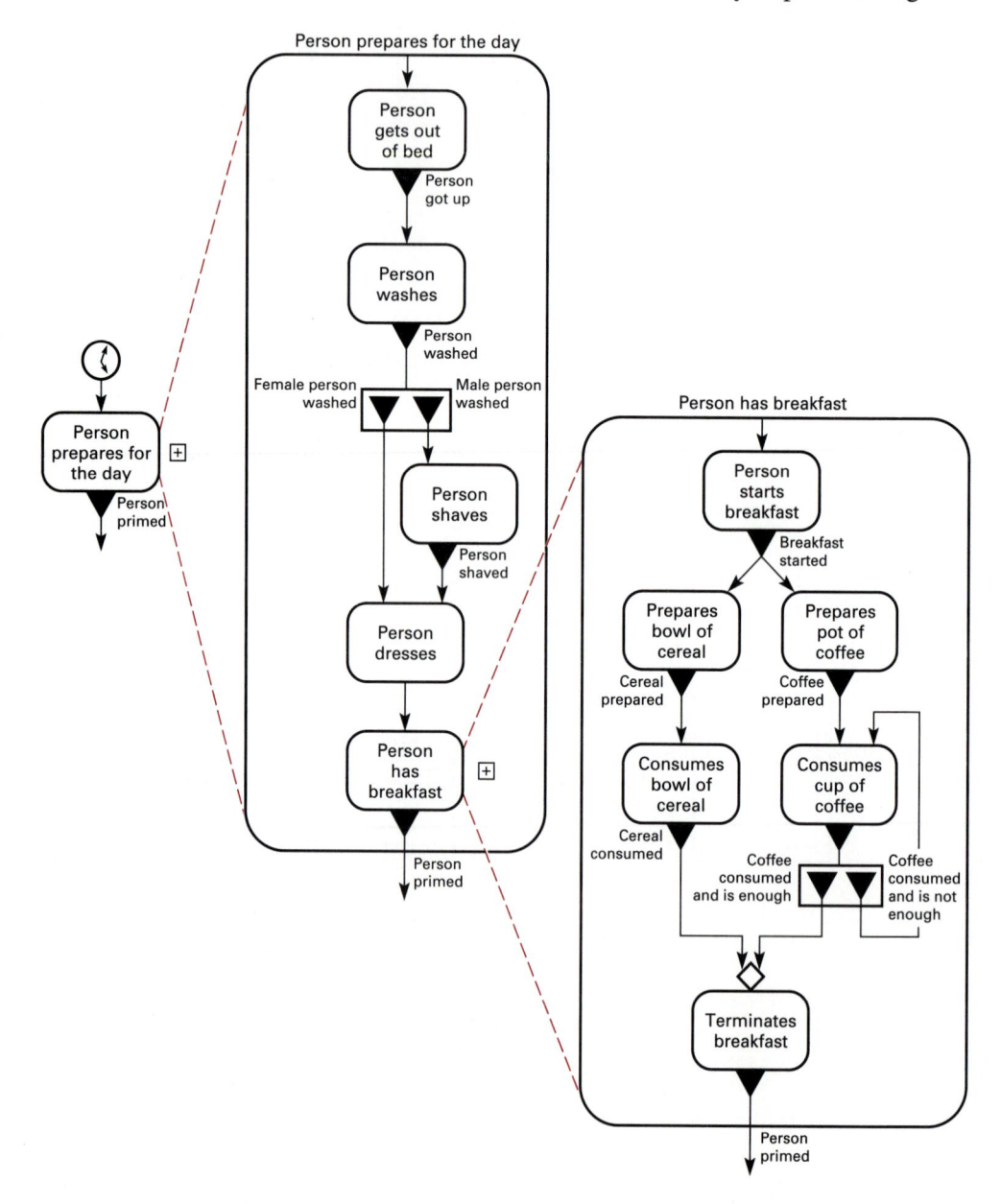

Figure A.18 Using the ⊞ symbol for expanding an event diagram.

Appendix A   Recommended Diagramming Standards   **403**

should be nested, that is, a box be put around a collection of boxes. They can be shown as one box and can be expanded when necessary.

To indicate that a line or block can be expanded to show more detail, the symbol "..." or " + " is used. Sometimes, the symbol " − " is used to indicate that a portion of the diagram can be contracted into one block or line.

The use of + symbols and corresponding expansions on an event diagram is shown in Fig. A.18, while Fig. A.19 shows them on a state-transition diagram. Diagrams should be designed for this type of CASE expansion and contraction.

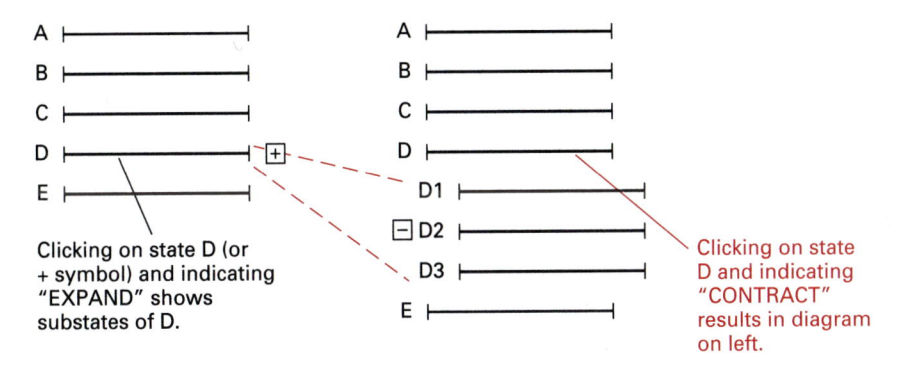

Figure A.19   An object can have many permissible states which may be drawn more closely by representing them as states and substates. When the substates of a particular state are not shown on a diagram, a "..." or " + " symbol is displayed next to the state. Clicking on this symbol prompts a display of its substates.

USING WINDOWS TO ACHIEVE CLARITY

Diagrams can be confusing if different types of ideas or types of representations are shown on the same diagram. To avoid this, the different types of representations should be separated into different windows. The user of a computerized tool can point to a node or line and indicate: SHOW DETAIL. A pop-on window will display the detail stored about the node or line. A window can be a diagram of a different type.

REFERENCE

1. James Martin, *Recommended Diagramming Standards for Analysts and Programmers,* Prentice Hall, Englewood Cliffs, NJ, 1987.

INDEX

A

Abstract data types (ADTs), 263
Action diagrams, 62, 225–26, 227, 228, 229, 289, 309, 310, 376
 code generation with, 226–28
Active databases, 308, 309
Activities, linking state changes and, 158–66
Actor, 270
Ada, 23, 62, 263, 329
Adapter, 344
ADT, 236
AEGIS Naval Weapon System, 43
Algol 60, 262, 326
Algol 68, 263
ANSI C++, 342. *See also* C++
Apple Computer Inc., 171
Arrows in diagrams, 88–89, 383, 392
Artificial intelligence, 6, 13
Attributes, 83, 155

B

Backward chaining, 10, 145
Beck, Kent, 171, 188, 190, 191
Behavior rules, 136, 137
Berg, H. K., 324
Binding, 275–76, 287
BLOBs (binary large objects), 23, 35, 308
Box diagrams, 74–75
Boxes, square-cornered and round-cornered, 377
Business area analysis (BAA), 244, 245, 251–52, 255, 256

C

CAD (computer-aided design), 308, 313, 315
CAE (computer-aided engineering), 308, 313

Cardinality constraints:
 crow's feet and, 83, 383–84
 minimum and maximum, 85–86, 385–87
 one-with-many, 83, 384
 one-with-one, 83, 384
 zero, 84, 384–85
CASE (Computer-Aided Software Engineering), 6, 7, 97, 156, 276–77, 282, 283, 322
 combining CRC cards and, 197–98
 future of, 298
Categorization diagrams, 235
CCITT X.500, 338
CD-ROMs, 350
Chief information officer (CIO), 38
C language, 9, 13, 37, 42, 61, 62, 222, 226, 227, 234, 270, 272, 287, 291, 327
Class(es), 30, 116, 145, 169, 171–72, 177, 187, 188, 263, 269
 definition of, 11, 23–24
 high in the hierarchy, 176
 naming, 191
 resembling actors, 188
Class communication diagrams, 195–97, 383
Class hierarchies, 169, 283
Class independency, 316
Class instance inheritance, 182
Class libraries, 10–11, 230, 239
Client, 10, 191, 338
Client-server technology, 10
Clock events, 117, 394
CLOS, 270
COBOL, 9, 13, 42, 61, 62, 185, 219, 221, 222, 224, 226, 231, 232, 270, 282, 287, 290, 291, 303, 304, 310, 326, 327, 329, 349, 350, 352, 371
CODASYL, 304
Codd, E. F., 305

405

Code Generation from the Enterprise Model
  (CGEM), 368
Code generators, 7–8, 169, 281, 282, 287, 328, 329
  design synthesis and, 285–86
Collaborators, responsibilities and, 188
Common Object Request Broker Architecture
  (COBRA), 338
Compilers, 273–74, 277, 328
Complex objects, 92
Composed-of diagrams, 89–92, 96, 144, 193, 196,
    216, 388–89, 391
  subtyping versus, 93
Composed-of hierarchies, 194, 287
Composed-of relationships, 90, 101
Computer Associates, 224, 226
Connection Machines, 363
Constellation project, 356
Construction, 244, 253
Contracts, 191–92, 196, 216
Control conditions, 120–21, 394, 396–97
Control structures, 328
Conventional diagrams, 376, 377–78
COOPERATION project, 40, 43
Core Model (ORB), 338
Corporate transparency, 293
C++, 5, 13, 37, 45, 53, 61, 171, 181, 219, 236, 270,
    271, 272, 276, 287, 291, 308, 310, 311, 326,
    327, 329, 342
CRC cards, 188–89, 190, 193, 206, 216
  combining with CASE, 197–98
CRC methods, 188
Cunningham, Ward, 188, 189, 190
Cyclometric complexity, 42

D

Dahl, Ole-Johan, 261
Data-analysis diagrams, 376
Database development:
  database management systems, 303–5
  file systems, 302–3
  relational database, 305–7
Database management systems (DBMSs), 303–5
Data definition language (DDL), 304, 311
Data-flow diagrams, 62, 130, 283, 309, 376
Data independence, 306–7, 314, 316
Data manipulation language (DML), 304, 305, 311
Data models, 82
Data-oriented methodologies, 187
Data structure, 20
Data structure diagrams, 289
Data types, 262, 328
Decision tables, 235
Decision trees, 235, 285, 376
Declarative languages, 134–35, 231–32
Declarative manipulation, 307
Declarative tables, 235–37, 289

Decomposition diagrams, 376
Default options, 231, 233
Dependency diagrams, 376
Derivation rules, 136, 137, 139
Diagram(s):
  executable, 52
  relationships among different, 149–54
  rules linked to, 166–67
Diagramming:
  consistency in, 293
  for OO development, 289–90
  precision in, 288
Diagramming standards:
  cardinality constraints, 383–87
  class communication diagrams, 383
  clock events, 394
  composed-of diagrams, 388–89, 391
  control conditions, 394, 396–97
  conventional diagrams, 376, 377–78
  easy to learn, 55
  event diagrams, 363, 393, 396
  events and, 392–93, 396–97
  expansion and contraction, 402–3
  external objects and operations, 382
  fern diagrams, 390
  labeling of lines in, 387
  lines and arrows in, 86, 87, 383, 387
  multiple sets of, 400–401
  mutual exclusivity, 399
  need for, 54–55
  nonmutually exclusive subtypes, 400
  object-oriented diagrams, 377, 380–81
  object-relationship diagrams, 387–88, 391
  parallel processing, 396
  reality and information about reality, 377, 382
  square-cornered and round-cornered boxes, 377
  standards for, 375–76
  states, 397–98
  subtypes and supertypes, 389–90
  supertype boxes, 399–400
  triangle arrows for subtyping, 392
  triggers, 394–96
  types and instances, 391–92
  using windows to achieve clarity, 403
Dialog-design diagrams, 376
Dialog-flow diagram, 104
Dialog painters, 231
Dictionary, 290–91
Dijkstra, E. W., 28, 322, 323, 324
Documentation, 292–93
Dynabook, 262
Dynamic compiler, 273

E

EDI (electronic data interchange), 30, 211, 301,
    321, 365, 367

Index

E

Eiffel, 270
Encapsulation, 19–21, 30, 172, 173, 263, 269, 301, 314, 315, 316, 364
   objects as, 264–65
Encyclopedia, 8, 55
End users, 51–52. *See also* Workshops
Enterprise model(s), 29, 201, 206
   code generation from, 367–68
   "intelligent," 53
Enterprise modeling, 57, 59, 186
Enterprise visualization, 52
Entities, 19
   objects and, 81–82
Entity-relationship diagrams, 62, 82, 83, 284, 309, 376
Entity types, 18, 284, 377
Event diagrams, 111, 122–23, 142, 144, 158, 163, 164, 166, 167, 168, 206, 216, 235, 236, 251, 283, 284, 285, 290, 293, 363, 393, 396
Events, 109, 111, 281, 392–93, 396–97
   clock, 117, 394
   external sources of, 117–18
   operations and, 112–13
   state changes and, 113–14
   subtypes and supertypes, 125–26
   types of, 118–19
Executive sponsor, workshop, 207
Expert systems, 145

F

Facilitated workshops, 201
Facilitators, workshop, 201, 207–9
   training, 209–10
Fern diagrams, 72–75, 155, 156, 176, 178–79, 390–91
File, 81
File management systems, 302–3
Finite-state machines, 107
FOCUS, 9, 222
FORTRAN, 13, 42, 62, 222, 262
Forward chaining, 10, 145
Fourth-generation languages (4GLs), 222, 282, 307
Fragment CASE, 283, 284
Frame-based techniques, 145
Functional decomposition, 62, 283, 284, 309

G

Gates, Bill, 4
Generalization, 71, 93, 174, 400
Generalization hierarchy, 71–72, 93
Generalization-specialization diagram, 93
Gensym Inc., 282
Goal-directed reasoning, 10, 146
Graphic user interface (GUI), 169, 231, 289

H

Hierarchical schemas, 127
Hoare, C. A. R., 322, 323, 324, 327, 328
Human Use of Human Beings, The, 352

I

IBM, 108, 292, 356, 357
I-CASE (Integrated CASE), 7, 243, 282–83, 284, 293, 294, 351, 352
ICM, 294
IDEAL, 222, 224, 226, 231
IE-CASE, 284
IEF-CASE, 226
IMS (Information Management System), 303, 304
Inference engine, 6, 10, 13, 145, 150, 235
Information engineering, 9, 53, 57, 64–66, 207, 241–43, 284
   analysis for reusability, 253–54
   business area analysis, 244, 245, 251–52, 255, 256
   characteristics of, 242
   commonality and, 257
   construction, 244, 253
   divide and conquer, 246–47
   enterprisewide planning, 249–50
   enterprisewide implementation, 255–56
   goals of, 247–49
   human coordination, 256–57
   object-oriented analysis, 254–55
   pyramid representing, 243–46, 257
   system design, 244, 252
Information hiding, 19
Inheritance, 24–25, 30, 101, 174–75, 266–69, 315, 389–90
   class instance, 182
   multiple, 24, 176, 177
Inheritance diagrams, 235
INMOS, 328
Input-directed reasoning, 10, 145
Instances, 18, 20, 83, 391–92
   types and, 73–74
Integrity rules, 136, 137, 138
INTELLECT, 239
IntelliCorp, 148, 149, 155, 157, 159, 178–79, 220, 234, 235
Intelligent database, 301, 308
Interface, 341
   to non-OO software, 344–45
Interface definition language (IDL), 341-42
Interpreters, 273-74, 277
ISAM (Indexed Sequential Access Method), 303
ISO (International Standards Organization), 367
I.S. project team, 39

J

JAD (joint application design), 201, 202, 203, 206, 207, 208, 209, 210, 211, 216, 252
   benefits of, 205
   duration of, 212
   group dynamics and, 213
JEM, 201, 202, 203, 206, 207, 208, 209, 216
   benefits of, 204
JOIN, 309
JRP (joint requirements planning), 201, 202, 203, 206, 207, 208, 209, 216, 252
   benefits of, 204
   duration of, 212
   group dynamics and, 213
   participants of, 210–11

K

Kay, Alan, 261, 262
Knowledgebases, 308, 309
Knowledge coordinator, 292
KnowledgeWare Inc., 292

L

Learning Research Group, 262
Legacy applications, 66, 197
Lines in diagrams, 86–87. 383, 387
LISP, 13, 270
Local area networks (LANs), 14, 363, 364
LOTUS 1-2-3, 39

M

MANTIS, 222
Mathematics, programming and, 9–10, 323–25
Matrices, 62
Maximum cardinality constraints, 85–86, 385–87
McCabe Cyclometric Complexity Metric, 42–43
Messages, 266
Metaphor Inc., 282, 356, 357
Methods, 18, 24, 26, 104, 112, 116, 145, 169, 171, 187, 207, 263, 264, 267, 269, 272, 277, 293, 326
   action diagrams, 225–29
   avoidance of procedural design, 229
   class libraries, 239
   decision trees and tables, 235
   declarative language, 231–32
   declarative tables, 235–37
   default options, 231, 233
   English and, 237–39
   event diagrams, 235
   from operations to, 172–74
   increasing the power of languages, 219–21
   inference engine, 235
   procedural versus nonprocedural techniques, 221–24
   report generators, 231
   rules, 233
   screen and dialog painters, 231
   selecting, 176–77, 181
Meyer, Bertrand, 116, 140
Minimum cardinality constraints, 85–86, 385–87
MO:DCA (Mixed Object Document Content Architecture), 367
Modula, 23, 263
Modules, 23, 263
Mutual exclusivity, 399

N

NATURAL, 9, 222
Navigation, 304, 305
NCR, 40, 43
Networks, intercorporate, 364–65
NOMAD, 222
Noma Industries, 184
Nonprocedural languages, 9
Nonprocedural techniques, 221–23, 229, 230
Normalization, 81–82, 307
Nygaard, Kristen, 261

O

Object(s), 19, 265–66
   definition of, 17–18
   as encapsulations, 264–65
   entities and, 81–82
   external, 382
   interface to, 341
   objects composed of, 193–95
Object Behavior Analysis (OBA), 61, 63–67, 136, 144, 169, 244
Object Behavior Design (OBD), 61, 63, 65
Object-behavior rules, 142
Object categorization, 69–70, 206, 216
   box diagrams, 74–75
   complete and incomplete sets of subtypes, 75
   determining subtypes, 79–80
   fern diagrams, 72–73
   generalization hierarchies, 71–72
   object as an instance of multiple subtypes, 75–77
   types and instances, 73–74
   various ways of, 77–78
Object COBOL, 270
Object Contents Architecture, 367
Object-flow diagrams, 128–32, 382
Objective-C, 181, 270

Index

Object Management Architecture, 335, 345
  Application Objects (AO), 336, 344
  Common Facilities (CF), 336
  Object Request Broker (ORB), 39, 337–40
  Object Services (OS), 336–37, 344
Object Management Group (OMG), 4, 15, 333–34, 357
  Object Management Architecture, 335–40
  object model, 334
Object Management Workbench (OMW), 148, 149
Object Method Architecture, 367
Object-oriented analysis, 254–55
Object-oriented CASE methodology (OOCM), 294
Object-oriented CASE (OO-CASE) tools, 53–54, 60–61, 281–82, 294
  categories of, 283–84
  code generators, 287
  consistency among diagrams, 293
  consistency among different projects, 293–94
  design synthesis and code generation, 285–86
  diagrams for OO development, 289–90
  dictionary, 290–92
  documentation, 292–93
  insightful models, 284–85
  instant CASE, 287
  intelligence in the repository, 292
  maximum reusability, 294–96
  precision in diagramming, 288
  pure OO and hybrid CASE, 283
  repository, 290
  sources of reusable components, 297–98
  variety of, 282–83
Object-oriented databases (OODBs), 9, 301, 302, 308–9, 329
  approaches to building, 313
  architecture of, 311–12
  avoiding redundancy, 315–16
  complexity of data structure, 314
  data independence versus encapsulation, 314
  development with, 312–13
  differences between relational databases and, 316–18
  Object Request Broker and, 342
  performance of, 315
  replacement of relational databases by, 314
  shared transactions of, 312
  unified conceptual model, 309–11
  versions of, 312
Object-oriented design, 11, 169–70
  class and, 171–72
  classes high in the hierarchy, 176
  class inheritance, 174–76
  components of, 170
  from operations to methods, 172–74
  polymorphism, 181–82
  reusability and, 182–86
  selecting a method, 176, 177, 181
  self-contained viewpoint of the object, 170–71
Object-oriented diagrams, 377, 380–81
Object-oriented models:
  accommodation of old systems, 66–67
  aspects of, 61
  information engineering, 64–66
  as models of reality, 59–60
  similarity of analysis and design, 62–64
  tools, 60–61
  understandability of, 51–52
Object-oriented programming languages (OOPL):
  abstract data types (ADTs), 263–65
  avoidance of CASE statements, 276–77
  canceling inherited features, 269
  characteristics of, 269–70, 278
  enforcement of discipline, 272
  environments and, 277, 278
  evolution from untyped to typed languages, 262
  genesis of, 261
  inheritance and polymorphism, 266–69
  interpreters versus compilers, 273–74
  objects and requests, 265–66
  pointers, 274–75
  pure versus hybrid, 270–72
  Smalltalk, 261–62
  static versus dynamic binding, 275–76
  user-defined types (UDTs), 263
Object-oriented techniques:
  benefits of, 32–39
  changes in thinking using, 46
  characteristics of, 31–32
  disadvantages of, 45–46
  enhanced creativity and, 44–45
  immediate feedback and, 45
  more like hardware engineering, 40–41
  orderly behavior, 41–42
  program complexity metrics, 42–43
  reliability needs simplicity of, 42
  reusability, 39–40
Object-PASCAL, 270
Object-relationship diagrams, 82, 96, 97, 144, 155, 156, 157, 158, 160, 166, 216, 287, 387–88, 391
Object Request Broker (ORB), 39, 337–38, 357
  diverse implementations of, 338, 340
  functions of, 339–40
  interface definition language and, 341
  multiple, 342–44
  object-oriented databases and, 342
  repositories, 342
Object schemas, 285
Object-state rules, 142
Object Structure Analysis (OSA), 61, 63–67, 136, 142, 144, 169, 171, 176, 244
Object Structure Design (OSD), 61, 63, 64, 65
Object-structure diagrams, 61, 206, 235, 251
Object types, 23, 69, 70, 71, 73, 377, 382, 391–92
  arrows indicating subtypes, 88–89
  attributes, 83
  cardinality constraints, 83–86

Object types, *(cont.)*
  composed-of diagrams, 89–92
  data models, 82
  definition of, 18–19
  entities and objects, 81–82
  instances and, 73–74, 83
  labeling of lines, 86–87
  object-relationship diagrams, 82
  Occam's Razor and, 95–96
  overview diagrams, 96–100
  reading associations like sentences, 87
  subtypes, 87–88
  subtyping and composition on the same diagram, 94–95
  subtyping versus composed-of diagrams, 93
OCCAM, 10, 328, 329, 330
Occam's Razor, 56, 95–96, 243
ODA (Office Document Architecture), 367
One-with-many association, 83, 384
One-with-one cardinality constraints, 83, 384
Operation(s), 19, 20, 21, 263, 269, 340, 341, 377
  cause-and-effect isolation, 114–15
  clear modularization, 117
  conditions for executing, 141–42
  control conditions, 120–21
  events and, 112–13
  external, 382
  from methods to, 172–74
  linking of, 114
  preconditions and postconditions, 115–17, 140–41, 326
  sequence of, 111–12
  simultaneous, 123–24
  subtypes and supertypes, 124–25
Operation identifier, 341
Operation name, 341
Optical disks, 350, 359
Overview diagrams, 96–100

P

Package, 23, 263
Parallelism, 362–63
Parallel processing, 396
Parametric polymorphism, 269
PASCAL, 42, 222, 263, 270
Patriot Partners, 356, 357
Persistent data, 308
PL/I, 42, 222
Pointers, 274
Polymorphism, 181–82, 183, 266–69, 276, 277
Postconditions, 115–17, 140–41, 326
Preconditions, 115–17, 140–41, 326
Private responsibility, 193
Procedural languages, 134–35
Procedural techniques, 221–24, 229, 230
Processes, 377

Process-oriented methodologies, 187
Production rules, 145, 150
Programming:
  mathematics and, 323–25
  problem with languages used in, 327–28
PROJECT, 309
ProKappa, 44, 155, 176, 178–79, 220
PROLOG, 13, 134, 363
Prototyping, 328
Public responsibility, 193

R

RAD (rapid application development), 202, 206, 253, 367
RAMIS, 222
RAMIS ENGLISH, 237, 239
Recommended Diagramming Standards for Analysts and Programmers, 55, 375, 377
Redundancy, 307, 315–16
Relation, 81
Relational databases (RDBs), 305–7, 310, 314
  avoiding redundancy in, 315–16
  differences between object-oriented databases and, 316–18
  performance of, 315
Reorganization, 304
Report generators, 13, 231, 232, 282
Repository, 6, 8, 12, 37, 55, 202, 206, 243, 257, 290, 291, 376
  intelligence in, 292
  Object Request Broker, 342
  standards for, 354–55
Repository-based methodologies, 8
Repository coordinator, 8, 292
Repository services, 292
Requests, 21–23, 104, 114, 187, 191, 193, 216, 265–66, 267, 326, 340
Responsibilities, 187–88, 206, 216
  collaborators and, 188
  public and private, 193
Responsibility-driven design, 252
  class communication diagrams, 195–97
  classes are actors, 188
  combining cards and CASE, 197–99
  contracts and, 191–92
  CRC cards, 188-89
  following the right wording, 191
  legacy applications, 197
  objects composed of objects, 193–95
  public and private responsibilities, 193
  responsibilities, 187–88
  responsibilities and collaborators, 188
  subtypes, 193
  thinking like an object, 189–90
Reusability, 39–40, 106–7, 182–86, 249, 253–54, 294–98, 350, 357–58, 367

RISC (Reduced Instruction Set Computing), 369, 371
Rules, 133, 206, 216, 233, 281, 285, 290, 293
   attached to other OO diagrams, 143
   behavior of, 136, 137
   categories of, 137, 151
   changing how businesses are run, 151, 153
   conditions for executing and operation, 141–42
   declarative versus procedural statements, 134–35
   derivation, 136, 137, 138
   diagrams linked to, 136
   executable diagrams and, 142, 143
   expressed in English, 133–34
   inference engine and, 145, 150
   integrity, 136, 137, 138
   linked to diagrams, 166–67
   making business knowledge explicit, 135–36
   operation condition, 140–41
   stimulus/response, 136, 140
   traceability, 150
   unnecessary, 150
   visible and nonvisible, 150, 152–53
Runtime repository, 341

S

Screen painters, 231
Scribe, workshop, 209, 214, 216
Server, 10, 191, 338
Signature, operation, 341
Simula I, 261
Simula 67, 261, 263
Smalltalk, 5, 13, 37, 53, 171, 181, 261–62, 270, 271, 272, 308, 310, 311
Soft pointers, 315
Software, 349–50
   automation of development of, 353–54
   bypassing controls, 327
   characteristics of future development of, 359–62
   code generation from enterprise model, 367–68
   combination of disciplines for building, 330–31
   evolution of production of, 351–52
   evolution of programming techniques, 368–70
   factory to produce, 37–38
   immediate feedback and, 327
   inhuman use of human beings and, 352–53
   intercorporate computer interaction, 364–65
   interface to non-OO, 344–45
   international standards for reusable classes, 367
   inventor of, 36–37
   killer technologies for development of, 5–11
   need for fast development, 366–67
   need for power tools for, 350–51
   networks and distribution of objects, 363–64
   optical disks and, 350, 359
   packaged, 355–57

   parallelism and, 362–63
   repository standards and, 354–55
   reusability of, 357–58
   revolution in, 4–5
   speed of interaction and, 365–66
   true engineering of, 321–23
   use of formal methods to build, 358, 362
SQL, 13, 282, 307, 309, 311, 318, 363
Standards, international, 367. *See also* Diagramming standards
State(s), 397–98
   lifecycles of, 103–4
   multiple simultaneous, 107, 109
   reusability in transitions, 106–7
State changes, 103, 119, 281, 289
   events and, 113–14
   linking activities and, 158–66
State-transition diagrams, 104–5, 114, 158, 160, 164, 165, 206, 216, 235, 285, 293, 376, 398
   complex, 107
Stimulus/response rules, 136, 140
Structure charts, 62, 283, 309
Substates, 105–6
Subsystems, 194–95
Subtypes, 87–88, 101, 193, 283, 287, 389–90
   arrows indicating, 88–89
   boxes indicating, 399–400
   complete and incomplete sets of, 75
   determining, 79–80
   event, 125–26
   multiple sets of, 400–401
   nonmutually exclusive, 400
   object as an instance of multiple, 75–77
   operation, 124–25
   triangle arrows for, 392
Subtyping, 96, 98
   composed-of diagrams versus, 93
   same diagram showing composition and, 94–95, 99
Supertypes, 73, 87, 389–90, 399–400
   event, 125–26
   operation, 124–25
Sybase, 308
System design, 244, 252–53
Systems integrator, 39
Systems Network Architecture (SNA), 107
System W, 228

T

Tables as presentation vehicles, 307
Taylor, David, 29
Texas Instruments, 226
Thinking Machines, Inc., 363
Third-generation languages, 222
Transparent mechanism, 24
Transputer, 328

Trigger rules, 119–20, 395
Triggers, 281, 394–96
   multiple, 120–21

U

User-defined types (UDTs), 263
User interface, 169

V

VDM, 323
Verification, 326
Virtual mechanism, 25
Visible rules, 152–53
Visual programming, 7
VSAM (Virtual Sequential Access Method), 303

W

Wall charting, workshops, 216–17
Whitehead, Alfred North, 221

Wiener, Norbert, 352
Williams, Mike, 44
Workshops, 201–2
   duration of, 212
   encouraging creativity, 202, 206
   executive sponsor, 207
   facilitator, 207–9
   facilitator training, 210
   five-minute rule, 213
   group dynamics, 212–13
   open issues in, 213
   participants of JRP, 210–11
   as repository, 206–7
   room for, 213–15
   scribe, 209–10
   team members in, 211
   training the participants, 215–16
   wall charting, 216–17
Wrapper, 344

X, Z

Xerox, 262
Zero cardinality constraints, 84, 384–85
Z language, 10, 323